Synthetic Data and Generative AI

Synthetic Data and Generative AI

Vincent Granville

MORGAN KAUFMANN PUBLISHERS

ELSEVIER AN IMPRINT OF ELSEVIER

ISBN: 978-0-443-21857-6

For information on all Morgan Kaufmann publications
visit our website at https://www.elsevier.com/books-and-journals

Publisher: Mara Conner
Acquisitions Editor: Chris Katsaropoulos
Editorial Project Manager: Shivangi Mishra
Production Project Manager: Jayadivya Saiprasad
Cover Designer: Greg Harris

Typeset by VTeX

Working together
to grow libraries in
developing countries

www.elsevier.com • www.bookaid.org

Contents

CHAPTER 1 Machine learning cloud regression and optimization................... 1

   1.1 Introduction: circle fitting... 1
      1.1.1 Previous versions of my method..................................... 2
   1.2 Methodology, implementation details, and caveats........................ 4
      1.2.1 Solution, R-squared, and backward compatibility............ 4
      1.2.2 Upgrades to the model.. 5
   1.3 Case studies... 6
      1.3.1 Logistic regression, two ways....................................... 7
      1.3.2 Ellipsoid and hyperplane fitting.................................... 8
      1.3.3 Nonperiodic sum of periodic time series: ocean tides......... 19
      1.3.4 Fitting a line in 3D, unsupervised clustering, and other generalizations... 24
   1.4 Connection to synthetic data: meteorites, ocean tides................. 33
      References.. 34

CHAPTER 2 A simple, robust, and efficient ensemble method........................ 35

   2.1 Introduction... 35
   2.2 Methodology.. 36
      2.2.1 How hidden decision trees (HDT) work......................... 37
      2.2.2 NLP case study: summary and findings......................... 38
      2.2.3 Parameters.. 39
      2.2.4 Improving the methodology.. 39
   2.3 Implementation details... 39
      2.3.1 Correcting for bias... 40
      2.3.2 Excel spreadsheet... 40
      2.3.3 Python code and dataset.. 41
   2.4 Model-free confidence intervals and perfect nodes..................... 46
      2.4.1 Interesting asymptotic properties of confidence intervals..................... 47
      References.. 47

CHAPTER 3 Gentle introduction to linear algebra – synthetic time series........ 49

   3.1 Power of a matrix... 49
   3.2 Examples, generalization, and matrix inversion.......................... 51
      3.2.1 Example with a noninvertible matrix.............................. 51
      3.2.2 Fast computations... 52
      3.2.3 Square root of a matrix... 52
   3.3 Application to machine learning problems.................................... 53
      3.3.1 Markov chains... 53

      3.3.2   Time series: autoregressive processes...................................... 53

      3.3.3   Linear regression.. 54

  3.4 Mathematics of autoregressive time series.. 54

      3.4.1   Simulations: curious fractal time series................................. 55

      3.4.2   Solving Vandermonde systems: a numerically stable method.............. 58

  3.5 Math for machine learning: must-read books..................................... 59

      References.. 60

CHAPTER 4 **Image and video generation**.................................. **61**

  4.1 Introduction... 61

  4.2 Applications.. 62

      4.2.1   Spatial time series.. 62

      4.2.2   Prediction intervals in any dimensions................................. 63

      4.2.3   Supervised classification of an infinite data set...................... 64

      4.2.4   Algorithms with chaotic convergence.................................. 67

  4.3 Python code.. 68

      4.3.1   Path simulation... 69

      4.3.2   Visual convergence analysis in 2D....................................... 72

      4.3.3   Supervised classification.. 74

  4.4 Visualizations... 77

      References.. 82

CHAPTER 5 **Synthetic clusters and alternative to GMM**.............. **83**

  5.1 Introduction... 83

  5.2 Generating the synthetic data.. 84

      5.2.1   Simulations with logistic distribution................................... 85

      5.2.2   Mapping the raw observations onto an image bitmap.............. 85

  5.3 Classification and unsupervised clustering...................................... 85

      5.3.1   Supervised classification based on convolution filters................ 87

      5.3.2   Clustering based on histogram equalization........................... 88

      5.3.3   Fractal classification: deep neural network analogy................. 89

      5.3.4   Generalization to higher dimensions.................................... 91

      5.3.5   Towards a very fast implementation..................................... 91

  5.4 Python code.. 92

      5.4.1   Fractal classification.. 93

      5.4.2   GPU classification and clustering.. 95

      5.4.3   Home-made graphic library.. 99

      References.. 102

CHAPTER 6 **Shape classification and synthetization via explainable AI**........... **103**

  6.1 Introduction... 103

  6.2 Mathematical foundations... 104

6.3 Shape signature... 105
   6.3.1 Weighted centroid.. 105
   6.3.2 Computing the signature.. 106
   6.3.3 Example... 106
6.4 Shape comparison.. 107
   6.4.1 Shape classification.. 108
6.5 Application.. 109
6.6 Exercises.. 110
   References.. 111

CHAPTER 7 Synthetic data, interpretable regression, and submodels.............. 113
7.1 Introduction... 113
7.2 Synthetic data sets and the spreadsheet............................ 114
   7.2.1 Correlation structure.. 115
   7.2.2 Standardized regression.. 115
   7.2.3 Initial conditions... 116
   7.2.4 Simulations and Excel spreadsheet......................... 117
7.3 Damping schedule and convergence acceleration................ 117
   7.3.1 Spreadsheet implementation................................. 118
   7.3.2 Interpretable regression with no overfitting............ 118
   7.3.3 Adaptive damping.. 119
7.4 Performance assessment on synthetic data......................... 119
   7.4.1 Results... 121
   7.4.2 Distribution-free confidence intervals..................... 123
7.5 Feature selection.. 124
   7.5.1 Combinatorial approach.. 124
   7.5.2 Stepwise approach... 126
7.6 Conclusion... 126
   References.. 128

CHAPTER 8 From interpolation to fuzzy regression............................ 131
8.1 Introduction... 131
8.2 Original version.. 132
8.3 Full, nonlinear model in higher dimensions........................ 133
   8.3.1 Geometric proximity, weights, and numerical stability...... 134
   8.3.2 Predicted values and prediction intervals................. 134
   8.3.3 Illustration, with spreadsheet............................... 135
8.4 Results.. 137
   8.4.1 Performance assessment.. 138
   8.4.2 Visualization... 138
   8.4.3 Amplitude restoration... 139
8.5 Exercises.. 139

8.6   Python source code and data sets.. 141

      References.. 145

CHAPTER 9   **New interpolation methods for synthetization and prediction**........ **147**

    9.1   First method.. 147

        9.1.1   Example with infinite summation.. 148

        9.1.2   Applications: ocean tides, planet alignment............................. 149

        9.1.3   Problem in two dimensions.. 152

        9.1.4   Spatial interpolation of the temperature data set....................... 154

    9.2   Second method.. 156

        9.2.1   From unstable polynomial to robust orthogonal regression.................. 156

        9.2.2   Using orthogonal functions.. 157

        9.2.3   Application to regression... 157

    9.3   Python code... 158

        9.3.1   Time series interpolation.. 158

        9.3.2   Geospatial temperature data set... 162

        9.3.3   Regression with Fourier series.. 167

      References.. 168

CHAPTER 10   **Synthetic tabular data: copulas vs enhanced GANs**...................... **169**

   10.1   Sensitivity analysis, bias reduction and other uses of synthetic data.............. 170

   10.2   Using copulas to generate synthetic data... 171

        10.2.1   The insurance data set: Python code and results............................ 172

        10.2.2   Potential improvements... 175

   10.3   Synthetization: GAN versus copulas... 176

        10.3.1   Parameterizing the copula quantiles combined with gradient descent... 176

        10.3.2   Feature clustering to break a big problem into smaller ones.............. 177

   10.4   Deep dive into generative adversarial networks (GAN)............................. 177

        10.4.1   Open source libraries and references... 177

        10.4.2   Synthesizing medical data with GAN.. 179

        10.4.3   Initial results.. 182

        10.4.4   Fine-tuning the hyperparameters... 184

        10.4.5   Enhanced GAN: methodology and results.................................... 185

        10.4.6   Feature clustering via hierarchical clustering or connected components 186

   10.5   Comparing GANs with the copula method.. 191

        10.5.1   Conclusion: getting the best out of copulas and GAN.................... 193

   10.6   Data synthetization explained in one picture.. 193

   10.7   Python code: GAN to synthesize medical data... 195

        10.7.1   Classification problem with random forests.................................. 195

        10.7.2   GAN method.. 196

        10.7.3   GAN evaluation and postclassification.. 200

      References.. 200

CHAPTER 11   **High quality random numbers for data synthetization**............... **203**
    11.1 Introduction... 203
    11.2 Pseudorandom numbers.................................. 204
        11.2.1 Strong pseudorandom numbers.................... 204
        11.2.2 Testing well-known sequences.................... 207
    11.3 Python code.. 212
        11.3.1 Fixes to the faulty random function in Python..... 212
        11.3.2 Prime test implementation to detect subtle flaws in PRNGs............... 213
        11.3.3 Special formula to compute 10 million digits of $\sqrt{2}$........................ 217
    11.4 Military-grade PRNG based on quadratic irrationals.............. 221
        11.4.1 Fast algorithm rooted in advanced analytic number theory................ 221
        11.4.2 Fast PRNG: explanations.......................... 222
        11.4.3 Python code..................................... 223
        11.4.4 Computing a digit without generating the previous ones................. 225
        11.4.5 Security and comparison with other PRNGs.............. 225
        11.4.6 Curious application: a new type of lottery................ 227
        References.. 227

CHAPTER 12   **Some unusual random walks**.......................... **229**
    12.1 Symmetric unbiased constrained random walks................ 229
        12.1.1 Three fundamental properties of pure random walks............ 229
        12.1.2 Random walks with more entropy than pure random signal............ 231
        12.1.3 Random walks with less entropy than pure random signal............ 234
    12.2 Related stochastic processes................................ 234
        12.2.1 From Brownian motions to clustered Lévy flights............ 235
        12.2.2 Integrated Brownian motions and special autoregressive processes...... 236
    12.3 Python code.. 238
        12.3.1 Computing probabilities and variances attached to S_n............ 238
        12.3.2 Path simulations................................. 239
        References.. 240

CHAPTER 13   **Divergent optimization algorithm and synthetic functions**.......... **243**
    13.1 Introduction.. 243
        13.1.1 The problem, with illustration.................... 244
    13.2 Nonconverging fixed-point algorithm........................ 245
        13.2.1 Trick leading to intuitive solution................ 245
        13.2.2 Root detection: method and parameters............ 246
        13.2.3 Case study: factoring a product of two large primes........ 247
    13.3 Generalization with synthetic random functions............... 249
        13.3.1 Example... 250
        13.3.2 Connection to the Poisson–binomial distribution............ 251
        13.3.3 Python code: finding the optimum................. 252

13.4 Smoothing highly chaotic curves.. 254

    13.4.1 Python code: smoothing... 254

13.5 Connection to synthetic data: random functions...................................... 257

    References.. 258

CHAPTER 14 Synthetic terrain generation and AI-generated art....................... **259**

14.1 Introduction.. 259

14.2 Terrain generation and the evolutionary process..................................... 262

    14.2.1 Morphing and nonlinear palette operations........................... 262

    14.2.2 The diamond-square algorithm... 262

    14.2.3 The evolutionary process... 263

    14.2.4 Finding optimum parameters... 263

    14.2.5 Mimicking real terrain: the synthesis step........................... 264

14.3 Python code.. 264

    14.3.1 Producing data videos with four subvideos in parallel............... 264

    14.3.2 Main program... 266

14.4 AI-generated art with 3D contours... 271

    14.4.1 Python code using Matplotlib... 272

    14.4.2 Python code using Plotly... 274

    14.4.3 Tips to quickly solve new problems................................... 275

    References.. 276

CHAPTER 15 Synthetic star cluster generation with collision graphs............... **277**

15.1 Introduction.. 277

15.2 Model parameters and simulation results... 278

    15.2.1 Explanation of color codes... 278

    15.2.2 Detailed description of top parameters............................... 278

    15.2.3 Interesting parameter sets... 280

15.3 Analysis of star collisions and collision graph................................... 280

    15.3.1 Weighted directed graphs: visualization with NetworkX................ 282

    15.3.2 Interesting findings: how the universe got started................... 283

15.4 Animated data visualizations... 284

15.5 Python code and computational issues.. 285

    15.5.1 Simulating the real and synthetic universes.......................... 285

    15.5.2 Visualizing collision graphs... 291

CHAPTER 16 Perturbed lattice point process: alternative to GMM................... **293**

16.1 Perturbed lattices: definition and properties..................................... 293

    16.1.1 Point counts distribution... 294

    16.1.2 Periodicity and amplitude of point count expectations................ 295

    16.1.3 Testing the independence of point counts............................. 296

16.2 Cluster processes and nearest neighbor graphs..................................... 298

    16.2.1 Synthetic, semirigid cluster structures.. 299

    16.2.2 Python code to generate cluster processes.................................... 301

    16.2.3 References on cluster processes... 302

    16.2.4 Superimposed perturbed lattices: an alternative to mixture models...... 303

  16.3 Statistical inference for point processes.. 310

    16.3.1 Estimation of core parameters.. 310

    16.3.2 Spatial statistics, nearest neighbors, clustering............................. 312

  16.4 Special topics.. 317

    16.4.1 Minimum contrast estimation and explainable AI.......................... 317

    16.4.2 Model identifiability, hard-to-detect patterns................................ 318

    16.4.3 Hidden model and random permutations....................................... 319

    16.4.4 Retrieving the F distribution.. 321

    16.4.5 Record distances between an observed point and its vertex.............. 323

    References.. 325

CHAPTER 17 **Synthetizing multiplicative functions in number theory**............. **329**

  17.1 Introduction.. 329

    17.1.1 Key concepts and terminology.. 330

    17.1.2 Orbits and holes.. 330

    17.1.3 Industrial applications... 331

  17.2 Euler products.. 331

    17.2.1 Finite Euler products.. 331

    17.2.2 Infinite Euler products.. 334

  17.3 Finite Dirichlet series and generalizations... 338

    17.3.1 Finite Dirichlet series... 338

    17.3.2 Nontrivial cases with infinitely many primes and a hole.................. 339

    17.3.3 Riemann Hypothesis with cosines replaced by wavelets.................. 343

    17.3.4 Riemann Hypothesis for Beurling primes..................................... 345

    17.3.5 Stochastic Euler products.. 346

  17.4 Exercises.. 348

  17.5 Python code... 352

    17.5.1 Computing the orbit of various Dirichlet series.............................. 353

    17.5.2 Creating videos of the orbit... 355

    References.. 359

CHAPTER 18 **Text, sound generation, and other topics**............................... **361**

  18.1 Sound generation: let your data sing!.. 361

    18.1.1 From data visualizations to videos to data music........................... 361

    18.1.2 References.. 362

    18.1.3 Python code.. 363

  18.2 Data videos and enhanced visualizations in R..................................... 364

    18.2.1 Cairo library to produce better charts.. 364

18.2.2 AV library to produce videos.. 365

18.3 Dual confidence regions... 366

18.3.1 Case study.. 367

18.3.2 Standard confidence region... 367

18.3.3 Dual confidence region.. 368

18.3.4 Simulations.. 368

18.3.5 Original problem with minimum contrast estimators....................... 369

18.3.6 General shape of confidence regions.. 371

18.4 Fast feature selection based on predictive power....................................... 372

18.4.1 How cross-validation works.. 373

18.4.2 Measuring the predictive power of a feature.................................. 374

18.4.3 Efficient implementation.. 375

18.5 NLP: taxonomy creation and text generation.. 376

18.5.1 Designing a keyword taxonomy... 376

18.5.2 Fast clustering algorithm for keyword data................................... 377

18.6 Automated detection of outliers and number of clusters............................. 380

18.6.1 Black-box elbow rule to detect outliers.. 381

18.7 Advice to beginners... 382

18.7.1 Getting started and learning how to learn..................................... 382

18.7.2 Automated data cleaning and exploratory analysis.......................... 384

18.7.3 Example of simple analysis: marketing attribution.......................... 385

References... 385

Glossary.. 387

Index... 391

Machine learning cloud regression and optimization

The Swiss army knife of optimization

This chapter is not about regression performed in the cloud. It is about considering your data set as a cloud of points or observations, where the concepts of dependent and independent variables (the response and the features) are blurred. It is a very general type of regression, offering backward-compatibility with existing methods. Treating a variable as the response amounts to setting a constraint on the multivariate parameter, and results in an optimization algorithm with Lagrange multipliers. The originality comes from unifying and bringing under the same umbrella a number of disparate methods, each solving a part of the general problem and originating from various fields. I also propose a novel approach to logistic regression, and a generalized R-squared adapted to shape fitting, model fitting, feature selection, and dimensionality reduction. In one example, I show how the technique can perform unsupervised clustering, with confidence regions for the cluster centers obtained via parametric bootstrap.

Besides ellipse fitting and its importance in **computer vision**, an interesting application is a non-periodic sum of periodic time series. While rarely discussed in machine learning circles, such models explain many phenomena, for instance ocean tides. It is particular useful in time-continuous situations where the error is not a white noise, but instead smooth and continuous everywhere, for instance, granular temperature forecast. Another curious application is modeling meteorite shapes. Finally, my methodology is model-free and data-driven, with a focus on numerical stability. Prediction intervals and confidence regions are obtained via bootstrapping. I provide Python code and synthetic data generators for replication purposes.

1.1 Introduction: circle fitting

The goal is to unify all regression techniques and present a simple, generic framework to solve most problems dealing with fitting an equation to a data set. Currently, there are dozens of types of regressions, each with its own methodology and algorithm. Here I propose a single methodology and a single algorithm to solve all these problems.

The originality of my technique resides in my approach and methodology, rather than in the type of math or algorithm being used. Like all generic methods, it is rather abstract and one would think more difficult to learn and describe. To the contrary, I believe it is actually more intuitive and easier to grasp. First, the dependent variable and independent features are interchangeable: the concept of dependent variables is even absent in my methodology. Thus I call it "cloud regression", as the data set is viewed as a cloud of points, with no particular axis or dimension being privileged unless explicitly required.

Synthetic Data and Generative AI. https://doi.org/10.1016/B978-0-44-321857-6.00005-9

Then the technique is model-free: it uses resampling and bootstrap to build prediction intervals, or confidence intervals for the regression coefficients.

A judicious choice of notations makes my methodology backward-compatible with all existing techniques. The concept of R-squared is slightly modified to offer extra possibilities: measuring the quality of the fit for the full model versus a submodel of your choice. In standard regression, the submodel is a constant and referred to as the base model. Here the submodel could be fitting a circle if the full model is about ellipses, or fitting a plane versus an hyperplane in standard linear regression.

All regression books and chapters for beginners start with fitting a line. Here the easiest example – the first one to be taught – is fitting a circle centered at the origin. Think about it for a moment: intuitively, the estimated radius is the average radius computed on the data points. Indeed, this is the solution produced by my technique. The second easiest case is then fitting a line involving a slope and an intercept. Both examples are a particular case of fitting a quadratic form (ellipsoid).

This presentation is intended to beginners. There are examples, just as in standard regression, where the solution is not unique. In my opinion, nonuniqueness should be embraced rather than avoided: in real life one would expect that multiple, different shapes can fit to a particular data set. Finding several of them provides more insights about your data. However, conditions needed for uniqueness are not discussed here: this is the topic of a more advanced presentation.

In many cases, thanks to an appropriate reparameterization, the solution is obtained using simple constrained optimization and Lagrange multipliers. It has more to do with elementary calculus than advanced matrix algebra. In particular, there is no explicit mention of **eigenvalues** [Wiki] or **singular value decomposition** [Wiki]. Also, the shape does not need to have derivatives, though if it does, a faster implementation is possible, with a Newton-like algorithm. Indeed, the shape may be differentiable nowhere: think about fitting a Brownian motion to a set of observations.

I provide examples using synthetic data [Wiki] and Python code. One of them involves time series forecasting with two periods p, q where p/q is not a rational number. Since p and q are among the parameters to be estimated, this is a true nonlinear problem that cannot be transformed into something linear via a link function [Wiki], unlike (say) logistic regression. A real-life application, to benchmark the performance of the method, is predicting ocean tides: large, granular geospatial data sets are available to test the prediction algorithm in this nonlinear context.

Finally, "cloud regression" encompasses the **general linear model** [Wiki], the **generalized linear model** [Wiki] (and thus logistic regression), as well as **weighted least squares** [Wiki] (and thus Bayesian regression). Via the mapping $z \mapsto w$ discussed in Section 1.1.1, it can accommodate splines as in **adaptive regression splines** [Wiki]. Both cloud regression and the **total least squares** method [Wiki] minimize the sum of the squared distances between the data points and the shape, though my method does not give the response (called the dependent variable by statisticians) a particular status: in other words, it also works in the standard situation where there is no response, but just a cloud of points instead. In addition, my technique handles truly nonlinear situations, unlike the generalized linear model. For that reason, I call it the mother of all regressions.

This is not the first time a regression technique does not discriminate between dependent and independent variables: **partial least squares** [Wiki] also allows for that. See also [5].

1.1.1 Previous versions of my method

The current version is much more general, simpler, and radically different from the first implementation. However, it may help to provide some historical context. Initially, the goal was to compute the sum of the squared distances between a set of points (the observations, or the "cloud"), and a prespecified shape Γ_θ (a line, plane, or circle) belonging to a parametric family driven by a multidimensional parameter θ.

The idea was as follows. Let P_∞ be a fixed point located extremely far away from the shape, and P be a point of the training set. Draw the line L_P that goes through P and P_∞, and find the intersection $\Gamma_\theta \cap L_P$ closest to P, between the shape and the line. Let Q_θ be this point. The point in question may not be unique or may not exist (depending on θ), but the distance $\Delta_\theta(P) = ||P - Q_\theta||$ is, assuming there is an intersection. Then find θ^* that minimizes the sum of $\Delta_\theta(P)$ computed over all training set points P. This θ^*, if unique, determines the shape that best fits the data. Traditional projection-based techniques compute the exact distance between a point and a shape, and therefore require the shape to be differentiable. The method based on P_∞ works with shapes that are not differentiable. Some particular cases in the new implementation produce similar or identical results to those obtained with the P_∞ method.

If the shape in question is a hyperplane and the context is traditional multivariate linear regression, then the shape is defined by $g(w, \theta) = 0$ where $w = (y, x_1, \ldots, x_m)$ and $g(w, \theta) = \theta_0 y + (\theta_1 x_1 + \cdots + \theta_m x_m)$. Here y corresponds to the dependent variable, $x_1, \ldots, x_m$ to the features, and $\theta_0, \theta_1, \ldots, \theta_m$ are the regression coefficients, with the constraint $\theta_0 = -1$. In the new methodology, the constraint $\theta_0 = -1$ is handled using a Lagrange multiplier, but other than that it leads to the same traditional solution. If there is an intercept, then $x_1 = 1$. In the end, the goal is to propose a technique that is both general and intuitive, following the modern trend of explainable AI [Wiki].

In a second version of my methodology (not the current version), I introduced a mapping system, which essentially is a change of coordinates associated to a link function. The goal was to transform the data so that after the mapping, it is more amenable to a simple solution. Also, it is an attempt at obtaining a scale-independent solution: whether your unit is a mile or a kilometer should have no impact on the solution. In its most general form, the observations and parameters are denoted as z and φ. The shape satisfies the equation $h(z, \varphi) = 0$. The mapping is defined as $g(w, \theta) = \xi(h(z, \varphi))$ where $\xi : \mathbb{R} \to \mathbb{R}$ is a strictly monotonic function, with $w = \nu(z)$ and $\theta = \phi(\varphi)$, for some multivariate one-to-one mappings ν and ϕ. All the computations are done in the (w, θ)-space, thought it is possible to revert back to the original (z, φ) when computations are done, if ever needed.

I eventually dropped both ξ and simply ignored φ and ϕ, leading to a less abstract model, yet covering all practical cases. Thus in the current version, $h(z, \varphi) = g(w, \theta)$, and we do not care about φ. We may as well use $\varphi = \theta$. The mapping ν gives rise to spline regression in the new method. However, when splines are used, they are prespecified rather than estimated, to avoid overfitting. Typically, they are chosen to simplify the computations.

Finally, I was interested in some original dimension-reduction technique. Not a true data-reduction technique, but it allows you to reduce the number of parameters by a factor of 2: consider w and θ to be complex, rather than real numbers, for instance, via a mapping $z \mapsto w$ from $\mathbb{R}^2$ to $\mathbb{C}$, with $w = \nu(z)$. A benefit is the possibility to use a **conformal map** [Wiki] for ν, thus preserving angles. Such an example is the **log-polar map** [Wiki] $z = \exp(w)$ with $g(w, \theta) = z^\theta = \exp(\theta w)$, which corresponds to using the polar coordinate system with $\theta, z, w \in \mathbb{C}$: it makes things easier when dealing with circular data. The next step was to look at quaternions to reduce the number of parameters by a factor of 4, but there are a number of challenges. Anyway, I promised to keep things simple in this introductory presentation, so I will not discuss complex or quaternion mappings here. This is the topic of future research.

It is interesting to note that the problem of circle fitting has been quite extensively studied, see [6]. Essentially, these methods solve the problem using φ and they are not trivial. The solution based on my method involves working with θ and leads to a very classic algorithm with a simple solution. The price to pay is that the θ parameters are less obvious to interpret: they are the coefficients of a quadratic form. To the contrary, the direct solution involves φ parameters that have obvious meaning: the radius of the circle, its center, and (in case of an ellipse) the rotation angle. However, my approach makes it a lot easier to generalize to ellipses and even far more complicated shapes, or hyperplanes for that matter, while at the same time having a solution that is even simpler than those discussed in [6] and applicable to the circle only. Of course, in this case there is a one-to-one mapping between φ and θ, see here. So you can always retrieve φ from θ.

1.2 Methodology, implementation details, and caveats

I encourage you to first read Section 1.1.1, as it provides a good amount of context. This section describes the details of the methodology. For simplicity, I do not describe the most general case, but a case that is general enough to cover all practical applications. I start by introducing the concept of data (called point cloud), parameter, and shape.

The **data** set is denoted as W, and consists of $m + 1$ variables and n observations. Thus W is an $n \times (m + 1)$ matrix as usual. The kth row corresponds to the kth observation $W_k = (W_{k,0}, W_{k,1}, \ldots, W_{k,m+1})$. For backward compatibility with traditional models, I use the notation $W_{k,0} = Y_k$ for the dependent variable or response (if there is one), and $(X_{k,1}, \ldots, X_{k,m}) = (W_{k,1}, \ldots, W_{k,m+1})$ for the independent variables of features. The column vector corresponding to the response is denoted as Y, and the $n \times m$ matrix representing the independent variables is denoted as X. The whole data set W is referred to as the point cloud.

The **parameter** is a multivariate column vector denoted as $\theta = (\theta_0, \theta_1, \ldots, \theta_d)$, with $d + 1$ components. Typically, $d = m$ and θ satisfies some constraint, specified by $\eta(\theta) = 0$ for some function η. The most common functions are $\eta(\theta) = \theta^T \theta - 1$, $\eta(\theta) = \theta_0 + 1$, and $\eta(\theta) = (\theta_0 + \cdots + \theta_d) - 1$. Here ^{T} denotes the matrix/vector transposition operator.

The purpose is to fit a **shape** to the point cloud. The most typical shapes, after proper mapping, are hyperplanes or quadratic forms (ellipsoids). The former is a particular case of the latter. The shape belongs to a parametric family of equations driven by the multivariate parameter θ. The equation of the shape is $g(w, \theta) = 0$, for some function g. Typical examples include $g(w, \theta) = w\theta$ and $g(w, \theta) = w\theta - 1$, with $d = m$. The former usually involves an intercept: $X_{k,1} = 1$ for all $k = 1, \ldots, n$. Keep in mind that w and θ are vectors, but $g(w, \theta)$ is a real number, not a vector. Thus $w\theta$ represents a **dot product** [Wiki].

1.2.1 Solution, R-squared, and backward compatibility

The shape that best fits the data corresponds to $\theta = \theta^*$, obtained by minimizing the squares:

$$\theta^* = \arg\min_{\theta} \sum_{k=1}^{n} g^2(W_k, \theta). \tag{1.1}$$

The solution may not be unique. Uniqueness and numerical stability will be addressed in a future article, but the basics are covered in this book. The constraint $\eta(\theta) = 0$ guarantees that the solution requires solving a (sometimes nonlinear) system of $d + 2$ equations with $d + 2$ unknowns. In some cases, $d \leq m$ to avoid **model identifiability** issues [Wiki]. Also, a large d may result in overfitting [Wiki]. Then, you want $n > d$ otherwise the solution may not be unique unless you add more constraints on θ. The solution θ^* is obtained by solving the system

$$\begin{cases} \sum_{k=1}^{n} \nabla_\theta [g^2(W_k, \theta)] = \lambda \nabla_\theta [\eta(\theta)], \\ \eta(\theta) = 0, \end{cases} \tag{1.2}$$

where ∇_θ is the gradient operator with respect to θ [Wiki], and λ is called the **Lagrange multiplier** [Wiki]. This is a classic constrained convex optimization problem. The top part of (1.2) consists of a system of $d + 1$ equations with $d + 2$ unknowns $\theta_0, \ldots, \theta_d$, and λ. The bottom part is a single equation with $d + 1$ unknowns $\theta_0, \ldots, \theta_d$. Combined together, it constitutes a system of $d + 2$ equations with $d + 2$ unknowns. Note the analogy with **Lasso regression** [Wiki] when $\eta(\theta) = \theta^T \theta - 1$, that is, when $\theta^T \theta = 1$.

The **mean squared error** (MSE) relative to a particular θ is defined as

$$\text{MSE}(\theta) = \frac{1}{n} \sum_{k=1}^{n} g^2(W_k, \theta) \geq \text{MSE}(\theta^*). \tag{1.3}$$

The inequality in (1.3) is an immediate consequence of (1.1). Now define the R-squared with respect to θ as

$$R^2(\theta) = 1 - \frac{\text{MSE}(\theta^*)}{\text{MSE}(\theta)}. \tag{1.4}$$

It follows immediately that $0 \leq R^2(\theta) \leq 1$. A perfect fit corresponds to $\text{MSE}(\theta^*) = 0$ (the whole cloud residing on the shape). In that case, if $\theta \neq \theta^*$ and the optimum θ^* is unique, then $R^2(\theta) = 1$.

In traditional linear regression, the R-squared is defined as $R^2(\theta_*)$ where θ_* is the optimum θ for the base model. The base model corresponds to all the coefficients θ_i attached to the independent variables set to zero, except the one attached to the intercept. In other words, in the base model, the predicted Y is constant, equal to the empirical mean of Y. As a result, $\text{MSE}(\theta_*) = \text{Var}[Y]$, the empirical variance of Y. A consequence is that $R^2(\theta_*)$ is the square of the correlation between the observed response Y, and the predicted response of the full model.

Backward compatibility with traditional linear regression works as follows. The standard univariate regression corresponds to $g(w, \theta) = w\theta = \theta_0 y + \theta_1 x + \theta_2$, with the constraint $\theta_0 = -1$. Thus $g(w, \theta) = 0$ if and only if $y = \theta_1 x + \theta_2$. This generalizes to multivariate regression as well. A more elegant formulation in the new methodology is to replace the constraint $\theta_0 = -1$ by the symmetric constraint $\theta_0^2 + \theta_1^2 + \theta_2^2 = 1$. Note that w is a row vector and θ is a column vector.

1.2.2 Upgrades to the model

By a model, I mean the general setting of the method: there is no probabilistic model involved in this discussion. **Prediction intervals** [Wiki] for the individual error $g(W_k, \theta^*)$ at each data point W_k (or for the estimated response attached to Y_k, if there is an independent variable) and confidence regions [Wiki] for θ^* can be obtained via resampling and bootstrapping [Wiki]. This is also true for points outside the training set.

Also, the squares can be replaced by absolute values, as in **quantile regression** [Wiki], to minimize the impact of outliers and for scale preservation: if a variable is measured in years, then squares are expressed in squared years, a metric that is meaningless. This leads to a modified, better metric to assess the quality of the fit, replacing the R-squared. See Section 7.4 about "performance assessment" in Chapter 7, for alternatives to the R-squared. The goodness-of-fit (say, the R-squared) should be measured on the validation set [Wiki] even though θ^* is computed on a subset of the training set: this is a standard practice, called cross-validation [Wiki], illustrated on synthetic data in Chapter 8 about fuzzy regression.

Now, let us get back to the R-squared. In standard linear regression, the R-squared is defined as $R^2(\theta_*)$ via formula (1.4), where θ_* is the optimum θ for the base model (the predicted response is constant, equal the mean of Y for the base model). In the new methodology, there may be no response. Still, the definition of R^2 extends to that situation, and is compatible with the traditional version. What is more, it leads to many possible R^2, one for each submodel (not just the base model), and this is true too for the standard regression. A submodel corresponds to adding constraints on the parameter vector θ or, in other words, working with a subset of the parameter space. Let θ_* be the optimum for a specific submodel, while θ^* is the optimum for the full model. Then the definition of R^2, depending on θ_*, is unchanged. It could not be any simpler!

Now you can use R^2 for model comparison purposes and even for feature selection [Wiki]. You can test the improvement obtained by using the full model over a submodel, with the metric $S(\theta_*) = R^2(\theta^*) - R^2(\theta_*)$. Here θ_* is the optimum θ attached to the submodel. Obviously, $0 \le S(\theta_*) \le 1$. The larger $S(\theta_*)$, the bigger the improvement. Conversely, the smaller, the better the performance of the submodel. Examples include fitting an ellipse (full model) versus fitting a circle (submodel) or using all the features (full model) versus using a subset (submodel). You can compare submodels and rank them according to $S(\theta_*)$. This allows you to identify the smallest set of features that achieve a good enough $S(\theta_*)$, for dimensionality reduction purposes [Wiki].

Finally, another update consists of using positive weights $\psi_k(\theta)$ in formula (1.1). This amounts to performing **weighted regression** [Wiki]. For instance, data points far away from the optimum shape, that is, observations with a large $g^2(W_k, \theta^*)$, may be discarded to reduce the impact of outliers. Or the weights can be used to balance the coefficients θ_i, in an effort to achieve scale-invariance in the expression $w\theta$. Then the top system in (1.2) becomes

$$\sum_{k=1}^{n} \psi_k(\theta) \nabla_\theta [g^2(W_k, \theta)] + \sum_{k=1}^{n} g^2(W_k, \theta) \nabla_\theta [\psi_k(\theta)] = \lambda \nabla_\theta [\eta(\theta)]. \tag{1.5}$$

1.3 Case studies

In Section 1.3.1, I show how to solve the logistic regression. The first version is standard least squares, to further illustrate backward compatibility with the traditional method. The second illustrates how it could be done if you want to follow the spirit of the new methodology. Then I discuss two fundamental examples based on synthetic data.

1.3.1 **Logistic regression, two ways**

In the traditional setting, $w = (y, x)$ where y is the response and x the features. For the logistic regression [Wiki], we have

$$g(w, \theta) = g(y, x) = y - F(x\theta), \quad \text{with } x\theta = \theta_1 x_1 + \cdots + \theta_m x_m.$$

Here $x_1 = 1$ corresponds to the intercept, thus we have $m - 1$ actual features $x_2, x_3, \ldots, x_m$. There is no constraint on the parameter θ, thus there is no function $\eta(\theta)$. In formula (1.2), $\eta(\theta) = 0$ should be ignored, and $\lambda = 0$. The function F is a cumulative distribution function with a symmetric density around the origin. In this case, $F(x\theta) = 1/(1 + \exp[-x\theta])$ is the standard **logistic distribution** [Wiki].

In the new methodology, one would proceed as follows. First, the original data is denoted as $z = (v, u)$. The logistic regression applies to the original data. Here v is the response, and u the feature vector. The parameter θ is unchanged (not subject to a mapping), and still denoted as θ. This regression can be stated as

$$g(z, \theta) = g(v, u) = v - F(u\theta), \quad \text{with } u\theta = \theta_1 u_1 + \cdots + \theta_m u_m.$$

The first step is to map $z = (v, u)$ onto $w = (y, x)$, with the hope of simplifying the problem, as discussed in Section 1.1.1. This is done via the link function $y = F^{-1}(v) = \log[v/(1 - v)]$ and $u = x$. Now we are back to

$$g(z, \theta) = g(w, \theta) = g(y, x; \theta) = y - x\theta, \quad \text{with } x\theta = \theta_1 x_1 + \cdots + \theta_m x_m.$$

This is how standard linear regression is expressed in the new framework. But it is still the traditional linear regression, with nothing new. The final step consists in extending θ, adding one component θ_0 to $\theta_1, \ldots, \theta_m$. With the new θ (still denoted as θ) we have $g(w, \theta) = w\theta = \theta_0 w_0 + \cdots + \theta_m w_m$. You need to add one constraint on θ. The constraint $\theta_0 = -1$, that is, $\eta(\theta) = \theta_0 + 1$, yields the exact same solution as traditional linear regression. But $\theta^T \theta = 1$, that is, $\eta(\theta) = \theta^T \theta - 1$, makes the problem somehow symmetric, and more elegant.

However, in many applications, the response v in the original space is either 0 or 1, such as cancer versus noncancer, or fraud versus nonfraud. In this case, the link function is undefined. The mapping with the link function works if the response is a proportion, strictly between zero and one. Otherwise, the standard logistic regression is the best approach. A possible workaround is to use for F a distribution with a finite support, such as uniform on $[a, b]$. After all, the observed values (the features) are always bounded anyway. Then, intuitively, given θ, estimates of a and b are proportional respectively to the minimum and maximum of $U_k\theta$, over $k = 1, \ldots, n$.

This suggests a new approach to logistic regression. First, use the model $v = F_\theta(u\theta)$ in the (v, u)-space, where $0 \le v \le 1$ and F_θ is the empirical distribution [Wiki] of $u\theta$ given θ. Then choose θ^* that minimizes the sum of squared residuals:

$$\theta^* = \arg\min_\theta \sum_{k=1}^{n} g^2(V_k, U_k; \theta) = \arg\min_\theta \sum_{k=1}^{n} (V_k - F_\theta(U_k\theta))^2.$$

Remember, U_k is a row vector, and θ is a column vector; the dot product $U_k\theta$ is a real number. Also, V_k is the binary response attached to the kth observation, while U_k is the corresponding m-dimensional feature vector, both in the original (v, u)-space. The empirical distribution F_θ is computed as follows:

$F_\theta(t)$ is the proportion of observed feature vectors, among $U_1, \ldots, U_n$, satisfying $U_k\theta \le t$. Such a method could be called **CDF regression**. You can use the methodology presented here to solve it, but it would be very computer-intensive, because F_θ depends on θ in a nonobvious way. The predicted value for V_k, is $F_{\theta*}(U_k\theta^*)$ in this case.

1.3.2 Ellipsoid and hyperplane fitting

This is a fundamental example, with hyperplanes being a particular case of ellipsoids. I illustrate the methodology with an example based on synthetic data, in a small dimension. The idea is to represent the shape with a quadratic form. In two dimensions, the equations is

$$\theta_0 x^2 + \theta_1 xy + \theta_2 y^2 + \theta_3 x + \theta_4 y + \theta_5 = 0.$$

The trick is to rewrite it with artificial variables $w_0 = x^2$, $w_1 = xy$, $w_2 = y^2$, $w_3 = x$, $w_4 = y$, $w_5 = 1$, so that we can use the general framework with $g(w, \theta) = w\theta$. Again, $w\theta$ is the dot product. To avoid the trivial solution $\theta^* = 0$, let us add the constraint $\theta^T \theta = 1$, that is, $\eta(\theta) = \theta^T\theta - 1$. Then, θ^* is solution of the system

$$\begin{cases} (W^T W - \lambda I)\theta = 0, \\ \qquad \theta^T\theta = 1. \end{cases} \tag{1.6}$$

The above solution is correct in any dimension. It is a direct application of (1.2). Here W is the $n \times 6$ matrix containing the n observations. Thus, $W_{k0} = X_k^2$, $W_{k1} = X_k Y_k$, $W_{k2} = Y_k^2$, $W_{k3} = X_k$, $W_{k4} = Y_k$, $W_{k5} = 1$. The Python code and additional details, for a slightly different version with a slightly different $\eta(\theta)$, can be found here. I use it in my own code, available on my GitHub repository, here, under the name `fittingEllipse.py`. It is based on Halir's article about fitting ellipses [2].

The Python code checks if the fitted shape is actually an ellipse. However, in the spirit of my methodology, it does not matter if it is an ellipse, a parabola, a hyperbola, or even a line. The uniqueness of the solution is unimportant: indeed, if two very different solutions (say, an ellipse and a parabola) yield the same minimum mean squared error and are thus both optimal, it says something about the data set, something interesting to know. However, it would be interesting to compute $R^2(\theta_*)$ using formula (1.4), where θ_* corresponds to a circle. It would tell whether the full model (ellipse) over a significant improvement over the circle submodel.

Ellipsoid fitting shares some similarities with multivariate polynomial regression [7]. The differences are:

- Ellipse fitting is a "full" model; in the polynomial regression $y = \theta_1 + \theta_2 x + \theta_3 x^2$, the terms y^2 and xy are always missing.
- Polynomial regression fits a curve that is unbounded, such as $y = x^2$, resulting in poor fitting; to the contrary, in ellipse fitting (if the solution is actually an ellipse) the solution is bounded.
- To get as many terms in polynomial regression as in ellipse fitting, the only way is to increase the degree of the polynomial, which further increases the instability of the solution.

Finally, Umbach [6] proposes a different approach to ellipse fitting. It is significantly more complicated, and indeed, they stopped at the circle. In short, their method directly estimates the center, semiaxis lengths, and rotation angle via least squares, as opposed to estimating the coefficients in the quadratic

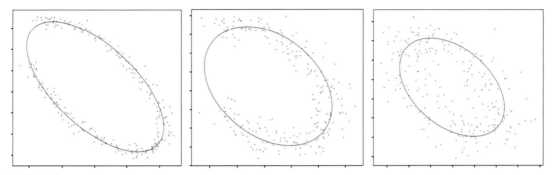

FIGURE 1.1

Fitted ellipse (blue; dark gray in print version), given the training set (red; light gray in print version) distributed around a partial arc.

form that represents the ellipse. More on parametric curves can be found in Chapter 6 on shape recognition.

1.3.2.1 *Curve fitting: 250 examples in one video*

Ellipse fitting is performed by setting `mode='CurveFitting'` in the Python code. The program automatically creates a number of ellipses, specified by their parameters (center, lengths of semiaxes, and rotation angle), then generates a different training set for each ellipse, and outputs the result of the fitting procedure as an image. The images are then bundled together to produce a video, and an animated gif. Each image features a particular ellipse and training set, as well as the fitted ellipse based on the training set. The ellipse parameters are set by the variable `params` in the code: it is an array with five components. The number of ellipses is set by the parameter `nframes`, which also determines the number of frames in the output video.

Actually, the program does a little more: it works with ellipse arcs. Using the centroid of the training set to estimate the center of the ellipse does not work in this case. So the program retrieves the original, unknown ellipse even if the training set consists of points randomly distributed around a portion of that ellipse. The arc in question is determined by a lower and upper angle in polar coordinates, denoted respectively as `tmin` and `tmax` in the code, with `tmin=0` and `tmax=`2π corresponding to the full ellipse.

The training set consists of n observations generated as follows. First sample n points on the ellipse (or the arc you are interested in). Then perturb these points by adding some noise. You have two options: `noise_CDF='Uniform'` and `noise_CDF='Normal'`. The amount of noise is specified by the parameter `noise` in the code. For the uniform distribution on the square $[-a, a] \times [-a, a]$, `noise` represents a. For the bivariate normal distribution with covariance matrix $\sigma^2 I$ where I is the identity matrix, it represents σ^2. There are various ways of sampling points on an ellipse. Three options are offered here, set by the parameter `sampling`. They are described in Section 1.3.2.3, in the paragraph "Sampling points on an ellipse arc". The option `'Enhanced'` is the only one performing stochastic sampling (points randomly picked up on the ellipse), and used in Fig. 1.2.

In Fig. 1.2, the size of the training set is $n = 30$ while in Fig. 1.1, $n = 250$. In the code, n is represented by the variable `npts`. The training set is colored in red (light gray in print version), the fitted ellipse in blue (dark gray in print version), and if present on the image as in Fig. 1.2, the true ellipse is in black. The latter appears as a polygon rather than an ellipse because the sampled points on the true ellipse are joined by segments, and n is small. Typically, the true and fitted ellipses are very close to each other, although there is a systematic bias too small to be noticed to the naked eye unless the ellipse eccentricity is high. More on this soon.

Table 1.1 compares the exact parameter values (set by the user) of the true ellipse in Fig. 1.2, to a few sets of estimated values obtained by least squares. Each set of estimates is computed using a different training set. All training sets are produced with same amount and type of noise, to give an idea of the variance of the parameter estimates at a specific level of noise. The five parameters are the ellipse center (x_0, y_0), the lengths of the semiaxes (a_p, b_p), and the ellipse orientation (the rotation angle ϕ).

In some cases, the solution may not be unique, or could be a hyperbola or parabola rather than an ellipse. For instance, if the ellipse is reduced to a circle, any value for the rotation angle is de facto correct, though the estimated curve is still unique and correctly identified. Also, if the true ellipse has a high eccentricity, the generated white (unbiased) noise forces the training set points inside the ellipse more often than they should, as opposed to outside the boundary. This is because inside the ellipse, the noise from the North side strongly overlaps with the noise from the South side, assuming the long axis is the horizontal one. The result is biased estimates for a_p and b_p, smaller than the actual ones. In the end, the fitted curve has a higher eccentricity than the true one. The effect is more pronounced the higher the eccentricity. If the variance of the noise is small enough, there is almost no bias.

I posted a video featuring 250 fitted ellipses with the associated training sets, here on YouTube. It is also on GitHub, here. The accompanying animated gif is also on GitHub, here. All were produced with the Python code. In the video, the transition from one ellipse to the next one is very smooth. While I use 250 different combinations of arcs, rotation angles, eccentricities, and noises to feature a large collection of very different cases, these configurations slowly progress from one frame to the next in the video. But the 250 frames eventually cover a large spectrum of situations. The last one shows a perfect fit, where the training set points are all on the true ellipse.

1.3.2.2 *Confidence region for the fitted ellipse: application to meteorite shapes*

The computation of confidence regions is performed by setting `mode='ConfidenceRegion'` in the Python code. This time the program automatically creates a number of training sets (determined by the parameter `nframes`), for the same ellipse specified by its parameters `params`: center, lengths of semiaxes, and rotation angle. Then it estimates the ellipse parameters, and thus the true ellipse, uniquely determined by the parameters in question. Fig. 1.2 shows the confidence region for the example outlined in Table 1.1.

Table 1.1 Estimated ellipse parameters vs true values ($n = 30$), for the shape in Fig. 1.2.

	x_0	x_1	a_p	b_p	ϕ
Exact values	3.00000	−2.50000	7.00000	4.00000	0.78540
Training set 1	2.61951	−2.41818	6.44421	3.82838	0.72768
Training set 2	2.77270	−2.32346	6.59185	4.24624	0.59971
Training set 3	3.29900	−2.60532	6.71834	4.15181	0.87760
Training set 4	2.71936	−2.42349	7.15562	4.52900	0.80404

Actually I decided to display a polygon instead of the fitted ellipse, by selecting the option `sampling='Enhanced'`. The polygon consists of the predicted locations of the $n = 30$ training set points on the fitted ellipse. These locations are obtained in the exact same way that predicted values are obtained in a linear regression problem and then shown on the fitted line. After all, ellipse fitting as presented in this section is a particular case of the general cloud regression technique. I then joined these points using segments, resulting in one polygon per training set. The superimposition of these polygons is the confidence region.

The reason for using polygons rather than ellipses is for a particular application: estimating the shape of a small, far away celestial body based on a low resolution image. This is particularly useful when creating a taxonomy of these bodies: the shape parameters are used to classify them and understand their history as well as gravity interactions, and can be used as features in a machine learning algorithm. Then, for a small meteorite, people expect to see it as a polyhedron (the 3D version of a polygon) rather than an ellipsoid. Of course, if the number n of points in the training set is large, then the polyhedron is indistinguishable from the fitted ellipsoid. But in practice, with low resolution images, n is usually pretty small.

FIGURE 1.2

Confidence region in blue (dark gray in print version), $n = 30$ training set points; 50 training sets (left) vs 150 (right).

1.3.2.3 *Python code*

The main parameters in the code are highlighted in red (light gray in print version) in this high level summary. The program is listed in this section and also available on GitHub here, under the name `fittingEllipse.py`.

The least square optimization is performed using an implementation of the Halir and Flusser algorithm [2], adapted from a version posted here by Christian Hill, the author of the book "Learning Scientific Programming with Python" [3]. The optimization – minimizing the sum of squared errors between the observed points and the fitted ellipse – is performed on the coefficients of the quadratic equation representing the ellipse. This is the easiest way to do it, and it is also the approach that I use elsewhere in this chapter. The function `fit_ellipse` does the job, while `cart_to_pol` converts these coefficients into meaningful features: the center, rotation angle, eccentricity, and the major and minor semiaxes of the ellipse [Wiki].

Sampling points on an ellipse arc

The Python code also integrates other components written by various authors. First, it offers three options to sample points on an ellipse or a partial arc of an ellipse, via the parameter `sampling` in the main section of the code:

- Evenly spaced on the perimeter, via the function `sample_from_ellipse_even`. The code is adapted from an anonymous version posted here. It requires the evaluation of **elliptic integrals** [Wiki]. The technique is identical to that described in Section 6.3.1 on "weighted centroid" in Chapter 6.
- Randomly chosen on the perimeter in such a way that on average the distance between two consecutive sampled points on the ellipse is constant. It involves sampling from a multinormal distribution, rescaling the points and then sorting the sampled points so that they are ordered on the perimeter. This also requires sorting an array according to another array. It is done in the function `sample_from_ellipse`.
- The standard, easiest, but notoriously skewed sampling. It consists of choosing equally spaced angles in the polar representation of the ellipse. For curve fitting, it is good enough with very little differences compared to the two other methods.

For sampling on a partial arc rather then the full ellipse, set the parameters `tmin` and `tmax` to the appropriate values, in the main loop. These are angles in the polar coordinate system, and should lie between 0 and 2π. The full ellipse corresponds to `tmin` set to zero, and `tmax` set to 2π.

Training set and ellipse parameters

Then, to create the training set, perturb the sampled points on the ellipse via uniform or Gaussian noise. The choice is set by the parameter `noise_CDF` in the main section of the code. The parameter `noise` determines the amount of noise, or in other words, the noise variance. Points, be it on the ellipse or in the training set, are arrays with names `x` and `y` (respectively for the X and Y coordinates). The number of points in the training set is determined by the parameter `npts`.

The shape of the ellipse is set by the 5-dimensional parameter vector `params`. Its components, denoted as `x0`, `y0`, `ap`, `bp`, `phi` throughout the code, are respectively the center of the ellipse, the length of the semiaxes, and the orientation of the ellipse (the rotation angle).

Confidence regions versus curve fitting

The program creates `nframes` ellipses, one at a time in the main loop. At each iteration, the created ellipse and training set is saved as a PNG image, for inclusion in a video or animated gif (see the next paragraph). This is why the variable controlling the main loop is called `frame`. At each iteration the true parameters of the ellipse (the ones you chose), and their least squares estimates are displayed on the screen.

If the parameter `mode` is set to `'ConfidenceRegion'`, then the amount of noise and all ellipse parameters are kept constant throughout the iterations. The fitted shapes varies from one iteration to the next depending on the training set (itself depending on the noise), creating a confidence region for a specific ellipse, given a specific amount of noise. New fitted ellipses keep being added to the image without erasing older ones, to display the confidence region under construction. Highly eccentric ellipses result in biased confidence regions. The method used to build the confidence region is known as **parametric bootstrap** [Wiki].

To the contrary, if `mode` is set to `'FittingCurves'`, a different ellipse with different parameters and different amount of noise is generated at each iteration, erasing the previous one in the new image. The purpose in this case is to assess the quality of the fit depending on the amount of noise and the shape of the ellipse (the eccentricity and whether you use a full or partial arc for training, in particular).

Creating videos and animated gifs

At each iteration in the main loop, the program creates and saves an image in your local folder, featuring the training set in red (light gray in print version) (a cloud of dots distributed around the true ellipse arc) and the fitted ellipse in blue (dark gray in print version). The name of the image is ellipsexxx.png, where xxx is the current frame number. At the last iteration (the last frame in the video), the true ellipse – that with the parameters set in the main loop – is added to the image, in black: it allows you to assess the bias when choosing the option mode='ConfidenceRegion'.

The video is saved as ellipseFitting.mp4, and the animated gif as ellipseFitting.gif. The parameter DPI (dots per inch) sets the resolution of the images. For videos, I recommend to set it to 300. For animated gifs, I recommend using 100. At the bottom of the code, when creating the video with a Moviepy function, you are free to change fps=20 to any other value. This parameter sets the number of frames per second. **Color transparency** [Wiki] is used throughout the plots, to improve the rendering when multiple curves overlap. The transparency level is denoted as alpha in the code. You are not supposed to play with it unless you do not like my choice. I mention it just in case you are wondering what alpha represents.

Finally, if the parameter ShowImage is set to True, each frame is also displayed on your screen. The default value is False. Turn it on only if you produce a very small number of frames, say nframes=10 or less.

```python
import numpy as np
import matplotlib.pyplot as plt
import moviepy.video.io.ImageSequenceClip # to produce mp4 video
from PIL import Image # for some basic image processing

def fit_ellipse(x, y):

    # Fit the coefficients a,b,c,d,e,f, representing an ellipse described by
    # the formula F(x,y) = ax^2 + bxy + cy^2 + dx + ey + f = 0 to the provided
    # arrays of data points x=[x1, x2, ..., xn] and y=[y1, y2, ..., yn].

    # Based on the algorithm of Halir and Flusser, "Numerically stable direct
    # least squares fitting of ellipses'.

    D1 = np.vstack([x**2, x*y, y**2]).T
    D2 = np.vstack([x, y, np.ones(len(x))]).T
    S1 = D1.T @ D1
    S2 = D1.T @ D2
    S3 = D2.T @ D2
    T = -np.linalg.inv(S3) @ S2.T
    M = S1 + S2 @ T
    C = np.array(((0, 0, 2), (0, -1, 0), (2, 0, 0)), dtype=float)
    M = np.linalg.inv(C) @ M
    eigval, eigvec = np.linalg.eig(M)
    con = 4 * eigvec[0]* eigvec[2] - eigvec[1]**2
    ak = eigvec[:, np.nonzero(con > 0)[0]]
    return np.concatenate((ak, T @ ak)).ravel()
```

```
def cart_to_pol(coeffs):

    # Convert the cartesian conic coefficients, (a, b, c, d, e, f), to the
    # ellipse parameters, where F(x, y) = ax^2 + bxy + cy^2 + dx + ey + f = 0.
    # The returned parameters are x0, y0, ap, bp, e, phi, where (x0, y0) is the
    # ellipse center; (ap, bp) are the semimajor and semiminor axes,
    # respectively; e is the eccentricity; and phi is the rotation of the
    # semimajor axis from the x-axis.

    # We use the formulas from https://mathworld.wolfram.com/Ellipse.html
    # which assumes a cartesian form ax^2 + 2bxy + cy^2 + 2dx + 2fy + g = 0.
    # Therefore, rename and scale b, d, and f appropriately.
    a = coeffs[0]
    b = coeffs[1] / 2
    c = coeffs[2]
    d = coeffs[3] / 2
    f = coeffs[4] / 2
    g = coeffs[5]

    den = b**2 - a*c
    if den > 0:
        raise ValueError('coeffs do not represent an ellipse: b^2 - 4ac must'
                    ' be negative!')

    # The location of the ellipse center.
    x0, y0 = (c*d - b*f) / den, (a*f - b*d) / den

    num = 2 * (a*f**2 + c*d**2 + g*b**2 - 2*b*d*f - a*c*g)
    fac = np.sqrt((a - c)**2 + 4*b**2)
    # The semimajor and semiminor axis lengths (these are not sorted).
    ap = np.sqrt(num / den / (fac - a - c))
    bp = np.sqrt(num / den / (-fac - a - c))

    # Sort the semimajor and semiminor axis lengths but keep track of
    # the original relative magnitudes of width and height.
    width_gt_height = True
    if ap < bp:
        width_gt_height = False
        ap, bp = bp, ap

    # The eccentricity.
    r = (bp/ap)**2
    if r > 1:
        r = 1/r
    e = np.sqrt(1 - r)

    # The angle of anticlockwise rotation of the major-axis from x-axis.
```

```
    if b == 0:
        phi = 0 if a < c else np.pi/2
    else:
        phi = np.arctan((2.*b) / (a - c)) / 2
        if a > c:
            phi += np.pi/2
    if not width_gt_height:
        # Ensure that phi is the angle to rotate to the semimajor axis.
        phi += np.pi/2
    phi = phi % np.pi

    return x0, y0, ap, bp, phi

def sample_from_ellipse_even(x0, y0, ap, bp, phi, tmin, tmax, npts):

    npoints = 1000
    delta_theta=2.0*np.pi/npoints
    theta=[0.0]
    delta_s=[0.0]
    integ_delta_s=[0.0]
    integ_delta_s_val=0.0
    for iTheta in range(1,npoints+1):
        delta_s_val=np.sqrt(ap**2*np.sin(iTheta*delta_theta)**2+ \
                    bp**2*np.cos(iTheta*delta_theta)**2)
        theta.append(iTheta*delta_theta)
        delta_s.append(delta_s_val)
        integ_delta_s_val = integ_delta_s_val+delta_s_val*delta_theta
        integ_delta_s.append(integ_delta_s_val)
    integ_delta_s_norm = []
    for iEntry in integ_delta_s:
        integ_delta_s_norm.append(iEntry/integ_delta_s[-1]*2.0*np.pi)

    x=[]
    y=[]
    for k in range(npts):
        t = tmin + (tmax-tmin)*k/npts
        for lookup_index in range(len(integ_delta_s_norm)):
            lower=integ_delta_s_norm[lookup_index]
            upper=integ_delta_s_norm[lookup_index+1]
            if (t >= lower) and (t < upper):
                t2 = theta[lookup_index]
                break
        x.append(x0 + ap*np.cos(t2)*np.cos(phi) - bp*np.sin(t2)*np.sin(phi))
        y.append(y0 + ap*np.cos(t2)*np.sin(phi) + bp*np.sin(t2)*np.cos(phi))

    return x, y

def sample_from_ellipse(x0, y0, ap, bp, phi, tmin, tmax, npts):
```

```
x=np.empty(npts)
y=np.empty(npts)
x_unsorted=np.empty(npts)
y_unsorted=np.empty(npts)
angle=np.empty(npts)

# sample from multivariate normal, then rescale
cov=[[ap,0],[0,bp]]
count=0
while count < npts:
    u, v = np.random.multivariate_normal([0, 0], cov, size = 1).T
    d=np.sqrt(u*u/(ap*ap) + v*v/(bp*bp))
    u=u/d
    v=v/d
    t = np.pi + np.arctan2(-ap*v,-bp*u)
    if t >= tmin and t <= tmax:
        x_unsorted[count] = x0 + np.cos(phi)*u - np.sin(phi)*v
        y_unsorted[count] = y0 + np.sin(phi)*u + np.cos(phi)*v
        angle[count]=t
        count=count+1

# sort the points x, y for a nice rendering with mpl.plot
hash={}
hash = dict(enumerate(angle.flatten(), 0)) # convert array angle to dictionary
idx=0
for w in sorted(hash, key=hash.get):
    x[idx]=x_unsorted[w]
    y[idx]=y_unsorted[w]
    idx=idx+1

return x, y

def get_ellipse_pts(params, npts=100, tmin=0, tmax=2*np.pi, sampling='Standard'):

    # Return npts points on the ellipse described by the params = x0, y0, ap,
    # bp, e, phi for values of the parametric variable t between tmin and tmax.

    x0, y0, ap, bp, phi = params

    if sampling=='Standard':
        t = np.linspace(tmin, tmax, npts)
        x = x0 + ap * np.cos(t) * np.cos(phi) - bp * np.sin(t) * np.sin(phi)
        y = y0 + ap * np.cos(t) * np.sin(phi) + bp * np.sin(t) * np.cos(phi)
    elif sampling=='Enhanced':
        x, y = sample_from_ellipse(x0, y0, ap, bp, phi, tmin, tmax, npts)
    elif sampling=='Even':
        x, y = sample_from_ellipse_even(x0, y0, ap, bp, phi, tmin, tmax, npts)
```

```
    return x, y

def vgplot(x, y, color, alpha, npts, tmin, tmax):

    plt.plot(x, y, linewidth=0.2, color=color,alpha=alpha) # plot exact ellipse
    # fill gap (missing segment in the ellipse plot) if plotting full ellipse
    if tmax-tmin > 2*np.pi - 0.01:
       gap_x=[x[npts-1],x[0]]
       gap_y=[y[npts-1],y[0]]
       plt.plot(gap_x, gap_y, linewidth=0.2, color=color,alpha=alpha)
    return()

def main(npts, noise, seed, tmin, tmax, params, sampling):

    # params = x0, y0, ap, bp, phi (input params for ellipse)

    # Get points x, y on the exact ellipse and plot them
    x, y = get_ellipse_pts(params, npts, tmin, tmax, sampling)
    if frame == nframes-1 and mode == 'ConfidenceRegion':
       vgplot(x, y,'black', 1, npts, tmin, tmax)

    # perturb x, y on the ellipse with some noise, to produce a training set
    np.random.seed(seed)
    if noise_CDF=='Normal':
      cov = [[1,0],[0,1]]
      u, v = np.random.multivariate_normal([0, 0], cov, size = npts).T
      x += noise * u
      y += noise * v
    elif noise_CDF=='Uniform':
      x += noise * np.random.uniform(-1,1,size=npts)
      y += noise * np.random.uniform(-1,1,size=npts)

    # get and print exact and estimated ellipse params
    coeffs = fit_ellipse(x, y) # get quadratic form coeffs
    print('True ellipse : x0, y0, ap, bp, phi = %+.5f %+.5f %+.5f %+.5f %+.5f' % params)
    fitted_params = cart_to_pol(coeffs) # convert quadratic coeffs to params
    print('Estimated values: x0, y0, ap, bp, phi = %+.5f %+.5f %+.5f %+.5f %+.5f' %
          fitted_params)
    print()

    # plot training set points in red
    if mode == 'ConfidenceRegion':
      alpha=0.1 # color transparency for Confidence Regions
    elif mode == 'CurveFitting':
      alpha=1
    plt.scatter(x, y,s=0.5,color='red',alpha=alpha)
```

```
# get points on the fitted ellipse and plot them
x, y = get_ellipse_pts(fitted_params,npts, tmin, tmax, sampling)
vgplot(x, y,'blue', alpha, npts, tmin, tmax)

# save plots in a picture [filename is image]
plt.savefig(image, bbox_inches='tight',dpi=dpi)
if ShowImage:
   plt.show()
elif mode=='CurveFitting':
   plt.close() # so, each video frame contains one curve only
return()

#--- Main Part: Initializations

noise_CDF='Normal' # options: 'Normal' or 'Uniform'
sampling='Enhanced' # options: 'Enhanced', 'Standard', 'Even'
mode='ConfidenceRegion' # options: 'ConfidenceRegion' or 'CurveFitting'
npts = 25          # number of points in training set

ShowImage = False # set to False for video production
dpi=100  # image resolution in dpi (100 for gif / 300 for video)
flist=[] # list of image filenames for the video
gif=[]   # used to produce the gif image
nframes=50 # number of frames in video

# initialize plotting parameters
plt.rcParams['axes.linewidth'] = 0.5
plt.rc('axes',edgecolor='black') # border color
plt.rc('xtick', labelsize=6) # font size, x axis
plt.rc('ytick', labelsize=6) # font size, y axis

#--- Main part: Main loop

for frame in range(0,nframes):

   # Global variables: dpi, frame, image
   image='ellipse'+str(frame)+'.png' # filename of image in current frame
   print("Creating image",image) # show progress on the screen

   # params = (x0, y0, ap, bp, phi) : first two coeffs is center of ellipse, last one
   # is rotation angle, the two in the middle are the semimajor and semiminor axes

   if mode=='ConfidenceRegion':
      seed=frame  # new set of random numbers for each image
      noise=0.8   # amount of noise added to to training set
      # 0 <= tmin < tmax <= 2 pi
      tmin=0      # training set: ellipse arc starts at tmin
      tmax = 2*np.pi # training set: ellipse arc ends at tmax
```

```
    params = 3, -2.5, 7, 4, np.pi/4 # ellipse parameters
elif mode=='CurveFitting':
    seed = 100      # same seed (random number generator) for all images
    p=frame/(nframes-1) # assumes nframes > 1
    noise=3*(1-p)*(1-p) # amount of noise added to the training set
    # 0 <= tmin < tmax <= 2 pi
    tmin= (1-p)*np.pi # training set: ellipse arc starts at tmin
    tmax= 2*np.pi   # training set: ellipse arc ends at tmax
    params = 4, -3.5, 7, 1+6*(1-p), 2*(p+np.pi/3) # ellipse parameters

# call to main function
main(npts, noise, seed, tmin, tmax, params, sampling)

# processing images for video and animated gif production (using pillow library)
im = Image.open(image)
if frame==0:
  width, height = im.size # determines the size of all future images
  width=2*int(width/2)
  height=2*int(height/2)
  fixedSize=(width,height) # even number of pixels for video production
im = im.resize(fixedSize) # all images must have same size to produce video
gif.append(im)   # to produce Gif image [uses lots of memory if dpi > 100]
im.save(image,"PNG") # save resized image for video production
flist.append(image)

# output video / fps is number of frames per second
clip = moviepy.video.io.ImageSequenceClip.ImageSequenceClip(flist, fps=20)
clip.write_videofile('ellipseFitting.mp4')

# output video as gif file
gif[0].save('ellipseFitting.gif',save_all=True, append_images=gif[1:],loop=0)
```

1.3.3 Nonperiodic sum of periodic time series: ocean tides

In this section I consider the problem of fitting a **nonperiodic trigonometric series** via least squares. One well-known example is the Dirichlet eta function with an infinite number of superimposed periods. Its modulus is pictured in Fig. 1.3. Practical applications are also numerous. A good exercise is to download ocean tide data, and use the methodology described in this section to predict low and high tides, at various locations: the tides are influenced mostly by two factors – gravitation from the moon and from the sun – each with its own period. But the combination is not periodic. The fitting technique allows you to quantify the effect of each hidden component (the sun and the moon in this case) and retrieve their respective periods. The tide data is available for free, here.

With my notation, the problem is defined by $w = (y, x)$ and

$$g(y, x; \theta) = y - \left[\theta_1 \cos(\theta_2 x + \theta_3) + \theta_4 \cos(\theta_5 x + \theta_6)\right]. \tag{1.7}$$

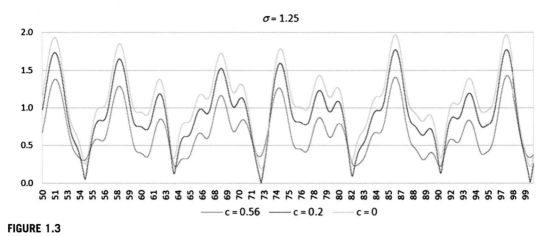

FIGURE 1.3

Three nonperiodic time series made of periodic terms (see Section 17.2.2.1).

There is no constraint on θ, and thus no η function and no λ in (1.2). Here y is the response, and x represents the time. For this reason, I also use the notation $y = f_\theta(x)$, equivalent to $g(y, x; \theta) = 0$. This type of problem is called **curve fitting** [Wiki] in scientific computing. There are libraries to solve it: in Python, one can use the optimize.curve_fit function from the Scipy library. For more details, see the Python documentation.

Finally, if you are only interested in predicting y given x, but not in estimating the parameter vector θ, then the following interpolation formula is sometimes useful:

$$y = f(x) \approx \frac{\sin \pi x}{\pi} \cdot \left[\frac{f(0)}{x} + 2x \sum_{k=1}^{n} (-1)^k \frac{f(k)}{x^2 - k^2} \right]. \tag{1.8}$$

I used it in Exercise 17.9 in Chapter 17 about the Riemann Hypothesis, to get a good approximation of $y = f_\theta(x)$ when y is known (that is, observed) at integer increments $x = 0, 1$, and so on, even though θ is not known. I applied it to a function $f_\theta(x)$ closely related to those pictured in Fig. 1.3. The function in question (namely, the real part of the Dirichlet eta function) can be expressed as an infinite sum of cosine terms with different amplitudes and different periods. Thus, in this case, the dimension of the unobserved θ is infinite, and θ remains an hidden parameter in the prediction experiment, hidden to the experimenter (as in a blind test). Its components are the various period and amplitude coefficients. The approximation formula (1.8) works under certain conditions: see Exercise 17.9 for details.

1.3.3.1 *Numerical instability and how to fix it*

Consider the simpler case where $\theta_3 = \theta_6 = 0$: let us drop these two coefficients from the model. Even then, the problem is **ill-conditioned** [Wiki]. In particular, if $\theta^* = (\theta_1^*, \theta_2^*, \theta_4^*, \theta_5^*)$ is an optimum solution, so is $(\theta_4^*, \theta_5^*, \theta_1^*, \theta_2^*)$. At the very least, without loss of generality, you need to add the constraint $|\theta_1| \geq |\theta_4|$.

In Python, I used the curve_fitting function from Scipy. It does a poor job for this problem, even if you specify bounds for the coefficients $\theta_1, \theta_2, \theta_4, \theta_5$ and start the algorithm with a vector θ close to an optimum θ^*. My test involved

- Finding an optimum θ if the fitting function is $y = f_\theta(x) = \theta_1 \cos \theta_2 x + \theta_4 \cos \theta_5 x$,
- Using a synthetic training set where $y = a_1 \cos a_2 x + a_4 \cos a_5 x + a_7 \cos a_8 x$.

The gray curve in Fig. 1.4, called the "model", is $y = a_1 \cos a_2 x + a_4 \cos a_5 x$, while the blue one is the fitted curve (not necessarily unique), and the dots represent the observations (training set in red, validation set in orange). The observations points do not lie exactly on the gray curve because I introduced some noise: the third term $a_7 \cos a_8 x$ between the model and the data. Note that the observations are equally spaced with respect to the X-axis, but absolutely not with respect to the Y-axis. It is possible to use a different sampling mechanism to address this issue. The figure was produced with the Python code in Section 1.3.3.2. The values of $a_1, \ldots, a_8$ are prespecified. Evidently, if $a_7 = 0$, then an obvious optimum solution is $\theta_i^* = a_i$ for $i = 1, 2, 4, 5$. It provides a perfect fit. Also, the coefficient a_7 specifies the amount of noise in the data.

Unfortunately, `curve_fitting` fails or performs very poorly in most cases. Fig. 1.4 shows one of the relatively rare cases where it works well in the presence of noise. This Python function is still very useful in many contexts, but not in our example. The default setting (`method='lm'`, to be avoided) uses a supposedly robust version of the Levenberg–Marquardt algorithm, dating back to 1977, see here. Essentially, it gets stuck in local minima or fails to converge, and may even reject a manually chosen initial condition close to an optimum as "not feasible". Surprisingly, increasing the amount of noise in the data can provide improvements.

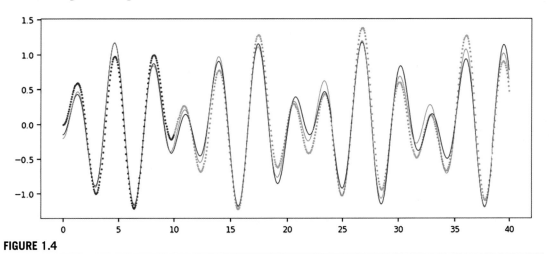

FIGURE 1.4

Training set (red), validation set (orange), fitted curve (blue), and model (gray).

To fix the numerical instability problem, one can use a more modern technique, such as **swarm optimization** [Wiki]. The `PySwarms` library documented here is the Python solution. For a tutorial, see here. A simpler home-made solution taking advantage of the fact that the fitting curve $f_\theta(x)$ (called regression function by statisticians) is linear both in θ_1 and θ_4, consists in splitting the problem as follows:

- Step 1: Sample (θ_2, θ_5) over a region large enough to encompass the optimum values.
- Step 2: Given θ_2, θ_5, find θ_1, θ_4 that minimizes $E(\theta) = \sum_{k=1}^{n} g^2(Y_k, X_k; \theta)$.

Here (Y_k, X_k) is the kth observation in the training set, and $\theta = (\theta_1, \theta_2, \theta_4, \theta_5)$. Both steps are straightforward. You repeat them until you reach a point where the minimum $E(\theta)$ computed over the past iterations almost never decreases anymore. Step 2 is just a simple standard two-dimensional linear regression with no intercept, with an exact solution. One of the benefits is that if there are multiple minima, you are bound to find them all, without facing convergence issues. It also reduces a 4D Monte Carlo simulation to a 2D one.

1.3.3.2 *Python code*

Despite the issues previously described, I decided to include the Python code. It shows how the `curve_fitting` function works, beyond using the default settings. It is still a good optimization technique for many problems such as polynomial regression. Unfortunately, not for our problem. If you decrease the amount of noise from `a7=0.2` to `a7=0.1` in the code below, there is a dramatic drop in performance. Likewise, if you change the initial θ_5 (the last component in θ_start) from 1.8 to 1.7, the performance collapses. The exact value in this example is $\theta_5 = 2$ by construction; the estimated (final) value produced by the Python code is about 1.995.

Table 1.2 First and last step of `curve_fitting`, approaching the model.

	θ_1	θ_2	θ_4	θ_5
Start	0.00000	1.00000	0.00000	1.80000
End	0.52939	1.42184	−0.67571	1.99526
Model	0.50000	1.41421	−0.70000	2.00000

Table 1.2 shows the quality of the estimation, for the parameter vector $\theta = (\theta_1, \theta_2, \theta_4, \theta_5)$. The procedure `curve_fitting` starts with an initial guess θ_start labeled "Start" in the table, and ends with the entry marked as "End" in the table: supposedly, close to an optimum θ^*. Because of the way the synthetic data is generated (within the Python code), the row marked "Model" and consisting of the value a_1, a_2, a_4, a_5 is always close to an optimum θ^*, unless the amount of noise introduced in the training set is too large. The "End" solution (the output of `curve_fitting`) is based exclusively on the training set points (the red dots in Fig. 1.4), not on the validation set (the orange dots). Yet the approximation is unusually good, given the amount of noise.

By noise, I do not mean a random or Gaussian noise. Here the noise is deterministic: the purpose of this test is to check how well we can predict a phenomena modeled by a superimposition of multiple cosine terms of arbitrary periods, phases, and amplitudes – for instance, ocean tides over time – if we only use a sum of two cosine terms as an approximation. This model (its generalization with more terms) is particular useful in situations where the error is not a **white noise** [Wiki], but instead smooth and continuous everywhere: for instance, in granular temperature forecast.

The curve fitting code, also producing Fig. 1.4, is on my GitHub repository, here, under the name `fittingCurve.py`, and also listed below. I use Greek letters in the code to represent the θ vector and its components, for consistency reasons. Python digests them with no problem.

```
import numpy as np
import matplotlib as mpl
from scipy.optimize import curve_fit
from matplotlib import pyplot, rc
```

```
# initializations, define functions

def fpred(x, θ1, θ2, θ4, θ5):
  y = θ1*np.cos(θ2*x)+ θ4*np.cos(θ5*x)
  return y

def fobs(x, a1, a2, a4, a5, a7, a8):
  y = a1*np.cos(a2*xobs)+a4*np.cos(a5*xobs)+a7*np.cos(a8*xobs)
  return y


n=800
n_training=200 # first n_training points is training set
x=[]
y_obs=[]
y_pred=[]
y_exact=[]

# create data set (observations)

a1=0.5
a2=np.sqrt(2)
a4=-0.7
a5=2
a7=0.2 # noise (e=0 means no noise)
a8=np.log(2)

for k in range(n):
  xobs=k/20.0
  x.append(xobs)
  y_obs.append(fobs(xobs, a1, a2, a4, a5, a7, a8))

# curve fitting between f and data, on training set

θ_bounds=((-2.0, -2.5, -1.0, -2.5),(2.0, 2.5, 1.0, 2.5))
θ_start=(0.0, 1.0, 0.0, 1.8)
popt, _ = curve_fit(fpred, x[0:n_training], y_obs[0:n_training],\
    method='trf',bounds=θ_bounds,p0=θ_start)
θ1, θ2, θ4, θ5 = popt
print('Estimates : θ1=%.5f θ2=%.5f θ4=%.5f θ5=%.5f' % (θ1, θ2, θ4, θ5))
print('True values: θ1=%.5f θ2=%.5f θ4=%.5f θ5=%.5f' % (a1, a2, a4, a5))
print('Initial val: θ1=%.5f θ2=%.5f θ4=%.5f θ5=%.5f' % \
   (θ_start[0], θ_start[1], θ_start[2], θ_start[3]))

# predictions

for k in range(n):
  xobs=x[k]
```

```
y_pred.append(fpred(xobs, θ1, θ2, θ4, θ5))
y_exact.append(fpred(xobs, a1, a2, a4, a5))

# show plot

mpl.rcParams['axes.linewidth'] = 0.5
rc('axes',edgecolor='black') # border color
rc('xtick', labelsize=6) # font size, x axis
rc('ytick', labelsize=6) # font size, y axis
pyplot.scatter(x[0:n_training],y_obs[0:n_training],s=0.5,color='red')
pyplot.scatter(x[n_training:n],y_obs[n_training:n],s=0.5,color='orange')
pyplot.plot(x, y_pred, color='blue',linewidth=0.5)
pyplot.plot(x, y_exact, color='gray',linewidth=0.5)
pyplot.show()
```

1.3.4 Fitting a line in 3D, unsupervised clustering, and other generalizations

In three dimensions, a line is the intersection of two planes A and B, respectively with equations $g_1(w, \theta_A) = 0$ and $g_1(w, \theta_B) = 0$. For instance, $g_1(w, \theta_A) = \theta_0 w_0 + \theta_1 w_1 + \theta_2 w_2 - \theta_3$. To fit the line,

- let $\theta_A = (\theta_0, \theta_1, \theta_2, \theta_3)^T$ and $\theta_B = (\theta_4, \theta_5, \theta_6, \theta_7)^T$,
- use $\theta = (\theta_A, \theta_B)$ and $g(w, \theta) = g_1^2(w, \theta_A) + g_1^2(w, \theta_B)$ in formula (1.1),
- use the constraints $\theta_A^T \theta_A + \theta_B^T \theta_B = 1$, or two constraints: $\theta_A^T \theta_A = 1$ and $\theta_B^T \theta_B = 1$.

With two constraints, we have two Lagrange multipliers λ_A and λ_B in formula (1.2).

Likewise, if the data points are either in plane A or plane B and you want to find these planes based on unlabeled training set observations, proceed exactly as for fitting a line in 3D (the previous paragraph), but this time use $g(w, \theta) = g_1(w, \theta_A)g_1(w, \theta_B)$ instead. By "unlabeled", I mean that you do not know which plane a training set point is assigned to. This is actually an unsupervised clustering problem. The training set points (called cloud) do not have to reside in two separate flat planes: the cloud consists of two subclouds A and B, possibly overlapping, each with its own thickness.

This generalizes in various ways: replacing planes by ellipsoids, working in higher dimensions, or with multiple subclouds A, B, C, and so on. One interesting example is as follows. Training set points are distributed in two clusters A and B, and you want to find the centers of these clusters. Typically, one uses a **mixture** [Wiki] to model this situation. In our model-free framework, with the convention that w is a row vector and θ_A, θ_B are column vectors, the problem is stated as

$$g(w, \theta) = ||w^T - \theta_A||^{p/2} \cdot ||w^T - \theta_B||^{p/2} \tag{1.9}$$

where w, θ_A, θ_B have same dimensions, and there is no constraint on $\theta = (\theta_A, \theta_B)$. Here, $p > 0$ is an hyperparameter [Wiki]. If you use an iterative algorithm to find an optimum solution $\theta^* = (\theta_A^*, \theta_B^*)$, that is, the two centers θ_A^*, θ_B^*, it makes sense to start with $\theta_A = \theta_B$ being the centroid of the whole cloud. The solution may not be unique. Obviously, the problem is symmetric in θ_A and θ_B, but there may be more subtle types of non-uniqueness.

A more general formulation, not discussed here, is to replace $w^T - \theta_A$ and $w^T - \theta_B$, respectively, by $\Lambda(w^T - \theta_A)$ and $\Lambda(w^T - \theta_B)$, where Λ is a square invertible matrix, considered and treated as

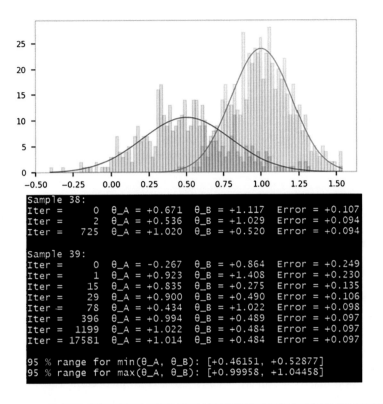

```
Sample 38:
Iter =       0   θ_A = +0.671   θ_B = +1.117   Error = +0.107
Iter =       2   θ_A = +0.536   θ_B = +1.029   Error = +0.094
Iter =     725   θ_A = +1.020   θ_B = +0.520   Error = +0.094

Sample 39:
Iter =       0   θ_A = -0.267   θ_B = +0.864   Error = +0.249
Iter =       1   θ_A = +0.923   θ_B = +1.408   Error = +0.230
Iter =      15   θ_A = +0.835   θ_B = +0.275   Error = +0.135
Iter =      29   θ_A = +0.900   θ_B = +0.490   Error = +0.106
Iter =      78   θ_A = +0.434   θ_B = +1.022   Error = +0.098
Iter =     396   θ_A = +0.994   θ_B = +0.489   Error = +0.097
Iter =    1199   θ_A = +1.022   θ_B = +0.484   Error = +0.097
Iter = 17581   θ_A = +1.014   θ_B = +0.484   Error = +0.097

95 % range for min(θ_A, θ_B): [+0.46151, +0.52877]
95 % range for max(θ_A, θ_B): [+0.99958, +1.04458]
```

FIGURE 1.5

Finding the two centers θ_A^*, θ_B^* in sample 39; $n = 1000$.

an extra parameter, part of the general parameter $\theta = (\theta_A, \theta_B, \Lambda)$. As a preprocessing step, one can normalize the data, so that its center is the origin and its covariance matrix – after a suitable rotation – is diagonal. My method preserves the norm $|| \cdot ||$, under such transformations.

1.3.4.1 *Example: confidence region for the cluster centers*

I tested model (1.9) in one dimension with $n = 1000$ observations, $p = 1$, and synthetic data generated as a mixture of two normal distributions. The purpose was to identify the cluster centers. The results are pictured in Fig. 1.5. The centers are correctly identified, despite the huge overlap between the two clusters (the purple area in the histogram; dark gray in print version). The histogram shows the point distribution in cluster A (blue; mid gray in print version) and B (red; light gray in print version), here for the test labeled "Sample 39" in the screenshot.

I computed confidence intervals for the centers, using **parametric bootstrap** [Wiki]. The theoretical values for the center locations are 0.50 and 1.00. The 95% confidence intervals are [0.46, 0.53] and [1.00, 1.04]. The small bias is due to the uneven point counts and variances in the generated clusters: 400 points and $\sigma = 0.3$ in A, versus 600 points and $\sigma = 0.2$ in B.

The bias visible in Fig. 1.6 could be exacerbated by the **Mersenne twister** pseudorandom number generator [Wiki] used in `numpy.random`, especially in extensive simulations such as this one: see

Chapter 11. In this experiment, the twister was called 800 million times. Then, I used the most extreme estimates based on 40 tests, to get the upper and lower bounds of the confidence intervals. This could have contributed to the bias as well, as it is not the most robust approach: running 400 tests and building the confidence intervals based on test percentiles is more robust. But it requires 10 times more computations.

Out of curiosity, I decided to plot the confidence region [Wiki] for (θ_A^*, θ_B^*), this time using 5000 tests, based on one trillion pseudorandom numbers: 5000 tests $\times$ 1000 points per test $\times$ 100,000 iterations per test $\times$ 2 coordinates. It took about two hours of computing time on my laptop. The result is displayed in Fig. 1.6. Not surprisingly, the confidence region is elliptic: see Section 18.3.6 for the explanation.

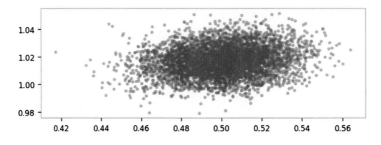

FIGURE 1.6

Biased confidence region for (θ_A^*, θ_B^*); same example as in Fig. 1.5; true value is $(0.5, 1.0)$.

The implementation details are in the short Python code in Section 1.3.4.4. This unsupervised center-searching algorithm is told that there are two clusters, but it does not know what proportion of points belong to A or B, or the variances attached to each distribution, or which one is labeled A or B. If the number of clusters is not specified, try different values. In Section 18.6, I describe a blackbox solution to find the optimum number of clusters.

1.3.4.2 *Exact solution and caveats*

Let W_k be the kth observation ($k = 1, \ldots, n$) stored as a row vector, W the data set (a matrix with n rows), and $\theta = (\theta_A, \theta_B)$ where θ_A, θ_B are column vectors, each with the same dimension as W_k. Then, according to (1.1), any optimum solution satisfies

$$(\theta_A^*, \theta_B^*) = \arg\min_{\theta} \sum_{k=1}^{n} g^2(W_k, \theta) = \arg\min_{\theta_A, \theta_B} \sum_{k=1}^{n} ||W_k^T - \theta_A||^p \cdot ||W_k^T - \theta_B||^p. \tag{1.10}$$

As usual, the **mean squared error** (MSE) is the sum in (1.10) computed at $\theta^* = (\theta_A^*, \theta_B^*)$, and divided by n. It follows immediately that if h is a distance-preserving mapping (rotation, symmetry, or translation) and θ^* is an optimum solution for the data set W, then $h(\theta^*)$ is optimum for $h(W)$, since MSE is invariant under such transformations. Thus, without loss of generality, one can assume that the data set W is centered at the origin.

You can choose a different p for each cluster – say, p_A, p_B – or a weighted sum as in formula (1.5). If $p = 2$ and there is only one cluster (thus no θ_B), then θ_A^* is the centroid of the point cloud (the W_k's). Now let the clusters be well separated to the point that each observation W_k coincides either with the center of A, or the center of B. Then there is only one unique optimum: θ_A^* is the centroid of one cluster, θ_B^* is the centroid of the other cluster, and the MSE is zero.

If there are three clusters, formula (1.10) becomes

$$(\theta_A^*, \theta_B^*, \theta_C^*) = \underset{\theta_A, \theta_B, \theta_C}{\arg\min} \sum_{k=1}^{n} ||W_k^T - \theta_A||^p \cdot ||W_k^T - \theta_B||^p \cdot ||W_k^T - \theta_C||^p. \tag{1.11}$$

If $p > 0$ is an even integer (or both p_A, p_B are even integers), then finding the optimum in (1.10) or (1.11) consists in solving a system of multivariate polynomials, where the unknowns are the components of θ_A and θ_B. The more clusters, the higher the degrees of the polynomials. In particular, in one dimension with $p = p_A = p_B = 2$, if the data set (the point cloud W) is centered at the origin, then the optimum (θ_A^*, θ_B^*) satisfies

$$\theta_A^* \theta_B^* = -\sigma_W^2, \quad \theta_A^* + \theta_B^* = \frac{1}{n\sigma_W^2} \sum_{k=1}^{n} W_k^3, \quad \text{with } \sigma_W^2 = \frac{1}{n} \sum_{k=1}^{n} W_k^2. \tag{1.12}$$

Formula (1.12) can easily be generalized to any dimension. It is obtained by vanishing the gradient to find the minimum in (1.10). Unfortunately, no exact formula exists for $p = 1$. However, in one dimension for $p = 1$, we have

$$|W_k - \theta_A| \cdot |W_k - \theta_B| = \frac{1}{2} \cdot |(W_k - \theta_A)^2 + (W_k - \theta_B)^2 - (\theta_A - \theta_B)^2|.$$

Based on the few tests done so far in one dimension, in general $p = 1$ works better than $p = 2$. If the two clusters are moderately unbalanced as in Fig. 1.5, then $p = 1$ still does well. However, if they are strongly unbalanced as in Fig. 1.7, the method fails. It is still fixable, by choosing two different p's, denoted as p_A and p_B. Then the optimum corresponds to the larger p attached to the smaller cluster: the blue one (dark gray in print version), in Fig. 1.7. In this case $p_A = 3$, $p_B = 1$ works just as well as $p_A = 1$, $p_B = 1$ does in Fig. 1.5. The blue cluster (dark gray in print version) has 1500 points in Fig. 1.7, the red one (mid gray in print version) 8500. The two centers are 0.5 and 1.0, and the standard deviations are 0.1 and 0.2, respectively, for the small and large cluster.

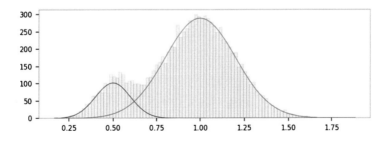

FIGURE 1.7

Challenging mixture, requiring $p_A = 3$, $p_B = 1$ to identify the two cluster centers.

It is a good practice to try $(1, 1)$, $(2, 1)$, and $(3, 1)$ for (p_A, p_B), to see which one provides the best fit as illustrated in Section 1.3.4.3. This is particularly useful in blackbox systems, when automatically processing thousands of data sets without a human being ever looking at any of them. Because the "best" solution – from a visual point of view – is sometimes a local rather than a global minimum, I recommend to list all the local minima found during the search for an optimum (θ_A^*, θ_B^*).

Of course, there is a limit to this methodology, as well as to any other classifiers or mode-searching algorithms: if the mixture has just one mode, it is impossible to find two distinct meaningful centers, no matter what method you use. This happens when the cluster centers are truly distinct, but the variances are huge, or if one cluster contains very few points. Another example is when the clusters have irregular, nonconvex shapes, with multiple centers and holes. In the latter case, the methodology is still useful to find the local modes.

1.3.4.3 *Comparison with K-means clustering*

I included the **K-means clustering** method [Wiki] in the Python code in Section 1.3.4.4. Here I compare Kmeans with my method, on two data sets, each with $n = 1000$ points and two overlapping clusters. The theoretical cluster centers based on the underlying mixture model are 0.5 and 1.0 respectively. The data sets are pictured in Figs. 1.5 and 1.7.

On challenging data with significant cluster overlapping, my method frequently outperforms Kmeans. However, on very skewed data, you need two exponents p_A, p_B in formula (1.10), rather than just p to get the best performance. When using $(p_A, p_B) = (3, 1)$, my method is denoted as (3, 1). Likewise, with $(p_A, p_B) = (1, 1)$ or $(p_A, p_B) = (2, 1)$, my method is denoted respectively as (1, 1) and (2, 1). Intuitively, model (3, 1) – compared to the default version (1, 1) – allows you to reduce the influence of a highly dominant cluster A, by penalizing its contribution to MSE, with a small p_A. Due to the symmetry of the problem, models (3, 1) and (1, 3) yield the same optimum centers with labels swapped, and the same MSE at the optimum. The reference model with one single cluster coinciding with the centroid of the whole data set, is called the "base" model. An alternative is to use the **medoid** [Wiki] rather than the centroid in the base model.

The remaining of this section, besides model comparison, focuses on automatically detecting whether the default model (1, 1) is good enough for a specific data set, or whether you should use the cluster centers generated by (2, 1) or (3, 1) instead. The decision is based on the MSE defined at the beginning of Section 1.3.4.2. However, comparing MSE(1, 1) and MSE(1, 3) even for the same θ and on the same data set is meaningless. This is the challenge that we face.

To solve this problem, I start by computing MSE(1, 1) and MSE(3, 1) for all methods and both data sets. I skipped MSE(2, 1) as it yields similar solutions to MSE(3, 1). The results are summarized in Table 1.3 for the first data set, and Table 1.4 for the second data set. The vector $\theta^*(1, 1) = (\theta_A^*(1, 1), \theta_B^*(1, 1))$ contains the two optimum centers according to model (1, 1), given a data set. The same notation $\theta^*(3, 1)$ is used for model (3, 1).

Table 1.3 MSE for different methods and θs, same data set as in Fig. 1.5.

Model	θ_A	θ_B	MSE(1, 1)	MSE(3, 1)
$\theta^*(1, 1)$	0.53554	1.02221	0.09804	0.02981
$\theta^*(3, 1)$	0.20602	0.94284	0.12986	0.02147
Kmeans	0.42525	1.01235	0.10086	0.03049
Base	0.80392	0.80392	0.11673	0.03661

Table 1.4 MSE for different methods and θs, same data set as in Fig. 1.7.

Model	θ_A	θ_B	MSE(1, 1)	MSE(3, 1)
$\theta^*(1, 1)$	0.72435	1.09296	0.05743	0.01092
$\theta^*(3, 1)$	1.06020	0.52378	0.06871	0.00686
Kmeans	0.65856	1.09833	0.05857	0.01340
Base	0.92682	0.92682	0.06812	0.01156

The red entries (light gray in print version) in Tables 1.3 and 1.4 correspond to an optimum for models (1, 1) and (3, 1). The centers for M(1, 1) in the first data set (Table 1.3), and for M(3, 1) in the second data set (Table 1.4), are much closer to the true values 0.5 and 1.0 than those produced by Kmeans. However, to claim that my method is better than Kmeans, you need a mechanism to decide when M(1, 1) or M(3, 1) is the best fit. This is still a work in progress. As a starting point, the following arguments provide empirical rules to decide.

- For the first data set, MSE(1, 1) evaluated at the centroid of the whole data set (the base model) is better (lower) than when evaluated at $\theta^*(3, 1)$, suggesting that $\theta^*(3, 1)$ is not a great solution here. Thus the default model (1, 1) should be preferred to (3, 1) in this case.
- For the second data set, MSE(1, 1) evaluated at the centroid is about the same as when evaluated at $\theta^*(3, 1)$, suggesting that $\theta^*(3, 1)$ is not that bad, at least not as bad as in the previous case. Thus model (3, 1) should not automatically be ruled out in this case. It is also an indicator that this data set is more challenging than the previous one.
- For the second data set, MSE(3, 1) evaluated at $\theta^*(3, 1)$ is better than when evaluated at $\theta^*(1, 1)$. This does not mean anything: of course, MSE(3, 1) is always best at $\theta^*(3, 1)$, by design. However, the ratio of these two MSEs, $\rho = 0.01092/0.00686 \approx 1.59$, is quite high here. To the contrary, for the first data set $\rho \approx 1.39$ is much smaller. Thus model (3, 1) is more justified for the second data set than for the first one.

Note that he computation of MSE(1, 1) or MSE(3, 1) is performed without knowing which cluster a point is assigned to. Indeed, point allocation is discussed nowhere in my method: you find the centers without allocating points to specific clusters. Once the two centers θ_A^*, θ_B^* have been computed, each point W_k is assigned to the closest cluster. Proximity is measured as the distance between the point and the cluster center. Then choose the model – (1, 1) or (3, 1) – minimizing the sum of these distances.

It is my guess that replacing $||W_k - \theta_A||^2$ and $||W_k - \theta_B||^2$ by $||W_k - \theta_A||^{p_A}$ and $||W_k - \theta_B||^{p_B}$ in the Kmeans procedure will yield better results similar to my method. Again, θ_A, θ_B are the two cluster centers, and W_k is the kth observation. Even $p_A = p_B = 1$ could lead to significant improvements in Kmeans in the presence of outliers (for instance, outliers from a large cluster spilling over to a nearby smaller cluster). This approach is somewhat similar to **K-medians clustering** [Wiki]. Using linear rather than power weights may have the same effect.

Conclusions

My method frequently works better than Kmeans to detect the centers when clusters strongly overlap and are unbalanced. However, this assumes that you have a mechanism to choose between models (1, 1), (2, 1), and (3, 1). If you know beforehand that your data is highly skewed as in Fig. 1.7, then model (3, 1) is a good candidate to begin with. When the clusters are well separated and one or two of the distributions are asymmetric, model $(1, 1)$ tends to correctly identify the cluster medians, rather than the standard centers (the mean).

The method is simple and fast: it does not perform point allocation. You can use it to find initial center configurations as first approximations in more complex algorithms, or in the context of "unsupervised" logistic regression to detect the two clusters when there is no independent variable. Exact solutions such as (1.12) are available in any dimension for two and more clusters, for instance, for the $(2, 2)$, $(2, 2, 2)$, and $(4, 2)$ models. Other original clustering algorithms are described in Chapter 5.

Next steps: test on asymmetric synthetic data modeled as a mixture of normal and gamma distributions with unequal cluster sizes and variances, reduce volatility, investigate the model $(1, \frac{1}{3})$ – the sister of $(3, 1)$ – and generalize the method to two or three dimensions and more than two clusters. One of the goals is to identify when my method performs better than Kmeans, to learn more about Kmeans and further improve it.

1.3.4.4 *Python code*

The Python code `mixture1D.py` for the one-dimensional case in Section 1.3.4.1 is also on GitHub here. Note that W_A, W_B, and W are vectors, respectively with n_A, n_B, and n elements. The vector operations (multiplications and so on) are implicitly performed component-wise, without using a loop on the elements. When $p = 2$, `Error` corresponds to the mean squared error. I use color transparency – the parameter `alpha` in the histogram function `plt.hist` – to visualize the overlap between the two components of the Gaussian mixture: see result in left plot, Fig. 1.5.

The optimum θ_A^*, θ_B^* (the cluster centers) are obtained via Monte Carlo simulations, using 100,000 sampled θ_A, θ_B per test. On the screenshot showing convergence to the optimum, you can see that θ_A and θ_B are randomly flipped back and forth within each test. The algorithm senses that there are two distinct centers; however, it cannot tell which one is labeled A or B. After all, this is **unsupervised learning**. To address this issue, when computing the confidence intervals, I use the notation θ_A for the center on the left, and θ_B for the other one. That is, $\theta_A < \theta_B$. Finally, I run 40 tests to determine a 95% confidence interval for the optimum values. Results are displayed in the screenshot in Fig. 1.5. Zoom in for a better view.

```
import numpy as np
import matplotlib.pyplot as plt
from scipy.stats import norm
from sklearn.cluster import KMeans


N_tests = 5 # number of data sets being tested
n_A = 1500 # number of points in cluster A
n_B = 8500 # number of points in cluster B
n = n_A + n_B
Ones = np.ones((n)) # array with 1's
p_A = 3
p_B = 1
np.random.seed(438713)
min_θ_A = 99999999
min_θ_B = 99999999
max_θ_A = -99999999
max_θ_B = -99999999
```

```
CR_x=[] # confidence region for (best_θ_A, best_θ_A), 1st coordinate
CR_y=[] # confidence region for (best_θ_A, best_θ_A), 2nd coordinate

def compute_MSE(θ_A, θ_B, p_A, p_B, W):
    n = W.size
    MSE = (1/n) * np.sum((abs(W - θ_A * Ones)**p_A) * (abs(W - θ_B * Ones)**p_B))
    return MSE


for sample in range(N_tests): # new dataset at each iteration

    # W_A = np.random.normal(0.5, 2, size=n_A)
    # W_B = 1 + np.random.gamma(8, 5, size=n_B)/4
    W_A = np.random.normal(0.5, 0.1, size=n_A)
    W_B = np.random.normal(1.0, 0.2, size=n_B)
    W   = np.concatenate((W_A, W_B))
    min_MSE=99999999
    print('Sample %1d:' %(sample))

    for iter in range(10000):

        θ_A = np.amin(W) + (np.amax(W)-np.amin(W))*np.random.rand()
        θ_B = np.amin(W) + (np.amax(W)-np.amin(W))*np.random.rand()
        MSE = compute_MSE(θ_A, θ_B, p_A, p_B, W) # MSE for my method
        if MSE < min_MSE:
            min_MSE=MSE
            print('Iter = %5d θ_A = %+8.4f θ_B = %+8.4f MSE = %+12.4f' \
                    %(iter,θ_A ,θ_B, MSE))
            best_θ_A = min(θ_A, θ_B)
            best_θ_B = max(θ_A, θ_B)

    if best_θ_A < min_θ_A:
        min_θ_A = best_θ_A
    if best_θ_A > max_θ_A:
        max_θ_A = best_θ_A
    if best_θ_B < min_θ_B:
        min_θ_B = best_θ_B
    if best_θ_B > max_θ_B:
        max_θ_B = best_θ_B
    CR_x.append(best_θ_A)
    CR_y.append(best_θ_B)
    print()

    # get centers and MSE from Kmeans method (for comparison purposes)
    V   = W.copy()
    km = KMeans(n_clusters=2)
    km.fit(V.reshape(-1,1))
    centers_kmeans=km.cluster_centers_
    kmeans_A=min(centers_kmeans[0,0],centers_kmeans[1,0])
```

```
kmeans_B=max(centers_kmeans[0,0],centers_kmeans[1,0])
MSE_kmeans = compute_MSE(centers_kmeans[0,0], centers_kmeans[1,0], p_A, p_B, V)

# get cluster centers, medians, global centroid and compute MSE on those,
# for comparison with my method and with Kmeans
centroid=(1/n)*np.sum(W)
centroid_A=(1/n_A)*np.sum(W_A)
centroid_B=(1/n_B)*np.sum(W_B)
median_A=np.median(W_A)
median_B=np.median(W_B)
MSE_base = compute_MSE(centroid, centroid, p_A, p_B, W) # MSE for base model
MSE_tc1 = compute_MSE(centroid_A, centroid_B, p_A, p_B, W)
MSE_tc2 = compute_MSE(centroid_B, centroid_A, p_A, p_B, W)
MSE_true_centers = min(MSE_tc1,MSE_tc2)
MSE_tm1 = compute_MSE(median_A, median_B, p_A, p_B, W)
MSE_tm2 = compute_MSE(median_B, median_A, p_A, p_B, W)
MSE_true_medians = min(MSE_tm1,MSE_tm2) # MSE for base model

print('True centers θ_A = %+8.4f θ_B = %+8.4f MSE = %+12.4f' \
    %(centroid_A,centroid_B,MSE_true_centers))
print('model (%1d,%1d) θ_A = %+8.4f θ_B = %+8.4f MSE = %+12.4f' \
    %(p_A,p_B,best_θ_A,best_θ_B,min_MSE))
print('Kmeans    θ_A = %+8.4f θ_B = %+8.4f MSE = %+12.4f' \
    %(kmeans_A,kmeans_B,MSE_kmeans))
print('True medians θ_A = %+8.4f θ_B = %+8.4f MSE = %+12.4f' \
    %(median_A,median_B,MSE_true_medians))
print('Base      θ_A = %+8.4f θ_B = %+8.4f MSE = %+12.4f' \
    %(centroid,centroid,MSE_base))
print()

print('95 %% range for min(θ_A, θ_B): [%+8.4f, %8.4f]' %(min_θ_A ,max_θ_A))
print('95 %% range for max(θ_A, θ_B): [%+8.4f, %8.4f]' %(min_θ_B ,max_θ_B))

# initialize plotting parameters
plt.rcParams['axes.linewidth'] = 0.2
plt.rc('axes',edgecolor='black') # border color
plt.rc('xtick', labelsize=7) # font size, x axis
plt.rc('ytick', labelsize=7) # font size, y axis

# plotting histogram and density
bins=np.linspace(min(W), max(W), num=100)
plt.hist(W_A, color = "blue", alpha=0.2, edgecolor='blue',bins=bins)
plt.hist(W_B, color = "red", alpha=0.3, edgecolor='red',bins=bins)
plt.hist(W, color = "green", alpha=0.1, edgecolor='green',bins=bins)
# plt.plot(bins, 8*norm.pdf(bins,0.5,0.3),color='blue',linewidth=0.6)
# plt.plot(bins, 12*norm.pdf(bins,1,0.2),color='red',linewidth=0.6)
plt.show()
```

```
# plotting confidence region
if N_tests > 50:
    plt.scatter(CR_x,CR_y,s=6,alpha=0.3)
    plt.show()
```

1.4 Connection to synthetic data: meteorites, ocean tides

The examples in this chapter are based on simulated data. Simulations are used in synthetic data as follows. Say you have a collection of meteorite images and the goal is to classify them based on their shape, summarized by the ellipse parameters discussed in Section 1.3.2.2. Each type of meteorite corresponds to a specific set of parameter values. For instance, elongated meteorites have a high eccentricity. The eccentricity is determined by the ration of the parameters `ap` and `bp` in the Python code (respectively the length of the semimajor and semiminor axes). To generate elongated meteorites, set a specific range in your simulations for the ratio in question. This generative model technique is referred to as **parametric bootstrap**.

Another approach is to generate a large collection of shapes, by sampling parameter values. Shapes that fit with the elongated type of meteorites constitute an artificial sample (synthetic data) representing this type, and can be added to your training set, creating what is called **augmented data**. In the context of neural networks, this technique is called **GAN**, an abbreviation for **generative adversarial networks**. To assess the quality of the fit, use a metric such as R-squared to measure the distance or similarity between a set of synthetic and a set of real shapes. With GANs, one uses a classifier: if it cannot discriminate between elongated synthetic shapes, and elongated meteorites in the real data, then your synthetic data for the category in question is deemed good. Implementation of GAN in Python is discussed in [1]. Some authors use a utility metric [4] to measure the quality of the fit between synthetic data and the real data that it represents.

In Section 1.3.4.3 dealing with clustering, I used a mixture of non-Gaussian distributions. The classic but less general approach is to use a **Gaussian mixture model** (GMM) and estimate the weights of each component using the **EM algorithm**.

Finally, to generate synthetic time series similar to those described in Section 1.3.3 (a typical example being ocean tides), proceed as for the meteorite problem. After standardization (for instance, trend removal) your real data set may consist of different categories: time series with 2, 3, or more periods, with large or small amplitudes, with high or low frequency (fast or slow oscillations), smooth of chaotic. Each category corresponds to a subset of parameter values in the parameter space. To add synthetic data to a specific category, simulate time series with parameter values in the parameter subset in question or simulate a large number of time series, and assign a category to each of them: the category that most closely matches a particular type of time series in your data set. Create new categories for simulated times series very different from anything you have in your training set. The comparison with real data is made based on the estimated parameter values in the training set, not with the time series themselves. The parameters summarize the time series and allows for easy clustering of time series. Their estimation is discussed in Section 1.3.3. This leads to explainable AI, as opposed to methods where no one can explain why a specific time series is assigned to a specific category.

References

[1] A. Géron, Hands-on Machine Learning with Scikit-Learn, Keras & TensorFlow, third edition, O'Reilly, 2023.

[2] R. Halir, J. Flusser, Numerically stable direct least squares fitting of ellipses, Preprint, pp. 1–8, 1998, [Link].

[3] C. Hill, Learning Scientific Programming with Python, Cambridge University Press, 2016, [Link].

[4] J. Snoke, et al., General and specific utility measures for synthetic data, Journal of the Royal Statistical Society Series A 181 (2018) 663–688, arXiv:1604.06651, [Link].

[5] C. Tofallis, Fitting equations to data with the perfect correlation relationship, Preprint, pp. 1–11, 2015, Hertfordshire Business School Working Paper, [Link].

[6] D. Umbach, K.N. Jones, A few methods for fitting circles to data, IEEE Transactions on Instrumentation and Measurement 52 (6) (2003) 1881–1885, [Link].

[7] D.A. Vaccari, H.K. Wang, Multivariate polynomial regression for identification of chaotic time series, Mathematical and Computer Modelling of Dynamical Systems 13 (4) (2007) 1–19, [Link].

A simple, robust, and efficient ensemble method

2

Application to natural language processing

The method described here illustrates the concept of ensemble methods, applied to a real-life NLP problem: ranking articles published on a website to predict performance of future blog posts yet to be written, and help decide on title and other features to maximize traffic volume and quality, and thus revenue. The method, called hidden decision trees (HDT), implicitly builds a large number of small usable (possibly overlapping) decision trees. Observations that do not fit in any usable node are classified with an alternate method, typically simplified logistic regression.

This hybrid procedure offers the best of both worlds: decision tree combos and regression models. It is intuitive and simple to implement. The code is written in Python, and I also offer a light version in basic Excel. The interactive Excel version is targeted to analysts interested in learning Python or machine learning. HDT fits in the same category as bagging, boosting, stacking, and **AdaBoost**. This chapter encourages you to understand all the details, upgrade the technique if needed, and play with the full code or spreadsheet as if you wrote it yourself. This is in contrast with using blackbox Python functions without understanding their inner workings and limitations. Finally, I discuss how to build model-free confidence intervals for the predicted values.

2.1 Introduction

The technique presented here, called **hidden decision trees**, blends nonstandard, robust versions of **decision trees** and regression. Compared to **adaptive boostingadaptive boosting** [Wiki], it is simpler to implement. I used it in credit card fraud detection while working at Visa, as well as for scoring Internet traffic quality and search keyword scoring and bidding at eBay. It is an **ensemble method** [Wiki], in the sense that it blends multiple techniques to get the best of each one, to make predictions. Here I describe an NLP (natural language processing) case study, namely optimizing website content. The purpose is to predict the performance of articles published in media outlets or blogs, in particular to predict which types of articles do well.

Here the response (that is, what we are trying to predict, also called dependent variable by statisticians) is the traffic volume, measured in page views, unique page views, or number of users who read the article over some time period. Page view counts can be influenced by robots, and "unique page views" is a more robust metric. Also, older articles have accumulated more page views over time, while the most recent ones have yet to build traffic. We need to correct for this bias. Correcting for time is explained in Section 2.3.1. A simple approach is to use articles published within the last two years but that are at least six month old, in the training set. Due to the highly skewed distribution, I use the logarithm of unique page views as the core metric.

Synthetic Data and Generative AI. https://doi.org/10.1016/B978-0-44-321857-6.00006-0

Table 2.1 List of potential features to use in the model.

Feature	Comment
Title keywords	binary
Article category	blog, event, forum
Publisher website or category	
Creation date	year/month
The title contains numbers	yes/no
The title is a question	yes/no
The title contains special characters	yes/no
Length of title	
Size of article	number of words
The article contains pictures	yes/no
Body keywords	binary
Author popularity	
First few words in the body	

The features, also called predictors or independent variables, are:

Each keyword is a binary feature in itself, also called **dummy variable** [Wiki]: it is set to "yes" if the keyword is found (say) in the title, and to "no" otherwise. I used a shortlist of top keywords (by volume) found in all the articles combined. Also, I used a subset, narrowed version of the features in Table 2.1: for instance, title keywords only, and whether the article is a blog or not.

The method takes into account at all potential **key–value pair** combinations, where "key" is a subset of features, and "value" is the vector of corresponding values, for instance, `key=(keyword1,keyword2,category)` and `value=('Python','tutorial','Blog')`. It is important to appropriately bin the features to prevent the number of key–value pairs from exploding, using **optimum binning** [Python]. See a recent article [1] on this topic. Another mechanism described later is also used to keep the key–value table, stored as an hash table or associate array, manageable. Finally, this can easily be implemented in a distributed environment. A key–value pair is also called a **node**, and plays the same role as a node in a decision tree.

2.2 Methodology

You want to predict p, the logarithm of unique page views for an article (over some time period), as a function of keywords found in the title, and whether the article in question is a blog or not. You start by creating a list of all one- and two-token keywords found in all the article titles, with the article category (blog versus nonblog), after cleaning the titles and eliminating some stop word such as "that", "and", or "the". Do not eliminate all keywords made up of one or two letters: the one-letter keyword "R", corresponding to the programming language R, has a high **predictive power**. For each key–value pair, get the number of articles matching it, as well as the average, minimum and maximum p across these articles.

For instance, say the key–value pair (`keyword1='R',keyword2 ='Python',category='Blog'`) has 6 articles and the following statistics: average p is 8.52, minimum is 7.41, and maximum is 10.45. If the average p across all articles in the training set is 6.83, then this specific key–value pair (also called node) generates $\exp(8.52 - 6.83) = 5.42$ times more traffic than an average article. It is thus a large node in terms of traffic.

Even the worst article among the six belonging to this node, with a p of 7.41, outperforms the average 6.83 across all nodes. So not only this is a large node, but a stable one. Some nodes have a higher variance $\text{Var}[p]$, for instance, when one of the keywords has different meanings, such as the word "training" in "training set" and in "courses and training".

2.2.1 How hidden decision trees (HDT) work

The nodes are overlapping, allowing considerable flexibility. In particular, nodes with two keywords are subnodes of nodes with one keyword. The general idea behind this technique is to group articles into buckets that are large enough to provide good predictions, without explicitly building decision trees. The nodes are simple and easy to interpret, and unstable ones (with high variance) can be discarded. There is no splitting/pruning involved as with classical decision trees, making this methodology simple and robust, and thus fit for artificial intelligence and blackbox implementation. The method is called **hidden decision trees** and abbreviated as **HDT** because you do not create decision trees, but you indirectly rely on a large number of small ones that are hidden in the algorithm.

Whether you are dealing with predicting the popularity of an article, or the risk for a client to default on a loan, the basic methodology is identical. It involves training sets, cross-validation, feature selection, binning, and populating hash tables of key–value pairs, referred to as the nodes. When you process a new observation outside the training set, you check which node(s) it belongs to. If the "ideal" nodes it belongs to are stable and not too small, you use a weighted average score computed over these nodes, as predictor. If this score (defined as p here) is significantly above the global average, and other constraints are met, then you classify the observation – in this case a potential article you want to write – as good. An ideal node has strong predictive power: its p is either very high or very low.

Also, you need to update your training set and the nodes table, including automatically discovered new nodes, every six months or so. Parameters must be calibrated to guarantee that the proportion of false positives remains small enough. Ideally, you want to end up with less than 3000 stable nodes, each with at least 10 observations (articles), covering 80% of the articles or more. I discuss the parameters of the technique, and how to fine-tune them, in Section 2.2.3. Fine-tuning can be automated or made more robust by testing (say) 2000 sets of parameters and identify regions of stability minimizing the error rate in the parameter space. Error rate is defined as the proportion of misclassification, and false positives in particular.

A big question is what to do with observations not belonging to any usable node: they cannot be classified. A **usable node** is one with enough articles, with average p within the mode far away from the global mean of p computed across all nodes. One way to address this issue is to use two algorithms: the one described so far, applied to usable or ideal nodes (let us call it algorithm A) and another one called algorithm B that classifies all observations. Observations that cannot be classified or scored with algorithm A are classified/scored with algorithm B. The resulting hybrid algorithm is called Hidden Decision Trees.

2.2.2 **NLP case study: summary and findings**

If you run the Python script listed in Section 2.3.3, besides producing the table of key–value pairs (the nodes) as a text file for further automated processing, it displays summary statistics that look like the following:

```
Average log pageview count (pv): 6.83
Avg pv, articles marked as Good: 8.09
Avg pv, articles marked as Bad : 5.95

Number of articles marked as Good: 223 (real number is 1079)
Number of articles marked as Bad : 368 (real number is 919)
Number of false positives   : 25 (Bad marked as Good)
Number of false negatives   : 123 (Good marked as Bad)
Total number of articles    : 2616

Proportion of False Positives: 11.2%
Proportion of Unclassified   : 77.4%

Aggregation factor (Good node): 29.1
Number of feature values: 16711 (marked as good: 49)

Execution time: 0.0630 seconds
```

In the code, p – the logarithm of the pageview count – is represented by pv. The number of nodes is the total number of key–value pairs found, including the small unstable ones, regardless as to whether they are classified as good, bad, or unclassified. An article with p above the arbitrary pv_thresh-old_good=7.1 (see source code) is considered as good. This corresponds to articles having about 1.3 times more traffic than average, since I use a log-scale and the average p is 6.83. Articles classified as good have an average p of 8.09, that is, about 3.3 times more traffic than average.

Two important metrics are:

- Aggregation factor: it is an indicator of the average size of a useful node, in this case classified as good. A value above 5 is highly desirable.
- The most important error rate is measured here as the number of bad articles wrongly classified as good. The goal is to detect very good articles and find the reasons that make them popular, to be able to increase the proportion of good articles in the future. Avoiding bad articles is the second most important goal, so I am also interested in identifying what makes them bad.

Also note that the method correctly identifies a proportion of the good articles, but leaves many unclassified. I explain in Section 2.3.3 how to improve this. Finally, an article is marked as good if it meets some criteria specified in Section 2.2.3.

Now I share some interesting findings revealed by these hidden decision tress, on the data set investigated in this study. First, articles with the following title features do well: contains a number as in "10 great deep learning articles", contains the current year, is a question (how to), is a blog post or belongs to the book category.

Then the following title keywords are a good predictor of popularity: everyone (as in "10 regression techniques everyone should know"), libraries, infographic, explained, algorithms, languages, amazing, must read, R Python, job interview questions, should know (as in "10 regression techniques everyone should know"), NoSQL databases, versus, decision trees, logistic regression, correlations, tutorials, code, free.

2.2.3 Parameters

Besides `pv_threshold_good` and `pv_threshold_bad`, the algorithm uses 12 parameters to identify a usable, stable node classified as good. You can see them in action in the Python code in Section 2.3.3, in the instruction

```
if n > 3 and n < 8 and Min > 6.9 and Avg > 7.6 or \
    n >= 8 and n < 16 and Min > 6.7 and Avg > 7.4 or \
    n >= 16 and n < 200 and Min > 6.1 and Avg > 7.2:
```

Here, n represents the size (number of observations) of a node, while Avg and Min are the average and minimum pv for the node in question. I tested many combinations of values for these parameters. Increasing the required size to qualify as usable node will do the following:

- Decrease the number of good articles correctly identified as good
- Increase the error rate
- Increase the stability of the system
- Decrease the predictive power
- Increase the aggregation factor

2.2.4 Improving the methodology

Some two-token keywords should be treated as one-token. For instance, "San Francisco" must be treated as a one-token keyword. It is easy to automatically detect this: when you analyze the text data, "San" and "Francisco" are lumped together far more frequently than dictated by pure chance. Also, I looked at nodes where the two keywords are adjacent in the text. If you allow the two keywords not to be adjacent, the number of key–value pairs (the nodes) increases significantly, but you do not get much more additional predictive power in return, and there is a risk of over-fitting.

Another improvement consists of favoring nodes containing articles spread over several years, as opposed to concentrated on a few weeks or months. The latter category may be popular articles at some time, that faded away. Finally, you cannot exclusively focus on articles with great potential. It is important to have many, less popular articles as well: they constitute the long tail. Without these less popular articles, you face excessive content concentration and readership attrition in the long term.

2.3 Implementation details

This section contains the Python code and details about the Excel spreadsheet. Both the decision trees and the regression part of HDT (referred to as "algorithm B" in Section 2.2.1) are implemented in the spreadsheet. The Python version, though more comprehensive in many regards, is limited to the decision trees. But first I start by discussing a possible improvement of the methodology, namely bias correction.

2.3.1 Correcting for bias

In online rankings, the most popular books, authors, articles, restaurants, products, and so on, are usually those that have been around for a long time. Here I address this issue by creating adjusted scores. It allows you to make fair comparisons between new and old items.

For top time-insensitive articles, page views peak in the first three days, but popularity remains high for many years. In short, page view decay is very low over time. Finally, the most popular topics (keywords) change over time; this type of analysis helps find the trends. It is also a good idea to use two different sources of data for pageview measurements, see how they differ, understand why, and check whether the discrepancy worsens over time.

The articles scored here span over a three-year period, covering over 2600 pieces of content totaling 6 million pageviews across three websites. The summary data is on GitHub, here. It features the top 46 articles ranked according to the time-adjusted score. The number in parenthesis attached to each article is the nonadjusted (old) score. The difference between the time-adjusted score and the old one, is striking.

2.3.1.1 *Time-adjusted scores*

You measure the page view count for a specific article, and your time period is $[t_0, t_1]$. Typical models use an **exponential decay** of rate λ. The adjustment factor is then

$$q = \frac{1}{\lambda} \cdot \left[\exp(-\lambda t_0) - \exp(-\lambda t_1) \right] > 0.$$

Now define the adjusted score as p/q, where p is the observed page view count in $[t_0, t_1]$. If $\lambda = 0$ (no decay) then $q = t_1 - t_0$.

2.3.2 Excel spreadsheet

The interactive spreadsheet named `HDTdata4Excel.xlsx` is on my GitHub repository, here. It uses a subset of 9 binary features. The first three are respectively "published after 2014", "article is a forum discussion", and "article is a blog post". The next six are indicators of whether or not the title contains a specific character string. The six strings in question are "python", "r", "machine learning", "data science", "data", and "analy". The last string captures words such as "analytic" or "analyst". These strings must be surrounded by spaces, so "r" clearly represents the R programming language. True/false are encoded as 1 and 0, respectively.

For instance, node `N-001-001110` in Table 2.2 corresponds to blog posts published in 2014, containing the keywords "machine learning", "data science", and "data" in the title, but not "python", "r", or "analy". The column "size" tells us that the node in question has only one article.

Nodes with fewer than 10 articles are classified using the regression method via the `LINEST` Excel function, rather than the mini decision trees. Instead of standard regression, you can use a simplified logistic regression, as described in Section 1.3.1. There are 2616 observations (articles) and 74 nodes in

Table 2.2 Statistics for selected HDT nodes (Excel version).

node	size	pv	index
N-000-000000	8	7.12	1.33
N-000-000001	5	6.87	1.04
N-000-000010	8	6.86	1.02
N-000-000011	3	6.49	0.71
N-000-000110	3	7.18	1.42
N-001-000000	313	6.88	1.05
N-001-000001	75	6.71	0.88
N-001-000010	276	7.14	1.35
N-001-000011	44	7.16	1.38
N-001-000110	130	7.68	2.34
N-001-000111	5	8.05	3.37
N-001-001000	5	8.07	3.45
N-001-001010	1	7.58	2.11
N-001-001110	1	7.35	1.67

the training set. By grouping all nodes with less than 10 observations into one node, we get down to 24 nodes. Correlations between individual features and the response p (logarithm of pageviews, denoted as pv in Table 2.2) is very low. Thus individual features have no predictive power. They must be combined together to gain predictive power. The full HDT method is superior to either the mini decision trees, or the regression model taken separately.

The index in Table 2.2 is the pv of the node in question, divided by the average pv across all nodes. It measures the performance of the node. Finally, an article is classified as good or bad depending on whether its index is significantly larger or lower than one. The thresholds are user-defined. (See Fig. 2.1.)

2.3.3 **Python code and dataset**

The input dataset HDTdata4.txt is on my GitHub repository, here. The Python program HDT.py is listed below and can also be found on my GitHub repository, here. The output file hdt-out2.txt contains the usable key–value pairs (nodes) corresponding to popular articles, and the list of article IDs for each of these nodes. Finally, the variable pv represents p, the logarithm of the pageview count. The bivariate combinations (title keyword, article category) constitute the keys of the hash table list_pv, while the pv are the hash table values. Keywords are either one- or two-token. For one-token keywords, the second token is marked as N/A. In short, keyword is a bivariate entity.

As for the error rate, since the focus is on producing good articles, I am interested only in minimizing the number of bad articles flagged as good: the false positives. To reduce error rates or the proportion of unclassified nodes, use more features (for instance, more of those listed in Table 2.1), three-token keywords, a larger training set, a better keyword cleaning mechanism, and fine-tune the parameters.

	Summary stats for (blue) binary features used in model, when value = 1								
	year > 2014 *	/forum	/blog	_python_	_r_	_machine_	_data_sci_	_data_	_analy
correl with pv	-0.11	-0.18	0.18	0.13	0.05	0.10	0.15	0.13	-0.09
avg pv (if val = 1)	6.71	6.35	6.95	8.23	7.27	7.53	7.33	7.00	6.56
pv index (if val = 1) *	0.88	0.62	1.13	4.04	1.54	2.01	1.65	1.18	0.76
count (val = 1)	1,499	487	2,081	39	65	85	357	1,309	424
percentage obs (val = 1)	57.3%	18.6%	79.5%	1.5%	2.5%	3.2%	13.6%	50.0%	16.2%

* average pv index is 1 (the higher the better; it is proportional to pageviews)

** more recent articles haven't accumulated as many pageviews (thus pv index < 1 for 'year > 2014')

	Cross-correlations table							
	/forum	/blog	_python_	_r_	_machine_	_data_sci_	_data_	_analy
year > 2014	-0.04	0.05	0.08	0.07	0.10	-0.04	-0.02	0.02
/forum		-0.94	0.05	0.02	-0.02	0.01	-0.05	0.05
/blog			-0.04	-0.02	0.03	0.00	0.05	-0.07
python				0.08	0.03	0.03	0.00	-0.02
_r_					0.00	-0.03	-0.08	0.00
_machine_learning_						-0.04	-0.11	-0.06
_data_science_							0.40	-0.12
data								-0.09

FIGURE 2.1

Output from the Excel version of HDT.

Of course, if you choose the option mode='perfect_fit' in the program, your false positive rate drops to 0% on the training set, but doing may lower the performance on the validation set, and may leave many nodes unclassified. On the plus side, you have much fewer parameters to fine-tune: pv_threshold_good, pv_threshold_bad, and the minimum size of a usable node (the variable n in the code). The first two can be set respectively to 5% above and 10% below the global average pv. The minimum node size should be set above 2, and ideally above 5, though a large value results in more unclassified nodes. For mode='robust method', the parameters in the conditional statements defining good_node and bad_node were set manually based on an average pv of 6.83. These choices can be automated.

In the end, unclassified nodes are classified via regression in the spreadsheet (see Section 2.3.2), but this has not yet been implemented in the Python code. But for my purpose (identifying what makes an article good), I did not need to add the regression part, as the mini decision trees alone (the nodes) provide enough valuable insights.

```
from math import log
import time

start = time.time()

# This method updates the dictionaries based on given ID, pv, and word
def update_pvs(word, pv, id, word_count_dict, word_pv_dict, min_pv_dict, max_pv_dict,
    ids_dict):
  if word in word_count_dict:
```

```python
            word_count_dict[word] += 1
            word_pv_dict[word] += pv
            if min_pv_dict[word] > pv:
                min_pv_dict[word] = pv
            if max_pv_dict[word] < pv:
                max_pv_dict[word] = pv
            ids_dict[word].append(id)
        else:
            word_count_dict[word] = 1
            word_pv_dict[word] = pv
            min_pv_dict[word] = pv
            max_pv_dict[word] = pv
            ids_dict[word] = [id]
# dictionaries to hold count of each key words, their page views, and the ids of the article
    in which used
List = dict()
list_pv = dict()
list_pv_max = dict()
list_pv_min = dict()
list_id = dict()
articleTitle = list() # Lists to hold article id wise title name and pv
articlepv = list()
sum_pv = 0
ID = 0
in_file = open("HDTdata4.txt", "r")


for line in in_file:
    if ID == 0: # excluding first line as it is header
        ID += 1
        continue
    line = line.lower()
    aux = line.split('\t') # Indexes will have: 0 - Title, 1 - URL, 2 - data and 3 - page views
    url = aux[1]
    pv = log(1 + int(aux[3]))
    if "/blogs/" in url:
        type = "BLOG"
    else:
        type = "OTHER"
#   #--- clean article titles, remove stop words
    title = aux[0]
    title = " " + title + " " # adding space at the ends to treat stop words at start, mid,
        and end alike
    title = title.replace('"', ' ')
    title = title.replace('?', ' ? ')
    title = title.replace(':', ' ')
    title = title.replace('.', ' ')
    title = title.replace('(', ' ')
    title = title.replace(')', ' ')
```

```
    title = title.replace(',', ' ')
    title = title.replace(' a ', ' ')
    title = title.replace(' the ', ' ')
    title = title.replace(' for ', ' ')
    title = title.replace(' in ', ' ')
    title = title.replace(' and ', ' ')
    title = title.replace(' or ', ' ')
    title = title.replace(' is ', ' ')
    title = title.replace(' in ', ' ')
    title = title.replace(' are ', ' ')
    title = title.replace(' of ', ' ')
    title = title.strip()
    title = ' '.join(title.split()) # replacing multiple spaces with one
    #break down article title into keyword tokens
    aux2 = title.split(' ')
    num_words = len(aux2)
    for index in range(num_words):
        word = aux2[index].strip()
        word = word + '\t' + 'N/A' + '\t' + type
        update_pvs(word, pv, ID - 1, List,list_pv, list_pv_min, list_pv_max, list_id) #
            updating single words

        if (num_words - 1) > index:
            word = aux2[index] + '\t' + aux2[index+1] + '\t' + type
            update_pvs(word, pv, ID - 1, List, list_pv, list_pv_min, list_pv_max, list_id) #
                updating bigrams

    articleTitle.append(title)
    articlepv.append(pv)
    sum_pv += pv
    ID += 1
in_file.close()

nArticles = ID - 1 # -1 as the increments were done post loop
avg_pv = sum_pv/nArticles
articleFlag = ["NA" for n in range(nArticles)]
nidx = 0
nidx_Good = 0
nidx_Bad = 0
pv_threshold_good = 7.1
pv_threshold_bad = 6.2
mode = 'robust method' # options are 'perfect fit' or 'robust method'
OUT = open('hdt-out2.txt','w')
OUT2 = open('hdt-reasons.txt','w')
for idx in List:
    n = List[idx]
    Avg = list_pv[idx]/n
    Min = list_pv_min[idx]
```

```
            Max = list_pv_max[idx]
            idlist = list_id[idx]
            nidx += 1
            if mode == 'perfect fit':
              good_node = n > 2 and Min > pv_threshold_good
              bad_node = n > 2 and Max < pv_threshold_bad
            elif mode == 'robust method':
                # below values are chosen based on heuristics and experimenting
                good_node = n > 3 and n < 8 and Min > 6.9 and Avg > 7.6 or \
                       n >= 8 and n < 16 and Min > 6.7 and Avg > 7.4 or \
                       n >= 16 and n < 200 and Min > 6.1 and Avg > 7.2
                bad_node = n > 3 and n < 8 and Max < 6.3 and Avg < 5.4 or \
                       n >= 8 and n < 16 and Max > 6.6 and Avg < 5.9 or \
                       n >= 16 and n < 200 and Max > 7.2 and Avg < 6.2
            if good_node:
                OUT.write(idx + '\t' + str(n) + '\t' + str(Avg) + '\t' + str(Min) + '\t' + str(Max) +
                     '\t' + str(idlist) + '\n')
                nidx_Good += 1
                for ID in idlist:
                    title=articleTitle[ID]
                    pv = articlepv[ID]
                    OUT2.write(title + '\t' + str(pv) + '\t' + idx + '\t' + str(n) + '\t' + str(Avg) +
                        '\t' + str(Min) + '\t' + str(Max) + '\n')
                    articleFlag[ID] = "GOOD"
            elif bad_node:
                nidx_Bad += 1
                for ID in idlist:
                    articleFlag[ID] = "BAD"
# Computing results based on Threshold values
pv1 = 0
pv2 = 0
n1 = 0
n2 = 0
m1 = 0
m2 = 0
FalsePositive = 0
FalseNegative = 0
for ID in range(nArticles):
    pv = articlepv[ID]
    if articleFlag[ID] == "GOOD":
        n1 += 1
        pv1 += pv
        if pv < pv_threshold_good:
            FalsePositive += 1
    elif articleFlag[ID] == "BAD":
        n2 += 1
        pv2 += pv
        if pv > pv_threshold_bad:
```

```
        FalseNegative += 1
  if pv > pv_threshold_good:
     m1 += 1
  elif pv < pv_threshold_bad:
     m2 += 1
#
# Printing results
avg_pv1 = pv1/n1
avg_pv2 = pv2/n2
errorRate = FalsePositive/n1
UnclassifiedRate = 1 - (n1 + n2) / nArticles
aggregationFactor = (nidx/nidx_Good)/(nArticles/n1)
print ("Average log pageview count (pv):","{0:.2f}".format(avg_pv))
print ("Avg pv, articles marked as Good:","{:.2f}".format(avg_pv1))
print ("Avg pv, articles marked as Bad :","{:.2f}".format(avg_pv2))
print()
print ("Number of articles marked as Good: ", n1, " (real number is ", m1,")", sep = "" )
print ("Number of articles marked as Bad : ", n2, " (real number is ", m2,")", sep = "")
print ("Number of false positives :",FalsePositive,"(Bad marked as Good)")
print ("Number of false negatives :", FalseNegative, "(Good marked as Bad)")
print ("Total number of articles :", nArticles)
print()
print ("Proportion of False Positives: ","{0:.1%}".format(errorRate))
print ("Proportion of Unclassified : ","{0:.1%}".format(UnclassifiedRate))
print()
print ("Aggregation factor (Good node):","{:.1f}".format(aggregationFactor))
print ("Number of feature values: ", nidx," (marked as good: ", nidx_Good,")", sep = "")
print ()
print("Execution time: ","{:.4f}".format(time.time() - start), "seconds")
```

2.4 Model-free confidence intervals and perfect nodes

Node N-100-000000 in the spreadsheet has an average pv of 5.85. It consists of 10 articles with the following pv: 5.10, 5.10, 5.56, 5.56, 5.66, 5.69, 6.01, 6.19, 6.80, 6.80. The 15th and 85th percentiles are 5.26 and 6.68, respectively, when computed with the Percentile function in Excel. Thus, [5.26, 6.68] is a 70% **confidence interval** (CI) for pv, for the node in question.

The whole CI including its upper bound is below the average pv of 6.83. In fact this node corresponds to articles posted after 2014, not a blog or forum question (it could be a video or event announcement), and with a title containing none of the keyword features in the spreadsheet (columns K:P in the data tab). This node has a maximum predictive power, in the sense that 100% of the articles that it contains are bad, and 0% are good. This would also be true if it was the other way around, with Good swapped with Bad. Such a node is called a **perfect node**. When selecting the option mode='Perfect fit' in the Python code, the method looks at perfect nodes only. The concept of **predictive power** is further discussed in Section 18.4.2.

2.4.1 Interesting asymptotic properties of confidence intervals

I focus here on traditional model-free confidence intervals, as computed in the above paragraphs. The reader should be aware that there are other ways to define them, for instance, **credible intervals** in the context of **Bayesian inference** [Wiki], or Bayesian-like **dual confidence intervals** as in Section 18.3.

Table 2.3 Order of magnitude for the expectation and standard deviation of the range R_n.

pv distribution	Type	$E[R_n]$	Stdev$[R_n]$
Uniform	short tail	1	$1/n$
Gaussian	medium tail	$\sqrt{\log n}$	$1/\sqrt{n}$
Exponential	fat tail	$\log n$	1

In almost all cases, as the number n of observations becomes large within a node, the length of the confidence interval, in this case for the expected pv, is asymptotically $L_n \sim \alpha n^\beta$. I discuss in an upcoming paper how to estimate α and β. The order of magnitude of the range $R_n = \max(\text{pv}) - \min(\text{pv})$ computed on a node with n observations, depends on the distribution of pv, and more specifically, on the type of this distribution. The result is summarized in Table 2.3, and discussed in the same upcoming article. In practice, pv may have a **mixture distribution**.

References

[1] G. Navas-Palencia, Optimal binning: mathematical programming formulation, Preprint, pp. 1–21, arXiv:2001. 08025, 2020, [Link].

Gentle introduction to linear algebra – synthetic time series

This simple introduction to matrix theory offers a refreshing perspective on the subject. Using a basic concept that leads to a simple formula for the power of a matrix, I show how it can solve time series, Markov chains, linear regression, linear recurrence equations, pseudoinverse and square root of a matrix, data compression, principal components analysis (PCA) or dimension reduction, and other machine learning problems. These problems are usually solved with more advanced matrix algebra, including eigenvalues, diagonalization, generalized inverse matrices, and other types of matrix normalization. My approach is more intuitive and thus appealing to professionals who do not have a strong mathematical background, or who have forgotten what they learned in math textbooks. It will also appeal to physicists and engineers, and to professionals more familiar or interested in calculus, than in matrix algebra. Finally, it leads to simple algorithms, for instance, for matrix inversion. The classical statistician or data scientist will find my approach somewhat intriguing. The core of the methodology is the characteristic polynomial of a matrix, and in particular, the roots with lowest or largest moduli. It leads to a numerically stable method to solve Vandermonde systems, and thus, many linear algebra problems. Simulations include a curious fractal time series that looks incredibly smooth.

3.1 Power of a matrix

This is not a traditional tutorial on linear algebra. The material presented here, in a compact style, is rarely taught in college classes. It covers a wide range of topics, while avoiding excessive use of jargon or advanced math. The fundamental tool is the power of a matrix, and its byproduct, the characteristic polynomial. It can solve countless problems, as discussed later in this chapter, with illustrations. It has more to do with calculus, than matrix algebra.

For simplicity, in this section, I illustrate the methodology for a 2×2 matrix denoted as A. The generalization is straightforward. I provide a simple formula for the nth power of A, where n is a positive integer. I then extend the formula to $n = -1$ (the most useful case) and to noninteger values of n. Using the notation

$$A = \begin{pmatrix} a & b \\ c & d \end{pmatrix}, \quad \text{with } A^n = \begin{pmatrix} a_n & b_n \\ c_n & d_n \end{pmatrix} = \begin{pmatrix} a & b \\ c & d \end{pmatrix} \cdot \begin{pmatrix} a_{n-1} & b_{n-1} \\ c_{n-1} & d_{n-1} \end{pmatrix},$$

Synthetic Data and Generative AI. https://doi.org/10.1016/B978-0-44-321857-6.00007-2

we obtain

$$\begin{cases} a_n = a \cdot a_{n-1} + b \cdot c_{n-1}, \\ b_n = a \cdot b_{n-1} + b \cdot d_{n-1}, \\ c_n = c \cdot a_{n-1} + d \cdot c_{n-1}, \\ d_n = c \cdot b_{n-1} + d \cdot d_{n-1}. \end{cases}$$

Using elementary substitutions, this leads to the following system:

$$\begin{cases} a_n = (a+d) \cdot a_{n-1} - (ad - bc) \cdot a_{n-2}, \\ b_n = (a+d) \cdot b_{n-1} - (ad - bc) \cdot b_{n-2}, \\ c_n = (a+d) \cdot c_{n-1} - (ad - bc) \cdot c_{n-2}, \\ d_n = (a+d) \cdot d_{n-1} - (ad - bc) \cdot d_{n-2}. \end{cases}$$

We are dealing with identical linear homogeneous recurrence relations. Only the initial conditions corresponding to $n = 0$ and $n = 1$ are different for these four equations. The solution to such equations is obtained as follows [Wiki]. First, solve the quadratic equation

$$x^2 - (a+d)x + (ad - bc) = 0. \tag{3.1}$$

The two solutions r_1, r_2 are

$$r_1 = \frac{1}{2}\left[a + d + \sqrt{(a+d)^2 - 4(ad - bc)}\right],$$
$$r_2 = \frac{1}{2}\left[a + d - \sqrt{(a+d)^2 - 4(ad - bc)}\right].$$

If the quantity under the square root is negative, then the roots are complex numbers. The final solution depends on whether the roots are distinct or not:

$$A^n = \begin{cases} r_1^n Q_1 + r_2^n Q_2 & \text{if } r_1 \neq r_2, \\ r_1^n Q_1 + n r_1^{n-1} Q_2 & \text{if } r_1 = r_2, \end{cases} \tag{3.2}$$

with

$$\begin{cases} Q_1 = (A - r_2 I)/(r_1 - r_2) & \text{if } r_1 \neq r_2, \\ Q_2 = (A - r_1 I)/(r_2 - r_1) & \text{if } r_1 \neq r_2, \\ Q_1 = I & \text{if } r_1 = r_2, \\ Q_2 = A - r_1 I & \text{if } r_1 = r_2. \end{cases} \tag{3.3}$$

Here the symbol I represents the 2×2 identity matrix. The last four relationships were obtained by applying formula (3.2) to A^n, with $n = 0$ and $n = 1$. It is easy to prove (by recursion on n) that (3.2), together with (3.3), is the correct solution. If none of the roots is zero, then the formula is still valid for $n = -1$, and thus it can be used to compute the inverse of A.

3.2 Examples, generalization, and matrix inversion

For a $p \times p$ matrix, the methodology generalizes as follows. The quadratic polynomial becomes a polynomial of degree p, known as the **characteristic polynomial**, and linked to the **Cayley–Hamilton theorem** [Wiki]. If its roots are distinct, we have

$$
A^n = \sum_{k=1}^{p} r_k^n Q_k, \quad \text{with} \quad
\begin{pmatrix} Q_1 \\ Q_2 \\ \vdots \\ Q_p \end{pmatrix}
= V^{-1}
\begin{pmatrix} I \\ A \\ \vdots \\ A^{p-1} \end{pmatrix}
=
\begin{pmatrix}
1 & 1 & \cdots & 1 \\
r_1 & r_2 & \cdots & r_p \\
\vdots & \vdots & \ddots & \vdots \\
r_1^{p-1} & r_2^{p-1} & \cdots & r_p^{p-1}
\end{pmatrix}^{-1}
\begin{pmatrix} I \\ A \\ \vdots \\ A^{p-1} \end{pmatrix}
\tag{3.4}
$$

The matrix V is a **Vandermonde matrix** [Wiki], so there is an explicit formula to compute its inverse, see [Wiki]. For a fast algorithm for the computation of its inverse, see [9]. However, inverting V should be avoided as it is a **numerically unstable** procedure. Instead, approximations methods based on selected roots of the characteristic polynomial – those with highest or lowest moduli – are preferred. They are discussed in Section 3.4.2.

The determinants of A and V are respectively equal to

$$
|A| = (-1)^p r_1 r_2 \cdots r_p,
$$

$$
|V| = \prod_{1 \le k < l \le p} (r_k - r_l).
$$

Note that the roots can be real or complex numbers, simple or multiple, or equal to zero. Usually, the roots are ordered by decreasing modulus, that is,

$$
|r_1| \ge |r_2| \ge |r_3| \ge \cdots \ge |r_p|.
$$

That way, a good approximation for A^n is obtained by using the first three or four roots if $n > 0$, and the last three or four roots if $n < 0$. In the context of linear regression, one of the main problems consists of inverting a matrix, that is, using $n = -1$ in formula (3.4). Working with the first three roots only is equivalent to performing a **principal component analysis** (PCA) [Wiki] as well as PCA-induced dimension reduction. This technique can be used for data compression.

If some roots have a multiplicity higher than one, the formulas must be adjusted. The solution can be found by looking at how to solve an homogeneous linear recurrence equation. See Theorem 4 in Section 8.2 of "Math 55 Lecture Notes" [3], taught at Berkeley University.

3.2.1 Example with a noninvertible matrix

Even if A is noninvertible, some useful quantities can still be computed when $n = -1$, not unlike using a **pseudoinverse matrix** [Wiki] in the **generalized linear model** [Wiki] in regression analysis. Let us look at the following example, using the methodology previously discussed:

$$
A = \begin{pmatrix} 1 & 2 \\ 2 & 4 \end{pmatrix} \implies A^n = 5^n \cdot \frac{1}{5} \begin{pmatrix} 1 & 2 \\ 2 & 4 \end{pmatrix} + 0^n \cdot \frac{1}{5} \begin{pmatrix} 4 & -2 \\ -2 & 1 \end{pmatrix}.
$$

Note that $0^n = 1$ if $n = 0$. The rightmost matrix attached to the second root 0 is of particular interest, and plays the role of a pseudoinverse matrix for A. If that second root was very close to zero rather than exactly zero, then the term involving the rightmost matrix would largely dominate in the expression of A^n, when $n = -1$. At the limit, some ratios involving the (nonexistent!) inverse of A still make sense. For instance,

- The sum of the elements of the inverse of A, divided by its trace, is $(4 - 2 - 2 + 1)/(4 + 1) = 1/5$.
- The arithmetic mean divided by the geometric mean of its elements, is $1/2$.

3.2.2 Fast computations

If n is large, one way to efficiently compute A^n is as follows. Let us say that $n = 100$. Do the following computations:

$$A^2 = A \cdot A, \quad A^4 = A^2 \cdot A^2, \quad A^8 = A^4 \cdot A^4, \quad A^{16} = A^8 \cdot A^8,$$
$$A^{32} = A^{16} \cdot A^{16}, \quad A^{64} = A^{32} \cdot A^{32}, \quad A^{100} = A^{64} \cdot A^{32} \cdot A^4.$$

This can be useful to quickly get an approximation of the largest root of the characteristic polynomial, by eliminating all but the first (largest) root r_1 in formula (3.4), and using $n = 100$. Once the first root has been found, it is easy to also get an approximation for the second, and then for the third. If, instead, you are interested in approximating the smallest roots, you can proceed the other way around, by using the formula for A^n, with $n = -100$ this time. Note that $A^{-100} = (A^{-1})^{100}$.

3.2.3 Square root of a matrix

Formula (3.4) works not only for integer values of n, but can be extended to fractional arguments, such as $n = 1/2$. Here, I illustrate how it works on an example. Thus, I show how to compute the **square root of a matrix** [Wiki], using the methodology developed so far. This problem has many applications, especially when the matrix A is symmetric **positive semidefinite** [Wiki]: then it has only one symmetric positive semidefinite square root, denoted as $A^{1/2}$. See, for instance, Chapter 7 on linear regression and synthetic data, especially Section 7.2.1 entitled "correlation structure". The square root is needed to generate synthetic data with a prespecified correlation matrix.

Now, using formula (3.4) with $n = 1/2$, let us compute the square root of the 2×2 matrix A defined as

$$A = \begin{pmatrix} 3 & 1 \\ 1 & 1 \end{pmatrix}.$$

Its characteristic polynomial, according to formula (3.1), is $x^2 - 4x + 2$. The roots are $r_1 = 1 + \sqrt{2}$ and $r_2 = 1 - \sqrt{2}$, and are both real and positive. According to formula (3.2), the matrices Q_1, Q_2 are respectively equal to

$$Q_1 = \frac{A - r_2 I}{r_1 - r_2} = \frac{1}{4} \cdot \begin{pmatrix} 2 + \sqrt{2} & \sqrt{2} \\ \sqrt{2} & 2 - \sqrt{2} \end{pmatrix}, \quad Q_2 = \frac{A - r_1 I}{r_2 - r_1} = \frac{1}{4} \cdot \begin{pmatrix} 2 - \sqrt{2} & -\sqrt{2} \\ -\sqrt{2} & 2 + \sqrt{2} \end{pmatrix}.$$

The matrix A has one positive definite square root, namely

$$A^{1/2} = \sqrt{r_1} \cdot Q_1 + \sqrt{r_2} \cdot Q_2 = \frac{1}{2} \begin{pmatrix} \sqrt{10 + \sqrt{2}} & \sqrt{2 - \sqrt{2}} \\ \sqrt{2 - \sqrt{2}} & \sqrt{2 + \sqrt{2}} \end{pmatrix}.$$

It is easy to show that $A^{1/2} \cdot A^{1/2} = A$. In higher dimensions, the Vandermonde system (3.4) is solved using the method described in Section 3.4.2.

3.3 Application to machine learning problems

I discussed principal component analysis (PCA), data compression via PCA, and pseudoinverse matrices in Section 3.2. Here I focus on applications to time series, Markov chains, and linear regression.

3.3.1 Markov chains

A **Markov chain** [Wiki] is a particular type of time series or stochastic process. At iteration or time n, a system is in a particular state i with probability $P_n(i)$. The probability to move from state i at time n to state j at time $n + 1$ is called a transition probability and denoted as p_{ij}. It does not depend on n, but only on i and j. The Markov chain is governed by its initial conditions $P_0(i)$, $1 \leq i \leq p$, and the transition probability matrix denoted as A, containing the elements p_{ij}. The size of the transition matrix is $p \times p$, where p is the number of potential states in the system. Thus $1 \leq i, j \leq p$. As n tends to infinity, A^n and the whole system reaches an equilibrium distribution. This is because

- The **characteristic polynomial** attached to A has a root equal to 1.
- The absolute value of any root is less than or equal to 1.

3.3.2 Time series: autoregressive processes

Autoregressive processes (AR) [Wiki] represent another basic type of time series. Unlike Markov chains, the number of potential states is infinite, and a state can any real value, not just an integer. Yet the time is still discrete. Time-continuous AR processes such as **Gaussian processes** [Wiki] are not included in this discussion. An AR(p) process is defined as follows:

$$X_n = a_1 X_{n-1} + \cdots + a_p X_{n-p} + e_n.$$

Its **characteristic polynomial** is

$$x^p = a_1 x^{p-1} + a_2 x^{p-2} + \cdots + a_{p-1} x + a_p. \tag{3.5}$$

Here $\{e_n\}$ is a **white noise** process (typically uncorrelated Gaussian variables with same variance) [Wiki]. We assume that all expectations are zero. We are dealing here with a nonhomogeneous linear (stochastic) recurrence relation. The most interesting case is when all the roots of the characteristic polynomial have absolute value less than 1. Processes satisfying this condition are called **stationary**. In that case, the **autocorrelations** are decaying exponentially fast.

The lag-k covariances satisfy the relation

$$\gamma_k = \text{Cov}[X_n, X_{n-k}] = \begin{cases} a_1\gamma(k-1) + \cdots + a_p\gamma(k-p) & \text{if } k \neq 0, \\ a_1\gamma(k-1) + \cdots + a_p\gamma(k-p) + \sigma^2 & \text{if } k = 0, \end{cases}$$

with

$$\sigma^2 = \text{Var}[e_n], \quad \text{Var}[X_n] = \gamma(0), \quad \rho(k) = \text{Corr}[X_n, X_{n-k}] = \gamma(k)/\gamma(0).$$

Thus the autocorrelations can be explicitly computed, and are also related to the characteristic polynomial. This fact can be used for model fitting, as the autocorrelation structure uniquely characterizes the (stationary) time series. Note that if the white noise is Gaussian, then the X_n's are also Gaussian.

More about the autocorrelation structure can be found in lecture notes from Marc-Andreas Muendler [7], who teaches economics at UCSD. His material is very similar to what I discuss here, but more comprehensive. See also Barbara Bogacka's lecture notes on time series [1], especially Chapter 6. Finally, Section 3.4 in this chapter explores the mathematical aspects in more details.

3.3.3 Linear regression

Linear regression problems can be solved using the **ordinary least squares** (OLS) method [Wiki]. The framework involves a response y, a data set X consisting of p features or variables and m observations, and p regression coefficients (to be determined) stored in a vector b. In matrix notation, the problem consists of finding b that minimizes the distance $||y - Xb||$ between y and Xb. Here X is an $m \times p$ matrix, and y, b are column vectors. The solution is

$$b = A^{-1}X^T y, \quad \text{with } A = X^T X.$$

The techniques discussed in Section 3.4.2 can be used to compute the inverse of A using formula (3.4) with $n = -1$, either exactly using all the roots of its **characteristic polynomial**, or approximately using the 2–3 roots with the lowest moduli. You need to use the recursion (3.8) backward when implementing the methodology in Section 3.4.2, that is, for $n = -1, -2$, and so on, rather than for $n = 1, 2$, and so on.

If A is not invertible, the methodology described in Section 3.2.1 can be useful: it amounts to working with a pseudoinverse of A. Note that A is a $p \times p$ matrix as in Section 3.2. Questions regarding confidence intervals can be addressed using model-free techniques as discussed in Chapter 8.

3.4 Mathematics of autoregressive time series

Here I connect the dots between the autoregressive **time series** described in Section 3.3.2, and the material in Section 3.2. For the AR(p) process in Section 3.3.2, we have

$$X_n = g(e_p, e_{p+1}, \dots, e_n) + \sum_{k=1}^{p} r_k^n q_k, \quad \text{with} \quad \begin{pmatrix} q_1 \\ q_2 \\ \vdots \\ q_p \end{pmatrix} = V^{-1} \begin{pmatrix} X_0 \\ X_1 \\ \vdots \\ X_{p-1} \end{pmatrix},$$

where V is the same matrix as in formula (3.4), the r_k's are the roots (assumed distinct here) of the **characteristic polynomial** defined by (3.5), and g is a linear function of $e_p, e_{p+1}, \ldots, e_n$. For instance, if $p = 1$, we have

$$g(e_p, e_{p+1}, \ldots, e_n) = \sum_{k=0}^{n-p} a_1^k e_{n-k}.$$

This allows you to compute $\mathrm{Var}[X_n]$ and $\mathrm{Cov}[X_n, X_{n-k}]$, conditionally to $X_0, \ldots, X_{p-1}$. The limit, when n tends to infinity, allows you to compute the unconditional variance and autocorrelations attached to the process, in the stationary case. For instance, if $p = 1$, we have

$$\mathrm{Var}[X_\infty] = \lim_{n \to \infty} \sum_{k=0}^{n-p} a_1^{2k} \mathrm{Var}[e_{n-k}] = \sigma^2 \sum_{k=0}^{\infty} a_1^{2k} = \frac{\sigma^2}{1 - a_1^2},$$

where $\sigma^2 = \mathrm{Var}[e_0]$ is the variance of the white noise $\{e_n\}$, and $|a_1| < 1$ because we assumed stationarity. For the general case (any p), the formula, if n is larger than or equal to p, is

$$g(e_p, e_{p+1}, \ldots, e_n) = \sum_{k=0}^{n-p} \alpha_k e_{n-k}, \text{ with } \alpha_0 = 1, \ \alpha_k = \sum_{t=1}^{p} a_t \alpha_{k-t} \text{ if } k > 0, \ \alpha_k = 0 \text{ if } k < 0.$$

In this case, we have

$$\mathrm{Var}[X_\infty] = \sigma^2 \sum_{k=0}^{\infty} \alpha_k^2.$$

The initial conditions for the coefficients α_k correspond to $k = 0, -1, -2, \ldots, -(p-1)$. Thus $\alpha_0 = 1$, and the remaining α_k's ($k < 0$) are zero. Thus, the recurrence relation for α_n can be solved using the same roots $r_1, \ldots, r_p$ solution of Eq. (3.5). Assuming the roots are distinct, we have

$$\alpha_n = \sum_{k=1}^{p} r_k^n q_k', \quad \text{with} \quad \begin{pmatrix} q_1' \\ q_2' \\ \vdots \\ q_p' \end{pmatrix} = W^{-1} \begin{pmatrix} 1 \\ 0 \\ \vdots \\ 0 \end{pmatrix}, \quad \text{and} \quad W = \begin{pmatrix} 1 & 1 & \cdots & 1 \\ r_1^{-1} & r_2^{-1} & \cdots & r_p^{-1} \\ \vdots & \vdots & \ddots & \vdots \\ r_1^{-(p-1)} & r_2^{-(p-1)} & \cdots & r_p^{-(p-1)} \end{pmatrix}. \quad (3.6)$$

Again, a direct computation of W^{-1} is numerically unstable, except in some special cases. Typically, a few of the r_k's are dominant. The others can be ignored, leading to approximations and increased stability. Finally, if two time series models, say an ARMA and an AR models, have the same variance and covariance structure, they are actually identical.

3.4.1 Simulations: curious fractal time series

To simulate the **autoregressive** time series described in Section 3.3.2, I proceed backwards: first, pick up the roots $r_1, \ldots, r_p$ of the **characteristic polynomial**, then compute the coefficients $a_1, \ldots, a_p$. This leads to interesting discoveries. I want at least one of the roots to have its modulus equal to one. The other roots must have a modulus strictly smaller than one. Roots can have a multiplicity greater than one. Depending on the roots, whether they are all real, whether some are complex, or whether some have a multiplicity greater than one, the pattern is very different. It falls into three categories:

- Type 1: A very smooth time series if the root(s) with largest modulus has a multiplicity greater than one.
- Type 2: A Brownian-like appearance if all the roots are real and distinct.
- Type 3: An highly oscillating time series that fills a dense area when complex roots with modulus equal to one, are present.

In Fig. 3.1, I have rescaled the horizontal and vertical axes so that the time series look time-continuous. With this transformation, Type 2 actually corresponds to a 1D **Brownian motion** [Wiki]. Type 3 has a curve that exhibits a **fractal dimension** [Wiki] strictly between 1 and 2. Type 1 looks very smooth. It seems like it has derivatives of any order, everywhere. Thus it cannot be a Brownian motion. Yet if you zoom in or out, the same statistical properties (smoothness, expected numbers of bumps, and so on) repeat themselves. This means that we are dealing with a strange mathematical function: one that cannot be approximated by a Taylor series, yet very smooth and chaotic with self-replicating features at the same time. Also, we need to keep in mind that it is a **stochastic function**.

The smoothness of a time series is typically measured using its **Hurst exponent** [Wiki]. The extreme, most chaotic case is a white noise, and the "middle case" is a Brownian motion. Here Type 3 seems more extreme than a white noise, and Type 1 is unusually smooth. Except for Type 3, the discrete version of these time series all have long-range autocorrelations.

3.4.1.1 *White noise: Fréchet, Weibull, and exponential cases*

I use one of the simplest distributions to sample from, to generate the white noise $\{e_n\}$. Using independent uniform deviates $U_1, U_2, \ldots$ on $[0, 1]$, I first generate the deviates

$$v_n = \tau\left(-\log(1 - U_n)\right)^\gamma, \quad n = 1, 2, \ldots \tag{3.7}$$

Then the noise e_n is produced using

$$e_n = v_n - \mathrm{E}[v_n], \quad \text{with } \mathrm{E}[v_n] = \tau\Gamma(1 + \gamma) \text{ and } \mathrm{Var}[e_n] = \mathrm{Var}[v_n] = \tau^2\left[\Gamma(1 + 2\gamma) - \Gamma^2(1 + \gamma)\right].$$

Here τ, γ are parameters, with $\gamma > -\frac{1}{2}$, and Γ is the **Gamma function** [Wiki]. We have the following cases:

- If $\gamma = 1$, then v_n has an exponential distribution.
- If $-1 < \gamma < 0$, then v_n has a **Fréchet distribution**. If in addition, $\gamma > -\frac{1}{2}$, then its variance is finite.
- If $\gamma > 0$, then v_n has a **Weibull distribution**, with finite variance.

It is surprising that this distribution has different names, depending on whether $\gamma < 0$ or $\gamma > 0$. This distribution is discussed in my book on stochastic processes [5, pages 41–42].

3.4.1.2 *Illustration*

The simulation results shown in Fig. 3.1 come from my spreadsheet `linear2-small.xlsx`, available on my GitHub repository, here. The cells highlighted in light yellow correspond to the model parameters, such as $\tau, \gamma, a_1, \ldots, a_4$: you can modify them, and it will automatically update the picture. A much

Category	a_1	a_2	a_3	a_4	Factored version
Type 1(a)	$\frac{11}{4}$	$-\frac{21}{8}$	1	$-\frac{1}{8}$	$(x-1)^2(x-\frac{1}{2})(x-\frac{1}{4})$
Type 1(b)	2	-2	2	-1	$(x-1)^2(x^2+1)$
Type 2	$\frac{15}{8}$	$-\frac{35}{32}$	$\frac{15}{64}$	$-\frac{1}{64}$	$(x-1)(x-\frac{1}{2})(x-\frac{1}{4})(x-\frac{1}{8})$
Type 3(a)	0	$-\frac{1}{2}$	0	$\frac{1}{2}$	$(x^2+1)(x^2-\frac{1}{2})$
Type 3(b)	0	2	0	-1	$(x-1)^2(x-\frac{1}{2})^2$

Table 3.1 Characteristic polynomials used in the simulations.

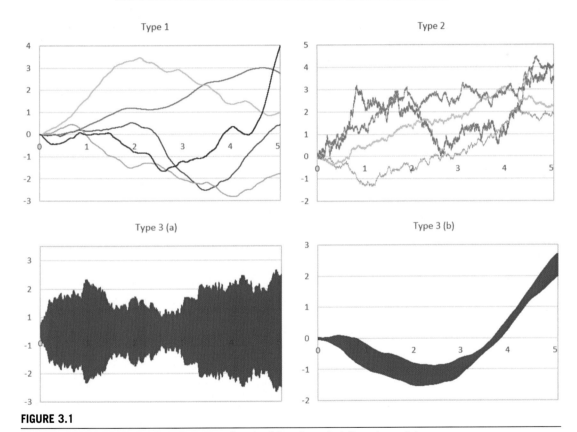

FIGURE 3.1

AR models, classified based on the types of roots of the characteristic polynomial.

larger spreadsheet `linear2.xlsx` (about 30 MB), containing many interesting simulations, each with 50,000 observations, is available here.

The simulations use $\tau = \gamma = 0.5$, and the characteristic polynomials $x^4 - (a_1x^3 + a_2x^2 + a_3x + a_4)$ listed in Table 3.1. The "Type 2" plot is a classic, while "Type 3 (a)" looks like an ordinary audio signal. In Types 3(a) and 3(b), the frequency of oscillations is extremely high: this explains while the curve seems to completely fill an area. The "Type 3(b)" time series is rather original. Its characteristic polynomial has two distinct real roots, each with multiplicity 2. Thus, you are unlikely to encounter it in college classes or textbooks.

But the truly spectacular plot, surprisingly, is "Type 1". These curves are very smooth, but no matter how much you zoom in, it never becomes a flat line, unlike polynomials or well-behaved math functions. The "Type 1" curves in Fig. 3.1 have this property: when differentiated, they become a "Type 2" curve. In short, these curves are the integral of Brownian motions, and called **Itô integrals** [Wiki]. The "Type 2" curves are continuous, and their derivatives are white noises. If the multiplicity of the root with largest modulus is 3, then the corresponding curve is even smoother and can be differentiated three times. Its first derivative is a "Type 1" curve, and its second derivative is a "Type 2" curve.

Other unusual Brownian motions, this time in two dimensions, are discussed in Section 12.2.1. They include a family of Brownian motions, exhibiting an extraordinary strong clustering structure, depending on model parameters. Some Gaussian processes can have a behavior similar to "Type 1" depending on parameters, see here. For Gaussian processes, see also [8], especially Chapter 4. Finally, the top parameter values (root modulus, multiplicity, and so on) can be grouped into clusters. Each cluster leads to a specific type of time series. It makes our time series simulator – called a generative model – useful to produce synthetic data with parameter values matching those estimated on real-life time series. See also Section 1.4 on how to accomplish this in a different context.

3.4.2 Solving Vandermonde systems: a numerically stable method

Vandermonde systems [Wiki] are notoriously **ill-conditioned** [Wiki]. This explains why nobody really solves them, and instead, uses other techniques. Yet they could potentially be used to solve many problems, including linear regression and **eigenvalues** [Wiki] via the characteristic polynomial, **Lagrange interpolation** [Wiki], Markov chains (computation of the **stationary distribution**), linear recurrence equations, principal component analysis (PCA), autoregressive time series, square root of a matrix, and more.

Using the methodology presented in this chapter, I propose a numerically stable algorithm to solve such systems, in a very indirect way. I illustrate my method on a particular example. Let us consider the autoregressive process

$$X_n = \frac{3}{4}X_{n-1} + \frac{7}{8}X_{n-2} - \frac{3}{4}X_{n-3} + \frac{1}{8}X_{n-4}, \tag{3.8}$$

with no white noise. In other words, let $\tau = 0$ in formula (3.7). The characteristic polynomial has roots $r_1 = 1, r_2 = -1, r_3 = \frac{1}{2}, r_4 = \frac{1}{4}$. Let the initial conditions be $X_0 = 1, X_{-1} = 0, X_{-2} = 0, X_{-3} = 0$ as in formula (3.6). Thus, I will be solving the Vandermonde system

$$\begin{pmatrix} 1 & 1 & 1 & 1 \\ 1 & -1 & 2 & 4 \\ 1 & 1 & 4 & 16 \\ 1 & -1 & 8 & 64 \end{pmatrix} \begin{pmatrix} q'_1 \\ q'_2 \\ q'_3 \\ q'_4 \end{pmatrix} = \begin{pmatrix} 1 \\ 0 \\ 0 \\ 0 \end{pmatrix}. \tag{3.9}$$

We know that

$$X_n = r_1^n q'_1 + r_2^n q'_2 + r_3^n q'_3 + r_4^n q'_4. \tag{3.10}$$

Computing X_n iteratively using formula (3.8), we find that $X_{30} \approx 1.6000$ and $X_{31} \approx 1.0667$. The influence of r_3, r_4 is negligible in formula (3.10), and we can reasonably ignore these two roots if n is large enough. Thus, if $n = 30$ we have $1.6000 \approx q_1' + q_2'$, according to (3.10). And $n = 31$ yields $1.0667 \approx q_1' - q_2'$. These two equations allow us to get a very good approximation both for q_1' and q_2'. We do not care about q_3' and q_4' as the associated roots r_3, r_4 have almost no impact on X_n when n is large.

However, we can still compute them if we want to. Consider the subrecursion $\{Y_n\}$ with characteristic polynomial $(x - r_3)(x - r_4)$, that is, $Y_n = \frac{3}{4}Y_{n-1} - \frac{1}{8}Y_{n-2}$. Let the initial conditions be

$$Y_n = X_n - (r_1^n q_1' + r_2^n q_2'), \quad \text{for } n = 0, -1. \tag{3.11}$$

Use the approximated values $q_1' = 1.333$ and $q_2' = 0.2667$ computed in the previous step. Clearly, by design,

$$Y_n = r_3^n q_3' + r_4^n q_4', \tag{3.12}$$

with $r_3 = \frac{1}{2}, r_4 = \frac{1}{4}$. Also, since r_3 dominates over r_4, for n large enough, we have $Y_n \approx r_3^n q'3$, that is, $q_3' \approx r_3^{-n} Y_n \approx 2^n Y_n$. Using formulas (3.11) and (3.12) combined with the approximated values of q_1', q_2' and $n = 15$, one eventually obtains $q_3' \approx 2^{15} Y_{15} \approx -0.6667$. Now we are left with finding the last coefficient q_4'. It can be done using the linear recurrence with characteristic polynomial $x - r_4$. The details are left as an exercise. The exact values are

$$q_1' = \frac{4}{3} = 1.3333\ldots, \quad q_2' = \frac{4}{15} = 0.2666\ldots, \quad q_3' = -\frac{2}{3} = -0.6666\ldots, \quad q_4' = \frac{1}{15} = 0.0666\ldots$$

If we have more than $p = 4$ unknowns, we can proceed iteratively in the same manner, obtaining approximate values successively for q_1', q_2', and so on, assuming the roots are ordered by modulus, with r_1 having the largest modulus. We accumulate inaccuracies at each new iteration, but the loss of accuracy is controlled: the biggest losses are on the coefficients with the lowest impact. Roots with same moduli must be treated jointly, as I did here for r_1 and r_2. If some roots have a multiplicity greater than 1, formula (3.10) must be adapted; see [3].

3.5 Math for machine learning: must-read books

In general, my methods are not traditional. I try to offer original content to the reader, presenting innovative methods explained in simple English, in a style that is pleasant to read. If you are looking for standard textbooks to learn the math of machine learning, I recommend "Mathematics for Machine Learning" [2] and "Introduction to Mathematical Statistics" [6]. The book "Deep Learning" [4] also covers the math of matrix algebra. Lectures notes from Zico Kolter at Stanford University (2015), covering linear algebra, are available here. The book "Linear Algebra for Data Science" by Shaina Bennett (2021) is available online here, and features examples in R. See also "Introduction to Probability for Data Science" by Stanley Chan (2021) available here, with Matlab® and Python code, especially the last chapter on random processes.

For hands-on references with Python code, StatsModels.org is a vast GitHub repository covering a lot of linear algebra and time series. Another one is Statistics and Machine Learning in Python, here.

See also the Python Scikit-learn.org guide about linear models, and Interpretable Machine Learning. You will not find the math or type of examples discussed here, in any of these books. However, they are useful, classic, yet modern references.

References

[1] B. Bogacka, Lecture Notes on Time Series, Queen Mary University of London, 2008, [Link].
[2] M. Deisenroth, A. Faisal, C.S. Ong, Mathematics for Machine Learning, Cambridge University Press, 2020, [Link].
[3] A. Farahmand, Math 55 Lecture Notes, University of Berkeley, 2021, [Link].
[4] I. Goodfellow, Y. Bengio, A. Courville, Deep Learning, MIT Press, 2016, [Link].
[5] V. Granville, Stochastic Processes and Simulations: A Machine Learning Perspective, MLTechniques.com, 2022, [Link].
[6] R.V. Hogg, J.W. McKean, A.T. Craig, Introduction to Mathematical Statistics, eighth edition, Pearson, 2016, [Link].
[7] M.-A. Muendler, Linear Difference Equations and Autoregressive Processes, University of Berkeley, 2000, [Link].
[8] C. Rasmussen, C. Williams, Gaussian Processes for Machine Learning, MIT Press, 2006, [Link].
[9] S. Yan, A. Yang, et al., Explicit algorithm to the inverse of Vandermonde matrix, in: 2009 International Conference on Test and Measurement, IEEE, 2009, [Link].

Image and video generation

The art of visualizing high-dimensional data

I discuss different techniques to produce professional data videos, animated GIFs, and other visualizations in Python, using the `pillow` and `moviepy` libraries. Applications include visualizing prediction intervals regardless of the number of features (also called independent variables), supervised classification applied to an infinite data set, convergence of machine learning algorithms, and animations featuring objects of various sizes moving at various speeds according to various paths. For instance, I show a video simulation of 300 comets circling the sun, to assess the risk of a collision.

The Python libraries in question allow for low-level image processing at the pixel level. This is particularly useful to build ad-hoc, original visualization algorithms. I also discuss optimization: amount of memory required, performance of compression techniques, numpy versus math library, antialiasing to depixelate an image, and so on. Some of the videos use the RGBA palette format. This 4-dimensional color encoding (red, green, blue, alpha) allows you to set the transparency level (also called "opacity") when objects overlap. It is particularly useful in models involving mixtures or overlapping groups in supervised classification. In that context, it not only helps with visualizations, but also actually solves the classification problem on its own.

4.1 Introduction

I start with Figs. 4.2 and 4.3. It is a simulation of comets orbiting the sun, at various velocities, with various orbit orientations and eccentricities. The goal is to assess the risk of collisions. The pictures do a poor job at rendering all the dimensions involved. Thus I created two videos, available here (showing the orbits) and here (featuring comet properties and collisions). The videos add far more than one dimension – the time – to understand the mechanics of the system.

The purpose of this chapter is to introduce you to enriched visualizations, with a focus on animated gifs and videos built in Python. For instance, the comet video can feature several dimensions that are difficult to show in a static picture: the comet locations at any given time, the relative velocity of each comet, the change in velocity (acceleration), the change in comet size when approaching the sun, the comet interactions (the apparent collisions), any change in the orbit (orientation or eccentricity), or any change in composition (the color assigned to a comet). The static images are good at showing the size, orbit path, and comet composition. We could make it a bit more general and represent the movements in 3D. Regardless we can easily display 17 dimensions. The 17 dimensions featured in the comet video are:

- location in space and time (3 or 4 dimensions)
- comet composition or type, and change in composition (2 dimensions, categorical variables)

- comet size and change in size (2 dimensions, categorical/binned variables here)
- comet velocity and acceleration, including change in acceleration (3 dimensions)
- orbit orientation (rotation angle) and eccentricity, and change in these metrics (4 dimensions)
- period of each orbit, and collisions (2 dimensions)
- the number of comets at any given time (1 dimension)

While it is possible to show all these features in traditional time series plots, the video conveys a more compelling message, providing strong visual insights. Note that in my video, the orbit, size, and composition of any given comet are static. I use colors to represent the velocity and eccentricity: red = fast, green = high eccentricity, purple = fast + high eccentricity, white = standard. Also, the size (big or small) is related to the maximum distance to the sun: small dots correspond to comets staying permanently close to the sun.

The remaining of this chapter focuses on four applications: prediction intervals in any dimension, supervised classification, convergence of algorithms such as gradient descent when dealing with chaotic functions, and spatial time series (the comets illustration). In some of these cases, using a video helps, and in other cases, it does not. All Python visualizations use the **RGB** (red / green / blue) color model [Wiki]. It can represent 3 dimensions. One of the videos uses the **RGBA** model [Wiki], allowing you to add transparency or opacity. This is particularly useful when displaying overlapping clusters: when a red cluster overlaps with a green one, the intersection looks yellow (red + green = yellow). I also use **antialiasing** [Wiki] to make contours look smooth instead of pixelated. Finally, I use a compression technique (**FFmpeg**, [Wiki]) to reduce the size of the animated gifs.

In a future article, I will add a soundtrack to the video, related to the behavior of the whole system. The sound (amplitude, frequency, texture) can easily add 3 dimensions. For instance, it can represent the local temperature, density, and size of the universe at any given time.

4.2 Applications

I discuss specifics of the code, such as Python instructions and libraries, in Section 4.3. This section focuses on high level concepts, including the math behind the visualizations. As much as possible, I use notations that are compatible with the names of the variables and arrays in the Python code.

4.2.1 Spatial time series

Here I discuss the comet visualization introduced in Section 4.1. All orbits are elliptic. The orbits are bivariate continuous time series or, in other words, spatial time series. This will become obvious when looking at the parametric equation of the ellipse. The cartesian equation of an unslanted ellipse centered at the origin is

$$\frac{x^2}{a^2} + \frac{y^2}{b^2} = 1,$$

with $a, b > 0$. The eccentricity is defined as $\epsilon = \sqrt{|a^2 - b^2|}$. It $\epsilon = 0$, the ellipse is a circle. If ϵ is large, the ellipse is elongated. In all cases, an "horizontal" ellipse has two focus points: $(g'_x, g'_y) = (0, \epsilon)$ and $(g_x, g_y) = (0, -\epsilon)$. Without loss of generality due to rotational symmetry, I only consider horizontal ellipses, and I ignore the second focus point. The parametric equation of the ellipse is

$$x_0(t) = a \cdot \cos(vt + \tau),$$
$$y_0(t) = b \cdot \sin(vt + \tau),$$

where v is the speed of the comet, t represents the time, and τ determines the initial position of the comet when $t = 0$. I then apply a rotation of angle θ. The parameter θ is referred to as the orientation of the orbit. Now the parametric equation of the ellipse becomes

$$x(t) = x_0(t) \cos \theta - y_0(t) \sin \theta,$$
$$y(t) = x_0(t) \sin \theta + y_0(t) \cos \theta,$$

and its focus point of interest becomes $(g_x, g_y) = (g'_x \cos \theta - g'_y \sin \theta, g'_x \sin \theta + g'_y \cos \theta)$.

Now, I want the sun to be at the origin, and have the comet rotates around the sun. This is accomplished by subtracting the vector (g_x, g_y) to $(x(t), y(t))$. Finally, there are m comets labeled $0, \ldots, m - 1$. The notation $(x_n(t), y_n(t))$ denotes the position of the nth comet at time t, with $0 \le n < m$. Time is sampled evenly: each sample value produces a frame in the video, with m dots, one per comet.

The parameters τ, θ, v, a, b, more precisely $\tau_n, \theta_n, v_n, a_n, b_n$, as there is one set for each orbit, are randomized. However, for a realistic simulation that complies with the laws of the universe (for instance, Kepler's laws), several constraints should be put on these parameters. For instance, the speed should increase when approaching the sun. Also the gravitational interactions are ignored. In fact, the real orbits are not truly periodic because of this, unlike in the simulations.

4.2.2 Prediction intervals in any dimensions

This application, including the accompanying Python code and Excel spreadsheet, is discussed in detail in Chapter 8, using synthetic data. There is no need for a video here: a simple scatterplot will do. I included this visualization because it works in any dimension, and it is rarely if ever mentioned elsewhere, despite its ease of interpretation. Also, it can be done in Excel, see Fig. 4.1, and the Excel implementation fuzzy4.xlsx, available here.

The purpose is to compute predictions and prediction intervals for data outside of a training set, typically in a regression problem (linear or not). I use a validation set [Wiki] to assess performance, comparing the true value with the predicted one. The validation set is a subset of the training set, not used to train the model, but rather, to test it. The observed response Z_{obs} – also called true value – depends on m features $X_1, \ldots, X_m$. All are column vectors, with each entry corresponding to an observation. Thus, the dimension is m. The predicted value at a specific location $x = (x_1, \ldots, x_m)$ in the m-dimensional feature space is denoted as $Z_{\text{pred}}(x)$, while the lower and upper bounds of (say) a 90% prediction interval are denoted as $Z_{0.05}(x)$ and $Z_{0.95}(x)$, respectively.

If $m > 2$, visualizing the prediction intervals becomes challenging. One way to do it is to create a scatterplot featuring the bivariate vectors $(Z_{\text{obs}}(x), Z_{\text{pred}}(x))$ colored in blue, for all x in the validation set. Thus $Z_{\text{obs}}(x)$ is on the horizontal axis, and $Z_{\text{pred}}(x)$ on the vertical axis. Then, add the points $(Z_{\text{obs}}(x), Z_{0.95}(x))$ in red, and the points $(Z_{\text{obs}}(x), Z_{0.05}(x))$ in green, on the scatterplot. The end result is Fig. 4.1. Of course, it works regardless of the dimension.

Interpreting the visualization is easy. If the observed and predicted values were identical, the point cloud, that is, the $(Z_{obs}(x), Z_{pred}(x))$'s, should all be located on the main diagonal. Deviations on the vertical axis from the main diagonal show the individual residual errors. It provides a much better picture of the goodness-of-fit [Wiki] than any single metric such as R-squared or root-mean-squared deviation **RMSE** [Wiki]. Note that metrics such as R-squared have several drawbacks, and alternatives are discussed in Chapter 8.

Another important feature of the visualization is the slope of the regression line going through the point cloud. If the fit was perfect and all the points aligned on the main diagonal, the slope would be equal to one. In practice, it is always between zero and one. A low slope, say 0.5, does not mean that the fit is bad. It means that the regression is smoothing out the spikes in the data, and acts as noise-removing filter. This is actually a good thing. It is easy to rescale the predicted values so that their variance is identical to that computed on the training set. This will restore the higher variations in the original data, while preserving the smoothness and the R-squared. Indeed, the R-squared, defined as the square of the correlation between the observed and predicted values, is invariant under scaling and/or translations.

4.2.3 Supervised classification of an infinite data set

In this problem, the visualization displays 9 dimensions: one for the time (in the video), one for the size of the dots, one for the category or group label, two for the physical location (state space), and four for the RGBA colors. The last frame of the video, showing raw data, is pictured in Fig. 4.5. The horizontal red line is the real axis (the X-axis). The black dot on the left, on the red line, is the origin $(0, 0)$ and the black dot on the right corresponds to $(0, 1)$. A version with bigger dots to actually perform the **fuzzy classification** of the whole state space is pictured in Fig. 4.6. This is the most insightful visualization in this case. The corresponding videos are found respectively here and here. Notice the huge overlap between the three groups (red, blue, yellow). Yet strong patterns emerge: the points are not randomly distributed.

The data set comes from number theory. It is not synthetic in the sense that it represents a real phenomenon. Yet, if it was possible to use the whole, infinite data set, the boundary of the clusters, the boundary of the holes, and the extend of the clusters overlap, would be known exactly. Theoretical considerations allow solving some of the mysteries. But the problem investigated here is related to the Riemann Hypothesis [Wiki], one of the most famous unsolved mathematical problems of all times. So machine learning techniques are still useful to gain more insights, and do a great job here. In math circles, the methods used here are described as **experimental mathematics** [Wiki].

4.2.3.1 *Machine learning perspective*

Before diving into the mathematical details, I explain the machine learning aspects of the problem. Color levels in each channel (red, green, blue) are represented by integer values between 0 and 255. The use of the **RGBA** color model helps visualize cluster overlap. Regions with a high density of yellow points and low density of blue points appear somewhat greenish, but with more yellow than blue in the color. Conversely, regions with a low density of yellow points and high density of blue points also appear somewhat greenish, but with more blue than yellow in the color. High point density results in brighter regions, while low density regions are almost transparent.

Indeed, the supervised classification is automatically performed based on that mechanism alone, with the size of a dot being the main hyperparameter. To find the label (red, yellow or blue) assigned to any location, one has to get its RGB color in Fig. 4.6. For instance, if RGB = (155, 105, 100) then the probability that the point is red, blue or yellow is respectively 50/255, 100/255, and 105/255. See Exercise 4.1 for this computation. Thus the name fuzzy classification sometimes used, but it is actually quite similar to Bayesian classification.

This is achieved thanks to the A component in the RGBA color scheme: it stands for the opacity or transparency of the color, allowing for color blending via the **α-compositing** algorithm [Wiki]. The letter A in RGBA is named after the α in question, and this component is sometimes referred to as the α channel. The technique also allows you to easily discriminate between areas of high and low density, determined by the brightness, that is, the cumulated transparency level computed over overlapping dots. In short, it performs density estimation on its own!

For similar applications, see the "glowing plot" in Fig. 18.5. Also see the fractal GPU-based classification technique described in Chapter 5, and its related video here.

Finally, the data points are located on a nonperiodic orbit that over time covers a dense area, see Fig. 4.4. So, the data points in Figs. 4.5 and 4.6 are sampled from that orbit (actually 3 orbits: red, blue, and yellow), in such a way as to be relatively equally spaced on the orbit. It is possible to obtain perfect spacing using a method similar to the reweighting technique described in Section 6.3.1. Without careful sampling, the points are distributed as in Fig. 4.7: the point density is higher where the curvature of the orbit is more pronounced, or when closer to the related hole. It becomes lower on average as the time increases, that is, as more and more video frames are displayed.

The orbits are displayed in Fig. 4.7. The related video can be found here. The added value provided by the video is that it shows how the points slowly fill a dense area over time. Also note the analogy with the comet video, where the sun plays the role of an attractor, yet comets never cross the sun (at least in the simulation). Here, the hole attached to an orbit plays the role of the sun. But a big difference is that the orbits are nonperiodic.

Exercise 4.1. *Point classification.* A point in Fig. 4.6 has the RGB components (155, 105, 100). What is the chance that it belongs to the red, blue, or yellow cluster?

Solution

Let p_r, p_b, p_y be the probabilities in question. They satisfy

$$M^T = \begin{pmatrix} 255 & 0 & 0 \\ 0 & 0 & 255 \\ 255 & 255 & 0 \end{pmatrix}^T \cdot \begin{pmatrix} p_r \\ p_b \\ p_y \end{pmatrix} = \begin{pmatrix} 155 \\ 105 \\ 100 \end{pmatrix}.$$

The solution $p_r = 50/255$, $p_b = 100/255$, $p_y = 105/255$ is obtained by solving the above system. The first row in the matrix M corresponds to red, the second to blue, and the third to yellow RGB vectors. $\square$

4.2.3.2 Six challenging problems

There are few other interesting machine learning problems worth investigating, raised by Fig. 4.6. I summarize them in the list below.

- Problem 1: The set of yellow points seems to be bounded. Is that also true for the blue and red dots?
- Problem 2: Assuming the set of yellow points is bounded, what is the shape of its boundary?
- Problem 3: There are holes in the blue and yellow point distributions. Can we characterize these holes?
- Problem 4: On the horizontal axis, some segments have no blue dots, some have no yellow dots. Can we characterize these segments?
- Problem 5: If we continue adding points indefinitely, will the holes eventually shrink to empty sets?
- Problem 6: If we continue adding points indefinitely, will the point distributions cover dense areas?

Keep in mind that the set of points is infinite, but only a finite number of points is shown in the picture. Before going into the mathematical details, I will mention this: if you solve Problem 4, you will probably win the Fields Medal in mathematics [Wiki] (the equivalent of the Nobel Prize of mathematics), and a $1 million award for solving one of the seven Millennium Problems [Wiki].

Partial solutions to the six problems are discussed in Section 4.2.3.4.

4.2.3.3 *Mathematical background: the Riemann hypothesis*

What I call data points are values of the Dirichlet eta function $\eta(\sigma + it)$ [Wiki] computed at sampled valued of $t > 0$, for $m = 3$ values of σ, namely $\sigma_0 = 0.50$ corresponding to the red dots, $\sigma_1 = 0.75$ corresponding to the blue dots, and $\sigma_2 = 1.25$ corresponding to the yellow dots. The notation $\sigma + it$ for the complex argument is well established in number theory, and I decided to keep it. There are mathematicians interested in the problem who will read this chapter, and using a different notation would make my presentation awkward and possibly confusing to them.

The η function returns a complex value defined by

$$\Re[\eta(\sigma + it)] = \sum_{k=1}^{\infty} (-1)^{k+1} \cdot \frac{\cos(t \log k)}{k^\sigma},$$

$$\Im[\eta(\sigma + it)] = \sum_{k=1}^{\infty} (-1)^{k+1} \cdot \frac{\sin(t \log k)}{k^\sigma},$$

(4.1)

where $\Re$, $\Im$ represent respectively the real and imaginary parts. For our purpose, no knowledge of complex number theory is required. The real and imaginary parts are just the two components of a 2D vector, with the real part on the horizontal axis (X-axis), and the imaginary part on the vertical axis (Y-axis). The notations used in the Python code in Sections 4.3.2 and 4.3.3, for the real and imaginary part of the η function, are respectively etax[n] and etay[n]. Here $n = 0$ corresponds to $\sigma = \sigma_0$, $n = 1$ to $\sigma = \sigma_1$, and $n = 2$ to $\sigma = \sigma_2$. The time argument t is a global variable in the Python code, incremented at each iteration, starting with $t = 0$.

Figures that show the orbit are based on fixed increments $\Delta t = 0.04$. Figures showing the points but not the orbit use variable increments. This is to correct for the fact that fixed increments do not produce points evenly spaced on the orbit. In that case, a separate timer is used for each value of σ. In the Python code in Section 4.3.3, it corresponds to t[0], t[1], and t[2], respectively, for the red, blue, and yellow points. The main loop is over the three colors (that is, the three values of σ), and the inner loop is over the time. The η function is computed by the Python function G, returning both the real and imaginary parts. It uses the first 10,000 terms of the sums in formula (4.1). These are slow converging series. I discuss convergence acceleration techniques, chaotic convergence, and numerical accuracy in Section 4.2.4.

4.2.3.4 *Partial solutions to the six challenging problems*

In machine learning, typically no mathematical proof is available to show that a model is exact. For instance, statistical models show that smoking increases the chances of getting lung cancer. The arguments are compelling. But there is no formal proof to this. Typically, it is difficult to establish causality. To the contrary, in mathematics, usually formal proofs are available, and they can be used to test and benchmark statistical models. One would think that there is a precise, mathematical answer to the six problems raised in Section 4.2.3.1. Unfortunately, this is not the case here. However, some partial answers are available. First, let me define what I mean by a "hole".

Definition. The T-hole $\Omega_T = \Omega_T(\sigma)$ is the largest circle centered at some location t_T on the real (horizontal) axis, for which $\eta(\sigma + it) \notin \Omega_T$ if $0 < t \leq T$. The hole Ω is the limit of Ω_T, as $T \to \infty$.

In short, η's orbit, given σ, never enters the hole if $0 < t < T$. Here $t_T = t_T(\sigma)$ is a function of σ, with $0 \leq t_T < 2$. Another important concept (see Problem 4) is the largest segment on the real axis, that is never crossed or hit by the orbit.

Now, let us focus on answering Problems 1–6. First, the series in formula (4.1) converge absolutely [Wiki]. Thus the yellow orbit is bounded: this is a trivial fact. The fact that the blue and red orbits are unbounded was proved long ago. See, for instance, the classic reference "The Theory of the Riemann-Zeta Function" [2]. This provides a full answer to Problem 1.

Then, it is also known that the orbits cover dense areas. And as you keep adding more and more points (thus increasing T), the holes eventually shrink to a set of Lebesgue measure zero: this is true if $0.5 < \sigma < 1$. It is a consequence of the universality property of the Riemann zeta function [Wiki]. This provides a partial answer to Problems 5 and 6. If σ is fixed and t is bounded, I presume that the holes associated to the blue and yellow orbits always exist. For the blue orbit, this statement, especially if applied to all σ in]0.5, 1[, is stronger than the Riemann Hypothesis (RH), and thus unproven to this day. Some argue that RH may be unprovable, but that is another story.

The red orbit ($\sigma = 0.5$) has no hole. As σ is decreased from 1.25 to 0.5, the hole shrinks and moves to the left on the real axis, towards the origin. It eventually shrinks to an empty set and becomes and attractor point when $\sigma = 0.5$. This is confirmed by the fact that the Riemann zeta function has infinitely many nontrivial zeros if $\sigma = 0.5$. And the roots of the Dirichlet eta and Riemann zeta functions are identical when $0.5 < \sigma < 1$. The hole of the blue orbit seems to encompass the origin, suggesting that if $\sigma = 0.75$, the Riemann zeta function has no zero. To this day, this conjecture, much weaker than RH, is unproven.

The concepts of repulsion and **attraction basin** [Wiki] are fundamental in dynamical systems. A hole is a repulsion basin, while the origin, for the red orbit, is an attractor point. One of my upcoming books will discuss these topics in detail, for a wide range of dynamical systems.

4.2.4 **Algorithms with chaotic convergence**

We are all familiar with pictures, even animated gifs, showing the gradient descent or some other optimization algorithm in action, converging to an optimum depending on initial conditions. In all cases, the surface (be it 2D or 3D) is smooth, though there are numerous examples with several local maxima and minima. See an example, with Mathematica code, here. The Wikipedia entry for the gradient descent (here) also features a nice 3D video.

Here I visually illustrate the convergence mechanism when the function much less smooth, in a general context. It is not optimization-related, unless you consider accelerating the convergence to be an optimization problem. Each new frame in the video shows the progress towards the final solution, given initial conditions. The convergence path, for this 2D problem, for six different initial conditions, is shown in Fig. 4.8. It is hard to tell where it starts and where it ends. This is straightforward if you look at the video, here.

The algorithm pictured in Fig. 4.8 computes the successive values of the η function in the complex plane, using formula (4.1). Each iteration adds one new term to the summation, and generates a new frame. It is possible to significantly improve the speed of convergence, using **convergence acceleration** techniques [Wiki] such as Euler's transform [Wiki], described on page 65 in my book [1]. I explain in my book (same page) why the convergence is so chaotic in this case. The same convergence acceleration techniques apply to gradient descent and other similar iterative algorithms, when successive iterations generate oscillating values. For the η function, Borwein's method [Wiki] may be the best approach.

I tested the numerical stability of the computations by introducing stochastic noise in formula (4.1). I describe the methodology in the section "Perturbed version of the Riemann Hypothesis", on page 20 in my book [1]. The holes described in Section 4.2.3.4 in this paper are very sensitive to minuscule errors in the computations, and are nonexistent when very small changes are introduced. This confirms that there is something really unique to the Riemann zeta function. For solutions to optimize highly chaotic functions (compute a global maximum or minimum), see my book [1], pages 17–18. I used a diverging **fixed-point algorithm** [Wiki] that emits a signal when approaching a global optimum. The technique will be described in detail in an upcoming article. A quick overview of the methodology is available here.

Finally, the visualization (Fig. 4.8 or the corresponding video here) uses a very large number of RGB colors. To produce the visual effect, I used sine functions to generate the colors. See Section 4.3.2 and page 85 in my book [1] for more details. Palette optimization (see here) will be the subject of an upcoming article.

4.3 Python code

The Python code, videos, and animated gifs are available on my GitHub repository, here. The videos are also on YouTube, here. For convenience, the Python code is also included in this section. Top variables include ShowOrbit (set to true if you want to display the orbit, not just the points), dot (the size of the dots), r (when iterating over time, it outputs a video frame once every r iterations), width and height (the dimensions of the image). The final image is eventually reduced by half due to the **antialiasing** procedure used to depixelate the curves. This is performed within img.resize in the code, using the Image.LANCZOS parameter [Wiki].

Ellipses and lines are produced using the Pillow library and its ImageDraw functions. Animated gifs are produced either with images[0].save (resulting in massive files), or with videoClip.write_gif, using the Moviepy library with the **ffmpeg** parameter [Wiki] for compression. When working with a large number of colors, ffmpeg causes considerable quality loss, not in the rendering of the shapes, but in the color palette. I suggest to use libraries other than Pillow to produce animated gifs, for instance openCV. Eventually, I converted some of the MP4 videos to gifs using the online tool ezgif, also based on ffmpeg.

Reducing the size of the image and the number of frames per second (FPS) will optimize the code and produce much smaller gifs. The biggest improvement, in terms of speed, is replacing all numpy calls (np.log, np.cos, and so on) by math calls (math.log, math.cos, and so on). If you use numpy for image production rather than Pillow, the opposite may be true (I did not test). Finally, the opacity level in the RGBA color model should be set to 127. Currently, it is set to 80; see the fourth parameter, for instance, in colp.append((0,0,255,80)).

4.3.1 **Path simulation**

On GitHub: image2.py. Produces the comet video. Description in Section 4.2.1.

```python
from PIL import Image, ImageDraw # ImageDraw to draw ellipses, etc.
import moviepy.video.io.ImageSequenceClip # to produce mp4 video
from moviepy.editor import VideoFileClip # to convert mp4 to gif
import numpy as np
import math
import random
random.seed(100)


#--- Global variables ---


m=300          # number of comets
nframe=1500    # number of frames in video
ShowOrbit=True # do not show orbit (default)


count=0        # frame counter

count1=0
count2=0
count3=0
count4=0

width = 1600
height = 1200

a=[]
b=[]
gx=[]     # focus of ellipse (x coord.)
gy=[]     # focus of ellipse (y coord.)
theta=[] # rotation angle of ellipse (the orbit)
v=[]      # speed of comet
tau=[]    # position of comet on the orbit path, at t = 0
col=[]    # RGB color of the comet
size=[]  # size of the comet
flist=[] # filenames of the images representing each video frame
```

```
a=list(map(float,a))
b=list(map(float,b))
gx=list(map(float,gx))
gy=list(map(float,gy))
theta=list(map(float,theta))
v=list(map(float,v))
tau=list(map(float,tau))
flist=list(map(str,flist))

#--- Initializing comet parameters ---

for n in range (m):
  a.append(width*(0.1+0.3*random.random()))
  b.append((0.5+1.5*random.random())*a[n])
  theta.append(2*math.pi*random.random())
  tau.append(2*math.pi*random.random())
  if a[n]>b[n]:
    gyy=0.0
    gxx=math.sqrt(a[n]*a[n]-b[n]*b[n]) # should use -gxx 50% of the time
  else:
    gyy=math.sqrt(b[n]*b[n]-a[n]*a[n]) # should use -gyy 50% of the time
    gxx=0.0
  gx.append(gxx*np.cos(theta[n])-gyy*np.sin(theta[n]))
  gy.append(gxx*np.sin(theta[n])+gyy*np.cos(theta[n]))
  if random.random() < 0.5:
    v.append(0.04*random.random())
  else:
    v.append(-0.04*random.random())
  if abs(a[n]*a[n]-b[n]*b[n])> 0.15*width*width:
    if abs(v[n]) > 0.03:
    # fast comet with high eccentricity
      red=255
      green=0
      blue=255
      count1=count1+1
    else:
    # slow comet with high eccentricity
      red=0
      green=255
      blue=0
      count2=count2+1
  else:
    if abs(v[n]) > 0.03:
    # fast comet with low eccentricity
      red=255
      green=0
      blue=0
```

```
      count3=count3+1
    else:
    # slow comet with low eccentricity
      red=255
      green=255
      blue=255
      count4=count4+1
  col.append((red,green,blue))
  if ShowOrbit:
    size.append(1)
  else:
    if min(a[n],b[n]) > 0.3*width: # orbit with large radius
      size.append(8)
    else:
      size.append(4)

sunx=int(width/2)  # position of the sun (x)
suny=int(height/2) # position of the sun (y)
if ShowOrbit:
  img = Image.new( mode = "RGB", size = (width, height), color = (0, 0, 0) )
  pix = img.load()
  draw = ImageDraw.Draw(img)
  draw.ellipse((sunx-16, suny-16, sunx+16, suny+16), fill=(255,180,0))

#--- Main Loop ---

for t in range (0,nframe,1): # loop over time, each t corresponds to a video frame
  print("Building frame:",t)
  if not ShowOrbit:
    img = Image.new( mode = "RGB", size = (width, height), color = (0, 0, 0) )
    pix = img.load()
    draw = ImageDraw.Draw(img)
    draw.ellipse((sunx-16, suny-16, sunx+16, suny+16), fill=(255,180,0))
  for n in range (m): # loop over asteroid
    x0=a[n]*np.cos(v[n]*t+tau[n])
    y0=b[n]*np.sin(v[n]*t+tau[n])
    x=x0*np.cos(theta[n])-y0*np.sin(theta[n])
    y=x0*np.sin(theta[n])+y0*np.cos(theta[n])
    x=int(x+width/2 -gx[n])
    y=int(y+height/2-gy[n])
    if x >= 0 and x < width and y >=0 and y < height:
      draw.ellipse((x-size[n], y-size[n], x+size[n], y+size[n]), fill=col[n])
  count=count+1
  fname='imgpy'+str(count)+'.png'

  # antialiasing mechanism
  img2 = img.resize((width // 2, height // 2), Image.LANCZOS) # antialiasing
  # output current frame to a png file
```

```
img2.save(fname,optimize=True,quality=30)
flist.append(fname)

clip = moviepy.video.io.ImageSequenceClip.ImageSequenceClip(flist, fps=20)
# output video file
clip.write_videofile('videopy.mp4')
# output gif image [converting mp4 to gif with ffmpeg compression]
videoClip = VideoFileClip("videopy.mp4")
videoClip.write_gif("videopy.gif",program='ffmpeg') #,fps=2)

print("count 1-4:",count1,count2,count3,count4)
```

4.3.2 Visual convergence analysis in 2D

On GitHub: image2R.py. Produces the successive approximations to the η function. Description in Section 4.2.4.

```
from PIL import Image, ImageDraw # ImageDraw to draw ellipses, etc.
import moviepy.video.io.ImageSequenceClip # to produce mp4 video
from moviepy.editor import VideoFileClip # to convert mp4 to gif
import numpy as np
import math
import random
random.seed(100)

#--- Global variables ---

m=6            # number of curves
nframe=4000    # number of images
count=0        # frame counter
start=2000     # must be smaller than nframe
r=20           # one out of every r image is included in the video

width = 3200
height =2400

images=[]
etax=[]
etay=[]
sigma=[]
t=[]
x0=[]
y0=[]
flist=[] # filenames of the images representing each video frame

etax=list(map(float,etax))
```

```
etay=list(map(float,etay))
sigma=list(map(float,sigma))
t=list(map(float,t))
x0=list(map(float,x0))
y0=list(map(float,y0))
flist=list(map(str,flist))

#--- Initializing comet parameters ---

for n in range (0,m):
  etax.append(1.0)
  etay.append(0.0)
  t.append(5555555+n/10)
  sigma.append(0.75)
sign=1

minx= 9999.0
miny= 9999.0
maxx=-9999.0
maxy=-9999.0

for n in range (0,m):
  sign=1
  sumx=1.0
  sumy=0.0
  for k in range (2,nframe,1):
    sign=-sign
    sumx=sumx+sign*np.cos(t[n]*np.log(k))/pow(k,sigma[n])
    sumy=sumy+sign*np.sin(t[n]*np.log(k))/pow(k,sigma[n])
    if k >= start:
      if sumx < minx:
        minx=sumx
      if sumy < miny:
        miny=sumy
      if sumx > maxx:
        maxx=sumx
      if sumy > maxy:
        maxy=sumy
sign=1
rangex=maxx-minx
rangey=maxy-miny

img = Image.new( mode = "RGB", size = (width, height), color = (255, 255, 255) )
pix = img.load()
draw = ImageDraw.Draw(img)

red=255
green=255
```

```
blue=255
col=(red,green,blue)
count=0

#--- Main Loop ---

for k in range (2,nframe,1): # loop over time, each t corresponds to a video frame
  if k%10 == 0:
   print("Building frame:",k)
  sign=-sign
  for n in range (0,m): # loop over curves
   x0.insert(n,int(width*(etax[n]-minx)/rangex))
   y0.insert(n,int(height*(etay[n]-miny)/rangey))
   etax[n]=etax[n]+sign*np.cos(t[n]*np.log(k))/pow(k,sigma[n])
   etay[n]=etay[n]+sign*np.sin(t[n]*np.log(k))/pow(k,sigma[n])
   x=int(width*(etax[n]-minx)/rangex)
   y=int(height*(etay[n]-miny)/rangey)
   shape = [(x0[n], y0[n]), (x, y)]
   red = int(255*0.9*abs(np.sin((n+1)*0.00100*k)))
   green= int(255*0.6*abs(np.sin((n+2)*0.00075*k)))
   blue = int(255*abs(np.sin((n+3)*0.00150*k)))

   if k>=start:
     # draw line from (x0[n],y0[n]) to (x_new,y_new)
     draw.line(shape, fill =(red,green,blue), width = 1)

  if k>=start and k%r==0:
   fname='imgpy'+str(count)+'.png'
   count=count+1
   # anti-aliasing mechanism
   img2 = img.resize((width // 2, height // 2), Image.LANCZOS) # antialiasing
   # output current frame to a png file
   img2.save(fname) # write png image on disk
   flist.append(fname) # add its filename (fname) to flist
   images.append(img2) # to produce gif image

# output video file
clip = moviepy.video.io.ImageSequenceClip.ImageSequenceClip(flist, fps=20)
clip.write_videofile('riemann.mp4')
```

4.3.3 Supervised classification

GitHub version: image3R_orbit.py. Produces the orbits of the η function. Description in Section 4.2.3.

```
from PIL import Image, ImageDraw # ImageDraw to draw ellipses, etc.
import moviepy.video.io.ImageSequenceClip # to produce mp4 video
from moviepy.editor import VideoFileClip # to convert mp4 to gif
```

```
import numpy as np
import math
import random
random.seed(100)

#--- Global variables ---

m=3            # number of orbits (one for each value of sigma)
nframe=20000   # number of images created in memory
ShowOrbit=True
ShowDots=False
count=0        # frame counter
r=50           # one out of every r image is included in the video
dot=2          # size of a point in the picture
step=0.04      # time increment in orbit

width = 3200   # width of the image
height =2400   # length of the image

images=[]
etax=[]  # real part of Dirichlet eta function
etay=[]  # real part of Dirichlet eta function
sigma=[]# imaginary part of argument of Dirichlet eta
x0=[]    # value of etax on last video frame
y0=[]    # value of etay on last video frame
#col=[]  # RGB color of the orbit
colp=[]  # RGP points on the orbit
t=[]     # real part of argument of Dirichlet eta (that is, time in orbit)
flist=[]# filenames of the images representing each video frame

etax=list(map(float,etax))
etay=list(map(float,etay))
sigma=list(map(float,sigma))
x0=list(map(float,x0))
y0=list(map(float,y0))
t=list(map(float,t))
flist=list(map(str,flist))

#--- Eta function ---

def G(tau,sig,nterms):
  sign=1
  fetax=0
  fetay=0
  for j in range(1,nterms):
    fetax=fetax+sign*math.cos(tau*math.log(j))/pow(j,sig)
    fetay=fetay+sign*math.sin(tau*math.log(j))/pow(j,sig)
    sign=-sign
```

```
    return [fetax,fetay]

#--- Initializing comet parameters ---

for n in range (0,m):
  etax.append(1.0)
  etay.append(0.0)
  x0.append(1.0)
  y0.append(0.0)
  t.append(0.0)  # start with t=0.0
sigma.append(0.50)
sigma.append(0.75)
sigma.append(1.25)
colp.append((255,0,0,80))
colp.append((0,0,255,80))
colp.append((255,180,0,80))

if ShowOrbit:
  minx=-2
  maxx=3
else:
  minx=-1
  maxx=2
rangex=maxx-minx
rangey=0.75*rangex
miny=-rangey/2
maxy=rangey/2
rangey=maxy-miny

img = Image.new( mode = "RGB", size = (width, height), color = (255, 255, 255) )
# pix = img.load() # pix[x,y]=col[n] to modify the RGB color of a pixel
draw = ImageDraw.Draw(img,"RGBA")

gx=width*(0.0-minx)/rangex
gy=height*(0.0-miny)/rangey
hx=width*(1.0-minx)/rangex
hy=height*(0.0-miny)/rangey
draw.ellipse((gx-8, gy-8, gx+8, gy+8), fill=(0,0,0,255))
draw.ellipse((hx-8, hy-8, hx+8, hy+8), fill=(0,0,0,255))
draw.rectangle((0,0,width-1,height-1), outline ="black",width=1)
draw.line((0,gy,width-1,hy), fill ="red", width = 1)

count=0

#--- Main Loop ---

for k in range (2,nframe,1): # loop over time, each t corresponds to an image
  if k %10 == 0:
```

```
    string="Building frame:" + str(k) + "> "
    for n in range (0,m):
      string=string+ " | " + str(t[n])
    print(string)
  for n in range (0,m): # loop over the m orbits
    if ShowOrbit:
      # save old value of etax[n], etay[n]
      x0.insert(n,width*(etax[n]-minx)/rangex)
      y0.insert(n,height*(etay[n]-miny)/rangey)
    (etax[n],etay[n])=G(t[n],sigma[n],10000) # 500 -> tau
    x= width*(etax[n]-minx)/rangex
    y=height*(etay[n]-miny)/rangey
    if ShowOrbit:
      if k>2:
        # draw line from (x0[n],y0[n]) to (x,y)
        draw.line((int(x0[n]),int(y0[n]),int(x),int(y)), fill =colp[n], width = 0)
        if ShowDots:
          draw.ellipse((x-dot, y-dot, x+dot, y+dot), fill =colp[n])
      t[n]=t[n]+step
    else:
      draw.ellipse((x-dot, y-dot, x+dot, y+dot), fill =colp[n])
      t[n]=t[n]+200*math.exp(3*sigma[n])/(1+t[n]) # 0.02
  if k%r==0: # this image gets included as a frame in the video
    draw.ellipse((gx-8, gy-8, gx+8, gy+8), fill=(0,0,0,255))
    draw.ellipse((hx-8, hy-8, hx+8, hy+8), fill=(0,0,0,255))
    fname='imgpy'+str(count)+'.png'
    count=count+1
    # antialiasing mechanism
    img2 = img.resize((width // 2, height // 2), Image.LANCZOS) # antialiasing
    # output current frame to a png file
    img2.save(fname) # write png image on disk
    flist.append(fname) # add its filename (fname) to flist
    images.append(img2) # to produce gif image

# output video file
clip = moviepy.video.io.ImageSequenceClip.ImageSequenceClip(flist, fps=20)
clip.write_videofile('riemann.mp4')

# output gif file - commented out because it is way too large
# images[0].save('riemann.gif',save_all=True, append_images=images[1:],loop=0)
```

4.4 **Visualizations**

The videos and animated gifs are available on my GitHub repository, here. The videos are also on YouTube, here. Below are selected frames from these videos: those that are referenced in this chapter.

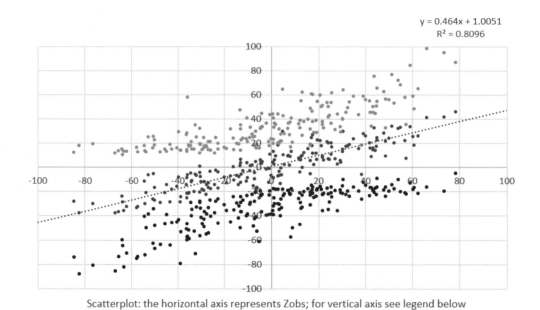

$y = 0.464x + 1.0051$
$R^2 = 0.8096$

Scatterplot: the horizontal axis represents Zobs; for vertical axis see legend below

• Zmedian   • Prediction Interval lower   • Prediction Interval upper

FIGURE 4.1

Scatterplot observations vs. predicted values, with prediction intervals (in any dimension).

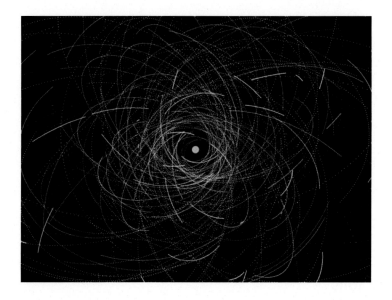

FIGURE 4.2

Comets orbiting the sun: Simulation.

FIGURE 4.3

Comets orbiting the sun: Snapshot in time.

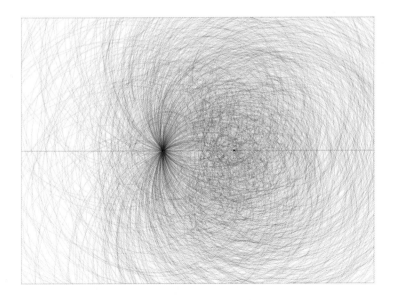

FIGURE 4.4

Three orbits of $\eta(\sigma + it)$: $\sigma = 0.5$ (red), 0.75 (blue), and 1.25 (yellow).

FIGURE 4.5

Sample orbit points of $\eta(\sigma + it)$: $\sigma = 0.5$ (red), 0.75 (blue), and 1.25 (yellow).

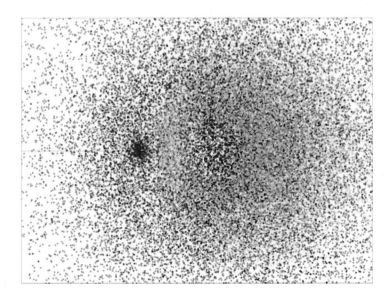

FIGURE 4.6

Sample orbit points of $\eta(\sigma + it)$: $\sigma = 0.5$ (red), 0.75 (blue), and 1.25 (yellow).

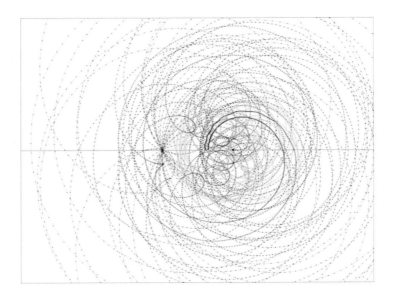

FIGURE 4.7

Raw orbit points of $\eta(\sigma + it)$: $\sigma = 0.5$ (red), 0.75 (blue), and 1.25 (yellow).

FIGURE 4.8

Convergence of partial sums of $\eta(z)$, for six $z = \sigma + it$ in the complex plane.

References

[1] V. Granville, Stochastic Processes and Simulations: A Machine Learning Perspective, MLTechniques.com, 2022, [Link].

[2] E.C. Titchmarsh, D.R. Heath-Brown, The Theory of the Riemann Zeta-Function, second edition, Oxford Science Publications, 1987.

Synthetic clusters and alternative to GMM

5

Fast classification and clustering via image convolution filters

Here I generate synthetic data using a superimposition of stochastic processes, comparing it to Bayesian generative mixture models (Gaussian mixtures or **GMM**). I explain the benefits and differences. The actual classification and clustering algorithms are model-free, and performed in GPU as image filters, after transforming the raw data into an image. I then discuss the generalization to 3D or 4D, and to higher dimensions with sparse tensors. The technique is particularly suitable when the number of observations is large, and the overlap between clusters is substantial.

It can be done using few iterations and a large filter window, comparable to a neural network, with pixels in the local window being the nodes, and their distance to the local center being the weight function. Or you can implement the method with a large number of iterations – the equivalent of hundreds of layers in a deep neural network – and a tiny window. This latter case corresponds to a **sparse network** with zero or one connection per node. It is used to implement fractal classification, where point labeling changes at each iteration, around highly nonlinear cluster boundaries. This is equivalent to putting a prior on class assignment probabilities in a Bayesian framework. Yet, classification is performed without underlying model. Finally, the clustering (unsupervised) part of the algorithm relies on the same filtering techniques, combined with a color equalizer. The latter can be used to perform hierarchical clustering.

The Python code, included in this document, is also on my GitHub repository. A data animation illustrates how simple the methodology is: each frame in the video represents one iteration, that is, a single application of the filter to all the data points. Indeed, the classifier can be used as a black box system. It follows the modern trend of interpretable machine learning, also called explainable AI. The video shows how the algorithm converges to an optimum, producing a classification of the entire observation space. Classifying a new point is then immediate: read its color. The whole system is time-efficient. It does not require the computation of all training set point intradistances. However it is memory-intensive. Large filters can be slow, though they require very few iterations. I discuss a simple technique to make them a lot faster.

5.1 Introduction

I explain, with Python code and numerous illustrations, how to turn traditional tabular data into images, to perform both clustering and supervised classification using simple image filtering techniques. I also explain how to generalize the methodology to higher dimensions, using tensors rather than images. In the end, image bitmaps are 2D arrays or matrices, that is, 2D tensors. By classifying the entire space

Synthetic Data and Generative AI. https://doi.org/10.1016/B978-0-44-321857-6.00009-6

(in low dimensions), the resulting classification rule is very fast. I also discuss the convergence of the algorithm, and how to further improve its speed.

This short chapter covers many topics and can be used as a first introduction to synthetic data generation, mixture models, boundary effects, explainable AI, fractal classification, stochastic convergence, GPU machine learning, deep neural networks, and model-free Bayesian classification. I use very little math, making it accessible to the layman, and certainly, to nonmathematicians. Introducing an original, intuitive approach to general classification problems, I explain in simple English how it relates to deep and very deep neural networks. In the process, I make connections to image segmentation, histogram equalization, hierarchical clustering, convolution filters, and stochastic processes. I also compare standard neural networks with very deep but sparse ones, in terms of speed and performance. The fractal classifier – an example of very deep neural network – is illustrated with a Python-generated video. It is useful when dealing with massively overlapping clusters and a large number of observations. Hyperparameters allow you to fine tune the level of cluster overlap in the synthetic data, and the shape of the clusters.

5.2 **Generating the synthetic data**

The data used in my examples is generated using a technique that bears some resemblance to **Gaussian mixture models** (GMM) in a Bayesian framework [Wiki]. Instead of mixtures, I used superimposed stochastic processes, also called interlacings. The differences with mixtures are subtle and can be detected with statistical tests, but unimportant and not visible to the naked eye. And rather than Gaussian distributions, I use arbitrary distributions. The mathematical model is that of stochastically perturbed lattice processes, also known as Poisson–binomial point processes.

Chapter 16 offers a more comprehensive survey on this topic, with numerous references, covering all aspects from simulation, graph properties, to theory. These processes have become popular recently, with applications to sensor data, cell networks, crystallography and chemistry. They are flexible and very easy to simulate. The three main parameters are the scale or diffusion factor s, the intensity λ (linked to the expected number of points per unit area), and the local distribution F which may be Gaussian or not. In this chapter, I do not discuss the theory. I only introduce the basic material necessary to generate the synthetic data. The reader is referred to Chapter 16 for details.

First, I use $\lambda = 1$ in the Python code included in this document. Then, if $s = 0$, the points are all located on a lattice: there is no randomness anymore. To the contrary, if s is large (say $s > 5$) then the points are nearly uniformly distributed, as in a Poisson point process. In that case, the simulated data has no clustering structure. The synthetic data here uses either $s = 0.05$ resulting in well separated clusters, or $s = 0.15$ resulting in significant cluster overlap.

For examples with five clusters, see the left plot in Fig. 5.3 (with $s = 0.15$) and Fig. 5.4 (with $s = 0.05$). For four clusters, see the left plot in Fig. 5.5 (with $s = 0.15$) and Fig. 5.6 (with $s = 0.05$). The number of clusters, denoted as m, is the number of components (stochastic processes) used in the superimposition.

Thus, the cluster structure is generated by interlacing multiple stretched and shifted perturbed lattices. The stretching factor and intensity may be different depending on the direction. A special case with $s = 0$ is the deterministic hexagonal lattice pictured in Fig. 5.1. A number of examples with various degrees of randomness are pictured in Chapter 16. If $s > 0$, the points of a single process are independently distributed with multivariate distribution F, around each lattice vertex. If $s = 0$, the data points are the lattice vertices, as in Fig. 5.1.

5.2.1 Simulations with logistic distribution

All simulations are in two dimensions. There is no particular reason to choose a logistic distribution for F, other than that it is the easiest to sample from. A Gaussian distribution would work, too. The distribution F has little impact on the final results. Indeed, it is not easy and sometimes impossible to reverse-engineer the system to identify the underlying distribution F. See Chapter 16 for a discussion on this topic. Finally, the algorithm is as follows:

Data generation: Algorithm
The data generated is 2D, but it is easy to generalize to any dimension. For each lattice vertex (h, k), where h, k are integers (positive or negative), and for each stochastic lattice process M_i with $0 \leq i < m$, generate the bivariate observation (x_{ih}, y_{ik}) as follows:

$$x_{ih} = \mu_i + \frac{h}{\lambda_i} + s \cdot \log\left(\frac{U_{ih}}{1 - U_{ih}}\right), \tag{5.1}$$

$$y_{ik} = \mu_i' + \frac{k}{\lambda_i'} + s \cdot \log\left(\frac{U_{ik}}{1 - U_{ik}}\right). \tag{5.2}$$

Formulas (5.1) and (5.2) are from Section 16.2.4. The U_{ih}, U_{ik} are independent uniform deviates on $[0, 1]$. In practice, we generate points in a finite rectangular window, and we only keep those inside a subwindow, to avoid the boundary effects described in my book. This is implemented in the Python code in Section 5.4, with $-25 \leq h, k \leq 25$. In the code, I use the arrays stretchX, stretchY to store the coefficients $1/\lambda_i, 1/\lambda_i'$, and shiftX, shiftY to store the shift vectors (μ_i, μ_i'). The shift vectors are the centers of the clusters. In the rectangular window, by design, the number of observed points from the process M_i (which plays the role of a mixture component in a mixture model) is proportional to $\lambda_i \times \lambda_i'$ in two dimensions. In my examples, I chose $\lambda_i = \lambda_i' = \lambda$, with $\lambda = 1$.

5.2.2 Mapping the raw observations onto an image bitmap

Eventually, due to the lattice nature of the stochastic processes involved (with point patterns exhibiting statistical tiling around each vertex), the points are transformed using a modulo operator (see xmod and ymod in the Python code) and then mapped onto an image bitmap (the bivariate array bitmap in the Python code). From there, image processing techniques are used to perform classification or clustering.

5.3 Classification and unsupervised clustering

I describe here a methodology for fast supervised and unsupervised classification. The data is first transformed into a two-dimensional array called *bitmap*. The points are referred to as pixels, and the array represents an image stored in **GPU** (the graphics processing unit) [Wiki]. The functions applied to the bitmap are standard image processing techniques such as high pass filtering or **histogram equalization** [Wiki].

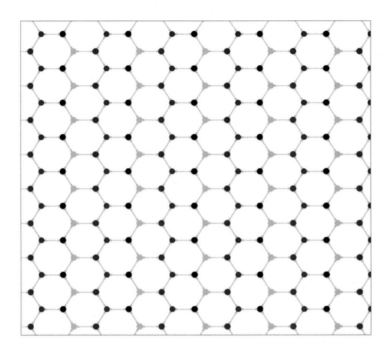

FIGURE 5.1

Special interlacing of 4 lattice processes with $s = 0$.

The input data consists of a realization (obtained by simulation in Sections 5.2.1 and 5.2.2) of an ***m*-interlacing** (that is, a superimposition of m shifted Poisson–binomial processes) with each individual process represented by a different color; see Figs. 5.2 and 5.3. The left plot shows the data points observed modulo $2/\lambda$. So, the point locations, after the modulo operation, are in $[0, 2/\lambda[\times [0, 2/\lambda[$. I chose $\lambda = 1$ for the intensity function, in the simulations.

The modulo operator magnifies the cluster structure, which is otherwise invisible to the naked eye. It is defined as $a \bmod b = a - b\lfloor a/b \rfloor$ where the brackets represent the integer part function. For your own simulations, you can use modulo $1/\lambda$, rather than $2/\lambda$: this will remove the apparent stochastic duplication in my pictures. The reason I chose $2/\lambda$ is due to boundary effects, with clusters extending beyond the window of observations and truncated because of the window, thus making the cluster structure much harder to see if using modulo $1/\lambda$. For the mathematically inclined reader, the methodology performs **classification on the torus** [Wiki] rather than on the plane: this is a standard technique when facing boundary effects. If all your data fits nicely in the observation window, you can ignore the modulo transformation.

The middle and right plots in Fig. 5.3 correspond to **unsupervised clustering**. The centers of the darkest areas provide an approximation to the unknown shift vectors (μ_i, μ_i') of formulas (5.1) and (5.2), with $i = 0, \ldots, m$ indicating the (unknown) cluster label. The shift vectors are the theoretical cluster centers. The approximation is far from perfect due to massive cluster overlapping. The situation is much better in Fig. 5.4 (right plot), where cluster overlapping is much less pronounced. See also Fig. 5.8. The methodology is described in Section 5.3.1.

The middle and right plots in Fig. 5.2 correspond to **supervised classification** of the entire space: the color of a point represents the individual point process or cluster it belongs to. In this case the data set is the training set. The methodology is described in Section 5.3.2.

5.3.1 Supervised classification based on convolution filters

Here the synthetic data set represents the training set. The algorithm consists of filtering the whole bitmap N times. Each time, a local filter is applied to each pixel (x, y). Initially, the color $c(x, y)$ attached to the pixel represents the cluster it belongs to, in the training set (or in other words, the individual point process it originates from in the m-mixture): its value is an integer between 0 and $m - 1$ if it is in the training set, and 255 otherwise. The new color assigned to (x, y) is

$$c'(x, y) = \arg\max_{j} \sum_{u=-w}^{w} \sum_{v=-w}^{w} \frac{\chi[c(x - u, y - v) = j]}{\sqrt{1 + u^2 + v^2}}, \tag{5.3}$$

that is, the value of j that maximizes (5.3). Here $\chi[A]$ is the indicator function [Wiki]: $\chi[A] = 1$ if A is true, and 0 otherwise. The boundary problem (when $x - u$ or $y - v$ is outside the bitmap) is handled in the source code.

 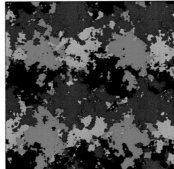 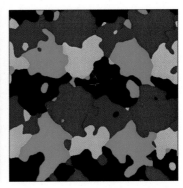

FIGURE 5.2

Classification of the left data set; $s = 0.15$, $w = 10$. One loop (middle) vs 3 (right).

In the Python code, N is the parameter `nloop`, and w is the parameter `window`. It is also referred to as w and *loops* in the figures. In particular, I used $N = 3$ and $w = 20$. Formula (5.3) corresponds to `method = 1` in the Python code. While slow, it provides granular cluster boundaries. A faster version, namely `method = 0`, does not make the division by $\sqrt{1 + u^2 + v^2}$. It is faster not only because it avoids the square-root computations, but also because it can be implemented very efficiently; see Section 5.3.5. Yet, the loss of accuracy when using the fast method, while noticeable, is smaller than expected. See Fig. 5.7 for comparisons.

Note that each cluster, even when the overlap is small, extends to the entire plane. So there is always some degree of overlap. But the overlap is much smaller when the diffusion factor s (the variable s in the Python code) is small. This is evident when comparing Fig. 5.2 with Fig. 5.4. Both figures have the same number of clusters, and the same cluster centers; only s – and thus the amount of cluster overlap – is different.

After filtering the whole bitmap $N = 3$ times, thanks to the large size of the local filtering window ($w = 20$), all pixels are assigned to a cluster. This means that any future point (not in the training set) can easily and efficiently be classified: first, find its location on the bitmap; then its cluster is the color assigned to that location. It is worth asking whether convergence occurs (and to what solution) if you were to filter the bitmap many times. I studied convergence for a similar type of filter, in my paper "Simulated Annealing: A Proof of Convergence" [1]. Empirical evidence suggests that additional loops (increasing N beyond $N = 3$) barely makes any difference.

5.3.2 Clustering based on histogram equalization

I use the same filter for unsupervised clustering. Indeed, both supervised and unsupervised clustering are implemented in parallel in the source code, within the same loop. The main difference is that the color (or cluster) $c(x, y)$ attached to a pixel (x, y) is not known. Instead of colors, I use gray levels representing the density of points at any location on the bitmap: the darker, the higher the density. I start with a bitmap where $c(x, y) = 1$ if (x, y) corresponds to the location of an observed point on the bitmap, and $c(x, y) = 0$ otherwise. Again, I filter the whole bitmap $N = 3$ times with the same filter size $w = 20$. The new gray level assigned to pixel (x, y) at loop t is now

$$c'(x, y) = \arg\max_{j} \sum_{u=-w}^{w} \sum_{v=-w}^{w} \frac{c(x-u, y-v) \cdot 10^{-t}}{\sqrt{1 + u^2 + v^2}}. \tag{5.4}$$

The first time this filter is applied to the whole bitmap, I use $t = 0$ in formula (5.4); the second time I use $t = 1$, and the third time I use $t = 2$. The purpose is to dampen the effect of successive filtering, otherwise the image (rightmost plots in Fig. 5.3) would turn almost black everywhere after a few loops, making it impossible to visualize the cluster structure. The second and third loops, with the damping factor, provide an improvement over using a single loop only.

 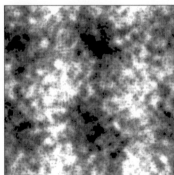 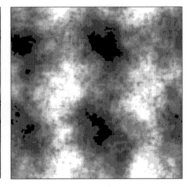

FIGURE 5.3

Clustering of the left data set; $s = 0.15$, 3 loops, $w = 10$ (middle) vs 20 (right).

After filtering the image, I use a final postprocessing step to enhance the gray levels: see Part 4 of the source code in the `GD_maps` function. It consists of binning and rescaling the histogram of gray levels to make the image sharper and easier to interpret, with 8 gray levels only. This step, called

histogram equalization, can be automated. The successive gray levels, starting with the darkest one, correspond to successive levels in an **hierarchical clustering** algorithm [Wiki]. To finalize the clustering procedure, one may use **image segmentation** techniques [Wiki] to identify the boundary of the clusters.

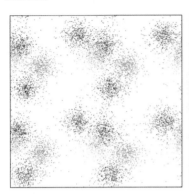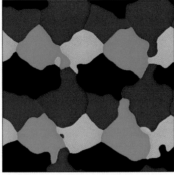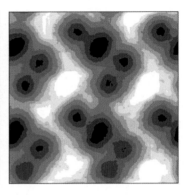

FIGURE 5.4

Classification ($w = 10$) and clustering ($w = 20$); $s = 0.05$, three loops.

The equalizer used in my code works on all the images tested. However, you may want to use one that is image-specific. The Python pillow library offers an easy way to do it, see here. You can also write your own Python code for full control. See the histogram equalization code in the gigantic Algorithms repository on GitHub, here. This type of algorithm, turning tabular data into an image or the other way around, or equalizing gray levels to perform clustering, is called a **transformer** [Wiki].

5.3.3 Fractal classification: deep neural network analogy

The filtering system is essentially a neural network [Wiki]. The image before the first loop (Figs. 5.2 and 5.4, left plot), consisting of the training set, is the input layer. The final image obtained after 3 loops is the output layer. The intermediate iterations correspond to the **hidden layers**. In each layer, the pixel color is a function of quantities computed on neighboring pixels, in the previous layer. The preprocessing step consists of transforming the data set into an image bitmap. In Section 5.3.2 about unsupervised clustering, the postprocessing step called "equalizer" plays the role of the sigmoid function in neural networks. See Luuk Spreeuwers' PhD thesis "Image Filtering with Neural Networks" defended in 1992 [2] (available online, here), for more about image filters used as neural networks.

In my video posted here (YouTube) and here (animated gif on GitHub), each frame represents a layer in a **very deep neural network**. In my methodology, I use the term "loop" or "iteration" instead of layer. It is represented by the Python variable `loop` in `PB_clustering_video.py` (Section 5.4.1). A pixel plays the role of a **neuron**, and the weight attached to the link between a pixel and one of its neighbors – as in formula (5.3) – is also called "weight", or parameter, in neural network terminology.

The fractal classifier described here, displayed in the video and also pictured in Figs. 5.5 and 5.6, is in some sense the opposite of the one described in Section 5.3.1: instead of using $N = 3$ loops (that is, 3 layers), it uses hundreds of them. But the local filter is extremely small, with $w \leq 1$, compared

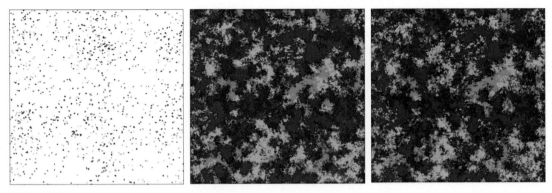

FIGURE 5.5

Fractal classification, $s = 0.15$; loops 6, 250, and 400.

to $w = 20$ in Section 5.3.1. Thus, each neuron (pixel) is connected to one neuron at most. Such neural networks are called "sparse". In the end, it produces similar results, compared to using few loops and a large local filtering window. The main difference is that cluster boundaries are less smooth, and appear fractal-like. The video (here) shows the successive image transformations taking place from one loop to the next one. By watching it, it is very easy to understand how the method works, making it a classic example of explainable AI [Wiki].

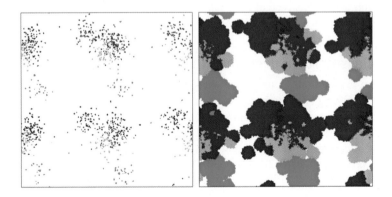

FIGURE 5.6

Fractal classification, $s = 0.05$; loops 6 and 60.

Once the whole state is classified (when no white area is left on the image), each subsequent loop randomly re-assigns the pixel labels (the cluster they belong to), around cluster borders. It allows you to compute, for a pixel on the border between two or more clusters, the a-posteriori probability that it belongs to any of these clusters. This makes the methodology similar to a **Bayesian classifier** [Wiki]. The borders between clusters are statistically stable over time: the algorithm converges, at least from a stochastic point of view.

5.3.4 **Generalization to higher dimensions**

All the examples featured in this chapter are in two dimensions. This makes it easy to use image processing techniques for classification or clustering. In three dimensions, images can be replaced by videos, and one can still use standard filtering techniques. It becomes more challenging in four dimensions. One way to handle the problem in higher dimensions (or even in two dimensions) is to use tensors [Wiki]. A 2D tensor is a standard rectangular matrix. A 3D tensor is a $p \times q \times r$ matrix, or in other words, a cubic matrix. Each "slice" of a 3D tensor can be treated as an image. The filters can be adapted to this type of data.

In higher dimensions, the training set occupies a tiny portion of the whole space. It does not make sense to try to classify the whole space: this becomes time-prohibitive in dimension 5 and above. Instead, the solution consists of working with sparse tensors. They can be represented as graph structures, with each point connected to its neighbors, then the neighbors of the neighbors and so on, with a depth or 4 or 5 levels. This is still a work in progress.

5.3.5 **Towards a very fast implementation**

The size w of the local filter window is the bottleneck. When filtering the image using the algorithm in Section 5.3.1, the window used at (x, y), and the next one at $(x + 1, y)$, both have $(2w + 1)^2$ pixels, but these two windows have $(2w + 1)^2 - 2 \times (2w + 1)$ pixels in common. So rather than visiting $(2w + 1)^2$ pixels each time, the overlapping pixels can be kept in a $(2w + 1)^2$ buffer. To update the buffer after visiting a pixel and moving to the next one to the right, one only has to update $2w + 1$ values in the buffer: overwrite the column corresponding to the old $2w + 1$ leftmost pixels, by the values derived from the new $2w + 1$ rightmost pixels.

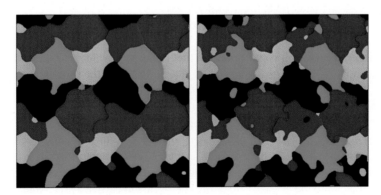

FIGURE 5.7

Fast (left) vs standard method (right), 3 loops, $s = 0.15$, $w = 10$.

This leads to a particularly efficient implementation when using `method = 0` (the fast filter). Then, the `GD_Maps` function in `GD_util.py` can be further optimized, since it only counts pixels (based on their color) in the local filter window, without computing distances to the center of the window. It will speed up the procedure by a factor proportional to w, both for supervised classification and clustering. Since I use $w = 20$ (the parameter `window` in the code), the improvement is significant.

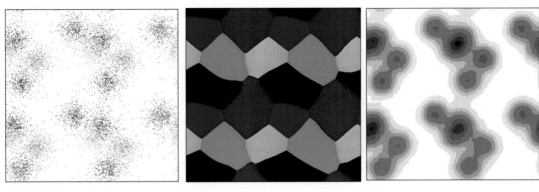

FIGURE 5.8

Fast method, $s = 0.05$, $w = 20$. Three loops (middle), one loop (right).

5.4 Python code

The Python code uses the `pillow` and `moviepy` libraries. To install Pillow, type `pip install pillow` on the Windows command prompt. The program `PB_clustering_video.py` in Section 5.4.1 is a self-contained and short, separate piece of code. It is also the only one that produces videos (MP4 files). You might want to look at it first. The parameter s, represented by the global variable s, is called the scaling or diffusion factor. It determines the amount of overlap between clusters. If $s = 0$, all the points are located on a lattice. If s is large (say $s > 5$) the points are almost uniformly distributed; clustering becomes meaningless, no matter what algorithm you use.

The main program `PB_NN.py` in Section 5.4.2 does not include any video / image processing. However, it requires `GD_util.py` (see Section 5.4.3), my home-made small library consisting of one function `GD_Maps`. All the image processing is performed in that function. The `GD_util.py` file is assumed to be in the same folder as `PB_NN.py`. Parts 3 and 4 in `PB_NN.py` deal with the time-intensive computation of all intradistances. You do not need it, and it is turned off by the global variable `NNflag`, set to `False`. It is provided only for compatibility with an older Perl version in the first edition of my book on stochastic processes. This Python version replaces the Perl code, in the new edition.

The output of `PB_NN.py` consists of PNG images, one for classification and one for clustering, per iteration. The input is the synthetic data created in Part 2, and transformed into a bitmap (array of colored pixels) also in Part 2. Image filtering, and thus classification and clustering, takes place in Part 5: it consists of a call to the `GD_maps` function. As discussed earlier, Parts 3 and 4 are skipped. The hyperparameter `window`, referred to as w in the figure captions, is the size of the local filter. To assign a cluster to a point (that is, a color to a pixel), the local filter consists of a $(2w + 1) \times (2w + 1)$ window centered at the point in question. Iterations (or layers, if it was a neural network) are referred to as "loops" in figure captions. The number of iterations is determined by the variable `nloop` in the code. Finally, `Nprocess` is the number of clusters, and `method` determines the type of filter. The methodology has been extensively tested with `method = 1`, which is time consuming if w is large. Note that `method = 0` still provides satisfactory results, and can be implemented in a very efficient way, as discussed in Section 5.3.5.

For colors, I use the **RGBA** model [Wiki]. However, for the time being, the A component or fourth element of the color vector, known as transparency level, is not used. A future version of the code may use it, in a way similar to the supervised classification technique described in Chapter 4.

5.4.1 Fractal classification

On GitHub: `PB_clustering_video.py`. Produces the fractal classification video with 400 frames or layers, using the smallest possible filter window. Short, self-sufficient code, using the `Pillow` and `Moviepy` libraries. The input data is synthetic and created in the code: it shares some features with Bayesian Gaussian mixtures. However the classification itself is model-free. Description in Section 5.3.3.

```python
# PB_clustering_video.py

import math
import random
from PIL import Image, ImageDraw # ImageDraw to draw rectangles, etc.
import moviepy.video.io.ImageSequenceClip # to produce mp4 video

Nprocess=4    # number of processes in the process superimposition
seed=82431    # arbitrary number
random.seed(seed) # initialize random generator
s=0.05 # scaling factor
shiftX=[]
shiftY=[]

for i in range(Nprocess) :
  shiftX.append(random.random())
  shiftY.append(random.random())
processID=0
height,width = (800, 800)
bitmap = [[255 for k in range(height)] for h in range(width)]

for h in range(-25,26):
  for k in range(-25,26):
    for processID in range(Nprocess):
      ranx=random.random()
      rany=random.random()
      ranID=random.random()
      if ranID < 0.20:
        processID=0
      elif ranID < 0.60:
        processID=1
      elif ranID < 0.90:
        processID=2
      else:
        processID=3
      x=shiftX[processID]+h+s*math.log(ranx/(1-ranx))
```

```
      y=shiftY[processID]+k+s*math.log(rany/(1-rany))
      if x>-3 and x<3 and x>-3 and x<3:
        xmod=1+x-int(x) # x modulo 2/lambda
        ymod=1+y-int(y) # y modulo 2/lambda
        pixelX=int(width*xmod/2)
        pixelY=int(height*(2-ymod)/2) # pixel (0,0) at top left corner
        bitmap[pixelX][pixelY]=processID

#---
img1 = Image.new( mode = "RGBA", size = (width, height), color = (0, 0, 0) )
pix1 = img1.load() # pix[x,y]=col[n] to modify the RGB color of a pixel
draw1 = ImageDraw.Draw(img1,"RGBA")

col1=[]
col1.append((255,0,0,255))
col1.append((0,0,255,255))
col1.append((255,179,0,255))
col1.append((0,179,0,255))
col1.append((0,0,0,255))
for i in range(Nprocess,256):
  col1.append((0,0,0,255))

for pixelX in range(0,width):
  for pixelY in range(0,height):
      topProcessID=bitmap[pixelX][pixelY]
      pix1[pixelX,pixelY]=col1[topProcessID]

draw1.rectangle((0,0,width-1,height-1), outline ="black",width=1)
fname="img_0.png"
img1.save(fname)

#---
nloop=400   # number of times the image is filtered

oldBitmap = [[255 for k in range(height)] for h in range(width)]
flist=[]

for loop in range(1,nloop+1):
  print("loop",loop,"out of",nloop+1)
  for pixelX in range(0,width):
    for pixelY in range(0,height):
      oldBitmap[pixelX][pixelY]=bitmap[pixelX][pixelY]
  for pixelX in range(1,width-1):
    for pixelY in range(1,height-1):
      x=pixelX
      y=pixelY
      topProcessID=oldBitmap[x][y]
      if topProcessID==255 or loop>50:
```

```
       r=random.random()
       if r<0.25:
         x=x+1
         if x>width-2:
           x=x-(width-2)
       elif r<0.5:
         x=x-1
         if x<1:
           x=x+width-2
       elif r<0.75:
         y=y+1
         if y>height-2:
           y=y-(height-2)
       else:
         y=y-1
         if y<1:
           y=y+height-2
       if loop>=50 and oldBitmap[x][y]==255:
         x=pixelX
         y=pixelY
     topProcessID=oldBitmap[x][y]
     bitmap[pixelX][pixelY]=topProcessID
     pix1[pixelX,pixelY]=col1[topProcessID]
   draw1.rectangle((0,0,width-1,height-1), outline ="black",width=1)
   fname="img_"+str(loop+1)+'.png'
   flist.append(fname)
   img1.save(fname)

clip = moviepy.video.io.ImageSequenceClip.ImageSequenceClip(flist, fps=20)
clip.write_videofile('img.mp4')
```

5.4.2 GPU classification and clustering

On GitHub: PB_NN.py. Produces the supervised classification and clustering using a large filter window and only 3 layers. Requires the small, home-made graphic library GD_util.py featured in Section 5.4.3. All image manipulations are performed in that library. The input data is synthetic and created in the code: it shares some features with Bayesian Gaussian mixtures. However the classification itself is model-free. Description in Sections 5.3.1 and 5.3.2.

```
# PB_NN.py
# lambda = 1

import numpy as np
import math
import random
```

```
#---
# PART 1: Initialization

Nprocess=5              # number of processes in the process superimposition
s=0.15                  # scaling factor
method=1                # method=0 is fastest
NNflag=False            # set to True if you need to compute NN distances
window=20               # determines size of local filter [the bigger, the smoother]
nloop=3                 # number of times the image is filtered [the bigger, the smoother]

epsilon=0.0000000001 # for numerical stability
seed=82431              # arbitrary number
random.seed(seed)       # initialize random generator

sep="\t"   # TAB character
shiftX=[]
shiftY=[]
stretchX=[]
stretchY=[]
a=[]
b=[]
process=[]
sstring=[] # string in Perl version

for i in range(Nprocess) :
  shiftX.append(random.random())
  shiftY.append(random.random())
  stretchX.append(1.0)
  stretchY.append(1.0)
  sstring.append(sep)
  # i TABs separating x and y coordinates in output file for points
  # originating from process i; Used to easily create a scatterplot in Excel
  # with a different color for each process
  sep=sep + "\t"

processID=0
m=0 # number of points generated
height,width = (400, 400)

bitmap = [[255 for k in range(height)] for h in range(width)]

#---
# PART 2: Generate point process, its modulo 2 version; save to bitmap and output files

OUT = open("PB_NN.txt", "w")        # the points of the process
OUT2 = open("PB_NN_mod.txt", "w") # the same points modulo 2/lambda both in x and y directions

for h in range(-25,26):
```

```
    for k in range(-25,26):
        for processID in range(Nprocess):
            ranx=random.random()
            rany=random.random()
            x=shiftX[processID]+stretchX[processID]*h+s*math.log(ranx/(1-ranx))
            y=shiftY[processID]+stretchY[processID]*k+s*math.log(rany/(1-rany))
            a.append(x) # x coordinate attached to point m
            b.append(y) # y coordinate attached to point m
            process.append(processID) # processID attached to point m
            m=m+1
            line=str(processID)+"\t"+str(h)+"\t"+str(k)+"\t"+str(x)+sstring[processID]+str(y)+"\n"
            OUT.write(line)
            # replace sstring[processID] by \t if you do not care about Excel

            if x>-20 and x<20 and x>-20 and x<20:
                xmod=1+x-int(x) # x modulo 2/lambda
                ymod=1+y-int(y) # y modulo 2/lambda
                pixelX=int(width*xmod/2)
                pixelY=int(height*(2-ymod)/2) # pixel (0,0) at top left corner
                bitmap[pixelX][pixelY]=processID
                line=str(xmod)+sstring[processID]+str(ymod)+"\n"
                OUT2.write(line)
                # replace sstring[processID] by \t if you do not care about Excel
OUT2.close()
OUT.close()

#---
# PART 3: Find nearest neighbor points, and compute nearest neighbor distances

if NNflag:

  OUT = open("PB_NN_dist_small.txt", "w") # the points of the process
  OUTf = open("PB_NN_dist_full.txt", "w") # the same points modulo 2/lambda both in x and y
      directions

  NNx=[]
  NNy=[]
  NNidx=[]
  NNidxHash={}

  for i in range(m):
    NNx.append(0.0)
    NNy.append(0.0)
    NNidx.append(-1)
    mindist=99999999
    flag=-1
    if a[i]>-20 and a[i]<20 and b[i]>-20 and b[i]<20:
      flag=0;
```

```
      for j in range(m):
        dist=math.sqrt((a[i]-a[j])**2 + (b[i]-b[j])**2) # taxicab distance faster to compute
        if dist<=mindist+epsilon and i!=j:
          NNx[i]=a[j] # x-coordinate of nearest neighbor of point i
          NNy[i]=b[j] # y-coordinate of nearest neighbor of point i
          NNidx[i]=j  # indicates that point j is nearest neighbor to point i
          # NNidxHash[i] is the list of points having point i as nearest neighbor;
          # these points are separated by "~" (usually only one point in NNidxHash[i]
          # unless the simulated points are exactly on a lattice, e.g., if s = 0)
          if abs(dist-mindist) < epsilon:
            NNidxHash[i]=NNidxHash[i]+"~"+str(j)
          else:
            NNidxHash[i]=str(j)
          mindist=dist
      if i % 100 == 0:
        print("Finding Nearest neighbors of point",i)
      line=str(i)+"\t"+str(mindist)+"\n"
      OUT.write(line)
      line=str(i)+"\t"+str(NNidx[i])+"\t"+str(NNidxHash[i])+"\t"+str(a[i])+"\t"
      line=line+str(b[i])+"\t"+str(NNx[i])+"\t"+str(NNy[i])+"\t"+str(mindist)+"\n"
      OUTf.write(line)

  OUTf.close()
  OUT.close()

#---
# PART 4: Produce data to use in R code that generates the nearest neighbors picture

if NNflag:

  OUT = open("PB_r.txt","w")
  OUT.write("idx\tnNN\tNNindex\ta\tb\taNN\tbNN\tprocessID\tNNprocessID\n")

  for idx in NNidxHash:
    NNlist=NNidxHash[idx]
    list=NNlist.split("~")
    nelts=len(list)
    for n in range(nelts):
      NNindex=int(list[n])
      line=str(idx)+"\t"+str(n)+"\t"+str(NNindex)+"\t"+str(a[idx])+"\t"+str(b[idx])
      line=line+"\t"+str(a[NNindex])+"\t"+str(b[NNindex])+"\t"+str(process[idx])
      line=line+"\t"+str(process[NNindex])+"\n"
      OUT.write(line)

  OUT.close()

#---
# PART 5: Creates density and cluster images
```

```
img_cluster="PB-cluster" # use for output image filenames
img_density="PB-density" # use for output image filenames

from GD_util import *
GD_Maps(method,bitmap,Nprocess,window,nloop,height,width,img_cluster,img_density)
```

5.4.3 Home-made graphic library

On GitHub: GD_util.py. Relies on the Pillow library, to perform various filtering processes directly in image bitmaps rather than on the initial data. The unsupervised clustering technique uses a color equalizer, as the main machine learning algorithm. The library has only one function GD_Maps that does both supervised classification at once.

```
import math
from PIL import Image, ImageDraw # ImageDraw to draw rectangles, etc.

def GD_Maps(method,bitmap,Nprocess,window,nloop,height,width,img_cluster,img_density):

  #---
  # PART 1: Allocate first image (clustering), including colors (palette)

  img1 = Image.new( mode = "RGBA", size = (width, height), color = (0, 0, 0) )
  pix1 = img1.load() # pix[x,y]=col[n] to modify the RGB color of a pixel
  draw1 = ImageDraw.Draw(img1,"RGBA")

  col1=[]
  col1.append((255,0,0,255))
  col1.append((0,0,255,255))
  col1.append((255,179,0,255))
  col1.append((0,0,0,255))
  col1.append((0,179,0,255))
  for i in range(Nprocess,256):
    col1.append((255,255,255,255))
  oldBitmap = [[255 for k in range(height)] for h in range(width)]
  densityMap= [[0.0 for k in range(height)] for h in range(width)]
  for pixelX in range(0,width):
    for pixelY in range(0,height):
      processID=bitmap[pixelX][pixelY]
      pix1[pixelX,pixelY]=col1[processID]
  draw1.rectangle((0,0,width-1,height-1), outline ="black",width=1)
  fname=img_cluster+'.png'
  img1.save(fname)

  #---
  # PART 2: Filter bitmap and densityMap
```

```
for loop in range(nloop): #

  print("loop",loop,"out of",nloop)
  for pixelX in range(0,width):
    for pixelY in range(0,height):
      oldBitmap[pixelX][pixelY]=bitmap[pixelX][pixelY]

  for pixelX in range(0,width):
    for pixelY in range(0,height):
      count=[0] * Nprocess
      density=0
      maxcount=0
      topProcessID=255 # dominant processID near (pixelX, pixelY)
      for u in range(-window,window+1):
        for v in range(-window,window+1):
          x=pixelX+u
          y=pixelY+v
          if x<0:
            x+=width   # boundary effect correction
          if y<0:
            y+=height # boundary effect correction
          if x>=width:
            x-=width   # boundary effect correction
          if y>=height:
            y-=height # boundary effect correction
          if method == 0:
            dist2=1
          else:
            dist2=1/math.sqrt(1+u*u + v*v)
          processID=oldBitmap[x][y]
          if processID < 255:
            count[processID]=count[processID]+dist2
            if count[processID]>maxcount:
              maxcount=count[processID]
              topProcessID=processID
            density=density+dist2
      density=density/(10**loop) # 10 at power loop (dampening)
      densityMap[pixelX][pixelY]=densityMap[pixelX][pixelY]+density
      bitmap[pixelX][pixelY]=topProcessID

  #---
  # PART 3: Some preprocessing; output cluster image

  densityCountHash={} # use to rebalance gray levels
  for pixelX in range(0,width):
    for pixelY in range(0,height):
      topProcessID=bitmap[pixelX][pixelY]
```

```
        density=densityMap[pixelX][pixelY]
        if density in densityCountHash:
          densityCountHash[density]=densityCountHash[density]+1
        else:
          densityCountHash[density]=1
        pix1[pixelX,pixelY]=col1[topProcessID]

draw1.rectangle((0,0,width-1,height-1), outline ="black",width=1)
fname=img_cluster+str(loop)+'.png'
img1.save(fname)

#---
# PART 4: Equalize gray levels in the density image; output image as a PNG file
# Also try https://www.geeksforgeeks.org/python-pil-imageops-equalize-method/

densityColorHash={}
col2=[]
size=len(densityCountHash) # number of elements in hash
counter=0

for density in sorted(densityCountHash):
  counter=counter+1
  quant=counter/size # always between zero and one
  if quant < 0.08:
    densityColorHash[density]=0
  elif quant < 0.18:
    densityColorHash[density]=30
  elif quant < 0.28:
    densityColorHash[density]=55
  elif quant < 0.42:
    densityColorHash[density]=90
  elif quant < 0.62:
    densityColorHash[density]=120
  elif quant < 0.80:
    densityColorHash[density]=140
  elif quant < 0.95:
    densityColorHash[density]=170
  else:
    densityColorHash[density]=254

# allocate second image (density image)

img2 = Image.new( mode = "RGBA", size = (width, height), color = (0, 0, 0) )
pix2 = img2.load() # pix[x,y]=col[n] to modify the RGB color of a pixel
draw2 = ImageDraw.Draw(img2,"RGBA")

# allocate gray levels (palette)
for i in range(0,256):
```

```
    col2.append((255-i,255-i,255-i,255))

# create density image pixel by pixel
for pixelX in range(0,width):
  for pixelY in range(0,height):
    density=densityMap[pixelX][pixelY]
    color=densityColorHash[density]
    pix2[pixelX,pixelY]=col2[color]

# output density image
draw2.rectangle((0,0,width-1,height-1), outline ="black",width=1)
fname=img_density+str(loop)+'.png'
img2.save(fname)

return()
```

References

[1] V. Granville, M. Krivanek, J.-P. Rasson, Simulated annealing: a proof of convergence, IEEE Transactions on Pattern Analysis and Machine Intelligence 16 (1996) 652–656.

[2] L. Spreeuwers, Image Filtering with Neural Networks: Applications and Performance Evaluation, PhD thesis, University of Twente, 1992.

Shape classification and synthetization via explainable AI

6

Here I define the mathematical concept of shape and shape signature in two dimensions, using parametric polar equations. The signature uniquely characterizes the shape, up to a translation or scale factor. In practical applications, the data set consists of points or pixels located on the shape, rather than the curve itself. If these points are not properly sampled – if they are not uniformly distributed on the curve – they need to be reweighted to compute a meaningful centroid of the shape, and to perform shape comparisons. I discuss the weights, and then introduce metrics to compare shapes (observed as sets of points or pixels in an image). These metrics are related to the Hausdorff distance. I also introduce a correlation distance between two shapes. Equipped with these metrics, one can perform shape recognition or classification using training sets of arbitrary sizes. I use synthetic data in the applications. It allows you to see how the classifier performs, to discriminate between two very similar shapes, or in the presence of noise. Rotation-invariant metrics are also discussed.

6.1 Introduction

A central problem in **computer vision** is to compare shapes and assess how similar they are. This is used, for instance, in text recognition. Modern techniques involve neural networks. Here, I revisit a methodology developed before computer even existed. With modern technology, it leads to an efficient, automated AI algorithm. The benefit is that the decision process made by this black-box system can be easily explained, and thus easily controlled.

To the contrary, neural networks use millions of weights that are impossible to interpret, potentially leading to overfitting. Why they work very well on some data and no so well on other data is a mystery. My "old-fashioned" classifier, adapted to modern data and computer architectures, leads to full control of the parameters. In other words, you know beforehand how fine-tuning the parameters will impact the output. Thus the word explainable AI [Wiki].

In an ideal world, one would want to blend both methods, to benefit from their respective strengths, and minimize their respective drawbacks. Such a blending is referred to as ensemble methods [Wiki]. Also, since we are dealing with sampled points located on a curve (the "shape"), the same methodology also applies to sound recognition.

Synthetic Data and Generative AI. https://doi.org/10.1016/B978-0-44-321857-6.00010-2

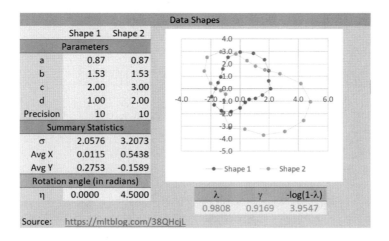

	Shape 1	Shape 2
Parameters		
a	0.87	0.87
b	1.53	1.53
c	2.00	3.00
d	1.00	2.00
Precision	10	10
Summary Statistics		
σ	2.0576	3.2073
Avg X	0.0115	0.5438
Avg Y	0.2753	-0.1589
Rotation angle (in radians)		
η	0.0000	4.5000

λ	γ	-log(1-λ)
0.9808	0.9169	3.9547

Source: https://mltblog.com/38QHcjL

FIGURE 6.1

Comparing two shapes.

6.2 Mathematical foundations

In this section, we are concerned with the mathematical concept of shape. Later on, I apply the methodology to shapes represented by sets of points or pixels, observed through a rectangular window – a digital image. The center of the window is the origin of the coordinate system. Shapes can be anything: they may represent a letter, an hieroglyph, or a combination of symbols. They may consist of multiple, nonconnected curves. We are only interested in the contour that defines the shape. It may or may not correspond to the boundary of a domain; the contour may not be closed and could consist of disconnected segments.

Furthermore, there is no color or gray scale involved. The mathematical shape model can be viewed as black on a white background, with no thickness. In practical applications, the rectangular image is centered around the shape, and the noise has been filtered out. See example in Fig. 6.1, comparing two shapes.

It is convenient, for illustrations purposes, to define a 2D mathematical shape using a parametric polar equation, as follows:

$$r_t = g(t), \quad \theta_t = h(t), \quad \text{with} \quad t \in T, \quad r_t \geq 0, \quad 0 \leq \theta_t \leq 2\pi.$$

Here g, h are real-valued functions, and T is the index domain. An example with $n = 20$ points is as follows:

$$\theta_t = (t + \eta) \bmod 2\pi, \quad r_t = c + d\sin(at)\sin(2\pi b - bt), \quad t = 2\pi k/n \text{ with } k = 0, \dots, n-1. \quad (6.1)$$

This example is pictured in Fig. 6.1. The parameter η controls the rotation angle or orientation of the shape. By definition, $\alpha \bmod \beta = \alpha - \beta \lfloor \alpha/\beta \rfloor$ where the brackets represent the integer part function. A more simple example, corresponding to an elliptic arc, is

$$r_t = \frac{p}{1 - \epsilon\cos t}, \quad \theta_t = t, \quad 0 \leq t \leq t_0,$$

where $0 < \epsilon < 1$, $p > 0$, and $0 < t_0 < 2\pi$ are the parameters. The parameter ϵ is the eccentricity. Since the functions $g(t)$ and $f(t)$ are arbitrary, can be discontinuous, and may contain infinitely many parameters (for instance, the coefficient of a Taylor or Fourier series), it covers all the possible shapes that exist in the universe.

6.3 Shape signature

The concept of shape signature is not new, see [1,3]. Each shape (or set of points) is uniquely described by a normalized set called **signature**. In our context, this set can be a curve, a set of points, multiple broken curves, or a combination of these elements. The signature does not depend on the location or center of gravity of the shape. It depends on the orientation, though it is easy to generalize the definition to make it rotation-invariant, or to handle 3D shapes. The first step is to use the center of gravity (centroid) for the origin, and then rescale the shape by standardizing the variance of the radius r_t.

The centroid is the weighted average of the points located on the shape. Typically, the weight is constant. However, if the points are not uniformly distributed on the shape, you may use appropriate weights to correct for this artifact. This is illustrated in Fig. 6.2. I now dive into the details of the reweighting procedure.

6.3.1 Weighted centroid

Let (x_t, y_t) be the standard coordinates of the observed points on the shape. In other words, $x_t = r_t \cos \theta_t$ and $y_t = r_t \sin \theta_t$. The centroid is defined as (G_x, G_y) with

$$G_x = \frac{1}{\mu} \int_T w_t x_t dt, \quad G_y = \frac{1}{\mu} \int_T w_t y_t dt, \quad \text{with } \mu = \int_T w_t dt. \tag{6.2}$$

Here $w_t > 0$ is the weight function, with $t \in T$. If t is discrete (for instance, the shape consists of observed data points), then the integrals are replaced by sums.

In most cases, the points are not evenly distributed on the curve. On a real data set, it translates by a curve that appears darker or thicker in locations with high point density; see Fig. 6.2. If this is not a desirable feature, it can be eliminated by proper reweighting. To get the points evenly distributed on the curve, when computing the centroid, proceed as follows. Using notations from infinitesimal calculus, you want Δs_t, the length of an infinitesimal curve segment encompassing (x_t, y_t), to be proportional to w_t. Since the proportion factor does not matter, we must have

$$\Delta s_t = \sqrt{(\Delta x_t)^2 + (\Delta y_t)^2} = w_t \Delta t.$$

This leads to

$$w_t = \sqrt{\left(\frac{dx_t}{dt}\right)^2 + \left(\frac{dy_t}{dt}\right)^2}.$$

It can be rewritten using polar coordinates as

$$w_t = \sqrt{\left(\frac{dr_t}{dt}\right)^2 + r_t^2 \left(\frac{d\theta_t}{dt}\right)^2}.$$

The formula assumes differentiability of the functions involved. In many cases, there are points (values of t) where the functions are either left- or right-differentiable [Wiki], but not both. Use the left or right derivative for these points.

6.3.2 Computing the signature

We want a mathematical object, easy to compute, that uniquely characterizes a shape, up to a translation vector and scaling factor. The set of all polar coordinates (r_t, θ_t), with $t \in T$, uniquely characterizes the shape. But it is not scale- or translation-invariant. To fix this problem, you first need to change the coordinate system to make the centroid (G_x, G_y) defined by formula (6.2), the origin. You may use the weight function w_t discussed in Section 6.3.1. Then, you need to rescale by a factor σ. Eventually, the new coordinates are

$$u_t = \sigma^{-1} \cdot (x_t - G_x) = \rho_t \cos \varphi_t,$$
$$v_t = \sigma^{-1} \cdot (y_y - G_y) = \rho_t \sin \varphi_t.$$

Here u_t, v_t are the new Cartesian coordinates replacing x_t, y_t, and ρ_t, φ_t the new polar coordinates replacing r_t, θ_t. For reasons that will become obvious when comparing two shapes in Section 6.4, the scaling factor is chosen as follows:

$$\sigma = \sqrt{\int_T (x_t - G_x)^2 + (y_t - G_y)^2 dt}.$$

It follows immediately that

$$\rho_t = \sigma^{-1} \cdot \sqrt{(x_t - G_x)^2 + (y_t - G_y)^2}, \quad \text{and} \quad \int_T \rho_t^2 dt = 1. \tag{6.3}$$

Now the signature is defined as the set of all (ρ_t, φ_t) with $t \in T$. By construction, $0 \leq \varphi_t \leq 2\pi$. When plotting the signature, to keep it bounded on $[0, 2\pi] \times [0, 1]$ regardless of the shape, one can use $\rho_t/(1 + \rho_t)$ instead of ρ_t on the vertical axis. An example of signature is shown in Fig. 6.2 (right plot).

6.3.3 Example

The shape illustrated in Figs. 6.2 and 6.3 is different from that defined by (6.1). This time, it is defined by the parametric polar equation

$$\theta_t = (2\pi + 2\pi \sin(ct) + \eta) \bmod 2\pi, \quad r_t = t^a (1-t)^b, \quad t \in T = [0, 1]. \tag{6.4}$$

Again, η is the angle determining the orientation of the shape. The point density, visible to the naked eye, is much higher on the right side of the shape on the left plot in Fig. 6.2. This is even more pronounced on the lower part. As a result, the centroid (orange dot; dark gray in print version) attracted to the dense area of the curve. Once this effect is corrected by the weight function, the new centroid (gray dot) now appears well "centered". Note that the weight function w_t, pictured in Fig. 6.3, is bimodal. It was chosen to integrate to one, thus it represents a probability distribution on $T = [0, 1]$.

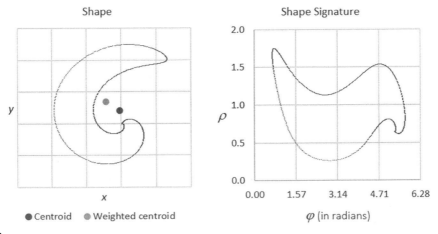

FIGURE 6.2

Weighted centroid, shape signature.

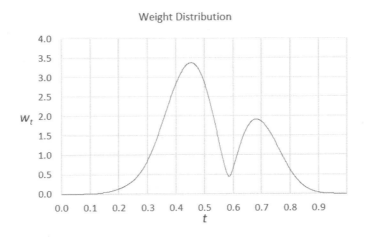

FIGURE 6.3

Weight function used in Fig. 6.2.

6.4 **Shape comparison**

I start with a correlation metric based on the mathematical theory developed so far. I then discuss its strengths and weaknesses, and how to improve it. A full implementation on a real data set is investigated in Section 6.5. I use the notation ρ_t, φ_t for the first shape, and ρ_t', φ_t' for the second. Assuming the parametric polar equations are such that (possibly after an appropriate transformation) $\varphi_t = \varphi_t'$ for $t \in T$, then define

$$\gamma = \int_T (\rho_t - \rho_t')^2 dt = \int_T \rho_t^2 dt + \int \rho_t'^2 dt - 2\int_T \rho_t \rho_t' dt = 2 - 2\lambda,$$

where

$$\lambda = \int_T \rho_t \rho_t' dt.$$

It follows from (6.3) that $0 \leq \lambda \leq 1$. Furthermore, the two shapes are identical (up to a scaling factor and translation vector) if and only if $\lambda = 1$. The correlation λ measures how close the two shapes are from each other. It relies on the fact that $\varphi_t = \varphi_t'$. It this assumption is mildly violated, the classifier may still work on simple data sets, for instance, to recognize the letters of the alphabet. But it may fail is the discrepancy between φ_t and φ_t' is significant.

It is not always possible to satisfy $\varphi_t = \varphi_t'$ for complicated shapes consisting of multiple arcs. But it can always be done for closed, convex shapes. Also, if the shapes are identical but rotated, usually $\lambda \neq 1$. The coefficient λ depends on the orientation angles η, η' of each shape, illustrated in formula (6.1). For this reason, λ is also denoted as $\lambda(\eta, \eta')$.

To circumvent this problem, one can use

$$\lambda^* = \min_{\eta, \eta'} \lambda(\eta, \eta').$$

Then the two shapes are identical, up to the scaling factors, translation vectors, and orientations, if and only if $\lambda^* = 1$. Due to symmetry, one can set $\eta = 0$. In practice, the metric $-\log(1 - \lambda)$ or $-\log(1 - \lambda^*)$ is used instead. See [4] for a general reference on shape correlation.

Of course, it is always possible to compare two shapes by comparing their signatures, see [2]. One way to do it is as follows. For each point P_t on the first shape signature, find its closest neighbor Q_t on the second shape signature, and compute the distance D_t between these two points. Then compute

$$D = \int_T D_t dt.$$

Repeat the operation by swapping the roles of the first and second shape: for each point Q_t' on the second shape signature, find its closest neighbor P_t' on the first shape signature, and compute the distance D_t' between these two points. Then compute

$$D' = \int_T D_t' dt.$$

If $D = 0$, the first shape is a subset of the second shape. If $D' = 0$, the second shape is a subset of the first shape. If $D = D' = 0$, the shapes are identical. Thus $\delta = \min(D, D')$ is a metric measuring shape similarity. It is closely related to the **Hausdorff distance** [Wiki], albeit less sensitive to outliers.

6.4.1 Shape classification

Now that we have a metric to compare two shapes, we can use it as a similarity measure to perform shape classification. If shapes S_1 and S_2 have $-\log(1 - \lambda) > \alpha$, we may write $S_1 \sim S_2$ to mean that they are equivalent (very similar). In this case, $\alpha = 8$ is a good threshold. In character recognition, if you have a training set with thousands of hieroglyphs, you can use this technique to classify any new hieroglyph as equivalent to one or more in your training set, or as yet uncategorized (a brand new one, or one so poorly written that it is not recognizable).

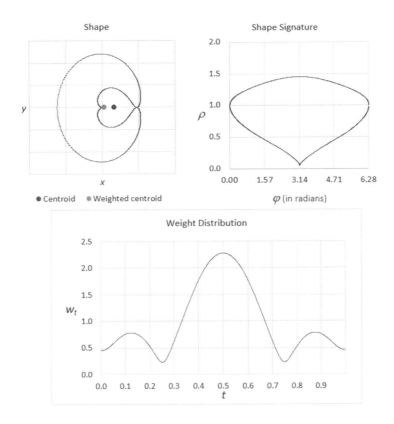

FIGURE 6.4

Another interesting shape.

6.5 Application

In all the cases investigated, including the mathematical ones, the computations were performed using sample points on the shape, corresponding to evenly spaced values of t. I used sums rather than integrals, and derivatives such as dx_t/dt were replaced by differences between successive values of x_t. You can find the computations in my spreadsheet Shapes4.xlsx, located on my GitHub repository, here.

Spreadsheet and data

The two main examples are:

- 20 points for the case pictured in Fig. 6.1. Here I tested 8 pairs of shapes; you can find the summary in the animated Gif, posted here. In addition, I introduced various levels of noise to test the discriminating power of the classifier. The amount of noise is controlled by the parameter Precision.
- 1000 points for the case pictured in Fig. 6.2. Details are in the Shape_Signature tab in the spreadsheet. In the same tab, you will find the computation of the weight function, the weighted centroid, and the computations related to the new coordinate system ρ_t, φ_t.

My simulations rely on synthetic data [Wiki]. In other words, I use mathematically-generated shapes. The benefit is that you can generate a large class of shapes (actually, infinitely many), mimicking any existing shape, and compare the performance of various shape classifiers. In particular, you can assess how well a specific metric can detect different, yet very similar shapes, or how it performs when various levels of noise are introduced. Modern methods combine real observations with synthetic data to further enrich training sets. This is known as **augmented data** [Wiki].

Several other machine learning techniques, tested on synthetic data and accompanied by professional summary spreadsheets, are available (along with the data sets and source code), in my book "Stochastic Processes and Simulations: A Machine Learning Perspective". Many are described in Chapter 16.

6.6 Exercises

The first exercise has an elegant solution. The second is an application of the principles discussed.

Exercise 6.1. Find the weight function satisfying $\Delta(w_t x_t) = \Delta(w_t y_t)$. This is related to the material presented in Section 6.3.1. It uses the same notations.

Solution

You need to find w_t satisfying $x_t \Delta w_t + w_t \Delta x_t = y_t \Delta w_t + w_t \Delta y_t$. Dividing by Δt, and letting $\Delta t \to 0$, we get

$$x_t \frac{dw_t}{dt} + w_t \frac{dx_t}{dt} = y_t \frac{dw_t}{dt} + w_t \frac{dy_t}{dt},$$

that is,

$$(x_t - y_t)\frac{dw_t}{dt} = \left(\frac{dy_t}{dt} - \frac{dx_t}{dt}\right) w_t.$$

This is successively equivalent to

$$\frac{d}{dt}(\log w_t) = \frac{1}{w_t}\frac{dw_t}{dt} = \frac{1}{x_t - y_t}\left(\frac{dy_t}{dt} - \frac{dx_t}{dt}\right),$$

$$\log w_t = \int \frac{1}{x_t - y_t}\left(\frac{dy_t}{dt} - \frac{dx_t}{dt}\right) dt + C,$$

$$w_t = C' \exp\left[-\int_0^t \frac{1}{y_\tau - x_\tau}\left(\frac{dy_\tau}{d\tau} - \frac{dx_\tau}{d\tau}\right) d\tau\right],$$

where C, C' are constants, with $C' > 0$. The value of C' is unimportant when using formula (6.2). However, you can choose it so that the weight function integrates to one. Or you can use $C' = 1$. I assumed, without loss of generality, that the integration domain T is an interval containing the origin $\tau = 0$.

You can test this formula on a line segment, defined by $x_t = t$, $y_t = a + bt$, with $t \in [0, 1]$. This is the most basic shape other than a finite set of points! A slightly more difficult exercise is to find the weight function satisfying $|\Delta(w_t x_t)| = |\Delta(w_t y_t)|$. Exercise 6.1 is a starting point to solve this problem.

Exercise 6.2. Compare the shape in Fig. 6.2 with that of Fig. 6.4, using the metrics presented in this chapter (D and λ). These shapes correspond to Eq. (6.4). The first has parameters $a = 7$, $b = 6$, $c = 8$. The second has parameters $a = b = 1$, $c = 2\pi$. In both cases, $\eta = 0$. Use 1000 sample points on each shape for comparison purposes. Order the points according to t, then according to φ_t, to see the impact on λ. Set $\eta = 0$, and choose η' (the orientation of the second shape) to maximize the similarity between the two shapes.

Solution

A starting point is my spreadsheet `Shapes4.xlsx`, available on my GitHub repository, here. This type of shape is analyzed in the `Shape_Signature` tab.

References

[1] S. Giannarou, T. Stathaki, Shape signature matching for object identification invariant to image transformations and occlusion, ResearchGate, 2007, [Link].
[2] K. Grauman, Shape Matching, University of Texas, Austin, 2008, [Link].
[3] F. Park, Shape descriptor / feature extraction techniques, 2011, UCI iCAMP 2011, [Link].
[4] Y. Vizilter, S. Zheltov, Geometrical correlation and matching of 2D image shapes, ResearchGate, 2012, [Link].

Synthetic data, interpretable regression, and submodels

Little known secrets about linear regression

The technique discussed here handles a large class of problems. In this article, I focus on a simple one, namely linear regression. I solve it with an iterative algorithm (fixed point) that shares some resemblance to gradient boosting, using machine learning methods and explainable AI, as opposed to traditional statistics. In particular, the algorithm does not use matrix inversion. It is easy to implement in Excel (I provide my spreadsheet) or to automate as a black-box system. Also, it is numerically stable, can generalize to nonlinear problems. Unlike the traditional statistical solution leading to meaningless regression coefficients, here the output coefficients are easier to understand, leading to better interpretation. I tested it on a rich collection of synthetic data sets: it performs just as well as the standard technique, even after adding noise to the data. I then show how to measure the impact of individual features, or groups of features (and feature interaction), on the solution. A model with m features has 2^m submodels. I show how to draw more insights by analyzing the performance of each submodel. Finally, I introduce a new metric called *score* to measure model performance. Based on comparison with the base model, it is more meaningful than R-squared or mean squared error.

7.1 Introduction

Here, X denotes the input. It is represented as a matrix with n rows and m columns; n is the number of observations, and m the number of features, also called dependent variables. The response (also called independent variable or output) is a column vector with n entries, and denoted as Y. The m regression coefficients (unknown, to be estimated) are stored in a column vector denoted as β. Thus we have

$$Y = X\beta + \epsilon, \tag{7.1}$$

where ϵ – also a column vector with n entries – is the error. The problem consists of finding a suitable β that, in some way, minimizes the error. If there was no error term, Eq. (7.1) could be rewritten as $X^T Y = X^T X\beta + \Lambda\beta - \Lambda\beta$, that is,

$$\beta = \Lambda^{-1} X^T Y + (I - \Lambda^{-1} X^T X)\beta.$$

Here Λ is any nonsingular (invertible) $m \times m$ matrix, and ^{T} denotes the matrix or vector transposition operator [Wiki]. This gives rise to the following iterative algorithm:

$$\beta_{k+1} = \Lambda^{-1} X^T Y + (I - \Lambda^{-1} X^T X)\beta_k, \tag{7.2}$$

Synthetic Data and Generative AI. https://doi.org/10.1016/B978-0-44-321857-6.00011-4
113

starting with some initial configuration β_0 for the parameter vector (the regression coefficients). I use a diagonal matrix for Λ, so the methodology does not involve complicated matrix inversions.

I also use the following notations: $M = X^T X$ and $S = I - \Lambda^{-1} M$. The convergence of this iterative algorithm, and how fast it converges, is entirely governed by how fast $S^k \to 0$ as $k \to \infty$. It requires a careful choice of Λ. I discuss later how to update Λ at each iteration k: in an adaptive version of this algorithm, Λ is replaced by Λ_k in (7.2), with the hope that it boosts convergence. The general term for this type of iteration, which also encompasses Newton optimization and gradient descent, is a **fixed point algorithm** [Wiki].

The remaining of this discussion focuses on the choice of Λ and β_0, with convergence implications and computational complexity, tested on **synthetic data** [Wiki]. I show that with very few iterations, one generally gets a very good predictor, even though the estimated parameter vector is quite different from the target one used in the simulations. In short, the R-squared arising from rough approximations, based on a few iterations of the fixed point algorithm, is very similar to that obtained using the full standard statistical apparatus. Despite the nonstatistical perspective and the absence of statistical model, I explain how to compute confidence intervals for the estimated regression coefficients and for the predicted values. The whole framework is designed to facilitate interpretation, and thus it falls in the category of explainable AI [Wiki].

Finally, I want to offer a simple version of this method, simple enough to easily be implemented in Excel. The choice $\beta_0 = 0$ and Λ minimizing the **Frobenius norm** of S [Wiki] (see also [2]) not only works well but also leads to simple formulas, and an interesting connection to **eigenvalues** [Wiki] (see also here). The last part of this chapter focuses on assessing the influence of each feature, and the impact of feature interaction. The synthetic training set data discussed in Section 7.2 allows you to simulate and test a large number of varied situations. Eventually, model performance is measured on a validation set, not on a training set.

7.2 Synthetic data sets and the spreadsheet

Rather than testing the methodology on a few real-life data sets, I tested it on a large number of very different synthetic data sets, each with its unique correlation structure. These data sets are generated via simulations, as follows. First, generate m column vectors $Z_1, \ldots, Z_m$, with Z_i consisting of n deviates Z_{ij} ($1 \le i \le m, 1 \le j \le n$). One of the simplest distributions to sample from is the **generalized logistic**. See examples in Chapter 16, to simulate cluster processes. In this case I used

$$Z_{ij} = -\log \frac{U_{ij}^{\gamma}}{1 - U_{ij}^{\gamma}},$$

where $\gamma > 0$ is a parameter, and U_{ij}'s are independently and identically distributed uniform deviates on $[0, 1]$. Then, I generated m column vectors $X_1, \ldots, X_m$ as random linear combinations of the Z_i's:

$$X_i = \sum_{j=1}^{m} w_{ij} Z_i, \quad i = 1, \ldots, m. \tag{7.3}$$

The $m \times m$ matrix $W = (w_{ij})$ is called the weight matrix. Here again, the w_{ij}'s are deviates from the same family of generalized logistic distributions. Finally, the simulated response is

$$Y = \sum_{i=1}^{m} \alpha_i X_i + \tau \epsilon, \quad i = 1, \dots, m,$$

where ϵ (a column vector with n independent entries) is an artificially generated white noise, and $\tau \geq 0$ controls the amount of noise. The α_i's can be prespecified or randomly generated. In any case, the exact, prespecified set of regression coefficients is the column vector $\alpha = (\alpha_1, \dots, \alpha_m)^T$. The estimated coefficients, at the kth iteration of the fixed point algorithm, using formula (7.2), comprise the column vector $\beta_k = (\beta_{k1}, \dots, \beta_{km})^T$. Thus in this setting, we are able to measure how close the estimate β_k is to the exact value α. In real-life applications, the exact value is never known. If it was, there would be no need to perform statistical inference.

7.2.1 Correlation structure

Let Ω_X (respectively Ω_Z) be the $m \times m$ **covariance matrix** [Wiki] attached to $X_1, \dots, X_m$ (respectively to $Z_1, \dots, Z_m$). Likewise, define the correlation matrices as R_X, R_Z, with

$$R_X = [D(\Omega_X)]^{-1/2} \Omega_X [D(\Omega_X)]^{-1/2} \quad \text{and} \quad R_Z = [D(\Omega_Z)]^{-1/2} \Omega_Z [D(\Omega_Z)]^{-1/2}.$$

Here $D(A)$ is the matrix consisting of the diagonal elements of the matrix A. We have

$$\Omega_X = W \Omega_Z W^T = (W \Omega_X^{1/2})(W \Omega_X^{1/2})^T, \quad \text{thus } W = \Omega_X^{1/2} \Omega_Z^{-1/2}.$$

These formulas allow you to easily compute R_X based on the weight matrix W and Ω_W. Though more difficult, it is possible to solve the inverse problem: prespecify the correlation structure R_X of the data set, and then find W that yields the desired, target R_X. This is best accomplished using an iterative algorithm similar to the fixed point discussed in Section 7.1, using the above formulas.

The formulas to solve the inverse problem involve the **square root** of **positive semidefinite matrices** [Wiki]. The solution is not unique. See how it is done, in Chapter 3 entitled "Gentle Introduction to Linear Algebra". Without loss of generality, a simplification consists of simulating standardized $Z_1, \dots, Z_m$ (from a distribution with zero mean and unit variance) so that $R_Z = \Omega_Z$ is the identity matrix. If, in addition, the observed $X_1, \dots, X_m$ are also standardized, then $R_X = \Omega_X$, and thus, $W = R_X^{1/2}$. Multiple square roots exist, in the same way that 2 and -2 are two "square roots" of 4.

7.2.2 Standardized regression

Under stable conditions, the predicted values for Y are very close to those obtained via standard statistical regression, even though the estimated regression coefficients may be quite different. The accompanying spreadsheet and computations are now stable. However, in previous tests, with a different damping schedule (the matrix Λ), sometimes the β_k diverged as $k \to \infty$. Yet after normalizing β_k, the instability was essentially removed and, again, the predicted Y was sound. I provide here the normalizing formula, to guarantee that the standard deviation of the response Y, denoted as σ_Y, is identical to that measured on the predicted Y. The new β_k, denoted as β_k^*, is computed as follows:

$$\beta_k^* = \frac{\sigma_Y}{\sqrt{\beta_k^T \Omega_X \beta_k}} \cdot \Omega_W \beta_k.$$

This may be useful if you modify Λ when doing some research, as a technique to stabilize the predictions. I also included the computation of β_k^* in the spreadsheet. However, it is best to avoid standardizing the regression coefficients when the algorithm is numerically stable. It results in more realistic variance in the predicted values as the uncorrected regression acts as a smoother, but it also comes with a price – a larger mean squared error.

To the contrary, shifting the predicted values so that their mean matches that of the observed values on the training set, is always useful. It is included in my computations (and in the spreadsheet) as a final, postprocessing step. It does not impact the R-squared. Also, it allows you to ignore the intercept parameter in the regression model. Indeed, this is an easy workaround to using an actual intercept parameter.

7.2.3 Initial conditions

The neutral choice $\beta_0 = 0$ as the starting vector of regression coefficients, for the iterative fixed point algorithm, works well. Another option consists of choosing regression coefficients that preserve the correlation sign between the response Y, and each feature $X_1, \ldots, X_m$. Here, X_i is the ith column of the matrix X. Let

$$c_i = \frac{\mathrm{Cov}[Y, X_i]}{\mathrm{Var}[X_i]}, \quad c = (c_1, \ldots, c_m)^T, \quad Q = \sum_{i=1}^{m} c_i X_i = Xc,$$

with ω a real number chosen to minimize the error $\epsilon^T \epsilon = (Y - \omega Q)^T (Y - \omega Q) = Y^T Y - 2 Q^T Y \omega + Q^T Q \omega^2$. We have

$$w = \frac{Y^T Q}{Q^T Q} = \frac{Y^T Xc}{c^T X^T Xc} \quad \text{and} \quad \mathrm{Var}[c_i X_i] = \mathrm{Var}[Y] \cdot \rho^2[X_i, Y] = \sigma_Y^2 \cdot \rho^2[X_i, Y],$$

where ρ denotes the correlation function. Now, $\beta_0 = \omega c$ is a starting point that makes sense, easy to interpret, and better then $\beta_0 = 0$. It significantly reduces the residual error, over the base model $\beta = 0$. In many cases, it yields a residual error almost comparable to that of the best predictors.

As an illustration, let us say that $X_2 = X_3$. You should avoid highly correlated features in your data set, but in some cases the interdependencies among several features are strong but much harder to detect, and result in the same problem. In my example, assuming both X_2 and X_3 are positively correlated to the response Y, a model with $+4$ and -2 for the regression coefficients attached to X_2 and X_3, performs just as well as -2, $+4$ or $+1$, $+1$. The β_0 proposed here addresses this issue: it guarantees that the regression coefficients attached to X_2 and X_3 are both positive in this example, and identical if $X_2 = X_3$. It makes the regression coefficients much easier to interpret. In addition, this technique is numerically stable and more robust.

7.2.4 **Simulations and Excel spreadsheet**

Formulas and computations described in Section 7.2 are implemented in my spreadsheet Regres-sion5.xlsx, available here on my GitHub repository. This material covers a large chunk of the spread-sheet, with the remaining explained in the next sections.

The Test and Results tabs in the spreadsheet contain the following:

- The random deviates $Z_1, \ldots, Z_m$ are in the Test tab in columns A:F. The zero-mean noise is in column H. The amount of noise in the response Y is controlled by the parameter Noise in cell E:5 in the Results tab. As a general rule, cells highlighted in light yellow in the Results tab correspond to parameters or hyperparameters that you can modify. The parameter γ just above in cell E:4 is the core parameter of the generalized logistic distribution used to simulate the column vectors $Z_1, \ldots, Z_m$.
- The flag in cell E:7 in the Results tab allows you to choose either $\beta_0 = 0$, or the special β_0 discussed in Section 7.2.3.
- By default, the regression uses the traditional β_k. If you want to use the normalized β_k^* instead, they are iteratively computed in cells AX2:ES7 in the Test tab. For instance, cells BL2:BL7 represent β_{15}^*, that is, the 15th iterate ($k = 15$) in the fixed point algorithm, stored as a column vector. The standard β_k are computed in cells AX20:ES25 in the same tab.
- Column I in the Test tab is the response Y. The features $X_1, \ldots, X_m$, also called independent variables, are in columns J:O in the same tab. They are generated as linear combinations of the random vectors $Z_1, \ldots, Z_m$. More precisely, $X = WZ$ as per Eq. (7.3), where W is the $m \times m$ weight matrix. The random weight matrix W is stored in cells B15:G20 in the Results tab. The actual, true (random) regression parameters are just above in the same tab, in cells B12:G12.
- Intermediary computations are in the Test tab. For instance, the $m \times m$ matrix $X^T X$ is stored in cells AP2:AU7, the vector $X^T Y$ in cells AN2:AN7, the correlation matrix R_X in cells AE3:AJ8, and the covariance matrix Ω_X in cells AE12:AJ17.

The interactive spreadsheet extensively uses the SumProduct and Transpose Excel functions, to easily multiply a row vector by a column vector with just one simple operation. It also makes matrix multiplications easier.

7.3 **Damping schedule and convergence acceleration**

The $m \times m$ diagonal matrix Λ^{-1} in Eq. (7.2) is called the damping parameter, or **preconditioner** [Wiki] of the fixed point iteration. It governs the rate of convergence. The fixed point algorithm converges if $|\varphi| < 1$, where $\varphi = \varphi(S)$ is the largest eigenvalue of $S = I - \Lambda^{-1} X^T X$, in absolute value. The smaller the $|\varphi|$, the faster the convergence. The convergence speed is eventually determined by how fast $S^k \to 0$ as $k \to \infty$, itself being a function of $|\varphi|$. Thus, it makes sense to choose Λ so that S is close to zero. One way to do it is to choose Λ that minimizes the Frobenius norm of S or, in other words, Λ that minimizes the sum of the square of the coefficients of S. This leads to

$$\lambda_i^{-1} = \frac{1}{m_{ii}} \sum_{j=1}^{m} m_{ij}^2, \quad i = 1, \ldots, m, \tag{7.4}$$

where $\lambda_1, \ldots, \lambda_m$ are the diagonal elements of the diagonal matrix Λ, and m_{ij} is the jth element in column i, of the matrix $M = X^T X$. In practice, with this choice of Λ, assuming M is not singular, the fixed point iteration always converges, and $m_{ii} > 0$. See discussion on this topic, here.

7.3.1 Spreadsheet implementation

The λ_i's are computed in cells AL2:AL7 in the Test tab. Also, $|\varphi|$ is iteratively computed in cells AY59:ES59 in the same tab. The method used in the spreadsheet to compute $|\varphi|$ is known as **power iteration** [Wiki]. See also here.

Now we have everything in place to compute the regression coefficients. They are found in cells K5:P5 (computation based on $k = 15$ iterations) and K6:P6 (based on $k = 100$ iterations) in the Results tab. The final value of $|\varphi|$ is in cell K21, also in the Results tab. Note that values of $|\varphi|$ above 0.95 means that the system is **ill-conditioned** [Wiki]. For instance, some features are almost linear combinations of other features. It typically results in poor performance. In this case, using a few iterations ($k = 15$), together with the initial β_0 suggested in Section 7.2.3, works best. It also avoids overfitting issues.

The predicted values of Y, obtained after $k = 15$ and $k = 100$ iterations, are in columns P and Q, respectively, in the Test tab. The predicted values obtained with β_0 alone (as computed in Section 7.2.3) are in column S, while those obtained with traditional regression are in column U and produced with the Linest Excel function. The filtered response, obtained by removing the artificial noise introduced in the observed (synthetic) data, is in column R. The computational complexity of the fixed point regression is the same as multiplying two $m \times m$ matrices, multiplied by the number of iterations in the fixed point algorithm.

7.3.2 Interpretable regression with no overfitting

The regression coefficient vector β_0 introduced in Section 7.2.3 is intuitive, robust, and preserves the correlation signs: by design, a feature positively correlated with the response Y gets assigned a positive correlation coefficient, as previously discussed. In addition, its performance is nearly as good as optimum regression coefficients, in many situations. It definitely performs well above the base model, unless the amount of noise is substantial. But in that case, all models perform badly, unable to improve over the base model. See Section 7.4.1 for performance comparison. If your problem is ill-conditioned (for instance, some features are nearly identical or linear combinations of other features), traditional techniques will lead to meaningless regression coefficients, or fail entirely. To the contrary, the β_0 in question handles this situation very well.

All of this makes the β_0 in question a good starting point for the fixed point iteration, if the goal is to obtain a robust solution, easy to interpret, and not prone to overfitting. It can be improved by using a few iterations of the fixed point algorithm. The more iterations, the closer you get to the standard "exact" solution, but you eventually lose interpretability. With fewer iterations, you may still get a good performance, yet avoid many of the aforementioned problems. One way to decide when to stop is to run many iterations, and compare your R-squared obtained after (say) 10 versus 100 iterations. If the difference is negligible, use the regression coefficients obtained at iteration $k = 10$. Instead of using R-squared, I suggest to use the metric s defined in Section 7.4.

7.3.3 Adaptive damping

A possible way to boost convergence is to use a matrix Λ that depends on k, and denoted as Λ_k. The most simple example is when $\Lambda_k = \lambda(k) \cdot I$ where $\lambda(k)$ is a real number and I is the $m \times m$ identity matrix. Then, choose $\lambda(k)$ that minimizes $||(I - \lambda^{-1})\beta_k||_2$, that is,

$$\lambda(k) = \arg\min_{\lambda} ||(I - \lambda^{-1})\beta_k||_2$$

$$= \arg\min_{\lambda} [(I - \lambda^{-1}M)\beta_k]^T (I - \lambda^{-1}M)\beta_k$$

$$= \arg\min_{\lambda} \beta_k^T \beta_k - 2\lambda^{-1}\beta_k^T M\beta_k + \lambda^{-2}(M\beta_k)^T M\beta_k$$

$$= \frac{(M\beta_k)^T M\beta_k}{\beta_k^T M\beta_k}.$$

Again, $M = X^T X$. Preliminary tests did not show large improvements over using a fixed Λ. Indeed, about 20% of the time, instead of converging, the successive iterates of the regression coefficients oscillate. Yet this issue is easy to address, and adaptive damping – where Λ depends on k – has potential to handle data sets with a larger m (the number of features). The worst case, by far in my 100 tests or so, is pictured in Fig. 7.1. The drawback, compared to using preconditioning only (a fixed Λ), is that it requires more computations. For a recent machine learning application of preconditioners in a similar context, see [1].

7.4 Performance assessment on synthetic data

I use three metrics to measure the goodness-of-fit between the observed (synthetic) response Y and the predicted response denoted here as P. These metrics are computed on a validation set, not on the training set: this is a standard cross-validation procedure to avoid overfitting and performance inflation. Thus, what I call R-squared is actually closer, but not identical, to "predictive R-squared" and PRESS statistics [Wiki]. The same applies to MSE. The synthetic control set is in the `Control` tab in the spreadsheet.

The three metrics are:

- The R-squared r, with $0 \le r \le 1$, is the square of the correlation between Y and P. It is also equal to $[\sigma_Y^2 - (Y - P)^T (Y - P)]/\sigma_Y^2$.
- The root mean squared error or RMSE [Wiki], defined as $e = \sqrt{(Y - P)^T (Y - P)}/n$, where n is the number of observations. It is a much better measure of the actual error, compared to the mean squared error (MSE). In particular, if Y is measured in (say) miles, then RMSE is measured in miles, while MSE is measured in square miles. Likewise, if Y is measured in years, RMSE is measured in years while MSE is measured in square years – a meaningless metric.
- The score s, with $0 \le s \le 1$, defined as $s = 1 - e(P)/e(P_0)$. Here, P_0 is the base model, corresponding to $\beta = 0$ (thus, the predicted value is constant after adjustment, equal to the mean value of Y computed on the training set). In particular, s measures the improvement over the base model, using RMSE ratios, while r does the same using MSE ratios instead. In my opinion, s is more intuitive and

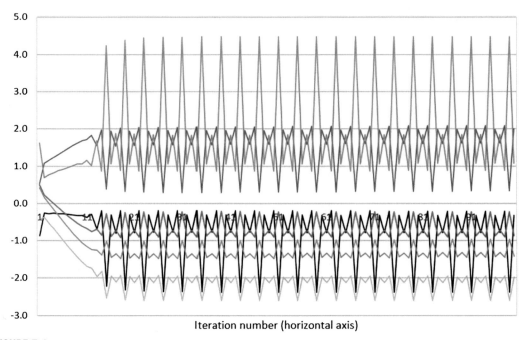

FIGURE 7.1

Regression coefficients oscillating when using adaptive damping.

more realistic than r. It is related to r via the formula $r = 2s - s^2$, or equivalently, $s = 1 - \sqrt{1-r}$. We always have $r \geq s$, so r is an inflated measure of goodness-of-fit.

Since the model is trained on the test data set, but model performance is measured on the validation set, the above performance metrics are hybrid. In particular, as a result, the relationship $r = 2s - s^2$ is almost satisfied, but not exactly. Also, on rare occasions (with very noisy data), r can be slightly negative. The performance results are shown in the `Results` tab, in cells `J13:R19`. I also included the performance metrics for the simple model consisting in using the regression coefficient vector $\beta = \beta_0$ defined in Section 7.2.3. In the spreadsheet, this model is referred to as "Predicted P_b".

In addition, the spreadsheet allows you to choose which features to include or not in the model, in the fixed point iteration. The feature selection flags are stored in cells `B4:B9` in the `Results` tab. The default value is 1, corresponding to inclusion. This is particularly useful to test how much model improvement is gained by using all features, versus a subset of them. On real data, some features are usually missing because the model developer was not aware of them, and they are not captured in the data set: in other words, they are unobserved. The feature selection flags allow you to compare the performance on observed data, versus the performance obtained with a dream data set that would include all the relevant features.

Finally, the use of synthetic data offers a big benefit: you can test and benchmark algorithms on millions of very different data sets, all at once. This assume that the synthetic data is properly generated. It is both an art and a science to design such data sets. It typically involves a decent amount of mathe-

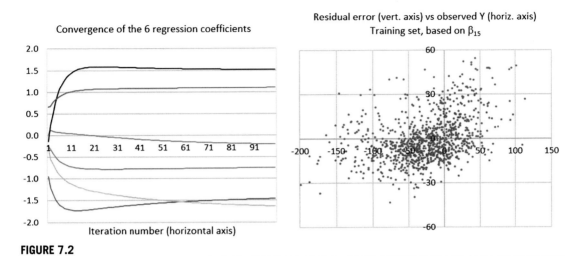

FIGURE 7.2

Convergence of regression coefficients (left) and distribution of residual error (right).

matics, sometimes quite advanced. It is my hope that this article will help the reader build good quality, rich synthetic data that covers a large spectrum of potential real life situations. Other synthetic data sets are found in Chapter 5 featuring synthetic clusters, and in Chapter 6 entitled "Computer Vision: Shape Classification via Explainable AI", featuring synthetic shapes.

7.4.1 **Results**

I tested the methodology on a synthetic data set with $n = 1000$ observations and $m = 6$ features. The validation set also has 1000 observations. Because the data is artificially generated, the exact regression coefficients are known. They are listed in the row labeled "Exact" in Table 7.1. The observed data Y is a mixture of the exact data and artificial noise. The amount of noise is controlled by the parameter Noise in the spreadsheet. The exact data is the vector $X\beta$, with β being the true, prespecified regression coefficients (also artificially generated). Note that X is also artificially generated, using the method described in Section 7.2.4.

The metric r in the Exact row in Table 7.1 measures the R-squared between the observed data Y and the exact data. In practice, the exact data is not known. But one of the benefits of using synthetic data is that we can simulate both the unobserved, exact data, and the observed, noisy, unfiltered version, denoted as Y.

The metric r in Table 7.1 is the R-squared, but measured on the validation set, not on the training set. By contrast, in Fig. 7.3, the R-squared on the right plot, attached to the blue dots and blue regression line, is computed on the training set. On the left plot, it is computed on the validation set, and it matches the r value attached to β_{15} in Table 7.1. The blue dots in Fig. 7.3 provide the scatterplot of Y versus the predicted values obtained with β_{15}. The orange dots form the scatterplot of Y versus the exact (unobserved) data.

Fig. 7.2 (left plot) shows how the six regression coefficients converge in the fixed point iterations, starting with the vector $\beta_0 = 0$. The same matrix Λ is used at all times, unlike in Fig. 7.1. The oscillating

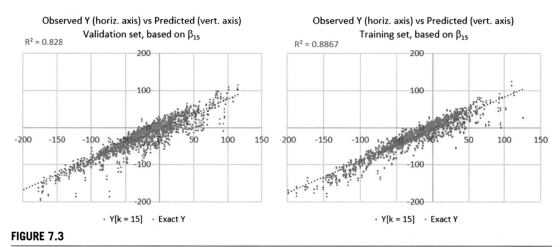

FIGURE 7.3

Goodness-of-fit: training set (right) versus validation set (left).

Table 7.1 Regression coefficients and performance metrics r, s based on methodology.

Method	r	s	Regression coefficients					
Exact	0.891	67.0%	−1.513	−0.202	1.514	−1.647	1.079	−0.799
β_{15}	0.828	58.5%	−1.726	0.025	1.544	−1.208	1.045	−0.758
β_{100}	0.830	58.8%	−1.460	−0.204	1.517	−1.631	1.103	−0.746
β_0	0.596	36.2%	−1.630	0.116	0.072	−0.947	0.627	−0.689
Excel	0.823	58.7%	−1.426	−0.236	1.542	−1.666	1.153	−0.669

behavior seen in Fig. 7.1 never occurs with the fixed Λ defined by Eq. (7.4). The right plot in Fig. 7.2 is a scatterplot of Y versus the residual error $\epsilon = Y - X\beta$, using $\beta = \beta_{15}$ measured on the training set. In idealized statistical models, ϵ is assumed to be a white noise. Clearly, this is not the case here, with larger observed values (on the horizontal axis) having a tendency to have a larger error. However, this data is very useful to simulate ϵ, to use in model-free confidence and prediction intervals, as discussed in Section 7.4.2.

The synthetic data set used in Tables 7.1 and 7.2 is different from that used in Section 7.4.2. In particular, I increased the amount of noise in the validation set, compared to the training set. I did it to better emulate real data, where performance is usually lower outside the training set. It explains why the R-squared is sensibly better when measured on the training set, as opposed to the validation set.

The performance metric s in Table 7.1 is discussed in Section 7.4. It is much more meaningful than the R-squared r. If measured on the training set, we would have $s = 1 - \sqrt{1-r}$. Here, it is measured on the validation set. Yet the equality is still almost satisfied. Also in Table 7.1, the row labeled β_0 corresponds to the special, basic regression method discussed in Section 7.2.3. The Excel row corresponds to the standard regression coefficients computed by any statistical package, in this case with the Excel Linest function. Note that β_{15}, β_{100} and the Excel regression yield different sets of regression coefficients. Yet the three of them have the same performance.

Table 7.2 Correlation matrix.

	Y	X_1	X_2	X_3	X_4	X_5	X_6
Y	1.000	−0.642	0.077	0.033	−0.481	0.404	−0.271
X_1	−0.642	1.000	−0.216	0.458	0.559	−0.266	−0.162
X_2	0.077	−0.216	1.000	−0.061	−0.840	−0.447	0.762
X_3	0.033	0.458	−0.061	1.000	0.048	−0.543	−0.088
X_4	−0.481	0.559	−0.840	0.048	1.000	0.281	−0.620
X_5	0.404	−0.266	−0.447	−0.543	0.281	1.000	−0.700
X_6	−0.271	−0.162	0.762	−0.088	−0.620	−0.700	1.000

The easiest to interpret is β_0, followed by β_{15}: in particular, they yield regression coefficients with the same sign as the correlations (the row labeled Y in Table 7.2). If you run the fixed point iteration long enough, eventually β_k will tend to the Excel solution, as $k \to \infty$. Because of the noise in the data set, even with infinitely many iterations, it is impossible to retrieve the exact, prespecified regression coefficients featured in the Exact row. However, β_{100} and Excel provide good approximations.

7.4.2 Distribution-free confidence intervals

This will be the topic of a future article. Here I provide a quick overview, using **resampling** [Wiki] and related data-driven techniques. Let $Y = P + \epsilon$, $P = X\beta$ be the regression model, with Y the observed (synthetic) response, P the predicted values, X the $n \times m$ matrix representing the features (with values synthetically generated; n is the sample size), β the regression coefficient vector, and ϵ the residual error vector. In other words, β is the vector minimizing $(Y - X\beta)^T (Y - X\beta)$, or its approximation using the fixed point algorithm.

The starting point is to randomly shuffle the n entries of ϵ, to create a new error vector ϵ'. Let $Y' = Y - \epsilon + \epsilon'$, that is, $Y' = X\beta + \epsilon'$. Now find β' that minimizes $(Y' - X\beta')^T (Y' - X\beta')$. Now you get a new set of regression coefficients, β'. Repeat this operation 100 times, and you get 100 sets of regression coefficients: β, β', β'', and so on.

This model-free procedure immediately provides confidence intervals for the regression coefficients, by looking at the empirical distribution [Wiki] of each regression coefficient across the 100 data sets. Now for a particular feature vector $(x_1, \ldots, x_m)$ – whether part of the training set or not – the predicted value can be obtained in 100 different ways: $p = x\beta$, $p' = x\beta'$, $p'' = x\beta''$, and so on. The empirical distribution of p, p', p'', and so on, provides a **prediction interval** for the predicted value of the response, at the arbitrary location x in the feature space. Another way to do it to resample ϵ with replacements (rather than by random permutations). This is then a bootstrapping technique [Wiki].

This methodology assumes that the individual residual errors are independently and identically distributed. I discuss how to address this issue in Section 7.4.2.1. Also it assumes that the error is additive, not multiplicative. In the latter case, one might want to work with a transformed version of Y rather than Y itself. For an Excel implementation, see the Regression5_Static spreadsheet on my GitHub repository, here. In the Test tab, column AD corresponds to $\epsilon' = \epsilon$, and column AE to ϵ''. Sort columns AE:AF by AF (uniform deviates) to reshuffle the residual error. Then Y is automatically replaced by Y'' in column I, and the new regression coefficient vector β'' is in cells K6:P6 in the Results tab.

7.4.2.1 *Parametric bootstrap*

Another option is to use Gaussian deviates for ϵ', ϵ'', and so on. They need to have the same variance as the one computed on the observed residual error ϵ. This approach is known as **parametric bootstrap**.

If ϵ is autocorrelated, for example, if you are dealing with time series and one of the features is the time, it is possible to use an autoregressive process that has the same autocorrelation structure as ϵ, to simulate ϵ', ϵ'', and so on. Likewise, if ϵ is correlated to Y, this can be handled with some appropriate parametric model. Parametric bootstrap for linear regression is discussed in [4]. Distribution-free predictive inference for regression is discussed in [5].

7.5 **Feature selection**

In Section 7.5.1, I compare the performance of the regression coefficients obtained for each of the potential feature combinations. The performance metric is a significantly improved version of the R-squared; also, it is applied to the validation set, not to the training set. Then, in Section 7.5.2, I discuss stepwise feature selection techniques (forward, backward), adding or removing one or two features at a time, based on the feature table built in Section 7.5.1. The comprehensive feature summary table allows you to quickly perform stepwise regression (which is more interpretable than a full fledged regression), and to assess whether or not this technique fails to catch good enough configurations, at least for the data set investigated here.

7.5.1 **Combinatorial approach**

Here I look at all the $2^m - 1$ possible configurations of features $X_1, \ldots, X_m$, to asses the importance of individual features and feature interaction, in a way that is more insightful than looking at cross-correlations between features. For each configuration, I computed the regression coefficient vector using three methods: fixed point with 15 iterations, fixed point with 100 iterations (starting with $\beta_0 = 0$ in both cases), and then the special β_0 alone (no iteration) defined in Section 7.2.3. All rankings, unless otherwise specified, are based on 100 iterations of the fixed point algorithm.

I use the score metric s defined in Section 7.4 – a meaningful, monotonic function of the R-squared – to measure performance. If you use the R-squared instead, the rankings would still be the same. The full model has $m = 6$ features. All other models are submodels, referred to as configurations: they miss one or more features. The metric s is computed on the validation set, not the training set.

The summary table in the `Regression5_Static.xlsx` spreadsheet, in the `Results` tab; see columns `U:AS`. The spreadsheet is available here. It has the same structure as the spreadsheet described in Sections 7.2, 7.2.4, and 7.3.1. The difference is that the data set is static in this case, so you cannot generate different data sets. The methodology is inspired by the book "Interpretable Machine Learning" [6], particularly Chapter 7 focusing on permutation feature importance and feature interactions. The higher the s, the better the performance. Note that if the performance was computed on the training set rather than the validation set, then we would have $0 \leq s \leq 1$.

Table 7.3 shows the top achievable performance given m (the number of features used in the computation) on a same (synthetic) data set. The three performance columns correspond respectively to 15 iterations, 100 iterations, and the special β_0. The table is also in the spreadsheet in cells `AP12:AS19`, where you can find the detailed computations. For the performance of each individual configuration,

Table 7.3 Best performance given m (number of features).

m	$s(\beta_{15})$	$s(\beta_{100})$	$s(\beta_0)$
1	0.2892	0.2892	0.2892
2	0.4080	0.4080	0.4075
3	0.4593	0.5019	0.4357
4	0.5175	0.5541	0.4382
5	0.5332	0.5865	0.4274
6	0.5243	0.5889	0.3597

see Tables 7.4 and 7.5: a configuration denoted as $3, 4, 6$ means that only X_3, X_4, and X_6 are used for the computation of the regression coefficients.

Below are some highlights, after ranking the feature configurations according to performance.

- The top 8 configurations include the simultaneous presence of features X_1, X_2, and X_6. While X_1 is strongly correlated to Y, the features X_2 and X_6 are not. Also, X_2 is negatively correlated to X_1.
- The worst configurations are X_2 alone, X_6 alone, and X_2, X_6 combined together. This is surprising, since X_2 and X_6 are both required in all top configurations. It shows that this type of feature interaction analysis is more powerful than looking at the feature cross-correlation structure.
- The worst configuration out of 63, consisting of X_2 alone, is so bad that it is the only one with a negative s when computed on the validation set. It is worse than using no feature at all (that is, using the mean value of Y for your predictions).
- The fourth configuration has only $m = 4$ features and does quite well. It is also the best possible configuration, among all configurations based on β_0 alone (defined in Section 7.2.3). It is thus the best configuration if you do not use a single iteration of the fixed point algorithm. With the full fixed point algorithm, only one configuration with fewer than 4 features, beats that performance (it needs 3 features only).
- The top configuration performs just as well as the classic statistical solution with $m = 6$, but it also requires all 6 features.
- The biggest improvement is from using two features, over one feature. Beyond two features, gains are smaller.
- The regression coefficient attached to X_5 is positive in the top configuration, but absent (zero) or negative in all the other top 8 configurations except the very top one. A negative value makes more sense, since the correlation between Y and X_5 is strongly negative.
- If, for whatever reason, the feature X_6 is not in your data set, you miss all the top 14 configurations, out of 63. This is really the feature that you cannot afford not to have. Surprisingly though, it is not highly correlated to Y, much less than X_1, X_3, or X_5. It shows its power not when left alone, but when combined with other features: a bit like charcoal that sounds inoffensive, but when combined with sulfur and saltpeter, makes gun powder.

Of course, identifying the ideal configuration is like cherry-picking. However, the goal is to minimize overfitting and favor simplicity and interpretability. In that regard, the fourth configuration is my favorite, as it uses only $m = 4$ features out of 6, and it is also the winner if you use the special β_0 alone with that same feature configuration. My second pick is the 15th configuration if you use the special β_0

alone. It is the second best configuration if using β_0 alone, it uses only 3 features, and it performs just as well (at that level) as using 100 iterations of the fixed point algorithm. It is also the best configuration without X_6.

7.5.2 Stepwise approach

Based on Tables 7.4 and 7.5, it is easy to reconstruct how **stepwise regression** progresses [Wiki]. This method is a stepwise feature selection procedure. Here (say) $\{2, 3\}$ denotes the configuration consisting of the two features X_2, X_3.

- Forward regression, adding one feature at a time:

$$1 \rightarrow \{1, 3\} \rightarrow \{1, 3, 6\} \rightarrow \{1, 2, 3, 6\} \rightarrow \{1, 2, 3, 4, 6\} \rightarrow \text{Full}.$$

  The scores $s(\beta_{100})$ are respectively $0.289, 0.408, 0.437, 0.554, 0.587, 0.589$, and the ranks are respectively $40, 23, 15, 4, 2, 1$.
- Backward regression, removing one feature at a time:

$$\text{Full} \rightarrow \{1, 2, 3, 4, 6\} \rightarrow \{1, 2, 3, 6\} \rightarrow \{1, 2, 6\} \rightarrow \{1, 2\} \rightarrow 1.$$

  The scores $s(\beta_{100})$ are respectively $0.589, 0.587, 0.554, 0.502, 0.318, 0.289$, and the ranks are respectively $1, 2, 4, 8, 33, 40$.
- Pairwise forward regression, adding two features at a time: $\{1, 3\} \rightarrow \{1, 2, 3, 6\} \rightarrow \text{Full}$.
- Pairwise backward regression, removing two features at a time: $\text{Full} \rightarrow \{1, 2, 3, 6\} \rightarrow \{1, 3\}$.

Note that the best configurations, respectively with $m = 5, 4, 3, 2, 1$ features, are $\{1, 2, 3, 4, 6\}$, $\{1, 2, 3, 6\}$, $\{1, 2, 6\}$, $\{1, 3\}$, $\{1\}$ scored respectively $0.587, 0.554, 0.502, 0.408, 0.289$, and ranked respectively $2, 4, 8, 23, 40$. So the stepwise procedures, while not fully optimum when involving only one configuration at a time, are nevertheless doing a rather decent job on this data set. The forward regression is easily interpretable if you stop at 4 features.

7.6 Conclusion

Using linear regression as an example, I illustrate how to turn the obscure output of a machine learning technique, into an interpretable solution. The method described here also shows the power of synthetic data, when properly generated. The use of synthetic data offers a big benefit: you can test and benchmark algorithms on millions of very different data sets, all at once.

I also introduce a new model performance metric, superior to R-squared in many respects, and based on cross-validation. The methodology leads to a very good approximation, almost as good as the exact solution on noisy data, with few iterations, natural regression coefficients easy to interpret, while avoiding overfitting. In fact, given a specific data set, many very different sets of regression coefficients lead to almost identical predictions. It makes sense to choose the ones that offer the best compromise between exactness and interpretability.

Table 7.4 Feature comparison table (top 32 feature combinations).

Rank	Configuration	m	$s(\beta_{15})$	$s(\beta_{100})$	$s(\beta_0)$	Regression coefficients attached to β_{100}					
1	1, 2, 3, 4, 5, 6	6	0.524	0.589	0.360	1.421	2.323	1.158	−1.296	0.211	2.221
2	1, 2, 3, 4, 6	5	0.533	0.587	0.427	1.419	2.411	1.013	−1.119		2.230
3	1, 2, 3, 5, 6	5	0.515	0.564	0.381	1.703	2.366	0.698		−0.405	1.873
4	1, 2, 3, 6	4	0.517	0.554	0.438	1.838	2.163	0.957			1.742
5	1, 2, 5, 6	4	0.488	0.549	0.323	1.672	2.909			−0.914	2.246
6	1, 2, 4, 5, 6	5	0.489	0.548	0.287	1.718	2.849		0.205	−0.961	2.141
7	1, 2, 4, 6	4	0.463	0.516	0.285	1.853	2.962		−0.872		2.566
8	1, 2, 6	3	0.459	0.502	0.308	2.165	2.747				2.170
9	2, 3, 4, 5, 6	5	0.407	0.501	0.273		1.751	2.177	−4.243	1.080	2.995
10	1, 3, 4, 5, 6	5	0.444	0.474	0.359	1.077		2.052	−1.527	1.011	0.898
11	2, 3, 4, 6	4	0.439	0.472	0.357		2.028	1.453	−3.138		2.886
12	1, 3, 4, 6	4	0.443	0.442	0.426	1.128		1.391	−0.306		0.565
13	1, 3, 5, 6	4	0.436	0.439	0.380	1.405		1.533		0.309	0.459
14	3, 4, 5, 6	4	0.366	0.437	0.272			2.784	−4.031	1.688	1.826
15	1, 3, 6	3	0.437	0.437	0.436	1.261		1.363			0.471
16	1, 2, 3, 4, 5	5	0.413	0.417	0.315	1.884	0.641	1.098	0.877	−0.246	
17	1, 2, 3, 4	4	0.414	0.416	0.367	1.879	0.550	1.268	0.646		
18	1, 2, 3, 5	4	0.412	0.415	0.345	1.692	0.360	1.512		0.254	
19	1, 2, 3	3	0.413	0.414	0.408	1.599	0.411	1.367			
20	1, 3, 5	3	0.408	0.411	0.344	1.570		1.607		0.347	
21	1, 3, 4, 5	4	0.408	0.411	0.314	1.582		1.549	0.135	0.274	
22	1, 3, 4	3	0.409	0.409	0.367	1.538		1.369	0.376		
23	1, 3	2	0.408	0.408	0.408	1.412		1.417			
24	1, 2, 4, 5	4	0.379	0.397	0.245	2.168	1.226		2.320	−1.384	
25	3, 4, 6	3	0.374	0.374	0.356			1.704	−2.066		1.319
26	2, 4, 5, 6	4	0.319	0.372	0.200		2.604		−2.077	−1.247	3.095
27	1, 4, 5, 6	4	0.337	0.343	0.286	1.516			1.448	−1.071	0.128
28	1, 2, 4	3	0.337	0.341	0.235	2.532	0.901		1.312		
29	1, 4, 5	3	0.336	0.341	0.244	1.593			1.649	−1.123	
30	1, 2, 5	3	0.332	0.335	0.292	1.597	0.731			−0.788	
31	1, 5, 6	3	0.330	0.330	0.321	1.122				−0.714	0.593
32	2, 4, 6	3	0.291	0.328	0.175		2.727		−3.738		3.756

My solution, which does not require matrix inversion, is also simple, compared to traditional methods. Indeed, it can easily be implemented in Excel, without requiring any coding. Despite the absence of statistical model, I also show how to compute confidence intervals, using parametric and nonparametric bootstrap techniques. Finally, I show how to generate multivariate data with a specific covariance matrix. An alternative is to use **copulas** [Wiki], which are a multidimensional generalization of **quantile functions**. The copula method has been used in the context of generative models for medical data; see page 98 in [3]. See also Section 10.2.

Table 7.5 Feature comparison table (bottom 31 feature combinations).

Rank	Configuration	m	$s(\beta_{15})$	$s(\beta_{100})$	$s(\beta_0)$	Regression coefficients attached to β_{100}					
33	1, 2	2	0.318	0.318	0.291	2.025	0.653				
34	1, 4, 6	3	0.309	0.311	0.283	1.681			0.350		0.494
35	1, 6	2	0.310	0.310	0.304	1.536					0.605
36	1, 5	2	0.304	0.305	0.291	1.320				−0.728	
37	1, 4	2	0.300	0.300	0.234	2.033			0.938		
38	2, 3, 5, 6	4	0.276	0.298	0.242		1.454	0.501		−1.711	1.878
39	2, 5, 6	3	0.276	0.293	0.205		1.845			−2.057	2.138
40	1	1	0.289	0.289	0.289	1.746					
41	3, 5, 6	3	0.252	0.252	0.242			1.076		−1.089	0.945
42	2, 3, 4, 5	4	0.227	0.249	0.200		−0.989	2.350	−1.997	0.477	
43	2, 3, 4	3	0.241	0.241	0.214		−0.820	2.022	−1.535		
44	4, 5, 6	3	0.216	0.216	0.199				−0.638	−1.340	1.119
45	3, 4	2	0.215	0.215	0.216			2.120	−1.879		
46	3, 4, 5	3	0.204	0.209	0.200			1.592	−1.070	−0.716	
47	5, 6	2	0.203	0.203	0.203					−1.642	0.972
48	2, 3, 5	3	0.188	0.188	0.178		−0.564	1.329		−1.029	
49	3, 6	2	0.180	0.180	0.179			1.891			1.198
50	3, 5	2	0.180	0.180	0.179			1.123		−1.384	
51	2, 3, 6	3	0.177	0.178	0.179		−0.242	1.910			1.019
52	4, 6	2	0.169	0.169	0.171				−2.353		1.730
53	5	1	0.139	0.139	0.139					−1.970	
54	2, 3	2	0.138	0.138	0.094		−1.132	2.086			
55	2, 5	2	0.137	0.137	0.139		−0.190			−1.887	
56	4, 5	2	0.135	0.134	0.126				0.487	−2.163	
57	2, 4, 5	3	0.135	0.133	0.126		−0.158		0.454	−2.081	
58	3	1	0.096	0.096	0.096			2.257			
59	4	1	0.071	0.071	0.071				−2.187		
60	2, 4	2	0.033	0.033	0.072		−1.073		−1.719		
61	2, 6	2	0.021	0.025	0.022		0.127				1.735
62	6	1	0.020	0.020	0.020						1.643
63	2	1	−0.057	−0.057	−0.057		−1.433				

References

[1] J. Ackmann, et al., Machine-learned preconditioners for linear solvers in geophysical fluid flows, Preprint, pp. 1–19, arXiv:2010.02866, 2020, [Link].

[2] O. Bröker, M.J. Groteb, Sparse approximate inverse smoothers for geometric and algebraic multigrid, Applied Numerical Mathematics 41 (1) (2002) 61–80.

[3] K. Emam, L. Mosquera, R. Hoptroff, Practical Synthetic Data Generation, O'Reilly, 2020.

[4] C. Kelechi, Towards efficiency in the residual and parametric bootstrap techniques, American Journal of Theoretical and Applied Statistics 5 (5) (2016), [Link].

[5] J. Lei, et al., Distribution-free predictive inference for regression, Journal of the American Statistical Association 113 (2018) 1094–1111, [Link].

[6] C. Molnar, Interpretable Machine Learning, ChristophMolnar.com, 2022, [Link].

From interpolation to fuzzy regression 8

The innovative technique discussed here does much more than regression. It is useful in signal processing, in particular spatial filtering and smoothing. Initially designed using hyperplanes, the original version can be confused with support vector machines or support vector regression. However, the closest analogy is fuzzy regression. A weighted version based on splines makes it somewhat related to nearest neighbor or **inverse distance interpolation**, and highly nonlinear. In the end, it is a kriging-like spatial regression, with many potential applications ranging from compression to signal enhancement and prediction. It comes with confidence intervals for the predicted values, despite the absence of a statistical model. A predicted value is determined by hundreds or thousands of splines. The splines play the role of nodes in neural networks. Unlike neural networks, all the parameters – the distances to the splines – have a natural interpretation.

The methodology was tested on synthetic data. The performance, depending on hyperparameters and the number of splines, is measured on the validation set, not on the training set. Despite (by design) nearly perfect predictions for training set points, it is robust against outliers, numerically stable, and does not lead to overfitting. There are no regression coefficients, no intercept, no matrix algebra involved, no calculus, no statistics beyond empirical percentiles, and even no square roots. It is accessible to high school students. Despite the apparent simplicity, the technique is far from trivial. In its simplest form, the splines are similar to multivariate Lagrange interpolation polynomials. Python code is included in this document.

8.1 Introduction

The original problem consisted of fitting a line to a set of points – a classic linear regression problem. I explored alternatives to the traditional **ordinary least squares** (OLS) solution [Wiki]. The line that yields the **least absolute residuals** (LAR) [Wiki] is such an example. It has the benefit of being more robust. The next step was to look at all potential line combinations. For a set of n points, there are $M = n(n-1)/2$ potential lines, as each pair of points determines a line. The LAR line is just one of them and in some sense, the best one.

The idea is that for any local location x on the real axis, one can choose between multiple lines $z = L_k(x)$ to compute the predicted response z, with $k = 1, \ldots, M$. Some lines provide a better fit than others, at the local level. Or in other words, each of the M lines has some unique, location-dependent probability to contribute to the predicted response computed at x. This perspective is very similar to the Bayesian approach. In the literature, this is known as the **Theil–Sen estimator** [Wiki]. In the simplest version, the median value of $L_k(x)$ computed across the M lines is the final point estimate of the response, at location x. An improved version uses different weights for each line, involving weighted averages or **weighted quantiles** [1]. Since there are M potential predicted values attached to each x – one for each line – you can define a 80% confidence interval for the response as follows: the lower (resp. upper) bound is the 10% (resp. 90%) **empirical quantile** [Wiki] (also called percentile) of the M predicted values computed at x.

The term **prediction interval** [Wiki], rather than confidence interval, is used in the literature. Note that the methodology to build these confidence intervals should not be confused with the **percentile bootstrap method** [Wiki]. Here, there is no resampling involved. The M lines are computed on the training set, while model performance is measured on the validation set [Wiki]. Note that I use the word "model" to represent the embodiment described in this chapter. There is no statistical or probabilistic model involved.

8.2 Original version

Before moving to the full, nonlinear model in higher dimensions, let us focus on the original method: the first version of my fuzzy regression technique. This version is easier to understand, more traditional, and leads to simple visualizations. It will help you better understand the new version, which is considerably more abstract and generic.

Let the n observed points be labeled as $(x_1, z_1), \ldots, (x_n, z_n)$. The line that contains (x_i, z_i) and (x_j, z_j) is denoted as $L_k = L_{i,j}$. Its equation is

$$L_{i,j}(x) = \frac{z_i - z_j}{x_i - x_j} \cdot x + \frac{x_i z_j - x_j z_i}{x_i - x_j}.$$

It immediately follows that

$$L_{i,j}(x_i) = z_i, \quad L_{i,j}(x_j) = z_j.$$

Note that if $x_i = x_j$, the equation does not make sense. I will address this issue in the general case. I also use the notation $z_{i,j} = L_{i,j}(x)$. It represents the predicted value of z at location x, based on line $L_{i,j}$ solely. In its simplest form, the predicted value at x is the median of the $z_{i,j}$.

Fig. 8.1 shows the result of this regression technique. To the naked eye, the regression curve is indistinguishable from the traditional regression line. It is also indistinguishable from a straight line, but it is actually a curve. The data set used here and pictured in Fig. 8.1 (the blue dots) comes from Chapter 7 on interpretable regression. It is a synthetic data set with $n = 1000$ observations.

The originality of the fuzzy regression procedure is that it allows you to compute prediction intervals without any underlying statistical model or bootstrap / resampling techniques. However, it requires the computation of $L_k(x)$ for $k = 1, \ldots, M$, for each sampled value of x. In higher dimensions, it is natural to replace the lines L_k by hyperplanes. However, this is not the path that I chose. Instead of hyperplanes, I used splines. The reason is that it leads to trivial computations and more flexibility. In particular, it does not involve matrix products or inversions. It does not involve matrices at all, or calculus, thus my claim that the methodology is accessible to high school students.

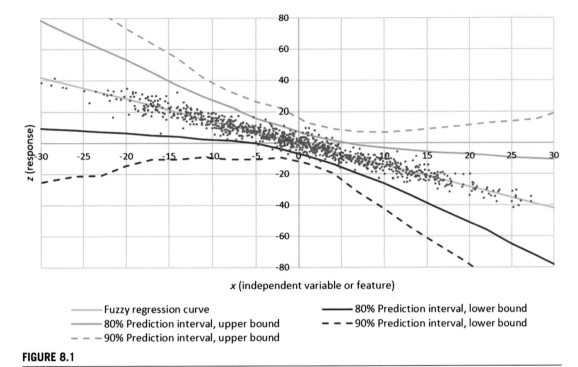

FIGURE 8.1

Fuzzy regression with prediction intervals, original version, 1D.

8.3 Full, nonlinear model in higher dimensions

I now discuss the general model. For the sake of simplicity, I focus on the 2-dimensional case: a response z, with two features x, y. It is an important case, with applications in **geostatistics** [Wiki]. The d-dimensional case is not more complicated, but the notations quickly become cumbersome. The line L_k is now replaced by a spline, also denoted as L_k. But this time, $k = (k_1, \ldots, k_r)$ is a vector, with $1 \le k_i \le n$ $(i = 1, \ldots, r)$. Just like a plane is uniquely determined by exactly 3 points, we want the spline L_k to be uniquely determined by exactly r points, in this case $(x_{k_1}, y_{k_1}, z_{k_1}), \ldots, (x_{k_r}, y_{k_r}, z_{k_r})$. That is, we want

$$z_{k_i} = L_k(x_{k_i}, y_{k_i}), \quad i = 1, \ldots, r.$$

There is very simple type of splines satisfying this property, namely

$$L_k(x, y) = \sum_{i=1}^{r} \frac{z_{k_i}}{2} \left[\prod_{j \neq i} \frac{\psi(x - x_{k_j})}{\psi(x_{k_i} - x_{k_j})} + \prod_{j \neq i} \frac{\psi(y - y_{k_j})}{\psi(y_{k_i} - y_{k_j})} \right], \tag{8.1}$$

where ψ is any real-valued function satisfying $\psi(0) = 0$. In practice, one can choose the identity function for ψ. The resulting splines are then similar to multivariate Lagrange polynomials of degree $r - 1$, used for interpolation [3]. I now discuss the various features, issues, capabilities, and potential implementations of this type of regression.

8.3.1 Geometric proximity, weights, and numerical stability

From now on, I assume that ψ is the identity function. A key concept is the proximity between a location (x, y) in the plane, and a spline. When predicting z, given (x, y), one has to compute $L_k(x, y)$ for each spline L_k. The number of splines quickly increases with r. For a specific location (x, y), some splines are more relevant than others. The following metric measures the proximity to L_k:

$$\delta_k(x, y) = \left(\prod_{i=1}^{r} \max(|x - x_{k_i}|, |y - y_{k_i}|) \right)^{1/r}. \tag{8.2}$$

It is the geometric mean of r Chebyshev distances [Wiki] in $\mathbb{R}^2$. In particular, it is zero if any of these distances is zero. This essential property cannot be satisfied with the arithmetic mean, but it is with the geometric mean. The relevance or importance of L_k, relative to (x, y), is then defined as the weight

$$w_k(x, y) = \exp[-s \cdot \delta_k(x, y)], \tag{8.3}$$

where $s > 0$ is the **smoothing parameter**. It is maximum when $\delta_k(x, y) = 0$. On the other side, some splines are always problematic, or may not even exist. These splines are identified by the accuracy metric

$$\epsilon_k = \prod_{i=1}^{r} \prod_{j=i+1}^{r} |x_{k_i} - x_{k_j}| \cdot |y_{k_i} - y_{k_j}|. \tag{8.4}$$

In particular, if $\epsilon_k = 0$, the spline L_k is undefined. It is a good practice to reject or ignore splines with $\epsilon_k < 10^{-5}$. It increases the numeral stability of the system.

In addition, some splines may produce outlier predictions, depending on the location (x, y). Such abnormal predictions should be ignored to boost performance, when blending the M predicted values $L_k(x, y)$ – one per spline – to compute the final predicted value and prediction interval at (x, y). This final predicted value is the median or weighted average computed across all splines at (x, y), after rejecting undesirable splines or predictions. Outlier predictions are detected and rejected in the Python code, via the **hyperparameter** `zzdevratio`.

There is no need to be overly aggressive when penalizing and rejecting undesirable individual splines or predicted values. The median does a good job at filtering out nonrobust measurements. The more aggressive, the fewer splines used, resulting in lower statistical confidence. At the extreme, some locations may end up with no predicted value at all: for such locations, the variable `count` in the Python code is equal to zero, and the counter `missing` is incremented by one. This may be a good thing, or not.

8.3.2 Predicted values and prediction intervals

In Section 8.2, I used the median predicted value computed across all $M = n(n-1)/2$ splines, as the final predicted value for the response z, at a specific location. Here n is the number of observations in the training set. Then I used the quantiles of these M values, computed at the same location, to build the prediction interval. The same applies to the general case, but now $M = \binom{n}{r}$ is a binomial coefficient. Note that the actual number of splines will depend on the location (x, y), and is smaller than M if some splines are rejected. In the Python code, each call to the function `F` generates a new, random spline. The number M is prespecified and is chosen to be large (> 500) but much smaller than $\binom{n}{r}$. Also, I mostly used $r = 2$.

An alternative to the median is to use a weighted average to compute a predicted value. For the weight attached to spline L_k, use formula (8.3). These weights and the whole system were designed to satisfy the following property. Let (x, y) be the location of a training set point. Then the predicted value at (x, y), using the weights in question with $s \to \infty$ and $M = n$ carefully chosen splines, is identical to the observed value. This is true, for instance, if the index k_1 in $k = (k_1, \ldots, k_r)$ covers all integer values between 1 and n, that is, all training set points. In that case, there is always at least one index vector k such that $\delta_k(x, y) = 0$, corresponding to a spline containing (x, y, z), with a weight equal to one, dwarfing all other weights. For a formal proof, see Exercise 8.1.

Indeed, when s is large, the weighted methodology is similar to **inverse distance weighting** (Shepard's method) [Wiki], or **nearest neighbor interpolation** [Wiki]. The weighted version is implemented in the Python code. Another way to include neighboring data in the predictions is to only use local splines determined by training set points close to the target location (x, y). Finally, an efficient implementation still needs to be developed. The methodology can easily be implemented using a parallel computer architecture.

8.3.3 Illustration, with spreadsheet

See Fig. 8.1 for an illustration of the original method. Here I focus on the general method discussed in Section 8.3, in two dimensions, and with nonlinear splines. Fig. 8.2 illustrates several aspects of this technique. Unlike in Fig. 8.1 (the one-dimensional case), it is difficult to show residual errors or prediction intervals for specific locations, because the locations (x, y) are now 2-dimensional. A workaround is to show a scatter plot of observed values z versus the predicted values z_m. These are the blue dots in Fig. 8.2. The notation z_m stands for the predicted value based on the median. The predicted value based on the weighted average is denoted as z_w, and not shown in the picture. The observed value z is also denoted as z_{obs}. The dashed blue line shows the quality of the fit between predicted and observed values. The R-squared is 0.8096.

However, the slope of the dashed line is only 0.4640. Maybe you expected it to be close to 1: after all, a perfect fit means all the blue dots are on the main diagonal. In practice, the slope will always be between 0 and 1. The explanation is as follows. The regression technique (spatial regression, to be precise), acts as a smoother or noise filtering technique, damping amplitudes. To eliminate the damping effect, you need to restore the amplitude. This is easily done by standardizing the predictions, so that their mean and variance corresponds to that of the original signal (observed response) z measured on the training set. Doing so will not change the R-squared, as it is invariant under translation and multiplication. Indeed, the R-squared is the square of the correlation between z and z_m.

The prediction levels are based on the 20% (lower bound) and 80% (upper bound) empirical quantiles. Thus, the confidence level is 60%. It is not possible to directly show prediction bands on a scatterplot in any meaningful way. Instead, to each blue dot in Fig. 8.2, corresponds one green and one red dot: the upper and lower bounds of the prediction interval. For each blue dot, the associated red and green dots are all on a same vertical line (not shown), parallel to the vertical axis. The details are unimportant; in the end, Fig. 8.2 still gives a good sense of how the methodology performs, and how the prediction intervals look like.

The detailed implementation is in the Fuzzy4.xlsx spreadsheet. Most of the heavy computations are done in Python. The spreadsheet provides the final steps: prediction intervals and visualizations. It also includes the output file `fuzzy_big.txt` produced by Python. Now, I am going to discuss the various fields in that spreadsheeet.

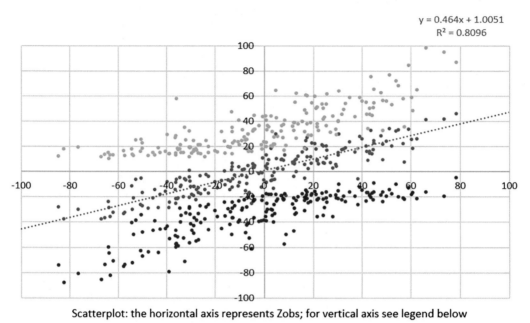

$$y = 0.464x + 1.0051$$
$$R^2 = 0.8096$$

Scatterplot: the horizontal axis represents Zobs; for vertical axis see legend below

• Zmedian   • Prediction Interval lower   • Prediction Interval upper

FIGURE 8.2

Fuzzy regression with prediction intervals, full model, 2D.

8.3.3.1 *Output fields*

I focus on the 2-D tab in the spreadsheet. It contains three separate sets of columns, organized as follows:

- Columns A, B, C, D correspond respectively to x, y, z and the traditional predicted z using standard regression. It has 1000 rows, corresponding to the $n = 1000$ training set points. Only the first 800 points are used for training, the remaining 200 are used for validation.
- Columns F to N correspond to the output fields of `fuzzy_big.txt` produced by the Python code. It features the 200 points of the validation set, with for each point, up to $M = 800$ entries, one per spline. These are used to build the prediction intervals. Some splines are rejected as discussed in Section 8.3.2, thus the actual number of rows is less than 800 per validation point. Columns F–I are trivial. Column J is the predicted value for the associated validation point in column I, arising from one single spline. The final predicted value for that point is the median of these values computed across all splines. It is stored in column R. Columns K and L correspond respectively to $\delta_k(x, y)$ and $w_k(x, y)$.
- Columns P to U correspond to summary statistics for each point of the validation set. Thus it has 200 rows, one per validation point. The median-based predicted value z_m is in column R, the weight-based predicted value z_w is in column U, the observed z is in column Q, and the lower and upper bounds of the prediction intervals are in columns S and T.

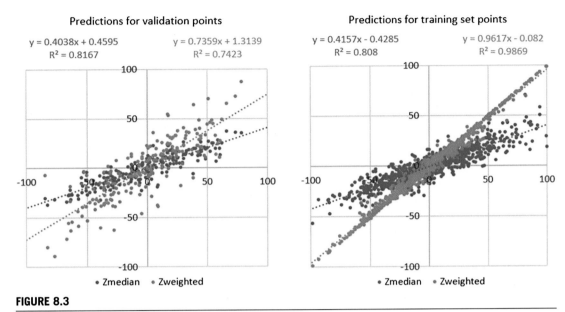

FIGURE 8.3

Scatterplots: median vs weighted method, on validation (left) vs training set (right).

The cells X2 and Y2 in the 2-D tab are the percentile levels for the prediction intervals. You can change these parameters, and it will automatically update Fig. 8.2 in the spreadsheet. The predicted z_w's could be computed using the AverageIf Excel function. However there is no MedianIf or PercentileIf function in Excel. There is an easy workaround: for instance, instead of using the nonexistent call MedianIf(F:F,P2,J:J), use Median(If(F:F=P2,J:J)). This instruction means "compute the median value of column J, but only for rows that have the element in column F equal to cell P2". The same applies to the Percentile function.

8.4 **Results**

In this section, I present the main results. I tested the methodology on the synthetic data described in Chapter 7. It consists of $m = 1000$ observations with known response. The first 800 points are used to train the "model", and the remaining 200 – the validation data – for testing and assessing performance. The data set is available in the spreadsheet fuzzyf2.xlsx, available on my GitHub repository. It corresponds to the small output file fuzzy_small.txt produced by the Python code in Section 8.6. Predictions intervals are discussed in Section 8.3.2 and illustrated in Fig. 8.2.

The main performance metric is the R-squared. It is certainly not the best metric for reasons discussed in Chapter 7, where I suggest alternatives. However, the data set is large enough, and relatively well behaved. Thus the R-squared is adequate enough in this case. Note that it is mostly measured on the validation set rather than the training set, so technically it is not the true R-squared in the typical sense. Also, it is defined here as the square of the correlation coefficient. This is discussed in Section 8.4.3.

8.4.1 Performance assessment

Table 8.1 summarizes my main experiment. The subscripts v, t, m, w stand respectively for the validation set, the training set, the median, and the weighted predicted value. Regardless of the number M of random splines used per location, the weighted predicted value does best with splines defined by $r = 1$ point. Such splines have a constant value everywhere. This is not surprising, since this method, with $r = 1$, is similar to kriging or inverse distance interpolation. Note that with $r = 1$, the maximum number of distinct splines is $M = n$. Thus, if $n = 800$ and $M = 5000$, some splines are used multiple times.

The median predicted value is less sensitive to outliers, but it tends to reduce the amplitude, resulting in β values well below one. This is not an issue, as predicted values can easily be scaled back without impacting the R-squared. The median method, for this particular 2D data set, works best with $r = 2$. Also, it performs equally well inside and outside the training set. To the contrary, the weighted method experiences a sharp drop of performance, outside the training set. Larger values of r do not lead to further improvement. This is encouraging, as you want to work with small values of r and M to speed up of the algorithm. The larger the r, the more potential splines to choose from, which leads to more accurate prediction intervals.

Table 8.1 R-squared ρ^2 and slope β, on training and validation sets, median vs weighted.

r	M	ρ^2_{vm}	ρ^2_{vw}	ρ^2_{tm}	ρ^2_{tw}	β_{vm}	β_{vw}	β_{tm}	β_{tw}
1	150	0.1922	0.6946	0.2490	0.7495	0.0916	0.7635	0.1066	0.7563
2	150	0.7688	0.4756	0.7525	0.7301	0.4128	0.6650	0.4210	0.7853
3	150	0.4272	0.3930	0.5601	0.5865	0.3032	0.6695	0.3306	0.7834
1	800	0.2600	0.7734	0.2936	0.8682	0.1025	0.7367	0.1039	0.8375
2	800	0.7941	0.6849	0.7913	0.9331	0.4058	0.7368	0.4154	0.9291
3	800	0.6838	0.5168	0.7204	0.9770	0.2986	0.6649	0.3392	0.9680
1	5000	0.2795	0.7876	0.4276	0.9294	0.1071	0.7421	0.1980	0.8945
2	5000	0.8167	0.7423	0.8080	0.9869	0.4038	0.7359	0.4157	0.9617
3	5000	0.7605	0.7203	0.7740	0.9988	0.3114	0.7063	0.3308	0.9892

8.4.2 Visualization

Figs. 8.2 and 8.3 further illustrate the methodology. The blue dots in the scatterplots represent the observed value (horizontal axis) versus the predicted value (vertical axis), computed using the median method. They provide a much better picture about the distribution of residual errors, than the R-squared alone. The orange dots show the same distribution of points, but computed using the weighted method instead. The fact that the slopes are different is not an issue: the predicted values need to go though a final rescaling step described in Section 8.4.3, to correct the damping effect caused by the fuzzy regression, acting as a smoothing, low pass filter. Once corrected, the slopes will be nearly identical, and the R-squared unchanged.

Fig. 8.2 is an original visualization, rarely seen. It allows you to look at individual residual errors and prediction intervals, regardless of the dimension of the problem.

8.4.3 Amplitude restoration

As mentioned a few times earlier, the fuzzy regression, especially the methodology based on the median, acts as a low-pass filter in signal processing. This is not surprising: after all it removes the noise. Indeed, it can be used as a data compression technique. As a result, predicted values have a lower variance than the observed ones, and the slope β in Table 8.1 or Fig. 8.3 is well below one. To correct this "issue", one has to standardize the predicted values, so that the mean and variance match that of the observed response in the training set. In short, the predicted values must be recalibrated. Because of this, the mean squared error is not a good metric to assess performance. Also, here the R-squared is the square of the correlation, but it is not equal to $1 - SS_{res}/SS_{tot}$, unlike in traditional regression where both agree.

The same phenomenon takes place when smoothing time series. A moving average can be used to predict or interpolate values. It also removes some noise, and reduces the amplitude of the signal. A scatterplot of exact values versus moving average will exhibit the same sharp drop in the slope. And it can be corrected using the same strategy, with no impact on the R-squared measured as the square of the correlation between observed and predicted (smoothed) values.

8.5 Exercises

The first exercise consists of proving a fundamental result: the fact that, under certain circumstances, the fuzzy regression technique described in this chapter is an exact interpolation technique. The proof does not involve math beyond elementary arithmetic, but rather out-of-the-box thinking. The second exercise is about another simple, numerically stable interpolation technique, this time based on partial fractions. The prerequisite is a first course in calculus, to understand and solve this problem. The third exercise explores an alternative to validation sets. The fourth exercise is a generalization to higher dimensions.

Exercise 8.1. Fuzzy regression for interpolation. Let $(x_1, y_1, z_1), \ldots, (x_n, y_n, z_n)$ be the training set points. We use a spline system with $M = n$ splines. Each spline is uniquely defined by r training set points. The kth spline ($k = 1, \ldots, n$) always contains (x_k, y_k, z_k). In other words, $L_k(x_k, y_k) = z_k$. Prove that as $s \to \infty$, the weight-based predicted value z_w evaluated at any training set location (x, y), is equal to the observed value z at that location.

Solution

When $s = \infty$, $w_k(x, y) = 1$ if $(x, y) = (x_k, y_k)$ is the location of a training set point, and 0 otherwise. If multiple training set points have the same (x, y) but different z's, then the predicted z_w at (x, y) will be the average of those z's. This is because at least one factor in the product formula (8.2) is equal to zero, and thus the product is zero.

To complete the proof, one has to carefully look at formula (8.1). Assume that $(x, y) = (x_k, y_k)$. If $i \neq k$, the ith term in formula (8.1) is zero, because at least one factor in each inner product if zero. But if $i = k$, both products are equal to one, and thus $L_k(x, y) = z_k$.

Exercise 8.2. Partial fractions for interpolation. This may be particularly useful for time series interpolation. Assume f is a smooth, slow growing even function, and $f(t)$ is known if t is a positive integer.

Then $f(t)$ is uniquely determined everywhere on the real axis. In short, there is an exact interpolation formula for the whole function, if we know $f(t)$ for $t = 0, 1, 2$ and so on. The formula is

$$f(t) = \frac{\sin \pi t}{\pi} \cdot \left[\frac{f(0)}{t} + \phi'(t) \sum_{k=1}^{\infty} (-1)^k \frac{f(k)}{\phi(t) - \phi(k)} \right], \tag{8.5}$$

and it works in particular if $\phi(t) = t^2$, $\phi'(t) = 2t$ is the derivative with respect to t, and

$$f(t) = \sum_{k=0}^{\infty} \alpha_k \cos \beta_k t, \text{ with } |\beta_k| < \pi. \tag{8.6}$$

The purpose of this exercise is to prove the validity of formula (8.5) under the right conditions, and to apply it to the real part of the Dirichlet eta function $\eta(\sigma + it)$ [Wiki], for (say) $\sigma = 0.8$ and $0 < t < 30$. Unlike the interpolation technique in Exercise 8.1, formula (8.5) provides only an approximation, albeit an excellent one. The approximation is exact if you include all the infinitely many terms. It can be used for **time series disaggregation** [2]. A potential application is to break down hourly temperature predictions into 5 minute increments.

Solution

A detailed discussion about this interpolation formula and its generalization, can be found here. Note that the real part of the Dirichlet eta function (closely linked to the **Riemann Hypothesis**) is

$$\Re[\zeta(\sigma + it)] = \sum_{k=1}^{\infty} (-1)^{k+1} \frac{\cos(t \log k)}{k^\sigma}, \quad \sigma > 0.$$

Fig. 8.4 shows how accurate the interpolation formula is, for this particular example. The full function was reconstructed, based on $f(k)$ computed at $k = 0, 1, \ldots, 249$. The horizontal axis represents t. Note that to estimate $f(t)$ beyond $t = 30$, more than 250 terms are needed in formula (8.5), to keep the error smaller than 3×10^{-4}. Interestingly, the interpolation formula seems to be working even though condition (8.6) is not satisfied. At integer arguments, the error is minimum in absolute value, and smaller than 10^{-6}.

For the imaginary part – an odd function –, you can multiply it by $\sin \lambda t$ to turn it into an even function, then apply the same methodology to the transformed function to interpolate it, then divide back by $\sin \lambda t$. Here $\lambda \neq 0$ is an arbitrary constant.

Exercise 8.3. A new type of validation set. Since we are dealing with a regression problem, it is natural to see how the methodology performs on a linear combination of training set points. In other words, a validation point could be a **convex linear combination** [Wiki] of two or more training set points. A convex combination guarantees that the validation point is inside the convex hull of the training set points, and is good for interpolation. Also try with nonconvex combinations, with validation points outside the convex hull. One would expect the performance to be lower for these points. It allows you to see how the method performs for **extrapolation**. Note that in d dimensions, the convex hull is obtained by computing all convex combinations of $d + 1$ points in the training set.

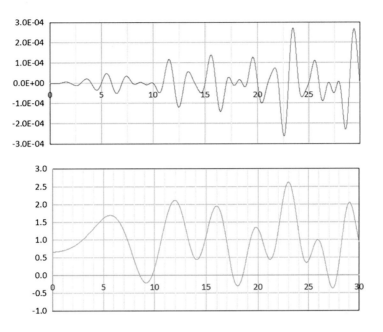

FIGURE 8.4

Dirichlet eta function (real part, bottom) and interpolation error (top).

Exercise 8.4. Fuzzy regression in higher dimensions. In three dimensions, (x, y) becomes (x, x', x'') and formula (8.1) has three inner products. The weighted method will continue to work best with $r = 1$, but my guess is that the median method will work best with $r = 3$. The response is still denoted as z. In formula (8.2), $\max(|x - x_{k_i}|, |y - y_{k_i}|)$ becomes $\max(|x - x_{k_i}|, |x' - x'_{k_i}|, |x'' - x''_{k_i}|)$. Formula (8.4) is updated accordingly.

8.6 Python source code and data sets

I described the input/output data of the Python code in the previous sections. The Python source code is available on my GitHub repository, here. Below, it is broken down into four parts: commented introduction and setting the hyperparameter values, reading the input file, the core function, and the main part.

Part 1: The hyperparameters

```
# Kriging-style spatial regression / inverse distance interpolation

import numpy as np
import random
random.seed(100)
```

```
# --- Highlights of this "fuzzy regression" code:

# Model-free; produces big output file to compute prediction intervals; Bivariate case,
    featuring nearest-neighbor approach (the weights); Exact predictions for training set,
    yet robust (no overfitting); Increasing M is "lazy way" to boost performance, but it
    slows speed
# Math-free (no matrix algebra, square root or calculus); Statistics-free (no statistical
    science involved at all); Requires no technical knowledge beyond high school, but far
    from trivial!
# Acts as low-pass, amplitude reduction, or signal compression filter; Also acts as noise
    filtering, signal enhancement. Amplitude restoration step not included, but easy to do.

# By Vincent Granville, www.MLTechniques.com

# --- Hyperparameters

# n (number of obs, called points) set after reading input file [n=1000 here]

P=0.8        # proportion of data allocated to training the remaining is for validation
M=5000       # max number of splines used per point; M=5000 offers modest gain over M=800
r=2          # number of points defining a spline; also works with r=1 or larger r
smoother=1.5 # smoothing param used in weighted predictions; try 0.5 for more smoothing (0 =
    max smoothing)
thresh1=25.0 # max distance allowed to nearby spline; increase to eliminate points with no
    predictions; decrease to narrow (improve) confidence intervals
thresh2=1.5 # max outlier level allowed for predicted values ; if < 1, predicted can't be
    more extreme than observed; if too low, may increase number of points with no prediction;
    if too large, may produce a few strong outlier predictions;
thresh3=0.001 # control numerical stability (keep 0.001)

# --- Output var (defined later)

# missing   : number of points not assigned a prediction
#
# count     : actual number of splines used for a specific point
# error     : code telling why a point is not assigned a prediction
# weight    : weight assigned to a spline, for a given point
# zpred     : predicted value for a point zz = (xx, yy)
# zpredw    : weighted predicted value

# Input var (defined later)
#
# xx, yy, zz: coordinates of a point
```

Part 2: Reading the input file

```
# --- Reading input file
```

```
x=[]
y=[]
z=[]

file=open('fuzzy2b.txt',"r")
lines=file.readlines()
for aux in lines:
   x.append(aux.split('\t')[0])
   y.append(aux.split('\t')[1])
   z.append(aux.split('\t')[2])
file.close()

x = list(map(float, x))
y = list(map(float, y))
z = list(map(float, z))

zmin=np.min(z)
zmax=np.max(z)
zavg=np.mean(z)
zdev=max(abs(zmin-zavg),abs(zmax-zavg))

n=len(x)
```

Part 3: The core function

```
# --- Core function: spline-based interpolator

def F(xx,yy,r):

  zz=0
  distmin=1
  error=0

  idx=[]
  A=[]
  B=[]

  for i in range(0,r):
    idx.insert(i,int(n*P*random.random()))

  prod=1.0:
  for i in range(0,r):
    for j in range(i+1,r):
      prod*=(x[idx[i]]-x[idx[j]])*(y[idx[i]]-y[idx[j]])
  if abs(prod)>thresh3:
    for i in range(0,r):
```

```
     A.insert(i,1.0)
     B.insert(i,1.0)
     for j in range(0,r):
       if j != i:
         A[i]*=(xx-x[idx[j]])/(x[idx[i]]-x[idx[j]])
         B[i]*=(yy-y[idx[j]])/(y[idx[i]]-y[idx[j]])
       zz+=z[idx[i]]*(A[i]+B[i])/2
       distmin*=max(abs(xx-x[idx[i]]),abs(yy-y[idx[i]]))
     distmin=pow(distmin,1/r)
   else:
     error=1;


   return [zz,distmin,error]
```

Part 4: Main step

```
# --- Main step: predictions for points in validation set

# For training set predictions, change range(int(P*n),n) to range(0,int(P*n))

file_small=open("fuzzy_small.txt","w")
file_big=open("fuzzy_big.txt","w")

for j in range(int(P*n),n): # loop over all validation points

  xx=x[j]
  yy=y[j]
  zobs=z[j]
  count=0
  missing=0
  sweight=0.0
  zpredw=0.0
  zpred=0.0

  for k in range(0,M): # inner loop over all splines

    list=F(xx,yy,r)
    zz=list[0]
    distmin=list[1]
    error=list[2]
    weight=np.exp(-smoother*distmin)
    zzdevratio=abs(zz-zavg)/zdev

    if distmin<thresh1 and zzdevratio<thresh2 and error==0:
      count+=1
      sweight+=weight
      zpredw+=zz*weight
```

```
      zpred+=zz
      row=[j,xx,yy,zobs,zz,distmin,weight,zzdevratio]
      for field in row:
        file_big.write(str(field)+"\t")
      file_big.write("\n")

  if count>0:
    zpredw=zpredw/sweight
    zpred=zpred/count
  else:
    missing+=1
    zpredw=""
    zpred=""

  row=[j,count,xx,yy,zobs,zpred,zpredw]
  for field in row:
    file_small.write(str(field)+"\t")
  file_small.write("\n")

file_big.close()
file_small.close()
print(missing,"ignored points\n")
```

References

[1] Weighted percentiles using numpy. Forum discussion, 2020. StackOverflow, [Link].

[2] V. Granville, R.L. Smith, Disaggregation of rainfall time series via Gibbs sampling, NISS Technical Report, 1996, pp. 1–21, [Link].

[3] K. Saniee, A simple expression for multivariate Lagrange interpolation, SIAM Undergraduate Research Online, 2007, [Link].

New interpolation methods for synthetization and prediction

I describe little-known original interpolation methods with applications to real-life data sets. These simple techniques are easy to implement and can be used for regression or prediction. They offer an alternative to model-based statistical methods. Applications include interpolating ocean tides at Dublin, predicting temperatures in the Chicago area with geospatial data, and a problem in astronomy, namely planet alignments and frequency of these events. In one example, the 5-min data can be replaced by 80-min measurements, with the 5-min increments reconstructed via interpolation, without noticeable loss. Thus, my algorithm can be used for data compression.

The first technique has strong ties to Fourier methods. In addition to the above applications, I show how it can be used to efficiently interpolate complex mathematical functions such as Bessel and Riemann zeta. For those familiar with MATLAB® or Mathematica, this is an opportunity to play with the MPmath library in Python and see how it compares with the traditional tools in this context. In the process, I also show how the methodology can be used to generate synthetic data [Wiki], be it time series or geospatial data.

Depending on the parameters, in the geospatial context, the interpolation is either close to nearest-neighbor methods, **kriging** [Wiki] (also known as Gaussian process regression), or a truly original and hybrid mix of additive and multiplicative techniques. There is an option not to interpolate at locations far away from the training set, where regression or interpolation results may be meaningless, regardless of the technique used.

The second technique is based on ordinary least squares – the same method used to solve polynomial regression – but instead of highly unstable polynomials leading to overfitting, I focus on generic functions that avoid these pitfalls, using an iterative **greedy algorithm** [Wiki] to find the optimum. In particular, a solution based on orthogonal functions leads to a particularly simple implementation with a direct solution.

9.1 First method

The general principle is simple. We want to interpolate a function $g(t)$ at certain points $t = \rho_1, \rho_2, \dots$ belonging to a set R called the root set. These points are the roots of some function ψ. We create a function $w(t, \rho)$ which is equal to zero only if $t = \rho$ and $\rho \in R$. The functions ψ and w are chosen so that when $t \to \rho \in R$, the limit $\psi(t)/w(t, \rho)$ – a quotient where both the numerator and denominator are zero – exists and is different from zero. The limit in question is denoted as $\lambda(\rho)$. The interpolated function, denoted as $f(t)$ and defined by (9.1), is by construction identical to $g(t)$ when $t \in R$. This

Synthetic Data and Generative AI. https://doi.org/10.1016/B978-0-44-321857-6.00013-8
147

leads to the formulation

$$f(t) = \psi(t) \cdot \sum_{\rho \in R} \frac{f(\rho)}{\lambda(\rho)} \cdot \frac{1}{w(t, \rho)}, \quad \text{with } \lambda(\rho) = \lim_{t \to \rho} \frac{\psi(t)}{w(t, \rho)}. \tag{9.1}$$

Here $w(t, \rho) = 0$ if and only if $t = \rho$. The functions ψ and w must be chosen so that the limit in formula (9.1) always exists and is different from zero. Typically, $w(t, \rho)$ measures how close t and ρ are to each other. If the summation is infinite and the series is **conditionally convergent** [Wiki] – as opposed to **absolutely convergent** – then the roots ρ need to be properly ordered. This is discussed in Section 9.1.1. Convergence of the series may also require that $w(t, \rho) \to \infty$ fast enough as $|\rho| \to \infty$ and t is fixed.

In one dimension, the limit can be computed using l'Hôpital's rule [Wiki]:

$$\lambda(\rho) = \frac{\psi'(\rho)}{w'(\rho, \rho)}, \quad \text{with } \psi'(t) = \frac{\partial \psi(t)}{\partial t} \text{ and } w'(t, \rho) = \frac{\partial w(t, \rho)}{\partial t}.$$

Multiple applications of l'Hôpital's rule may be required for **roots with multiplicity** [Wiki]. The symbol ∂ stands for the **partial derivative** [Wiki], here with respect to t. In higher dimensions, the limit usually does not exist except under certain circumstances, see [1] and Section 9.1.3.

9.1.1 Example with infinite summation

I start with some mathematics leading to interesting formulas. Then I use the formulas to interpolate time series, with a cool application. Let $\psi(t) = \sin \pi t$ and $R = \{\rho_0, \rho_1, \dots\} = \mathbb{N}$ so that $\rho_k = k$. With $w(t, \rho) = t^2 - \rho^2$, you get

$$f(t) = \frac{\sin \pi t}{\pi} \cdot \left[\frac{f(0)}{t} + 2t \sum_{k=1}^{\infty} (-1)^k \frac{f(k)}{t^2 - k^2} \right]. \tag{9.2}$$

Formula (9.2) is valid for any even function f that can be written as

$$f(t) = \sum_{k=0}^{\infty} \alpha_k \cos \beta_k t \text{ with } |\beta_k| < \pi, \text{ or } f(t) = \int_{-\infty}^{\infty} \alpha(u) \cos(\beta(u)t) du \text{ with } |\beta(u)| < \pi. \tag{9.3}$$

Convergence and the fact that the left-hand side of (9.2) matches the right-hand side is rooted in the theory of Fourier series. For details, see here. A similar formula exists for odd functions. Note that f is even if $f(-t) = f(t)$, and f is odd if $f(-t) = -f(t)$. By combining the two formulas for odd and even functions, you get a formula that works for all functions regardless of parity. Again, limitations apply for convergence towards $f(t)$: the function f must be a sum of two terms, one involving cosines as in (9.3), and a similar one involving sines. In my general solution, you must replace π by $\pi/2$ in (9.3) – and the same in the sine term – for the generalized version of formula (9.2) to be valid.

The formula assumes that the **interpolation nodes** are integers. But a different grid could be used with a transformation such as $t' = a + bt$. You then interpolate f using known values of $f(t')$ where $(t' - a)/b$ is an integer, rather than interpolating f using known values of $f(t)$ where t is an integer. With an appropriate choice for a, you can extend the interpolation formula beyond the limitation previously discussed. For unevenly spaced nodes, use a nonlinear mapping $\varphi(t)$ instead of $a + bt$. The function φ should be strictly monotonic, and thus invertible.

The Python implementation is in Section 9.3.1, and available as `interpol_fourier.py` on my GitHub repository, here. With the linear transformation $a + bt$, I use nodes that are not integers to interpolate the math functions. I included advanced complex-valued math functions (Bessel, Riemann zeta) with complex arguments for those interested in scientific computing. It also illustrates how to use the mpmath library in Python, which is an alternative to Matlab.

Fig. 9.1 shows the interpolation of the real part of the **Riemann zeta function** $\zeta(\sigma + it)$ [Wiki] on the **critical line** [Wiki], that is, when $\sigma = \frac{1}{2}$. According to the famous **Riemann Hypothesis**, that is where all the nontrivial zeros lie. Actually, the first time I used my interpolation formula was in this context, with integer nodes. The approximation here is based on a more granular grid, and more accurate. See details in Chapter 17.

Interestingly, this function looks quite similar to many real-life time series: in the end, it just a special combination of sine and cosine terms with various amplitudes and incompatible periods. It is thus a good candidate for time series synthetization, able to mimic many real examples by choosing the right interval and mapping for t. The ocean tide data and the distance between Earth and Venus (Section 9.1.2) fit in that category, though they involve a small number of terms (the number is infinite for ζ).

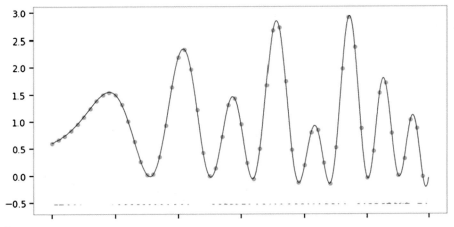

FIGURE 9.1

Interpolating the real part of $\zeta(\frac{1}{2} + it)$ based on orange points.

9.1.2 Applications: ocean tides, planet alignment

The framework introduced in Section 9.1.1 and the corresponding Python code can handle both math functions and time series data sets. In the code, I use the notation g for the exact function. The interpolated version is denoted as `interpolate`. Each interpolated value $f(t)$ is based on $2n + 1$ integer nodes where the exact value $g(t)$ is assumed to be known, on both sides of t on the horizontal axis representing the time (left and right).

Here the data set (time series) consists of ocean tides at Dublin, measured in 5-min increments. The small data extract `tides_Dublin.txt` is on my GitHub repository, here. You can download the full version here, on DigitalOcean.ie. I used it to test the methodology, since tides are easy to forecast without any statistical model. The conclusions are as follows:

- You only need data in 80-min increments to reconstruct the 5-min time series. So you can compress the data set by a factor 16 (keeping a small fraction of it), almost without loss of information.
- The 5-min data and the 5-min interpolated values are very close to each other. When they differ, the interpolated values seem better than the observed ones. The interpolation removes the noise.
- What I did is known as time series **disaggregation** in the literature. It is useful to recover unobserved 5-min pollution levels and rainfall data from hourly observations, and in other contexts.
- What I did also amounts to generating 16 shifted subsets of 80-min interpolated tides, the shift being 5 minutes. Each subset is a synthetic data set in itself. It would be very useful if the 5-min data was not known, offering various synthetic copies of the 80-min data set. The reason I did it despite the fact that the 5-min data is known, is to test the accuracy of the interpolated values. All of them (regardless of time) were generated using one single subset of real observations with 80-min increments, as if no intermediate values were known.

The data set is stored in the table `temp`. It is equivalent to an array where the index, rather than being an integer, is a multiple of 1/16. For that reason, I used a dictionary rather than an array in Python. Interpolated values are computed using observations where the index – representing the time – is an integer (one out of 16 observations). This is also true for interpolating the math functions in Section 9.1.1. Finally, each interpolated value is based on $2n + 1$ nodes (exact values where the index is an integer) with $n = 8$, spread over a $(8 + 8) \times 80$-min time period (that is, about 21 hours). By design, every 80 minutes – when the index is an integer – the interpolated and exact values are perfectly identical: this corresponds to the orange dots in Fig. 9.2.

In Fig. 9.2, the red curve represents the observed (exact) 5-min tides. The blue curve represents the interpolated values. Except in a few instances, they are indistinguishable to the naked eye. The small black bars at the bottom represents the error, in absolute value. The same black bars are found in Fig. 9.1 related to the Riemann zeta function. However, in that case the error is so small that the minuscule bars look like a glitch in the picture.

Note that no statistical model is involved in my method. It is still possible to compute various confidence or prediction intervals for the interpolated values, using bootstrapping techniques. It is discussed at length in my articles and books, and in the literature in general. For a parametric model to predict ocean tides, see Section 1.3.3.

The whole method can be seen as a regression technique to predict values within the range of observations, for time series or for observations ordered in a certain way (here by time). In some sense, it is a model-free regression that uses only one feature – the time. Can it be generalized to handle multiple features, or in other words, multivariate data? The answer is yes. See Sections 9.1.3 and 9.1.4 for an application to temperature interpolation based on two features, longitude and latitude.

Exercise 9.1. – When are planets aligned?
We first create a data set with daily measurements of the distance between Earth and Venus, and interpolate the distance to test how little data is needed for good enough performance: can you reconstruct daily data from monthly observations? What about quarterly or yearly observations? Then, the purpose is to assess how a specific class of models is good at synthetizing not only this type of data, but at the same time other types of data sets like the ocean tides in Fig. 9.2 or the Riemann zeta function in Fig. 9.1.

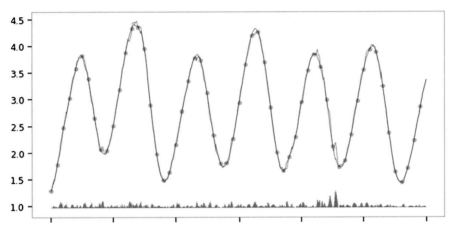

FIGURE 9.2

Tides at Dublin (5-min data), with 80 mins between interpolating nodes.

The planetary fact sheet published by the NASA contains all the information needed. It is available here. I picked up Venus and Earth because they are among the planets with the lowest eccentricities in the solar system. For simplicity, assume that the two orbits are circular. Also assume that at a time denoted as $t = 0$, the Sun, Venus, and Earth were aligned and on the same side (with Venus between Earth and the Sun).

Note that all the major planets revolve around the Sun in the same direction. Let $\theta_V, \theta_E, R_V, R_E$ be respectively the orbital periods of Venus and Earth, and the distances from the Sun for Venus and Earth. From the NASA table, these quantities are respectively 224.7 days, 365.2 days, 108.2×10^6 km, and 149.6×10^6 km. Let $d_V(t)$ be the distance at time t, between Earth and Venus. You first need to convert the orbital periods into angular velocities $\omega_V = 2\pi/\theta_V$ and $\omega_E = 2\pi/\theta_E$ per day. Then elementary trigonometry leads to the formula

$$d_V^2(t) = R_E^2 \left[1 + \left(\frac{R_V}{R_E} \right)^2 - 2\frac{R_V}{R_E} \cos\left((\omega_V - \omega_E)t \right) \right]. \tag{9.4}$$

The distance is thus periodic and minimum, and equal to $R_E - R_V$ when $(\omega_V - \omega_E)t$ is a multiple of 2π. This happens roughly every 584 days.

Steps to complete

The exercise consists of the following steps:

Step 1: Use formula (9.4) to generate daily values of $d_V(t)$, for 10 consecutive years, starting at $t = 0$.

Step 2: Use the Python code in Section 9.3.1 applied to your data. Interpolate daily data using one out of every 30 observations. Conclude whether or not using one measurement per month is good enough to reconstruct the daily observations. See how many nodes (the variable n in the code) you need to get a decent interpolation.

Step 3: Add planet Mars. The three planets (Venus, Earth, Mars) are aligned with the Sun and on the same side when both $(\omega_V - \omega_E)t$ and $(\omega_M - \omega_E)t$ are almost exact multiples of 2π, that is, when both the distance $d_M(t)$ between Earth and Mars, and $d_V(t)$ between Earth and Venus, are minimum. In short, it happens when $g(t) = d_V(t) + d_M(t)$ is minimum. Assume it happened at $t = 0$. Plot the function $g(t)$, for a period of time long enough to see a global minimum (thus, corresponding to an alignment). Here ω_M is the angular velocity of Mars, and its orbit is approximated by a circle.

Step 4: Repeat Steps 1 and 2 but this time for $g(t)$. Unlike $d_V(t)$, the function $g(t)$ is not periodic. Alternatively, use Jupiter instead of Venus, as this leads to alignments visible to the naked eye in the night sky: the apparent locations of the two planets coincide.

Step 5: A possible general model for this type of time series is

$$f(t) = \sum_{k=1}^{m} A_k \sin(\theta_k t + \varphi_k) + \sum_{k=1}^{m} A_k' \cos(\theta_k' t + \varphi_k') \qquad (9.5)$$

where the $A_k, A_k', \theta_k, \theta_k', \varphi_k, \varphi_k'$ are the parameters, representing amplitudes, frequencies, and phases. Show that this parameter configuration is redundant: you can simplify while keeping the full modeling capability, by setting $\varphi_k = \varphi_k' = 0$ and reparameterize. Hint: use the angle sum formula (Google it).

Step 6: Try 10^6 parameter configurations of the simplified model based on formula (9.5) with $\varphi_k = \varphi_k' = 0$, to synthetize time series via Monte Carlo simulations. For each simulated time series, measure how close it is to the ocean tide data (obtained by setting mode='Data' in the Python code), the functions $g(t)$ and $d_V(t)$ in this exercise, and the Riemann zeta function pictured in Fig. 9.1 (obtained by setting mode='Math.Zeta' in the Python code). Use a basic proximity metric of your choice to asses the quality of the fit, and use it on the transformed time series obtained after normalization (to get zero mean and unit variance). A possible comparison metric is a combination of lag-1, lag-2, and lag-3 autocorrelations.

Step 7: Because of the **curse of dimensionality** [Wiki], Monte Carlo is a very poor technique here as we are dealing with 8 parameters. On the other hand, you can get very good approximations with just 4 parameters, with a lower risk of overfitting. Read Section 1.3.3 about a better inference procedure, applied to ocean tides. Also read Chapter 13 on synthetic universes featuring nonstandard gravitation laws to generate different types of synthetic time series. Finally, read Chapter 6 on shape generation and comparison: it features a different type of metric to measure the distance between two objects, in this case the time series (their shape: real versus synthetic version).

9.1.3 **Problem in two dimensions**

In this section I discuss a basic example with a finite summation, where everything works nicely. However, it is a fundamental and very important case, as it applies to all regression problems. Also, it easily generalizes to higher dimensions. I use the notation $t = (x, y)$ and $z = f(t) = f(x, y)$. Let us assume that $\psi(x, y)$ has n roots $\rho_k = (x_k, y_k)$ with $k = 1, \ldots, n$. The setting is as follows: we have a data set with n observations (z_k, x_k, y_k) for $k = 1, \ldots, n$. Here z_k is the response or dependent variable, and x_k, y_k are the two features, also called independent variables or predictors. I use

$$\psi(t) = \psi(x, y) = \prod_{k=1}^{n} w_k(x, y), \quad \lambda(\rho_k) = \lambda(x_k, y_k) = \prod_{i \neq k} w_i(x, y),$$

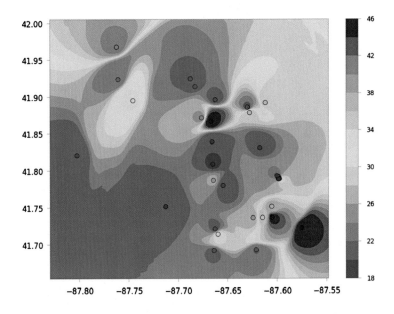

FIGURE 9.3

Temperature data: interpolation with my method (observed values at dots).

with the notation $w_k(x, y) = w(t, \rho_k) = w(x, y; x_k, y_k)$. I provide a specific example in formula (9.7). For now, let us keep in mind that by construction, $w(x, y; x', y') = 0$ if and only if $(x, y) = (x', y')$. It follows that

$$z = f(x, y) = \sum_{k=1}^{n} \gamma_k f(x_k, y_k), \quad \text{with } \gamma_k = \prod_{i \neq k} \frac{w_i(x, y)}{w_i(x_k, y_k)} = \prod_{i \neq k} \frac{w(x, y; x_i, y_i)}{w(x_k, y_k; x_i, y_i)}. \quad (9.6)$$

Thus, $z_k = f(x_k, y_k)$, for $k = 1, \ldots, n$. Given a new observation (x, y), the predicted response z, based on the n data points in the training set, is provided by formula (9.6). If (x, y) is already in the training set, then the predicted z will be exact.

Unlike in traditional kernel-based methods, here the choice of the "distance" or "kernel" function w is critical. Some adaptations preserve the fact that $z_k = f(x_k, y_k)$ for $k = 1, \ldots, n$, while providing significantly better predictions and smoothness for observations outside the training set. This makes the method a suitable alternative to regression techniques. In particular, I implemented the following upgrades:

- Replacing γ_k by $\gamma_k' = \gamma_k / (1 + \gamma_k)$. It guarantees that these coefficients lie between 0 and 1.
- Replacing γ_k' by $\gamma_k^* = \gamma_k' / w_k^{\kappa}(x, y)$ where $\kappa \geq 0$ is a hyperparameter. This reduces the impact of the point (x_k, y_k) if it is too far away from (x, y).
- Normalizing γ_k^* so that their sum is equal to 1. This eliminates additive bias outside the training set.

These transformations make the technique somewhat hybrid: a combination of multiplicative, additive, and nearest-neighbor methods. Further improvement is obtained by completely ignoring a point (x_k, y_k) when interpolating $f(x, y)$, if $w_k(x, y) > \delta$. Here $\delta > 0$ is a hyperparameter. It may result in

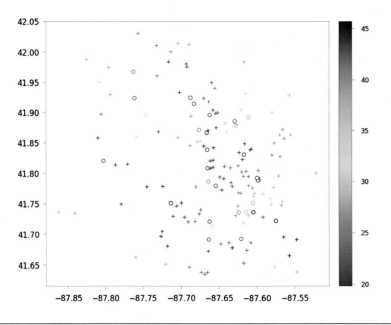

FIGURE 9.4

My method: round dots represent observed values, "+" are interpolated.

the inability to make a prediction for a point (x, y) far away from all training set points: this is actually a desirable feature, not a defect.

9.1.4 Spatial interpolation of the temperature data set

To test the method presented in Section 9.1.3, I used the streaming high frequency temperature data in Chicago, retrieved from Array of Things. The data was analyzed here in 2019 using CyberGISX, a set of **GIS** tools [Wiki] developed in Python by the University of Illinois. They used ordinary kriging; see code here. The data set has 3 fields: latitude (shown on the vertical axis), longitude (horizontal axis), and temperature (the color).

Figs. 9.3 and 9.5 show the results: my method versus ordinary kriging. The picture corresponding to kriging covers a larger area, with vast regions without training locations. This is extrapolation rather than interpolation, and the deep blue well and strong red dome are artifacts of the method. They are much less pronounced in my picture (Fig. 9.3). Indeed, I had to force my technique to cover an area away from the training set, beyond what is reasonable, to avoid blank (noninterpolated) zones in my image.

Fig. 9.4 used a smaller interpolation window: the green "+" are noninterpolated locations due to their distance to the training set. Interpolating so far away from the training set, without additional information on how the real data behaves (heat domes, cold atmospheric depressions) is meaningless and does not generalize to other fields. The 32 training set locations are represented by circular dots in all three pictures. In Fig. 9.3, the color of these dots (exact temperature) does not match the color of the background (interpolated value on nearby location) despite the appearance. There are tiny differences,

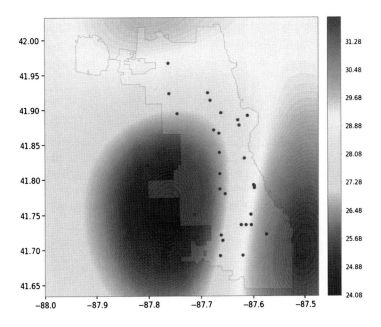

FIGURE 9.5

Temperature data set: interpolation using ordinary kriging.

not visible to the naked eye: it proves that the method works! One location in the South East corner has four training set points in very close proximity, with vastly different temperatures (the red dot is almost hidden): there you can see that the interpolation averaged out the four temperatures in question.

For $w_k(x, y)$, I used the function defined by (9.7), with $\alpha = 1$, $\beta = 2$. I did not make any efforts to find ideal parameter values, as this would defeat the purpose of designing a generic algorithm that works in many settings with as little fine-tuning as possible. For the same reason, the parameter κ in Section 9.1.3 is set to 2, and δ is automatically computed as the smallest value that guarantees all the tested locations can be interpolated so that

$$w_k(x, y) = \left(|x - x_k|^\beta + |y - y_k|^\beta \right)^\alpha, \text{ with } \alpha, \beta > 0. \tag{9.7}$$

The parameters α, β control the smoothness of the interpolated function. Choosing a small value for δ amounts to using a nearest neighbor type of interpolation. Choosing a high value for κ amounts to performing kriging. Thus the method is eclectic and encompasses various types of interpolation. The Python implementation in Section 9.3.2 follows best practices: the data is first normalized before interpolation, divisions by zero are properly handled, and you can choose not to interpolate at locations too far away from the training set by adjusting δ.

As seen in Fig. 9.4, the Python code also generates 4 copies of the training set; the number of copies is specified by the variable `ppo` in the code. In each copy, the location of each point is uniformly distributed in a circle around the original training set location that it represents. The radius of that circle is determined by the variable `radius` in the code. This synthetic data is used to test the performance of the algorithm. It allows you to play with different values of the radius. The final line of code computes the average distance (temperature discrepancy) between exact values in the training set and the associated values in the synthetic data, interpolated at sampled locations.

9.2 Second method

So far I managed to hide the underlying mathematics quite well to make the presentation easier to understand, without limiting its depth. Here the mathematics are significantly more visible. Again, Fourier series make their apparition. I cover interpolation and regression in this section, both univariate and multivariate, not just for data sets but also for mathematical functions. There is no novelty in terms of mathematical research: the originality is in the angle took to present and use the methodology. It leads to remarkably simple, elegant, and robust multivariate regression methods.

9.2.1 From unstable polynomial to robust orthogonal regression

A classic approach to approximate a function is to use **ordinary least squares** [Wiki]. Indeed, regression techniques often rely, in one way or another, on this optimization technique. When the response is denoted as $f(x)$, and the feature vector denoted as x, the problem consists of finding coefficients $\alpha_1, \ldots, \alpha_n$ such that

$$f_n(x) \equiv \sum_{k=0}^{n} \alpha_k p_k(x) \tag{9.8}$$

is the "best" approximation to $f(x)$. As in the time series application in Section 9.1.2, the function f can be a mathematical function, or represent observed values in a data set. In the latter case, f is known only for a finite number of arguments x corresponding to an entry in the data set. Either way, the problem consists of interpolating f. This is usually called a regression problem when dealing with real data, and the function f allows you to predict the response, given a new observation x not in the training set, via formula (9.8). Also, n is not the number of observations, but the index in an iterative loop associated with an optimization algorithm.

Traditionally, $p_k(x) = x^k$ in polynomial regression. In classic multivariate regression, $p_k(x)$ is the kth component of the feature vector x, possibly after some transformation such as normalization, with $p_0(x) = 1$ corresponding to the intercept. Here, I am approaching the problem from a different angle. The idea is to build a sequence of functions (f_n) converging to f as $n \to \infty$, starting with $f_{-1}(x) = 0$. At iteration n, the function f_n is chosen to minimize

$$\delta(\alpha_n) \equiv \int_D \left(f_n(x) - f(x) \right)^2 dx = \int_D \left(\alpha_n p_n(x) + f_{n-1}(x) - f(x) \right)^2 dx, \tag{9.9}$$

where D is the domain where we want the approximation to be best. If f is known only for integer values or we are dealing with a data set, the integral is replaced by a sum, and D is the discrete set of interpolation nodes (the integers), or the set of observed features in case of a data set. It is convenient to introduce the following notations:

$$\beta_k = \int_D p_k(x) f(x) dx, \quad \gamma_k = \int_D p_k^2(x) dx, \quad \beta_{ij} = \int_D p_i(x) p_j(x) dx.$$

Then we have $\alpha_0 = \beta_0/\gamma_0$ and for $n > 0$,

$$\alpha_n = \frac{1}{\gamma_n}\left[\beta_n - \sum_{k=0}^{n-1}\alpha_k\beta_{kn}\right].$$

9.2.2 Using orthogonal functions

If the coefficients β_{ij} are all zero, the formulas considerably simplify. This is the case if (p_k) is a sequence of **orthogonal functions** [Wiki]. The most well-known example is $p_{2k}(x) = \cos(k\pi x/L)$ combined with $p_{2k+1}(x) = \sin(k\pi x/L)$ for $k = 0, 1$, and so on. If $D = [-L, L]$, it corresponds to approximating or interpolating a periodic function f on D using its **Fourier series** [Wiki]. In this case, $\gamma_k = L$ if $k > 0$, with $\gamma_0 = 2L$.

Unfortunately, the polynomials $p_x(x) = x^k$ are not orthogonal on any interval. However, there is a process called **Gram–Schmidt orthogonalization** [Wiki] that turns any sequence of linearly independent functions into orthogonal ones. When applied to $1, x, x^2, x^3$, and so on, it leads to **Legendre polynomials** [Wiki] for the $p_k(x)$'s. They are orthogonal on $D = [-1, 1]$.

As usual, rather than minimizing the distance between f and f_n in formula (9.9), it is possible to use a weighted distance. All the results can be adapted. In particular, many orthogonal functions involve a weight. For instance, the **Hermite polynomials** [Wiki] involve the weight $w(x) = \exp(-x^2/2)$, and satisfy

$$\int_{-\infty}^{\infty} p_i(x)p_j(x)w(x)dx = 0 \quad \text{if } i \neq j.$$

In this case, D is the entire real line, infinite in both directions. Finally, it is also possible to directly work with a discrete set D and **discrete orthogonal functions** [Wiki]. The integrals become sums as usual. The general framework related to all these concepts is the **Sturm–Liouville theory** [Wiki].

9.2.3 Application to regression

You can apply the Fourier series method to multivariate regression as follows. It works best with continuous features. For discrete features, I advise to look at **discrete Fourier series** [Wiki] instead. You want to transform each continuous feature separately so that the values are – as closely as possible – distributed uniformly on the interval $[-1, 1]$ after the transformation. This is accomplished in two steps: first apply the transformation F_k to the kth component of the feature vector. Then apply the transformation Q. Do this for each component $k = 1, \ldots, n$. Here

- F_k is the empirical distribution function [Wiki] attached to feature k. In Python, use the function ECDF from the statsmodel library.
- Q is the **quantile function** [Wiki] of a uniform distribution on $[-1, 1]$. Thus $Q(u) = -1 + 2u$.

Now use formula (9.8) on the transformed data, with the p_k and α_k from the first paragraph in Section 9.2.2, together with $L = 1$. Note that there is no matrix inversion in this procedure. It is a particular type of **spline regression** [Wiki]. See Python code in Section 9.3.3. For a different type of spline regression based on exact interpolation similar to the method discussed in Section 9.1.3, see Chapter 8.

For polynomial regression, use Legendre polynomials, after transforming the features so that values stay within $[-1, 1]$, and uniformly distributed. Again, there is no matrix inversion and the procedure is fast and simple. For another example of regression with Legendre polynomials, see [3].

The methods presented here have their roots in interpolating math functions, where successive terms in the summation formula – in this case formula (9.8) – have on average a decreasing impact. Otherwise, the sum, usually involving an infinite number of terms, would not converge. So it makes sense to order the features by decreasing importance. The first feature with coefficient α_1 may be chosen as that with least residual error. The second feature with coefficient α_2 being the one yielding the best improvement to the residual error, and so on.

Also, for the same reason, in multivariate regression, the method is suited for data sets with a large n (number of features) well approximated by model (9.8), even with a small number of observations, see [4]. Such data sets are sometimes referred to as **wide data**. A more general version uses **multidimensional Fourier series** [2].

9.3 Python code

This section contains the code, both for the time series interpolation, and the geospatial temperature data set. The time series version deals with the ocean tide data set, as well as interpolating advanced math functions (with complex values and complex arguments), using the MPmath library. You can use the code for your own data sets, and for synthetization purposes. In addition, I added some minimal code for the multivariate regression based on Fourier series.

9.3.1 Time series interpolation

This program deals with the interpolation method in one dimension. The code is also on my GitHub repository, here. For parameter description, see Sections 9.1.1 and 9.1.2. The code can interpolate a math function or a time series (data set with observations ordered by time, with fixed time increments) depending on the `mode` parameter. Either way, the "object" to be interpolated (function or data) is represented by the function g in the code. The program computes nonlinear moving averages, to interpolate the value of $g(t)$ at fractional arguments of the time, say $t = 1/16, 2/16, 3/16$, and so on, when the value is known only for integer arguments.

When t is an integer, the interpolated and observed values are identical. In the case of math functions, under certain general conditions, the interpolated values are also exact when the number of nodes (determined by variable n) is infinite. In practice, very good approximations are obtained already with $n = 8$.

The parameter $1/16$ is represented by the variable `incr` in the code. You can change it to the inverse of a power of two, say $1/8, 1/4$, or $1/2$. Other values such as $1/7$ may cause problems: due to computer arithmetic, the instruction `7*1/7` or `9*1/9` does not return an exact integer; however, `8*1/8` does. It is easy to correct this issue if you need to.

Finally, one way to reduce the number of operations is to use a hash table (dictionary in Python) to store values of $g(t)$ each time a new t is encountered. Due to the moving average, the same value $g(t)$ may be computed multiple times on different occasions. The hash table will avoid double computations, and can save time especially when computing the Zeta function.

```
# interpol_fourier.py (author: MLTechniques.com)
import numpy as np
import mpmath
import matplotlib as mpl
from matplotlib import pyplot as plt

# https://www.digitalocean.ie/Data/DownloadTideData

mode = 'Data' # options: 'Data', 'Math.Bessel', 'Math.Zeta'

#--- read data

if mode == 'Data':

    # one column: observed value
    # time is generated by the algorithm; integer for interpolation nodes

    IN = open("tides_Dublin.txt","r")
    table = IN.readlines()
    IN.close()

    temp={}
    t = 0
    # t/t_unit is an integer every t_unit observations (node)
    t_unit = 16 # use 16 for ocean tides, 32 for planet data discussed in the classroom
    for string in table:
        string = string.replace('\n', '')
        fields = string.split('\t')
        temp[t/t_unit] = float(fields[0])
        t = t + 1
    nobs = len(temp)

else:
    t_unit = 16

#--- function to interpolate

def g(t):
    if mode == 'Data':
        z = temp[t]
    elif mode == 'Math.Bessel':
        t = 40*(t-t_min)/(t_max-t_min)
        z = mpmath.besselj(1,t)
        z = float(z.real) # real part of the complex-valued function
    elif mode == 'Math.Zeta':
        t = 4 + 40*(t-t_min)/(t_max-t_min)
        z = mpmath.zeta(complex(0.5,t))
```

```
        z = float(z.real) # real part of the complex-valued function
    return(z)

#--- interpolation function

def interpolate(t, eps):
    sum = 0
    t_0 = int(t + 0.5) # closest interpolation node to t
    pi2 = 2/np.pi
    flag1 = -1
    flag2 = -1
    for k in range(0, n):
        # use nodes k1, k2 in interpolation formula
        k1 = t_0 + k
        k2 = t_0 - k
        tt = t - t_0
        if k != 0:
            if k %2 == 0:
                z = g(k1) + g(k2)
                if abs(tt**2 - k**2) > eps:
                    term = flag1 * tt*z*pi2 * np.sin(tt/pi2) / (tt**2 - k**2)
                else:
                    # use limit as tt --> k
                    term = z/2
                flag1 = -flag1
            else:
                z = g(k1) - g(k2)
                if abs(tt**2 - k**2) > eps:
                    term = flag2 * tt*z*pi2 * np.cos(tt/pi2) / (tt**2 - k**2)
                else:
                    # use limit as tt --> k
                    term = z/2
                flag2 = -flag2
        else:
            z = g(k1)
            if abs(tt) > eps:
                term = z*pi2*np.sin(tt/pi2) / tt
            else:
                # use limit as tt --> k (here k = 0)
                term = z
        sum += term
    return(sum)

#--- main loop and visualizations

n = 8
    # 2n+1 is number of nodes used in interpolation
    # in all 3 cases tested (data, math functions), n >= 8 works
```

```python
if mode=='Data':
    # restrictions:
    #     t_min >= n, t_max <= int(nobs/t_unit - n)
    #     t_max > t_min, at least one node between t_min and t_max
    t_min = n # interpolate between t_min and t_max
    t_max = int(nobs/t_unit - n) # must have t_max - t_min > 0
else:
    t_min = 0
    t_max = 100
incr = 1/t_unit # time increment between nodes
eps  = 1.0e-12

OUT = open("interpol_tides_Dublin.txt","w")

time = []
ze = []
zi = []

fig = plt.figure(figsize=(6,3))
mpl.rcParams['axes.linewidth'] = 0.2
mpl.rc('xtick', labelsize=6)
mpl.rc('ytick', labelsize=6)

for t in np.arange(t_min, t_max, incr):
    time.append(t)
    z_interpol = interpolate(t, eps)
    z_exact = g(t)
    zi.append(z_interpol)
    ze.append(z_exact)
    error = abs(z_exact - z_interpol)
    if t == int(t):
        plt.scatter(t,z_exact,color='orange', s=6)
    print("t = %8.5f exact = %8.5f interpolated = %8.5f error = %8.5f %3d nodes" %
        (t,z_exact,z_interpol,error,n))
    OUT.write("%10.6f\t%10.6f\t%10.6f\t%10.6f\n" % (t,z_exact,z_interpol,error))
OUT.close()

plt.plot(time,ze,color='red',linewidth = 0.5, alpha=0.5)
plt.plot(time,zi,color='blue', linewidth = 0.5,alpha=0.5)
base = min(ze) - (max(ze) -min(ze))/10
for index in range(len(time)):
    # plot error bars showing delta between exact and interpolated values
    t = time[index]
    error = abs(zi[index]-ze[index])
    plt.vlines(t,base,base+error,color='black',linewidth=0.2)
plt.savefig('tides2.png', dpi=200)
plt.show()
```

9.3.2 Geospatial temperature data set

The Python code interpol.py is also on my GitHub repository, here. The functions and parameters are described in Sections 9.1.3 and 9.1.4. The main function, performing interpolation on a 2-dimensional grid applied to temperatures in the Chicago area, is rather simple. The data is stored into the data array, mapped to the npdata Numpy array. It is then mapped onto a grid, represented by the zgrid array. The grid is used only to produce contour plots.

Four copies of the training set are generated (using ppo=4). They can be viewed as four synthetized versions of the training set, with locations and temperatures distributed just like in the original training set. The synthetized locations are stored in the arrays xa and ya (latitude and longitude); the synthetized temperatures obtained by interpolation are stored in the array za.

Interpolated values computed on locations identical to a training set location are exact, by design. Note that before interpolating, the data is transformed: it is normalized to have zero mean and unit variance, a standard practice. It is denormalized at to end to produce the contour plots. Each interpolated value is computed using a variable number of nodes. That number depends on how many nodes are close enough to the target location. A node is a location in the training set with known temperature.

The number of nodes, for each synthetized location, is stored in the npt array. Using the default parameter value for alpha guarantees that there is always at least one node (the nearest neighbor) to compute the interpolated value. This can lead to meaningless interpolated values for locations far away from the training set. Reducing the default alpha results in some noninterpolated values marked as NaN, and it is actually recommended. The uncomputed values show up as a green "+" in Fig. 9.4.

Finally, the interpolate function accepts locations x, y that are either a single location or an array of locations. Accordingly, the returned value z – the temperature – can be a single value or an array. The audit parameter is used internally for testing and monitoring purposes.

```python
import numpy as np
import matplotlib as mpl
from matplotlib import pyplot as plt
from matplotlib import colors
from matplotlib import cm # color maps

data = [
# (latitude, longitude, temperature)
# source = https://cybergisxhub.cigi.illinois.edu/notebook/spatial-interpolation/
(41.878377,-87.627678,28.24),
(41.751238,-87.712990,19.83),
(41.736314,-87.624179,26.17),
(41.722457,-87.575350,45.70),
(41.736495,-87.614529,35.07),
(41.751295,-87.605288,36.47),
(41.923996,-87.761072,22.45),
(41.866786,-87.666306,45.01), # 125.01 outlier changed to 45.01
(41.808594,-87.665048,19.82),
(41.786756,-87.664343,26.21),
(41.791329,-87.598677,22.04),
```

```
(41.751142,-87.712990,20.20),
(41.831070,-87.617298,20.50),
(41.788979,-87.597995,42.15),
(41.914094,-87.683022,21.67),
(41.871480,-87.676440,25.14),
(41.736593,-87.604759,45.01), # 125.01 outlier changed to 45.01
(41.896157,-87.662391,21.16),
(41.788608,-87.598713,19.50),
(41.924903,-87.687703,21.61),
(41.895005,-87.745817,32.03),
(41.892003,-87.611643,28.30),
(41.839066,-87.665685,20.11),
(41.967590,-87.762570,40.60),
(41.885750,-87.629690,42.80),
(41.714021,-87.659612,31.46),
(41.721301,-87.662630,21.35),
(41.692703,-87.621020,21.99),
(41.691803,-87.663723,21.62),
(41.779744,-87.654487,20.88),
(41.820972,-87.802435,20.55),
(41.792543,-87.600008,20.41)
]
npdata = np.array(data)

#--- top parameters

n = len(npdata) # number of points in data set
ppo = 4        # create ppo new points around each observed point
new_obs = n * ppo
alpha = 1.0   # small alpha increases smoothing
beta = 2.0    # small beta increases smoothing
kappa = 2.0   # high kappa makes method close to kriging
eps  = 1.0e-8 # make it work if sample locations same as observed ones
np.random.seed(6)
radius = 1.2
audit = True # so log monitoring info about the interpolation

xa = []          # latitude
ya = []          # longitude
da = []          # dist between observed and interpolated value
zd = []          # observed z
za = np.empty(new_obs) # interpolated z

#--- transform data: normalization

mu = npdata.mean(axis=0)
stdev = npdata.std(axis=0)
npdata = (npdata - mu)/stdev
```

```
#--- interpolation for sampled locations

def w(x, y, x_k, y_k, alpha, beta):
    # distance function
    z = (abs(x - x_k)**beta + abs(y - y_k)**beta)**alpha
    return(z)

# create random locations for interpolation purposes
for h in range(ppo):
    # sample points in a circle of radius "radius" around each obs
    xa = np.append(xa, npdata[:,0] + radius * np.random.uniform(-1, 1, n))
    ya = np.append(ya, npdata[:,1] + radius * np.random.uniform(-1, 1, n))
    da = np.append(da, w(xa[-n:],ya[-n:],npdata[:,0],npdata[:,1],alpha,beta))
    zd = np.append(zd, npdata[:,2])

delta = eps + max(da) # to ignore obs too far away from sampled point
npt = np.empty(new_obs) # number of points used for interpolation at location j

def interpolate(x, y, npdata, delta, audit):
    # compute interpolated z at location (x, y) based on npdata (observations)
    # also returns npoints, the number of data points used in the interpolation
    # data points (x_k, y_k) with w[(x,y), (x_k,y_k)] >= delta are ignored
    # note: (x, y) can be a location or an array of locations

    sum = 0.0
    sum_coeff = 0.0
    npoints = 0
    for k in range(n):
        x_k = npdata[k, 0]
        y_k = npdata[k, 1]
        z_k = npdata[k, 2]
        coeff = 1
        for i in range(n):
            x_i = npdata[i, 0]
            y_i = npdata[i, 1]
            if i != k:
                numerator = w(x, y, x_i, y_i, alpha, beta)
                denominator = w(x_k, y_k, x_i, y_i, alpha, beta)
                coeff *= numerator / (eps + denominator)
        dist = w(x, y, x_k, y_k, alpha, beta)
        if dist < delta:
            coeff = (eps + dist)**(-kappa) * coeff / (1 + coeff)
            sum_coeff += coeff
            npoints += 1
            if audit:
                OUT.write("%3d\t%3d\t%8.5f\t%8.5f\t%8.5f\n" % (j,k,z_k,coeff,dist))
        else:
```

```
            coeff = 0.0
        sum += z_k * coeff
    if npoints > 0:
        z = sum / sum_coeff
    else:
        z = 'NaN' # undefined
    return(z, npoints)


OUT=open("audit.txt","w") # output file for auditing / detecting issues
OUT.write("j\tk\tz_k\tcoeff\tdist\n")


for j in range(new_obs):
    (za[j], npt[j]) = interpolate(xa[j], ya[j], npdata, 0.5*delta, audit=True)


OUT.close()

#--- inverse transform (unnormalize) and visualizations

steps = 140 # to create grid with steps x steps points, to generate contours
xb = np.linspace(min(npdata[:,0])-0.50, max(npdata[:,0])+0.50, steps)
yb = np.linspace(min(npdata[:,1])-0.50, max(npdata[:,1])+0.50, steps)
xc = mu[0] + stdev[0] * xb
yc = mu[1] + stdev[1] * yb
xc, yc = np.meshgrid(xc, yc)
zgrid = np.empty(shape=(len(xb),len(yb)))

# create grid and get interpolated values at grid locations
for h in range(len(xb)):
    for k in range(len(yb)):
        x = xb[h]
        y = yb[k]
        (z, points) = interpolate(x, y, npdata, 2.2*delta, audit=False)
        if z == 'NaN':
            zgrid[h,k] = 'NaN'
        else:
            zgrid[h,k] = mu[2] + stdev[2] * z
zgridt = zgrid.transpose()

# inverse transform
xa = mu[0] + stdev[0] * xa
ya = mu[1] + stdev[1] * ya
za = mu[2] + stdev[2] * za
xb = mu[0] + stdev[0] * xb
yb = mu[1] + stdev[1] * yb
npdata = mu + stdev * npdata

def set_plt_params():
    # initialize visualizations
```

```
    fig = plt.figure(figsize =(4, 3), dpi=200)
    ax = fig.gca()
    plt.setp(ax.spines.values(), linewidth=0.1)
    ax.xaxis.set_tick_params(width=0.1)
    ax.yaxis.set_tick_params(width=0.1)
    ax.xaxis.set_tick_params(length=2)
    ax.yaxis.set_tick_params(length=2)
    ax.tick_params(axis='x', labelsize=4)
    ax.tick_params(axis='y', labelsize=4)
    plt.rc('xtick', labelsize=4)
    plt.rc('ytick', labelsize=4)
    plt.rcParams['axes.linewidth'] = 0.1
    return(fig,ax)

# contour plot
(fig, ax) = set_plt_params()
cs = plt.contourf(yc, xc, zgridt,cmap='coolwarm',levels=16)
cbar = plt.colorbar(cs)
cbar.ax.tick_params(width=0.1)
cbar.ax.tick_params(length=2)
plt.scatter(npdata[:,1], npdata[:,0], c=npdata[:,2], s=8, cmap=cm.coolwarm,
    edgecolors='black',linewidth=0.3,alpha=0.8)
plt.show()
plt.close()

# scatter plot
(fig, ax) = set_plt_params()
my_cmap = cm.get_cmap('coolwarm')
my_norm = colors.Normalize()
ec_colors = my_cmap(my_norm(npdata[:,2]))
plt.scatter(npdata[:,1], npdata[:,0], c='white', s=5, cmap=cm.coolwarm,
    edgecolors=ec_colors,linewidth=0.4)
sc=plt.scatter(ya[npt>0], xa[npt>0], c=za[npt>0], cmap=cm.coolwarm,
    marker='+',s=5,linewidth=0.4)

# show in green points not interpolated as they were too far away
plt.scatter(ya[npt==0], xa[npt==0], c='lightgreen', marker='+', s=5,
    linewidth=0.4)

cbar = plt.colorbar(sc)
cbar.ax.tick_params(width=0.1)
cbar.ax.tick_params(length=2)
# plt.ylim(min(npdata[:,0]),max(npdata[:,0]))
# plt.xlim(min(npdata[:,1]),max(npdata[:,1]))
plt.show()

#--- measuring quality of the fit
```

```
error = np.mean(abs(za[npt>0] - zd[npt>0]))
print("Error=",delta)
```

9.3.3 Regression with Fourier series

The basic code here is provided to illustrate the methodology in Section 9.2.3, for multivariate regression with sine and cosine splines. It is a minimal workable piece of code. The data is made up, and no transformer is necessary because the observed values are already in $[-1, 1]$ for the feature vector, by construction. The code is also on my GitHub repository, here. Look for `interpol_ortho.py`.

```python
import numpy as np
import random

#---- make up data

data = []
nobs = 100
random.seed(69)
for i in range(nobs):
    x1 = -1 + 2*random.random()  # feature 1
    x2 = -1 + 2*random.random()  # feature 2
    z = np.sin(0.56*x1) - 0.5*np.cos(1.53*x2) # response
    obs = [x1, x2, z]
    data.append(obs)

npdata = np.array(data)
transf_npdata = npdata # no data transformer needed here

#--- the p_k functions

def p_k(x, k):

    # if input x is an array, output z is also an array

    if k % 2 == 0:
        z = np.cos(k*x*np.pi)
    else:
        z = np.sin(k*x*np.pi)
    return(z)

#--- beta_k, alpha_k, gamma_k coefficients

intercept = np.ones(nobs)
p_0 = p_k(intercept, k = 0)
p_1 = p_k(transf_npdata[:,0], k = 1) # feature 1
p_2 = p_k(transf_npdata[:,1], k = 2) # feature 2
```

```python
gamma_0 = np.dot(p_0, p_0) # dot product
gamma_1 = np.dot(p_1, p_1)
gamma_2 = np.dot(p_2, p_2)

observed_temp = npdata[:,2]
beta_0 = np.dot(p_0, observed_temp)
beta_1 = np.dot(p_1, observed_temp)
beta_2 = np.dot(p_2, observed_temp)

alpha_0 = beta_0 / gamma_0
alpha_1 = beta_1 / gamma_1
alpha_2 = beta_2 / gamma_2

#--- interpolation

predicted_temp = alpha_0 * p_0 + alpha_1 * p_1 + alpha_2 * p_2

#--- print results: predicted vs observed

for i in range(nobs):
    print("%8.5f %8.5f" %(predicted_temp[i],observed_temp[i]))

correlmatrix = np.corrcoef(predicted_temp,observed_temp)
correlation = correlmatrix[0, 1]
print("corr between predicted/observed: %8.5f" % (correlation))

#--- interpolate for new observation (with intercept = 1)

x1 = 0.234
x2 = -0.541

z_predicted = alpha_0 * p_k(1,k=0) + alpha_1 * p_k(x1,k=1) + alpha_2 * p_k(x2,k=2)
print("test interpolation: z_predict = %8.5f" %(z_predicted))
```

References

[1] G.R. Lawlor, A l'Hospital's rule for multivariable functions, Preprint, pp. 1–13, arXiv:1209.0363, 2013, [Link].

[2] A.R. Osborne, Multidimensional Fourier series, International Geophysics 97 (2010) 115–145, [Link].

[3] M. Shivanand, et al., Fitting random regression models with Legendre polynomial and B-spline to model the lactation curve for Indian dairy goat of semi-arid tropic, Journal of Animal Breeding and Genetics (2022) 414–422, [Link].

[4] F. Wang, et al., Bivariate Fourier-series-based prediction of surface residual stress fields using stresses of partial points, Mathematics and Mechanics of Solids (2018), [Link].

Synthetic tabular data: copulas vs enhanced GANs

10

I covered many methods leading to interpretable machine learning and explainable AI throughout this book. For the sake of completeness, in this chapter, I describe copulas and GAN for data synthetization, as well as additional explainable AI topics and other usages of synthetic data.

A key concept is **feature attribution**. It indicates how much each feature in your model contributed to the predictions, for each individual observation. It is different from global feature attribution, applied to the data set as a whole and measured using predictive power or percentage of total variance attributed to specific features in **principal component analysis**, or based on combinatorial methods such as in Section 7.5. In the context of computer vision, it is sometimes called pixel attribution and represents the most influential pixels that explain the result of image classification performed by neural networks or other means. In this context, each pixel of an image is considered as a feature. See the book "Interpretable Machine Learning" [8], page 254. For an introduction to feature attribution, comparing different methods, see here.

For regression, additive models and tabular data (as opposed to images), a popular feature attribution method referred to as SHAP is based on the **Shapley value** [Wiki], originating from game theory. More about SHAP can be found here, in the document "An introduction to explainable AI with Shapley values" posted in 2018 by Scott Lundberg, Senior Researcher at Microsoft Research. A simple example in the context of linear regression is posted here. Another key concept is **feature importance**. It is used to score input features based on how useful they are at predicting a target variable. The term, possibly coined around 2020 by machine learning practitioners, is a different name for the predictive power of a feature, used throughout this book and covering many different metrics. It has become popular among Python developers; see, for instance, here.

In addition to feature attribution and importance, another way to understand how a black-box system works (to increase explainability) is to assess the contribution of a subset of observations, and its predictive impact either on the whole system or on a specific observation. In particular, one would want to detect the observations with the greatest impact on specific predictions, to understand how these predictions were made, especially outside the training set. For instance, to see how a specific prediction is impacted by individual observations, you can remove the observation that least impacts that prediction, in your training set. Then rerun the model, and again remove the observation with minimum impact on that prediction. And again and again recursively until you are left with a tiny training set, yet big enough to compute with great precision the predicted value in question. Then see if the observations left in your tiny training set share common patterns.

Another way to understand how your black-box works is to use rich synthetic or hand-made data to find observations that are not properly handled. For instance, a specific word such as 2:39 pronounced

Synthetic Data and Generative AI. https://doi.org/10.1016/B978-0-44-321857-6.00014-X

with an accent. Alexa always confuses it with 2:59 when I ask her, with my French accent, to set an alarm at 2:39 to go pick up my son at school. A simple fix in this case would be for Alexa to learn directly from me, recognize her error as I train her, and then get it fixed for good. This has the benefit to let Alexa adapt to each customer, offering customized chats rather than relying only on a central training set. Finding counterexamples to your system, to make it fail, in essence to crack it, is referred to as **adversarial learning** [Wiki]. It helps you better understand how your black-box works, and by integrating these tricky cases, it helps you improve your system.

Finally, **generative adversarial networks** (GANs) [Wiki] are popular in computer vision. Given a training set, this technique learns to generate new data with the same statistics as the training set. For example, a GAN trained on photographs can generate new photographs that look at least superficially authentic to human observers, having many realistic characteristics. How to identify a fake GAN-generated picture from a real one of the same person based on iris parameters, see [4].

10.1 Sensitivity analysis, bias reduction and other uses of synthetic data

Synthetic data was originally developed as a method to replace missing values with synthetic ones: this is known as **imputation** [Wiki]. It did not work well as the missing values typically do not follow the underlying statistical model. A potential solution is as follows. Use real or synthetic data (ideally, both) and remove some values to emulate a data set with missing values. Then replace the missing values by synthetic ones. Try with a large number of parameter-driven simulations to see which parameter values are best at producing meaningful missing values. Another benefit of synthetic data is its ability to test model resilience: replace some real observations in your validation set with synthetic ones, and see how your predictions are sensitive to this change. Eliminate models that show lack of resilience. This is an easy way to reduce overfitting.

Another use of synthetic data is for **bootstrapping** [Wiki] or to compute **confidence regions** based on **parametric bootstrap**. Numerous examples are included in this book: see the keywords in question in the index. This simulation-heavy technique requires a large amount of data generated with the same parameter values as those estimated on your original data set. Also, synthetic data is used to benchmark and test algorithms. Again, this book features numerous examples. It is also used to correct for imbalanced data or to reduce algorithm biases, by oversampling from groups or segments with few observations or representing minorities. The example in Section 10.2 shows how to generate synthetic data at the group level, rather than globally. It allows you to choose how many observations you want to generate, for each group.

The technique must be properly implemented to reduce **algorithmic bias** [Wiki] that penalizes minorities. When using copulas, see the issues in Section 10.2.1. A solution is to add extra features (say, education level) to your real data to better capture the nuances of a population segment that is consistently penalized as a whole (high crime area), to detect subsegments that do well. Then you can compute a separate copula for subsegments such as college-educated in high crime area.

Finally, for authors and publishers, synthetic images can mimic and replace copyrighted ones, eliminating licensing fees and authorization issues. Synthesized art is called **AI art**. The question is: who owns it? Can you own randomly generated patterns or numbers?

10.2 **Using copulas to generate synthetic data**

One method to generate data with the exact same correlation structure and same marginal distributions as in your real data set is to use **copulas** [Wiki]. The algorithm to produce n synthesized observations is as follows:

- Step 1: Compute the correlation matrix W associated to your real data.
- Step 2: Generate n deviates from a multivariate Gaussian distribution with zero mean and covariance matrix W. Each deviate is a vector Z_i ($i = 1, \ldots, n$), with the components matching the features in the real data set.
- Step 3: For each generated Z_{ij} (the jth feature in your ith vector) compute $U_{ij} = \Phi(Z_{ij})$, where Φ is the CDF (cumulative distribution function) of a univariate standard normal distribution. Thus $0 \le U_{ij} \le 1$.
- Step 4: Compute $S_{ij} = Q_j(U_{ij})$ where Q_j is the univariate **empirical quantile distribution** (the inverse of the empirical distribution) attached to the jth feature, and computed on the real data.

Assuming W is nonsingular, your set of feature vectors S_i ($i = 1, \ldots, n$) is your synthesized data, mimicking your real data set. I implicitly used the **Gaussian copula** here, but other options exist, such as the **Frank copula**. This method is a direct application of **Sklar's theorem** [Wiki]. There are various ways to measure the similarity or distance between the synthetic and real version of the data. In this context, the **Hellinger distance** [Wiki] is popular. See also Section 6.4 on comparing two data sets. However, these metrics lead to overfitting: the best synthetic data being an exact replica of the real data. Having statistical summaries matching those in the real data as in Table 10.1, combined with the worst Hellinger score, leads to richer synthetic data. In the end, the quality should be measured by the improvement obtained when making predictions for the validation set, after adding your synthetic data to the training set.

The Hellinger distance is popular because it takes values between 0 and 1, with 0 being a perfect fit, and 1 being the worst case. It is based on the PDF (probability density function) instead of the CDF (cumulative distribution function). This leads to a bumpier metric more sensitive to noise, compared to (say) the **Kolmogorov–Smirnov distance** [Wiki] between two CDFs. Also, while the Hellinger distance can be computed globally by working with the joint, multivariate PDF involving all the features, it is based on observed frequencies measured over a large number of small multivariate bins in the feature vector, each with very few observations and thus unstable. A better solution is to compute the distance separately for each feature, and then take the maximum of these distances. In short, considering the best synthetization as that minimizing the maximum distance across all features. On the plus side, the Hellinger distance can handle categorical data very well.

The formula to compare two probability density functions P and P' is as follows, illustrated for discrete distributions with n levels or categories. In practice, it is applied to frequencies (the empirical PDF measured on each feature):

$$H(P, P') = \frac{1}{\sqrt{2}} \sqrt{\sum_{k=1}^{n} \left(\sqrt{p_i} - \sqrt{p_i'} \right)^2}.$$

In Python, the four steps of the synthetization algorithm are respectively performed with the functions `np.corrcoef`, `np.random.multivariate_normal`, `norm.cdf`, and `np.quantile`. Except for norm.cdf (CDF of standard Gaussian distribution) which comes from the Scipy library, the others are implemented in Numpy. To generate the exact same synthetic data each time you run the program, use np.random.seed with the same **seed**.

Finally, a few Python libraries deal with copulas, for instance, Copulalib and Copulas. See also SDV (the Synthetic Data Vault, in Python) for more options including deep learning. The Python program copula.py on my GitHup repository (main folder) shows how it works. It is also possible to avoid copulas and deal directly with the correlation matrix, as in Section 7.2.1. Or ignore correlations altogether, and simply add uncorrelated white noise to each feature: this may be the easiest way to generate synthetic data. This approach is significantly superior to copulas to generate synthetic values outside the range observed in the real data. It also preserves the correlation structure, and in some sense, generates richer data. Another popular method is **rejection sampling** [Wiki].

10.2.1 The insurance data set: Python code and results

I used the algorithm in Section 10.2 to synthesize the insurance data set shared on Kaggle, here. The spreadsheet insurance.xlsx on GitHub (main folder) summarizes all the findings, and contains three data sets: the real data, synthetic data that I produced with insurance.py (same folder), and synthetic data generated by Mostly.ai. The data set has the following fields: age, sex, bmi (body mass index), number of children covered by plan, smoker (yes or no), region (Northeast, and so on), and charges incurred by the insurer for the customer in question.

I do not know what algorithm Mostly.ai uses, but their synthetic copy of the real data is strikingly similar to mine. Both have all the hallmarks (quality and defects) of being copula-generated. My version is slightly better because I generated a different copula (and thus, a different correlation matrix) for each group of observations. I grouped the observations by sex, smoker status, and region, while Mostly.ai applied the same copula across all these groups. Automatically detecting the groups as large homogeneous **nodes** in a decision tree, combined with using a separate copula for each node, would lead to an **ensemble method** not unlike the **boosted trees** described in Chapter 2. By a large node, I mean a node with many observations (enough to compute a meaningful correlation matrix and empirical quantiles) but little depth to avoid overfitting. The nodes are detected on the real data.

Table 10.1 provides some high-level summary statistics: Synthetic 1 is produced by Mostly.ai, and Synthetic 2 using the methodology described here. The correlation structure is well reconstituted. Synthetic 2 is better than Synthetic 1 for "Max charges" (the maximum computed over all observations) because it generates separate copulas for each group. Also, this feature has a bimodal distribution.

The sore point is that copulas are unable to generate values outside the range observed in the real data set: this is evident when looking at the maxima and minima. All data sets have the same number of observations. Even when I increase the number of synthesized observations by a factor 100, I am still stuck with a maximum charge less than \$63,770, even though this ceiling is not an outlier in the real data. The same is true with "age", although this is compounded by the fact that ages 18 and 64 are cut-off points. The issue is that the quantile functions Q_j in Section 10.2 generate values between the minimum and maximum observed in the real data, for each feature j. A workaround is to introduce uncorrelated white noise either in the real or synthetic data; see Section 10.2.2.

The Python code in this section can be optimized for speed as follows: precompute the empirical quantiles functions associated to each feature in the real data set, as well as the CDF of the standard Gaussian distribution. In other words, use a table of precomputed values. Note that the empirical quantiles in my method need to be computed separately for each group. Except for "bmi", the features in the

Table 10.1 Comparing real data with two different synthetic copies.

Statistic	Real data	Synthetic 1	Synthetic 2
Mean age	39.21	39.21	38.61
Min age	18	18	18
Max age	64	64	64
Mean bmi	30.66	30.97	30.79
Min bmi	15.96	17.29	16.11
Max bmi	53.13	47.74	52.98
Mean charges	13,270	13,516	13,253
Min charges	1122	1137	1126
Max charges	63,770	49,993	59,588
Stdev charges	12,110	12,330	12,132
Correl age, bmi	0.11	0.06	0.09
Correl age, children	0.04	0.02	0.03
Correl age, charges	0.30	0.29	0.30
Correl bmi, charges	0.20	0.14	0.18
Stdev children	1.21	1.19	1.20

insurance data set are highly non-Gaussian: "charges" is bimodal, "number of children" has a geometric (discrete) distribution, and "age" is uniform except for the extremes.

```
import csv
from scipy.stats import norm
import numpy as np

filename = 'insurance.csv' # make sure fields do not contain commas
# source: https://www.kaggle.com/datasets/teertha/ushealthinsurancedataset
# Fields: age, sex, bmi, children, smoker, region, charges

with open(filename, 'r') as csvfile:
    reader = csv.reader(csvfile)
    fields = next(reader) # Reads header row as a list
    rows = list(reader) # Reads all subsequent rows as a list of lists

#-- group by (sex, smoker, region)

groupCount = {}
groupList = {}
for obs in rows:
    group = obs[1] +"\t"+obs[4]+"\t"+obs[5]
    if group in groupCount:
        cnt = groupCount[group]
        groupList[(group,cnt)]=(obs[0],obs[2],obs[3],obs[6])
        groupCount[group] += 1
```

```
    else:
        groupList[(group,0)]=(obs[0],obs[2],obs[3],obs[6])
        groupCount[group] = 1

#-- generate synthetic data customized to each group (Gaussian copula)

seed = 453
np.random.seed(seed)
OUT=open("insurance_synth.txt","w")
for group in groupCount:
    nobs = groupCount[group]
    age = []
    bmi = []
    children = []
    charges = []
    for cnt in range(nobs):
        features = groupList[(group,cnt)]
        age.append(float(features[0])) # uniform outside very young or very old
        bmi.append(float(features[1])) # Gaussian distribution?
        children.append(float(features[2])) # geometric distribution?
        charges.append(float(features[3])) # bimodal, not Gaussian
    mu = [np.mean(age), np.mean(bmi), np.mean(children), np.mean(charges)]
    zero = [0, 0, 0, 0]
    z = np.stack((age, bmi, children, charges), axis = 0)
    corr = np.corrcoef(z) # correlation matrix for Gaussian copula for this group

    print("------------------")
    print("\n\nGroup: ",group,"[",cnt,"obs ]\n")
    print("mean age: %2d\nmean bmi: %2d\nmean children: %1.2f\nmean charges: %2d\n"
          % (mu[0],mu[1],mu[2],mu[3]))
    print("correlation matrix:\n")
    print(np.corrcoef(z),"\n")
    nobs_synth = nobs # number of synthetic obs to create for this group
    gfg = np.random.multivariate_normal(zero, corr, nobs_synth)
    g_age = gfg[:,0]
    g_bmi = gfg[:,1]
    g_children = gfg[:,2]
    g_charges = gfg[:,3]

    # generate nobs_synth observations for this group
    print("synthetic observations:\n")
    for k in range(nobs_synth):
        u_age = norm.cdf(g_age[k])
        u_bmi = norm.cdf(g_bmi[k])
        u_children = norm.cdf(g_children[k])
        u_charges = norm.cdf(g_charges[k])
        s_age = np.quantile(age, u_age)     # synthesized age
        s_bmi = np.quantile(bmi, u_bmi)     # synthesized bmi
```

```
    s_children = np.quantile(children, u_children) # synthesized children
    s_charges = np.quantile(charges, u_charges) # synthesized charges
    line =
        group+"\t"+str(s_age)+"\t"+str(s_bmi)+"\t"+str(s_children)+"\t"+str(s_charges)+"\n"
    OUT.write(line)
    print("%3d. %d %d %d %d" %(k, s_age, s_bmi, s_children, s_charges))
OUT.close()
```

10.2.2 Potential improvements

The copula method as implemented in Section 10.2.1 has some limitations: it does not generate synthetic data outside the observed range in the real data. A simple solution is to add some parametric noise to each feature. The parameter can be the amount of noise added to a specific feature, or in other words, the variance attached to the added noise. See Section 7.2 for an application of this method. For Gaussian-like features, it makes sense to use a white noise (uncorrelated Gaussian noise with zero mean). For some features, a noise generated using a two-parameter distribution may be a better fit. Noise can also be generated jointly for more than one feature at a time, with correlations among the noise components replicating those found in the real data, for the features in question. Again, this is discussed in Section 7.2.

Also, rather than using the empirical quantiles in Step 4 (see beginning of Section 10.2), you may use the quantiles of some known distribution: one that is a good fit for the feature in question. The parameters attached to the distribution in question are estimated on the real data. So, when performing the simulation in Step 4 for a specific feature, you use the distribution in question with its parameter(s) estimated on the real data. For instance, in the insurance data set, the BMI feature (body mass index) is well approximated by a Gaussian distribution, while the number of children is well approximated by a geometric distribution. The "charges" feature (cost to the insurance company for each policy holder) is bimodal: in this case, a mixture of two Gaussians may be a good fit. Such mixtures are referred to as **Gaussian mixture models** (GMM) in this context.

Finally, you can produce a very large number of synthetic data sets to mimic the same real data set. This is accomplished by using a different seed each time in the Python code. However, it is rather inefficient as each new synthetized version does not make any progress towards improving the fit with the real data: you need to try a very large number of seeds. A better solution consists in using parametric noise or prespecified distributions: Gaussian, geometric, or Gaussian mixture depending on the feature, as described earlier for this particular data set. Thus you introduce parameters that can be estimated or fine-tuned based on the real data, rather than using parameter-free empirical quantiles. Remember that the quantile distribution is the inverse of the cumulative distribution, whether empirical or parametric and model-based.

Now, when moving from one synthetized version to the next one, this approach allows you to fine-tune the parameters in such a way that the fit with the real data – measured via Hellinger, or a discriminator function if using GAN – improves over time. This approach can use a gradient-descent path, where the target function to optimize is (say) the Hellinger distance, and the domain of this function (its arguments) is the parameter space. By optimization, I mean finding the minimum in the case of the Hellinger distance, as it corresponds to the best fit. This is illustrated in Fig. 10.9. It can be done without neural networks unlike traditional GAN. It may be a lot faster than training a neural network, easier to control, leading to more explainable AI and lower risk of overfitting. In short, you get all the benefits of **generative adversarial networks**, without the drawbacks.

10.3 Synthetization: GAN versus copulas

Generative adversarial networks (GAN) have been very successful in some applications such as computer vision. Many computer-intensive AI platforms rely on them, partly because of its benefits, partly for marketing purposes as it tends to sell well. Here I describe my point of view. There are many good things in GAN, and many features that can be dropped or improved. In particular, it can be done outside of neural networks (and then renamed accordingly). But what is GAN to begin with?

In this context, GAN is used to mimic real data sets, create new ones, and blend them with real data, to improve predictions, classification, or any machine learning algorithm. Think about text generation in ChatGPT. It has two parts: data generation (the synthesizer) and checking how good the generated data is (the discriminator). In the process, it uses an iterative optimization algorithm to move from one set of synthetized data, to the next one: a better one hopefully, using a gradient technique minimizing a cost function involving many parameters. The cost function tells you how good or bad you are at mimicking the real data.

10.3.1 Parameterizing the copula quantiles combined with gradient descent

The immediate drawbacks of GAN are the risk of overfitting, the time it takes to train the algorithm, and the lack of explainability. There are solutions to the latter, based on feature importance. But if you work with traditional data (transactional, digital twins, tabular data), what are the benefits? Or more specifically, can you get most of the benefits without using an expensive, slow or full GAN implementation? The answer is yes. Replicating the feature distribution and correlation structure present in your real data can be done efficiently with copulas. Indeed, many GAN systems also use copulas. Parameter-free empirical quantiles used in copulas can be replaced by parametric probability distributions fit to your real data. If a feature is bimodal, try a mixture of Gaussian distributions: now you are playing with GMMs (**Gaussian mixture models**), a technique sometimes incorporated in GAN. The parameters of your GMM (centers, variance, and weight attached to each component) are estimated on the real data with the **EM algorithm**. It also allows you to sample outside the range in your real data.

But one of the big benefits of GAN is its ability to navigate through a high-dimensional parameter space to eventually get closer and closer to a good minimum (a good representation of the original data), albeit very slowly due to the curse of dimensionality. Parameter-free, copula-based methods would require a tremendous number of simulations, each using a different seed from a random generator, to compete with GAN. What GAN could do in several hours, these simulations may require months of computing power to achieve similar results. This true especially if the number of features is large.

But there is a solution to this, outside of GAN. First, use a parametric technique with your copula method (or other method such as noise injection). If you have many features, you may end up with as many parameters as a large GAN system, so you are stuck again. One workaround is to compress the feature space: use selected features for selected groups in your data. Another way is to optimize 2–3 parameters at a time (carefully selected) in a stepwise procedure. Start from various configurations as in swarm optimization and do it separately for data segments (groups) as in ensemble methods such as XGBoost. You may not reach a global optimum, but the difference with extensive neural network processing (GAN) may be very small. And then you have a more interpretable technique, faster and requiring fewer resources than GAN, and thus less expensive. And possibly home-made, so you have full control of the algorithm.

10.3.2 Feature clustering to break a big problem into smaller ones

One way to identify subsets of features to apply a separate copula to each of them is as follows. The method is called **feature clustering** [6], as opposed to traditional clustering aimed at grouping observations. A Python implementation can be found here. Start by computing the correlation matrix attached to your real data. Rank all pairs of features $\{A, B\}$ by correlation between A and B, starting with the largest correlation in absolute value, down to the lowest one that is statistically significant and/or at least above (say) 0.30. The top pair constitutes your first group of features. Look at the second pair. If it contains a feature from the first group, merge the two groups to obtain a single group with 3 features. If not, you have two groups of features at this stage, each containing 2 features. Proceed iteratively until all pairs of features have been visited.

However, the correlation structure may not always represent all the dependencies in the data: points distributed on a circle are not correlated, yet they are highly dependent! In this case, use 1 dimension (the angular position) rather than the 2 Cartesian coordinates. More generally, appropriate data transformations and reduction can fix the issue.

10.4 Deep dive into generative adversarial networks (GAN)

In this section I discuss GAN in details, with a Python implementation to synthesize tabular data. Unlike many neural networks, my code can generate replicable outputs. Other solutions and references are provided in Section 10.4.1. Later on, I discuss enhancements to the original model. Finally, I show how to blend GAN with copulas to get the best of both worlds.

10.4.1 Open source libraries and references

One of the most popular libraries for synthetization is SDV, which stands for **synthetic data vault**. You can check it out on GitHub, here. For sample code, see here and here. SDV comes with 28 real-life data sets. To see the list, with the number of tables, rows, and columns for each data set, run the code below.

```python
from sdv.demo import get_available_demos
from sdv.demo import load_tabular_demo
from sdv.tabular import CopulaGAN

demos = get_available_demos()
print(demos) # show list of demo datasets

metadata, real_data = load_tabular_demo('student_placements_pii',metadata=True)
print("\nReal data:\n",real_data.head())
model = CopulaGAN()
```

```
model = CopulaGAN(primary_key='student_id',anonymize_fields={'address': 'address' })
model.fit(real_data)
synth_data1 = model.sample(200)
print("\nSynth. set 1:\n",synth_data1.head())

model.save('my_model.pkl')      # this shows how to save the model
loaded = CopulaGAN.load('my_model.pkl') # load the model, and
synth_data2 = loaded.sample(200) # get new set of synth. data
print("\nSynth. set 2\n:",synth_data2.head())
```

The first example is a YouTube data set with 2 tables, 2735 rows, and 10 columns. The number of rows ranges from 83 to over 6 million, and some data sets have over 300 features. The code in question also loads one data set (`'student_placements_pii'`), and shows how to use a GAN model based on **Gaussian copulas**. See output in Fig. 10.1. The code is on GitHub, here. Some of the fields such as the address are anonymized rather than synthesized. This is performed by implicitly calling the Python library Faker, described here. Also, you can choose the option `FAST_ML` for the optimizer (the gradient descent algorithm), for faster processing but with lower accuracy. This is done using the instruction `TabularPreset(name='FAST_ML', metadata=metadata)` as explained here.

```
Real data:
   student_id                                          address gender  ...  start_date   end_date duration
0       17264         70304 Baker Turnpike\nEricborough, MS 15086      M  ...  2020-07-23 2020-10-12      3.0
1       17265     805 Herrera Avenue Apt. 134\nMaryview, NJ 36510      M  ...  2020-01-11 2020-04-09      3.0
2       17266         3702 Bradley Island\nNorth Victor, FL 12268      M  ...  2020-01-26 2020-07-13      6.0
3       17267                  Unit 0879 Box 3878\nDPO AP 42663      M  ...         NaT        NaT      NaN
4       17268 96493 Kelly Canyon Apt. 145\nEast Steven, NC 3...      M  ...  2020-07-04 2020-09-27      3.0

[5 rows x 18 columns]

Synth. set 1:
   student_id                                          address gender  ...  start_date   end_date duration
0           0 17907 Salinas Street Apt. 677\nPort Alexander,...      M  ...         NaT        NaT      NaN
1           1             36658 Shirley Rapid\nOrtizfort, MO 91102      M  ...         NaT 2020-07-29      5.0
2           2        66408 Walters Tunnel\nNorth Edward, GA 92486      F  ...  2020-01-26 2020-11-12      4.0
3           3        1278 Sergio Village\nNew Bryanland, KY 62563      M  ...  2020-01-15 2020-11-06      6.0
4           4                       USNV White\nFPO AE 74466      F  ...  2020-02-26        NaT      6.0

[5 rows x 18 columns]

Synth. set 2
:    student_id                                          address gender  ...  start_date   end_date duratio
0           0           94143 Banks Crescent\nDavidberg, NJ 29268      F  ...  2020-02-25 2020-07-11      NaN
1           1         62754 Ford Inlet\nSouth Amberland, AK 08157      F  ...         NaT        NaT     12.0
2           2 13622 Schwartz Villages\nNorth Tiffanyside, NY...      M  ...  2020-03-21 2020-09-02     12.0
3           3       86891 Black Burg Apt. 641\nPageshire, OK 90448      M  ...  2020-03-05 2020-11-12      NaN
4           4      11438 Jason Parks Apt. 610\nHuberfort, MN 32078      M  ...         NaT 2020-11-09      6.0

[5 rows x 18 columns]
```

FIGURE 10.1

Synthetic versus real data, produced by SDV GAN + copula.

SDV is a black-box, so to illustrate the various steps of GAN in details, I use an implementation based on the Keras library instead. Keras is easier to use than **Tensorflow** [Wiki], though it requires Tensorflow to be installed on your system. Another black-box alternative, allowing you to implement GAN for tabular data synthetization with just 3 lines of code, is **TabGAN**, available here. See [1] for a discussion. I had to install the most recent version of Numpy to get it to work. More generally, installing these libraries may also require the most recent version of pip, which you can get via the command `pip` `install -upgrade pip`. TabGAN uses **LightGBM** [Wiki], a fast version of gradient boosting, and it is thus a bit faster than my step-by-step version in Section 10.7.

Another implementation very similar to mine and illustrated on time series, is discussed here. Mine includes a new version of **correlation matrix distance** to assess quality; see here and [5] for a standard definition. It also uses a seed for every single source of randomness in the algorithm, allowing for full replicability, as well as other specific features. If you run the code in GPU, there might be additional sources of randomness that you cannot control. You can run the code (say `mycode.py`) with the following command line in that case, if replicability is important for your application:

```
> CUDA_VISIBLE_DEVICES="" PYTHONHASHSEED=0 python mycode.py
```

Finally, there are various libraries to assess the quality of the synthetized data. I use TableEvaluator in my code in Section 10.7, along with home-made metrics that are more useful to me. TableEvaluator is described here. There is not much documentation about it, but you can check out the full source code on GitHub, here. That is how I found out that the output metric called "Base Statistics" is a correlation distance between the real versus synthesized data, computed on various bivariate indicators as data points (mean, median, correlation between features, and so on, both for real and synthesized).

Additional reading on the subject includes the book "Synthetic Data for Deep Learning" [9], "Pros and Cons of GAN Evaluation Measures" [2], "Survey on Synthetic Data Generation, Evaluation Methods and GANs" [3], and "Are GANs Created Equal? A Large-Scale Study" by Google Brain [7]. See also Lei Xu's master thesis (MIT, 2017) available here and the related article on ArXiv [10], as well as this article. For the Keras models used in my implementation, see here.

10.4.2 Synthesizing medical data with GAN

Here I summarize my implementation of GAN applied to the Kaggle diabetes data set. First, I discuss the hyperparameters, then the main steps in the methodology. The data is processed "as is", without normalization or transformation. Possible transformations (preprocessing) are discussed in Section 10.5.1. However, I removed all the observations with missing values, for better comparison with the copula method. Anyway, it makes sense to treat these observations separately, as a different segment, by rerunning GAN on them only. Indeed, it produces better results when they are separated from the complete observations. After removing observations with missing values, we are left with 392 rows.

The data set has 9 features. One of them called `Outcome` is the response: it indicates whether or not the patient had cancer. Thus the problem is predicting – based on the remaining 8 features – the chance of getting cancer. It is a supervised classification problem with two groups: cancer versus noncancer.

The first part of the code (Section 10.7.1) imports the libraries, reads the data, removes observations with missing values, and then performs the classification with the **random forest** algorithm [Wiki]. It also defines some global variables such as the **learning rate** [Wiki] in the Adam gradient descent, and `seed` which allows for replicability by using the same value in each run. The quality of the classification is displayed on the screen, as the `Base Accuracy` metric.

The last part of the code (Section 10.7.3) evaluates the quality of the synthetic data. It also performs the classification on the synthetic data, for comparison with the results obtained on the real data. It would be interesting to augment the real data by adding the synthetic data into it, and see if we get more robust predictions. The augmented data is not expected to increase accuracy; instead it is expected to increase robustness and reduce overfitting.

The data set `diabetes.csv` is on my GitHub directory, here. The original can be found on Kaggle, here. It should be noted that all the features are treated as continuous, even the binary `Outcome`. Thus the number of pregnancies (an integer) or the "outcome" generated by GAN are real numbers, that must be mapped onto integers to make sense. Other implementations such as copulas or copula-based GANs do not have this limitation. An alternative is to use one GAN for `Outcome==0`, and another one for `Outcome==1`. Also, categorical features (absent here except for Outcome) can be replaced by **dummy variables** [Wiki].

10.4.2.1 *Hyperparameters*

There is a surprisingly large number of hyperparameters that can be fine-tuned. This is one of the reasons why these systems take a lot of time to train and optimize. In addition, the gradient descent present in all GANs (with its own parameters) is the bottleneck. Self-identification of good parameters by the algorithm itself – and possibly adjusted over time – is one way to at least automate the process. But it can lead to overfitting. The best solution is to use standard hyperparameters that work well in many contexts, without trying to overadjust.

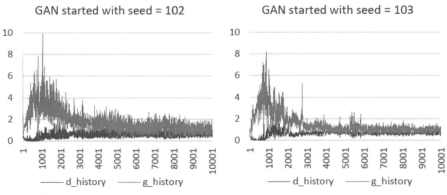

FIGURE 10.2

Loss function (in orange) for 10^4 successive epochs; enhanced GAN on the right plot.

All these parameters are set and used in the GAN part of the code, in Section 10.7.2. The only exception is the learning rate parameter.

- Epochs. One iteration of GAN consists of processing the full data set: this is done using a number of small samples (batches), one at a time. The number of iterations is the number of **epochs**, set to `n_epochs=10000` (a typical value) in the `train` function used to train the GAN.
- Batch size. See Epochs. Here it is set to `n_batch=128` in the `train` function. Half of the batch is used to sample from the real data, and the other half to generate latent data.
- Latent data. Here **latent variables** [Wiki] are univariate random Gaussian deviates with zero mean and unit variance; typically their number matches the number of features. Their role is similar to the Gaussian deviates in the copula method. However, using a uniform distribution on $[-1, 1]$ is worth exploring as many GAN functions (for instance, ReLU) return values between 0 and 1. Such restrictions are also used in Fourier regression in Section 9.3.3.

- Activation function. In neural network, the **activation function** [Wiki] decides whether a **neuron** should be activated or not. Classic examples used in the code are **ReLU** [Wiki] and **sigmoid** [Wiki].
- Kernel initializer. It defines the way to set the initial random weights of Keras layers. See documentation here.
- Number of layers. The neural networks (both the generator and discriminator) use 3 layers. A layer is added via the instruction `model.add`, with a number of options: activation function, kernel initializer, and so on. See `define_generator`, `define_discriminator` and `define_gan` (the combination of both) in the code. With 3 layers, we are dealing with a **deep neural network**.
- Learning rate. It is attached to the gradient descent. I tried 0.01 and 0.001, and settled for the latter. Small values result in quite chaotic, faster behavior (at the beginning) and somewhat reduced accuracy. Large values result in slow steady progress but you can end up stuck in a bad local optimum. Think of it as the cooling schedule in a simulated annealing algorithm.
- Gradient descent method. I use `Adam`. The alternative `SGD` (**stochastic gradient descent** [Wiki]) did no do well here, but does well in computer vision.
- Loss function. In gradient descent or any optimization problem, the **loss function** [Wiki] specifies the type of distance to the optimum vector, used for minimization. Think of it as a regression problem solved by least squares – the loss function being quadratic in this case. It is sometimes called the error function.
- Accuracy. It calculates how often predictions equal labels in the context of classification. In this context, classification means assigning an observation to either real (truly real or excellent synthetization) or fake (poor synthetic data not close to the reality). See Keras documentation here. There are various options to choose from, to measure accuracy.
- Architecture. It is the type of neural network. In this example, set to `Sequential`.

10.4.2.2 *GAN: main steps*

The steps in this section corresponds to the actual GAN procedure in Section 10.7.2. It does not include the preprocessing step: checking how good the real training set is at predicting cancer in a cross-validation framework (Section 10.7.1). It does not cover the postprocessing step either: GAN evaluation and how good the synthesized training set is at predicting cancer in the same cross-validation framework. This part of the code is covered in Section 10.7.3. It is assumed that all the GAN models have been created and compiled, with the hyperparameters discussed in Section 10.4.2.1. So this section only covers the `train` function used to train GAN. That said, it is the most important part of the code.

The following steps are repeated for each epoch in the `train` function:

- Step 1: Update the discriminator. Get a new sample (half batch) from the real data and assign these points to `label=1`; get a new latent data sample (half batch, random Gaussian vectors) to generate fake data and assign these points to `label=0`. The fake sampling function also maps the latent data into the space of the real data via the instruction `X=generator.predict(x_input)`. Here `x_input` represents the latent data, and `X` the mapped version. The `train_on_batch` function (one call for the real sample, one call for the fake one) also returns the losses for each data label (fake / real). Note that the discriminator is set to "nontrainable".
- Step 2: Update the generator. Get a full sample (full batch) of latent data, assigned this time to `label=1` to train the generator. Training aims at minimizing over time (on average) the loss function `g_loss` (an average of the `d_loss` values returned by the discriminator) until an equilibrium is reached: a local minimum in all likelihood. Note that `g_loss` oscillates over time in order to not get

		Pregnanci	Glucose	BloodPres	SkinThickr	Insulin	BMI	DiabetesP	Age	Outcome
AVG	synth 1	1.82	119.34	68.49	27.25	141.86	33.52	1.53	30.40	0.46
	synth 2	3.00	124.20	73.55	28.89	137.10	35.70	1.54	34.26	0.42
	copula	3.07	121.30	70.64	29.30	153.85	33.29	0.50	30.13	0.33
	real	3.30	122.63	70.66	29.15	156.06	33.09	0.52	30.86	0.33
MIN	synth 1	-5.01	26.22	13.35	4.04	14.41	7.72	0.20	2.29	0.00
	synth 2	-3.08	16.41	14.94	7.16	1.69	9.15	-0.71	8.03	0.00
	copula	0.00	62.37	28.42	7.48	17.49	18.76	0.09	21.00	0.00
	real	0.00	56.00	24.00	7.00	14.00	18.20	0.09	21.00	0.00
MAX	synth 1	13.31	355.83	194.77	86.79	662.69	95.30	4.22	75.99	1.00
	synth 2	15.67	304.61	154.16	91.65	745.49	89.84	3.63	87.25	1.00
	copula	14.83	197.93	110.00	60.03	602.11	58.01	2.30	72.57	1.00
	real	17.00	198.00	110.00	63.00	846.00	67.10	2.42	81.00	1.00
Stdev	synth 1	2.85	56.02	35.53	16.54	115.73	17.46	0.63	13.74	0.50
	synth 2	3.37	46.89	25.06	13.88	96.11	13.36	0.73	14.99	0.49
	copula	2.85	31.57	11.52	10.41	112.60	7.13	0.32	9.22	0.47
	real	3.21	30.86	12.50	10.52	118.84	7.03	0.35	10.20	0.47
p.25	synth 1	0.04	79.11	42.47	14.71	58.77	20.15	1.09	20.40	0.00
	synth 2	0.62	88.09	55.71	18.13	66.24	25.77	1.02	23.42	0.00
	copula	1.00	97.75	64.00	21.00	76.00	28.70	0.27	23.00	0.00
	real	1.00	99.00	62.00	21.00	76.75	28.40	0.27	23.00	0.00
p.75	synth 1	3.64	149.07	88.13	36.65	187.51	43.08	1.88	38.94	1.00
	synth 2	4.94	156.80	88.59	38.04	185.61	44.81	2.01	42.15	1.00
	copula	4.02	142.25	78.00	36.37	192.27	37.22	0.67	35.03	1.00
	real	5.00	143.00	78.00	37.00	190.00	37.10	0.69	36.00	1.00

FIGURE 10.3

Summary statistics, medical data set (synth 1 and 2 correspond to GAN).

stuck too quickly in a local minimum. The steepest gradient descent can result in this problem. So we use the **Adam gradient descent** (adaptive moment estimation) instead to avoid this issue.

- Step 3. If the epoch iteration is a multiple of 200, output the summary statistics to show progress, in particular how g_loss is decreasing over time, on average.

Note that the output layer of the discriminator is activated by the sigmoid function to discriminate between real and fake samples.

10.4.3 Initial results

The first synthetized data using GAN on the medical data set was disappointing. While GAN was able to replicate the mean, variance, and percentiles attached to each of the 9 features, it failed at replicating the correlation structure. In addition, GAN was very sensitive to the **seed** (denoted as seed in the code). Also, even for a single gradient path started with a specific seed, the oscillations in the loss function over successive epochs, and thus the quality of the synthetized data, were still volatile even after 5000 epochs. I present the initial results here. They originate from a piece of code widely

Correl		Pregnanci	Glucose	BloodPres	SkinThickr	Insulin	BMI	DiabetesP	Age	Outcome
Correl	Pregnanci	1.00	0.38	0.20	0.23	0.17	0.32	0.14	0.82	0.17
synth 2	Glucose	0.38	1.00	0.64	0.63	0.72	0.75	0.82	0.67	0.67
	BloodPres	0.20	0.64	1.00	0.48	0.35	0.75	0.52	0.70	0.51
	SkinThickr	0.23	0.63	0.48	1.00	0.45	0.92	0.18	0.44	0.44
	Insulin	0.17	0.72	0.35	0.45	1.00	0.55	0.63	0.43	0.66
	BMI	0.32	0.75	0.75	0.92	0.55	1.00	0.37	0.68	0.55
	DiabetesP	0.14	0.82	0.52	0.18	0.63	0.37	1.00	0.43	0.56
	Age	0.82	0.67	0.70	0.44	0.43	0.68	0.43	1.00	0.46
	Outcome	0.17	0.67	0.51	0.44	0.66	0.55	0.56	0.46	1.00

		Pregnanci	Glucose	BloodPres	SkinThickr	Insulin	BMI	DiabetesP	Age	Outcome
Correl	Pregnanci	1.00	0.13	0.22	0.05	0.00	-0.06	-0.02	0.56	0.25
copula	Glucose	0.13	1.00	0.27	0.25	0.62	0.25	0.20	0.36	0.57
	BloodPres	0.22	0.27	1.00	0.23	0.15	0.29	-0.02	0.26	0.21
	SkinThickr	0.05	0.25	0.23	1.00	0.22	0.67	0.13	0.15	0.26
	Insulin	0.00	0.62	0.15	0.22	1.00	0.25	0.21	0.16	0.33
	BMI	-0.06	0.25	0.29	0.67	0.25	1.00	0.13	0.12	0.25
	DiabetesP	-0.02	0.20	-0.02	0.13	0.21	0.13	1.00	0.05	0.22
	Age	0.56	0.36	0.26	0.15	0.16	0.12	0.05	1.00	0.36
	Outcome	0.25	0.57	0.21	0.26	0.33	0.25	0.22	0.36	1.00

		Pregnanci	Glucose	BloodPres	SkinThickr	Insulin	BMI	DiabetesP	Age	Outcome
Correl	Pregnanci	1.00	0.20	0.21	0.09	0.08	-0.03	0.01	0.68	0.26
real	Glucose	0.20	1.00	0.21	0.20	0.58	0.21	0.14	0.34	0.52
	BloodPres	0.21	0.21	1.00	0.23	0.10	0.30	-0.02	0.30	0.19
	SkinThickr	0.09	0.20	0.23	1.00	0.18	0.66	0.16	0.17	0.26
	Insulin	0.08	0.58	0.10	0.18	1.00	0.23	0.14	0.22	0.30
	BMI	-0.03	0.21	0.30	0.66	0.23	1.00	0.16	0.07	0.27
	DiabetesP	0.01	0.14	-0.02	0.16	0.14	0.16	1.00	0.09	0.21
	Age	0.68	0.34	0.30	0.17	0.22	0.07	0.09	1.00	0.35
	Outcome	0.26	0.52	0.19	0.26	0.30	0.27	0.21	0.35	1.00

FIGURE 10.4

Correlation matrix, real vs synthetic: GAN (synth 2) and copula-based.

distributed over the Internet. I show in Section 10.4.5 how to significantly improve the algorithm using front-end modifications, with little changes to the hyperparameters.

The left plot in Fig. 10.2 shows the volatility in the loss function – the orange curve. In the same figure, the contrast between the left and right plot shows the huge impact of the seed on the final results. In Figs. 10.3, 10.4, and 10.5, "synth 1" represents the initial version of GAN, while "synth 2" corresponds to the enhanced version. Even the enhanced version is inferior to copulas to reconstruct the correlation structure. However, GAN, even with the initial version, does a decent job at reconstructing the statistical summaries of most features (mean, variance, percentiles $p_{0.25}$ and $p_{0.75}$). More results are in the spreadsheet `diabetes_synthetic.xlsx`, available here on GitHub.

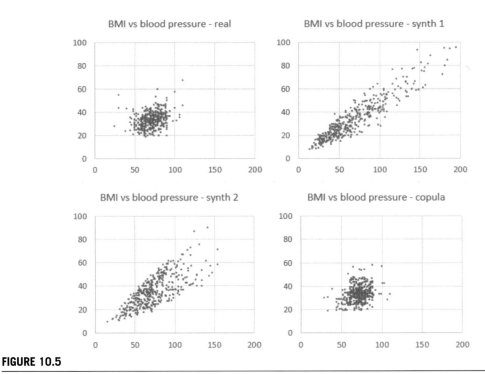

FIGURE 10.5

Copulas superior to GANs (synth 1, 2) to capture correlations in real data.

10.4.4 Fine-tuning the hyperparameters

You can use a back-end or front-end approach to fine-tune the hyperparameters and other GAN components, or a combination of both. The back-end strategy consists of modifying components that are buried deeper in the architecture, such as the loss function, the number and type of layers, the type of neural network (sequential here), the gradient descent method (Adam here), the size of the batches and the ratio when splitting batches into real versus fake, the dimension and type of random deviates for the latent variables (Gaussian here, with dimension about the same as the number of features), the Keras metric used in the compile step, the learning rate, the type of activation function, and so on. I kept the original settings as found here and elsewhere, except for the learning rate and number of epochs.

Instead, I focused on front-end modifications. In particular, the enhanced version of my implementation produces a full synthetic data set at each epoch, and computes the fit with the real data each time. It barely increases the amount of time needed to run a full GAN cycle. The fit is measured as the correlation matrix distance between the real and synthesized data. This metric is always between 0 and 1, with 0 being the best. The goal was to replicate the correlation structure in the real data set, thus the choice of this particular metric. The final synthetic data is the one obtained at the epoch where the correlation matrix distance is the best (minimum). In addition, it must not come from an early epoch. For instance, if the number of epochs is 10,000, I check the correlation matrix distance starting at epoch 7500.

In addition, the **seed** is an integral and important part of my algorithm. I made the results replicable, so if you run the program twice with the same seed, you will get the same results, unlike in most other implementations. Then, I test various seeds and pick up the one that produces the best results.

10.4.5 Enhanced GAN: methodology and results

To achieve better results, I explained how to process missing data separately, or applying a different GAN to specific segments of your population. Or a different GAN for each group of features resulting from **feature clustering**, as discussed in Section 7.2.1.

Transforming or normalizing your data (for instance, decorrelating) may also lead to better synthetization. For instance, say your real data X is an $n \times m$ array with n rows (the observations) and m columns (the features). Assume that all the features have been normalized, thus having zero mean and unit variance. You can transform X to obtain $Y = XW$, where $\mathrm{Cov}[Y] = W^T C_X W$ is an $m \times m$ diagonal matrix, ^{T} denotes the transposition operator, $C_X = \mathrm{Cov}[X]$, and W has size $m \times m$. The transformed data Y consists of uncorrelated features. To achieve this goal, take $W = C^{-1/2}$. There are multiple possible square roots, and this transformation is discussed in Section 10.3.2. You can use an iterative algorithm to compute the **matrix square root**. Then synthesize Y (instead of X) and let Z be the resulting data. Your final (untransformed) synthesized data is $X' = ZW^{-1}$, with the exact same correlation matrix as your real data X. This procedure is known as **decorrelation** [Wiki], followed by recorrelation.

However, the easiest solution is as follows. The GAN algorithm is very sensitive to the **seed**, which determines the initial configuration. In Fig. 10.2, I compare two trajectories of the gradient descent based on two different seeds. Clearly, `seed=103` does a much better job than `seed=102`, attaining and staying in regions of lower loss much faster than `seed=102`. Thus the solution consists in trying different seeds. Not only that, even with a same seed the iterates (called **epochs**) oscillate wildly. In short, you could get a much better synthetization if you stop after 9800 epochs rather than (say) 10,000. The problem is further compounded by the fact that the **loss function** may achieve an optimization goal different from what you are looking for.

I address these issues in my enhanced version of GAN. To use it, set `mode='Enhanced'` in the Python code in Section 10.7.2. Given one instance of GAN corresponding to a specific seed, it will retain the best synthetic data (in other words, the best model produced by Keras) based on a distance function of your choice, rather than that obtained at the last epoch and very dependent on the loss function. In my code, I was interested in synthetic data, good a mimicking the correlation structure present in the real data set, so I wrote my own function `gan_distance`, measuring the correlation distance between real and synthetic data at each epoch. It is based on the **correlation matrix distance**. Of course, you can modify that function to meet your own needs.

The enhancement techniques described so far are front-end: they do not modify the internal components of GAN. They are also easy to understand and implement, contributing to explainable AI. But you can also dig into the GAN black-box internals and modify some of the low-level components. This is facilitated to some extend by the Keras library, which offers some tools, for instance, to customize the loss function. These back-end enhancements require more knowledge about how GANs work. You can write your own function `custom_distance` and have Keras "digest" it by choosing the option `model.compile(metrics=[custom_distance])` in your GAN model. See additional documentation here and here. Another possibility is to use an adaptive **learning rate**; see how to do it here.

Finally, being able with **reinforcement learning** [Wiki] to reward configurations minimizing your own front-end distance function (rather than the default loss function) would be helpful, see [11]. By configuration, I mean the updated model and its set of updated weights obtained at the end of each epoch.

To summarize, the enhanced version of my implementation has the following upgrades:

- Replicable results
- Missing data treated separately
- Run multiple versions each with a different seed, use the best version
- Binary data: 0 and 1 processed with two different GANs (available in future version)
- Stop when your customized distance between real and synthetic data is minimum

The last feature requires mode='Enhanced' in the Python code. The increased performance of the enhanced version can be seen in the Fig. 10.2, comparing standard (left) with enhanced mode (right). Also, the GAN synthetization in Fig. 10.7 (right plot) uses the enhanced mode. It features an example on tabular data where GAN outperforms copulas. An additional upgrade is to blend copula methods with GAN. This is done in the SDV library; see code in Section 10.4.1. Finally, applying GAN on decorrelated data (followed by a recorrelation step) as discussed at the beginning of this section, is guaranteed to preserve the exact correlation structure in the real data. This operation is fully reversible.

10.4.6 Feature clustering via hierarchical clustering or connected components

For those interested in the **feature clustering** algorithm, the topic is well covered in the literature; see, for instance, [6]. Here I provide a simple method, consisting of finding the **connected components** [Wiki] in the correlation matrix. The main program is a slight adaptation of the version used to detect connected components in nearest neighbor graphs in Section 16.2.4.3. Two features are connected if their correlation is above some parameter named threshold in the Python code. A cluster of features is just a connected component of the **undirected graph** in question.

I applied the method to the medical data set (the real data), using the correlation matrix at the bottom of Fig. 10.4 with threshold=0.4. Five feature clusters are detected: $\{0, 7\}, \{1, 4, 8\}, \{3, 5\}, \{2\}, \{6\}$. For instance, feature 0 corresponds to pregnancies, 1 to glucose, 2 to blood pressure, and so on. It means, thanks to the low correlations between these 5 clusters, that a separate copula or GAN can be applied to each of them, thus splitting a 9D problem into a number a small-dimensional problems, each with a dimension no larger than 3. The Python code featureClustering.py is also on GitHub, here.

Feature clustering via the correlation matrix is scale-invariant. You can also use this methodology for traditional clustering, by swapping features and observations. For instance, with **wide data**, that is, a small number of observations (say, less than 10,000) with a large number of features, as in clinical trials.

I provide two implementations of the feature clustering procedure. The first uses **hierarchical clustering** with the Scipy library. In Fig. 10.6, ρ is the correlation, the X-axis is the feature label. The code is available on GitHub, here. The second is based on the connected components. The code is also available here.

```
# feature correlation with hierarchical clustering and dendograms
# featureClusteringScipy.py

import matplotlib.pyplot as plt
```

```
import numpy as np
import scipy.spatial.distance as ssd
import scipy.cluster.hierarchy as hcluster

correlMatrix = [
    [1.0000,0.1983,0.2134,0.0932,0.0790,-0.0253,0.0076,0.6796,0.2566],
    [0.1983,1.0000,0.2100,0.1989,0.5812,0.2095,0.1402,0.3436,0.5157],
    [0.2134,0.2100,1.0000,0.2326,0.0985,0.3044,-0.0160,0.3000,0.1927],
    [0.0932,0.1989,0.2326,1.0000,0.1822,0.6644,0.1605,0.1678,0.2559],
    [0.0790,0.5812,0.0985,0.1822,1.0000,0.2264,0.1359,0.2171,0.3014],
    [-0.0253,0.2095,0.3044,0.6644,0.2264,1.0000,0.1588,0.0698,0.2701],
    [0.0076,0.1402,-0.0160,0.1605,0.1359,0.1588,1.0000,0.0850,0.2093],
    [0.6796,0.3436,0.3000,0.1678,0.2171,0.0698,0.0850,1.0000,0.3508],
    [0.2566,0.5157,0.1927,0.2559,0.3014,0.2701,0.2093,0.3508,1.0000]]

simMatrix = correlMatrix - np.identity(len(correlMatrix))
distVec = ssd.squareform(simMatrix)
linkage = hcluster.linkage(1 - distVec)

plt.figure()
axes = plt.axes()
axes.tick_params(axis='both', which='major', labelsize=8)
for axis in ['top','bottom','left','right']:
   axes.spines[axis].set_linewidth(0.5)
with plt.rc_context({'lines.linewidth': 0.5}):
   dendro = hcluster.dendrogram(linkage,leaf_font_size=8)
plt.show()
```

The following implementation is based on connected components. It provides the same results as the previous one based on hierarchical clustering and dendograms. Fig. 10.6 illustrates the hierarchical clustering version.

```
# feature correlation with connected components
# featureClustering.py

correlMatrix = [
    [1.0000,0.1983,0.2134,0.0932,0.0790,-0.0253,0.0076,0.6796,0.2566],
    [0.1983,1.0000,0.2100,0.1989,0.5812,0.2095,0.1402,0.3436,0.5157],
    [0.2134,0.2100,1.0000,0.2326,0.0985,0.3044,-0.0160,0.3000,0.1927],
    [0.0932,0.1989,0.2326,1.0000,0.1822,0.6644,0.1605,0.1678,0.2559],
    [0.0790,0.5812,0.0985,0.1822,1.0000,0.2264,0.1359,0.2171,0.3014],
    [-0.0253,0.2095,0.3044,0.6644,0.2264,1.0000,0.1588,0.0698,0.2701],
    [0.0076,0.1402,-0.0160,0.1605,0.1359,0.1588,1.0000,0.0850,0.2093],
    [0.6796,0.3436,0.3000,0.1678,0.2171,0.0698,0.0850,1.0000,0.3508],
    [0.2566,0.5157,0.1927,0.2559,0.3014,0.2701,0.2093,0.3508,1.0000]]

dim = len(correlMatrix)
```

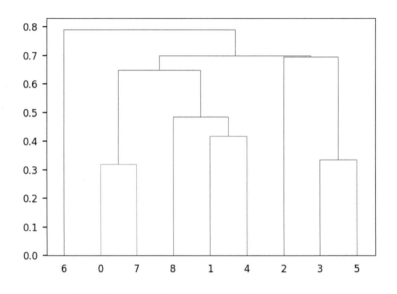

FIGURE 10.6

Feature clustering using Scipy; Y-axis is $1 - |\rho|$.

```
threshold = 0.4 # two features with |correl| > threshold are connected
pairs = {}

for i in range(dim):
    for j in range(i+1,dim):
        dist = abs(correlMatrix[i][j])
        if dist > threshold:
            pairs[(i,j)] = abs(correlMatrix[i][j])
            pairs[(j,i)] = abs(correlMatrix[i][j])

# connected components algo to detect feature clusters on feature pairs

#---
# PART 1: Initialization

point=[]
NNIdx={}
idxHash={}

n=0
for key in pairs:
    idx = key[0]
    idx2 = key[1]
    if idx in idxHash:
        idxHash[idx]=idxHash[idx]+1
    else:
```

```
        idxHash[idx]=1
    point.append(idx)
    NNIdx[idx]=idx2
    n=n+1


hash={}
for i in range(n):
    idx=point[i]
    if idx in NNIdx:
        substring="~"+str(NNIdx[idx])
    string=""
    if idx in hash:
        string=str(hash[idx])
    if substring not in string:
        if idx in hash:
            hash[idx]=hash[idx]+substring
        else:
            hash[idx]=substring
    substring="~"+str(idx)
    if NNIdx[idx] in hash:
        string=hash[NNIdx[idx]]
    if substring not in string:
        if NNIdx[idx] in hash:
            hash[NNIdx[idx]]=hash[NNIdx[idx]]+substring
        else:
            hash[NNIdx[idx]]=substring

#---
# PART 2: Find the connected components

i=0;
status={}
stack={}
onStack={}
cliqueHash={}

while i<n:

    while (i<n and point[i] in status and status[point[i]]==-1):
        # point[i] already assigned to a clique, move to next point
        i=i+1

    nstack=1
    if i<n:
        idx=point[i]
        stack[0]=idx; # initialize the point stack, by adding $idx
        onStack[idx]=1;
```

```
size=1 # size of the stack at any given time

while nstack>0:
    idx=stack[nstack-1]
    if (idx not in status) or status[idx] != -1:
        status[idx]=-1 # idx considered processed
        if i<n:
            if point[i] in cliqueHash:
                cliqueHash[point[i]]=cliqueHash[point[i]]+"~"+str(idx)
            else:
                cliqueHash[point[i]]="~"+str(idx)
        nstack=nstack-1
        aux=hash[idx].split("~")
        aux.pop(0) # remove first (empty) element of aux
        for idx2 in aux:
            # loop over all points that have point idx as nearest neighbor
            idx2=int(idx2)
            if idx2 not in status or status[idx2] != -1:
                # add point idx2 on the stack if it is not there yet
                if idx2 not in onStack:
                    stack[nstack]=idx2
                    nstack=nstack+1
                onStack[idx2]=1

#---
# PART 3: Save results

clusterID = 1
for clique in cliqueHash:
    cluster = cliqueHash[clique]
    cluster = cluster.replace('~', ' ')
    print("Feature Cluster number %2d: features %s" %(clusterID, cluster))
    clusterID += 1
clusteredFeature = {}
for feature in range(dim):
    for clique in cliqueHash:
        if str(feature) in cliqueHash[clique]:
            clusteredFeature[feature] = True
for feature in range(dim):
    if feature not in clusteredFeature:
        cluster = " "+str(feature)
        print("Feature Cluster number %2d: features %s" %(clusterID, cluster))
        clusterID += 1
```

10.5 Comparing GANs with the copula method

On the medical data set, the copula method performs better as illustrated in Figs. 10.3 and 10.4, and it is a lot faster. Unlike my copula method in Section 10.2.1, many GAN implementations do not produce replicable results. However, this problem is solved in my implementation in Section 10.7. Also GAN is very sensitive to the initial configuration (the seed), and oscillations from one epoch to the next one are rather large, even after 10,000 epochs. This latter issue may actually be an advantage: trying different seeds and/or using a stopping rule based on the quality of the synthetization in any given epoch leads to substantial improvements.

GAN has many hyperparameters that can be fine-tuned, even the loss function. This can lead to overfitting and makes the method less suitable as a black-box, compared to the parameter-free copula technique. Copulas are also less sensitive to outliers and small modifications of the real data, at least in this context (tabular data) and when using a parameter-free method based on empirical quantiles. But unlike GAN, they may not be able to generate synthetic data outside the range of observations. There are solutions to this problem: noise injection, or using parametric rather than empirical quantiles. Parametric quantiles are obtained by fitting a feature or pair of features to a known probability distribution such as a mixture of Gaussians (GMM). This can also lead to overfitting. A nice feature of copulas is that they easily work with a mix of categorical, ordinal, and continuous features.

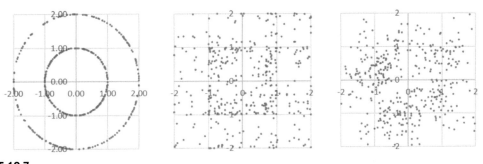

FIGURE 10.7

Real data (left), copula (middle), and GAN synthetization (right).

Another issue with GAN, on this particular data set, is the fact that the feature correlations in the synthetic data are exaggerated. This is true in the early epochs, and this phenomenon is attenuated in the last epochs, but it is still strongly noticeable, for instance, on the left plot in Fig. 10.2.

The superiority of copulas, as seen in Fig. 10.3 and 10.4, is due to the goal being achieved here: mimicking the correlation structure in the real data. Indeed, copulas are perfect at that. But what if the goal is different, or if the correlation matrix fails to capture the patterns in the real data? I tried with an artificial example, where most of the feature correlations are zero, but with strong nonlinear dependencies instead. The data set in question has 9 features; the last one is also a binary response for classification purposes, as in the medical data set. The first two features represent points lying on two concentric circles; see Fig. 10.7. It is trivial to synthesize the whole 9D data set with any method. However, I use it for illustration purposes as some real-life data sets have similar undetected or invisible patterns buried in very high dimensions.

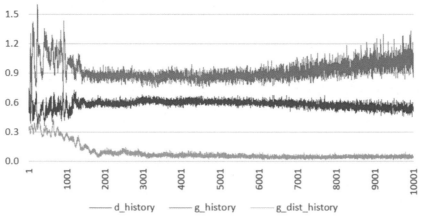

FIGURE 10.8

Loss function (orange) and distance (gray), circle data set.

In this case, it turns out that GAN does a better job. Both GAN and copula generate the correct correlation structure, though copula fails to recognize the circular patterns. Also, GAN iterations are very stable in this example, compared to the medical data set. The copula method used in this example is based on two copulas, one for each group: the two concentric circles correspond to the two groups. This is not the case for GAN which is somewhat at a disadvantage, because of using the same model for both groups.

I computed the correlation between $X_1^2 + X_2^2$ (based on the first two features) and the binary response X_9. In the real data consisting of 400 observations, by design it is exactly 1 even though the correlation between X_1 and X_2 is zero. The copula method yields 0.014, and GAN yields a dramatic improvement with a value of 0.723, much closer to 1. Even when using a separate copula for each group, copula yields a much better correlation of 0.676 but still worse than GAN, even though GAN is based on a single model for both groups. Another interesting correlation is between X_1 and the response X_9. In the real data set, the value is 0.067. The copula yields 0.128, and GAN yields 0.070. So GAN is slightly better. Given the way the real data set was built, the true value would be zero if it had an infinite number of observations. More correlations are displayed in Table 10.2, and the full list is easy to obtain from the Excel spreadsheet.

I stopped GAN at epoch 7727 which achieves the minimum overall **correlation matrix distance** of 0.017, a very good performance since the best possible value is zero, and the worst case is one. Epoch 10001 (the last one) yields 0.036 and epoch 9998 yields 0.057: it shows the benefit of using the enhanced version of GAN to capture the 0.017 minimum. The evolution of this GAN system is pictured in Fig. 10.8. The labels d_history, g_history, g_dist are as in the Python code, with "d" standing for the discriminator model, and "g" standing for the generator model in GAN (the one that creates the synthetization). The details are in my spreadsheet circle8d.xlsx on GitHub, here.

Note that even if GAN is not as good as copulas at replicating the correlation structure in the medical data set, it is possible to first **decorrelate** the data, then apply GAN (or any method!), and finally recorrelate, as explained in Section 10.4.5. With this transformation, any synthetization algorithm that

Table 10.2 Correlations on 9D circle data set: real vs copula and GAN.

Feature pair	Real data	Copula synth.	GAN synth.
$X_9, X_1^2 + X_2^2$	1.0000	0.0136	0.7235
X_1, X_9	0.0662	0.1281	0.0700
X_1, X_2	0.0641	0.1069	0.0660
X_1, X_3	1.0000	1.0000	0.9976
X_2, X_3	0.0641	0.1069	0.0495
$X_1, X_1^2 + X_2^2$	0.0662	0.1906	0.1186
X_1, X_5	−0.0278	−0.0278	−0.0047

generates uncorrelated data will perfectly replicate the correlations found in the real data, after the recorrelation step.

10.5.1 Conclusion: getting the best out of copulas and GAN

I already discussed how to improve GANs in the context of tabular data, for instance, by applying GAN to the **decorrelated** real data, or using your own distance metric or **loss function**, fine-tuning the **learning rate**, or using a faster version of the gradient descent such as **LightGBM**. Some improvements apply both to GANs and copulas: using a separate GAN model or copula for specific groups of observations, or for specific groups of features based on **feature clustering**. Or testing 10 different GANs (using different seeds) or 10 different copulas: the latter is a lot faster. Some implementations blend GAN and copulas. See, for instance, the CopulaGAN module in the **SVD** library.

To improve copulas methods specifically, you can replace the parameter-free **empirical quantiles** by quantiles from a parametric family of distributions, fit to the data, with parameters estimated on the real data. For instance, a **Gaussian mixture model** (GMM) for features with multimodal distribution. Then generate synthetic data using an iterative process based on the **Hellinger distance**. This distance measures the fit between the real data and the current synthesized version. And proceed iteratively as in GAN: successive iterations are obtained following the gradient path of the Hellinger distance, viewed as multivariate function of the parameters of your model. In essence, this is very similar to the GAN approach, and can be done with or without neural networks.

In other words, you can improve GANs by integrating them with copulas and follow a gradient path that leads to an optimum of some discriminating function. And you can improve copulas by using a gradient descent algorithm (or stepwise procedure focusing on 2 parameters at a time) to navigate the parameter space until you optimize the Hellinger distance. In the end, the two techniques with the respective improvements may not be that different, especially when using multivariate parametric distributions spanning across multiple features, for the copula.

10.6 Data synthetization explained in one picture

Fig. 10.9, summarizing many of the elements discussed in this book, is organized as follows. Dashed blue lines (dark gray in print version) are associated to GANs (**generative adversarial networks**),

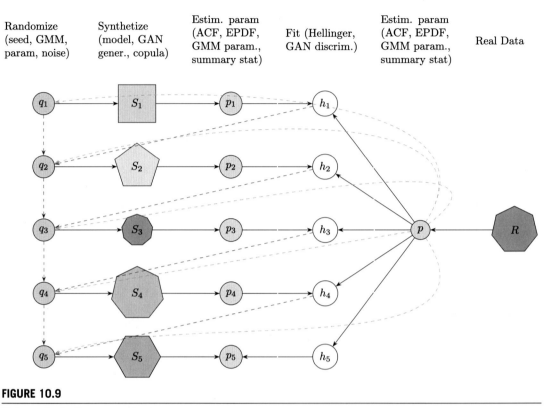

Randomize (seed, GMM, param, noise)   Synthetize (model, GAN gener., copula)   Estim. param (ACF, EPDF, GMM param., summary stat)   Fit (Hellinger, GAN discrim.)   Estim. param (ACF, EPDF, GMM param., summary stat)   Real Data

FIGURE 10.9

Data synthetization: general schema.

where the goal is to produce a sequence of synthetic data sets that get better and better at mimicking the structure present in the real data, over successive iterations. The diagram features 5 such iterations, with the synthetized data sets denoted as $S_1, S_2, \ldots, S_5$. Typically, GANs follow the gradient of h to reach an optimum configuration q that cannot be classified as nonreal anymore. Synthetic data that gets closer to the real data gets rewarded in this **reinforcement learning** technique. Like any simulation-intensive method, training the neural network can be time-consuming, and this black-box approach may lack **explainability**.

Dashed pink lines (light gray in print version) are associated to modeling techniques (generative model, GMM) where synthetic data is obtained by simulating the underlying model using the parameter values estimated on the real data, that is, $q_k = p$ for all k. In case of GMM (**Gaussian mixture models**), the parameters are the cluster centers, the covariance matrix attached to each cluster, and the proportions of the mixture. For stationary time series, the parameter is typically the autocorrelation function (ACF). In some applications including when using **copulas**, the EDPD (empirical probability density function) is used instead. For GANs, the q_k's are the weights attached to neuron connections.

The goal is to mimic the structure in the real data, not the real data itself. The structure is represented by a parametric configuration denoted as p in the real data. I use the notation $p_1, \ldots, p_5$ for the structures found in the 5 synthetic data sets. The quality h_k of the synthetic data set k is the distance between p_k and p, based on the **Hellinger metric** or some discriminating function in the case of GAN. It is assumed that the real data has been normalized (transformed) before synthesizing. Also "Estim. param." stands for estimated parameters in the diagram, though sometimes the parameters can be a function or matrix rather than a set of elements.

10.7 **Python code: GAN to synthesize medical data**

I broke down the program into three pieces. First, reading the data and removing observations with missing values. During this step, I also run a classification algorithm (random forest) on the real data, as the goal is to discriminate between patients likely to get cancer, from the others. The rightmost column in the tabular data set, called Outcome, is the cancer indicator (1 = yes, 0 = no).

The second step is the core of the GAN procedure, including the production of synthetic data. Finally, the last part performs model evaluation – the fit between real and synthetic data – using the TableEvaluator library my matrix correlation distance defined in Step 2. In the last part, I classify again the data with the random classifier, but this time the synthesized data, for comparison purposes with the classification on the real data obtained in the first step.

To run in enhanced mode, set mode='Enhanced'. The full program named GAN_diabetes.py is also on my GitHub repository, here. The real dataset diabetes.csv can be found here.

10.7.1 **Classification problem with random forests**

This step reads the data, removes observations with missing values, and performs a classification on the real data. It also imports all the libraries needed. and eliminates all sources of uncontrollable randomness by using a seed for all the random number generators involved (native Python, TensorFlow, Numpy). This leads to replicable results. The hyperparameter learning_rate is also initialized here.

```
import numpy as np
import pandas as pd
import os
import matplotlib.pyplot as plt
import random as python_random
from tensorflow import random
from keras.models import Sequential
from keras.layers import Dense
from keras.optimizers import Adam # type of gradient descent optimizer
from numpy.random import randn
from matplotlib import pyplot
from sklearn.model_selection import train_test_split
from sklearn.ensemble import RandomForestClassifier
from sklearn import metrics

data = pd.read_csv('diabetes.csv')
# data located at https://github.com/VincentGranville/Main/blob/main/diabetes.csv
```

```
# rows with missing data must be treated separately: I remove them here
data.drop(data.index[(data["Insulin"] == 0)], axis=0, inplace=True)
data.drop(data.index[(data["Glucose"] == 0)], axis=0, inplace=True)
data.drop(data.index[(data["BMI"] == 0)], axis=0, inplace=True)
# no further data transformation used beyond this point
data.to_csv('diabetes_clean.csv')

print (data.shape)
print (data.tail())
print (data.columns)

seed = 102 # to make results replicable
np.random.seed(seed) # for numpy
random.set_seed(seed) # for tensorflow/keras
python_random.seed(seed) # for python

adam = Adam(learning_rate=0.001) # also try 0.01
latent_dim = 10
n_inputs = 9 # number of features
n_outputs = 9 # number of features


#--- STEP 1: Base Accuracy for Real Data Set

features = ['Pregnancies', 'Glucose', 'BloodPressure', 'SkinThickness', 'Insulin', 'BMI',
    'DiabetesPedigreeFunction', 'Age']
label = ['Outcome'] # OutCome column is the label (binary 0/1)
X = data[features]
y = data[label]

# Real data split into train/test data sets for classification with random forest

X_true_train, X_true_test, y_true_train, y_true_test = train_test_split(X, y, test_size=0.30,
    random_state=42)
clf_true = RandomForestClassifier(n_estimators=100)
clf_true.fit(X_true_train,y_true_train)
y_true_pred=clf_true.predict(X_true_test)
print("Base Accuracy: %5.3f" % (metrics.accuracy_score(y_true_test, y_true_pred)))
print("Base classification report:\n",metrics.classification_report(y_true_test, y_true_pred))
```

10.7.2 GAN method

The main function is `train`. Adding layers to the networks, combining the discriminator and generator models of GAN, selecting the loss functions, and so on, and compiling the models is done in the satellite functions defined here. In addition, my matrix correlation distance function is defined in this step. It is heavily used in the enhanced version, when mode=='Enhanced'. The last instruction saves the synthesized data data_fake to a CSV file.

```python
#--- STEP 2: Generate Synthetic Data

def generate_latent_points(latent_dim, n_samples):
    x_input = randn(latent_dim * n_samples)
    x_input = x_input.reshape(n_samples, latent_dim)
    return x_input

def generate_fake_samples(generator, latent_dim, n_samples):
    x_input = generate_latent_points(latent_dim, n_samples) # random N(0,1) data
    X = generator.predict(x_input,verbose=0)
    y = np.zeros((n_samples, 1)) # class label = 0 for fake data
    return X, y

def generate_real_samples(n):
    X = data.sample(n) # sample from real data
    y = np.ones((n, 1)) # class label = 1 for real data
    return X, y

def define_generator(latent_dim, n_outputs):
    model = Sequential()
    model.add(Dense(15, activation='relu', kernel_initializer='he_uniform',
        input_dim=latent_dim))
    model.add(Dense(30, activation='relu'))
    model.add(Dense(n_outputs, activation='linear'))
    model.compile(loss='mean_absolute_error', optimizer=adam, metrics=['mean_absolute_error'])
        #
    return model

def define_discriminator(n_inputs):
    model = Sequential()
    model.add(Dense(25, activation='relu', kernel_initializer='he_uniform',
        input_dim=n_inputs))
    model.add(Dense(50, activation='relu'))
    model.add(Dense(1, activation='sigmoid'))
    model.compile(loss='binary_crossentropy', optimizer=adam, metrics=['accuracy'])
    return model

def define_gan(generator, discriminator):
    discriminator.trainable = False # weights must be set to not trainable
    model = Sequential()
    model.add(generator)
    model.add(discriminator)
    model.compile(loss='binary_crossentropy', optimizer=adam)
    return model
```

```python
def gan_distance(data, model, latent_dim, nobs_synth):

    # generate nobs_synth synthetic rows as X, and return it as data_fake
    # also return correlation distance between data_fake and real data

    latent_points = generate_latent_points(latent_dim, nobs_synth)
    X = model.predict(latent_points, verbose=0)
    data_fake = pd.DataFrame(data=X, columns=['Pregnancies', 'Glucose', 'BloodPressure',
        'SkinThickness', 'Insulin', 'BMI', 'DiabetesPedigreeFunction', 'Age', 'Outcome'])

    # convert Outcome field to binary 0/1
    outcome_mean = data_fake.Outcome.mean()
    data_fake['Outcome'] = data_fake['Outcome'] > outcome_mean
    data_fake["Outcome"] = data_fake["Outcome"].astype(int)

    # compute correlation distance
    R_data     = np.corrcoef(data.T) # T for transpose
    R_data_fake = np.corrcoef(data_fake.T)
    g_dist = np.average(abs(R_data-R_data_fake))
    return(g_dist, data_fake)

def train(g_model, d_model, gan_model, latent_dim, mode, n_epochs=10000, n_batch=128,
    n_eval=200):

    # determine half the size of one batch, for updating the discriminator
    half_batch = int(n_batch / 2)
    d_history = []
    g_history = []
    g_dist_history = []
    if mode == 'Enhanced':
        g_dist_min = 999999999.0

    for epoch in range(0,n_epochs+1):

        # update discriminator
        x_real, y_real = generate_real_samples(half_batch) # sample from real data
        x_fake, y_fake = generate_fake_samples(g_model, latent_dim, half_batch)
        d_loss_real, d_real_acc = d_model.train_on_batch(x_real, y_real)
        d_loss_fake, d_fake_acc = d_model.train_on_batch(x_fake, y_fake)
        d_loss = 0.5 * np.add(d_loss_real, d_loss_fake)

        # update generator via the discriminator error
        x_gan = generate_latent_points(latent_dim, n_batch) # random input for generator
        y_gan = np.ones((n_batch, 1))          # label = 1 for fake samples
        g_loss_fake = gan_model.train_on_batch(x_gan, y_gan)
        d_history.append(d_loss)
        g_history.append(g_loss_fake)
```

```
    if mode == 'Enhanced':
        (g_dist, data_fake) = gan_distance(data, g_model, latent_dim, nobs_synth=400)
        if g_dist < g_dist_min and epoch > int(0.75*n_epochs):
            g_dist_min = g_dist
            best_data_fake = data_fake
            best_epoch = epoch
    else:
        g_dist = -1.0
    g_dist_history.append(g_dist)

    if epoch % n_eval == 0: # evaluate the model every n_eval epochs
        print('>%d, d1=%.3f, d2=%.3f d=%.3f g=%.3f g_dist=%.3f' % (epoch, d_loss_real,
            d_loss_fake, d_loss, g_loss_fake, g_dist))
        plt.subplot(1, 1, 1)
        plt.plot(d_history, label='d')
        plt.plot(g_history, label='gen')
        # plt.show() # un-comment to see the plots
        plt.close()

OUT=open("history.txt","w")
for k in range(len(d_history)):
    OUT.write("%6.4f\t%6.4f\t%6.4f\n" %(d_history[k],g_history[k],g_dist_history[k]))
OUT.close()

if mode == 'Standard':
    # best synth data is assumed to be the one produced at last epoch
    best_epoch = epoch
    (g_dist_min, best_data_fake) = gan_distance(data, g_model, latent_dim, nobs_synth=400)

return(g_model, best_data_fake, g_dist_min, best_epoch)

#--- main part for building & training model

discriminator = define_discriminator(n_inputs)
discriminator.summary()
generator = define_generator(latent_dim, n_outputs)
generator.summary()
gan_model = define_gan(generator, discriminator)

mode = 'Enhanced' # options: 'Standard' or 'Enhanced'
model, data_fake, g_dist, best_epoch = train(generator, discriminator, gan_model, latent_dim,
    mode)
data_fake.to_csv('diabetes_synthetic.csv')
```

10.7.3 GAN evaluation and postclassification

Evaluates the quality of the synthetic data with the TableEvaluator library and `g_dist`, the matrix correlation distance obtained in the previous step. Also, performs classification, but this time on the synthetic data, to compare with the results obtained on the real data in Step 1.

```
#--- STEP 3: Classify synthetic data based on Outcome field

features = ['Pregnancies', 'Glucose', 'BloodPressure', 'SkinThickness', 'Insulin', 'BMI',
    'DiabetesPedigreeFunction', 'Age']
label = ['Outcome']
X_fake_created = data_fake[features]
y_fake_created = data_fake[label]
X_fake_train, X_fake_test, y_fake_train, y_fake_test = train_test_split(X_fake_created,
    y_fake_created, test_size=0.30, random_state=42)
clf_fake = RandomForestClassifier(n_estimators=100)
clf_fake.fit(X_fake_train,y_fake_train)
y_fake_pred=clf_fake.predict(X_fake_test)
print("Accuracy of fake data model: %5.3f" % (metrics.accuracy_score(y_fake_test,
    y_fake_pred)))
print("Classification report of fake data
    model:\n",metrics.classification_report(y_fake_test, y_fake_pred))


#--- STEP 4: Evaluate the Quality of Generated Fake Data with g_dist and Table_evaluator

from table_evaluator import load_data, TableEvaluator

table_evaluator = TableEvaluator(data, data_fake)
table_evaluator.evaluate(target_col='Outcome')
# table_evaluator.visual_evaluation()

print("Avg correlation distance: %5.3f" % (g_dist))
print("Based on epoch number: %5d" % (best_epoch))
```

References

[1] I. Ashrapov, Tabular GANs for uneven distribution, Preprint, pp. 1–11, arXiv:2010.00638, 2020, [Link].

[2] A. Borji, Pros and cons of GAN evaluation measures: new developments, Preprint, pp. 1–35, arXiv:2103.09396, 2021, [Link].

[3] A. Figueira, B. Vaz, Survey on synthetic data generation, evaluation methods and GANs, New Insights in Machine Learning and Deep Neural Networks, MDPI, 2022, [Link].

[4] H. Guo, et al., Eyes tell all: irregular pupil shapes reveal GAN-generated faces, Preprint, pp. 1–7, arXiv:2109.00162, 2021, [Link].

[5] M. Herdin, Correlation matrix distance, a meaningful measure for evaluation of non-stationary MIMO channels, in: Proc. IEEE 61st Vehicular Technology Conference, 2005, pp. 1–5, [Link].

[6] H. Liu, et al., A new model using multiple feature clustering and neural networks for forecasting hourly PM$_{2.5}$ concentrations, Engineering 6 (2020) 944–956, [Link].

[7] M. Lucic, et al., Are GANs created equal? A large-scale study, in: Proc. NeurIPS Conference, 2018, pp. 1–10, [Link].

[8] C. Molnar, Interpretable Machine Learning, ChristophMolnar.com, 2022, [Link].

[9] S.I. Nikolenko, Synthetic Data for Deep Learning, Springer, 2021.

[10] L. Xu, K. Veeramachaneni, Synthesizing tabular data using generative adversarial networks, Preprint, pp. 1–12, arXiv:1811.11264, 2018, [Link].

[11] C. Zheng, et al., Reward-reinforced generative adversarial networks for multi-agent systems, IEEE Transactions on Emerging Topics in Computational Intelligence 6 (2021) 479–488, arXiv:2103.12192, [Link].

High quality random numbers for data synthetization

High quality random numbers are critical in large-scale simulations such as data synthetization. I discuss a new test of randomness for pseudorandom number generators (PRNG), to detect subtle patterns in binary sequences. The test shows that congruential PRNGs, even the best ones, have flaws that can be exacerbated by the choice of the seed. This includes the Mersenne twister used in many programming languages including Python. I also show that the digits of some numbers such as $\sqrt{2205}$, conjectured to be perfectly random, fail this new test, despite the fact that they pass all the standard tests. I propose a methodology to avoid these flaws, implemented in Python. The test is particularly useful when high quality randomness is needed. This includes cryptographic and military-grade security applications, as well as synthetic data generation and simulation-intensive **Markov chain Monte Carlo** methods. The origin of this test is in number theory and connected to the Riemann Hypothesis. In particular, it is based on Rademacher stochastic processes. These random multiplicative functions are a number-theoretic version of Bernoulli trials. This chapter features state-of-the-art research on this topic, as well as an original, simple, integer-based formula to compute square roots to generate random digits. It is offered with a Python implementation that handles integers with millions of digits.

11.1 Introduction

Let $\chi(\cdot)$ be a function defined for strictly positive integers, with $\chi(1) = 1$ and $\chi(ab) = \chi(a)\chi(b)$ for any integers $a, b > 0$. Such a function is said to be **completely multiplicative** [Wiki]. Here we are interested in the case where χ takes on two possible values, $+1$ and -1. The core of my methodology is based on the following, well-known identity:

$$\sum_{k=1}^{\infty} \chi(k)k^{-z} = \prod_{p \in P} \frac{1}{1 - \chi(p)p^{-z}}. \tag{11.1}$$

The product is over all prime integers ordered by increasing values: $P = \{2, 3, 5, 7, 11, \dots\}$ is the set of all primes. Such a product is called an **Euler product** [Wiki]. The series on the left-hand side is called a **Dirichlet series** [Wiki]. The argument $z = \sigma + it$ is a complex number. You do not need to know anything about complex numbers to understand this chapter. The only important fact is that the series or product converges only if σ – the real part of z – is large enough, typically larger than 0, $\frac{1}{2}$, or 1, depending on χ. If χ is a constant function, thus equal to 1, then the product and series converge to the **Riemann zeta function** $\zeta(z)$ [Wiki] if $\sigma > 1$.

For primes p, let the $\chi(p)$'s be independent random variables, with $P[\chi(p) = 1] = P[\chi(p) = -1] = \frac{1}{2}$. The product, denoted as $L_P(z, \chi)$, is known as a **Rademacher random multiplicative function**,

Synthetic Data and Generative AI. https://doi.org/10.1016/B978-0-44-321857-6.00015-1

see [5], [6], and [9]. If z is a complex number, we are dealing with **complex random variables** [Wiki]. From the product formula and the independence assumption, it is easy to obtain

$$\mathrm{E}[L_P(z, \chi)] = \prod_{p \in P} \mathrm{E}\left[\frac{1}{1 - \chi(p)p^{-z}}\right] = \prod_{p \in P} \frac{1}{1 - p^{-2z}} = \zeta(2z). \tag{11.2}$$

Thus the expectation is finite if $\sigma = \Re(z) > \frac{1}{2}$. A similar argument can be used for the variances.

Now let us replace the random variables $\chi(p)$ by pseudorandom numbers, taking the values $+1$ or -1 with probability $\frac{1}{2}$. If these generated numbers are "random enough", free of dependencies, then one would expect them to satisfy the laws of Rademacher random multiplicative functions. The remaining of this chapter explores this idea in details, with a focus on applications.

11.2 Pseudorandom numbers

There is no formal definition of pseudorandom numbers. Intuitively, a good set of pseudorandom numbers is a deterministic binary sequence of digits that satisfies all statistical tests of randomness. Of course, it makes no sense to talk about randomness if the sequence contains very few digits, say one or two. So pseudorandom numbers (PRN) are associated with infinite sequences, even though in practice one only uses finite subsequences.

A rigorous definition of PRN sequences requires the convergence of the multivariate empirical distribution [Wiki] of any finite subsequence of m digits, to the known theoretical value under the assumption of full randomness. Let the PRN sequence be denoted as $\{d(k)\}$ with $k = 1, 2$, and so on. A subsequence of m digits is defined by its indices, denoted as $i_1, i_2, \ldots, i_m$. The convergence of the empirical distribution means that regardless of the indices $0 \le i_1 < i_2 < \cdots$ we have

$$\lim_{n \to \infty} \frac{1}{n} \sum_{k=1}^{n} I\left[d(k + i_1) = k_1, d(k + i_2) = k_2, \ldots, d(k + i_m) = k_m\right] = 2^{-m} \tag{11.3}$$

for any $(k_1, k_2, \ldots, k_m)$ in $\{-1, +1\}^m$. Here I is the indicator function: $I[A] = 1$ if A is true, otherwise $I[A] = 0$. The following number λ is of particular interest:

$$\lambda = \sum_{k=1}^{\infty} d'(k) \cdot 2^{-k}, \quad \text{with } d'(k) = \frac{1 + d(k)}{2} \in \{0, 1\}. \tag{11.4}$$

Thus the $d'(k)$'s are the binary digits of the number λ, with $0 \le \lambda \le 1$.

The connection between the multiplicative function $\chi(\cdot)$ in formula (11.1) and the $d(k)$'s is as follows. Denote the kth prime as p_k, with $p_1 = 2$. Then $d(k) = \chi(p_k)$. The traditional definition of PRNs is equivalent to requiring λ be a **normal number** in base 2 [Wiki]. I introduce a stronger criterion of randomness in Section 11.2.1.

11.2.1 Strong pseudorandom numbers

Convergence of the empirical joint distributions, as defined by formula (11.3), has a few important implications. The **Kolmogorov–Smirnov test** [Wiki], the **Berry–Esseen inequality** [Wiki] and the

law of the iterated logarithm [Wiki] can be applied to the PRN sequence $\{d(k)\}$. These three fundamental results provide strong limitations on the behavior of finite PRN sequences. If a sequence $\{d(k)\}$ or its representation by the number λ does no stay within these limits, then it does not emulate pure randomness. However, some quasirandom PRN sequences, with weak dependencies, meet these requirements, yet are not truly "random". For instance, a number can be normal in base 2, yet have digits that exhibit some dependencies, see here. The purpose of this section is to introduce stronger requirements in order to catch some of these exceptions. This is where the multiplicative function $\chi(\cdot)$ comes into play.

The function $\chi(\cdot)$, initially defined for primes p, is extended to all strictly positives integers via $\chi(ab) = \chi(a)\chi(b)$. Because the $\chi(p)$'s are independent among prime numbers (by construction), the full sequence $\{\chi(k)\}$ over all k must behave in a certain way. Obviously, if k is a square integer, $\chi(k) = 1$. But if k is not a square, we still have $P[\chi(k) = 1] = P[\chi(k) = -1] = \frac{1}{2}$. For instance, $\chi(4200) = \chi(4)\chi(25)\chi(6)\chi(7) = \chi(6)\chi(7)$. Since the product of two independent random variables with **Rademacher distribution** [Wiki] has a Rademacher distribution, it follows that $\chi(6) = \chi(2)\chi(3)$ has a Rademacher distribution, and thus $\chi(4200) = \chi(6)\chi(7)$ also has a Rademacher distribution. So, the $\chi(k)$'s are identically distributed with zero mean, unless k is a square integer. However, they are not independently distributed, even after removing square integers, or even if you only keep **square-free integers** [Wiki].

I now define three fundamental functions, which are central to my new test of randomness. First, define the following sets:

- $S_1(n)$ contains all prime integers $\leq n$.
- $S_2(n)$ contains all positive square-free integers $\leq n$.
- $S_3(n)$ contains all positive nonsquare integers $\leq n$.

So each of these sets contains at most n elements. Then, define the three functions as

$$L_1(n) = \sum_{k \in S_1(n)} \chi(k), \quad L_2(n) = \sum_{k \in S_2(n)} \chi(k), \quad L_3(n) = \sum_{k \in S_3(n)} \chi(k). \tag{11.5}$$

Now, I can introduce my new test of randomness.

11.2.1.1 *New test of randomness for PRNGs*

Let $d(1), d(2), \ldots$ be a sequence of integer numbers, with $d(k) \in \{-1, 1\}$ and $P = \{p_1, p_2, \ldots\}$ be the set of prime numbers. The goal is to test how random the sequence $\{d(k)\}$ is, based on the first n elements $d(1), \ldots, d(n)$. The algorithm is as follows:

- Step 1. Set $\chi(p_k) = d(k)$, where p_k is the kth prime number ($p_1 = 2$).
- Step 2. For $k \notin P$ with prime factorization $k = p_1^{a_1} p_2^{a_2} \cdots$, set $\chi(k) = \chi^{a_1}(p_1)\chi^{a_2}(p_2)\cdots$, with $\chi(1) = 1$.
- Step 3. Using formula (11.5), compute $L_3^*(n) = |L_3(n)|/\sqrt{n \log\log n}$.
- Step 4. If $L_3^*(n) < 0.5$ or $L_3^*(n) > 1.5$, the sequence $\{d(k)\}$ (the first n elements) lacks true randomness.

This test is referred to as the "**prime test**". Let us illustrate Step 2 with $k = 4200$: since $4200 = 2^3 \cdot 3 \cdot 5^2 \cdot 7$, we have $\chi(4200) = \chi^3(2)\chi(3)\chi^2(5)\chi(7) = \chi(2)\chi(3)\chi(7)$.

Some nonrandom sequences may pass the prime test. So you should never use this test alone to decide whether a sequence is good enough. Also, the standardization of $L_3(n)$, using the $\sqrt{n \log\log n}$

denominator, is not perfect, but good enough for all practical purposes, assuming $10^4 < n < 10^{15}$. This test can detect departure from randomness that no other test is able to uncover. I discuss practical examples and a Python implementation later in this chapter.

A PRN sequence that satisfies (11.3) and passes all the existing tests, including the prime test, is called **strongly pseudorandom**. The corresponding real number λ defined by formula (11.4) is called **strongly normal**. It should not be difficult to prove that almost all numbers are strongly normal. Thus almost all PRN sequences are strongly pseudorandom. Yet creating one that can be proved to be strongly pseudorandom is as difficult as proving that a given number is normal (and a fortiori, strongly normal). Interestingly, none of the sequences produced by **congruential random number generators** [Wiki] are strongly pseudorandom, for the same reason that no rational number is normal: in both cases, $d(k)$ is periodic.

Modern test batteries include the **Diehard tests** [Wiki] published in 1995, and the **TestU01** framework [Wiki], introduced in 2007.

11.2.1.2 *Theoretical background: the law of the iterated logarithm*

The prime test checks whether the multiplicative function $\chi(k)$ derived from $\{d(k)\}$ satisfies a particular version of the **law of the iterated logarithm** [Wiki]. Truly random sequences $\{d(k)\}$ satisfy that law. Since $\{\chi(k)\}$ is multiplicative and thus nonrandom, the law of the iterative algorithm must be adapted to take care of the resulting dependencies. In particular, the $\sqrt{n \log \log n}$ weight used to standardize $L_3(n)$ provides only an approximation, good enough for all practical purposes. The exact weight is discussed in [6] and [9].

Many sequences $\{d(k)\}$ satisfy the basic law of the iterated logarithm without the prime number / Euler product apparatus introduced in this chapter. This is the case for most of the sequences studied here. However, by looking at $\chi(k)$ rather than the original $d(k)$, we are able to magnify flaws that are otherwise undetectable by standard means. An example is the Mersenne twister implemented in Python, passing the standard test, but failing the prime test when the seed is set to 200.

11.2.1.3 *Connection to the Generalized Riemann Hypothesis*

The **Generalized Riemann Hypothesis** (GRH) [Wiki] is one of the most famous unsolved problems in mathematics. It states that the function $L(z, \chi)$ defined by formula (11.1) has no root if $\frac{1}{2} < \sigma = \Re(z) < 1$. Here $z = \sigma + it$ is a complex number, and $\sigma = \Re(z)$ is its real part. It applies to a particular class of functions $\chi(\cdot)$, those that are "well behaved". Of course, without any restriction on $\chi(\cdot)$, there are **completely multiplicative functions** [Wiki] known to satisfy GRH. For instance, the function defined by $\chi(p_{2k}) = -1$, $\chi(p_{2k+1}) = 1$ where p_k is the kth prime number. The corresponding $L(z, \chi)$ has no root if $\sigma > \frac{1}{2}$ because the product converges for $\sigma > 0$, and, of course, the product has no root. The sequence $\{\chi(p_k)\}$ is obviously nonrandom as it perfectly alternates, and thus I labeled it CounterExample in Table 11.1.

If the Euler product in formula (11.1) converges for some $\sigma > \sigma_0$, it is equal to its series expansion when $\sigma > \sigma_0$, it converges for all $\sigma > \sigma_0$, and $L(z, \chi)$ satisfies GRH when $\sigma > \sigma_0$. When $\sigma < 1$, the convergence is **conditional** [Wiki], making things more difficult. Another example that trivially satisfies GRH if $\sigma > \frac{1}{2}$ is when $\chi(\cdot)$ is a random variable with $P[\chi(p) = 1] = P[\chi(p) = -1] = \frac{1}{2}$ for primes p. In this case convergence means that $L(z, \chi)$ has finite expectation as proved by formula (11.2), and finite variances. This function $\chi(\cdot)$ is called a **random Rademacher multiplicative function**, see

[7]. Here the $\chi(p)$'s are identically and independently distributed over the set of all primes, and the definition is extended to all strictly positive integers with the formula $\chi(ab) = \chi(a)\chi(b)$.

So, if we were able to find a "nice enough" pseudorandom, yet deterministic function $\chi(\cdot)$ with convergence of the Euler product when $\sigma > \sigma_0$ for some $\sigma_0 < 1$, a function $\chi(\cdot)$ that is random enough over the primes (like its sister, the truly stochastic version) to guarantee the convergence of the product, then it would be a major milestone towards proving GRH. Convergence of the product would imply that:

- $L(z, \chi)$ is **analytic** [Wiki], because the product is equal to its series expansion, which trivially satisfies the **Cauchy–Riemann equations** [Wiki],
- $L(z, \chi)$ has no root if $\sigma > \sigma_0$ since the product has no root.

As discussed, examples that are "not so nice" exist; "nice enough" means that $L(z, \chi)$ satisfies a **Dirichlet functional equation** [Wiki]. Typically, "nice enough" means that $L(z, \chi)$ is a **Dirichlet-L function** [Wiki]. Besides the **Riemann zeta function** where $\chi(p) = 1$ is the trivial Dirichlet character, the most fundamental example is when $\chi = \chi_4$ is the nontrivial **Dirichlet character modulo** 4 [Wiki]. This example is featured in Fig. 11.1 where $\sigma = \frac{1}{2}$ (left plot) and contrasted with a not so nice example on the right plot, corresponding to a pseudorandom sequence $\{\chi(p_k)\}$. The χ_4 example is referred to as `Dirichlet4` in Table 11.1. Note that for $\sigma = \frac{1}{2}$, $L(z, \chi_4)$ has infinitely many roots just like the Riemann zeta function, though its roots are different: this is evident when looking at the left plot in Fig. 11.1. The (conjectured) absence of root is when $\frac{1}{2} < \sigma < 1$.

I went as far as to compute the Euler product for $L(z, \chi_4)$ when $z = \sigma = 0.99$. It nicely converges to the correct value, without the typical growing oscillations associated to lack of convergence, agreeing with the value computed using the series expansion in formula (11.1). It means that the product converges at least for all z with $\sigma = \Re(z) \geq 0.99$. Thus there is no root for $L(z, \chi_4)$ if $\sigma \geq 0.99$. This would be an immense milestone compared to the best known result (no root if $\sigma \geq 1$) if it was theoretically possible to prove the convergence in question, supported only by empirical evidence. Convergence implies that the sequence $\{\chi_4(p_k)\}$ is random enough over the primes p_1, p_2, and so on. That is, the gap between $+1$ and -1 in the sequence never grows too large (that is, runs of same value can only grow so fast), and the proportion of $+1$ and -1 tends to $\frac{1}{2}$ fast enough, despite the known **Chebyshev's bias** [Wiki]. The fact that the proportion eventually converges to $\frac{1}{2}$ when using more and more terms in the sequence, is a consequence of **Dirichlet's theorem** [Wiki]. This is how close we are – or you may say how far – to proving GRH.

There are other "nice functions" $\chi(\cdot)$ that fit within the GRH framework. For instance, with primes that are not integers, such as Beurling primes [8] (discussed later in this chapter) or **Gaussian primes** [Wiki]. For a general family of such functions, see the **Dedekind zeta function** [Wiki]. For a general introduction to the Riemann zeta function and related topics, see [2] and [10].

11.2.2 Testing well-known sequences

The binary sequences analyzed here are denoted as $\{d(k)\}$, with $d(k) \in \{-1, +1\}$ and $k = 1, 2$, and so on. The tests, restricted to $d(k) \leq n$, are based on $L_3^*(n) = L_3(n)/\sqrt{n \log \log n}$, with $L_3(n)$ defined by (11.5). Again, $\chi(p_k) = d(k)$ for prime numbers, and $\chi(\cdot)$ is extended to nonprime positive integers via $\chi(ab) = \chi(a)\chi(b)$. Finally, p_k is the kth prime with $p_1 = 2$. In my examples, $n = 20,000$ in Table 11.1, and $n = 80,000$ in Figs. 11.2 and 11.3.

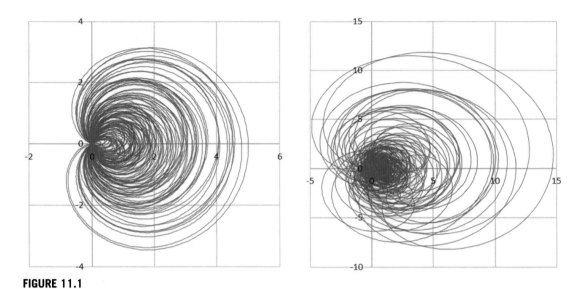

FIGURE 11.1

Orbit of $L(z, \chi)$ at $\sigma = \frac{1}{2}$, with $0 < t < 200$ and $\chi = \chi_4$ (left) versus pseudorandom χ (right).

The fact that a sequence fails the test for a specific n does not mean it fails for all n. The success or failure also depends on the seed (the initial conditions). Some seeds require many iterations – that is, a rather large n – before randomness kicks in. The test should not be used for small n, say $n < 1000$. Finally, passing the test does not mean that the sequence is random enough. I provide examples of poor PRNGs that pass the test. Typically, to assess the randomness character of a sequence, one uses a battery of tests, not just one test. However, the prime test can detect patterns that no other one can. In some sense, it is a last resort test.

The sequences investigated here fall into four types:

- Discrete chaotic **dynamical systems** [Wiki]. In one dimension, many of these systems are driven by a recursion $x_{k+1} = g(x_k)$, where g is a continuous mapping from [0, 1] onto [0, 1]. The initial value x_0 is called the seed. Typically, $d(k) = 1$ if $x_k < 0.5$, otherwise $d(k) = -1$. The **logistic map** [Wiki], with $g(x) = 4x(1 - x)$, is labeled `Logistic` in Table 11.1 as well as in the Python code in Section 11.3.2. The **shift map** in base b, defined by $g(x) = bx - \lfloor bx \rfloor$ where the brackets represent the integer part function, here with $b = 3$, is labeled `Base3`. The case $b = 2$ is known as the **dyadic map** [Wiki]. The number $\lfloor bx_k \rfloor$ is the k-digit of the seed x_0, in base $b > 1$. In particular, if x_0 is a rational number, then the sequence $\{d(k)\}$ is periodic, and thus nonrandom. Even in the best-case scenario (using a random seed), the sequence $\{d(k)\}$ is autocorrelated. These dynamical systems are studied in detail in my book on chaotic dynamical systems [4].
- **Mersenne twister** [Wiki] as implemented in the Python function `random.random()`. This congruential PRNG is also another type of dynamical system, though technically "nonchaotic" because the sequence $\{x_k\}$ is periodic. It emulates randomness quite well as the period is very large. Likewise, the shift map with a large base b and a bad seed x_0 (a rational number resulting in periodicity) will emulate randomness quite well if $x_0 = q/p$, where p, q are integers and p is a very large prime.

Both in the table and in the figures, I use the label `Python` for the Mersenne twister. It fails the prime test for various seeds, especially if the seed is set to 200. See also Section 11.3.1.

- Number-theoretic sequences related to the distribution of prime numbers or **Beurling primes**. Sequences of this type are labeled `Dirichlet4`. The main one, with the seed set to 3, corresponds to $\chi(p_k) = +1$ if $p_k \equiv 1 \mod 4$ and $\chi(p_k) = -1$ if $p_k \equiv 3 \mod 4$. Here $\chi(2) = 0$. This function, denoted as χ_4, is the nontrivial **Dirichlet character modulo 4** [Wiki]. The sequence barely fails the L_3^* test; the full function χ_4 defined over all positive integers (not just the nonsquare integers) is periodic. The sister sequence (with the seed set to 1) has $\chi(p) = -\chi_4(p)$ if p is prime. Sequences based on Beurling primes (a generalization of prime numbers to nonintegers) are not included here, but discussed in Chapter 17. The Python code in Section 11.3.2 can easily be adapted to handle them. The `DirichletL.py` code posted here on my GitHub repository, includes Beurling primes. These numbers are studied in Diamond [3] and Hilberdink [8].
- Binary digits of **quadratic irrational** numbers. I use a simple, original recursion to compute these digits: see code description in Section 11.3.3. The Python code painlessly handles the very large integers involved in these computations. Surprisingly, $\sqrt{2}$ passes the prime test as expected, but $\sqrt{2205}$ does not. Sequences based on these digits are labeled `SQRT` in this document.

The dyadic map is impossible to implement in Python due to the way computations are performed in the CPU: the iterates $\{x_k\}$ are (erroneously) all equal to zero after about 45 iterations. This is why I chose the shift map with $b = 3$. In this case, the iterates are also all wrong after 45 iterations due to propagating errors caused by limited machine precision (limited to 32 bits). Even with 64 or any finite number of bits, the problem persists. However, with $b = 3$, the x_k's keep oscillating properly and maintain their statistical properties forever (including randomness or lack of), due to the **ergodicity** [Wiki] of the system. The result is identical to using a new seed every 45 iterations or so.

The dyadic map with $b = 2$, in principle, could be used to compute the binary digits of the seed $x_0 = \sqrt{2}$, but because of the problem discussed, it does not work. Instead, I use a special recursion to compute these digits. If you replace $b = 2$ by $b = 2 - 2^{-31}$ (the closest you can get to avoid complete failure) the x_k's produced by the Python code, even though also completely wrong after 45 iterations, behave as expected from a statistical point of view: this is a workaround to using $b = 2$. The same problem is present in other programming languages.

11.2.2.1 *Reverse-engineering a pseudorandom sequence*

Many of the sequences defined by a recursion $x_{k+1} = g(x_k)$, where x_0 is the seed, can be reverse-engineered, and are thus unsafe to use when security is critical. This includes sequences produced by congruential PRNGs. By reverse engineering, I mean that if you observe m consecutive digits, you can easily compute all the digits, and thus correctly "guess" the whole sequence. In the case of the Mersenne twister, $m = 624$ is conjectured to be the smallest possible value even though the period is $2^{19,937} - 1$, see here. For the shift map in base b, while x_k is asymptotically uniformly distributed on $[0, 1]$ if x_0 is random, the vectors (x_k, x_{k+1}) lie in a very specific configuration: $x_{k+1} - x_k$ is a small integer, making the sequence $\{x_k\}$ anything but random. As a result, for any positive integer q, the empirical **autocorrelation** [Wiki] between $(x_1, x_2, x_3, \dots)$ and $(x_{q+1}, x_{q+2}, x_{q+3}, \dots)$ computed on the infinite sequence, is equal to $1/b^q$ if b is an integer ≥ 2. A good sequence should have zero autocorrelations for all q.

It is possible to significantly improve the base sequence $\{x_k\}$, to make it impossible to reverse-engineer. In the case of the shift map, using $d(k) = \lfloor bx_k \rfloor$ instead of x_k, results in zero autocorrelations

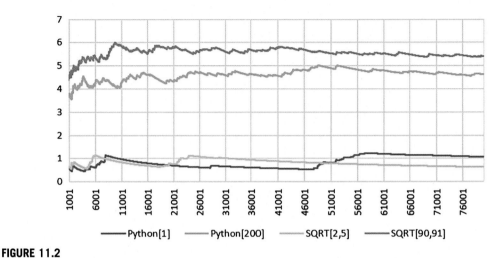

FIGURE 11.2

$L_3^*(n)$ test statistic for four sequences: Python[200] and SQRT[90,91] fail.

and perfect randomness if the seed x_0 is random. A seed such as $x_0 = \sqrt{2}/2$ or $x_0 = \log 2$ is conjectured to achieve this goal. The explanation is as follows: $d(k)$ is the kth digit of x_0 in base b. Even if you were to observe $m = 10^{50,000}$ consecutive digits of $\sqrt{2}/2$, there is no way to predict what the next digit will be, if you do not know that $x_0 = \sqrt{2}/2$. Actually, even if you have that information, it is still impossible to predict the next digit. Any sequence of m digits is conjectured to occur infinitely many times at arbitrary locations for a seed such as $\sqrt{2}/2$. So given any such string of m digits (no matter how large m is), it is impossible to tell where it takes place in the infinite sequence of digits, and thus impossible to correctly predict all the subsequent digits.

However, because of machine precision (the problem discussed in Section 11.2.2), the x_k's generated by a computer for the shift map (or any map for that matter) eventually become periodic. Thus $\{d(k)\}$ becomes periodic, too. A workaround is the use exact arithmetic to compute $d(k)$, as in my Python code in Section 11.3.3. Another solution is to use **Bailey–Borwein–Plouffe formulas** [Wiki] to compute the digits. There are many BBP formulas for various good **transcendental** seeds [Wiki] such as $x_0 = \frac{\pi}{4}$, but as far as I know, none for the subset of **algebraic numbers** [Wiki] such as $x_0 = \sqrt{2}/2$.

11.2.2.2 Illustrations

Figs. 11.2 and 11.3 show the core statistics of the prime test, defined by formula (11.5): $L_3^*(n)$ and $|L_3(n)|$, for n between 1000 and 80,000. If $L_3^*(n) < 0.5$ or $L_3^*(n) > 1.5$, the sequence $\{d(k)\}$ (the first n elements) lacks true randomness; it is not **strongly pseudorandom**. Table 11.1 summarizes these findings for a larger collection of sequences, computed at $n = 20,000$. The notation Python[200] corresponds to the Python implementation of the Mersenne twister, using the random.random() function and the seed 200, that is, random.seed(200). Similarly, SQRT[90,91] is for the binary digits of $\sqrt{2205}$, obtained using the bivariate seed $y = 90, z = 91$ in the code in Section 11.3.3. Not surprisingly, the sequence Base3[0.72] fails, as $0.72 = 18/25$ is a rational number with a small denominator. Thus $d(k) = \chi(p_k)$ is periodic with a rather small period. The column labeled Status in Table 11.1 indicates if the sequence in question fails or passes the prime test.

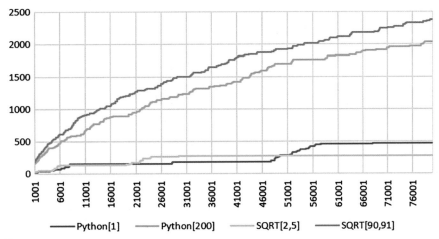

FIGURE 11.3

$|L_3(n)|$ test statistic for four sequences: Python[200] and SQRT[90,91] fail.

For convenience, I also included a type of sequences called `CounterExample`. For this type of sequences, $\chi(p_k)$ perfectly alternates between -1 and $+1$. One of the two resulting sequences $\{d(k)\}$ barely passes the test, the other fails. Now, the `Dirichlet4` sequence with seed set to 3, has perfectly alternating $d(k)$'s and is thus nonrandom. It fails the prime test, but barely. This means that passing this test is not a guarantee of randomness. Only failing the test is a guarantee of nonrandomness.

The prime test can be extended using the option `All` in the Python code. To do so, define the L_4 statistics as follows:

$$L_4(n) = \sum_{k=1}^{n} \chi(k), \quad L_4^*(n) = \frac{|L_4(n)|}{\sqrt{n \log \log n}}. \tag{11.6}$$

Now with L_4^* rather than L_3^*, the `Dirichlet4` sequence with the seed set to 3 would dramatically fail the prime test, rather than just barely failing. It would reveal that despite the appearances, there is something definitely nonrandom about this sequence. Indeed, it satisfies $\chi(4k+1) = 1$, $\chi(4k+3) = -1$, and $\chi(2k) = 0$. The details of the L_4^* version of the prime test still need to be worked out, thus I did not include it in this chapter.

Finally, if you swap $-1/+1$ in the $\{d(k)\}$ sequence, the new sequence may pass the test even if the original fails (or the other way around). This is the case for the sequence `SQRT[90,91]`. Also, the L_3^* scale should be interpreted as an earthquake scale: an increase from 0.35 to 0.45, or from 1.3 to 1.8, represents a massive difference. A sequence with a low L_3^* alternates too frequently compared to a random sequence, resulting in a ratio $+1$ versus -1 too close to 50% among the $d(k)$'s. The ratio in question corresponds to the column labeled $P[d(k) = 1]$ in Table 11.1.

Exercise 11.1. – Pseudorandom sequence generated by rational numbers. Let $q_k = 2^{-\{k \log_2 3\}}$ be a rational number ($k = 1, 2$, and so on), where the brackets represent the **fractional part function** [Wiki]. For instance, $q_6 = 512/729$. Let M_n be the median of $\{q_1, \ldots, q_n\}$. Thus if n is odd, then M_n is the middle term after rearranging the q_k's in increasing order. Prove that (1) $M_n \to \sqrt{2}/2$ as $n \to \infty$,

Table 11.1 $L_3^*(n)$, **for various sequences** ($n = 20,000$); **"Fail" means failing the prime test.**

Sequence	Seed	$|L_3(n)|$	$P[d(k)=1]$	$L_3^*(n)$	Status
Base3	0.181517	239	49.49%	1.1202	Pass
Base3	0.72	81	49.93%	0.3796	Fail
CounterExample	1	137	49.69%	0.6421	Pass
CounterExample	0	91	49.80%	0.4265	Fail
Dirichlet4	1	113	50.11%	0.7611	Pass
Dirichlet4	3	70	49.65%	0.4715	Fail
Logistic	0.181517	115	49.82%	0.539	Pass
Logistic	0.72	254	49.37%	1.1905	Pass
Python	0	220	49.71%	1.0311	Pass
Python	1	150	50.03%	0.7031	Pass
Python	2	279	49.46%	1.3077	Pass
Python	4	365	50.81%	1.7108	Fail
Python	100	386	49.10%	1.8092	Fail
Python	200	922	52.29%	4.3214	Fail
Python	500	258	49.67%	1.2093	Pass
SQRT	(2, 5)	146	49.63%	0.6843	Pass
SQRT	(90, 91)	1236	53.07%	5.7932	Fail

(2) the binary digit expansion of q_k has period $2 \cdot 3^{k-1}$, and (3) the proportion of 0 and 1 among these digits is exactly 50/50.

Solution

Solution to (2) and (3) is found here; (3) follows from the **equidistribution modulo** 1 [Wiki] of the sequence $\{k \log_2 3\}$. This implies that the q_k's are distributed like 2^{-U} where U is uniformly distributed on $[0, 1]$.

11.3 Python code

The code in Section 11.3.3 focuses on big integers and computing the binary digits for a class of quadratic irrational numbers, using an original, not well-known recursion, possibly published here for the first time. This code is very short, and the description is accompanied by pretty cool math. I recommend that you start looking at it, before digging into the main program in Section 11.3.2.

The main program deals with the prime test. Before that, Section 11.3.1 discusses some generalities related to Python and other languages, pertaining to PRNG issues and fixes.

11.3.1 Fixes to the faulty random function in Python

The default Python function to generate pseudorandom numbers is `random.random()`, available in the `random` library. It is based on the **Mersenne twister** congruential generator [Wiki], and documented here. As discussed in Section 11.2.2, it is not suitable for cryptographic and other applications where pure randomness is critical. Indeed, the documentation comes with the following warning: "The pseudorandom generators of this module should not be used for security purposes".

One way to improve `random.random()` is to avoid particularly bad seeds, such as 200 or 4, in the `random.seed()` call. You may also use binary digits of some **quadratic irrational numbers** [Wiki], using the Python code in Section 11.3.2. Again, it is a good idea to check, using the prime test proposed in this chapter, which irrational numbers to avoid. Also this method may be slow, as it involves working with very big integers. A workaround is to store large tables of precomputed digits in a secure location. The number of quadratic irrationals you can choose from is infinite. Also, your digit sequence should never start with the first binary digit of such numbers, but rather at a random position, to make hacking more difficult.

For instance, to generate your sequence $\{d(k)\}$, set $d(3k)$ to $\delta(g_1(k), \alpha_1)$, set $d(3k+1)$ to $\delta(g_2(k), \alpha_2)$, and set $d(3k+2)$ to $\delta(g_3(k), \alpha_3)$ where

- The numbers $\alpha_1, \alpha_1, \alpha_3$ are three quadratic irrationals, say $\sqrt{2}, \sqrt{10}, \sqrt{41}$,
- The number $(\delta(k, \alpha) + 1)/2$ is the kth binary digit of the quadratic irrational α,
- The functions g_1, g_2, g_3 are used for scrambling: for instance, $g_1(k) = 5 \cdot 10^5 + 2k$, $g_2(k) = 3 \cdot 10^5 + 3k$, and $g_3(k) = 7 \cdot 10^6 - k$.

Another solution is to use for your sequence $\{d(k)\}$ a **bitwise XOR** [Wiki] on two pseudorandom sequences: the binary digits of (say) $\sqrt{2}$ and $\sqrt{41}$, starting at arbitrary positions.

There are also Python libraries that provide solutions suitable for cryptographic applications. For instance, `os.urandom()` uses the operating system to create random sequences that cannot be seeded, and are thus not replicable. See here and here.

11.3.2 Prime test implementation to detect subtle flaws in PRNGs

The code presented here performs the prime test, computing $L_3(n)$. The variable `nterms` represents n, and it is set to 10,000. Rather than directly computing $L_3(n)$, the code iteratively computes more granular statistics, namely `minL` and `maxL`; $L_3(n)$ is the maximum between `-minL` and `maxL`, obtained at the last iteration.

The seeds and the sequences are initialized in the main part, at the bottom. The default category `nonSquare` is used for L_3. The other categories, `Prime` and `All`, are respectively for L_1 defined in formula (11.5) and L_4 defined in formula (11.6). If you use the function `createSignHash()` rather than the default `createSignHash2()`, you can easily compute L_2. The code is somewhat long only because it covers all the options discussed in Section 11.2.2, and more. It heavily relies on hash tables (dictionaries in Python) rather than arrays, because the corresponding arrays would be rather sparse, consume a lot of memory, and slow down the computations. In addition, the code can easily handle Beurling primes (noninteger primes) thanks to the hash tables. A lengthier version named `dirichletL.py`, computing the orbit of $L_P(z, \chi)$ for z in the complex plane when $\sigma = \Re(z) \geq \frac{1}{2}$ is fixed, for any set of primes P (finite or infinite) including Beurling primes, is available on GitHub, here.

The Python code does not use any exotic library other than `primePy`. To install this library, type in the command `pip install primePy` on the Windows command prompt or its Unix equivalent, as you would to install any library. There is a possibility that some older versions of Python would require the

BigNumber library. The code was tested under Python 3.10. The source code, featured below, is also on GitHub: look for randomNumbersTesting.py.

```python
# Test randomness of binary sequences via the law of the iterated logarithm
# By Vincent Granville, www.MLTechniques.com

import math
import random
import numpy as np
from primePy import primes

#--
def createRandomDigits(method,seed):
  primeSign={}
  idx=0
  if method=='SQRT':
   y=seed[0]
   z=seed[1]
  elif method=='Python':
   random.seed(seed)
  else:
   x=seed
  start=2
  if method=='Dirichlet4':
   start=3
  for k in range(start,nterms):
   if k%2500==0:
    print(k,"/",nterms)
   if primes.check(k):
    primeSign[k]=1
    if method=='SQRT':
     if z<2*y:
      y=4*y-2*z
      z=2*z+3
     else:
      y=4*y
      z=2*z-1
      primeSign[k]=-1
    elif method=='Dirichlet4':
     if k%4==seed:
      primeSign[k]=-1
    elif method=='CounterExample':
     idx=idx+1
     if idx%2==seed:
      primeSign[k]=-1
    elif method=='Python':
     x=random.random()
    elif method=='Logistic':
```

```
      x=4*x*(1-x)
    elif method=='Base3':
      x=3*x-int(3*x)
    if method in ('Python','Logistic','Base3') and x>0.5:
      primeSign[k]=-1
  return(primeSign)

#--
def createSignHash2():
  signHash={}
  signHash[1]=1
  for p in primeSign:
    oldSignHash={}
    for k in signHash:
      oldSignHash[k]=signHash[k]
    for k in oldSignHash:
      pp=1
      power=0
      localProduct=oldSignHash[k]
      while k*p*pp<nterms:
        pp=p*pp
        power=power+1
        new_k=k*pp
        localProduct=localProduct*primeSign[p]
        signHash[new_k]=localProduct
  return(signHash)

#--
def createSignHash():
  # same as createSignHash() but for square-free integers only
  signHash={}
  signHash[1]=1
  for p in primeSign:
    oldSignHash={}
    for k in signHash:
      oldSignHash[k]=signHash[k]
    for k in oldSignHash:
      if k*p<nterms:
        new_k=k*p
        signHash[new_k]=oldSignHash[k]*primeSign[p]
  return(signHash)

#--
def testRandomness(category):
  signHash=createSignHash2()
  isSquare={}
  sqr=int(math.sqrt(nterms))
  for k in range(sqr):
```

```
  isSquare[k*k]=1
count=0
count1=0
sumL=0
minL= 2*nterms
maxL=-2*nterms
argMin=-1
argMax=-1
for k in sorted(signHash):
  selected=False
  if category=='Prime' and k in primeSign:
    selected=True
  elif category=='nonSquare' and k not in isSquare:
    selected=True
  elif category=='All':
    selected=True
  if selected==True:
    if signHash[k]==1:
      count1=count1+1
    count=count+1
    sumL=sumL+signHash[k]
    if sumL<minL:
      minL=sumL
      argMin=count
    if sumL>maxL:
      maxL=sumL
      argMax=count
  return(minL,argMin,maxL,argMax,count,count1)

#--
# Main Part. Requirements:
#  0 < seed < 1 for 'Base3' and 'Logistic'; rational numbers not random
#  seed=(y,z) with z>y, z!=2y, y!=2x and x,y>0 are integers for 'SQRT'
#  swapping -1/+1 for seed=(90,91) in 'SQRT' does well, the original does not

seedMethod={}
seedMethod['Python']=(0,1,2,4,100,200,500)
seedMethod['Logistic']=(0.181517,0.72)
seedMethod['Base3']=(0.181517,0.72)
seedMethod['SQRT']=((2,5),(90,91))
seedMethod['Dirichlet4']=(1,3)
seedMethod['CounterExample']=(1,0)
categoryList=('Prime','nonSquare','All')

nterms=10000

OUT=open("prngTest.txt", "w")
for method in seedMethod:
```

```
for seed in seedMethod[method]:
  for category in categoryList:

    primeSign=createRandomDigits(method,seed)
    [minL,argMin,maxL,argMax,count,count1]=testRandomness(category)

    string1=("%14s %9s|%5d %5d|%5d %5d|%5d %5d|" % (method,category,\
      minL,maxL,argMin,argMax,count1,count))+str(seed)
    print(string1)
    string2=("%s\t%s\t%d\t%d\t%d\t%d\t%d\t%d\t" % (method,category,\
      minL,maxL,argMin,argMax,count1,count))+str(seed)+'\n'
    OUT.write(string2)

OUT.close()
```

11.3.3 Special formula to compute 10 million digits of $\sqrt{2}$

The purpose of this code is twofold: to show you how to process integers with millions of digits in Python, and to offer a simple mechanism to compute the binary digits of some quadratic irrational numbers such as $\sqrt{2}/2$. The first problem is solved transparently with no special code or library in Python 3.10. In short, this is a nonissue. With older versions of Python, you might have to install the BigNumber library. See documentation here. Nevertheless, it would be a good idea to track the size of the integers that you are working with (y and z in my code), as eventually their size will become the bottleneck, slowing down the computations.

As for the actual computation of the digits, it is limited here to 10,000 digits, but I compare these digits with those obtained from an external source: Sagemath, see here. It shows, as it should, that both methods produce the same digits, for the number $\sqrt{2}/2$ in particular.

The special recursion used for the digit computation is as follows:

If $z_k < 2y_k$ **then**
$\quad y_{k+1} = 4y_k - 2z_k$
$\quad z_{k+1} = 2z_k + 3$
$\quad d(k) = 1$
else
$\quad y_{k+1} = 4y_k$
$\quad z_{k+1} = 2z_k - 1$
$\quad d(k) = 0.$

The bivariate seed (the initial condition) is determined by the values of y_0 and z_0. You need $z_0 > y_0$ and $z_0 \neq 2y_0$. Then the binary digits $d(k)$ are those of the number

$$x_0 = \frac{-(z_0 - 1) + \sqrt{(z_0 - 1)^2 + 8y_0}}{4},$$

see here. In particular, if $y_0 = 2, z_0 = 5$, then $x_0 = -1 + \sqrt{2}$. Using the change of variables $u_k = 2y_k - z_k$ and $v_k = 2z_k + 3$, the recurrence can be rewritten as:

If $u_k > 0$ then
$$u_{k+1} = 4u_k - v_k$$
$$v_{k+1} = 2v_k + 3$$
$$d(k) = 1$$
else
$$u_{k+1} = 4u_k + v_k - 2$$
$$v_{k+1} = 2v_k - 5$$
$$d(k) = 0.$$

Now $v_k - 5$ is divisible by 8. Let $w_k = (v_k - 5)/8$. We have $d(k) = 1$ if w_{k+1} is odd, otherwise $d(k) = 0$. We also have the following one-dimensional backward recursion, allowing you to compute the digits backward all the way down to the first digit:

If w_{k+1} is odd, then
$$v_k = (v_{k+1} - 3)/2$$
$$d(k) = 1$$
else
$$v_k = (v_{k+1} + 5)/2$$
$$d(k) = 0.$$

These recursions are reminiscent of the unsolved **Collatz conjecture** [Wiki]. Below is the source code, also available on GitHub: look for randomNumbers-sqrt2.py.

```
# Comparing binary digits of SQRT(2) obtained with two different methods

# Method 1:
# 10,000 binary digits of SQRT(2) obtained via https://mltblog.com/3uMZQ4s
# Using sagemath.org. Sagemath command: N(sqrt(2),prec=10000).str(base=2)

sqrt2='0110101000001001111001100110011111110011101111001100100100001000101100101111110110\
0010011011001101110101010010101011111010011111000111010110111101100000101110101000100100\
1110111010100001001100111011010001011110101100100000101100000110011001110011001000010101\
0010101111110010000011000001000011101010111000101000010110000111010100010110001111111001\
1011111101110010000011110110110011001000001110111010010101000010111100100000111001110001\
1110110100101001110000000010010000110011011000111101111101000100111011010001101001000\
1000000010111010000111010000101010111100011111010011100101001100000101100111000110000000\
0100011011110000110011011110111100101010110001101111001001000100010110100010000100010110\
0010100100011000001010101110001110010001011110101111100010011100011001111000110110101010\
1010001010001110001011101101111110100110111001100100101100101010011000110100001100110001111\
1100111100100000100110111110101001011110001001000001111100000110110111001011000000101110\
1010101010100100101000001000100110010000010000001100101001001010100000010011100101001010\
1101101101100011111101000011101011111011111010011010011010000000101100111010111100100100\
1111100000110001000010011001001101101010111100110101010010100010110110010100011011100011\
0011100110100000110110110111110000010001101101100011100000001000001001101110000000000111\
1111100011001000110101001011110011001100101010010101110100111110111110111101101000011110\
1111111111011010100001101111100011111111001010001000100001001100000111110111101010000001\
1000100100000111110111101010101000000011100001011000001111111001011110111011101010001011\
1101111101110000100110011000110001000001110001010001011101010111111110101111100111011001011\
```

```
0100100100111101001010011011000111111101011001011100010000010111111011111111000010111000\
0011111101001110110001111101111000000011111001101011001100111001000001011110010111111100\
1010000000010111000010010001100111100001011110100100101001010101011000000100011010111111\
0011111000111101111011110010100011111010100011001110110101001101011110001100000101001011\
1001100011001111100001111100001010010000101111100111011010010010100110110000010101110001\
1000001000010110101100001001111101101001000011111001001001001001111010110110110111000111111\
0000010110111001101001010010000001101100000100111011110111010001001000100101001100000111\
1010100111010101010101101000011011101010001100100001111101110100100010011111010100011010100\
1111110100100000011000010111110001000001111101101101101010010100111011111011010101000011001\
0011001100001001100110111010111000010100001101101010010000010001011100001111010000100110\
0111010000001101000010000100011110101101110001110000011000000111101100100000000110111010\
0011101101000110100011011001101000010001110010110110001011100110101010011001011100101011011\
1000000111111100110101010000000110000110100000100101001010000101101011001000000011000010\
0000001111011101101011111100011011011110100100010001010010100010101011001111100100100100010001\
1000110100010011000110000000010111011010000001010100010110101011010110000010000011111\
1010101110111100110111000000110111010000110001100110110101001000001100011111111100111111111\
1111111010101101010101111100010001110001000010011000000110011011011110101010111000010011011\
0000100100001011011010010111101001000110110011111000101110010000000101101101110010011110\
0100101101110010111000111010110000010100001111100010001000111100001000101000001010001101\
1100001000000001100110011011011000010110011100101101111011001100010010111011100111000111\
1100100001011000100110100011010011011110100110000001100101111001000100000000110011101000\
1100001001111111111100001000100100010100110100001110011110101010001011110101001100110011\
0110110110010011110001111001110011000111111001010011010110000010010010101011001110000010\
0100000101010111000110010101010000110000011010101010100010000101101000100001100011100010\
1110111100011001111011000000011010100001101000000101111110100000101111100101001111011001\
0001011111001011100011001010110000000011110101110101011011100011011100000100101101100\
0110000101000001110011110000011011101101010100100011100000010001100110101001111111100001\
1111000111100110010001110110011011000101000000111010010001001010110100001001110000010110\
1011010100000010000001000111110110111001100010011111011000111010100010100110010011101000\
1010001100110111100000011010000110000011110001000100010100000000010010001001101100101001\
1110100111110011011101100111101010010110011000111010100100010011101011101010010001100011\
0110101110001000110011110001001000000110010010110101111100101010010011011111101010111011\
0010110011001110001011010011010010110001001101101101010000110011101111011101100011100100111\
0000000010100111111110101010001100100000010111001101010110011111000010101101010001111010\
0111100111010011011111111000001011110100011011010011011101011101110001000101110000000000\
1010111011011010010101101101111101010111100011011000001011000010001011001000110101011\
1111110111010111010000011101111111111011001001011011011011000111101101011110001111111000\
0011100001010111011011100111000011011010010011110101111101011010101110100010001100001\
0001000001010010101100010110111010000000111001010011111110001101101101011110000010110\
1111110110000011011100011011100000101001011101101101101110001100111111110000101101100100\
1110100111000001000010000110110011101000010011011110101011000110110001011001010100100\
0000111001111010010000100011100111010101010111001101001101100000000011110010101011110010\
1000100010110111100011000001010001111100000101001001111110110001001011010001110101101111\
0010100101111011100011100000010110101101001010001011101101010010100101100000100101001000\
1000000110010101011100100101000011000011111000011110100100110111111010000111100111011111\
1101000101011110110001100000101101001010011010000010111011100101000100010101100101000010\
0111111101101000000011011001001100000101001000101011101100000111011101000001101001101010\
1011000110110000000111011101000100010101100111101001011001000011111010101010001001111111101\
```

```
0110111011101010111010001000000101001010010111010110110110111101001010100010001001111100\
0111101000010010010101110110001110001101000010101001000000011011100001011101001100110010\
1000111101100110111001011011110110110100000010111100010000110010010111110010101101100011\
0111001001001100101000100101011010000000100110000110011000110000001110101100100101000110\
1011001101010001001101101101111100010000110010011100111101010101110101001100011001001100\
1011001101010100011000011000100101011110101001001110100101011110100101100101101011101010\
1000111111110100000111011000000110110011000011001011011101101010100001001110111101110010\
0000011110100101101001011010101011110110110110000010101001101001011111001011111100001010\
1000111011111111100010100100101000110100110010000110110010100101000110000111010101110000\
1000001010110001011001111001101101101100011001001010110111100001111001000011000110100010\
0111000101101101111011111001110011000001011011010001101111011111111110000010111100011100\
1010100111111110011111101100000001000010101110110110010000010110110011001001011001100100\
1010010001010101000011110111000011001000011110001110100010111000011100001111100011000\
0100101101101011001011110000000110000011010101010110111000001011111010100011101101001110\
1110011111000010101100010010010101101011010101001000110110000110000010110010110010100000\
0110001111101000100110010100010011110101101000110100110010111111101010101011011111101100\
0101001101001111100011110101001001111100100001001111001101010100001001011010100011000010\
0100000110101001001010010010101101101101011111001001101110001100111011011011111001011010\
1101110100000001010100111011111100001000101101100011010011000010111101010001011101110010\
1001000000000011101011101000000110000011001100100001000111101111110010000010001011000000\
1001000000001010010011101110110110001011010100000010000100111010010011011100001100001110\
1111111101111000010010000110100111101111100100001101001111100000111010000101010101011100\
1111011110111100101001100011111011010010111010111110110101111000010110101011111011111010\
1001100000001011001100101101101101101110111011100011111011101011000110011011011010001010\
1011000111001001011001111011110000000111100010110010010000111100000000110100111010010000\
0111110110011111011000011001000110000101110001001111010110010001111101101010101001000011\
1110110001010100110010010110011100011111010111010001010011010001001111110110110101010001\
1101111110001010110111101000011110101011100110101010001010110000111010011111011010100000\
0011110110100110110001011101101100110101110000001101111110111010000100011110110101010\
0100100000101011010111111011100011111001010011111110010101100001011001010001101011101100\
0100000100000010110000101111000000001011001100101101000000001011011101101010011111001110\
0100111100101101111011000110011110010011101000100111111011011000001011100101100001110101\
1111110001101000000000110100011001011101001100110111101011010100010010001111110001001111\
0010110000000010100011111101011100000010011001100100011010011001010101001010001101010\
0000000000011111111111000001001000010101011111110111100001011011000101001001010100010000\
0010100010110011110110100010010011110100101010011001100111011001011011000111100111101100\
0110111001101001110001000111001001110011111001000010101011001101100001110010111101100101\
0000010011110001010011111110000101110110001011101111000100010100010110110111011110010101\
0110000111011011101001010101011101000100100011110010011111011101011100000011110110101101\
0011111100110100101101010010010111000111011000001110011001110000000111011111100111011011\
0111000101011001110111011111010100011011011001110001111100111000100110111001000010101\
0100101100110000100110101001101101110010101011000010010111011000101001010001010001001000\
1011111100111101000011110110110011011101010101111110000101000001010000111111100001001001\
1111110001000011000111101000101101100011000001110010000010010000010000000100010010110010\
0110010111100111000110001000000001100101111000111000011101010111000100101110001110111010\
1001111011110010110011011011110110010111011000010100101110101110100011010111100101111010\
0001000010010001011000111010101100111111011011000100110111110100011’
```

```
size=len(sqrt2)

# Method2:
# 10,000 binary digits of SQRT(2) obtained via formula at https://mltblog.com/3REtOB9
# Implicitly uses the BigNumber Python library (https://pypi.org/project/BigNumber/)

y=2
z=5
for k in range(0,size-1):
    if z<2*y:
        y=4*y-2*z
        z=2*z+3
        digit=1
    else:
        y=4*y
        z=2*z-1
        digit=0
    print(k,digit,sqrt2[k])
```

11.4 Military-grade PRNG based on quadratic irrationals

If you produce simulations or create synthetic data that requires billions or trillions of random numbers (such as in Section 1.3.4.1), you need a pseudorandom number generator (PRNG) that is not only fast, but in some cases truly emulates randomness. Usually you cannot have both. Congruential PRNGs are very fast and can be pretty good at emulating randomness. The Mersenne twister available in Python and in other languages has a very large period, more than enough for any practical need. Yet, depending on the seed, it has flaws caused by the lack of perfect randomness in the distribution of prime numbers. These were revealed by the **prime test** in Section 11.2.2. To the contrary, PRNGs based on irrational numbers exhibit stronger randomness if you skip the first few digits and carefully choose your numbers. But they tend to be very slow.

In this section I propose a new approach to obtain billions of trillions of digits from combinations of **quadratic irrationals** [Wiki] such as $\sqrt{2}$ or $\sqrt{7583}$, based on the algorithm in Section 11.3.3. The goal is to produce replicable random numbers. If you want to use them for strong encryption, you need to use a seed that is hardware-generated so that the same seed is never used more than once.

11.4.1 Fast algorithm rooted in advanced analytic number theory

The idea to get a fast algorithm is simple. Instead of producing n digits from a single number, I generate r digits from m different numbers, with $n = rm$. While the Python code relies only on basic additions and very few operations, the computation of n binary digits of a single irrational number involves very large integers. The **computational complexity** is $O(n^2)$. If instead you generate r digits from m numbers, the computational complexity drops to $O(rm^2)$. In the most extreme and very interesting case where $r = n$ and $m = 1$, the computational complexity is $O(n)$, just as fast as the Mersenne twister. The method is based on two deep results in number theory:

- The binary digits of a quadratic irrational behave as an infinite realization of independent Bernoulli trials with equal proportions of 0 and 1. This unproven conjecture is one of the most difficult unsolved problems in mathematics. Very strong empirical results involving trillions of digits, support this hypothesis.
- Two sequences of digits from irrational numbers that are linearly independent over the set $\mathbb{Q}$ of rational numbers have zero cross-correlation. The correlation is defined as the empirical correlation in this case.

The latter is a consequence of the following theorem: the correlation $\rho(p, q)$ between the sequences $(\{pb^k\alpha\})$ and $(\{qb^k\alpha\})$ indexed by $k = 0, 1$, and so on, where p, q are positive integers with no common divisors, $b > 1$ is an integer, and α is a positive irrational, is equal to $\rho(p, q) = (pq)^{-1}$. Here $\{\cdot\}$ denotes the fractional part function.

A proof (by William Huber) of this unpublished theorem can be found here, with additional discussion on this topic, here. Note that $\lfloor b \cdot \{b^k\alpha\} \rfloor$ is the kth digit of α in base b. The brackets represent the integer part function. Thus, if $\alpha_1 = p\alpha$ and $\alpha_2 = q\alpha$, the correlation between the sequences $(\{b^k\alpha_1\})$ and $(\{b^k\alpha_2\})$ is $\rho(p, q) = (pq)^{-1}$. If α_1, α_2 are irrational and linearly independent over $\mathbb{Q}$, then the only way you can write $\alpha_1 = p\alpha, \alpha_2 = q\alpha$ is by letting p, q tend to infinity, thus the correlation vanishes. It implies that the correlation between the digit sequences of α_1 and α_2 is zero.

There is more number theory involved. In particular, the method uses the new algorithm described in Section 11.3.3 to compute the binary digits of quadratic irrationals. It is also connected to **square-free integers**, and approximations of irrational by rational numbers which is linked to continued fractions. Square-free integers [Wiki] are also discussed in Sections 11.2.1 and 17.2.2.2. They represent 61% of all positive integers: the exact proportion is $6/\pi^2$.

11.4.2 Fast PRNG: explanations

Each positive integer c can be written as $c = ab$, where a is a square, and b is square-free. For instance, if $c = 3^5 \times 13^6 \times 19$, then $a = 3^4 \times 13^6$ and $b = 3 \times 19$. If c is a square, then $c = a$ and $b = 1$.

The quadratic irrationals used here are characterized by a bivariate **seed** (y_0, z_0). Given a seed, the successive iterations produce the binary digits of the number

$$x_0 = \frac{-(z_0 - 1) + \sqrt{(z_0 - 1)^2 + 8y_0}}{4}. \tag{11.7}$$

The connection to square-free integers is as follows: $c = (z_0 - 1)^2 + 8y_0$ cannot be a square. I use the notation $c = ab$, where a is the square part of c and b is the square-free part. Thus, we must have $b > 1$. I use a large number of seeds to generate a large number of quadratic irrationals. The cross-correlation between the two digit sequences in any pair of quadratic irrationals must be zero. Based on the theory in Section 11.4.1, it means that once a seed produces a specific b, any future seed with the same b must be rejected. This is accomplished using the variable `accepted` in the code, along with the **hash table** (dictionary in Python) `squareFreeList`. The key for this hash table is actually b.

The number of digits produced for each quadratic irrational is specified by the parameter `size`. The total number of quadratic irrationals is determined by `Niter`. Not all of them are used: a few are rejected for the reason just mentioned. All the binary digits of all the accepted quadratic irrationals are stored in the hash table `digits`. For instance, `digits[(b,k)]` is the kth digit of the quadratic irrational with square-free part b. The seed (y_0, z_0) corresponding to this number is `squareFreeList[b]`.

Due to the particular choice of seeds in the Python code (with $y_0 = 1$), many quadratic irrationals are close to zero. More specifically, formula (11.7) yields the following approximation: $x_0 \approx y_0/(z_0 - 1)$. So the first few digits are biased and should be skipped. This is accomplished via the parameter offset. There are other problematic quadratic irrationals such as those with $z_0 - 1$ being a power of 2. A future version of this algorithm can reject these quadratic irrationals, and also reject those that are too close to a number already in the hash table. However, increasing the parameter offset is the easiest option to eliminate these problems. The next step is to run a standard battery of tests such as the **Diehard tests**, and check whether this PRNG passes all of them depending on the parameters and configuration.

I have not tested yet the algorithm with size=1: this is the fastest way to generate many digits (assuming Niter is increased accordingly), and possibly the best choice assuming offset is large enough. In particular, if you extract just one digit of each quadratic irrational, there is a faster way to do it, see Section 11.4.4.

11.4.3 Python code

Now that I explained all the details about the algorithm, here is the Python code. It is also available on GitHub, here, under the name stronprng.py.

```
# By Vincent Granville, www.MLTechniques.com

import time
import random
import numpy as np

size = 400        # number of binary digits in each number
Niter = 5000      # number of quadratic irrationals
start = 0         # first value of (y, z) is (1, start)
yseed = 1         # y = yseed
offset = 100      #   skip first offset digits (all zeroes) of each number
PRNG = 'Quadratic' # options: 'Quadratic' or 'Mersenne'
output = True     # True to print results (slow)

squareFreeList = {}
digits = {}
accepted = 0 # number of accepted seeds

for iter in range(start, Niter):

    y = yseed # you could use a nonfixed y instead, depending on iter
    z = iter
    c = (z - 1)**2 + 8*y

    # represent c as a * b where a is square and b is square-free
    d = int(np.sqrt(c))
    a = 1
    for h in range(2, d+1):
        if c % (h*h) == 0: # c divisible by squared h
```

```
        a = h*h
    b = c // a # integer division

    if b > 1 and b not in squareFreeList:
        q = (-(z - 1) + np.sqrt(c)) / 4 # number associated to seed (y, z); ~ y/(z-1)
        squareFreeList[b]=(y,z)  # accept the seed (y, z)
        accepted += 1

start = time.time()

for b in squareFreeList:

    y = squareFreeList[b][0]
    z = squareFreeList[b][1]

    for k in range(size):

        # trick to make computations faster
        y2 = y + y
        y4 = y2 + y2
        z2 = z + z

        # actual computations
        if z < y2:
            y = y4 - z2
            z = z2 + 3
            digit = 1
        else:
            y = y4
            z = z2 - 1
            digit = 0
        if k >= offset:
            digits[(b,k)] = digit

end = time.time()
print("Time elapsed:",end-start)

if output == True:
    OUT=open("strong4.txt","w")
    separator="\t" # could be "\t" or "" or "," or " "
    if PRNG == 'Mersenne':
        random.seed(205)
    for b in squareFreeList:
        OUT.write("["+str(b)+"]")
        for k in range(offset, size):
            key = (b, k)
            if PRNG == 'Quadratic':
                bit = digits[key]
```

```
    elif PRNG == 'Mersenne':
        bit = int(2*random.random())
    OUT.write(separator+str(bit))
  OUT.write("\n")
OUT.close()

print("Accepted seeds:",accepted," out of",Niter)
```

11.4.4 Computing a digit without generating the previous ones

If offset is large, you spend time computing digits (at the beginning of the binary expansion of each quadratic irrational) that you will use only to get the subsequent digits. There is a more efficient approach: use a different seed (y_0', z_0'). The new seed has the benefit of keeping the square-free part b unchanged. To get the digit in position k in one shot (assuming the first position corresponds to $k = 0$), use the seed $y_0' = 2^{2k}y_0$, $z_0' = 2^k(z_0 - 1) + 1$. Then $x_0' = 2^k x_0$, so your quadratic irrational is multiplied by 2^k. This is a direct consequence of formula (11.7). However, this will not work if $y_0' \geq z_0'$, which is always the case when k is large enough. So you need to work with a different (y_0', z_0'), one that leads to $x_0' = \lfloor 2^k x_0 \rfloor$. I describe how to do it efficiently in Section 5.3.3 in my book on chaotic dynamical systems [4].

Finally, by digits, I mean the binary digits on the right starting after the decimal point. The position k that you select for the starting digit may be randomized: it can depend on the quadratic irrational. This makes it very difficult to reverse-engineer your sequence of random digits.

11.4.5 Security and comparison with other PRNGs

The spreadsheet strongprng.xlsx (on GitHub) compares the quadratic irrational PRNG with the Mersenne twister. The test involves 5000 quadratic irrationals, one per row. Based on the acceptation rule, only 4971 were used. For each of them, I computed 400 binary digits and skipped the first 100 as suggested in the methodology. So in total, there are 4971 blocks, each with 300 digits. The tab corresponding to the Mersenne twister has the same block structure with the same number of digits: it was produced using the option PRNG='Mersenne' in the Python code. The numbers in brackets in column D represent the block ID: the number b in the case of the quadratic irrational PRNG, and nothing in particular in the case of the Mersenne twister.

I computed some summary statistics: digit expectation and variance for each column and for each row, as well as cross-correlations between rows, and also between columns. The results are as expected and markedly similar when comparing the two PRNGs. You would expect any decent PRNG to pass these basic tests, so this is not a surprise. You need more sophisticated tests to detect hard-to-find departure from randomness; that was the purpose of Section 11.2.2 with the prime test. Fig. 11.4 shows 5000 correlation values. They are not statistically different from zero, and independent despite the fact that they correspond to seeds produced in chronological order. Indeed, their joint distribution is identical to that produced with the Mersenne twister (not shown in the picture, but included in the spreadsheet).

Whether using the Mersenne twister or quadratic irrationals, the compression factor – based on the zip tool applied to the 1.5 million raw digits – is about the same and equal to almost 8. This is the worst achievable compression factor: each character (8 bits) representing a digit is turned into 1 bit of

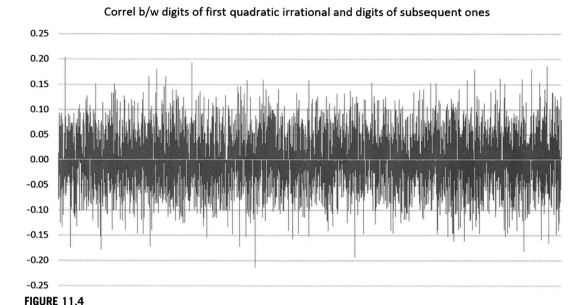

FIGURE 11.4

Correlations are computed on sequences consisting of 300 binary digits.

information. It means that the zip tool is unable to detect any pattern in the digits that would allow for any amount of real compression.

11.4.5.1 *Important comments*

There are very few serious articles in the literature dealing with digits of irrational numbers to build PRNGs. It seems that this idea was abandoned long ago due to the computational complexity and the erroneous belief that it defeats the nondeterministic nature of randomness. It is my hope that my quadratic irrational PRNG debunks all these myths. Note that there has been attempts to use chaotic dynamical systems to build PRNGs. See, for instance, [11] and [1]. My upcoming book on dynamical systems explores many new related methods in great details.

Also, my PRNGs, by combining thousands to billions of quadratic irrationals, present some similarity to **combined linear congruential generators** [Wiki]. They avoid the drawbacks that these generators are facing. In the context of congruential generators, combining is used to increase the period and randomness. In the case of quadratic irrational PRNGs, the period is always infinite, and the goal is to increase security, but not randomness which is already maximum with just one number. Also using many quadratic irrationals each with a few digits runs a lot faster than one number with many digits. In addition, using many quadratic irrationals leads to a very efficient implementation using a distributed architecture.

Finally, while it sounds like a cave-man idea to publish a table of random digits, it servers a very important purpose that has been forgotten in modern scientific research and benchmarking – replicability. You are free to reuse my Excel spreadsheet if you want your research to be replicable. Of course, you would get the same digits if you use the Python code with the same seeds. This is not true with the Mersenne twister: the digits may depend on which version of Python you use. Also, one advantage of the quadratic irrational PRNG is its portability, and the fact that you will get the same digits regardless of your programming language. Time permitting, I will publish a much larger table with at least a trillion digits. In the meanwhile, if you need such a table, feel free to email me at vincentg@MLTechniques.com.

11.4.6 Curious application: a new type of lottery

The following application requires a very large number of pseudorandom numbers generated in real-time, as fast as possible. The digits must emulate randomness extremely well. It would benefit from using the quadratic irrational PRNG. The idea consists of creating a virtual, market-neutral stock market where people buy and sell stocks with tokens. In short, a synthetic stock market where you play with synthetic money (tokens). Another description is a lottery or number guessing game. You pay a fee per transaction (with real money), and each time you make a correct guess, you are paid a specific amount, also in real money. The participant can select different strategies ranging from conservative and limited to small gains and low volatility, to aggressive with a very small chance to win a lot of money.

The algorithm that computes the winning numbers is public; it requires some data input, also publicly published (the equivalent of a public key in cryptography). So you can use it to compute the next winning number and be certain to win each time, which would very quickly result in bankruptcy for the operator. However, the public algorithm necessitates billions of years of computing time to obtain any winning number with certainty. But you can guess the winning number: your odds of winning by pure chance (in a particular example) is 1/256.

The operator uses a private algorithm that very efficiently computes the next winning number. From the public algorithm, it is impossible to tell – even if you are the greatest computer scientist or mathematician in the world – that there is an alternative that could make the computations a lot faster: the private algorithm is the equivalent of a private key in cryptography. The public algorithm takes as much time as breaking an encryption key (comparable to factoring a product of two very large primes), while the private version is equivalent to decoding a message if you have the private key (comparable to finding the second factor in the number in question if you know one of the two factors – the private key).

Needless to say, any very slight deviation resulting from flaws in the PRNG will quickly lead to either the bankruptcy of the operator, or the operator enriching itself and being accused of lying about the neutrality of the simulated market. I made a presentation on this topic at the Operations Research Society conference (INFORMS) in 2019, in a session exploring biases in algorithms. See the abstract here. The full paper will be included in my upcoming book "Experimental Math and Probabilistic Number Theory".

References

[1] D. Bailey, R. Crandall, Random generators and normal numbers, Experimental Mathematics 11 (2002) 527–546, Project Euclid, [Link].
[2] K. Conrad, L-functions and the Riemann Hypothesis, 2018 CTNT Summer School, 2018, [Link].
[3] H.G. Diamond, W.-B. Zhang, Beurling Generalized Numbers, Mathematical Surveys and Monographs, vol. 213, American Mathematical Society, 2016, [Link].

[4] V. Granville, Gentle Introduction to Chaotic Dynamical Systems, MLTechniques.com, 2023, [Link].

[5] A.J. Harper, Moments of random multiplicative functions, II: high moments, Algebra and Number Theory 13 (10) (2019) 2277–2321, [Link].

[6] A.J. Harper, Moments of random multiplicative functions, I: low moments, better than square-root cancellation, and critical multiplicative chaos, Forum of Mathematics, Pi 8 (2020) 1–95, [Link].

[7] A.J. Harper, Almost sure large fluctuations of random multiplicative functions, Preprint, pp. 1–38, 2021, arXiv, [Link].

[8] T.W. Hilberdink, M.L. Lapidus, Beurling zeta functions, generalised primes, and fractal membranes, Preprint, pp. 1–31, 2004, arXiv, [Link].

[9] Y.-K. Lau, G. Tenenbaum, J. Wu, On mean values of random multiplicative functions, Proceedings of the American Mathematical Society 142 (2) (2013) 409–420, [Link].

[10] E.C. Titchmarsh, D.R. Heath-Brown, The Theory of the Riemann Zeta-Function, second edition, Oxford Science Publications, 1987.

[11] L. Wang, H. Cheng, Pseudo-random number generator based on logistic chaotic system, Entropy 21 (10) (2019) 960, [Link].

Some unusual random walks
Testing and leveraging quasirandomness

This is a follow-up to Chapter 11 about "Detecting Subtle Departures from Randomness", where I introduced the prime test to identify very weak violations of various laws of large numbers. Pseudorandom sequences failing this test usually pass most test batteries, yet are unsuitable for a number of applications, such as security, strong cryptography, or intensive simulations. The purpose here is to build such sequences with very low, slow-building, long-range dependencies, but that otherwise appear as random as pure noise. They are useful not only for testing and benchmarking tests of randomness, but also in their own right to model almost random systems, such as stock market prices. I introduce new categories of random walks (or quasi-Brownian motions subject to constraints), and discuss the peculiarities of each category. For completeness, I included related stochastic processes discussed in some of my previous articles, for instance integrated and 2D clustered Brownian motions. All the processes investigated here are drift-free and symmetric, yet not perfectly random. They all start at zero.

12.1 Symmetric unbiased constrained random walks

The standard symmetric 1D **random walk** [Wiki] fundamental to this chapter is a sequence $\{S_n\}$ with $n \geq 0$, starting at $S_0 = 0$, and recursively defined by $S_n = X_n + S_{n-1}$, for $n > 0$. Here X_1, X_2, and so on, are independent random variables with $P[X_n = 1] = P[X_n = -1] = \frac{1}{2}$. Thus $\{S_n\}$ is a time-discrete stochastic process, and indeed the most basic one. In Sections 12.1.2 and 12.1.3, I drop the assumption of independence, leading to modified random walks such as those described in [6,9]. More general references include [1,8].

With proper rescaling, a random walk becomes a time-continuous stochastic process S_t called **Brownian motion** [Wiki], with $t \in \mathbb{R}^+$. See the time series in gray in Fig. 12.1, displaying a particular instance: it shows the first 50,000 values of S_n in a short window, giving the appearance of a Brownian motion. By contrast, each of the orange, red, and gray time series represents one instance of a specific type of non-Brownian motion. Sections 12.1.2 and 12.1.3 focus on these three types of processes, which are quasi-, but not fully random.

12.1.1 Three fundamental properties of pure random walks

The standard random walk $\{S_n\}$ (illustrated in gray in Fig. 12.1) is the base or reference process, used to build more sophisticated models. It has too many properties to list in this short chapter. However, the following are the most relevant to our discussion:

- **Law of the iterated logarithm** [Wiki]. In our context, it is stated as follows:

$$\limsup \frac{|S_n|}{\sqrt{2n\nu \log \log n}} = 1 \quad \text{as } n \to \infty. \tag{12.1}$$

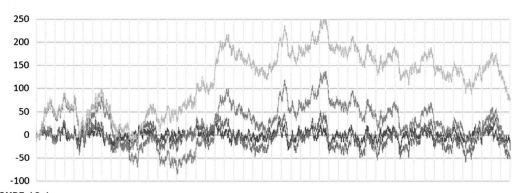

FIGURE 12.1

Typical path S_n with $0 \le n \le 50{,}000$ for four types of random walks.

Here, as per **Hartman–Wintner theorem** [Wiki], $v = \text{Var}[X_1] = 1$. See [8], pages 118–123, for a version adapted to Brownian motions.

- Expected number of **zero crossings** in $S_1, \ldots, S_n$, denoted as N_n. Here a zero-crossing is an index $0 < k \le n$ such that $S_k = 0$. For $n > 0$, we have (see here)

$$\mathrm{E}[N_{2n}] = -1 + \frac{2n+1}{4^n}\binom{2n}{n} \sim \frac{2}{\sqrt{\pi}} \cdot \sqrt{n} \quad \text{as } n \to \infty.$$

- Distribution of **first hitting time** to zero [Wiki], or first zero crossing after $S_0 = 0$, also called time of first return. The random variable in question is denoted as T. It is defined as follows: $T = n$ (with $n > 0$) if and only if $S_n = 0$ and $S_k \neq 0$ if $0 < k < n$. We have $P[T = n] = 0$ if n is odd, and $\mathrm{E}[T] = \text{Var}[T] = \infty$. Yet, our random walks cross the X-axis infinitely many times. We also have the following **probability generating function** [Wiki] (see here):

$$\sum_{n=1}^{\infty}(2x)^{2n}\, P[T = 2n] = 1 - \sqrt{1 - 4x^2} \quad \text{if } x \le \frac{1}{4}.$$

From this one can obtain

$$P[T = 2n] = \frac{1}{(2n-1)4^n}\binom{2n}{n} \sim \frac{1}{\sqrt{4\pi}} \cdot n^{-3/2} \quad \text{as } n \to \infty,$$

$$\mathrm{E}[T^{-1}] = \int_0^{1/2} \frac{1 - \sqrt{1 - 4x^2}}{x}\, dx = 1 - \log 2.$$

Note that $\mathrm{E}[T^{-1}]$ is finite, while $\mathrm{E}[T]$ is infinite. The fact that $\mathrm{E}[T] = \infty$ explains why the sequence S_n can stay above or below the X-axis for incredibly long time periods, as shown in Fig. 12.1 for the gray curve.

The above three statistics $|S_n|/\sqrt{2n \log\log n}$, N_{2n}, and T^{-1} can be used to design tests of randomness for pseudorandom number generators. Indeed, the **prime test** in Chapter 11 relies on a number-theoretic version of the law of the iterated logarithm (LIL). The purpose is to detect very weak departures from randomness, even in sequences that are random enough to pass the classic LIL test, yet not fully random. In this chapter, the goal is to simulate quasirandom sequences, rather than creating new tests of randomness.

I now describe special types of modified random walks that lack true independence in the sequence $\{X_n\}$. In particular, I discuss why they are special and of great interest, with a focus on applications.

12.1.2 Random walks with more entropy than pure random signal

One way to introduce dependencies in the sequences is to increase the frequency of oscillations (and thus the entropy) in the gray curve in Fig. 12.1. The gray curve represents a realization of a pure random walk. To achieve this goal, you may want the sequence to violate the law of the iterated logarithm: you want to build a sequence that would satisfy a modified law of the iterated logarithm with $\sqrt{2n \log \log n}$ in formula (12.1) replaced by (say) $n^{2/5}$.

To accomplish this, you need to add constraints when simulating the sequence in question. Yet you want to preserve quasirandomness – the absence of drifts and autocorrelations in the sequence $\{X_n\}$ – even though there is some modest lack of independence. So modest indeed that most statistical tests would fail to catch it, even though it can made highly visible to the naked eye: see the red, and especially the blue curve in Fig. 12.1.

12.1.2.1 *Applications*

Such sequences can be used to generate synthetic data (see Chapter 7) or to model barely-constrained stochastic processes, such as stock price fluctuations in an almost perfect market. See also [4]. Another application is to introduce an undetectable backdoor in some encryption systems without third parties (government or hackers) being able to notice it, depending on the strength of the dependencies. This type of backdoor can help the encryption company decrypt a message when requested by a legitimate user who lost his key, even though the encryption company has no standard mechanism to store or retrieve keys (precisely to avoid government interference).

This assumes that there is a mapping between the type of weak dependencies introduced in a specific sequence, and the type of algorithm (or the key) used to decrypt the sequence in question. The mapping can be made too loose for full decryption even by the parent company, but helpful to retrieve partial data, such as where the sequence originates from: in this case, the type of dependencies is a proxy for a signature. All that is needed is to add some extra bits so that the sequence has the desired statistical behavior.

Ironically, you need a very good, industrial-grade **pseudorandom number generator** (PRNG) to generate almost perfectly random sequences. PRNGs that are not good enough – such as the **Mersenne twister** – may introduce irregularities that can interfere with those you want to introduce. This is discussed in detail in Chapter 11 on PRNGs.

12.1.2.2 *Algorithm to generate quasirandom sequences*

One way to generate such sequences is as follows:

$S = 0$
For $n = 1, 2, \ldots$
    Generate random deviate U on $[0, 1]$
    $M = g(n)$

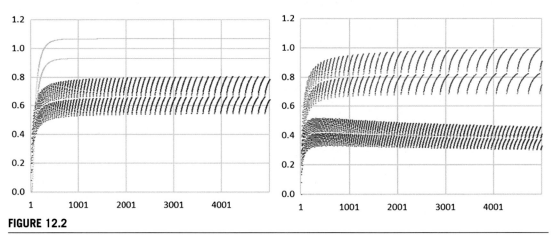

FIGURE 12.2

$\delta_n = 1 - \text{Var}[S_{n+1}] + \text{Var}[S_n]$ for four types of random walks, with $0 \le n \le 5000$.

If $(S < -M$ and $U < \frac{1}{2} - \epsilon)$ or $(S > M$ and $U < \frac{1}{2} + \epsilon)$ or $(|S| \le M$ and $U < \frac{1}{2})$
Then
   $X_n = -1$
Else
   $X_n = 1$
$S = S + X_n$
$S_n = S$

Here $0 < \epsilon < \frac{1}{2}$ and $\alpha > 0$. The function $g(n)$ is positive and growing more slowly than $\sqrt{n}$. Typically, $g(n) = \alpha n^\beta$ with $0 \le \beta \le \frac{1}{2}$, or $g(n) = \alpha(\log n)^\beta$ with $\beta \ge 0$. The Python code in Section 12.3.2 performs this simulation: choose the option `deviations='Small'`. You can customize the function $g(n)$, denoted as G in the code. The option `mode='Power'` corresponds to $g(n) = \alpha n^\beta$, while `mode='Log'` corresponds to $g(n) = \alpha(\log n)^\beta$.

Results are displayed in Fig. 12.1. The color scheme is as follows:

- Gray curve: $\epsilon = 0$, corresponding to a pure random walk.
- Blue curve: $g(n) = \log n$, $\epsilon = 0.05$.
- Red curve: $g(n) = n^\beta$ with $\beta = 0.35$, $\epsilon = 0.05$.

The yellow curve represents a very different type of process, discussed in Section 12.1.3.

12.1.2.3 *Variance of the modified random walk*

The symmetric nature of the modified random walk $\{S_n\}$ defined in Section 12.1.2.2 results in several identities. Let $p_n(m) = P(S_n = m)$, with $-n \le m \le n$. Also, let $S_0 = 0$ and $p_0(0) = 1$. Then $p_n(m)$ can be recursively computed using some modified version of the Pascal triangle recursion:

$$p_{n+1}(m) = \left[\frac{1}{2} + \epsilon \cdot A_n(m-1)\right]p_n(m-1) + \left[\frac{1}{2} - \epsilon \cdot A_n(m+1)\right]p_n(m+1), \tag{12.2}$$

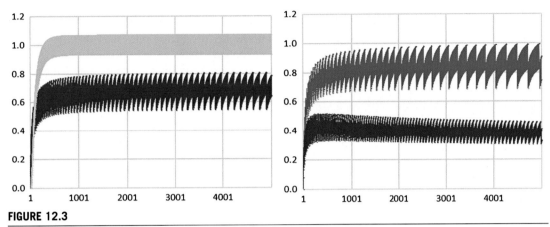

FIGURE 12.3

Same as Fig. 12.2, using a more aesthetic but less meaningful chart type.

where $A_n(m) = \chi[m < -g(n)] - \chi[m > g(n)]$. Here χ is the indicator function: $\chi(\omega) = 1$ if ω is true, otherwise $\chi(\omega) = 0$. Some of the identities in question include:

$$\sum_{m=-n}^{n} m \cdot p_n(m) = E[S_n] = 0, \quad \sum_{m=-n}^{n} A_n(m) p_n(m) = 0, \quad \sum_{m=-n}^{n} m^2 A_n(m) p_n(m) = 0,$$

$$\sum_{m=-n}^{n} m^2 \Big[A_{n-1}(m-1) p_{n-1}(m-1) + A_{n-1}(m+1) p_{n-1}(m+1) \Big] = 0.$$

From these identities, it is easy to establish a recursion for the variance:

$$\text{Var}[S_{n+1}] = \text{Var}[S_n] + 1 - \delta_n, \quad \text{with } \delta_n = 8\epsilon \cdot \sum_{m>g(n)} m \cdot p_n(m). \tag{12.3}$$

The sum for δ_n is finite since $p_n(m) = 0$ if $m > n$. Of course, $\text{Var}[S_0] = 0$. Also, if $\epsilon = 0$, the sequence is perfectly random: $\delta_n = 0$, $\text{Var}[S_n] = n$, and $S_n/\sqrt{n}$ converges to a normal distribution. In turn, the law of the iterated logarithm is satisfied. Conversely, this is violated if $\epsilon > 0$. Formula (12.3), combined with **Hoeffding's inequality** [Wiki], may provide some bounds for $\text{Var}[S_n]$.

Fig. 12.3 shows δ_n for four types of modified random walks, using the following color scheme:

- Yellow: $g(n) = 10$, $\epsilon = 0.05$
- Red: $g(n) = n^\beta$, $\beta = 0.50$, $\epsilon = 0.05$
- Blue: $g(n) = n^\beta$, $\beta = 0.45$, $\epsilon = 0.05$
- Purple: $g(n) = n^\beta$, $\beta = 0.55$, $\epsilon = 0.05$

The curve that coincides with the X-axis ($\delta_n = 0$) corresponds to $\epsilon = 0$, that is, to pure randomness regardless of $g(n)$. It is not colored in Fig. 12.3. Finally, the Python code in Section 12.3.1 computes $\text{Var}[S_n]$ exactly (not via simulations) using two different methods, proving that formula (12.3) is correct.

12.1.3 **Random walks with less entropy than pure random signal**

In Section 12.1.2, I focused on creating sequences with higher oscillation rates than dictated by randomness, resulting in lower amplitudes. Doing the opposite – decreasing the oscillation rate – is more difficult. For instance, using $g(n) = n^\beta$ with $\beta > \frac{1}{2}$ will not work. You cannot do better than $\sqrt{n}$ because of the law of the iterated logarithm: boosting β beyond the threshold $\frac{1}{2}$ is useless.

A workaround is to use the following algorithm:

$S = 0$
For $n = 1, 2, \ldots$
    Generate random deviate U on $[0, 1]$
    $M = g(n)$
    If $(-M < S < 0$ and $U < \frac{1}{2} + \epsilon)$ or $(0 < S < M$ and $U < \frac{1}{2} - \epsilon)$ or $(S = 0$ and $U < \frac{1}{2})$
    Then
        $X_n = -1$
    Else
        $X_n = 1$
    $S = S + X_n$
    $S_n = S$

The Python code in Section 12.3.2, with the option `deviations='Large'`, performs this simulation. The yellow time series in Fig. 12.1 is a realization of such a modified random walk, in this case with $g(n) = \alpha n^\beta$, with $\alpha = 0.30$, $\beta = 0.54$, and $\epsilon = 0.01$. It is unclear if the yellow curve will ever cross again the horizontal axis after 50,000 iterations, but it is expected to do so. To the contrary, the other three curves (gray, red, blue) are guaranteed to cross the horizontal axis infinitely many times, even though the random variable T measuring the spacing between two crossings (referred to as the **hitting time** in Section 12.1.1) has infinite expectation.

For pure random walks (the gray curve in Fig. 12.1), the average number of times that $S_k = 0$ when $0 < k \leq 2n$ is asymptotically equal to $\sqrt{4n/\pi}$, as discussed in Section 12.1.1. One would expect this value to be about 178 when $2n = 50,000$. For the gray curve, the observed value is 243. Keep in mind that huge variations are expected between different realizations of the same random walk, due to the fact that $E[T] = \infty$. Indeed, averaged over three realizations, the value 243 was down to 185. Also, a faulty pseudorandom number generator could easily lead to results that are off, in this case.

One would expect much larger values for the "nonrandom" red and blue curves. The observed values are respectively 747 and 1783, based on a single realization in each case. Likewise, the yellow curve is expected to have a much smaller value: in Fig. 12.1, that value is 105.

12.2 **Related stochastic processes**

There are countless types of random walks or quasi-Brownian motions that are – on purpose and by design – not perfectly random. One could write an encyclopedia on this topic. A good reference is the book by Mörters and Peres [8], published in 2010. My goal in this section is to present two examples (one in two dimensions) that are very recent, interesting, and related to the material discussed in Section 12.1. I built these stochastic processes in the last two years, to address modeling issues with fintech applications in mind.

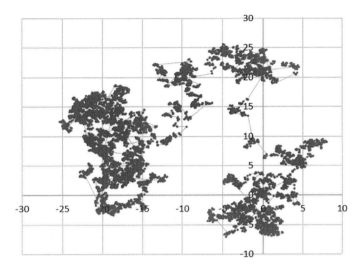

FIGURE 12.4

Clustered Brownian process.

12.2.1 **From Brownian motions to clustered Lévy flights**

Here I discuss a 2D Brownian motion generated using some specific probability distributions. Depending on the parameters, these distributions may or may not have an infinite expectation or variance. Things start to get interesting when the expectation becomes infinite (and the Brownian motion is no longer Brownian), resulting in a system exhibiting a strong clustering structure.

In some sense, it is similar to the examples studied earlier, where moving away from the law of the iterated logarithm resulted in unusual patterns: either very strong or very weak oscillations. Note that all the simulations performed here consist of discrete random walks rather than time-continuous Brownian motions. They approach Brownian motions very well, but since modern computers (at least to this date) are "digital" as opposed to "analog", everything is broken down into bits, and is thus discrete, albeit with a huge granularity.

In one dimension, we start with $S_0 = 0$ and $S_n = S_{n-1} + R_n \theta_n$, for $n = 1, 2$, and so on. If the R_n's are independently and identically distributed (iid) with an exponential distribution of expectation $1/\lambda$ and $\theta_n = 1$, then the resulting process is a stationary **Poisson point process** [Wiki] with intensity function λ on $\mathbb{R}^+$; the R_n's are the successive **interarrival times**. If the θ_n's are iid with $P(\theta_n = 1) = P(\theta_n = -1) = \frac{1}{2}$, and independent from the R_n's, then we get a totally different type of process, which, after proper rescaling, represents a time-continuous **Brownian motion** in one dimension. For general references, see [2,3].

I generalize it to two dimensions, as follows. Start with $(S_0, S_0') = (0, 0)$. Then generate the points (S_n, S_n'), with $n = 1, 2$, and so on, using the recursion

$$S_n = S_{n-1} + R_n \cos(2\pi \theta_n), \tag{12.4}$$

$$S_n' = S_{n-1}' + R_n \sin(2\pi \theta_n), \tag{12.5}$$

where θ_n is uniform on $[0, 1]$, and the radius R_n is generated using the formula

$$R_n = \frac{1}{\lambda}\left(-\log(1 - U_n)\right)^{\gamma}, \tag{12.6}$$

where U_n is uniform on $[0, 1]$. Also, $\lambda > 0$, and the random variables U_n, θ_n are all independently distributed. If $\gamma > -1$, then $E[R_n] = \frac{1}{\lambda}\Gamma(1 + \gamma)$ where Γ is the **gamma function** [Wiki]. In order to standardize the process, I use $\lambda = \Gamma(1 + \gamma)$. Thus, $E[R_n] = 1$ and if $\gamma > -\frac{1}{2}$,

$$\text{Var}[R_n] = \frac{\Gamma(1 + 2\gamma)}{\Gamma^2(1 + \gamma)} - 1.$$

We have the following cases:

- If $\gamma = 1$, then R_n has an exponential distribution.
- If $-1 < \gamma < 0$, then R_n has a **Fréchet distribution**. If in addition, $\gamma > -\frac{1}{2}$, then its variance is finite.
- If $\gamma > 0$, then R_n has a **Weibull distribution**, with finite variance.

Interestingly, the Fréchet and Weibull distributions are two of the three **attractor distributions** in **extreme value theory**.

The two-dimensional process consisting of the points (S_n, S_n') is a particular type of random walk. The random variables R_n represent the (variable) lengths of the successive increments. Under proper rescaling, assuming the variance of R_n is finite, it tends to a time-continuous two-dimensional Brownian motion. However, if $\text{Var}[R_n] = \infty$, it may not converge to a Brownian motion. Instead, it is very similar to a **Lévy flight** [Wiki], and produces a strong cluster structure, with well separated clusters. See Fig. 12.4, based on $\gamma = -\frac{1}{2}$, $\lambda = 8$, and featuring the first 10,000 points of the bivariate sequence $\{(S_n, S_n')\}$.

The Lévy flight uses a **Lévy distribution** [Wiki] for R_n, which also has infinite expectation and variance. Along with the **Cauchy distribution** (also with infinite expectation and variance), it is one of the few **stable distributions** [Wiki]. Such distributions are attractors for an adapted version of the **Central Limit Theorem** (CLT), just like the Gaussian distribution is the attractor for the CLT. A well-written, seminal book on the topic is "Limit Distributions for Sums of Independent Random Variables", by Gnedenko and Kolmogorov [5].

For a simple introduction to Brownian and related processes, see the website RandomServices.org by Kyle Siegrist, especially the chapter on standard Brownian motions, here. The processes discussed in Section 12.2.1 are further investigated in my book "Stochastic Processes and Simulations: A Machine Learning Perspective" [7].

12.2.2 Integrated Brownian motions and special autoregressive processes

The Brownian motions pictured in Fig. 12.5 are generated by simple time-discrete **autoregressive time series** [Wiki]. Thus, the base process is autocorrelated, but the limit (after rescaling) is still a standard Brownian motion and thus perfectly random, if the autocorrelation structure is weak enough.

This autoregressive (AR) model is driven initial conditions $S_1, \ldots, S_p$ and the recursion

$$S_n = a_1 S_{n-1} + \cdots + a_p S_{n-p} + e_n,$$

where $a_1, \ldots, a_p$ are real coefficients satisfying some conditions to guarantee **stationarity**. By choice, the sequence $\{e_n\}$ is a **white noise**: $E[e_n] = 0$, $Var[e_n] = \sigma^2$ is fixed (it does not depend on n), and the e_n's are independently and identically distributed.

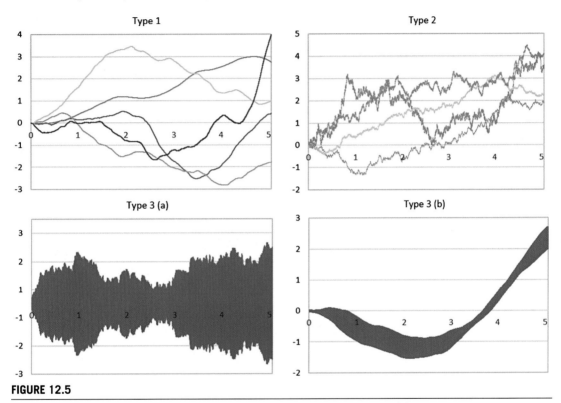

FIGURE 12.5

AR models, classified based on the types of roots of the characteristic polynomial.

The behavior of this process, and thus of the resulting Brownian motions pictured in Fig. 12.5, is determined by the roots of its **characteristic polynomial** of degree p,

$$x^p = a_1 x^{p-1} + a_2 x^{p-2} + \cdots + a_{p-1} x + a_p.$$

These roots can be real or complex, and simple or multiple. A borderline case, as far as stationarity is concerned, is when the root with highest modulus has a **modulus** equal to 1. If the modulus in question is above 1, the process is no longer stationary. The modulus of a real number a is its absolute value $|a|$, and for a complex number $a + bi$, it is defined as $\sqrt{a^2 + b^2}$. If in addition the root with largest modulus is multiple, then something unusual happens: the resulting Brownian motion is very smooth and is not a Brownian motion anymore. It becomes is an integrated Brownian motion; its derivative is a Brownian motion. See the top left plot in Fig. 12.5. The other plots in the same figure correspond to other awkward situations, regarding the roots of the characteristic polynomials and the resulting behavior. This is discussed in detail in Chapter 3 on linear algebra.

12.3 Python code

Section 12.3.1 covers the exact computation of the variances, while Section 12.3.2 focuses on simulations: generating realizations of the sequence $\{S_n\}$, for various types of quasirandom walks described in Section 12.1.

12.3.1 Computing probabilities and variances attached to S_n

This Python code is related to Section 12.1.2.2, where you can find more details. It computes the variance of S_n for $n = 1, 2$, and so on, using two different methods: one based on the standard definition of the variance (denoted as var1 in the code), and the other based on formula (12.3). The latter is denoted as var2 in the code. Also, the variable delta represents δ_n. The output δ_n is featured in Fig. 12.2. Finally, the function G represents $g(n)$. The code below is also available on Github, here. Program name is brownian_var.py.

```python
import math

epsilon=0.05
beta=0.45
alpha=1.00
nMax=5001

Prob={}
Exp={}
Var={}
Prob[(0,0)] =1
Prob[(0,-1)]=0
Prob[(0,1)] =0
Prob[(0,-2)]=0
Prob[(0,2)] =0

def G(n):
 return(alpha*(n**beta))

def psi(n,m):
  p=0.0
  if m>G(n):
    p=-1
  if m<-G(n):
    p=1
  return(p)

Exp[0]=0
Var[0]=0
OUT=open("rndproba.txt","w")
for n in range(1,nMax):
  Exp[n]=0
```

```
     Var[n]=0
     delta=0
     for m in range(-n-2,n+3,1):
       Prob[(n,m)]=0
     for m in range(-n,n+1,1):
       Prob[(n,m)]=(0.5+epsilon*psi(n-1,m-1))*Prob[(n-1,m-1)]\
         +(0.5-epsilon*psi(n-1,m+1))*Prob[(n-1,m+1)]
       Exp[n]=Exp[n]+m*Prob[(n,m)]
       Var[n]=Var[n]+m*m*Prob[(n,m)]
       if m>G(n-1) and m<n:
         delta=delta+8*epsilon*m*Prob[(n-1,m)]
     var1=Var[n]
     var2=Var[n-1]+1-delta
     string1=("%5d %.6f %.6f %.6f" % (n,var1,var2,delta))
     string2=("%5d\t%.6f\t%.6f\t%.6f\n" % (n,var1,var2,delta))
     print(string1)
     OUT.write(string2)
OUT.close()
```

12.3.2 Path simulations

This Python code performs all the simulations discussed in Sections 12.1.2.2 and 12.1.3 and shown in Fig. 12.1. The option deviations='Small' is discussed in detail in Section 12.1.2.2, while deviations='Large' is explained in Section 12.1.3. The function G in the code corresponds to $g(n)$. Also, if you want to simulate a perfectly random walk, set ϵ (the parameter eps in the code) to zero. Finally, the code generates multiple realizations for any type of random walk. The number of realizations is determined by the parameter Nsample. The code below is also available on Github, here. Program name is brownian_path.py.

```
import random
import math
random.seed(1)

n=50000
Nsample=1
deviations='Large'
mode='Power'

if deviations=='Large':
  eps=0.01
  beta=0.54
  alpha=0.3
elif deviations=='Small':
  eps=0.05
  beta=0.35 #beta = 1 for log
  alpha=1
```

```
def G(n):
  if mode=='Power':
    return(alpha*(n**beta))
  elif mode=='Log' and n>0:
    return(alpha*(math.log(n)**beta))
  else:
    return(0)

OUT=open("rndtest.txt","w")
for sample in range(Nsample):
  print("Sample: ",sample)
  S=0
  for k in range(1,n):
    x=1
    rnd=random.random()
    M=G(k)
    if deviations=='Large':
      if ((S>=-M and S<0 and rnd<0.5+eps) or (S<=M and S>0 and rnd<0.5-eps) or
        (abs(S)>=M and rnd<0.5) or (S==0 and rnd<0.5)):
        x=-1
    elif deviations=='Small':
      if (S<-M and rnd<0.5-eps) or (S>M and rnd<0.5+eps) or (abs(S)<=M and rnd<0.5):
        x=-1
    print(k,M,S,x)
    S=S+x
    line=str(sample)+"\t"+str(k)+"\t"+str(S)+"\t"+str(x)+"\n"
    OUT.write(line)
OUT.close()
```

References

[1] R. Bhattacharya, E. Waymire, Random Walk, Brownian Motion, and Martingales, Springer, 2021.

[2] D.J. Daley, D. Vere-Jones, An Introduction to the Theory of Point Processes. Volume 1 – Elementary Theory and Methods, second edition, Springer, 2002.

[3] D.J. Daley, D. Vere-Jones, An Introduction to the Theory of Point Processes. Volume 2 – General Theory and Structure, second edition, Springer, 2014.

[4] P.A. Van Der Geest, The binomial distribution with dependent Bernoulli trials, Journal of Statistical Computation and Simulation (2004) 141–154, [Link].

[5] B.V. Gnedenko, A.N. Kolmogorov, Limit Distributions for Sums of Independent Random Variables, Addison-Wesley, 1954.

[6] M. González-Navarrete, R. Lambert, Non-Markovian random walks with memory lapses, Preprint, pp. 1–14, 2018, arXiv, [Link].

[7] V. Granville, Stochastic Processes and Simulations: A Machine Learning Perspective, MLTechniques.com, 2022, [Link].

[8] P. Mörters, Y. Peres, Brownian Motion, Cambridge Series in Statistical and Probabilistic Mathematics, vol. 30, Cambridge University Press, 2010, [Link].

[9] L. Wua, Y. Qi, J. Yang, Asymptotics for dependent Bernoulli random variables, Statistics & Probability Letters (2012) 455–463, [Link].

Divergent optimization algorithm and synthetic functions

13

When all else fails

In this chapter, I discuss an unusual optimization algorithm. Why would anyone be interested in an algorithm that never converges to the solution you are looking for? This version of the fixed-point iteration, when approaching a zero or an optimum, emits a strong signal and allows you to detect a small interval likely to contain the solution: the zero or global optimum in question. It may approach the optimum quite well, but subsequent iterations do not lead to convergence: the algorithm eventually moves away from the optimum, or oscillates around the optimum without ever reaching it.

The **fixed-point iteration** [Wiki] is the mother of all optimization and root-finding algorithms. In particular, all **gradient-based** optimization techniques [Wiki] are a particular version of this generic method. In this chapter, I use it in a very challenging setting. The target function may not be differentiable or may have a very large number of local minima and maxima. All the standard techniques fail to detect the global optima. In this case, even the fixed-point method diverges. However, somehow, it can tell you the location of a global optimum with a rather decent precision. Once an approximation is obtained, the method can be applied again, this time focusing around a narrow interval containing the solution to achieve higher precision. Also, this method is a lot faster than brute force such as **grid search**.

I first illustrate the method on a specific problem. Then, generating synthetic data that emulates and generalizes the setting of the initial problem, I illustrate how the method performs on different functions or data sets. The purpose is to show how synthetic data can be used to test and benchmark algorithms, or to understand when they work, and when they do not. This, combined with the intuitive aspects of my fixed-point iteration, illustrates a particular facet of explainable AI. Finally, I use a smoothing technique to visualize the highly chaotic functions involved here. It highlights the features of the functions that we are interested in, while removing the massive noise that makes these functions almost impossible to visualize in any meaningful way.

13.1 Introduction

While the technique discussed here is a last resort solution when all else fails, it is actually more powerful than it seems at first glance. First, it also works in standard cases with "nice" functions. However, there are better methods when the function behaves nicely, taking advantage of the differentiability of the function in question, such as the **Newton algorithm** [Wiki] (itself a fixed-point iteration). It can be generalized to higher dimensions, though I focus on univariate functions here.

Perhaps the attractive features are the fact that it is simple and intuitive, and quickly leads to a solution despite the absence of convergence. However, it is an empirical method and may require working

Synthetic Data and Generative AI. https://doi.org/10.1016/B978-0-44-321857-6.00017-5

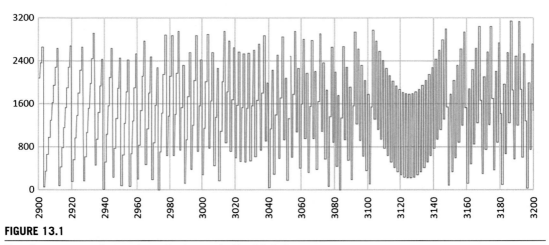

FIGURE 13.1

Function $f(b)$ as a better alternative to $g(b)$ in Fig. 13.2. Root at $b = 3083$.

with different parameter sets to actually find a solution. Still, it can be turned into a black-box solution by automatically testing different parameter configurations. In that respect, I compare it to the empirical **elbow rule** to detect the number of clusters in unsupervised clustering problems. I discuss the elbow rule and its automation in Section 18.6. Another fixed-point algorithm leading to explainable AI in the context of linear regression is discussed in Section 7.1.

13.1.1 The problem, with illustration

The method can solve two types of problems: finding the zeros of a function, or its optima (maxima or minima). Optima correspond to a zero of the derivative, so finding them is a root-finding problem. In my example, the functions typically have multiple global minima that we want to detect. The initial problem is to find a factor b of a large integer number a. Here a is fixed, and the function is denoted as $f(b)$ with $f(b) = 0$ if and only if b is such a factor (integer number) different from 1 and a. If b is not a factor, then $f(b) > 0$. Initially, the interest was to factor a number that is a product of two large primes, as this has implications in cryptography. However, the technique led to a much larger class of applications where it has much more value than for factoring integers.

The first step was to change the problem setting: extending the function $f(b)$ which accepts an integer argument b, into a continuous function where b is a real number. Here $f(b) = a \bmod b$. So to get a continuous extension, one has to define the modulo operator for arguments b that are not integer numbers. Finally, it led to

$$f(b) = a - \lfloor b + \epsilon \rfloor \left\lfloor \epsilon + \frac{a}{\lfloor b + \epsilon \rfloor} \right\rfloor, \quad b > 0. \tag{13.1}$$

The brackets represent the integer part function, and $\epsilon = 0$. However, in the code, $\epsilon = 10^{-8}$ to avoid problems caused by numerical precision. Formula (13.1) defines the base function, denoted as `fmod` in the Python code. It is a piecewise constant function, pictured in Fig. 13.1 between $b = 2900$ and $b = 3200$, using $a = 3083 \times 7919$. Thus the interval $[2900, 3200]$ contains the root $b = 3083$. There

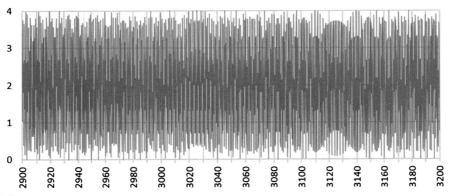

FIGURE 13.2

Function $g(b) = 2 - \cos(2\pi b) - \cos(2\pi a/b)$, with $a = 3083 \times 7919$.

are no other roots besides 3083 and 7919 since these two integers are prime numbers. Also note that $0 \le f(b) < b$. Optimization methods based on the gradient are guaranteed not to work here.

Note that instead of $f(b)$, I could have used $g(b) = 2 - \cos(2\pi b) - \cos(2\pi a/b)$. This function is also positive and equal to zero only if b is an integer number that divides the integer a. In addition, g is bounded with $0 \le g(b) \le 4$, and infinitely differentiable. Yet it has a very large number of local minima and maxima: the frequency of oscillations is insanely high. For all purposes, g is just as chaotic of f, indeed worse than f, and no standard optimization algorithm could handle it. The function g is pictured in Fig. 13.2.

13.2 Nonconverging fixed-point algorithm

In this section, I start with the function $f(b)$ defined by formula (13.1). I investigate a larger class of functions in Section 13.3. The trick is to massively amplify the zero, creating ripple effects that the fixed point iteration can leverage to narrow down on the solution. In the end, instead of looking at convergence (absent here), you look at the strength of a signal ρ_n at iterations $n = 1, 2$, and so on. The value of ρ_n is typically close to 1, but high values (above 2) indicate that something unusual is happening. Typically, such high values are created when stepping over a root.

13.2.1 Trick leading to intuitive solution

Let us assume that f is positive and that its minimum value is zero. If f takes on negative values, replace $f(b)$ by the absolute value $|f(b)|$ or by the square $f^2(b)$. This works both in root-finding and optimization problems. In optimization, f is the derivative of the target function. The base function f (or its absolute value or square) is denoted as f_0.

The goal is to apply successive transformations to make the function f_0 more amenable to root detection. The first transformation consists of taking the logarithm, thus creating a vertical bottomless abyss in the graph of the function, around any root. In practice, it is implemented as follows: the new

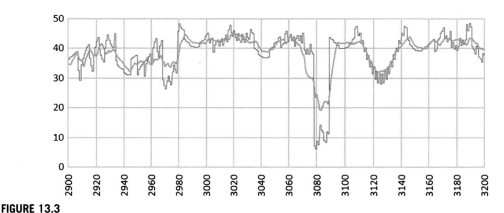

FIGURE 13.3

Transformed function f_3, amplifying the root at $b = 3083$.

function is simply

$$f_1(b) = \max \left[\log(f_0(b)), \delta \right],$$

where δ is a negative number, large enough in absolute value. In the Python code, δ is represented by `logeps`, and set to -10. This parameter controls the depth of the abyss, that now has a bottom. It helps discriminate between a value very close to zero, and a value exactly equal to zero. For instance, if $f_0(b) = 0.01$, then $f_1(b) = -4.61$, while if $f_0(b) = 0$, then $f_1(b) = -10$.

The second step consists in enlarging the abyss. Its walls will change from vertical to inclined. The width of the abyss, and the slope of its walls, is controlled by the parameter `window` in the Python code, and referred to here as w. In a nutshell, this transformation is a **moving average** applied to f_1. The resulting function is

$$f_2(b) = \frac{1}{2w+1} \sum_{k=-w}^{w} f_1(b + kh).$$

The increment h is set to 1 as it makes sense in my particular problem. I did not test other values.

The third step is a linear transformation, turning f_2 into f_3, with $f_3(b) = p + qf_2(b)$. The parameters p and q are respectively denoted as `offset` and `slope` in the Python code. The functions f_0, f_1, and f_3 are respectively denoted as `fmod`, `fmod2`, and `fresidue` in the Python code. The blue curve (dark gray in print version) in Fig. 13.3 is the f_3 transform associated to the f_0 function pictured in Fig. 13.1, with $p = -100$ and $q = 20$. Subsequent transformations discussed in Section 13.4 are done only for embellishment, and are irrelevant to the fixed point algorithm.

13.2.2 Root detection: method and parameters

The fixed-point algorithm starts with an initial value b_0, and then proceeds iteratively as follows:

$$b_{n+1} = b_n + \mu f(b_n). \tag{13.2}$$

If the sequence (b_n) converges, the function f is continuous and $\mu \neq 0$, then b_n must converge to some b^* such that $f(b^*) = 0$, thus b_n converges to a root of f. You can allow μ to depend on n, and in one example I successfully used $\mu = 1/\sqrt{b_n}$. The function f used here is actually the function f_3 defined in Section 13.2.1 and pictured in blue (dark gray in print version) in Fig. 13.3. This function is not even continuous, and the fixed point iteration does not converge. Other functions are investigated in Section 13.3. Here, the purpose is to explain how the fixed point iteration can help find a root despite the lack of convergence.

Many of the parameters in the Python code are described in Section 13.2.1, including offset, slope, and logeps. The parameter eps corresponds to ϵ in Section 13.1.1. The main parameters driving the fixed-point iteration are:

- mu, corresponding to μ in formula (13.2). A large value results in bigger jumps in the fixed point iteration, allowing you to find a root faster, but with an increased risk of missing all roots when μ becomes too large.
- window, corresponding to w in Section 13.2.1. A large w increases your chances of finding a root. The price to pay is reduced precision. If b^* is a root and the fixed point iteration succeeds in locating it, it will not find b^*, but instead, it will tell you that there might be a root in the interval $[b^* - w, b^* + w]$, without knowing what the actual b^* is. Thus a large w is useful to get a rough approximation of where a root is located.

I illustrate these features, as well as how fast this algorithm is compared to brute force, on a real example in Section 13.2.3. The algorithm does not converge with the type of functions discussed here: the successive iterates b_n become larger and larger as n increases, or they may oscillate without ever converging. Of course, if the function is smooth enough and with the right parameters, it will converge. But we are not interested in that case.

Since there is no convergence in my examples, how can the algorithm detect a root? Now I explain how it works. First, define $\Delta_n = b_n - b_{n-1}$. Then let $\rho_n = \Delta_n/\Delta_{n-1}$. The number ρ_n is called the **signal** at iteration n. Usually, $\rho_n \approx 1$. If ρ_n is unusually low or high, we say that the signal is strong. In my examples, a value $\rho_n > 2$ usually means that there is a root close to b_{n-1}. Details are discussed in Section 13.2.3.

Finally, the functions investigated here have many values close to zero. The brute force method consisting of testing a very large number of values may not even work. In most cases, finding b such that $f_0(b) = 0.001$ does not mean that there is a b^* close to b such that $f_0(b^*) = 0$. For the same reason, the efficient but naive **bisection method** [Wiki] will also fail. Note that my method is empirical: a strong signal does not always correspond to a root, and the absence of strong signal does not mean that there is no root. Testing with different parameter sets helps.

13.2.3 Case study: factoring a product of two large primes

The goal here is to find at least one of the two roots of the function $f_0(b)$ pictured in Fig. 13.1, and defined by (13.1). Using the transformations described in Section 13.2.1, I will actually work with the third transform $f_3(b)$ in the fixed point iteration (formula (13.2)), starting with $b_0 = 2000$. The two roots are the two prime factors of $a = 7919 \times 3083$, that is, $b^* = 3083$ and $b^* = 7919$. So finding one root makes it straightforward to find the other.

Finding the roots of f_0 is the same as finding the roots of $g(b) = 2 - \cos(2\pi b) - \cos(2\pi a/b)$ pictured in Fig. 13.2. The parameters values are those in the Python code in Section 13.3.3. The results

Table 13.1 High ρ_n at iterations $n = 31$ and $n = 127$ points to roots 3083 and 7919.

n	b_n	Δ_n	ρ_n	n	b_n	Δ_n	ρ_n	n	b_n	Δ_n	ρ_n
1	2033.70	33.70	–	46	3740.11	48.99	0.79	91	5940.08	58.20	0.89
2	2070.73	37.02	0.91	47	3787.29	47.18	1.04	92	5996.05	55.97	1.04
3	2105.69	34.96	1.06	48	3833.88	46.58	1.01	93	6044.88	48.83	1.15
4	2143.15	37.47	0.93	49	3880.82	46.95	0.99	94	6094.87	50.00	0.98
5	2177.58	34.43	1.09	50	3929.45	48.62	0.97	95	6158.31	63.43	0.79
6	2211.57	33.98	1.01	51	3974.72	45.27	1.07	96	6200.89	42.58	1.49
7	2234.25	22.68	1.50	52	4021.53	46.81	0.97	97	6257.29	56.40	0.75
8	2263.00	28.75	0.79	53	4066.34	44.81	1.04	98	6308.72	51.43	1.10
9	2300.72	37.72	0.76	54	4109.76	43.42	1.03	99	6368.62	59.90	0.86
10	2332.77	32.05	1.18	55	4146.40	36.64	1.18	100	6426.70	58.08	1.03
11	2372.61	39.84	0.80	56	4196.55	50.15	0.73	101	6482.41	55.70	1.04
12	2396.52	23.91	1.67	57	4240.43	43.88	1.14	102	6538.13	55.72	1.00
13	2435.08	38.56	0.62	58	4283.13	42.70	1.03	103	6593.53	55.40	1.01
14	2469.07	33.99	1.13	59	4339.39	56.26	0.76	104	6651.41	57.89	0.96
15	2503.82	34.75	0.98	60	4379.64	40.25	1.40	105	6705.05	53.64	1.08
16	2536.48	32.65	1.06	61	4427.22	47.58	0.85	106	6760.28	55.23	0.97
17	2572.00	35.53	0.92	62	4475.73	48.51	0.98	107	6816.19	55.91	0.99
18	2609.43	37.42	0.95	63	4525.94	50.22	0.97	108	6873.41	57.22	0.98
19	2650.28	40.86	0.92	64	4575.57	49.63	1.01	109	6931.39	57.98	0.99
20	2692.95	42.67	0.96	65	4627.85	52.28	0.95	110	6980.78	49.39	1.17
21	2731.07	38.12	1.12	66	4674.64	46.79	1.12	111	7039.95	59.18	0.83
22	2771.50	40.43	0.94	67	4721.67	47.04	0.99	112	7108.67	68.72	0.86
23	2802.76	31.26	1.29	68	4771.85	50.17	0.94	113	7168.63	59.96	1.15
24	2844.27	41.51	0.75	69	4813.86	42.01	1.19	114	7220.86	52.23	1.15
25	2889.18	44.90	0.92	70	4871.29	57.43	0.73	115	7274.43	53.57	0.98
26	2924.68	35.50	1.26	71	4901.82	30.53	1.88	116	7336.46	62.02	0.86
27	2961.03	36.35	0.98	72	4957.42	55.60	0.55	117	7390.45	53.99	1.15
28	3001.25	40.22	0.90	73	4996.69	39.27	1.42	118	7449.19	58.74	0.92
29	3046.38	45.13	0.89	74	5061.62	64.93	0.60	119	7510.73	61.55	0.95
30	3086.18	39.80	1.13	75	5101.22	39.59	1.64	120	7565.90	55.17	1.12
31	3094.62	8.44	4.72	76	5149.52	48.30	0.82	121	7628.20	62.30	0.89
32	3135.72	41.10	0.21	77	5206.31	56.79	0.85	122	7688.69	60.49	1.03
33	3172.01	36.29	1.13	78	5255.88	49.57	1.15	123	7750.83	62.15	0.97
34	3216.43	44.42	0.82	79	5306.17	50.30	0.99	124	7802.41	51.58	1.20
35	3259.84	43.41	1.02	80	5365.49	59.31	0.85	125	7855.95	53.54	0.96
36	3303.38	43.54	1.00	81	5416.54	51.06	1.16	126	7915.67	59.72	0.90
37	3343.08	39.70	1.10	82	5472.24	55.69	0.92	127	7945.56	29.89	2.00
38	3384.42	41.34	0.96	83	5524.53	52.30	1.06	128	8008.42	62.85	0.48
39	3422.90	38.48	1.07	84	5577.40	52.87	0.99	129	8072.94	64.52	0.97
40	3468.43	45.53	0.85	85	5629.32	51.92	1.02	130	8131.86	58.93	1.09
41	3510.77	42.34	1.08	86	5672.84	43.52	1.19	131	8194.84	62.98	0.94
42	3565.04	54.26	0.78	87	5724.36	51.52	0.84	132	8258.05	63.21	1.00
43	3603.60	38.57	1.41	88	5777.10	52.74	0.98	133	8312.50	54.45	1.16
44	3652.45	48.85	0.79	89	5829.89	52.79	1.00				
45	3691.12	38.66	1.26	90	5881.87	51.98	1.02				

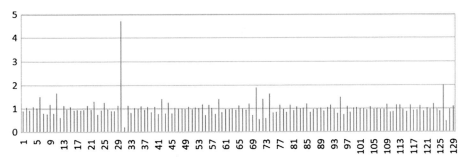

FIGURE 13.4

Signal strength ρ_n, first 130 fixed-point iterations; $n = 31$ leads to a root.

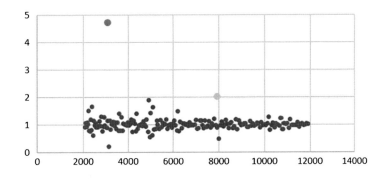

FIGURE 13.5

Plot of (b_n, ρ_n). Yellow (light gray in print version) and orange (mid gray in print version) dots linked to roots.

are displayed in Table 13.1, Fig. 13.4 and 13.5. The root $b^* = 3083$ is detected at iteration $n = 31$. Since $\rho_{31} = 4.72$ is exceptionally high, there is a strong possibility that the algorithm stepped over a root in the previous iteration ($n = 30$). Indeed, $b_{30} = 3086.18$ is close to the root $b^* = 3083$. What the algorithm tells is that there is probably a root in the interval $[b_{30} - w, b_{30} + w]$ where w is the size of the window (the parameter `window` in the Python code) set to 5 here.

At this point, after testing $b = 3081, 3082$, and 3083 to find the root, one can stop the algorithm. It does not converge anyway: b_n is getting bigger and bigger, faster and faster, as shown in Table 13.1. The second root is simply $b^* = 7919 = a/3083$. Surprisingly though, at iteration $n = 127$, there is another spike, namely $\rho_{127} = 2.00$. Again, $b_{126} = 7915.67$ is close to the second root $b^* = 7919$. There is another, weaker spike at $n = 71$, with $\rho_{71} = 1.88$. This one is a false positive.

13.3 Generalization with synthetic random functions

Perhaps the synthetic example most closely resembling $f_0(b) = a \bmod b$ discussed in Section 13.2.2 is $f_0(b) = \lfloor bU_b \rfloor$ where the U_b's are independent random deviates on $[0, 1]$. The major difference is the independence assumption. For $a \bmod b$, the residues somewhat behave as if they were independent (assuming the b's are integers and a is fixed), but they are not really independent. To use $f_0(b) = \lfloor bU_b \rfloor$, set `mode='Random'` in the Python code.

13.3.1 Example

Unlike in the example based on a product of two primes, now the **random function** $f_0(b)$ has infinitely many roots. They are more and more spaced out as b increases. In this example, with the seed of the random generator set to `seed=105`, the first few roots are

$$5646, \quad 15156, \quad 59004, \quad 122345, \quad 689987, \quad 1021037, \quad 1186047, \quad 2829138.$$

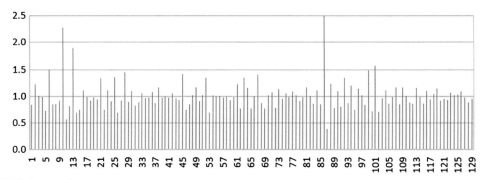

FIGURE 13.6

Signal strength ρ_n, first 130 fixed-point iterations; $n = 87$ leads to a root.

The statistical distribution of the roots and the number of expected roots in any given interval is studied in Section 13.3.2. I used the same Python code with same parameters as in Section 13.2.3, also starting with $b_0 = 2000$. This time, at iteration $n = 87$, we have $\rho_n = 2.52$ which is extremely high. Again, this points to a root at iteration $n - 1$, with $b_{86} = 5650.48$. The actual root is $b^* = 5646$. It could be anywhere between $b_{86} - w$ and $b_{86} + w$, with w set to 5 in this case, via `window=5`. So it suffices to test $b = 5645$ and $b = 5646$ to find the root. The values of ρ_n for successive iterations of the fixed point algorithm, between $n = 1$ and $n = 130$, are displayed in Fig. 13.6.

With the current parameters, the algorithm misses the next root $b^* = 15156$. Decreasing μ or increasing w (or a combination of both that minimizes the number of required iterations) may lead to that root, most likely in more than 100 iterations. Note that high values of ρ_n are also found at $n = 11$ and $n = 14$, respectively $\rho_{11} = 2.28$ and $\rho_{14} = 1.90$. These are false positives and can easily be ruled out. It is unusual to reach a root in as few as 20 iterations for this kind of problem, especially when starting far away from the root.

Fig. 13.7 features the random function discussed in this section, with a visible absolute minimum around $b = 5646$ both for the blue (dark gray in print version) and orange (mid gray in print version) curves, but invisible (although present) for the initial function f_0 in red (light gray in print version). Here $b \in [5500, 5800]$. The blue (dark gray in print version) curve is the transformed version of f_0, referred to as f_3, while the orange (mid gray in print version) curve is the result after additional smoothing discussed in Section 13.4. The vertical axis for the blue (dark gray in print version) and orange (mid gray in print version) curves is on the left. For the red (light gray in print version) curve, it is on the right.

13.3.2 Connection to the Poisson–binomial distribution

Depending on the sequence of random deviates (U_b), the new function f_0 may have zero, one, or more than one integer root in any specific interval $[s, t]$. The expected number of integer roots is a random variable $N(s, t)$ with a **Poisson–binomial distribution** [Wiki]. Assuming s and t are integers, the expectation, variance, and probability of no root are respectively

$$\mathrm{E}[N(s,t)] = \sum_{k=s}^{t} \frac{1}{k}, \quad \mathrm{Var}[N(s,t)] = \sum_{k=s}^{t} \frac{1}{k}\left(1 - \frac{1}{k}\right), \quad P[N(s,t) = 0] = \prod_{k=s}^{t} \left(1 - \frac{1}{k}\right).$$

When s, t are very large and $t/s \to \lambda$, the Poisson–binomial distribution is well approximated by a Poisson distribution of expectation $\log \lambda$. A proof of this advanced result (not even taught in graduate classes) can be found in my book on stochastic processes [1], in Section 2.3.1. This result generalizes the well-known convergence of Binomial to Poisson distribution under some assumptions. It is a particular case of **Le Cam's inequality** [Wiki]; see also [2].

Applied to the problem in Section 13.2.2 with $f_0(b) = a \bmod b$, with $b \in [2900, 3200]$, the chance to find at least one root in that interval is approximately $1 - \exp(-\log \lambda) = 1 - 1/\lambda$. Since $\lambda = t/s$ with $s = 2900$, $t = 3200$, the chance in question is about 9.4%. Note that $t < \sqrt{a}$. In general, this condition is required for the result to be valid. The absence of root in the interval $[2, \sqrt{a}]$ would mean that a is a prime number.

13.3.2.1 *Location of the next root: guesstimate*

Let T_s be the location of the first root larger than s. I am interested in the ratio $R_s = T_s/s > 1$. From the previous discussion, the distribution of successive roots approximately follows a **nonhomogeneous Poisson process** when s is large. It is easy to prove that R_s has an infinite expectation. However, $\log R_s$ has a finite expectation. Let us compute it, using the Poisson approximation. We have

$$P(\log R_s > \tau) = P[T_s > s \exp(\tau)] = \exp(-\tau).$$

Thus,

$$\mathrm{E}[\log R_s] = \int_0^{\infty} \exp(-\tau)d\tau = 1.$$

So, given a root $b^* > 2000$, one would expect the next one to be of the order $e \cdot b^*$, with $e = 2.718\ldots$ This is consistent with the successive roots displayed at the beginning in Section 13.3.1.

13.3.2.2 *Integer sequences with high density of primes*

The Poisson–binomial distribution, including its Poisson approximation, can also be used in this context. The purpose is to find fast-growing integer sequences with a very high density of primes, see here.

The probability for a large integer a to be prime is about $1/\log a$, a consequence of the prime number theorem [Wiki]. Let $a_1, a_2, \ldots$ be a strictly increasing sequence of positive integers, and N

denote the number of primes among $a_n, a_{n+1}, \ldots, a_{n+m}$ for some large n. Assuming the sequence is independently and congruentially equidistributed, then N has a Poisson–binomial distribution of parameters $p_n, \ldots, p_{n+m}$, with $p_k = 1/\log a_k$. It is unimportant to know the exact definition of congruential equidistribution. Roughly speaking, it means that the joint empirical distribution of residues across the a_k's, is asymptotically indistinguishable from that of a sequence of random integers. Thus a sequence where 60% of the terms are odd integers does not qualify (that proportion should be 50%).

This result is used to assess whether a given sequence of integers is unusually rich, or poor, in primes. If it contains far more large primes than the expected value $p_n + \cdots + p_{n+m}$, then we are dealing with a very interesting, hard-to-find sequence, useful both in cryptographic applications and for its own sake. One can build confidence intervals for the number of such primes, based on the Poisson–binomial distribution under the assumption of independence and congruential equidistribution. A famous example of such a sequence (rich in prime numbers) is $a_k = k^2 - k + 41$ [Wiki]. If $n, m \to \infty$ and $p_n^2 + \cdots + p_{n+m}^2 \to 0$, then the distribution of N is well approximated by a Poisson distribution, thanks to Le Cam's theorem.

13.3.3 Python code: finding the optimum

This Python code performs the transformations from f_0 to f_3 as described in Section 13.2.1 and run the fixed point algorithm on f_3 to find a minimum of f_3, and thus a root of f_0. The parameters are described in Section 13.2.2. The case `mode='Prime'` corresponds to the example discussed in Section 13.2.3, while the case `mode='Random'` corresponds to the random function studied in Section 13.3.1. The results are saved in a tab-separated text file `rmodb.txt`. The full version with curve smoothing, tabulation, and saving the values of the various transforms is in Section 13.4.

A potential improvement is to handle the situation when b_n decreases to the point of becoming negative. Also, the values of $f_0(b)$ and $f_3(b)$ are not stored in some array or hash table, but instead computed on the fly. Some may be computed multiple times, and the code is not efficient in that regard. This is particularly true if the parameter `window` is large.

```
# realmod.py | MLTechniques.com | vincentg@MLTechniques.com
# Find b such that fresidue(b) = 0, via fixed-point iteration
# Here, fresidue(b) = a mob b (a is a fixed integer; b is a real number)


import math
import random

a = 7919*3083      # product of two prime numbers (purpose: find factor b = 3083)
logeps = -10       # approximation to log(0) = - infinity
eps = 0.00000001   # used b/c Python sometimes fails to compute INT(x) correctly
offset = -100      # offset of linear transform, after log transform
slope = 20         # slope of linear transform, after log transform
mu = 1             # large mu --> large steps between successive b in fixed-point
b0  = 2000         # initial b in fixed-point iteration
window = 5         # size of window search
mode = 'Prime'     # Options: 'Prime' or 'Random'

def fresidue(b):
```

```
    # function f_3
    sum=0
    sumw=0
    for w in range(-window,window+1):
        sumw = sumw+1
        sum += fmod2(b+w)
    ry=offset + slope*sum/sumw
    return(ry)

def fmod2(b):
    # function f_1
    ry=fmod(b)
    if ry==0:
        ry=logeps
    else:
        ry=math.log(ry)
    return(ry)

def fmod(b):
    # function f_0
    if mode=='Prime':
        ry=a-int(b+eps)*int(eps+a/int(b+eps))
    elif mode=='Random':
        ry=res[int(b+eps)]
    return(ry)

if mode=='Random':
    # precompute f_0(b) for all integers b
    seed = 105
    random.seed(seed)
    res={}
    for b in range(1,40000):
        res[b]=int(b*random.random());
        if res[b]==0 and b >= b0:
            print("zero if b =", b)

# fixed-point iteration
OUT=open("rmodb.txt","w")
b = b0
for n in range(1,190):
    old_b = b
    b = b + mu*fresidue(b)
    delta = b - old_b
    line=str(n)+"\t"+str(b)+"\t"+str(delta)+"\n"
    OUT.write(line)
OUT.close()
```

13.4 Smoothing highly chaotic curves

All the functions discussed so far are piecewise constant. The purpose here is to beautify these functions to make them look smooth and continuous, while preserving the key feature: the roots, corresponding to massive dips in the graph of these functions. This is best illustrated in Fig. 13.7, where the original function f_0 in red is impossible to interpret, while the blue (dark gray in print version) curve f_3 clearly features the minimum. The orange (mid gray in print version) curve is the final result obtained after smoothing the blue (dark gray in print version) curve, using the three transformations `fresidue2`, `fresidue3` and `fresidue4` in the Python code in Section 13.4.1, in that order.

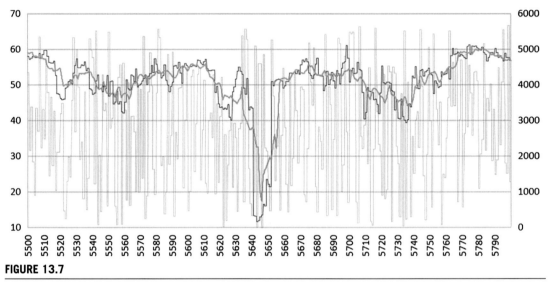

FIGURE 13.7

Random function from Section 13.3.1, with root at $b = 5646$.

13.4.1 Python code: smoothing

The code is also available on my GitHub repository, here. In addition to smoothing, it also produces a tab-separated text file `rmod.txt`. This files contains the tabulated values of the function f_0 and its successive transforms, for b in a range specified by the user.

```
# realmod_full.py | MLTechniques.com | vincentg@MLTechniques.com
# Find b such that fresidue(b) = 0, via fixed-point iteration
# Here, fresidue(b) = a mob b (a is a fixed integer; b is a real number)

import math
import random

a = 7919*3083     # product of two prime numbers (purpose: find factor b = 3083)
logeps = -10      # approximation to log(0) = - infinity
eps = 0.00000001  # used b/c Python sometimes fails to compute INT(x) correctly
```

```
offset = -100      # offset of linear transform, after log transform
slope = 20         # slope of linear transform, after log transform
mu = 1             # large mu --> large steps between successive b in fixed-point
b0  = 2000         # initial b in fixed-point iteration
window = 5         # size of window search
mode = 'Random'    # Options: 'Prime' or 'Random'

# -- transformation needed for fixed-point iteration
def fresidue(b):
    # function f_3
    sum=0
    sumw=0
    for w in range(-window,window+1):
        sumw = sumw+1
        sum += fmod2(b+w)
    ry=offset + slope*sum/sumw
    return(ry)


def fmod2(b):
    # function f_1
    ry=fmod(b)
    if ry==0:
        ry=logeps
    else:
        ry=math.log(ry)
    return(ry)


def fmod(b):
    # function f_0
    if mode=='Prime':
        ry=a-int(b+eps)*int(eps+a/int(b+eps))
    elif mode=='Random':
        ry=res[int(b+eps)]
    return(ry)

#-- smooth the curve f_3
def fresidue4(b):
    left = fresidue3(b)
    right = fresidue3(b+1)
    weight = b - int(eps+b)
    ry = (1-weight)*left + weight*right
    return(ry)


def fresidue3(b):
    f1 = fresidue2(b-5)
    f2 = fresidue2(b-6)
    f3 = fresidue2(b+4)
    ry = (f1+f2+f3)/3
```

```
    return(ry)

def fresidue2(b):
    flag1=0
    flag2=0
    ry = fresidue(b)
    ry2 = ry
    if ry2 > fresidue(b+5):
        ry2 = ry2 - 0.20*(ry2-fresidue(b+5))
        flag1 = 1
    if ry2 > fresidue(b+4):
        ry2 = ry2 - 0.20*(ry2-fresidue(b+4))
        flag1=1
    if ry2 > fresidue(b+3):
        ry2 = ry2 - 0.20*(ry2-fresidue(b+3))
        flag1=1
    if ry2 > fresidue(b+2):
        ry2 = ry2 - 0.50*(ry2-fresidue(b+2))
        flag1=1
    if ry2 > fresidue(b+1):
        ry2 = ry2 - 0.50*(ry2-fresidue(b+1))
        flag1=1
    ry3 = ry;
    if ry3 < fresidue(b+5):
        ry3 = ry3 - 0.30*(ry3-fresidue(b+5))
        flag2 = 1
    if ry3 < fresidue(b+4):
        ry3 = ry3 - 0.30*(ry3-fresidue(b+4))
        flag2 = 1
    if ry3 < fresidue(b+3):
        ry3 = ry3 - 0.30*(ry3-fresidue(b+3))
        flag2 = 1
    if ry3 < fresidue(b+2):
        ry3 = ry3 - 0.30*(ry3-fresidue(b+2))
        flag2 = 1
    if ry3 < fresidue(b+1):
        ry3 = ry3 - 0.50*(ry3-fresidue(b+1))
        flag2 = 1
    if flag1==1 and flag2==0:
        ry = ry2
    if flag1==0 and flag2==1:
        ry = ry3
        if flag1==1 and flag2==1:
            gap2 = abs(ry2-ry)
            gap3 = abs(ry3-ry)
            if gap3 > gap2:
                ry = ry3
            else:
```

```
            ry = ry2
    return(ry)

#-- preprocessing if mode=='Random'
if mode=='Random':
    # precompute f_0(b) for all integers b
    seed = 105
    random.seed(seed)
    res={}
    for b in range(1,40000):
        res[b]=int(b*random.random());
        if res[b]==0 and b >= b0:
            print("zero if b =", b)

#-- fixed-point iteration
OUT=open("rmodb.txt","w")
b = b0
for n in range(1,390):
    old_b = b
    b = b + mu*fresidue(b)
    delta = b - old_b
    line=str(n)+"\t"+str(b)+"\t"+str(delta)+"\n"
    OUT.write(line)
OUT.close()

#-- save tabulated function f (transforms and smoothed versions)
import numpy as np
OUT=open("rmod.txt","w")
for b in np.arange(5500, 5800, 0.1):
    r0 = fmod(b)
    r1 = fmod2(b)
    r2 = fresidue(b)
    r3 = fresidue2(b)
    r4 = fresidue3(b)
    r5 = fresidue4(b)
    line=str(b)+"\t"+str(r0)+"\t"+str(r1)+"\t"+str(r2)+"\t"+str(r3)+"\t"
    line=line+str(r4)+"\t"+str(r5)+"\n"
    OUT.write(line)
OUT.close()
```

13.5 Connection to synthetic data: random functions

First, there is a strong similarity between the various transforms used to magnify the roots and beautify the curves, and the concept of **transformers** in **Seq2seq neural networks** [Wiki]. But the true connection to synthetic data is about how the simulations can be used to generate random functions mimicking the deterministic ones that we deal with in real life. This also applies to the random Rademacher functions discussed in Section 17.3.5, mimicking deterministic multiplicative functions, also related to prime numbers as in this section.

The functions discussed here have a variable number of roots, a certain behavior (piecewise constant, roots are spaced out) and a certain potential range of values depending on the argument. These values, for a specific argument, are typically equally likely to show up. There is also some relative independence between (say) $f(b)$ and $f(b+1)$. These are the parameters of the real-life functions $f(b) = a \bmod b$ where a is a large fixed integer number with few divisors. Remember that the initial goal was to factor a product a two very large primes – a very hard problem of considerable interest in cryptography. Here the product in question is the number a.

To study the divergent fixed-point algorithm, and to benchmark and improve it in this context, I used synthetic random functions that mimic the properties of the original functions. Each random function is uniquely determined by the seed parameter. Thus, we have access to an infinite collection of functions, both for the real (determined by a) and the random ones. Assessing whether the synthetic functions are a good fit or not, as a proxy to represent the real-life functions, is the central "synthetic data" problem. The functions can be categorized in different types, depending on the number of roots and other parameter values. The problem is to simulate functions that can be used as substitutes, in each category.

To achieve this goal, some random functions must be ruled out from some categories, as being too different from the target functions that they try to emulate. Comparing two functions (a random one with a set of real-life functions within a specific category) is done by comparing their core parameters (number of roots and so on). In particular, random functions with no root below some threshold, are rejected. The mechanism that produces the suitable random functions is called a generative model. It is discussed in its most general form in Section 1.4.

References

[1] V. Granville, Stochastic Processes and Simulations: A Machine Learning Perspective, MLTechniques.com, 2022, [Link].

[2] J.M. Steele, Le Cam's inequality and Poisson approximations, The American Mathematical Monthly 101 (1) (1994) 48–54, [Link].

Synthetic terrain generation and AI-generated art

14

This chapter provides an introduction to **agent-based modeling** [Wiki] and computer vision techniques in Python, diving into the technical details of a specific class of problems. I show how to use generative models based on synthetic data, to simulate terrain evolution or other natural phenomena such as cloud formation or climate change. The material is accessible and targeted to software engineers interested in understanding and applying the machine learning and probabilistic background behind the scene, as well as to machine learning professionals interested in the programming aspects and scientific computing. The end-goal is to help the reader design and implement his own models and generate his own data sets, by showcasing an interesting application with all the details. My Python code can also be used as an end in itself. This type of application is referred to as **generative AI**.

From a machine learning perspective, the stochastic processes involved can be compared to spatial time series or time-continuous **chaotic dynamical systems**. There is a similarity with **constrained Brownian motions**, where at each time, rather than observing a typical observation (say a vector of stock prices), the observation consists of a particular configuration of the entire space (for instance, a moving storm system at a given time). In this chapter, the focus is on stationary-like processes. I briefly discuss the probabilistic models behind my algorithms, to explain when they work, and when they do not. However, I limit theoretical discussions to the essential, so that software engineers and other professionals lacking a strong mathematical background, can easily read and benefit from my presentation.

A possible use of my methodology is to automatically generate and label a large number of different landscapes (mountains, sea, land, combinations, and so on) to create a large training set. The training set can be used as **augmented data** for landscape classification, or to generate more landscape within a specific category to further enrich the classifier. The methodology can also be used to simulate transitions and reconstruct the hidden statistical behavior over short periods of time, when granular observations are not available. Finally, in addition to modeling and simulating uncontrolled evolutionary processes, the animated data visualizations also feature image morphing, both in the state space (coalescing physical shapes) and the spectral space (palette and color morphing).

14.1 Introduction

Watch the video posted here on YouTube to get a quick overview of the problems discussed in this chapter. For a better visual experience, you can download the MP4 file from my GitHub repository, here. Fig. 14.1 represents six frames from this video: the first one (top, left), the last one (bottom, right), as well as four intermediate frames in-between. Each frame consists of four images, evolving over time. So there are four subvideos playing in parallel in the **animated data visualization**. Now I describe the four images found in each frame. The details in the bullet list below apply to any specific video frame.

- The two images at the top, given a specific time (that is, the frame number), represent the same landscape with the same physical shapes. They illustrate the concept of **morphing** [Wiki]: over time, one terrain is turned into an entirely different terrain. The top left corner of each frame features morphing applied independently both to the landscape, and the **color palette** [Wiki]. To the contrary, in the image in the top right corner of each frame, only the terrain is morphed, not the color scheme.
- The two images at the bottom represent an **evolutionary process**. Unlike morphing, this involves statistical modeling. In this case, we know where it starts, but we can not predict its random path. The stochastic process behind the scene is stationary [Wiki]. An actual realization of this evolutionary process (as featured in the video) is similar to a time-continuous time series, more precisely to a **reflected Brownian motion** [Wiki], where each observation at a given time consists of an image – the terrain – rather than a finite vector of numerical observations.
- The difference between the left and right side, in the two bottom plots in each of the six video frames, is as follows. First, a different palette is used in each picture, to simulate cloud formation on the left, and terrain evolution on the right. Then the left picture is based on a **mixture model**, while the right one is based on blending. These two methods are described later in this chapter. In short, **blending** is less subject to wild oscillations, and in some sense less chaotic than the mixture approach. To the contrary, there is no chaos in morphing: the transitions are always smooth, nonstochastic, and one-directional.

Before diving into the details, in this section I describe a few general features. First, I focus on **stationary processes** only: the distribution of the colors, the granularity of the images, and any other pattern – while somewhat varying over time – are stochastically stable. An **equilibrium probability distribution** is attached to the evolutionary process, as in many other **stochastic dynamical systems** [Wiki]. For instance, colliding gas molecules or the successive binary digits of a number such as π have their own equilibrium distribution: in the latter case, independent Bernoulli trials that mimic flipping a fair coin. Another way to describe the situation is **stochastic convergence** of the images, or **ergodicity** [Wiki].

Then, the color palette plays an important role. It is referred to as the **spectral domain** in statistical theory, as opposed to the physical layout called the **state space**. The choice of the color scheme determines whether you are modeling landscape (a terrain), clouds, or a crystalline structure as in the picture in the top left corner. The roughness of the contours is another important parameter of the system. I kept it constant throughout the video. In the Python code, it is represented by the variable ds.

Morphing is a trivial procedure, unlike the simulation of model-based evolutionary processes. However, generating a terrain is far from obvious. In particular, finding a good palette color requires an algorithm on its own. The colors must be ordered in a certain way. The difference between two adjacent colors in the palette must be small, with one exception: the transition from sea to land, which is sharp, hence giving rise to sharp coast lines. Of course, you can always extract or compute palettes from existing real-life images. For details, see [1–3]. The physical layout of the terrain is created using the **diamond-square algorithm** [Wiki], described in Section 14.2. This Wikipedia entry features an application to plasma fractals.

Since a **palette** M is rectangular array with values between 0 and 1, palettes can be multiplied element-wise, or you can compute the power M^{α} with $\alpha \geq 0$, and still obtain a valid palette. These element-wise operations are done with just one line of code, when using numpy arrays in Python. It

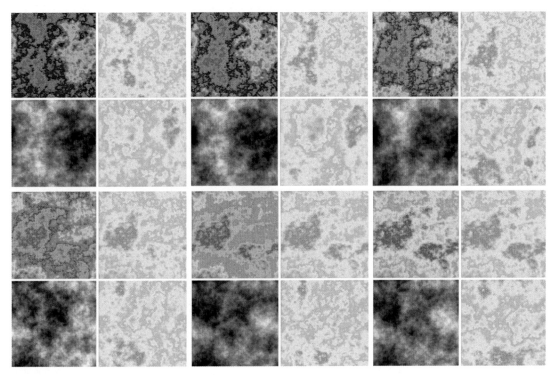

FIGURE 14.1

Six frames from the terrain video, each containing four images.

leads to interesting results, and I use it in my code. Typically, each row of M is a color entry, with three components: red, green, and blue. You may add a fourth component called alpha, representing **color transparency** or opacity [Wiki].

The algorithm offers an infinite number of terrains that you can choose from, as starting point for the video, or end point in case of morphing. A terrain is identified by a unique number: the **seed** [Wiki] used in the pseudorandom number generator (PRNG) when building the terrain. The video discussed here has 100 frames, each frame composed of 4 images, and each image requiring 750,000 calls to the Python function called `random`. So you need 3×10^8 pseudorandom numbers to produce one video. Python uses the **Mersenne twister** [Wiki] as its PRNG, with a period equal to $2^{19937} - 1$. However, as discussed in Chapter 11, this PRNG has flaws: some seeds must be avoided.

Finally, you can use the methodology as a generative model technique to automatically generate and label a large number of different landscapes (mountains, sea, land, combinations, and so on) to create a large training set of synthetic data. The training set, blended with real-life data, can then be used as **augmented data** for landscape classification, or to generate terrains within a specific category to further enrich the classifier; see Section 1.4 on how to do it in a similar context. The choice of the palette makes clustering and classification easy. Possible applications include modeling climate evolution, weather patterns, or tectonic plate movements, on Earth and elsewhere. You can also use it for AI-generated art or when designing video games. While I focus mostly on 2D simulations, I briefly discuss 3D contours in Section 14.4.

14.2 Terrain generation and the evolutionary process

When you watch the video here, you may think that the two images at the top – especially the one on the right side – are not changing, compared to the two at the bottom. This is an optical illusion, caused by the fact that transitions are very smooth when morphing alone takes place. The evolutionary transitions at the bottom seem to happen much faster, because they are chaotic and involve both backward and forward steps. But in the end, the transformation between the first and last frame in the video, is just as dramatic for the slow-moving scene.

Now I discuss the three main components of my method.

14.2.1 Morphing and nonlinear palette operations

Morphing is straightforward. But there is something interesting in the way I do it. It is accomplished using numpy arrays in Python, both for the palette M and the terrain W. Both M and W are matrices. The elements of M are between 0 and 1. The morphing involves element-wise operations [Wiki]. For instance, the terrain at time t is computed with one line of code: $W_t = (1 - r_t)W_0 + r_t W_T$, where $r_t = t/T$, W_0 is the initial terrain configuration corresponding to $t = 0$, and W_T is the final, target configuration corresponding to $t = T$.

To obtain better results, I use a nonlinear morphing for the palette, $M_t = M_0^{1-r_t} \cdot M_T^{r_t}$. Again, this element-wise operation is accomplished with just one line of code, thanks to the way numpy arrays work. The resulting intermediary palette M_t is a valid one, with all elements between 0 and 1.

14.2.2 The diamond-square algorithm

I use the **diamond-square** algorithm [Wiki] for terrain generation. My implementation is adapted from a recent version published in 2022 by Philipp Janert, here. The main difference is that I use Gaussian rather than uniform deviates whenever I need random numbers in the blending method. The reason is that the blending method in the evolutionary process preserves Gaussian distributions and thus results in a **stable distribution** [Wiki] over time, while uniform distributions (and all non-Gaussian distributions with finite variance) do not have this property.

The diamond-square algorithm successively populates an array (the terrain), at increasing levels of detail. Initially, only the corners need to be initialized; the remaining cells in the array are then populated by averaging over the four nearest populated neighbors, and adding a small random amount. At each step, the amplitude of the random noise initially set to s, is reduced by some factor ds. This factor controls the roughness of the terrain. The number of points being updated (and thus number of calls to the random number generator) exponentially increases with each subsequent step, by a factor close to 4. So very few steps are needed. Here s and ds are the names of the variables in the Python code.

There are two ways to improve the algorithm. First, instead of averaging values across nearest neighbors, use a median value. Then, in the evolutionary process, do not update the random deviates in the early steps corresponding to small s, but only in the final steps. This may eliminate rare but abrupt transitions over time, especially when using the mixture method. Unless you really want these rare, unpredictable "cataclysms" of various amplitudes (the larger the rarer): after all, they are present in real-life situations such as the evolution of life on Earth. The parameter jump in the code also controls how frequently they occur.

14.2.3 The evolutionary process

The terrain at time t is an image represented by an $n \times n$ matrix of pixels W_t, each pixel representing a level or elevation on a map. Here $n = 1 + 2^9$. The diamond-square algorithm requires n to be a power of two, plus one. The time is represented by the integer variable frame in the code. The total number of (video) frames is denoted as Nframes. The terrain is stored as a numpy array named d.

Initially, at time $t = 0$, the terrain is built incrementally using a few number of steps, with each subsequent step being more granular and updating about 4 times more pixels than the previous step, with exponentially decreasing noise amplitudes from one step to the next. This is performed by the function make_terrain in the code. At step s, let $W_0(s)$ be the partially built terrain. It is a function of some random numbers $u_0(s, 1), u_0(s, 2)$, and so on, generated either with the function random.gauss(0,s) or random.uniform(-s,s) depending on whether the global parameter distribution is set to 'Gaussian' or 'Uniform'. The step s is represented by the variable s in the code.

A time $t + 1$, the new terrain W_{t+1} is a function of W_t. The only quantities that are updated are the numbers $u_t(s, 1), u_t(s, 2)$, and so on, at each step s during the construction of W_{t+1}. Two options are offered to update these numbers, via the global parameter mode. This parameter can be set either to 'Blending' or 'Mixture'. I now describe these two options:

- The mixture option. We either have $u_{t+1}(k, s) = u_t(k, s)$ with probability p, or $u_{t+1}(k, s)$ is a new deviate with probability $1 - p$, generated from a Uniform$[-s, s]$ or Normal$(0, s)$ distribution depending on the parameter distribution, for $k = 1, 2$, and so on. Typically, p is small and represented by the global parameter jump in the code.
- The blending option. It is allowed only when distribution is set to 'Gaussian' in the code. Again, either $u_{t+1}(k, s) = u_t(k, s)$ is unchanged with probability p, or $u_{t+1}(k, s)$ is updated with probability $1 - p$. When an update takes place, it is performed as follows: $u_{t+1}(k, s) = u_t(k, s) + \omega z$, where ω is a weight, and z is a Normal$(0, s)$ deviate. Either way, by construction, $u_{t+1}(k, s)$ is a Gaussian deviate with zero mean. The weight ω is represented by the global parameter weight in the code.

Now if you are familiar with the theory of stochastic processes, you will quickly recognize the analogy with Brownian motions and **random walks** when using the blending option. Indeed, the quantity ωz corresponds to the independent increments in a random walk. And since many frames are packed into the video (5 per second, determined by the parameter fps), the random walk appears time-continuous, and thus more like a Brownian motion than a time-discrete process.

14.2.4 Finding optimum parameters

There are some rules to comply with to produce good-looking terrain. For instance, the palette cannot be arbitrary. The choice of the parameters, even the seed in the random number generator, has a significant impact on the results. When fine-tuning a small number of parameters, you can try all possible combinations out of a set of prespecified values. This is known as a **grid search** [Wiki]. It is typically used to find optimum hyperparameters. You need a criterion to compare the visual quality of two terrains. For instance, you want enough water and snow-covered areas, a good granularity, and a clear delimitation between ocean and land. Some of the parameters can be tested separately, while others (the palette parameters) have cross-interactions and must be tested jointly.

14.2.5 Mimicking real terrain: the synthesis step

Given some observed terrain or terrain animation, the first step is to estimate the top parameters used in the Python code, using proxy estimators, also known as **minimum contrast estimators**, as in Section 18.3.5. For instance, the parameter ds, measuring the granularity of the terrain, can be substituted by the average color variance in a 3×3 window. This is easy to estimate. Then, based on simulations, you can build a table that maps the estimated variance in question to an actual ds value. The quality of the fit between the true parameter ds and the proxy estimate – measured using **R-squared** or related metrics – tells you how good your proxy estimator is. You want to find a proxy estimator that minimizes R-squared.

Another example is the parameter jump, that controls how frequently massive changes from one video frame to the next, occur in the evolutionary process. It is easy to estimate it via a proxy estimator: the number of video frames where some distance measurement between the current image and the previous one, is much larger than the median. Again, you will need to build a table that maps these measurements to actual values of jump, based on simulations. The same applies to the parameter weight, or the speed of evolution, controlled here by fps, jump, and weight. It can be measured by the average distance between video frames occurring taking place around the same time.

Then, once the top parameters are estimated based on real terrains and proxy estimation techniques, you can synthesize terrains that are stochastically similar (that is, have the same statistical properties) to the real terrains used in your training set. Note that in my example, the proxy estimators are natural and intuitive. It illustrates what explainable AI is about, and represents an alternative to **generative adversarial networks** discussed in chapter 10.

14.3 Python code

I divided the code section into two parts, corresponding to two separate programs. The first combines input images to produce a video with four subplots, each subplot consisting of a video of its own. The second part is the main program, producing the images in question, as well as independent videos.

14.3.1 Producing data videos with four subvideos in parallel

This code is also on GitHub, here. It is a simple application of the subplot functionality in matplotlib. However, there are a few things to watch out. You want to remove the axes and labels, and reduce the amount of space between the subplots. Then, by default, the savefig function adds a border in the output image. Here I configured the parameters `bbox_inches` and `pad_inches` to remove the border in question.

You also want to make sure that all the input images are properly numbered and present in your local folder. These images are produced by the program in Section 14.3.2. They must have the same physical size (height and width expressed in number of pixels or inches). In addition the number of pixels must be an even number, otherwise the video may not be properly rendered. I used the main program four times, each time with a different set of parameters, to produce the four sets of input images.

```python
# twoImages.py | www.MLTechniques.com | vincentg@MLTechniques.com

import matplotlib.pyplot as plt
import matplotlib.image as mpimg
import moviepy.video.io.ImageSequenceClip # to produce mp4 video

my_dpi = 300
Nframes=100
fps=5
flist=[]

for frame in range(0,Nframes):
    image ='output'+str(frame)+'.png'
    print('Creating image',image)
    image1='terrainA'+str(frame)+'.png' # subplot 1 (input)
    image2='terrainB'+str(frame)+'.png' # subplot 2 (input)
    image3='terrainC'+str(frame)+'.png' # subplot 3 (input)
    image4='terrainD'+str(frame)+'.png' # subplot 4 (input)
    imgs=[]
    imgs.append(mpimg.imread(image1))
    imgs.append(mpimg.imread(image2))
    imgs.append(mpimg.imread(image3))
    imgs.append(mpimg.imread(image4))

    fig, axs = plt.subplots(2, 2,figsize=(6,6))
    axs = axs.flatten()
    for img, ax in zip(imgs, axs):
        ax.set_axis_off()
        ax.set_xticklabels([])
        ax.imshow(img)
    plt.subplots_adjust(wspace=0.025, hspace=0.025)
    plt.savefig(image,bbox_inches='tight',pad_inches=0.00,dpi=my_dpi)
    plt.close()
    flist.append(image)

# output video
clip = moviepy.video.io.ImageSequenceClip.ImageSequenceClip(flist, fps=fps)
clip.write_videofile('terrainx4.mp4')
```

14.3.2 **Main program**

I discussed many of the global parameters and options in the previous sections. The parameter method allows you to choose between morphing and simulating an evolutionary process. In case of morphing, the first and last terrain configurations are specified by the parameters start and end as described in Section 14.1. In addition to terrain morphing, the parameter col_morphing, if set to True, allows you to perform color morphing.

The parameters n, fps, Nframes, mode, jump, weight, distribution, and method are described in Section 14.2.3. In the same section, I also describe important variables such as s and d (the terrain itself). For ds, see Section 14.2.2. Also, you can choose from three different prespecified palettes, determined by the parameter palette.

Some of the comments in Section 14.3.1 are also relevant to the code presented here. In particular, the discussion about the image size and the associated parameter my_dpi, where dpi stands for dots per inch. The other video parameter, fps, is the number of frames per second. As for bdry and anything else not discussed in this chapter, see the documentation in an earlier implementation, here. This code is also on my GitHub repository, here.

```
# terrain8.py | www.MLTechniques.com | vincent@MLTechniques.com | 2022

import random
import numpy as np

def fixed( d, i, j, v, offsets ):
    # For fixed bdries, all cells are valid. Define n so as to allow the
    # usual lower bound inclusive, upper bound exclusive indexing.
    n = d.shape[0]

    res, k = 0, 0
    for p, q in offsets:
        pp, qq = i + p*v, j + q*v
        if 0 <= pp < n and 0 <= qq < n:
            res += d[pp, qq]
            k += 1.0
    return res/k

def periodic( d, i, j, v, offsets ):
    # For periodic bdries, the last row/col mirrors the first row/col.
    # Hence the effective square size is (n-1)x(n-1). Redefine n accordingly!
    n = d.shape[0] - 1

    res = 0
    for p, q in offsets:
        res += d[(i + p*v)%n, (j + q*v)%n]
    return res/4.0

def update_random_table(rnd_table, s, frame):
```

```
    global counter

    if distribution == 'Uniform' and mode == 'Blending':
        print("Error: Blending allowed only with Gaussian distribution.")
        exit()

    if frame < 1:
        if distribution == 'Gaussian':
            rnd_table[counter]=random.gauss(0,s)
        elif distribution == 'Uniform':
            rnd_table[counter]=random.uniform(-s,s)
    else:
        if random.uniform(0,1) > 1 - jump:
            if mode == 'Blending':
                rnd_table[counter] += weight*random.gauss(0,s) # update random number table # 0.5
                    * ..
                rnd_table[counter] /= np.sqrt(1+weight*weight)
            elif mode == 'Mixture':
                if distribution == 'Gaussian':
                    rnd_table[counter] = random.gauss(0,s)
                elif distribution == 'Uniform':
                    rnd_table[counter] = random.uniform(-s,s)

def single_diamond_square_step(d, w, s, avg, frame):
    # w is the dist from one "new" cell to the next
    # v is the dist from a "new" cell to the nbs to average over

    global counter
    n = d.shape[0]
    v = w//2

    # offsets:
    diamond = [ (-1,-1), (-1,1), (1,1), (1,-1) ]
    square = [ (-1,0), (0,-1), (1,0), (0,1) ]

    # (i,j) are always the coords of the "new" cell

    # Diamond Step
    for i in range( v, n, w ):
        for j in range( v, n, w ):
            update_random_table(rnd_table, s, frame)
            d[i, j] = avg( d, i, j, v, diamond ) + rnd_table[counter]
            counter=counter+1

    # Square Step, rows
    for i in range( v, n, w ):
        for j in range( 0, n, w ):
            update_random_table(rnd_table, s, frame)
```

```
            d[i, j] = avg( d, i, j, v, square ) + rnd_table[counter]
            counter=counter+1

    # Square Step, cols
    for i in range( 0, n, w ):
        for j in range( v, n, w ):
            update_random_table(rnd_table, s, frame)
            d[i, j] = avg( d, i, j, v, square ) + rnd_table[counter]
            counter=counter+1

def make_terrain( n, ds, bdry, frame):
    # Returns an n-by-n landscape using the Diamond-Square algorithm, using
    # roughness delta ds (0..1); bdry is an averaging fct, including the
    # bdry conditions: fixed() or periodic(); n must be 1+2**k, k integer.

    global counter

    d = np.zeros( n*n ).reshape( n, n )

    w, s = n-1, 1.0
    counter = 0
    while w > 1:
        single_diamond_square_step(d, w, s, bdry, frame)

        w //= 2
        s *= ds

    return d

def set_palette(palette):
    # Create a colormap (palette with ordered RGB colors)

    color_table_storm = []
    for k in range(0,29):
        color_table_storm.append([k/28, k/28, k/28])

    color_table_vincent = []
    for k in range(0,29):
        red  = 0.9*abs(np.sin(0.20*k)) # 0.9 | 0.20
        green= 0.6*abs(np.sin(0.21*k)) # 0.6 | 0.21
        blue = 1.0*abs(np.sin(0.54*k)) # 1.0 | 0.54
        color_table_vincent.append([red, green, blue])

    color_table_terrain = [
            (0.44314, 0.67059, 0.84706),
            (0.47451, 0.69804, 0.87059),
            (0.51765, 0.72549, 0.89020),
            (0.55294, 0.75686, 0.91765),
```

```
            (0.58824, 0.78824, 0.94118),
            (0.63137, 0.82353, 0.96863),
            (0.67451, 0.85882, 0.98431),
            (0.72549, 0.89020, 1.00000),
            (0.77647, 0.92549, 1.00000),
            (0.84706, 0.94902, 0.99608),
            (0.67451, 0.81569, 0.64706),
            (0.58039, 0.74902, 0.54510),
            (0.65882, 0.77647, 0.56078),
            (0.74118, 0.80000, 0.58824),
            (0.81961, 0.84314, 0.67059),
            (0.88235, 0.89412, 0.70980),
            (0.93725, 0.92157, 0.75294),
            (0.90980, 0.88235, 0.71373),
            (0.87059, 0.83922, 0.63922),
            (0.82745, 0.79216, 0.61569),
            (0.79216, 0.72549, 0.50980),
            (0.76471, 0.65490, 0.41961),
            (0.72549, 0.59608, 0.35294),
            (0.66667, 0.52941, 0.32549),
            (0.67451, 0.60392, 0.48627),
            (0.72941, 0.68235, 0.60392),
            (0.79216, 0.76471, 0.72157),
            (0.87843, 0.87059, 0.84706),
            (0.96078, 0.95686, 0.94902)
        ]
    if palette == 'Storm':
        color_table = color_table_storm
    elif palette == 'Terrain':
        color_table = color_table_terrain
    elif palette == 'Vincent':
        color_table = color_table_vincent
    return(color_table)

def morphing(start, end):
    # create all the images for the video
    # morphing from 'start' to 'end' image

    size = (n - 1) / 64

    random.seed(start)
    frame=0
    start_terrain = make_terrain( n, ds, bdry, frame)
    random.seed(end)
    frame=-1
    end_terrain = make_terrain( n, ds, bdry, frame)
    if col_morphing:
```

```
        col_table_start = np.array(set_palette('Terrain'))**1.00 *
            np.array(set_palette('Vincent'))**0.50
        col_table_end = np.array(set_palette('Terrain'))**1.50

    for frame in range(0,Nframes):
        A = frame/(Nframes - 1)
        B = 1 - A
        tmp_terrain = B * start_terrain + A * end_terrain
        if col_morphing: # both palettes must have same size
            tmp_col_table = col_table_start**B * col_table_end**A
            tmp_cm = matplotlib.colors.LinearSegmentedColormap.from_list('temp',tmp_col_table)
        else:
            tmp_cm = cm
        image='terrainM'+str(frame)+'.png' # filename of image in current frame
        print("Creating image",image) # show progress on the screen
        plt.figure( figsize=(size, size), dpi=my_dpi ) # create n-by-n pixel fig
        plt.tick_params( left=False, bottom=False, labelleft=False, labelbottom=False )
        plt.imshow( tmp_terrain, cmap=tmp_cm )
        plt.savefig(image,bbox_inches='tight',pad_inches=0,dpi=my_dpi) # Save to file
        plt.close()
        flist.append(image)


def evolution(start):
    # create all the images for the video

    random.seed(start)
    for frame in range(0,Nframes):
        image='terrainE'+str(frame)+'.png' # filename of image in current frame
        print("Creating image",image) # show progress on the screen
        size = (n - 1) / 64
        plt.figure( figsize=(size, size), dpi=my_dpi ) # create n-by-n pixel fig
        plt.tick_params( left=False, bottom=False, labelleft=False, labelbottom=False )
        terrain = make_terrain( n, ds, bdry, frame )
        plt.imshow( terrain, cmap=cm )
        plt.savefig(image,bbox_inches='tight',pad_inches=0,dpi=my_dpi) # Save to file
        plt.close()
        flist.append(image)


#--- Main

import matplotlib.colors
import matplotlib.pyplot as plt
import moviepy.video.io.ImageSequenceClip # to produce mp4 video



n        = 1 + 2**9 # Edge size of the resulting image in pixels
ds       = 0.7      # Roughness delta. 0 < ds < 1 : smaller ds => smoother results
bdry     = periodic # One of the averaging routines: fixed or periodic
```

```
Nframes    = 100      # must be > 10
my_dpi     = 300      # dots per inch (image resolution)
fps        = 5        # frames per second
mode       = 'Blending' # options: 'Blending' or 'Mixture'
jump       = 0.5 #0.01   # the lower, the smoother the image transitions (0 < jump < 1)
weight     = 0.2      # used in Gaussian mixture: low weight keeps pixel color little changed
start      = 134      # seed for random number generator, for initial image
end        = 143      # seed for target image, used in morphing only
distribution = 'Gaussian' # option: 'Gaussian' or 'Uniform'
palette    = 'Terrain' # options: 'Storm', 'Terrain' or 'Vincent'
method     = 'Evolution' # options: 'Morphing' or 'Evolution'
col_morphing = False # available in morphing method only

flist    = []        # list of image filenames for the video
rnd_table = {}       # dynamic list of random numbers for simulations

color_table = set_palette(palette)
cm = matplotlib.colors.LinearSegmentedColormap.from_list('geo-smooth',color_table)

if method == 'Evolution':
   evolution(start)
elif method == 'Morphing':
   morphing(start,end)

# output video
clip = moviepy.video.io.ImageSequenceClip.ImageSequenceClip(flist, fps=fps)
clip.write_videofile('terrain.mp4')
```

14.4 AI-generated art with 3D contours

Of course, the 2D terrains created in this chapter may be perceived as **AI art** [Wiki] or a computer vision problem. But doing it in 3D brings a different perspective and more possibilities, especially when animated. It is definitely at the intersection of machine learning, scientific computing, automated art, cartography, and video games. It is easy to image a game based on the video presented here, entitled "flying above menacingly rising mountains".

While both **surface plots** [Wiki] and 2D **contour plots** [Wiki] are very popular and easy to make, it is a lot more difficult, mathematically speaking, to produce 3D contour plots, also called contour maps. Surface plots are helpful in multivariate regression problems. Unlike surface plots, contour plots come with horizontal curves called **contour levels**. They represent **confidence regions** of various levels – a generalization of confidence intervals – when the underlying function is a probability distribution.

In practice, contour plots are easy to generate using standard libraries. Here I compare Matplotlib with Plotly, in Python. Since **Plotly** [Wiki] is a generic library used in different programming languages, the code discussed here can easily be adapted to R or Julia. The contour plots in this section also show that a **mixture** of Gaussian-like distributions is typically non-Gaussian-like, and may or may not be unimodal. Then the associated **data video**, through various rotations, give you a much better view of your data. It is also perfect to show systems that evolve over time: a time series where each observation is an image. You can watch the video here. The last frame pictured in Fig. 14.2 and produced with Plotly, corresponds to the same distribution mixture featured in Fig. 18.6 in Section 18.3.6, this time produced with **Mathematica**.

The data set used to produce the video consists of 300 images (video frames), representing some mixture of distributions evolving over time. It is based on synthetic data: there are about 20 parameters that drive the evolution and govern the behavior of these mountains, including a rising volcano. One of the parameters governs the decaying rate of growth of the volcano. In short, the whole video can be summarized by 20 numbers, called features in machine learning. The model used to produce the data is called a generative model.

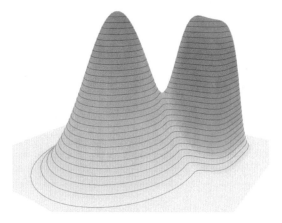

FIGURE 14.2

Contour plot, 3D mixture model, produced with Plotly.

And in the same way that images (say, pictures of hand-written digits) can be summarized by 10 parameters to perform text recognition, here 20 parameters allow you to perform topography classification. Not just of static terrain, but terrain that changes over time, assuming you have access to 50,000 videos representing different topographies. You can produce the videos needed for supervised classification with the code in Section 14.4.2. The next step is to use data (videos) from the real world, and leverage the model trained on synthetic data for classification.

14.4.1 Python code using Matplotlib

The source code is also available on my GitHub repository, here. Look for filenames starting with `contour`. This folder also contains the video and an animated gif version. I was unable to fix the issue visible in Fig. 14.3 in the Matplotlib version, despite my experience with **color opacity** and transparency. This glitch results in a nice optical illusion: if you watch Fig. 14.3 long enough, it switches back and forth between the mountains perceived as seen from above, and seen from underground (revealing the inside of the mountains).

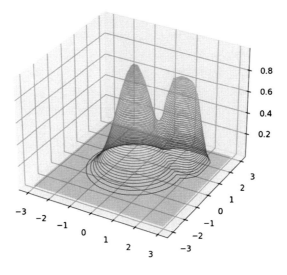

FIGURE 14.3

Same as Fig. 14.2, produced with Matplotlib.

This issue is addressed in the Plotly version. This library is more comprehensive and harder to master, but offers more possibilities. The code in this section corresponds to the Plotly version, including the production of the video. The choice of the colors is determined by the parameter `colorscale`, set to "Peach" here. The list of available palettes is posted here. You can easily add axes and labels, change font sizes, and so on. The parameters to handle this are present in the source code, but turned off in the present version.

```
import numpy as np
import plotly.graph_objects as go
import matplotlib

def create_3Dplot(frame):

    param1=-0.15 + 0.65*(1-np.exp(-3*frame/Nframes)) # height of small hill
    param2=-1+2*frame/(Nframes-1) # rotation, x
    param3=0.75+(1-frame/(Nframes-1)) # rotation, y
    param4=1-0.7*frame/(Nframes-1) # rotation z

    X, Y = np.mgrid[-3:2:100j, -3:3:100j]
    Z= 0.5*np.exp(-(abs(X)**2 + abs(Y)**2)) \
       + param1*np.exp(-4*((abs(X+1.5))**4.2 + (abs(Y-1.4))**4.2))

    fig = go.Figure(data=[
        go.Surface(
            x=X, y=Y, z=Z,
            opacity=1.0,
```

```
        contours={
            "z": {"show": True, "start": 0, "end": 1, "size": 1/60,
                "width": 1, "color": 'black'} # add <"usecolormap": True>
        },
        showscale=False, # try <showscale=True>
        colorscale='Peach')],
    )

    fig.update_layout(
        margin=dict(l=0,r=0,t=0,b=160),
        font=dict(color='blue'),
        scene = dict(xaxis_title='', yaxis_title='',zaxis_title='',
            xaxis_visible=False, yaxis_visible=False, zaxis_visible=False,
            aspectratio=dict(x=1, y=1, z=0.6)),        # resize by shrinking z
        scene_camera = dict(eye=dict(x=param2, y=param3, z=param4))) # change vantage point

    return(fig)

#-- main

import moviepy.video.io.ImageSequenceClip # to produce mp4 video
from PIL import Image # for some basic image processing

Nframes=300 # must be > 50
flist=[] # list of image filenames for the video
w, h, dpi = 4, 3, 300 # width and height in inches
fps=10 # frames per second

for frame in range(0,Nframes):
    image='contour'+str(frame)+'.png' # filename of image in current frame
    print("Creating image",image) # show progress on the screen
    fig=create_3Dplot(frame)
    fig.write_image(file=image, width=w*dpi, height=h*dpi, scale=1)
    # fig.show()
    flist.append(image)

# output video / fps is number of frames per second
clip = moviepy.video.io.ImageSequenceClip.ImageSequenceClip(flist, fps=fps)
clip.write_videofile('contourvideo.mp4')
```

14.4.2 Python code using Plotly

Below is the Matplotlib version. It is also available on GitHub, here. I did not include the code for the video production in the Matplotlib version.

```
import numpy as np
```

```
from mpl_toolkits.mplot3d import axes3d
import matplotlib.pyplot as plt

plt.rcParams['lines.linewidth']= 0.5
plt.rcParams['axes.linewidth'] = 0.5
plt.rcParams['axes.linewidth'] = 0.5

SMALL_SIZE = 6
MEDIUM_SIZE = 8
BIGGER_SIZE = 10

plt.rc('font', size=SMALL_SIZE) # controls default text sizes
plt.rc('axes', titlesize=SMALL_SIZE) # fontsize of the axes title
plt.rc('axes', labelsize=MEDIUM_SIZE) # fontsize of the x and y labels
plt.rc('xtick', labelsize=SMALL_SIZE) # fontsize of the tick labels
plt.rc('ytick', labelsize=SMALL_SIZE) # fontsize of the tick labels
plt.rc('legend', fontsize=SMALL_SIZE) # legend fontsize
plt.rc('figure', titlesize=BIGGER_SIZE) # fontsize of the figure title

fig = plt.figure()
ax = fig.add_subplot(111, projection="3d")
X, Y = np.mgrid[-3:3:30j, -3:3:30j]
Z= np.exp(-(abs(X)**2 + abs(Y)**2)) + 0.8*np.exp(-4*((abs(X-1.5))**4.2 + (abs(Y-1.4))**4.2))

ax.plot_surface(X, Y, Z, cmap="coolwarm", rstride=1, cstride=1, alpha=0.2)
# ax.contourf(X, Y, Z, levels=60, colors="k", linestyles="solid", alpha=0.9, antialiased=True)
ax.contour(X, Y, Z, levels=60, linestyles="solid", alpha=0.9, antialiased=True)

plt.savefig('contour3D.png', dpi=300)
plt.show()
```

14.4.3 Tips to quickly solve new problems

Assume you are asked to produce good quality, 3D contour plots in Python – not surface plots – and you have no idea how to start. Yet, you are familiar with Matplotlib, but rather new to Python. You have 48 hours to complete this project (two days of work at your office, minus the regular chores eating your time every day). How would you proceed? Here I explain how I did it, as I was in the same situation (self-imposed onto myself). I focus on the 3D contour plot only, as I knew beforehand how to quickly turn it into a video, as long as I was able to produce a decent single plot. My strategy was broken down into the following steps:

- I quickly realized it would be very easy to produce 2D contour or surface plots, but not 3D contour plots. I googled "contour map 3d matplotib". Not satisfied with the results, I searched images, rather than the web. This led me to a Stackoverflow forum question here, which in turn led me to some page on the Matplotlib website, here.

- After tweaking some parameters, I was able to produce Fig. 14.3. Unsatisfied with the result and spending quite a bit of time trying to fix the glitch, I asked for a fix on Stackoverflow. You can see my question, and the answers that were posted, here. One participant suggested to use color transparency, but this was useless, as I had tried it before without success. The second answer came with a piece of code, and the author suggested that I used Plotly instead of Matplotlib. I trusted his advice, and got his code to work after installing Plotly (I got an error message asking me to install Kaleido, but that was easy to fix). Quite exciting, but that was far from the end.

- I googled "Matplotlib vs Plotly", to make sure it made sense using Plotly. I was convinced, especially given my interest in scientific computing. Quickly though, I realized my plots were arbitrarily truncated. I googled "plotly 3d contour map" and "plotly truncated 3d contour", which led me to various websites including a detailed description of the `layout` and `scene` parameters. This webpage was particularly useful, as it offered a solution to my problem.

- I spent a bit of time to figure out how to remove the axes and labels, as I feared they could cause problems in the video, changing from one frame to the next, based on past experience. It took me 30 minutes to find the solution by trial and error. But then I realized that there was one problem left: in the PNG output image, the plot occupied only a small portion, even though it looked fine within the Python environment. Googling "plotly write_image" did not help. I tried to ask for a fix on Stackoverflow, but was not allowed to ask a question for another 24 hours. I asked my question in the Reddit Python forum instead.

- Eventually, shrinking the Z axis, modifying the orientation of the plot, the margins, and the dimensions of the images, I got a substantial improvement. By the time I checked for a potential answer to my Reddit question, my post had been deleted by an admin. But I had finally solved it. Well, almost.

- My concern at this point was using the correct DPI (dots per inch) and FPS (frames per second) for the video, and make sure the size of the video was manageable. Luckily, all the 300 frames (the PNG images, one per plot), now automatically generated, had the exact same physical dimension. Otherwise I would have had to resize them (which can be done automatically). Also, the rendering was good, not pixelized. So I did not have to apply antialiasing techniques. And here we are, I produced the video and was happy!

- So I thought. I realized, when producing the animated gif, that there was still a large portion of the images unused (blank). Not as bad as earlier, but still not good enough for me. Now I know how to crop hundreds of images automatically in Python, but instead I opted to load my video on Ezgif, and use the crop option. The final version posted in this chapter is this cropped version. I then produced another video, with 4 mountains, rising up, merging or shrinking according to various schedules. This might be the topic of a future article, as it is going into a new direction – video games.

References

[1] C. Beckham, C. Pal, A step towards procedural terrain generation with GANs, Preprint, pp. 1–5, arXiv:1707. 03383, 2017, [Link].

[2] A. Zeileis, et al., Colorspace: a toolbox for manipulating and assessing colors and palettes, Preprint, pp. 1–45, arXiv:1903.06490, 2019, [Link], [R Library].

[3] M. Wu, Y. Sun, Y. Li, Adaptive transfer of color from images to maps and visualizations, Cartography and Geographic Information Science (2021) 289–312, [Link].

Synthetic star cluster generation with collision graphs

The N-body problem consists of predicting the evolution of celestial bodies bound by gravity. Here I go one step further: up to 1000 stars and star clusters are simulated using various initial conditions, to produce videos that show how these synthetic universes evolve. It tells a lot about the past and future of our current universe, corroborating the theory that it is expanding, albeit more and more slowly. In addition, stars with negative masses and gravity laws other than the standard inverse square, when allowed, lead to the most bizarre systems and spectacular videos. Star collisions are studied in details and lead to interesting graph theory applications. I provide the Python code for these simulations, including the production of animated data visualizations (videos) and graph representations. This type of simulations is at the intersection of **agent-based modeling** [Wiki] and **generative AI**.

15.1 Introduction

This project started as an attempt to generate simulations for the **three-body problem** [Wiki] in astronomy: studying the orbits of three celestial bodies subject to their gravitational interactions. There are many illustrations available online, and after some research, I was intrigued by Philip Mocz's version of the N-body problem: the generalization involving an arbitrary number of celestial bodies. These bodies are referred to as stars in this chapter. Philip is a computational physicist at Lawrence Livermore National Laboratory, with a PhD in astrophysics from Harvard University. The Python code for his simulations can be found here.

My simulations are based on his code, which I have significantly upgraded. The end result is the three-galaxy problem: small star clusters, each with hundreds of stars, coalescing due to gravitational forces of the individual stars. It simulates the merging of galaxies. In addition, I added a birth process, with new stars constantly generated. I also allow for star collisions, resulting in fewer but bigger stars over time. Finally, my simulations allow for stars with negative masses, as well as unusual gravitation laws, different from the classic **inverse square law** [Wiki].

These bizarre universes lead to spectacular data animations (MP4 videos), but, perhaps most importantly, they may help explain what could cause our universe to expand, including the different stages of compression and expansion over time. Depending on the initial configuration, very different outcomes are possible. Negative masses, with cluster centroids based on the absolute value of the mass while gravitational forces are based on the signed mass, could lead to a different model of the universe. Many well-known phenomena, such as rogue stars escaping their cluster at great velocity, black holes and twin stars formation, star filaments, and star clusters becoming less energetic over time (decreasing expansion, smaller velocities) are striking features visible in my videos. Star collisions lead to an interesting graph problem.

Synthetic Data and Generative AI. https://doi.org/10.1016/B978-0-44-321857-6.00019-9

The implementation uses a discrete approximation to Newton's law of gravity. A previous version based on elliptic orbits, but not complying with the laws of our universe, can be found in Section 4.3.1. Other spectacular orbit visualizations, which have been compared to the 3-body problem but are indeed related to the Riemann Hypothesis in number theory, can be found in Section 4.3.3. For 3D visualizations, see here. The simulations in this chapter are 2D and correspond to a projection on one of the 2D planes.

15.2 Model parameters and simulation results

The evolving star systems featured in the videos start with an initial configuration, consisting of the location, velocity, and mass of the stars. These vectors are stored in three numpy arrays in the Python code, named `pos`, `vel`, and `mass`, with one entry per star. The position and velocity have three components, corresponding to the X, Y, and Z axis. Initial values are randomly generated. A typical video requires about a billion pseudorandom numbers. Thus it is important to use a good pseudorandom number generator (PRNG). How to choose a good seed for the Python PRNG – the Mersenne twister – is discussed in Chapter 11.

The location, velocity, and mass of each star is updated at each iteration, based on the current proximity, speed, and velocity of the other stars, according to gravitation laws. Negative masses, star collisions, new star generation, and star grouping (star clusters) are allowed. In addition to `pos`, `vel`, and `mass`, there is one additional array named `col` that stores the color of each star, when displayed in the video. Individual colors can change over time, as explained in Section 15.2.1.

15.2.1 Explanation of color codes

Unless the user selects a model with multiple star clusters via the option `threeClusters=True`, a star with positive mass is blue, and one with negative mass is red. If collisions are allowed, a star will turn and stay orange after absorbing another star. The losing star (the one that gets eaten) has its mass set to zero and will not be visible anymore in the video: the size of a star pictured in the video is proportional to its mass at any given time. When a new star is generated after the initialization step, its color is set to dark violet, regardless of the mass sign. Again, it will turn orange if it collides with another star.

If choosing a system with three star clusters, the star color will be blue, green, or magenta, depending on which clusters it initially belongs to. Negative masses or new star creation are not yet allowed in these systems, mostly to avoid conflicts with the color scheme. Again, upon collision, the star color turns to orange.

15.2.2 Detailed description of top parameters

Now I describe all the parameters and features available in my implementation, in Table 15.1. I recommend to read this table, as it shows all the options offered in the Python program. Finding a great set of parameters to illustrate a particular type of system is not easy. In Section 15.2.3, I describe eight hand-picked sets of parameter configurations covering a large variety of situations. With a bit of practice and common sense, it becomes easier to predict the behavior of the system based on the parameter selection.

Table 15.1 Description of top parameters used in the star cluster simulator.	
starBoost	Create one massive star in the system if value larger than 1 in absolute value. For instance, star-Boost=-5 means that the star in position 0 in the star tables has a negative mass which is (in absolute value) 5 times larger than any other star.
law	The classic law of gravity uses $r/||r||^3$ in its formula, where $||r||$ is the distance between two interacting bodies. This corresponds to law=3, but you can try other values for the exponent.
speed	Increase or decrease the initial velocities of the stars. It has a big impact on the evolution of the system, with high speeds potentially above escape velocity or preventing cycling orbits from happening. You can choose speed=0, meaning that all stars are initially at rest.
zoom	Specifies the visualization window. For instance, zoom=2 means that the portion of the sky displayed in the video is $[-2, 2] \times [-2, 2]$.
negativeMass	When set to True, the star masses follow some Gaussian rather than exponential distribution upon creation, and some masses will be negative.
collisions	By default, collisions are not allowed. If set to True, stars getting very close to each other are deemed to have collided: one star adsorbs the other and its mass is updated accordingly; the other star gets its mass adjusted to zero.
collThresh	Determines how close to each other two stars must be to result in a collision. The lower the collThresh, the more collisions. The maximum value is collThresh=1, resulting in no collision. Requires collisions=True.
expand	Some configurations result in the star cluster expanding over time, with fewer and fewer stars in the observation window. A value higher than expand=1 offers a zoom-out, with the window of observations becoming larger over time, giving the impression that your observation point is moving away from the star cluster, with stars seemingly shrinking over time, allowing you to see the full cluster at all times despite its expansion. To the contrary, a negative value corresponds to zoom-in.
origin	There is no "center of the universe", that is, there is no absolute origin. Set origin='Centroid' to focus your vision around the moving centroid of the system (it will be static on the video). If you added a massive star with the parameter starBoost, it makes sense to consider this big star as your origin, by setting origin='Star_0'. Another option is origin='Zero'.
threeClusters	The Python code simulates one star cluster. You can expand the possibilities with threeClusters=True. Presently, not implemented with negative masses or new star generation.
p, Nstars, N	Initially start with Nstars active stars, out of a potential of N stars. The active stars are the first in the star tables. The inactive stars have their mass set to 0. At each new video frame, it turns an inactive star into an active one with probability p, thus increasing the Nstars counter. Great to start with very few stars and see how the system evolves until it has hundreds of stars, some colliding, and some becoming larger and larger after eating smaller ones. Not implemented with negative masses. The reliance on all interdistances between stars is the bottleneck in the current implementation.
dt, t, tend	The parameter dt represents time increments, with a large dt resulting in a fast-moving video. Initial and end times are respectively t and tend. The number of frames in the resulting video is (tend-t)/dt.
G	The gravitation parameter. The default value is 1. I tested smaller values as well.
softening	Increase distance between two stars to avoid division by zero if the distance vanishes.
createVideo	May slow down the simulations if createVideo=True. Set it to False when testing parameters, until you are ready to produce the video.
saveData	The output file nbody.txt contains N rows per video frame, each with 13 columns. It can be very large and slow to produce. Set saveData=False if you do not need it. Regardless, the much smaller file nbody_graph.py, summarizing the collisions (if any), is always produced.
fps, my_dpi	Respectively the number of frames per second, and dots per each in the video. A value above 240 for my_dpi produces high resolution, but a bigger file. A value above 20 for fps produces much shorter videos than (say) fps set to 3.
adjustVel	If True, converts velocities to centroid frame. For compatibility with original version.

15.2.3 Interesting parameter sets

In other to show the possibilities of the algorithm, I created a table featuring eight parameter sets covering a wide range of situations. These sets are broken down into the following categories:

- The first two sets feature a universe with a nonstandard law of gravity (law=0.5). In addition, negative masses are allowed. The first set has a massive red star with a negative mass (starBoost=-30): the star cluster expands and contracts regularly, with wilder oscillations and subclusters forming over time. In the second set, oscillations are even faster, but much more predictable.
- The third set is the standard universe. It starts very much like the second set, but never contracts. Instead, it expands more and more, but the expansion pace and star velocities considerably slow down over time.
- The fourth set, again with a massive red star (negative mass) at the center, has the most spectacular behavior, thanks to law=-0.5. Oscillations become incredibly fast over time, with significant expansion and scattered stars rotating wildly around the massive red star, seemingly ending in a singularity.
- The fifth set is similar to the third (standard universe), but this time star collisions are allowed. Orange stars are those that have collided, with a few of them growing bigger by eating more stars over time. There are many collisions initially, but eventually, due to expansion, collisions become very rare and even absent. There is a visible drift in the video. Occasionally, rogue stars escape at high speed. There are a number of stars that have a companion star for some time until the paths diverge.
- The sixth and seventh sets also correspond to the standard universe with collisions, but they start with three star clusters that coalesce over time. In the sixth set, I zoom-in (expand=-0.2) on a specific location during the course of the video, while on the identical system in the seventh set, I zoom out (expand=0.2).
- The seventh set corresponds to a standard universe with collisions allowed, as well as new star creation over time. It is not realistic in the sense that the mass of the whole system is not constant over time. But the addition of new stars prevent the single star cluster from expanding, creating some stability. Also, it starts with just one star and ends with several hundreds: it allows you to see the behavior when the number of stars is smaller, with more regular patterns partly caused by a massive star at the center, this time with positive mass.

At the top of Table 15.2, the clickable blue (light gray in print version) links (one per parameter set) point to the corresponding videos on YouTube, featuring the evolution of the star systems in question. It is surprising to see that sometimes, even some of the biggest stars can be ejected from the system. The parameters in Table 15.2 characterize the type of universes that our generative model can produce.

15.3 Analysis of star collisions and collision graph

Before diving into the analysis of star collisions, I provide details about the nbody.txt data set generated by the Python code when saveData=True. It consists of one row per star per time frame, with 13 fields in the following order: time, star ID, mass, color, and position of the star at the time in question, centroid of the global star cluster, and velocity of the star at the same time. The last three features (star

Table 15.2 Eight selected parameter sets covering various situations.

Parameter	Set 1	Set 2	Set 3	Set 4	Set 5	Set 6	Set 7	Set 8
N	100	100	100	100	500	1000	1000	500
t	0	0	0	0	0	0	0	0
tEnd	20	20	20	15	40	40	40	20
dt	0.01	0.01	0.01	0.01	0.02	0.02	0.02	0.01
softening	0.1	0.1	0.1	0.1	0.01	0.1	0.1	0.1
G	1	1	1	1	0.1	0.1	0.1	0.1
starBoost	−30	0	0	−30	0	0	0	5
law	0.5	0.5	3	−0.5	3	3	3	3
speed	0.2	0.2	0.2	0.8	0.8	0.8	0.8	0
zoom	40	3	3	5	10	10	4	2
seed	58	58	58	58	58	58	58	58
adjustVel	False	False	False	False	True	False	False	False
negativeMass	True	False	False	True	False	False	False	False
collisions	False	False	False	False	True	True	True	True
collThresh	0.0	0.0	0.0	0.0	0.1	0.9	0.9	0.9
expand	1.0	0.0	2.0	0.0	0.0	−2.0	2.0	0.0
origin	'Centroid'	'Centroid'	'Centroid'	'Star_0'	'Centroid'	'Centroid'	'Centroid'	'Star_0'
threeClusters	False	False	False	False	False	True	True	False
p	0.0	0.0	0.0	0.0	0.0	0.0	0.0	0.2
Nstars	0	0	0	0	0	0	0	1
fps	20	20	20	20	20	20	20	20
my_dpi	240	240	240	240	240	240	240	240

position, centroid, and star velocity) are 3D vectors, with components corresponding to the X, Y, and Z axis. Each time frame corresponds to a video frame.

This rather large collection of synthetic data can be used to perform various analyses and benchmark predictive algorithms. It can be split into multiple subsets of stars or time periods, for cross-validation purposes. Subsets used to train a predictive model are called training sets, while those used to test the model are called validation sets. Due to the chaotic nature of the star system – it is indeed a **chaotic dynamical system** – some features such as individual star paths or drift of the whole system (similar to **Brownian motion**) may be difficult to predict, especially long-term. However, some general features may be easier to predict such as the decreasing expansion rate of the star cluster, the number of rogue and twin stars over time, the average distance between neighboring stars, or the decaying rate of star collisions. Patterns such as star filaments or star clustering may be identifiable. In most cases, the stochastic processes at play are not **stationary** [Wiki]: they clearly exhibit trends.

In this section, I focus on star collisions and the **collision graph**, attached to the star system corresponding to the seventh parameter set in Table 15.2. In particular, three distinct star clusters are initially created. All the data needed for this analysis is stored in a smaller data set named nbody_collisions.txt. It contains the following fields: collision ID (the key to this table), the collision time or video frame, the IDs of the two stars involved, the cluster IDs the stars were assigned to at creation time (represented by the color), the masses of the two stars involved in the collision, and the distance between the impact location and the centroid of the whole system at the time of impact. The collision data set is available on my GitHub repository, here. The larger data set nbody.txt, not analyzed in this chapter, is available here (87 MB compressed, 2 million rows).

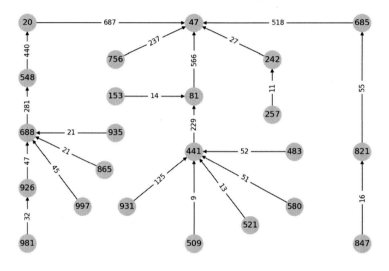

FIGURE 15.1

Collisions graph for the biggest star eater (star 47) in video 7.

15.3.1 **Weighted directed graphs: visualization with NetworkX**

The **directed graph** in Fig. 15.1 is produced with the **NetworkX** library in Python. The code is listed in Section 15.5.2. The numbers in the pink circles represent a star ID. The weight attached to each arrow represents the time frame when the collision happened. The last collision for star 47 happens at time $t = 687$ (that is, in video frame 687, out of 2000 frames for the whole video). Note the chain of collisions $509 \mapsto 441 \mapsto 81 \mapsto 47$, starting at video frame 9. Star 47 ends up with a mass of 59.21, while star 509 has a mass of 2.90 before being eaten: the mass has grown by a factor 20 after all the collisions!

The total number of collisions across all stars is 349. At creation time ($t = 0$) there were 1000 stars. Mass accumulation resulting from collisions happens very fast in the early days, but rapidly reaches a maximum. In this case, star 47 becomes the largest one with the largest number of collisions, thus the reason to choose it for illustration. There are a few other stars with many collisions, though most stars experience zero or one collision.

Detecting all the collision graphs amounts to detecting all the **connected components** of the whole graph [Wiki]. To that effect, I used the PB_NN_graph.py program described in Section 16.2.4.3. The Python code in question is also available on GitHub, here. Make sure that you input file is symmetric: if A, B is one of the collisions (between stars A and B), also include B, A in the input file. The subgraph associated to star 47 in Fig. 15.1 represents one of these connected components, namely the largest one. The list of all connected components, ordered by size, can be found here, with the star 47 merger series at the top; each number in each component represents a star.

There are several tools such as **GraphViz** [Wiki] to visualize the type of graph displayed in Fig. 15.1. Here I used the **NetworkX** library in Python [Wiki]. However, it is not trivial to make nice visualizations. The `draw` function offers many different layouts, illustrated here: spectral, spring, random, or **Fruchterman–Reingold** [Wiki]. Each layout chooses some optimum locations for the nodes, but none of them produces good results. In the end, I manually computed the locations of the nodes, though this process can be automated. Note that the graph in question is actually a **tree** [Wiki], with 47 being the root node. See here for an alternative solution to visualize this type of graph.

15.3.2 Interesting findings: how the universe got started

Fig. 15.2 illustrates the behavior of the collisions when using the seventh parameter set in Table 15.2. The X-axis represents the time frame, each instance of time corresponding to a specific video frame. The time axis is truncated in the top left image as collisions become very rare over time. In the two other images, it is not on a linear scale but compacted to the right, for the same reason.

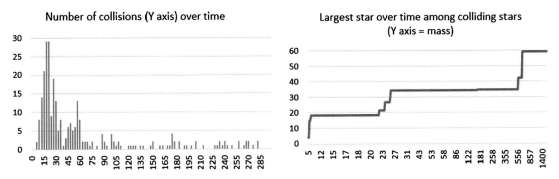

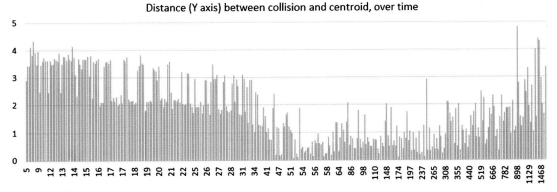

FIGURE 15.2

Summary statistics for the whole collision structure: the X axis represents the time.

The behavior is typical for a standard universe. In particular, while collisions become rare over time, they come in waves, with each new wave being less intense than previous ones, and increased spacing between successive waves over time. The plot on the top right corner shows how quickly the star masses increase at the beginning due to collisions, with the largest mass 6 times above what it was at the beginning, in less than 30 video frames. The video has 2000 frames: 20 per second, and thus, it lasts one minute and 40 seconds. So 30 frames represents the first 1.5 second of the video.

The picture at the bottom of Fig. 15.2 shows the complexity of the process. The Y axis represents the distance between a collision site and the evolving centroid of the global star cluster, for all the collisions occurring during the time frame. At the beginning, by design we have three star clusters, and collisions happen locally within each cluster. The collisions take place relatively far away from the global centroid, which is outside the three clusters. But very quickly, these three clusters coalesce, thus the distances to the centroid change, and many collisions eventually take place near the new centroid where larger stars are forming. The result is a decrease in the average distance to the centroid. But after a while (about 54 time frames, that is less than 3 seconds in the video), the distances start increasing again, as the universe expands and many collisions are not taking place near the centroid.

15.4 Animated data visualizations

The pictures in this section feature snapshots taken from the various synthetic universes generated using the parameter sets in Table 15.2. The full videos are on GitHub, here. Look for the MP4 files starting with `nbody` in the filename. The videos are also on YouTube, here. The parameter sets that I tested are described in Section 15.2.3.

Common themes for standard universes (positive star masses with `law=3`) include decreasing expansion and reduced star velocities over time, twin stars that remain bonded only for so long, filaments, rogue stars ejected at high speed from a central location, small local clusters of stars moving around, drift of the whole system, and the creation of massive stars over time when collisions are allowed. Another question worth addressing is whether or not there is a dominant rotation sign, clockwise or anticlockwise, depending on the initial configuration. In other words, are these systems **anisotropic** [Wiki]?

Fig. 15.3 shows snapshots for two different universes, corresponding to parameter sets 4 and 7. The full videos can be watched respectively here and here. I encourage you to zoom in on the pictures to get a better view.

Universe 4 has a massive central star of negative mass, in red. In addition, the law of gravity is not inverse-square: instead, I use `law=-0.5` rather than the standard `law=3` in the Python code. Blue stars have a positive mass, and the whole system starts with one single star cluster. However, it ends up with multiple clusters. The cluster in the top right corner, formed in the early stages, moves around the red star at wildly increasing speeds and eventually breaks apart. This pulsating universe exhibits a fast-growing **entropy** [Wiki] and ends up in a **singularity** [Wiki]: it actually crashed the Python program in the end, before completing the 2000 video frames. This explains why the corresponding video is 25 seconds shorter than the others. If you zoom in, you will notice that there are a few small stars with negative mass, besides the central one: they are pictured in red.

To the contrary, universe 7 is the classic, well-behaved version as we know it in real life. It starts with three separate clusters, but ends up with just one, as the clusters quickly coalesce. Entropy decreases over time, as the universe expands, albeit more and more slowly in the end. The green, blue, and magenta colors indicate which cluster a star originally belongs to. The snapshot, taken in the middle of the video, shows that the three clusters are already well blended, forming a single cluster at this

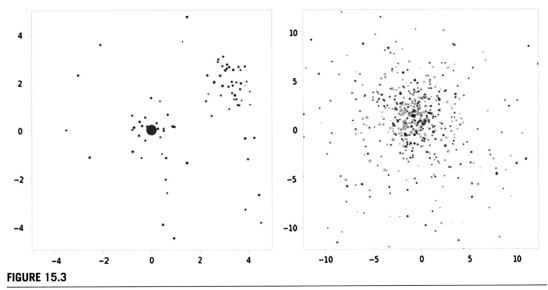

FIGURE 15.3

Snapshots of universe 4 (left) and universe 7 (right).

point. A number of twin stars can be seen, and may involve stars from different clusters. Once two stars collide, the color of the resulting star turns orange, explaining the concentration of orange stars (typically larger) near the center.

15.5 Python code and computational issues

There are two separate pieces of code: the main program for the simulations and video production in Section 15.5.1, and the auxiliary program for graphs representation (visualizing the collision tree) in Section 15.5.2.

15.5.1 Simulating the real and synthetic universes

The Python code is also on GitHub, here. The main parameters are described in Section 15.2.2.

The bottleneck is the computation of all pairwise interactions. One way to dramatically improve performance is to ignore stars that are far away from each other. Instead of using a square matrix to store all the distances between stars, one could use a **hash table** [Wiki], where the key is a pair of stars and the value is the separating distance. If the number of stars is n, the size of the distance matrix is $n \times n$, but the hash table (a dictionary in Python) could be limited to (say) $20 \times n$ entries if $n > 200$. The use of a very coarse grid for star locations can help detect when two stars are getting closer to each other, requiring to add a new entry in the hash table, and possibly delete some entries.

Another improvement consists of embedding multiple universe simulations (each with its own video) as "subplots" into a single video. I describe how to do it with an example, in Chapter 14. Also, when the number of stars is very small, you could join the locations of a same star on adjacent frames with line segments, to show the orbit in the video. See how to do this in Section 4.3.3.

Finally, I resize all images (the PNG files) before inclusion in the video. The video generator requires that they all have the same size.

```python
# nbody.py | www.MLTechniques.com | vincent@MLTechniques.com | 2022

import numpy as np
import matplotlib.pyplot as plt
from PIL import Image
import moviepy.video.io.ImageSequenceClip # to produce mp4 video

def getAcc( pos, mass, G, law, softening, col ):

    # Calculate the acceleration on each particle due to Newton's Law
    # pos is an N x 3 matrix of positions
    # mass is an N x 1 vector of masses
    # G is Newton's gravitational constant
    # softening is the softening length
    # a is N x 3 matrix of accelerations
    #
    # Also: update collisionTable

    global ncollisions

    # positions r = [x,y,z] for all particles
    x = pos[:,0:1]
    y = pos[:,1:2]
    z = pos[:,2:3]

    # matrix that stores all pairwise particle separations: r_j - r_i
    dx = x.T - x
    dy = y.T - y
    dz = z.T - z

    # matrix that stores 1/r^(law) for all particle pairwise particle separations
    inv_r3 = np.sqrt(dx**2 + dy**2 + dz**2 + softening**2)
    inv_r3 = inv_r3**(-law)

    # detect collisions
    if collisions:
        threshold = collThresh * softening**(-law)
        for i in range(N):
            for j in range(i+1,N):
                if inv_r3[i][j] > threshold and mass[i] != 0 and mass[j] !=0:
                    print("Collision between body",i,"and",j)
                    dist=np.linalg.norm(pos[i] - centroid) # distance to centroid
                    collData = str(ncollisions)+ " "+str(frame)+" "+str(i)+" "+str(j)
```

```
              collData = collData + " "+col[i]+" "+col[j]
              collData = collData +" "+str(mass[i])+" "+str(mass[j])+" "+str(dist)
              # collData = collData +" "+str(centroid)
              collisionTable.append(collData)
              ncollisions += 1
              mass[i]=mass[i]+mass[j]
              mass[j]=0
              col[i]='orange'
              col[j]='white'

    ax = G * (dx * inv_r3) @ mass
    ay = G * (dy * inv_r3) @ mass
    az = G * (dz * inv_r3) @ mass

    # pack together the acceleration components
    a = np.hstack((ax,ay,az))
    return a

def vector_to_string(vector):
    # turn numpy array entry into string of tab-separated values
    string = str(vector)
    string = " ".join(string.split()) # multiple spaces replaced by one space
    string = string.replace('[ ','').replace('[','')
    string = string.replace(' ]','').replace(']','')
    string = string.replace(' ',"\t") ## .replace("\t\t","\t")
    return string


#--- main

# Simulation parameters
N           = 1000    # Number of stars
t           = 0       # current time of the simulation
tEnd        = 40.0    # time at which simulation ends
dt          = 0.02    # timestep
softening   = 0.1     # softening length
G           = 0.1     # Newton's gravitational constant
starBoost   = 0.0     # create one massive star in the system, if starBoost > 1 or < -1
law         = 3       # exponent in denominator, gravitation law (should be set to 3)
speed       = 0.8     # high initial speed, above 'escape velocity', results in dispersion
zoom        = 10      # output on [-zoom, zoom] x [-zoom, zoom ] image
seed        = 58      # set the random number generator seed
adjustVel   = False   # always True in original version
negativeMass = False # if true, bodies are allowed to have negative mass
collisions  = True    # if true, collisions are properly handled
collThresh  = 0.9     # < 1 and > 0.05; fewer collisions if close to 1
expand      = -2.0    # enlarge window over time if expand > 0
origin      = 'Centroid' # options: 'Star_0', 'Zero', or 'Centroid'
```

```python
threeClusters = True # if true, generate three separate star clusters
p         = 0.0     # add one new star with proba p at each new frame if p > 0
Nstars    = 0       # if p > 0, start with Nstars; will add new stars up to N, over time
fps       = 20      # frames per second in video
my_dpi    = 240     # dots per inch in video
createVideo = True  # set to False for testing purposes (much faster!)
saveData  = False   # save data to nbody.txt if True (large file!)

# Handle configurations that are not supported
if threeClusters and p > 0:
    print("Error: adding new stars not supported with threeClusters set to True.")
    exit()
if Nstars >= N:
    print("Error: Nstars must be <= N.")
    exit()

# Generate Initial Conditions
np.random.seed(seed)
if negativeMass:
    mass = 1.25 + 0.75*np.random.randn(N,1)
else:
    mass = np.random.exponential(2.0,(N,1))
adjustedMass = 1
if starBoost > 1 or starBoost < 0:
    mass[0]= starBoost * np.max(abs(mass))
col=[] # bodies with positive mass in blue; others in red
for k in range(N):
    if mass[k] > 0:
        col.append('blue')
    else:
        col.append('red')
    if p > 0 and k >= Nstars:
        mass[k] = 0 # make room for future stars
        col[k] = 'darkviolet' # newly added stars appear in pink

pos = np.random.randn(N,3) # randomly selected positions and velocities
if threeClusters:
    for k in range(int(N/3)):
        pos[k] += [5.0, 0.0, 0.0]
        col[k] = 'green'
    for k in range(int(N/3),int(2*N/3)):
        pos[k] += [0.0, 5.0, 1.0]
        col[k] = 'magenta'
vel = speed * np.random.randn(N,3)

# Convert to Center-of-Mass frame
if adjustVel:
    for k in range(N):
```

```python
        vel[k] -= np.mean(abs(mass[k]) * vel[k]) / np.mean(abs(mass))

# calculate initial gravitational accelerations
frame=-1
acc = getAcc( pos, mass, G, law, softening, col )

# number of timesteps (or frames in the video)
Nt = int(np.ceil(tEnd/dt))

# prep figure
fig = plt.figure(figsize=(4,5),dpi=80)
ax1 = fig.gca() # or ax1 = plt.subplot() ??
plt.setp(ax1.spines.values(), linewidth=0.1)
plt.rc('xtick', labelsize=5) # fontsize of the tick labels
plt.rc('ytick', labelsize=5) # fontsize of the tick labels
ax1.xaxis.set_tick_params(width=0.1)
ax1.yaxis.set_tick_params(width=0.1)

flist=[]      # list of image filenames for the video
collisionTable=[] # collision table
ncollisions=1

if Nt > 2000:
    print("About to generate", Nt, "images.")
    answer = input ("Type y to proceed: ")
    if answer != 'y':
        exit()

# Simulation Main Loop

if saveData:
    OUT=open("nbody.txt","w")

for frame in range(Nt):
    if p > 0 and Nstars < N: # add new star with proba p
        if np.random.uniform() < p:
            mass[Nstars] = np.random.exponential(2.0,1)
            Nstars += 1

    vel += acc * dt/2.0 # (1/2) kick
    pos += vel * dt # drift
    acc = getAcc( pos, mass, G, law, softening, col ) # update accelerations
    vel += acc * dt/2.0 # (1/2) kick
    t += dt # update time

    image='nbody'+str(frame)+'.png' # filename of image in current frame
    if frame % 10 == 0:
        print("Creating image",image) # show progress on the screen
```

```
plt.sca(ax1)
plt.cla()
centroid = np.zeros(3)
totalMass=np.sum(abs(mass))
if origin == 'Star_0':
    centroid = pos[0]
elif origin == 'Centroid':
    for k in range(N):
        centroid += abs(mass[k]) * pos[k] / totalMass

# save results
if saveData:
    for k in range(N):
        line=str(frame)+"\t"+str(k)+"\t"+str(float(mass[k]))+"\t"+str(col[k])+"\t"
        string1 = vector_to_string(pos[k])
        string2 = vector_to_string(centroid)
        string3 = vector_to_string(vel[k])
        line=line+string1+"\t"+string2+"\t"+string3+"\n"
        OUT.write(line)

adjustedMass /= (1.0 + expand/Nt) # for visualization only
plt.scatter(pos[:,0]-centroid[0],pos[:,1]-centroid[1],
                    s=adjustedMass*abs(mass),color=col)
zoom *= (1.0 + expand/Nt)

ax1.set(xlim=(-zoom, zoom), ylim=(-zoom, zoom))
ax1.set_aspect('equal', 'box')

if createVideo and frame>0:
    # plt.axis('off')
    plt.savefig(image,bbox_inches='tight',pad_inches=0.2,dpi=my_dpi)
    im = Image.open(image)
    if frame == 1:
        width, height = im.size
        width=2*int(width/2)
        height=2*int(height/2)
        fixedSize=(width,height)
    im = im.resize(fixedSize)
    im.save(image,"PNG")
    flist.append(image)
    plt.pause(0.001)
if saveData:
    OUT.close()

# output collision table
OUT2=open("nbody_collisions.txt","w")
for entry in collisionTable:
```

```
        OUT2.write(vector_to_string(entry)+"\n")

# output video / fps is number of frames per second
if createVideo:
    clip = moviepy.video.io.ImageSequenceClip.ImageSequenceClip(flist, fps=fps)
    clip.write_videofile('nbody.mp4')
```

15.5.2 Visualizing collision graphs

This code is also on GitHub, here. For explanations, see Section 15.3.1.

```
# nbody_graph.py | www.MLTechniques.com | vincent@MLTechniques.com | 2022
# collision history for star # 47 (biggest star eater) using parameter set # 7

import networkx as nx
# https://www.python-graph-gallery.com/322-network-layout-possibilities
# graph layouts: https://networkx.org/documentation/stable/auto_examples/index.html

# importing matplotlib.pyplot
import matplotlib.pyplot as plt

G = nx.DiGraph(directed=True)

# define the graph; each entry is (node, next node, weight)
E = [(509, 441, 9),
    (257, 242, 11),
    (521, 441, 13),
    (153, 81, 14),
    (847, 821, 16),
    (821, 685, 55),
    (865, 688, 21),
    (935, 688, 21),
    (242, 47, 27),
    (981, 926, 32),
    (997, 688, 45),
    (926, 688, 47),
    (580, 441, 51),
    (483, 441, 52),
    (821, 685, 55),
    (931, 441, 125),
    (441, 81, 229),
    (756, 47, 237),
    (688, 548, 281),
    (548, 20, 440),
    (685, 47, 518),
    (81, 47, 566),
    (20, 47, 687)]
```

```
G.add_weighted_edges_from(E)

# specify locations of the nodes on the graph
pos = {441: (3, 2.6),
       931: (1.8, 2),
       483: (4.8, 2.6),
       580: (4.8, 2),
       521: (4, 1.8),
       509: (3, 1.6),
       81: (3, 3.2),
       153: (1.6, 3.2),
       47: (3, 4),
       756: (1.6, 3.6),
       685: (6, 4),
       821: (6, 2.6),
       847: (6, 1.6),
       20: (0,4),
       548: (0, 3.4),
       688: (0, 2.8),
       997: (1, 2),
       935: (1.6, 2.8),
       865: (1.4, 2.4),
       926: (0, 2.2),
       981: (0, 1.6),
       242: (4.4, 3.6),
       257: (4.4, 3.0)}

nx.set_node_attributes(G, pos, 'coord')

nx.draw(G, pos, with_labels=True, node_size=700, node_color='pink') ### , font_weight="bold")
edge_weight = nx.get_edge_attributes(G,'weight')
nx.draw_networkx_edge_labels(G, pos, edge_labels = edge_weight)
plt.savefig("graph.png")
plt.show()
```

Perturbed lattice point process: alternative to GMM

16

Inference, nearest neighbor graph

This chapter covers additional topics most relevant to modern machine learning, from my book "Stochastic Processes and Simulations: A Machine Learning Perspective" [20]. The purpose is to introduce you to a new type of **stochastic point processes** [Wiki] with applications to sensor data, chemistry, physics (crystallography in particular) and cellular networks: for instance, to optimize the locations of cell towers or **Internet-of-Things** (IOT) devices.

The processes in question are known as **perturbed lattices**, and referred to here as Poisson–binomial processes for reasons that will soon become obvious. It is different both from Poisson and binomial processes. This chapter covers more advanced material, especially pertaining to statistical and probability theory. Most of the mathematical developments such a theorems are mentioned without proof. The interested reader is referred to [20] for the details. Emphasis is still on data-driven inference, empirical distributions, **quantile functions** (the inverse of a probability distribution) and inference techniques including a new test of independence. The topics discussed here include 2D cluster processes, nearest neighbor graphs, lattice-based structures, statistical inference, and a simple alternative to **Gaussian mixture models** (GMM) typically used in **generative adversarial models** (GAN). In recent years, there has been a considerable interest in perturbed-lattice point processes, see [34,38].

16.1 Perturbed lattices: definition and properties

Stochastically perturbed lattices are referred to here as Poisson–binomial processes. They are based on a lattice structure and on a location–scale family of probability distributions. They are characterized either by the joint distribution of point counts in arbitrary nonoverlapping sets, or the distribution of distances between **nearest neighbor** points. In one dimension, the latter is called **interarrival times**, while the former (the point counts) have a joint **Poisson–binomial distribution**. Similarly, the nearest neighbor distances have a joint **Poisson–exponential distribution**. In one dimension, the point process is a time series.

The underlying lattice is the infinite 2D square grid [Wiki] with square of area λ^2 and integer coordinates for the lattice locations (the **vertices**). The parameter $\lambda > 0$ is called the **intensity** of the process: it determines the average number of points per unit. To each location (h, k) on the lattice, we associate a random variable (X_h, Y_k) which represents the coordinates of the random point attached to the vertex (h, k), with $h, k \in \mathbb{Z}$. The random variables (X_h, Y_k) are independently distributed, with a distribution F_s depending on a parameter s called the **scale**. More specifically, we have

$$P[(X_h, Y_k) < (x, y)] = F_s\left(\frac{\lambda x - h}{\lambda}\right) F_s\left(\frac{\lambda y - k}{\lambda}\right) = F\left(\frac{x - h/\lambda}{s}\right) F\left(\frac{y - k/\lambda}{s}\right). \tag{16.1}$$

Synthetic Data and Generative AI. https://doi.org/10.1016/B978-0-44-321857-6.00020-5

A fundamental result similar to the **central limit theorem** is the convergence of the process to a homogeneous **Poisson process** of intensity λ^2 [Wiki] as $s \to \infty$. The proof is found in [20]. The approximation is very good even if $s \approx 20$. To the contrary, if $s = 0$, the points (X_h, Y_k) coincide with the fixed locations (h, k) of the underlying lattice. Typically, the lattice locations are not known and not easy to retrieve: the lattice plays the role of a deterministic **hidden process**. All of this, including generalization to lattices on the sphere, hexagonal lattices, or random points replaced by random lines, is discussed in my book [20].

Typical choices for F leading to easy simulations via the quantile function are

$$\text{Uniform: } F(x) = \frac{1}{2} + \frac{x}{2} \text{ if } -1 \leq x \leq 1, \text{ with } F(x) = 1 \text{ if } x > 1 \text{ and } F(x) = 0 \text{ if } x < -1$$

$$\text{Laplace: } F(x) = \frac{1}{2} + \frac{1}{2}\text{sgn}(x)(1 + \exp(-|x|))$$

$$\text{Logistic: } F(x) = \frac{1}{1 + \exp(-x)}$$

$$\text{Cauchy: } F(x) = \frac{1}{2} + \frac{1}{\pi}\arctan(x)$$

where $\text{sgn}(x)$ is the sign function [Wiki], with $\text{sgn}(0) = 0$. Table 16.1 establishes the connection between the scaling factor s and the variance of F_s.

Table 16.1 Variance attached to F_s, as a function of s.

F	Uniform	Logistic	Laplace	Cauchy	Gaussian
$\text{Var}[F_s]$	$s^2/3$	$\pi^2 s^2/3$	$2s^2$	∞	s^2

16.1.1 Point counts distribution

Let $B = [a, b] \times [c, d]$ define a rectangle, with $a < b$, $c < d$, and $p_{h,k} = P[(X_h, Y_k) \in B]$. We have

$$p_{h,k} = \left[F\left(\frac{b - h/\lambda}{s}\right) - F\left(\frac{a - h/\lambda}{s}\right)\right] \cdot \left[F\left(\frac{d - k/\lambda}{s}\right) - F\left(\frac{c - k/\lambda}{s}\right)\right]. \tag{16.2}$$

As a consequence, the integer-valued random variable $N(B)$ counting the number of points of the process in a set B, known as the **counting measure** [Wiki] or point count, has a **Poisson–binomial distribution** of parameters $p_{h,k}$ with $h, k \in \mathbb{Z}$ [Wiki]. The only difference with a standard Poisson–binomial distribution is that here we have infinitely many parameters (the $p_{h,k}$'s). Basic properties of that distribution yield

$$E[N(B)] = \sum_{h,k=-\infty}^{\infty} p_{h,k}, \tag{16.3}$$

$$\text{Var}[N(B)] = \sum_{h,k=-\infty}^{\infty} p_{h,k}(1 - p_{h,k}), \tag{16.4}$$

$$P[N(B) = 0] = \prod_{h,k=-\infty}^{\infty} (1 - p_{h,k}), \tag{16.5}$$

$$P[N(B) = 1] = \left\{ \prod_{h,k=-\infty}^{\infty} (1 - p_{h,k}) \right\} \cdot \sum_{h,k=-\infty}^{\infty} \frac{p_{h,k}}{1 - p_{h,k}}. \qquad (16.6)$$

It is more difficult, though possible, to obtain the higher moments $E[N^r(B)]$ or $P[N(B) = r]$ in closed form if $r > 2$. This is due to the combinatorial nature of the Poisson–binomial distribution. But you can easily obtain approximated values using simulations. Note that as $s \to \infty$, the process tends to a Poisson process. Thus the point count distribution tends to a Poisson distribution. The convergence of the Poisson–binomial distribution to the Poisson distribution is known as **Le Cam's theorem** [Wiki].

16.1.2 **Periodicity and amplitude of point count expectations**

For the sake of simplicity, I consider the one-dimensional case here. In short, the lattice is $\mathbb{Z}$, and (X_h, Y_k) is replaced by X_k with $k \in \mathbb{Z}$. The results extend to the 2D case, with double periodicity: one for each component.

Let (X_k), with $k \in \mathbb{Z}$, represents the points of a one-dimensional Poisson–binomial process of intensity λ and scaling factor s. We are interested in point counts $N_\tau(t) = N[B_\tau(t)]$ in the interval $B_\tau(t) = [t, t + \tau[$. Let

$$\phi_\tau(t) = E[N_\tau(t)].$$

By virtue of Theorem 4.1 in [20] (page 50), we have $\phi_\tau(t) = 1$ if $\tau = 1/\lambda$. More generally, regardless of τ, the function $\phi_\tau(t)$ is periodic of period $1/\lambda$. That is, $\phi_\tau(t) = \phi_\tau(t + 1/\lambda)$. This latter statement is also true for $\text{Var}[N_\tau(t)]$, $P[N_\tau(t) = 0]$, and $P[N_\tau(t) = 1]$. This fact is trivial if you look at formulas (16.3), (16.4), (16.5), and (16.6), used to compute the four quantities in question.

The amplitude of the oscillations is extremely small even with a scaling factor as low as $s = 0.3$ (assuming F is logistic). It quickly tends to zero as $s \to \infty$. So the process is almost stationary, unless s is very close to zero. Thus, in most inference problems, the choice of the (nonoverlapping) intervals has very little impact. In particular, $\phi_\tau(t) \approx \lambda\tau$. The small amplitude of $\phi_\tau(t)$ is pictured in Fig. 16.1.

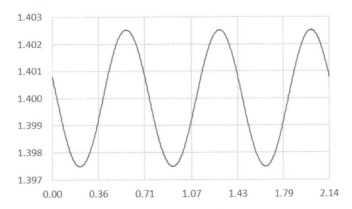

FIGURE 16.1

Period and amplitude of $\phi_\tau(t)$; here $\tau = 1$, $\lambda = 1.4$, $s = 0.3$.

The point counts divided by the length τ of the interval, especially averaged over a number of nonoverlapping intervals represent an excellent estimator of the intensity λ, regardless of the scaling factor s. In this simulation, $\tau = 1$, the true theoretical value is $\lambda = 1.4$, and the estimated value oscillates between 1.39975 and 1.4025. The **boundary effects** are ignored here, by focusing on intervals that are not too close to the observation window. Otherwise the estimator would be biased. In two dimensions, the interval is replaced by a square, and the length is replaced by the square root of the area, to estimate λ.

16.1.3 Testing the independence of point counts

As in Section 16.1.2, I illustrate the method in the one-dimensional case. Generalization to 2D is straightforward. I want to assess whether the point count distribution $N(B)$ in various nonoverlapping domains B are independent or not. Generally, one works with domains of same area. The most popular test of independence is the χ^2 (**Chi-squared**) test [Wiki]. One drawback of χ^2 is that it requires binning the data. The bin size cannot be too small, and the bins may be arbitrary. My approach is different, and avoids this problem. It is also well suited to detect small deviations from independence.

It works as follows. I compare the empirical distribution of count frequencies with what it should be if the counts were independent. I offer two solutions: one based on the R-squared [Wiki], and one based on the **Kolmogorov–Smirnov statistic** [Wiki]. The latter is similar to the approach discussed by Zhang in his article "A Kolmogorov–Smirnov type test for independence between marks and points of marked point processes" [45], available online here.

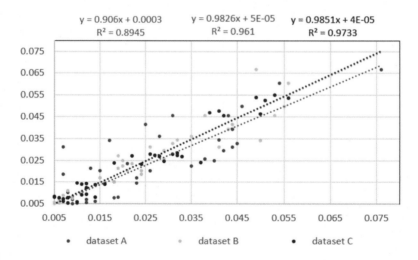

FIGURE 16.2

A new test of independence (R-squared version).

Let (X_k) be the points of a Poisson–binomial process M_A of intensity $\lambda = 1$ and scale factor $s = 0.7$, with a logistic F. Exercise 10 in [20] (page 60) shows – using theoretical arguments – that the point counts are not independent. This proves that Poisson–binomial processes are different from Poisson processes. Here I establish the same conclusion via statistical testing. The purpose is to illustrate how the test works, so that you can use it in other contexts. I chose three intervals $B_1 = [-1.5, -0.5[$, $B_2 = [-0.5, 0.5[$, and $B_3 = [0.5, 1.5[$. The data consists of $m = 1000$ realizations of the process in question, each one consisting of 41 points X_k, $k = -20, \ldots, 20$. The number 41 is large enough in this case, to eliminate **boundary effects**. The data, computations and results are in the spreadsheet `PB_independence.xlsx`, described later in this section.

The point counts attached to a realization ω of the point process, is denoted as N_ω. The aggregated point count over the m realizations is denoted as N, and the set of m realizations is denoted as Ω. Now, for $i = 1, 2, 3$ and $j_1, j_2, j_3 \in \mathbb{N}$, I can define the following quantities:

$$p_i(j) = \frac{1}{m} \sum_{\omega \in \Omega} \chi[N_\omega(B_i) = j],$$

$$p(j_1, j_2, j_3) = \frac{1}{m} \sum_{\omega \in \Omega} \prod_{i=1}^{3} \chi[N_\omega(B_i) = j_i], \tag{16.7}$$

$$p'(j_1, j_2, j_3) = \frac{1}{m^3} \prod_{i=1}^{3} \sum_{\omega \in \Omega} \chi[N_\omega(B_i) = j_i], \tag{16.8}$$

where χ is the indicator function [Wiki]. For instance, $p_1(3) = 0.043$ means that in 43 realizations out of $m = 1000$, the domain B_1 contained exactly 3 points. Also, $p'(j_1, j_2, j_3) = p_1(j_1) p_2(j_2) p_3(j_3)$. The three point counts $N(B_1)$, $N(B_2)$, $N(B_3)$ are independently distributed if and only if formulas (16.7) and (16.8) represent the same quantity when $m = \infty$. In other words, the three point counts are independently distributed if $p \to p'$ pointwise [Wiki], as $m \to \infty$.

To avoid future confusion, p and p' are denoted as p_A and p'_A to emphasize the fact that they are attached to the process M_A. To test for independence, I simulated m realizations of a sister point process M_B: one with the same marginal distributions for the three point counts, using the estimates $p_i(j)$ obtained from M_A, but this time with guaranteed independence of the point counts, by design. Likewise, I define the functions p_B and p'_B. Let ρ_A be the correlation between p_A and p'_A, computed across all triplets satisfying

$$\min\{p_A(j_1, j_2, j_3), p'_A(j_1, j_2, j_3)\} > \epsilon.$$

I chose $\epsilon = 0$. In my example, there were fewer than $7 \times 7 \times 7 = 343$ such triplets. Finally, the statistic of the test is ρ_A^2.

16.1.3.1 *Results and interpretation*

In the spreadsheet `PB_independence.xlsx`, the tab `Dataset_A` corresponds to M_A, and `Dataset_B` corresponds to M_B. The same computations are done in tab `Dataset_C` for another point process M_C, identical to M_A except that this time $s = 4$. With such a "large" s, M_C is not that different from a stationary Poisson point process: in particular, the point counts are almost independent (no statistical test could detect that they are not, unless using extremely large samples).

The main findings are displayed in Fig. 16.2. Blue represents the M_A process, gray represents M_B, and red represents M_C. Each blue dot corresponds to a vector (p_A, p'_A) attached to a particular (j_1, j_2, j_3). In case of perfect independence, all the dots should be on the main diagonal. Blue dots are two far away from the main diagonal, and thus the point counts in M_A are not independent. To the contrary, M_B (supposed to exhibit independence by construction) and M_C (known from theory to exhibit near-independence) are close enough to each other and to the main diagonal. If you repeat the experiment with M_B a hundred times, you will get a hundred gray regression lines, generating a confidence curve for the test. Note that the R^2 displayed for the three regression lines in Fig. 16.2, are identical to $\rho_A^2, \rho_B^2, \rho_C^2$, confirming the somewhat poor performance of M_A. The slope of the regression line is also an indicator of lack of independence, if it is not close enough to one. Again, M_B is the loser here, when measured against the slope. The intercept of the regression line (when different enough from zero) further confirms this.

A version of this test, available in the spreadsheet, relies on the Kolmogorov–Smirnov statistics instead of the R-squared. It works with aggregated rather than raw frequencies. In short, you replace the empirical probabilities p_A, p_A' (the frequencies) by empirical aggregated probabilities P_A, P_A', that is, the empirical distributions. The statistic of the test is the uniform norm [Wiki] $\delta_A = ||P_A - P_A'||_\infty$. It leads to the same conclusion. Since the argument of the functions p_A, p_A' are the triplets (j_1, j_2, j_3) and are unordered, there are many different ways to build the empirical distribution. However, the differences among these constructions are minuscule. See also the section "Interactions in Point Pattern Analysis" in [22].

16.1.3.2 *About the spreadsheet*

The interactive spreadsheet is on my GitHub repository; see `PB_independence.xlsx`. The `Summary` tab controls the parameters s, λ, and the upper/lower bounds of the intervals B_1, B_2, B_3. It also contains the results: the R-squared's $\rho_A^2, \rho_B^2, \rho_C^2$ respectively in cells `B11`, `C11`, `D11`, and the Kolmogorov–Smirnov statistics $\delta_A, \delta_B, \delta_C$ respectively in cells `B12`, `C12`, `D12`. Columns `J`, `K`, `L` represent the triplets (j_1, j_2, j_3), also available in concatenated format in column `I`. For the M_A process, the empirical probabilities p_A, p_A' are in columns `Q`, `R`, and the empirical distributions P_A, P_A' are in columns `S`, `T`. For M_B and M_C, the corresponding values are in columns `Z` to `AD` and `AI` to `AM`, respectively.

In the `Dataset_A` and `Dataset_C` tabs, each row (except the first one) represents a realization of the underlying point process, respectively M_A and M_C. The 41 points of each realization are in columns `F` to `AT`. The first row (same columns) stores the indices of the points in question. I used the logistic distribution for `F`.

The `Dataset_B` tab corresponds to M_B. It is organized differently. The actual points of each realization are not computed as they are not needed this time. Thus they are not in the spreadsheet. Instead, point counts summarizing each "unobserved" realization are in columns `I`, `J`, `K`, corresponding respectively to B_1, B_2, B_3. Columns `Q` and `R`, representing the values of p_B and p_B' (with the argument in column `F`), are derived from these counts. Remember that M_B was designed so that (1) $p_B' = p_A'$ and (2) the point counts $N(B_1)$, $N(B_2)$, $N(B_3)$ are independent.

16.2 Cluster processes and nearest neighbor graphs

Poisson–binomial processes and compound systems derived from these processes are used to model cluster structures. Here, I discuss radial **cluster processes** associated to perturbed lattices, and potential applications. The examples are produced as follows. First, I generate a 2D realization of a Poisson–binomial process, called the parent process. Then around each point (X_h, Y_k) of the parent process, I generate a random number of points (up to 15 per location) radially distributed around the parent center (X_h, Y_k). The collection of all the "child" points constitute the cluster process, as pictured in green in Figs. 16.3 and 16.4. The points of the parent process – the centers – are in blue.

16.2.1 Synthetic, semirigid cluster structures

To simulate radial distributions (also called radial intensities in this case), I use a **generalized logistic distribution** (see Section 2.1.1 in [20]) instead of the Gaussian one, for the child process. The generalized logistic distribution has nice features: easy to simulate, easy to compute the cumulative distribution function (CDF), and it has many parameters, offering a lot of flexibility for the shape of the density. The peculiarity of the Poisson–binomial process offers two options:

- Classic option. Child processes are centered around the points of the parent process, with exactly one child process per point.
- Ad-hoc option. Child processes are centered around the bivariate lattice locations $(h/\lambda, k/\lambda)$, with exactly one child process per location, and $h, k \in \mathbb{Z}$.

In the latter case, if s is small, the child process attached to the index (h, k) has its points distributed around (X_h, X_k) – a point of the parent process – thus it will be similar to the classic option. This is because if s is small, then $(h/\lambda, k/\lambda)$ is close to (X_h, X_k) on average. It becomes more interesting when s is neither too small nor too large.

Figs. 16.3 and 16.4 show two extreme cases. The parent process modeling the cluster centers, is Poisson–binomial. It is simulated with intensity function $\lambda = 1$, using a uniform distribution for F. The **scaling factor** is $s = 0.2$ in Fig. 16.3, and $s = 2$ in Fig. 16.4. The left plot is a zoom-in. Around each center (marked with a blue cross in the picture), up to 15 points are radially distributed, creating the overall cluster structure. These points are the actual, observed points of the process, referred to as the child process. The distance between a point (X', Y') and its cluster center (X, Y) has a **half-logistic distribution** [Wiki]. The simulations shown here are performed using formulas (16.9) and (16.10):

$$X' = X + \log\left(\frac{U}{1 - U}\right)\cos(2\pi V), \tag{16.9}$$

$$Y' = Y + \log\left(\frac{U}{1 - U}\right)\sin(2\pi V). \tag{16.10}$$

Here U and V are independent uniform deviates on $[0, 1]$. The **quantile function** $Q(U) = \log\frac{U}{1-U}$ corresponds to a standard logistic distribution.

The contrast between Figs. 16.3 and 16.4 is due to the choice of the scaling factor s. The value $s = 0.2$, close to zero, strongly reveals the underlying lattice structure. Here this effect is strong because of the choice of F (it has a very thin tail), and the relatively small variance of the distance between a point and its associated cluster center. It produces repulsion among neighbor points: we are dealing with a **repulsive process**. When $s = 0$, all the randomness is gone. Modeling applications include optimum distribution of sensors (for instance, cell towers), crystal structures, and bonding patterns of molecules in chemistry.

By contrast, $s = 2$ makes the cluster structure much more apparent. This time, there is **attraction** among neighbor points: we are dealing with an **attractive process**. It can model many types of structures, associated to human activities or natural phenomena, such as the distribution of galaxies in the universe. Fig. 16.5 provides an example, related to the manufacture of kitchen countertops.

Fig. 16.5 shows luxury kitchen countertops called "Inverness bronze Cambria quartz", on the left. While the quality (and price) is far superior to all other products from the same company, the rendering of marble veins is not done properly. It looks man-made: not the kind of patterns you would find in real

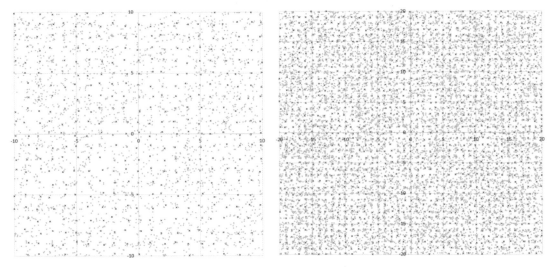

FIGURE 16.3

Radial cluster process ($s = 0.2$, $\lambda = 1$) with centers in blue; zoom in on the left.

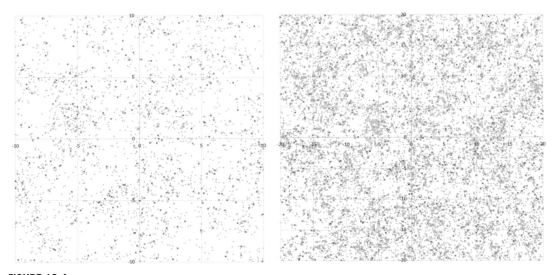

FIGURE 16.4

Radial cluster process ($s = 2$, $\lambda = 1$) with centers in blue; zoom in on the left.

stones. The pattern is too regular, as if produced using a very small value of the scaling factor s. An easy fix is to use patterns generated by the cluster processes described here. To increase randomness, increase s. The picture on the right shows a more realistic rendering of randomness.

FIGURE 16.5

Manufactured marble lacking true lattice randomness (left).

16.2.2 **Python code to generate cluster processes**

The Python code for the simulations is also on my GitHub repository, here.

```
# PB_radial.py [www.MLTechniques.com] -- simulate a realization of a cluster process

import math
import random
random.seed(100)


s=10
pi=3.14159265358979323846264338

file=open('PB_radial.txt',"w")
for h in range(-30,31):
    for k in range(-30,31):

        # Create the center (parent Poisson-binomial process, F uniform)
        ranx=random.random()
        rany=random.random()
        x=h+2*s*(ranx-1/2)
        y=k+2*s*(rany-1/2)
        line=str(h)+"\t"+str(k)+"\tCenter\t"+str(x)+"\t"+str(y)+"\n"
        file.write(line)

        # Create the child, radial process (up to 15 points per center)
        M=int(15*random.random())
        for m in range(M):
            ran1=random.random()
```

```
ran2=random.random()
factor=math.log(ran2/(1-ran2))
x1=x+factor*math.cos(2*pi*ran1);
y1=y+factor*math.sin(2*pi*ran1);
line=str(h)+"\t"+str(k)+"\tLocal\t"+str(x1)+"\t"+str(y1)+"\n"
file.write(line)
file.close()
```

16.2.3 **References on cluster processes**

Typical examples of cluster point processes include **Neyman–Scott** (see here) and **Matérn** (see here). Useful references include Baddeley's textbook "Spatial Point Processes and their Applications" [4], Sigman's course material (Columbia University) on one-dimensional **renewal processes** for beginners, entitled "Notes on the Poisson Process" [39], Last and Kenrose's book "Lectures on the Poisson Process" [27], and Cressie's comprehensive 900-page book "Statistics for Spatial Data" [11]. Cluster point processes are part of a larger field known as **spatial statistics**, encompassing other techniques such as geostatistics, kriging, and tessellations. For lattice-based processes known as **perturbed-lattice point processes**, more closely related to the theme of this chapter (lattice processes), and also more recent with applications to cellular networks, see the following references:

- "On Comparison of Clustering Properties of Point Processes" [9]
- "Clustering and percolation of point processes" [8]
- "Clustering comparison of point processes, applications to random geometric models" [10]
- "Stochastic Geometry-Based Tools for Spatial Modeling and Planning of Future Cellular Networks" [26]
- "Hyperuniform and rigid stable matchings" [28]
- "Rigidity and tolerance for perturbed lattices" [38]
- "Cluster analysis of spatial point patterns: posterior distribution of parents inferred from offspring" [37]
- "Recovering the lattice from its random perturbations" [42]
- "Geometry and Topology of the Boolean Model on a Stationary Point Processes" [44]
- "On distances between point patterns and their applications" [29]

More general references include two comprehensive volumes on point process theory by Daley and Vere-Jones [12,13], a chapter by Johnson [23], books by Møller and Waagepetersen, focusing on statistical inference for spatial processes [32,33], and "Point Pattern Analysis: Nearest Neighbor Statistics" by Anselin [3] focusing on point inhibition/aggregation metrics. See also [31] by Møller, and "Limit Theorems for Network Dependent Random Variables" [24], available online here.

There are different ways to simulate **radial processes**; the most popular method uses a bivariate Gaussian distribution for the child process. Poisson point processes with **nonhomogeneous** radial intensities are discussed in my article "Estimation of the Intensity of a Poisson Point Process by Means of Nearest Neighbor Distances" [19]. The focus is on radial, and thus nonhomogeneous intensity functions: in this case λ depends on the location, as opposed to a stationary Poisson process where λ is constant. Estimating the **intensity function** of such a process is equivalent to a **density estimation** problem, using kernel density estimators [Wiki].

16.2.4 Superimposed perturbed lattices: an alternative to mixture models

When the points of m independent Poisson–binomial processes with same distribution F are bundled together, we say that the processes are **superimposed**. The result may no longer be Poisson–binomial, unlike the superimposition of standard Poisson processes (itself a special case of Poisson–binomial, with $s = \infty$). Indeed, if the scaling factor s is small and $m > 1$ is not too small, the resulting process exhibits clustering around each lattice location. Also, the intensities or scaling factors of each individual point process may be different, and the resulting process may not be homogeneous. Superimposed point processes also called **interlaced** processes.

I first describe mixtures before moving to interlaced processes. The two models share many similarities, but also some differences. A **mixture** of m point processes, denoted as M, is defined as follows:

- We have m independent point processes $M_1, \ldots, M_m$ with same distribution F.
- The intensity and scaling factor attached to M_i are denoted respectively as λ_i and s_i ($i = 1, \ldots, m$).
- The points of M_i ($i = 1, \ldots, m$) are denoted as (X_{ih}, Y_{ik}).
- The point (X_h, Y_k) of the mixture process M is equal to (X_{ih}, Y_{ik}) with probability $\pi_i > 0$, $i = 1, \ldots, m$.

The π_i's are the mixture proportions, and their sum is equal to one. While mixing or superimposing Poisson–binomial processes seem like the same operation, which is true for stationary Poisson processes, in the case of Poisson–binomial processes, these are distinct operations resulting in significant differences when the scaling factors are very small. The difference is most striking when $s = 0$. In particular, superimposed processes are less random than mixtures. This is due to the discrete nature of the underlying lattice. However, with larger scaling factors, the behavior of mixed and superimposed processes tend to be similar.

Fig. 16.6 represents a realization of m superimposed shifted stretched Poisson–binomial processes, called **m-interlacing**. For each individual process M_i, $i = 1, \ldots, m$, the distribution attached to the point (X_{ih}, X_{ik}) (with $h, k \in \mathbb{Z}$) is

$$P(X_{ih} < x, Y_{ik} < y) = F\left(\frac{x - \mu_i - h/\lambda}{s}\right) F\left(\frac{y - \mu_i' - k/\lambda'}{s}\right), \quad i = 1, \ldots, m.$$

This generalizes formula (16.1). The parameters used for the model pictured in Fig. 16.6 are:

- Number of superimposed processes: $m = 4$; each one displayed with a different color,
- Color: red for M_1, blue for M_2, orange for M_3, black for M_4,
- Scaling factor: $s = 0$ (left plot) and $s = 5$ (right plot),
- Intensity: $\lambda = 1/3$ (X-axis) and $\lambda' = \sqrt{3}/3$ (Y-axis),
- Shift vector, X-coordinate: $\mu_1 = 0$, $\mu_2 = 1/2$, $\mu_3 = 2$, $\mu_4 = 3/2$,
- Shift vector, Y-coordinate: $\mu_1' = 0$, $\mu_2' = \sqrt{3}/2$, $\mu_3' = 0$, $\mu_4' = \sqrt{3}/2$,
- F distribution: standard centered **logistic distribution** with zero mean and variance $\pi^2/3$.

For simulation purposes, the points (X_{ih}, Y_{ik}) of the ith process M_i ($i = 1, \ldots, m$), are generated as follows:

$$X_{ih} = \mu_i + \frac{h}{\lambda} + s \cdot \log\left(\frac{U_{ih}}{1 - U_{ih}}\right), \tag{16.11}$$

$$Y_{ik} = \mu_i' + \frac{k}{\lambda'} + s \cdot \log\left(\frac{U_{ik}}{1 - U_{ik}}\right), \tag{16.12}$$

where U_{ij} are uniformly and independently distributed on $[0, 1]$ and $-n \leq h, k \leq n$. I chose $n = 25$ in the simulation – a window much larger than that of Fig. 16.6 – to avoid **boundary effects** in the picture. The boundary effect is sometimes called **edge effect**. The unobserved data points outside the window of observations, are referred to as **censored data** [Wiki]. Of course, in my simulations their locations and features (such as which process they belong to) are known by design. But in a real data set, they are truly missing or unobservable, and statistical inference must be adjusted accordingly [15].

Formulas (16.11) and (16.12) are also used in Section 5.2.1 in the context of clustering and supervised classification. A simple introduction to mixtures of ordinary Poisson processes is found on the Memming blog, here. In Section 16.3.2, I discuss statistical inference: detecting whether a realization of a point process is Poisson or not, and detecting the number of superimposed processes (similar to estimating the number of clusters in a **cluster process**, or the number of components in a **mixture model**). In Section 16.3, I discuss a black-box version of the **elbow rule** to detect the number of clusters or mixture components, or the number of superimposed processes.

16.2.4.1 *Hexagonal lattice, nearest neighbors*

The source code to produce Fig. 16.6 is on my GitHub repository: `PB_NN.py` for the nearest neighbor graph, and `av_demo.r` for the visualizations.

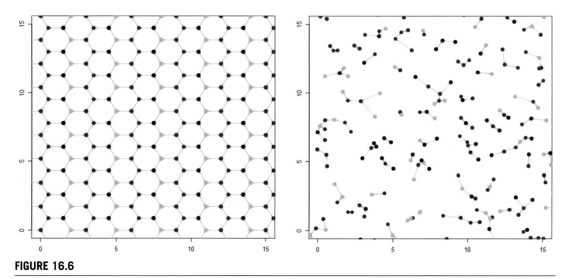

FIGURE 16.6

Four superimposed Poisson–binomial processes: $s = 0$ (left), $s = 5$ (right).

Surprisingly, it is possible to produce a point process with a regular **hexagonal lattice** using simple operations on a small number ($m = 4$) of square lattices: superimposition, stretching, and shifting. A **stretched lattice** is a square lattice turned into a rectangular lattice, by applying a multiplication factor to the X and/or Y coordinates. A **shifted lattice** is a lattice where the grid points have been shifted via a translation.

Each point of the process almost surely (with probability one) has exactly one nearest neighbor. However, when the scaling factor s is zero, this is no longer true. On the left plot in Fig. 16.6, each point (also called **vertex** when $s = 0$) has exactly 3 nearest neighbors. This causes some challenges when plotting the case $s = 0$. The case $s > 0$ is easier to plot, using arrows pointing from any point to its unique nearest neighbor. I produced the arrows in question with the `arrow` function in R [Wiki]. A bidirectional arrow between points A and B means that B is a nearest neighbor of A, and A is a nearest neighbor of B. All arrows on the left plot in Fig. 16.6 are bidirectional. Boundary effects are easily noticeable, as some arrows point to nearest neighbors outside the window. Four colors are used for the points, corresponding to the 4 shifted stretched Poisson–binomial processes used to generate the hexagon-based process. The color indicates which of these 4 process, a point is attached to.

The source code handles points with multiple nearest neighbors. It produces a list of all points with their nearest neighbors, using a **hash table**. A point with 3 nearest neighbors has 3 entries in that list: one for each nearest neighbor. A group of points that are all connected by arrows is called a **connected component** [Wiki]. A path from a point of a connected component to another point of the same connected component, following arrows while ignoring their direction, is called a **path** in **graph theory**.

In my definition of connected component, the direction of the arrow does not matter: the underlying **graph** is considered **undirected** [Wiki]. An interesting problem is to study the size distribution, that is, the number of points per connected component, especially for standard Poisson processes. See Exercise 16.1. In graph theory, a point is called a **vertex** or **node**, and an arrow is called an **edge**. More about nearest neighbors is discussed in Exercises 18 and 19 in [20].

Finally, if you look at Fig. 16.6, the left plot seems to have more points than the right plot. But they actually have roughly the same number of points. The plot on the right seems to be more sparse, because there are large areas with no points. But to compensate, there are areas where several points are in close proximity.

16.2.4.2 *Exercises: nearest neighbor graphs, size of connected components*

These exercises complement the material introduced in Section 16.2.4, offering a deeper dive in some aspects of graph theory. They are not designed to test your knowledge, but instead, to expand it. Rather than trying to solve them, read the solution. I also mention open (unsolved) questions linked to these problems, in particular regarding **random graphs**.

Exercise 16.1. Nearest neighbors and size distribution of connected components. Simulate 10 realizations of a stationary Poisson process of intensity $\lambda = 1$, each with $n = 10^3$ points distributed over a square window. Identify the **connected components** [Wiki] and their size (the number of points in each connected component). The purpose of the exercise is to study the distribution of the size, denoted as S. In particular, what is the proportion of connected components with only 2 points ($P[S = 2]$), 3 points ($P[S = 3]$), and so on? For connected components, use the **undirected graph**, that is, points V_i, V_j (also called vertices) are connected if V_i is nearest neighbor to V_j, or the other way around. The questions are:

- Estimate the probabilities in question via simulations. When computing the proportions using multiple realizations of the same process, do we get a similar empirical distribution for S, across all realizations? Does the empirical distribution seem to convergence, when increasing n, say from $n = 10^3$ to $n = 10^4$ or $n = 10^5$?

- Do the same experiment with a Poisson–binomial process, with $\lambda = 1$ and $s = 0.15$. Do we get the same distribution for S? What about $P[S = 2]$?
- Generate a particular type of **random graph**, called **random NN graph**, as follows. Let $V_1, \ldots, V_n$ be the n **vertices** of the graph (their locations do not matter). For the "nearest neighbor" to vertex V_k ($k = 1, \ldots, n$), randomly pick up one of the n vertices except V_k itself. Two points (vertices) can have the same nearest neighbor. Now study the distribution of S via simulations. Is it the same as for the graph generated by the nearest neighbors in a stationary Poisson point process?
- This is the most difficult part. Let $P(S = k)$, $k = 2, 3, \ldots$ be the size distribution for connected components of a stationary Poisson process; S is a random variable. Of course, it does not depend on λ. Does it uniquely characterize the Poisson process, in the same way that the exponential distribution for interarrival times uniquely characterizes the Poisson process in one dimension? Do we have $P(S = 2) = \frac{1}{2}$, not only for Poisson processes, but also for a much larger class of point processes?

Useful references about random graphs [Wiki] include "The Probabilistic Method" by Alon and Spencer [1], and "Random Graphs and Complex Networks" by Hofstad [41]. See also here.

Hints

Beware of the **boundary effect**; to minimize the impact, use a uniform distribution for F (the distribution attached to the points of the Poisson–binomial process) and $n > 10^3$. When the scaling factor s is zero, there is only one connected component of infinite size ($P[S = \infty] = 1$): this is a singularity, as illustrated on the left plot in Fig. 16.6. But as soon as $s > 0$, all the connected components are of finite size and rather small. The smallest ones have two points as each point has a nearest neighbor, thus $P[S < 2] = 0$. When $s = \infty$, the process becomes a stationary Poisson process.

    I conjecture that stationary Poisson processes and some other (if not all) Poisson–binomial processes share the exact same discrete probability distribution for the size of connected components defined by nearest neighbors, and abbreviated as CCS distribution. Thus, unlike the point count distribution or nearest neighbor distance distributions, the CCS distribution can not be used to characterize a Poisson process. For random graphs, the CCS distribution is different from that of a Poisson process. I used a **Kolmogorov–Smirnov test** [Wiki] (see also [17]) to compare the two empirical CCS distributions – the one attached to Poisson processes versus the one attached to random NN graphs – and concluded, based on my sample size ($n = 10^4$ points or vertices), that they were statistically different.

    To conclude, it appears that the CCS distribution cannot be arbitrary. Many point processes seem to have the same CCS distribution, called **attractor distribution**, and these processes constitute the **domain of attraction** of the attractor. The concepts of domain of attraction and attractor is used in other contexts such as **dynamical systems** [Wiki] or extreme value theory [Wiki] (also, see [5], page 317). The most well known analogy is the **Central Limit Theorem**, where the Gaussian distribution is the main attractor, and the Cauchy distribution is another. In Chapter 11 of "The Probabilistic Method" [1], dealing with the size of connected components in random graphs, the author introduces a random variable T_c, also counting a number of vertices (called **nodes** in the book). Its distribution has all the hallmarks of an attractor. See Theorem 11.4.2 (page 202) in the book in question.

    To find the connected components, you can use the source code in Section 16.2.4.3. To simulate point processes, you can use the program PB_NN.py available on GitHub and described in section 6.4 in [20]: it produces an output file PB_NN_dist_full.txt that can be used as input, without any change, to the connected components algorithm in section 16.2.4.3. Exercise 16.2 features a similar problem, dealing with cliques rather than connected components.

Exercise 16.2. Maximum clique problem. In **undirected graphs** [Wiki], a **clique** is a set of vertices (also called nodes) all connected to each other. In **nearest neighbor** graphs, two points are connected if one of them is a closest neighbor to the other. How would you identify a clique of maximum size in such a graph? No need to design an algorithm from scratch; instead, search the literature. Finding the maximum clique [Wiki] is NP-hard [Wiki], and the problem is related to the "P versus NP" conjecture [Wiki]. The maximum clique problem has many applications, in particular in social networks. Probabilistic properties of cliques in **random graphs** are discussed in "Cliques in random graphs" [6] and "On the evolution of random graphs" [16]. See also the **Erdős–Rényi model** [Wiki]. More recent articles include [18,30].

Solution

In two dimensions, in an **undirected nearest neighbor graph**, the minimum size of a maximum clique is 2 (as each point has a nearest neighbor), and the maximum size is 3. A maximum clique must be a **connected component**. See definition of connected component in Exercise 16.1. If each point has exactly one nearest neighbor, then a connected component of size $n > 1$ has n or $n - 1$ edges (the arrows on the right plot in Fig. 16.6), while a clique of size n has exactly $\frac{1}{2}n(n - 1)$ edges. This is why maximum cliques of size larger than 3 do not exist. But in d dimensions, a maximum clique can be of size $d + 1$. The maximum clique can be found using the **MaxCliqueDyn algorithm** [Wiki].

16.2.4.3 Python code to compute connected components

The Python code PB_NN_graph.py is also on GitHub. I also used it to produce the connected components in the problem described in Section 15.3. There are many implementations available online. The algorithm presented here does not use recursions unlike most others. Instead, it relies on a data structure called stack. It is just as fast as any efficient alternative, and was tested on nearest neighbor graphs. Two points are considered connected if one of the two points is the nearest neighbor to the other one. The first column of the input file represents the index idx of a point, and NNidx[idx] (in the second column) is the index of a point that has point idx as nearest neighbor.

The algorithm works as follows. Browse the list of points. If a point idx has not yet been assigned to a connected component, create a new connected component cliqueHash[idx] containing idx; find the points connected to idx, add them to the stack (stack). Find the points connected to the points connected to idx, and so on recursively, until no more points can be added. Each time a point is added to cliqueHash, decrease the stack size by one. It takes about $2n$ steps to find all the connected components, where n is the number of points. This algorithm does not use recursive functions; it uses a stack instead, which emulates recursivity.

The first part of the code creates the undirected graph hash, as follows: if a point with index k is nearest neighbor to a point with index idx, add point idx to hash[k], and add point k to hash[idx]. Thus hash[idx] contains all the points (their indices) directly connected to point idx; the points are separated by the tilde symbol.

```
# PB_NN_graph.py -- Compute connected components of nearest neighbor graph.
#
# Input file has two tab-separated columns: idx and idx2; idx is the index of a point,
```

```
#    idx2 is the index of a nearest neighbor to idx
# Output file has two fields, for each principal component: the list of points it is
#    made up (separated by ~), and the number of points

# Example.

# Input:

# 100 101
# 100 103
# 101 100
# 101 102
# 103 100
# 103 102
# 102 101
# 102 100
# 102 103
# 102 104
# 104 102
# 106 105
# 105 107

# Output:

# ~100~103~102~104~101 5
# ~106~105~107 3

#---
# PART 1: Initialization

point=[]
NNIdx={}
idxHash={}

n=0
file=open('cc_input.txt',"r") # input file
lines=file.readlines()
for aux in lines:
   idx =int(aux.split('\t')[0])
   idx2=int(aux.split('\t')[1])
   if idx in idxHash:
      idxHash[idx]=idxHash[idx]+1
   else:
      idxHash[idx]=1
   point.append(idx)
   NNIdx[idx]=idx2
   n=n+1
file.close()
```

```
hash={}
for i in range(n):
    idx=point[i]
    if idx in NNIdx:
        substring="~"+str(NNIdx[idx])
    string=""
    if idx in hash:
        string=str(hash[idx])
    if substring not in string:
        if idx in hash:
            hash[idx]=hash[idx]+substring
        else:
            hash[idx]=substring
    substring="~"+str(idx)
    if NNIdx[idx] in hash:
        string=hash[NNIdx[idx]]
    if substring not in string:
        if NNIdx[idx] in hash:
            hash[NNIdx[idx]]=hash[NNIdx[idx]]+substring
        else:
            hash[NNIdx[idx]]=substring

#---
# PART 2: Find the connected components

i=0;
status={}
stack={}
onStack={}
cliqueHash={}

while i<n:

    while (i<n and point[i] in status and status[point[i]]==-1):
        # point[i] already assigned to a clique, move to next point
        i=i+1

    nstack=1
    if i<n:
        idx=point[i]
        stack[0]=idx; # initialize the point stack, by adding $idx
        onStack[idx]=1;
        size=1 # size of the stack at any given time

        while nstack>0:
            idx=stack[nstack-1]
            if (idx not in status) or status[idx] != -1:
```

```
            status[idx]=-1 # idx considered processed
            if i<n:
                if point[i] in cliqueHash:
                    cliqueHash[point[i]]=cliqueHash[point[i]]+"~"+str(idx)
                else:
                    cliqueHash[point[i]]="~"+str(idx)
            nstack=nstack-1
            aux=hash[idx].split("~")
            aux.pop(0) # remove first (empty) element of aux
            for idx2 in aux:
                # loop over all points that have point idx as nearest neighbor
                idx2=int(idx2)
                if idx2 not in status or status[idx2] != -1:
                    # add point idx2 on the stack if it is not there yet
                    if idx2 not in onStack:
                        stack[nstack]=idx2
                        nstack=nstack+1
                    onStack[idx2]=1

#---
# PART 3: Save results

file=open('cc_graph.txt',"w")
for clique in cliqueHash:
    count=cliqueHash[clique].count('~')
    line=cliqueHash[clique]+"\t"+str(count)+"\n"
    file.write(line)
file.close()
```

16.3 Statistical inference for point processes

This section covers the following topics: estimation of the core parameters of Poisson–binomial processes (intensity and scaling factor), and the Rayleigh test to assess – based on the distribution of nearest neighbor distances – whether or not a spatial data set exhibits patterns not expected in a random distribution. Minimum contrast estimation, predicting extreme distances between neighboring points, and retrieving the underlying, hidden distribution F attached to a Poisson–binomial process are discussed in Section 16.4. Testing the independence of points counts is covered in Section 16.1.3. Detecting clusters and estimating their number in a cluster process similar to a mixture are discussed in Chapter 5.

16.3.1 Estimation of core parameters

It is assumed that the point process covers the entire space $\mathbb{R}$ or $\mathbb{R}^2$ with infinitely many points, and that only a finite number of points are observed through a finite (typically rectangular) window or interval. Here I focus on the one-dimensional case. For processes in two dimensions, see Section 16.3.2.1.

In one dimension, the two most fundamental parameters are the intensity λ and the scaling factor s. The standard estimator of λ proposed here is asymptotically unbiased [Wiki]. For a more generic, model-free method yielding an unbiased estimator simultaneously for s and λ, along with confidence regions, see Section 18.3. The goal of this section is to offer efficient estimators, easy to compute, and taking advantage of the properties of the underlying model.

16.3.1.1 *Intensity*

There are various ways to estimate the intensity λ (more specifically, λ^d in d dimension) using **interarrival times** (one dimension), nearest neighbors distances (in two dimensions) or the point count distribution $N(B)$ computed on some interval B. A good estimator with small variance, assuming boundary effects are mitigated, is the total number of observed points divided by the area (or length, in one dimension) of the window of observations.

The expected value of the interarrival times is $1/\lambda$. Thus, if you average all the interarrival times across all the observed points (called events in one dimension), you get an unbiased estimator of $1/\lambda$. Its multiplicative inverse will be a slightly biased estimator of λ; if the number of points is large enough (say > 50), the bias is negligible.

16.3.1.2 *Scaling factor*

Once λ has been estimated, the scaling factor s can be estimated by leveraging the fact that $\mathrm{E}[T^r(\lambda, s)] = \mathrm{E}[T^r(1, \lambda s)]/\lambda^r$ for any $r > 0$. Here $T(\lambda, s)$ is the interarrival time (a random variable) or, in other words, the distance between a point and its nearest neighbor to the right on the X axis, in one dimension. This result does not depend on the distribution F. For a proof, see Theorem 4.2 in my book "Stochastic Processes and Simulations: A Machine Learning Approach".

With $r = 2$, let

- τ_0 be your estimate of $T^2(\lambda, s)$ (the average value computed on your data set),
- $\tau' = (\lambda_0)^r \cdot \tau_0$, where λ_0 is your estimate of λ (see Section 16.3.1.1),
- s' be the solution to $\mathrm{E}[T^r(1, s')] = \tau'$.

Then $s_0 = s'/\lambda_0$ is an estimate of s.

Example. Here F is the logistic distribution, and I chose $r = 2$. Any $r > 0$ except $r = 1$ would work. If $\lambda_0 = 1.45$ and $\tau_0 = 0.77$, then $\tau' = (\lambda_0)^2 \tau_0 = 1.61$. Looking at the $\mathrm{E}[T^2(1, s')]$ table, to satisfy $\mathrm{E}[T^2(1, s')] \approx 1.61$, you need $s' = 0.65$. Thus $s_0 = s'/\lambda_0 = 0.45$. These numbers match those obtained by simulation. To view or download the table, look at the $\mathrm{E}[T^2]$ tab in `PB_inference.xlsx`.

The equation $\mathrm{E}[T^2(1, s')] = \tau'$, where s' is the unknown, can be solved using numerical methods. The easiest way is to build a granular table of $\mathrm{E}[T^2(1, s)]$ for various values of s, by simulating Poisson–binomial processes of intensity $\lambda = 1$ and scaling factor s. Then finding s' consists in browsing and interpolating the table in question the old fashioned way, to identify the value of s closest to satisfying $\mathrm{E}[T^2(1, s)] = \tau'$. This can, of course, be automated. There are two ways to perform the simulations in question:

- Generating one realization of each process with a large number of points (that is, one realization for each $0 < s < 20$ with $\lambda = 1$ and s increments equal to 0.01),
- Or generating many realizations of each process, each one with a rather small number of points.

Either way, the results should be almost identical due to **ergodicity** if the same F is used in both cases. The simulations also allow you to compute the theoretical variance of the estimators in question (at least a very good approximation). This is useful when multiple estimators (based on different statistics) are available, to choose the best one: that with minimum variance. Simulations also allow you to compute **confidence intervals** for your estimators.

16.3.1.3 *Alternative estimation method*

It is also possible to use the point count $N(B)$ to estimate s. The idea is to partition the state space (the real line in one dimension, where the points reside) into short intervals $B_k = [k/\lambda, (k+1)/\lambda[$, $k = 0, \pm 1, \pm 2$, and so on, covering the observed points; beware of the **boundary effect**. This assumes that λ is known or estimated. Let $N_k = N(B_k)$ be the random variable counting the number of observed points in B_k. We have $E[N_k] = 1$. Also $\text{Var}[N_k] \leq 1$ does not depend on k thanks to the choice of B_k (see Section 16.1.2). The variance is maximum and equal to 1 when $s = \infty$.

It is possible, for any value of s and λ, to compute the theoretical variance $v(\lambda, s) = \text{Var}[N_k]$ using either simulations or formula (16.4) with $a = 0$ and $b = 1/\lambda$. It slightly depends on F, but barely. Now compute the empirical variance of N_k as the average $(N_k - 1)^2$ across all the B_k's, based on your observations, assuming λ is known or estimated. This empirical variance is denoted as $v_0(\lambda)$. The estimated value of s is the one that makes the empirical and theoretical variances identical, that is, the *unique* value of s that solves the equation $v(\lambda, s) = v_0(\lambda)$. This method easily generalizes to higher dimensions, see Section 16.3.2.1. The fact that $E[N_k] = 1$ is a direct consequence of Theorem 4.1 in the same book.

See the N_k tab in `PB_inference.xlsx` for a Poisson–binomial process simulation with a **generalized logistic** F and computation of $E[N_k]$ and $\text{Var}[N_k]$ in Excel.

16.3.2 **Spatial statistics, nearest neighbors, clustering**

Here the focus is on 2D point processes. Section 16.3.2.3 features an original test to determine whether the point distribution – more precisely the nearest distances – in a particular data set is consistent with that of a Poisson process. In short, it tests whether you are dealing with a realization of a **Poisson process**, or a more complex process such as an m-mixture: a superimposition of Poisson–binomial processes.

16.3.2.1 *Inference for two-dimensional processes*

Let us assume for now that we are dealing with a single two-dimensional Poisson–binomial point process. Some of the methodology discussed in Section 16.3.1 for the one-dimensional case can be generalized to higher dimensions. The point count distribution in a square of side $1/\lambda$ has expectation equal to 1. So, one way to estimate λ is to partition the window of observations W into small squares $B_{h,k}(\lambda) = \left[\frac{h}{\lambda}, \frac{h+1}{\lambda}\right[\times \left[\frac{k}{\lambda}, \frac{k+1}{\lambda}\right[$ for various values of the (unknown) λ, compute the number of points $N_{h,k}(\lambda)$ (called **point count**) in each of these squares, and find λ that minimizes the empirical variance

$$v(\lambda) = \sum_{h,k} \left(N_{h,k}(\lambda) - 1\right)^2$$

computed on the observations. The sum is over $h, k \in \mathbb{Z} \cap W'$, where W is the window of observation, and W' is slightly smaller than W to mitigate **boundary effects**. In short, your estimate of the **intensity** λ is defined as $\lambda_0 = \arg \min_{\lambda} v(\lambda)$.

The benefit of this approach is that it also allows you to easily estimate the **scaling factor** s. Since $v(\lambda)$ also depends on the unknown s, let us denote it as $v(\lambda, s)$. Also, let $V(\lambda, s)$ be the theoretical variance of the point count $N(B)$ in $B = \left[0, \frac{1}{\lambda}\right[\times \left[0, \frac{1}{\lambda}\right[$, computed using simulations or via formula (16.4). The estimated value of s, assuming λ_0 is the estimate of λ, is the solution to the equation $v(\lambda_0, s) = V(\lambda_0, s)$.

Another simple estimator, this time for λ^d, is the total number of observed points in the observation window W, divided by the area of W. Here $d = 2$ is the dimension. Estimators of λ and s may also be obtained using **nearest neighbor** distances, in a way similar to using interarrival times in one dimension as in Section 16.3.1.1. I have not checked if the random variable S, defined as the size of the **connected components** associated to the undirected **nearest neighbor graph** (see Exercise 16.1), is of any use to estimate s. confidence regions for (λ, s) can be built using the methodology in Section 16.4.1.

16.3.2.2 *Other possible tests*

Besides estimating the core parameters, many other properties or features can be tested. They are too numerous to be treated in details here, so I only provide a quick summary.

- **Anisotropy** – testing if the point distribution is statistically identical in all directions. This is the case for all the examples discussed in this chapter. Testing for anisotropy can be done using $\rho(z, r) = N[B(z, r)]/(\pi r^2)$ where $B(z, r)$ is a circle of radius r centered at z, and N is the point count distribution. In case of anisotropy, and assuming r is not too small so that each circle has at least 20 points, there should be only little variations among the $\rho(z, r)$'s computed at different (z, r). Simulate a truly anisotropic process (stationary Poisson) with the same number of points in the window of observations, to find exactly what "only little variations" means.
- **Stationarity** – testing whether $N[B(z, r + t)] - N[B(z, r)]$ depends only on t, and not on r. In our context, using squares centered at z and of side r for $B(z, r)$, would show lack of stationarity if s is small and you try different values of t, say $t = 1/(2\lambda)$ and $t = 1/\lambda$.
- Independence – this test (discussed in Section 16.1.3) is used, for instance, to assess whether the point counts $N(B)$ in various nonoverlapping domains B are independent or not. In our context, this is not generally the case.
- **Ergodicity** – for some statistics based on simulations (as opposed to a real-life data set), one can use a single realization of the process with many points or a large window of observations, to make inference. Or one can use many realizations, each with a few points or small window, to compute the same statistic and average the observed values across all the realizations. If the results are statistically the same in both cases, the statistic in question is ergodic, for the point process model in question. A good example is the **nearest neighbor distance**, between two neighbor points of the process.
- Repulsion (or attraction) – an **attractive point process** is one where points tend to cluster together, leaving large areas empty, and some areas filled high point density. An example is a **cluster process**. The opposite is a repulsive process: points tend to stay as far away as possible from each other. The most extreme case is when the scaling factor s is zero, as in the left plot in Fig. 16.6. Typically, the degree of attraction is determined by s. However, a cluster process can be both: for instance,

if the unobserved cluster centers come from a parent point process with a very small s, such as in Fig. 16.3.

- Number of clusters – determining the number m of clusters in an m-interlacing (superimposition of m Poisson–binomial point processes), or the number of components in a mixture of m processes, is not easy and usually not feasible if cluster overlap is substantial, at least not exactly. This is discussed in Section 5.3.2. A black-box version of the **elbow rule** (the traditional tool to estimate the number of clusters) is discussed in Section 18.6.

- Shift vectors – the parameters μ_i, μ'_i in formulas (16.11) and (16.12), or "centers" associated to m-**interlacings** (a superimposition of m Poisson–binomial processes). Each of the m individual processes has a shift vector attached to it: it determines the position of a cluster center modulo $1/\lambda$. If these vectors are well separated and s is small, they can be retrieved. This is a clustering problem; see Section 5.3.2 and Fig. 16.8 featuring 5 different shift vectors ($m = 5$) and thus 5 clusters.

- To decide whether you are dealing with a mixture rather than a superimposition of m point processes, one has to look at the point count distribution on a square B_λ of area $1/\lambda^2$. The theoretical expectation of the point count is $E[N(B_\lambda)] = m$ if the process is an m-interlacing; in that case, the number of points in each B_λ is also very stable. The first thing to do is to estimate λ, then look at the empirical variance of $N(B_\lambda)$ computed on the observations. When s is small enough, $N(B_\lambda)$ is almost constant (equal to m) for an m-interlacing; it almost has a **binomial distribution** for a **mixture**.

- Size of **connected components** – an interesting problem is to identify the connected components in the **undirected graph** of nearest neighbors associated to a point process, see Exercise 16.1. These connected components are featured in Fig. 16.6. Their size distribution is of particular interest: for instance, on the left plot in Fig. 16.6, corresponding to $s = 0$, there is only one connected component of infinite size; on the right plot, there are infinitely many small connected components (about 50% only have two points). It is still an open question as to whether or not this statistic can be used to discriminate between different types of point processes, or whether its theoretical distribution is exactly the same for a large class of point processes (that is, it is an **attractor distribution**) and thus of little practical value.

16.3.2.3 *Rayleigh test*

The **Rayleigh test** is a generic statistical test to assess whether two data sets consisting of points in two dimensions arise from the same type of stochastic point process. It assumes that the underlying point process model is uniquely characterized by the distribution of nearest neighbor distances. The most popular use is when the assumed model is a stationary Poisson process: in that case, the statistic of the test has a **Rayleigh distribution**. It generalizes to higher dimensions; in that case the Rayleigh distribution becomes a **Weibull distribution**. In short, what the test actually does is comparing the empirical distributions of nearest neighbor distances computed on the two data sets, possibly after standardization, to assess if from a statistical point of view they are indistinguishable.

The test is performed as follows. Let us say you have two data sets consisting of points in two dimensions, observed through a window. You compute the empirical distribution of the nearest neighbor distances for both data sets, based on the observations, after taking care of **boundary effects**. Let $\eta_1(u)$ and $\eta_2(u)$ be the two distributions in question. The statistic of the test is

$$V = \int_{-\infty}^{\infty} |\eta_1(u) - \eta_2(u)| du = \int_0^1 |v_1(u) - v_2(u)| du, \tag{16.13}$$

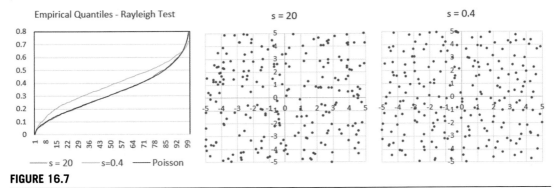

FIGURE 16.7

Rayleigh test to assess if a point distribution matches that of a Poisson process.

where v is the empirical **quantile function**, that is, the inverse of the empirical distribution. An alternative test is based on $W = \sup_u |\eta_1(u) - \eta_2(u)|$, or on $W' = \sup_u |v_1(u) - v_2(u)|$. The test based on W is the traditional Kolmogorov–Smirnov test [Wiki] with known tabulated values. In Excel, it is easier to use the empirical quantile function, readily available as the PERCENTILE Excel function. In practice, the integral in formula (16.13) is replaced by a sum computed over 100 equally spaced value of $u \in [0, 1]$. The advantage of W is that it is known (asymptotically) not to depend on the underlying (possibly unknown) point process model that the data originates from.

I provide an illustration in PB_inference.xlsx: see the "Rayleigh test" tab in the spreadsheet. I compare two data sets, one from a simulation of a two-dimensional Poisson–binomial process with $s = 20$, and one with $s = 0.4$. In both cases, λ is set to 1.5 in the simulator; its estimated value on the generated data set is close to 1.5. I then compare the **nearest neighbor distances** (their empirical quantile function) with the theoretical distribution of a two-dimensional stationary Poisson process of intensity λ^2. The theoretical distribution is Rayleigh of expectation $1/(2\lambda)$. The data set with $s = 20$ is indistinguishable, at least using the Rayleigh test, from a realization of a stationary Poisson process. This was expected: as $s \to \infty$, the Poisson–binomial process converges to a Poisson process, and the convergence is very fast. But the data set with $s = 0.4$ is markedly different from a Poisson point process realization, as seen by looking at the statistic V or W'.

Tabulated values for the statistics V and W' can be obtained by simulations. For W, they have been known since at least 1948, since W is the Kolmogorov–Smirnov statistic [17]. Here I simply used tabulated values of the Rayleigh distribution since I was comparing the simulated data with a realization of stationary Poisson process. **Confidence bands** [Wiki] for the empirical quantile function can be obtained using **resampling** methods [Wiki] such as bootstrapping or **parametric bootstrap**. See also Section 18.3.

Fig. 16.7 illustrates the result of my test, using the empirical quantile function of the nearest neighbor distances, and the statistic V for the test. No resampling or confidence bands were needed, the conclusion is obvious: $s = 0.4$ provides a simulated data set markedly different from a Poisson point process realization (the gray curve is way off) while $s = 20$ is indistinguishable from a Poisson point process (the red and blue curves, representing the empirical quantile function of the **nearest neighbor distances**, are almost identical). Interestingly, the scatterplot corresponding to $s = 0.4$ (rightmost in Fig. 16.7) seems more random than with $s = 20$ (middle plot), but actually, the opposite is true. The plot with $s = 0.4$ corresponds to a **repulsive process**, where points are more away from each other than pure chance would dictate; thus it exhibits fewer big empty spaces and less clustering, falsely giving the impression of increased randomness.

16.3.2.4 *Exercises*

The following exercises are a useful complement to the theory, and should be considered part of the core material. This section provides a simple introduction to **covering problems** [Wiki] and stochastic geometry.

Exercise 16.3. Distribution of nearest neighbor distances. In two dimensions, $T = T(\lambda, s)$ represents the distance between a point of the process and its **nearest neighbor**.

- Prove that when $s \to \infty$, the limiting distribution of T is **Rayleigh** [Wiki] of mean $\frac{1}{2\lambda}$.
- Show by simulations or logical arguments, that unlike in the one-dimensional case, E[T] depends on s.
- Also, show that depending on F, the maximum **nearest neighbor distance**, computed over the infinitely many points of the process, can have a finite expectation. Is this true too when $s \to \infty$, that is, for stationary Poisson point processes?
- Finally, what is T's distribution if T is replaced by the distance between an arbitrary location in $\mathbb{R}^2$, and its closest neighbor among the points of the process?

Solution

In two dimensions, the fact that E[$T(\lambda, s)$] depends on s, is obvious: if $s = 0$, it is equal to $\frac{1}{\lambda}$, and if $s = \infty$, it is equal to $\frac{1}{2\lambda}$. Between these two extremes, there is a continuum of values, of course depending on s. The maximum nearest neighbor distance (over all the infinitely many points) always has a finite expectation if F is uniform, regardless of $s < \infty$. To the contrary, for a Poisson point process, the maximum is infinite, see here.

Now let us prove that T has a Rayleigh distribution when $s = \infty$, corresponding to a Poisson process of intensity λ^2. We have $P(T > y) = P[N(B) = 0]$, where B is a disc of radius y centered at an arbitrary point of the process, and N is the **point count**, with an exponential distribution of mean $\lambda^2 \mu(B)$ with $\mu(B) = \pi y^2$ being the area of B. Thus $P(T > y) = \exp(-\lambda^2 \pi y^2)$, that is, $P(T < y) = 1 - \exp(-\lambda^2 \pi y^2)$. This is the CDF of a Rayleigh distribution of mean $\frac{1}{2\lambda}$.

Exercise 16.4. Cell networks: coverage problem. Points are randomly distributed on the plane, with an average of λ points per unit area. A circle of radius R is drawn around each point. What is the proportion of the plane covered by these (possibly overlapping) circles? What if R is a random variable, so that we are dealing with random circles? Such **stochastic covering problems** are part of **stochastic geometry** [Wiki] [14,40]. See also Hall's book on coverings [21]. Applications include wireless networks [Wiki].

Solution

The points are distributed according to a Poisson point process of intensity λ. The probability that an arbitrary location x in the plane is not covered by any circle is the probability that there is zero point from the process, in a circle of radius R centered at x. This is equal to $\exp(-\lambda \pi R^2)$. Thus the proportion of the plane covered by the circles is $1 - \exp(-\lambda \pi R^2)$. Now, let us say that we have two types of circles: one with radius R_1, and one with radius R_2, each type equally likely to be picked up. This is like having two independent, superimposed Poisson processes, each with intensity $\lambda/2$, one for each type of circle. Now the probability p that x is not covered by any circle is thus a product of two probabilities:

$$p = \exp\left(-\frac{\lambda}{2}\pi R_1^2\right) \times \exp\left(-\frac{\lambda}{2}\pi R_1^2\right) = \exp\left(-\lambda\pi \frac{R_1^2 + R_2^2}{2}\right).$$

You can generalize to m types of circles, each type with a radius R_k and probability p_k to be picked up, with $1 \le k \le m$. It leads to

$$1 - p = 1 - \exp\left[-\lambda\pi \sum_{k=1}^{m} p_k R_k^2\right], \tag{16.14}$$

which is the proportion of the plane covered by at least one circle. If R, the radius of the circle, is a continuous random variable, the sum in formula (16.14) must be replaced by $E[R^2]$. A related topic is the smallest circle problem [Wiki]. See also [36].

16.4 Special topics

This section covers special topics of interest, that do not fit well in the previous sections. Minimum contrast estimation is a powerful, yet simple, inference technique applicable to many problems, especially when the true parameters are impossible to compute, buried into some hidden layer, or face identifiability problems. This topic is discussed in Chapter 18 (Section 18.3.5). Here I focus on the specifics related to perturbed-lattice point processes. Identifiability issues and the hidden model (the lattice) are also discussed in this section.

16.4.1 Minimum contrast estimation and explainable AI

The idea behind **minimum contrast estimation** is to use proxy statistics as substitutes for the parameter estimators. It makes sense here as it is not clear what combination of variables represents s. The goal is to estimate (λ, s) using proxy parameters (p, q) to be defined shortly, then map (p, q) back to (λ, s) to get the estimates that we are interested in. In particular, (λ, s) – the intensity and scaling factor – is easy to interpret while (p, q) is rather obscure. Thus estimates of (λ, s) lead to explainable AI, while (p, q) do not.

For simplicity, I consider one-dimensional Poisson–binomial processes. The observations consist of $2n + 1$ points X_k ($k = -n, \dots, n$), realization of a one-dimensional Poisson–binomial process of intensity λ and scaling factor s, obtained by simulation. I chose a logistic F in the simulation. Unless F has an unusually thick or thin tail, it has little impact on the point distribution. Let

$$R = \frac{1}{2n+1}\left[\max_{|k| \le n} X_k - \min_{|k| \le n} X_k\right], \tag{16.15}$$

$$B_k = \left[\frac{k}{R}, \frac{k+1}{R}\right[, \quad k = -n, \dots, n-1, \tag{16.16}$$

and

$$p = \frac{1}{2n} \sum_{k=-n}^{n-1} \chi[N(B_k) = 0], \quad q = \frac{1}{2n} \sum_{k=-n}^{n-1} \chi[N(B_k) = 1], \tag{16.17}$$

where χ is the indicator function [Wiki] and $N(B_k)$ is the number of points in B_k. If there is a one-to-one mapping between (λ, s) and (p, q), then one can easily compute (p, q) using formula (16.17) applied to the observed data, and then retrieve (λ, s) via the inverse mapping. It is even possible to build 2D confidence regions for the bivariate parameter (λ, s). The method is highly generic (not specific to point processes) and thus, all the details are found in Sections 18.3 (confidence regions) and 18.3.5 (minimum contrast estimation).

16.4.2 Model identifiability, hard-to-detect patterns

Poisson–binomial and related point processes such as **m-interlacings**, exhibit many hard-to-detect patterns. Some cannot even be detected with statistical tests. Depending on model parameters, many are not visible to the naked eye. In some cases, this is due to **identifiability**: two apparently different models, with different sets of parameters, are statistically identical and indistinguishable from each other. Most of the times though, the differences are real but subtle or imperceptible. To the contrary, on occasions, the naked eye perceives differences when there are none, akin to visual illusions. Examples of hard-to-detect differences include:

- Discriminating between two different F's (the distribution attached to the points), for instance, logistic versus Gaussian or Cauchy, unless s is very small.
- If s is large, the process is hard to distinguish from a stationary Poisson process.
- Point count statistics (expectation, variance and so on) are periodic, but amplitudes are extremely small.
- The cluster structure in m-interlacings may be invisible unless some transformation is applied: see the left plot in Fig. 16.8. **Nearest neighbor distances** are generally better at detecting differences, compared to point counts.
- Unless s is very small, it may be impossible to detect if the underlying lattice is square or hexagonal, or if we are dealing with an m-interlacing or a mixture of Poisson–binomial processes.

To the contrary, in some cases, the naked eye perceives nonexistent differences, for instance, the fact that the right plot in Fig. 16.6 has fewer points than the left, when in fact they both have the same number. In fact, the Poisson–binomial model is a good framework to test and benchmark statistical techniques in contexts that require a very high level of precision. For instance, those aimed at detecting exoplanets, early signs of cancer, or subtle patterns in the stock market.

16.4.2.1 Stochastic residues

Each individual process of an m-interlacing has its own shift vector, which determines the center of a cluster. By translation, the cluster is stochastically replicated around each lattice location. As a result, for statistical inference, it is customary to study the process (the observed data) modulo $2/\lambda$ or $1/\lambda$, where statistical patterns are magnified and easier to detect. By modulo $2/\lambda$, I mean the following: instead of studying the original points (X, Y), we focus on $(X \bmod 2/\lambda, Y \bmod 2/\lambda)$. The transformed data, after the modulo operation, is called the residual data, or **stochastic residues**. The fact that there

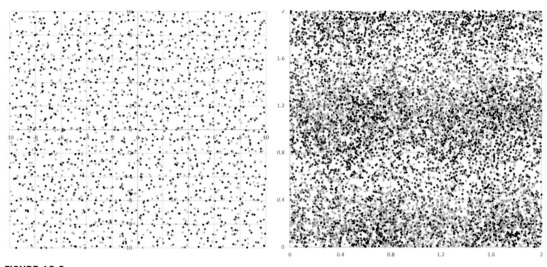

FIGURE 16.8

Realization of a 5-interlacing with $s = 0.15$ and $\lambda = 1$: original (left), modulo $2/\lambda$ (right).

are $m = 5$ clusters (albeit with huge overlap) in Fig. 16.8 is apparent on the right plot featuring the residues, but not on the left plot. Typically, in the context of unsupervised clustering, we do not known which individual process a point m-interlacing belongs to.

Remark. The modulo operator is defined as $\alpha \bmod \beta = \alpha - \beta \cdot \lfloor \alpha/\beta \rfloor$, where the brackets represent the floor function (also called integer function [Wiki]). It is identical to that used in modular arithmetic [Wiki], except that here α, β are usually real numbers rather than integers.

16.4.3 Hidden model and random permutations

In one dimension, the unobserved index k attached to any point X_k of the Poisson–binomial point process gives rise to an interesting random process called the **hidden process** or index process. It can be used to generate infinite, locally random permutations (here in one dimension), using the following algorithm:

Algorithm. Generate a locally random permutation of order m.

> Step 1: Generate a 1D realization of a Poisson–binomial process with $2n + 1$ points $X_{-n}, \ldots, X_n$.
> Let $L(X_k) = k$, for $-n \le k \le n$. The function L is stored as a **hash table** [Wiki] in your source code; the keys of your hash table are the X_k's. In practice, no two X_h, X_k with $h \ne k$ have the same value $X_h = X_k$, so this collision problem will not arise.
> Step 2: Sort the $2n + 1$ points X_k, with $-n \le k \le n$.
> Denote as $X_{(k)}$ the kth point after ordering.
> Step 3: Select m consecutive ordered points, say $X_{(1)}, \ldots, X_{(m)}$ with m much smaller than n.
> Retrieve their original indices: $\sigma(k) = L(X_{(k)})$, $k = 1, \ldots, m$.
> Set $\tau(k) = L(X_{(k+1)})$, $k = 1, \ldots, m$ (so $X_{\tau(k)}$ is the closest point to $X_{\sigma(k)}$, to the right).

Now σ is a **random permutation** on $\{1, \ldots, m\}$ [Wiki]. To produce the plots in Fig. 16.9, I used $m = 10^3$, $n = 3 \times 10^4$, and a Poisson-0binomial process with $\lambda = 1$, $s = 3$, and a logistic distribution for F. Since the theory is designed to produce infinite rather than finite permutations, **boundary effects** can take place. To minimize them, take both m and n large. The boundary effects, if present (for instance when using a thick tail distribution for F such as Cauchy, or when using a large s) will be most noticeable for $\sigma(k)$ when k is close to 1 or close to m.

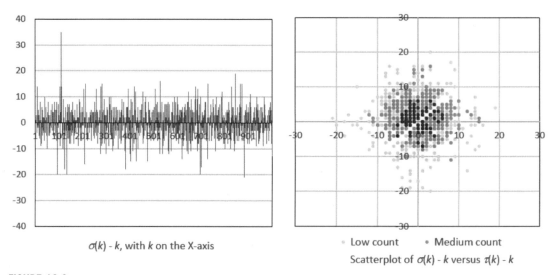

o(k) - k, with k on the X-axis

• Low count   • Medium count

Scatterplot of σ(k) - k versus τ(k) - k

FIGURE 16.9

Locally random permutation σ; $\tau(k)$ is the index of X_k's closest neighbor to the right.

These permutations can be used to model local reshuffling in a long series of events. Effects are mostly local, but tend to spread to longer distances on average, when s is large or F has a thick tail. For instance, in Fig. 16.9, the biggest shift in absolute value is $\sigma(k) - k = 35$, occurring at $k = 108$ (see the peak on the left plot). However, peaks (or abysses) of arbitrary height will occur if m is large enough, unless you use a uniform distribution for F, or any distribution with a finite support domain.

The right plot in Fig. 16.9 shows the joint empirical distribution (data-based as opposed to theoretical) of the discrepancies $\sigma(k) - k$ and $\tau(k) - k$ in the index space $\mathbb{Z} \times \mathbb{Z}$. Of course, since the index $\tau(k)$ points to the closest neighbor of $X_{\sigma(k)}$ to the right, that is, to $X_{\tau(k)}$, we have $\tau(k) \geq 1 + \sigma(k)$, which explains why the main diagonal is blank. Other than that, the plot shows independence, symmetry, and **anisotropy** (absence of directional trend in the scattering). It means that

- Given a point X_k, the index $\tau(k)$ of its nearest neighbor to the right is randomly distributed around k, according to some radial distribution;
- Given a point X_k, its order $\sigma(k)$ once the points are ordered, is randomly distributed around k, according to the same radial distribution;
- There is independence between the two.

Two metrics used to compare or describe these permutations are the average and maximum **index discrepancy**, measured as the average and maximum value of $|\sigma(k) - k|$ for $1 \leq k \leq m$. It gets larger as s increases. Another metric of interest, related to the **entropy** of the permutation [Wiki] [43], is the correlation between the integer numbers k and $\sigma(k) - k$, computed over $k = 1, \dots, m$. While the example featured in Fig. 16.9 exhibits essentially a zero correlation, some other cases not reported here, exhibit a strong correlation. See also [2]. For an elementary introduction to permutations, see [7].

16.4.4 Retrieving the F distribution

For simplicity, let us assume that we are dealing with a one-dimensional Poisson–binomial process. It is difficult if not impossible to retrieve the common distribution F attached to each point X_k. However, see Section 16.4.4.2. In many cases, two different F's result in essentially the same model, causing **identifiability** issues. The situation if much easier if s is very small, small enough that $|X_k - \frac{k}{\lambda}| < \frac{1}{2\lambda}$ for most $k \in \mathbb{Z}$. Then the index attached to a point X, usually unknown, is now equal to

$$L(X) = \arg\min_{k \in \mathbb{Z}} \left| X - \frac{k}{\lambda} \right|.$$

That is, $X = X_k$ with $k = L(X)$. See definition of arg min here. This assumes that λ and s are known or estimated. In this particular situation, empirical distribution of $sX - sL(X)$ computed over many points X, converges to F as the number of observed points tends to infinity.

A more practical situation is when one has to decide which F provides the best fit to the data, given a few potential candidates for F. In that case, one may compute (using simulations) the theoretical expectation $\eta(r, \lambda, s, F) = \mathrm{E}[T^r(\lambda, s)]$ as a function of $r > 0$ for various F's, and find which F provides the best fit to the estimated $\mathrm{E}[T^r(\lambda, s)]$, denoted as $\eta_0(r, \lambda, s, F)$ and computed on the data (the expectation being replaced by an average when computed on the data). By best fit, I mean finding F that minimizes (say)

$$\gamma(F) = \int_0^2 |\eta(r, \lambda, s, F) - \eta_0(r, \lambda, s, F)| dr. \tag{16.18}$$

Again, s and λ should be estimated first. The statistic $T(\lambda, s)$ is the **interarrival time** or distance between a point and its closest neighbor the right (in one dimension). However, a simultaneous estimation of λ, s, F is feasible and consists of finding the parameters λ, s, F minimizing $\gamma(F)$, now denoted as $\gamma(\lambda, s, F)$. See Section 16.3.1 to estimate λ and s separately: this stepwise procedure is simpler and less prone to **overfitting** [Wiki].

The estimation technique introduced here, especially formula (16.18), is sometimes referred to as **minimum contrast estimation**. See slides 114–116 in the presentation entitled "Introduction to Spatial Point Processes and Simulation-Based Inference", by Jesper Møller [31].

16.4.4.1 *Theoretical values obtained by simulations*

This section highlights some simulation results obtained with `PB_main.py` to compute moments $\mathrm{E}[T^r]$ of the interarrival times $T = T(\lambda, s)$ for various λ, s, as well as statistics related to the point count (random variable) $N(B)$, where $B = [a, b]$ is an interval. The goal is to:

- Show that except if F has a finite support or s is very small, the choice of F has very little impact;
- Show how fast the Poisson–binomial process converges to a stationary Poisson process as s increases;

- Show that any point of the process can be used to compute the *theoretical distribution* of T, thus choosing X_0 or any X_k, or averaging over many points, yields the same theoretical distribution;
- Show that you can use one realization of the process with many points, or many realizations of the process, each with few points, to compute the theoretical distribution of T.

The last fact illustrates the **ergodicity** of T.

Table 16.2 Poisson process ($s = \infty$) versus $s = 39.85$.

	Formula	Value	Uniform	Logistic	Cauchy
	$s = \infty$	$s = \infty$	$s = 39.85$	$s = 39.85$	$s = 39.85$
$E[N(B)]$	$\lambda\mu(B)$	3/2	1.5019	1.5000	1.4962
$Var[N(B)]$	$\lambda\mu(B)$	3/2	1.4738	1.4906	1.4872
$P[N(B)=0]$	$e^{-\lambda\mu(B)}$	0.2231	0.2196	0.2221	0.2230
$E[T]$	$1/\lambda$	1	1.0003	0.9999	1.0010
$Var[T]$	$1/\lambda^2$	1	0.9680	0.9888	1.0029
$E[\sqrt{T}]$	$\frac{1}{2}\sqrt{\pi/\lambda}$	0.8862	0.8865	0.8862	0.8873

Table 16.2 shows simulation results based on $\lambda = 1$, $r = 1/2$ and $B = [a, b]$ with $a = -0.75$ and $b = 0.75$. Three different F were tested: uniform, logistic, and Cauchy. The notation $\mu(B)$ stands for $b - a$. In two dimensions, it represents the area of the set B (typically, a square or a circle). In one dimension, when $s = \infty$, $N(B)$ has a Poisson distribution of expectation $\lambda\mu(B)$, and T has an exponential distribution of expectation $1/\lambda$. The limiting process is a stationary Poisson process of intensity λ. The exact formula for $E[\sqrt{T}]$, when $s = \infty$, was obtained with the online version of Mathematica: you can check the computation, here. In general, convergence to the Poisson process, when $s \to \infty$, is slower and more bumpy if F is uniform, compared to using a logistic or Cauchy distribution for F.

16.4.4.2 *Retrieving F from the interarrival times distribution*

I assume here that F has a density f, and we are dealing with a one-dimensional Poisson–binomial process. The random variable $T(\lambda, s)$ measuring the distance between a point and the closest neighbor to the right on the X axis is called the interarrival time. Given the limit distribution of the standardized interarrival times, the purpose is to retrieve the distribution of F. If you are familiar with the concept of **characteristic function** [Wiki], this exercise is easy. If not, you should first get familiar with this concept. The theorems referred to are from my book "Stochastic Processes and Simulation: A Machine Learning Approach".

The **standardized interarrival times** is defined as $\frac{1}{s}[T(\lambda, s) - \frac{1}{\lambda}]$ and has zero expectation by virtue of Theorem 4.3. By virtue of Theorem 4.2, it can be rewritten as $\frac{1}{\lambda s}[T(1, \lambda s) - 1]$. Its limit, as $s \to 0$, is denoted as T^*. One of the simplest cases, besides Gaussian and Cauchy, is the following: If T^* has a standard **Laplace distribution** [Wiki] (that is, symmetric centered at zero, and with variance $\pi^2/3$), show that F is a **modified Bessel distribution** of the second kind [35]. Note that as a consequence of L'Hôpital's rule [Wiki], T^* is the derivative of $T(\lambda, s)$ with respect to s, evaluated at $s = 0$.

By virtue of Theorem 4.4, we have

$$P(T^* < y) = \int_{-\infty}^{\infty} F(y - x) f(x) dx,$$

which is a **convolution** of F with itself. Thus T^* has the distribution of the sum of two independent random variables, say Z_1, Z_2, of distribution F. Its characteristic function is therefore

$$E[\exp(-itT^*)] = \frac{1}{1+t^2} = E[\exp(-itZ_1)] \times E[\exp(-itZ_2)] = \left(E[\exp(-itZ_1)]\right)^2.$$

Thus $E[\exp(-itZ_1)] = (1+t^2)^{-1/2}$. Taking the inverse **Fourier transform** to retrieve the density of Z_1, which is the density attached to F, one finds

$$f(x) = \frac{1}{2\pi} \int_{-\infty}^{\infty} \frac{\cos(tx)}{\sqrt{1+t^2}} dt = \frac{1}{\pi} K_0(x),$$

where K_0 is the modified **Bessel function** of the second kind [Wiki]. More about the Laplace distribution and its generalization can be found in [25]. The cases when T^* is Gaussian or Cauchy are easy because these distributions belong to **stable families of distributions** [Wiki]: in that case, F is respectively Gaussian or Cauchy.

16.4.5 Record distances between an observed point and its vertex

Fig. 16.10 shows the points (X_h, Y_k) of a Poisson–binomial process with a logistic F, in blue. Their lattice vertices $(h/\lambda, k/\lambda)$ are shown with little red crosses. The arrows connected both. Here, $\lambda = 1$. This picture shows how far away a point can be from the **vertex** it is attached to. If $s = 0$, both locations coincide, but when s is large, the distances can be arbitrarily large.

Note that both plots (left and right in Fig. 16.10) have the same number of points. But points are clustered in some areas, and sparse in other areas on the right plot, giving the impression that there are fewer of them. Clearly, the empirical distribution of the distance between nearest neighbors (especially extreme distances), or the average area of the largest empty zone, can be used to estimate the **scaling factor** s once λ is known or estimated.

This brings me to my next discussion, namely **extreme values**, or **records**. This is part of a field know as **order statistics** [Wiki] or extreme value theory [Wiki]. Extreme values are different from **outliers** [Wiki]: they can be predictable, with known distribution. To the contrary, outliers are usually considered as errors, glitches, or data points obeying a different model. In any case, both have an impact on the window of observations, delimited by the "boundary", and have the potential to introduce biases.

One question is how far a point can be from its vertex, and how frequently such "extremes" occur. Even more interesting is the reverse question, associated to the inverse or **hidden model**: can a point (X_h, Y_k) close to the origin, well within the small window of observations, have its vertex very far away? Such a point will not be generated by the point process simulator. It will be unaccounted for, introducing a bias. This happens with increased frequency as s increases, requiring a larger and larger observation window.

Unless F has a finite support domain (for instance, if F is uniform), unobserved points in the small window of observations – even though their expected number is finite and rather small – can be attached to any arbitrary vertex, no matter how far away. In two dimensions, the probability $P[R > r]$ that the distance R between a point and its lattice location is greater than r is

$$P(R > r) = \int_{-\infty}^{\infty} \int_{-\infty}^{\infty} \chi(x^2 + y^2 > r) F\left(\frac{x}{s}\right) F\left(\frac{y}{s}\right) dxdy,$$

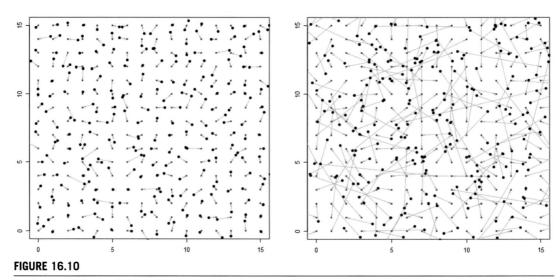

FIGURE 16.10

Each arrow links a point (blue) to its vertex (red): $s = 0.2$ (left), $s = 1$ (right).

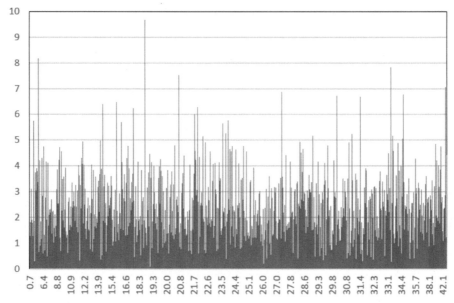

FIGURE 16.11

Distance between a point and its vertex ($\lambda = s = 1$).

where $\chi(A)$ is the indicator function, equal to one if A is true, and to zero otherwise.

The distance R corresponds to the length of the arrow, in Fig. 16.10. If F is Gaussian, then R has a **Rayleigh distribution** [Wiki]. In two dimensions, the distance between two nearest neighbor points, for a stationary Poisson point process, also has a Rayleigh distribution, see Section 16.3.2.3 and Exercise 16.3.

16.4.5.1 *Distribution of records*

Now let M_n be the maximum distance between a point and its vertex, measured over n points of the process, randomly selected. In other words $M_n = \max(R_1, \ldots, R_n)$ where R_i ($i = 1, \ldots, n$) is the distance between the ith point, and its vertex. Depending on F, the standardized distribution of M_n is asymptotically **Weibull**, Gumbel, or Fréchet: these are the tree potential **attractor distributions** in the context of extreme value theory [Wiki]. The Rayleigh distribution is a particular case of the Weibull distribution. Surprisingly, in d dimensions, the distribution of the **nearest neighbor distances**, for a stationary Poisson point process, is also Weibull, see Section 16.3.2.

Fig. 16.11 shows (on the Y-axis) the distance R between a point (X_h, Y_k) and its vertex $(h/\lambda, k/\lambda)$. These are the same points as on the right plot in Fig. 16.10; R represents the length of the arrows. The points are ordered by how close they are to the origin $(0, 0)$, and the X-axis represents their distance to the origin, that is, their norm. By looking at Fig. 16.11, it is easy to visualize the extreme values of R, and when they occur on the X-axis.

16.4.5.2 *Distribution of arrival times for records*

Now let us assume that n is infinite, and let us look at the arrival times of the successive records in the sequence R_1, R_2, R_3, and so on. The ith arrival time is denoted as L_i with $L_1 = 1$, and defined as follows: $L_{i+1} = \min\{j : R_j > R_{L_i}\}$. In other words, the ith record is R_{L_i}. The random variable L_i has the following properties:

- The distribution of L_i does not depend on F.
- Let η_i be the probability that R_i is a record. The η_i's are independent Bernoulli random variables, and $P(\eta_i = 1) = 1/i$.
- $P(L_i \geq m) = P(\eta_1 + \eta_2 + \cdots + \eta_m \leq i)$. We are again dealing with a **Poisson–binomial distribution** [Wiki].
- $E[L_i] = \infty$ if $i > 1$. However, $E[\log L_i] \sim i - \gamma$ as $i \to \infty$, where $\gamma = 0.5772\ldots$ is the Euler–Mascheroni constant [Wiki].
- $\text{Var}[\log L_i] \sim i - \pi^2/6$ as $i \to \infty$.

These results, and many others, are found in Chapter 19 (*A Record of Records*) in Balakrishnan handbook entitled "Order Statistics: Theory & Methods" [5]; see pages 517–525.

References

[1] N. Alon, J.H. Spencer, The Probabilistic Method, fourth edition, Wiley, 2016, [Link].
[2] J. é, M. Amigó, R. Dale, P. Tempesta, A generalized permutation entropy for random processes, Preprint, pp. 1–9, arXiv:2003.13728, 2012, [Link].
[3] L. Anselin, Point Pattern Analysis: Nearest Neighbor Statistics, The Center for Spatial Data Science, University of Chicago, 2016, Slide presentation, [Link].
[4] A. Baddeley, Spatial point processes and their applications, in: W. Weil (Ed.), Stochastic Geometry, in: Lecture Notes in Mathematics, Springer, Berlin, 2007, pp. 1–75, [Link].

[5] N. Balakrishnan, C.R. Rao (Eds.), Order Statistics: Theory and Methods, North-Holland, 1998.

[6] B. Bollobás, P. Erdős, Cliques in random graphs, Mathematical Proceedings of the Cambridge Philosophical Society 80 (3) (1976) 419–427, [Link].

[7] M. Bona, Combinatorics of Permutations, second edition, Routledge, 2012.

[8] B. Błaszczyszyn, D. Yogeshwaran, Clustering and percolation of point processes, Preprint, pages 1–20, 2013, Project Euclid, [Link].

[9] B. Błaszczyszyn, D. Yogeshwaran, On comparison of clustering properties of point processes, Preprint, pp. 1–26, arXiv:1111.6017, 2013, [Link].

[10] B. Błaszczyszyn, D. Yogeshwaran, Clustering comparison of point processes with applications to random geometric models, Preprint, pp. 1–44, arXiv:1212.5285, 2014, [Link].

[11] N. Cressie, Statistic for Spatial Data, revised edition, Wiley, 2015.

[12] D.J. Daley, D. Vere-Jones, An Introduction to the Theory of Point Processes – Volume I: Elementary Theory and Methods, second edition, Springer, 2013.

[13] D.J. Daley, D. Vere-Jones, An Introduction to the Theory of Point Processes – Volume II: General Theory and Structure, second edition, Springer, 2014.

[14] David Coupier (Ed.), Stochastic Geometry: Modern Research Frontiers, Wiley, 2019.

[15] D.-G. Chen, J. Sun, K.E. Peace (Eds.), Interval-Censored Time-to-Event Data: Methods and Applications, Chapman and Hall/CRC, 2012.

[16] P. Erdős, A. Rényi, On the evolution of random graphs, in: Publication of the Mathematical Institute of the Hungarian Academy of Sciences, vol. 5, 1960, pp. 17–61, [Link].

[17] W. Feller, On the Kolmogorov–Smirnov limit theorems for empirical distributions, Annals of Mathematical Statistics 19 (2) (1948) 177–189, [Link].

[18] M. Gjoka, E. Smith, C. Butts, Estimating clique composition and size distributions from sampled network data, Preprint, pp. 1–9, arXiv:1308.3297, 2013, [Link].

[19] V. Granville, Estimation of the intensity of a Poisson point process by means of nearest neighbor distances, Statistica Neerlandica 52 (2) (1998) 112–124, [Link].

[20] V. Granville, Stochastic Processes and Simulations: A Machine Learning Perspective, MLTechniques.com, 2022, [Link].

[21] P. Hall, Introduction to the Theory of Coverage Processes, Wiley, 1988.

[22] K. Hartmann, J. Krois, B. Waske, Statistics and Geospatial Data Analysis, Freie Universität, Berlin, 2018, E-Learning Project SOGA, [Link].

[23] T.D. Johnson, Introduction to spatial point processes, Preprint, page 2008, NeuroImaging Statistics Oxford (NISOx) group, [Link], [Mirror].

[24] D. Kojevnikov, V. Marmer, K. Song, Limit theorems for network dependent random variables, Journal of Econometrics 222 (2) (2021) 419–427, [Link].

[25] S. Kotz, T. Kozubowski, K. Podgorski, The Laplace Distribution and Generalizations: A Revisit with Applications to Communications, Economics, Engineering, and Finance, Springer, 2001.

[26] F. Lagum, Stochastic Geometry-Based Tools for Spatial Modeling and Planning of Future Cellular Networks, PhD thesis, Carleton University, 2018, [Link].

[27] Gü. Last, M. Penrose, Lectures on the Poisson Process, Cambridge University Press, 2017.

[28] G. Last, M.A. Klatt, D. Yogeshwaran, Hyperuniform and rigid stable matchings, Random Structures & Algorithms 2 (2020) 439–473, [Link], [PowerPoint].

[29] J. Mateu, F.P. Schoenberg, D.M. Diez, On distances between point patterns and their applications, Preprint, pp. 1–29, 2010, [Link].

[30] N. Meghanathan, Distribution of maximal clique size of the vertices for theoretical small-world networks and real-world networks, Preprint, pp. 1–20, arXiv:1508.01668, 2015, [Link].

[31] J. Møller, Introduction to spatial point processes and simulation-based inference, in: International Center for Pure and Applied Mathematics (Lecture Notes), Lomé, Togo, 2018, [Link], [Mirror].

[32] J. Møller, R.P. Waagepetersen, An Introduction to Simulation-Based Inference for Spatial Point Processes, Springer, 2003.

[33] J. Møller, R.P. Waagepetersen, Statistical Inference and Simulation for Spatial Point Processes, CRC Press, 2007.

[34] S. Ghosh, N. Miyoshi, T. Shirai, Disordered complex networks: energy optimal lattices and persistent homology, Preprint, pp. 1–44, arXiv:2009.08811, 2020.

[35] S. Nadarajah, A modified Bessel distribution of the second kind, Statistica 67 (4) (2007) 405–413, [Link].

[36] H. Nasab, M. Tavana, M. Yousefu, A new heuristic algorithm for the planar minimum covering circle problem, Production & Manufacturing Research (2014) 142–155, [Link].

[37] Y. Ogata, Cluster analysis of spatial point patterns: posterior distribution of parents inferred from offspring, Japanese Journal of Statistics and Data Science 3 (2020) 367–390.

[38] Y. Peres, A. Sly, Rigidity and tolerance for perturbed lattices, Preprint, pp. 1–20, arXiv:1409.4490, 2020, [Link].

[39] K. Sigman, Notes on the Poisson process, New York NY, 2009. IEOR 6711: Columbia University course, [Link].

[40] D. Stoyan, W.S. Kendall, S.N. Chiu, J. Mecke, Stochastic Geometry and Its Applications, Wiley, 2013.

[41] R. van der Hofstad, Random Graphs and Complex Networks, Cambridge University Press, 2016, [Link].

[42] O. Yakir, Recovering the lattice from its random perturbations, Preprint, pp. 1–18, arXiv:2002.01508, 2020, [Link].

[43] R. Yan, Y. Liub, R. Gao, Permutation entropy: a nonlinear statistical measure for status characterization of rotary machines, Mechanical Systems and Signal Processing 29 (2012) 474–484.

[44] D. Yogeshwaran, Geometry and topology of the boolean model on a stationary point processes: a brief survey, Preprint, pp. 1–13, 2018, Researchgate, [Link].

[45] T. Zhang, A Kolmogorov–Smirnov type test for independence between marks and points of marked point processes, Electronic Journal of Statistics 8 (2) (2014) 2557–2584.

Synthetizing multiplicative functions in number theory

New perspective on the Riemann Hypothesis

Machine learning relies on mathematics to solve real-life problems. But what if you switched the roles and relied on machine learning to solve or at least explore pure mathematical problems? This is the subject of **experimental mathematics**. Over the years, I made considerable progress tackling famous conjectures using this approach. In addition, I leveraged mathematical objects such as functions or numbers, to build infinite **synthetic data sets** with an infinite number of features, to test and benchmark new machine learning techniques, and to produce new types of animated data videos. Here I share the culmination of this research, to address one of the most famous mathematical problems in number theory. Some of this material is used in Section 11.2.1 to design a strong test of randomness. Also, the number-theoretic "synthetic data" discussed here is used in Section 4.2.3 to illustrate a simple, yet efficient, probabilistic clustering method in machine learning, to handle massive cluster overlap.

This chapter provides a solid introduction to the Generalized Riemann Hypothesis and related functions, including Dirichlet series, Euler products, noninteger primes (Beurling primes), Dirichlet characters, and Rademacher random multiplicative functions. The topic is usually explained in obscure jargon or inane generalities. To the contrary, this presentation will intrigue you with the beauty and power of this theory. The summary style is very compact, covering much more than traditionally taught in a first graduate course in analytic number theory. The choice of the topics is a little biased, with an emphasis on probabilistic models. My approach, discussing the "hole of the orbit" – called the eye of the Riemann zeta function in a previous article – is particularly intuitive.

The accompanying Python code covers a large class of interesting functions to allow you to perform as many different experiments as possible. If you are interested in knowing a lot more than the basics and possibly investigating this conjecture using machine learning techniques, this chapter is for you. The Python code also shows you how to produce beautiful videos of the various functions involved, in particular their orbits. This visual exploration shows that the Riemann zeta function (based on the trivial character χ), and a specific Dirichlet-L function (based on the nontrivial character χ_4), behave very uniquely and similarly, explaining the connection between the Riemann and the Generalized Riemann Hypothesis, in pictures and videos rather than words.

17.1 Introduction

Let $z = \sigma + it$ be a complex number: σ is the real part, and t is the imaginary part. Let P be a set of numbers, called primes: an element of P cannot be factored into a product of elements of P. In some sense, numbers are to molecules what primes are to atoms. Typically, but not always, P is the standard set of all prime numbers, or a subset of it, either finite or infinite. Finally, p represents an element of P

Synthetic Data and Generative AI. https://doi.org/10.1016/B978-0-44-321857-6.00021-7

and $\chi(p)$ is any function taking on two possible values: $+1$ or -1 depending on p. The function $\chi(\cdot)$ is extended outside P using the formula $\chi(ab) = \chi(a)\chi(b)$, with $\chi(1) = 1$.

This chapter summarizes known properties and conjectures about various functions of z that can be represented by the following product, called Euler product:

$$\prod_{p \in P} \frac{1}{1 - \chi(p)p^{-z}}.$$

The most well-known example is when the function $\chi(\cdot)$ is constant (thus equal to 1) and P is the full set of prime integers: this corresponds to the Riemann zeta function $\zeta(z)$. When expanded into a series, the Euler product becomes what is called a Dirichlet series. The series and product may not convergence on the same domain; when the series is conditionally but not **absolutely convergent** [Wiki] the product can diverge. This typically happens if $\sigma < 1$. It is the source of considerable difficulties, and the reason why the Generalized Riemann Hypothesis (GRH) is unproven to this day. Also, this explains why all the action takes place when $\frac{1}{2} \leq \sigma < 1$.

I will not discuss complex analysis in details here. It is sufficient to know that if $z = \sigma + it$, then $p^{-z} = \exp(-z \log p) = p^{-\sigma} \cos(t \log p) - ip^{-\sigma} \sin(t \log p)$. Also, the factors in the Euler product are ordered by increasing values of p. Without this specification, the product may be subject to multiple interpretations with different values, when convergence is conditional but not absolute. An introduction to the Riemann zeta and Dirichlet functions can be found in [4] and [18]. Finally, I occasionally use the term conditionally or absolutely convergent product. This intuitive concept is defined here.

17.1.1 Key concepts and terminology

The complex plane is the standard two-dimensional space: the real axis is the horizontal or X-axis; the imaginary axis is the vertical or Y-axis. The Riemann Hypothesis (RH) states that the Riemann zeta function $\zeta(z)$ defined earlier, has no root (that is, $\zeta(z) \neq 0$) if $\frac{1}{2} < \sigma < z$. I use the notation $\sigma = \Re(z)$ to indicate that σ is the real part of the complex number $z = \sigma + it$. Throughout this text, a positive number is a number ≥ 0. A number > 0 is called strictly positive.

The Generalized Riemann Hypothesis (GRH) makes the same statement as RH, for a larger class of well behaved functions, not just $\zeta(z)$. In short, it applies to Dirichlet functions where $\chi(\cdot)$ is completely multiplicative and periodic; these are called Dirichlet-L functions. Here, we limit ourselves to $\chi(p) \in \{-1, +1\}$. However, we also consider $\chi(\cdot)$'s that are not periodic. The classic nontrivial periodic $\chi(\cdot)$ is $\chi = \chi_4$, the nontrivial Dirichlet character modulo 4. It leads to an Euler product suspected to converge if $\sigma > \frac{1}{2}$. Proving the convergence, even only at $\sigma = 0.99$, would be a major milestone towards proving GRH. Of course, the product converges if $\sigma > 1$. If $\chi(\cdot)$ is allowed not to be periodic, there are known cases, discussed in this chapter, that meet the requirements of GRH. Typically, these functions are much less interesting and do not satisfy a Dirichlet-like functional equation.

17.1.2 Orbits and holes

An original concept, the hole of the orbit of a Dirichlet function, is introduced in this chapter for the first time. It is epitomized in Fig. 17.1 dealing with finite Euler products, and in Fig. 17.5 featuring the orbit of truncated Dirichlet series (the truncated expansion of an infinite product or, in other words, the partial sums). In the RH and GRH contexts, the hole is present if $\frac{1}{2} < \sigma < 1$ is fixed and $0 < t < T$ is bounded.

But as $T \to \infty$, the hole shrinks to a singleton at the origin in the absence of roots ($\frac{1}{2} < \sigma < 1$), or to an empty set if roots are present ($\sigma = \frac{1}{2}$). Studying modified Dirichlet functions that always have a hole may be key to making progress towards RH and GRH. In particular, it is interesting to study the behavior at their limit as they approach standard Dirichlet functions, and the hole slowly evaporates. This is the topic of Sections 17.3.1 and 17.3.3.

The hole is a circle of maximum radius, with center on the X-axis (due to symmetry), that the orbit never crosses. The center of the hole may not be at the origin (see Section 17.2.2.1 for examples), even when there is no root. The absence of root can be caused by a hole, or because the orbit never gets too close to the Y-axis. The orbit on a fixed domain $0 < t < T$, for a fixed σ, is defined as the set of all possible values of the corresponding Dirichlet function in the complex plane, as t (called the "time"), varies continuously between $t = 0$ and $t = T$. Here, t is the imaginary part of the argument $z = \sigma + it$. The full orbit corresponds to $T = \infty$. The size of the hole, as well as its presence/absence and location, depends on σ, and of course on T, P, and $\chi(\cdot)$.

Finally, the hole is called a repulsion basin in the context of dynamical systems. The orbit may be bounded if $\sigma > 1$ or unbounded otherwise (in that case, typically extending to the entire complex plane).

17.1.3 Industrial applications

While not discussed in this chapter, there are very interesting industrial applications of GRH. See Section 11.2.1.1 on the prime test used to test and design better pseudorandom number generators for cryptography purposes, based on Rademacher random multiplicative function and the Dirichlet character modulo 4. See also Section 4.2.3 featuring synthetic data in machine learning applications, based on the orbits of Dirichlet functions and used to benchmark classification algorithms.

17.2 Euler products

I start with finite Euler products, where everything works fine: here the set P is a finite subset of the prime integers; there is no convergence issue, and orbits always have a hole. I first introduce the Dirichlet version $\eta(z)$ of the Riemann function $\zeta(z)$, as we need it to extend the convergence domain from $\sigma > 1$ to $\sigma > 0$ in order to study the behavior (presence of a hole and/or roots) when $0 < \sigma < 1$. For $\zeta(z)$, the function $\chi(\cdot)$ is constant and equal to 1. I then move to arbitrary $\chi(\cdot)$'s including Dirichlet characters modulo 4, and to infinite products. The function χ is extended to all integers via the formula $\chi(ab) = \chi(a)\chi(b)$: this extension leads to the fundamental formulas (17.4), (17.5), and (17.6), linking the Euler product to its Dirichlet series expansion whenever both converge. The Euler product establishes the connection between the analytic properties of Dirichlet functions, and the distribution of prime numbers.

17.2.1 Finite Euler products

Let $p_1 = 2$ and $P = \{p_1, p_2, \ldots, p_d\}$ be a set of primes, listed in increasing order. Let $Q = \{q_1, q_2, q_3, \ldots\}$ be the set of all $p_1^{a_1} p_2^{a_2} p_3^{a_3} \cdots$ where the a_i's are positive integers (including zero). The elements $q_1, q_2, \ldots$ are also listed in increasing order. Thus $q_1 = 1$ and $q_2 = 2$.

The Dirichlet eta function $\eta_P(z)$ induced by P is then defined as

$$\eta_P(z) = \sum_{k=1}^{\infty} \delta_k q_k^{-z} = (1 - 2^{1-z}) \prod_{p \in P} \frac{1}{1 - p^{-z}}, \tag{17.1}$$

where $\delta_k = 1$ if q_k is odd, and $\delta_k = -1$ otherwise. The **Euler product** [Wiki] in formula (17.1) is finite and has d factors, while the infinite series always converges. Indeed, it can be proved (see Exercise 17.1) that

$$q_k \sim \exp\left[k^{1/d}\left(d! \prod_{p \in P} \log p\right)^{1/d}\right] \quad \text{as } k \to \infty. \tag{17.2}$$

If P is the set of all prime numbers, and thus $d = \infty$, then the product in formula (17.1) converges if $\sigma > 1$ while the **alternating series** [Wiki] converges if $\sigma > 0$. This can be proved using the **Dirichlet test** [Wiki], see here. For this reason, the series is called the **analytic continuation** of the product [Wiki]. This is the reason why we are interested in the alternating series, where $\delta_k \in \{-1, +1\}$, rather than in the series with $\delta_k = 1$: the latter, equal to the infinite product, diverges if $\sigma \leq 1$. This issue occurs only if $d = \infty$. See Exercise 17.3 for details. When the product diverges, the alternating series converges, but it is not **absolutely convergent** [Wiki].

Now let $\tau_z = |1 - 2^{1-z}|$. Assuming $z = \sigma + it$, the distance between $\eta_P(z)$ and the origin is equal to

$$|\eta_P(z)| = \tau_z \prod_{p \in P} \frac{1}{|1 - p^{-z}|} = \tau_z \prod_{p \in P} \frac{1}{|1 - 2p^{-\sigma}\cos(t \log p) + p^{-2\sigma}|} > \tau_z \prod_{p \in P} \frac{1}{1 + p^{-\sigma}}. \tag{17.3}$$

Here $|\cdot|$ stands for the distance to the origin, and referred to as the **modulus** [Wiki] in complex analysis. An immediate consequence of formula (17.3) is this: if $\sigma \neq 1$ is fixed and strictly positive, and if P only has a finite number of primes, then there is always a zone around the origin, with a strictly positive area, that the orbit of $\eta_P(z)$ will never hit or cross. This is illustrated in Fig. 17.1. The zone in question corresponds to a hole in the orbit, also called **repulsion basin** [Wiki] in dynamical systems, for the red ($\sigma = 0.5$) and blue orbit ($\sigma = 0.75$). For the yellow orbit ($\sigma = 1.25$), the origin is outside the boundary of the orbit. The origin in Fig. 17.1 is the black dot in the white area. Note that the "center" of the hole, in all three cases, is not the origin, but further to the right on the X-axis. See here the video corresponding to $P = \{2, 3, 5, 7\}$, and here for $P = \{2, 3, 5\}$.

As you add more and more primes in P, the hole shrinks. In the end, when $d = \infty$, the hole shrinks to a single point (the origin) if we plot the whole orbit, rather the restricted orbit to $t \in [0, T]$ with $T = 1000$, as in Fig. 17.1. Also, the center of the hole moves to the left on the X-axis (real axis) as σ is decreased from (say) 1.25 to 0.55.

For a fixed T, the center of the hole is denoted as z_0. It lies on the X-axis, and depends both on T and σ. It is tempting to scale the η function and replace it by $\sqrt{t} \cdot (\eta_P(z) - z_0)$, in the hope that when P is the full set of prime numbers and $T \to \infty$, the hole does not shrink to a singleton or an empty set. However, no matter how fast growing the scaling factor is (as a function of t), the **universality property** [Wiki] of the Dirichlet eta function implies that this goal cannot be achieved. Generally speaking, working on finite Euler products and taking the limit $d \to \infty$, while very tempting, does not seem to lead to a proof of the Riemann Hypothesis, despite numerous attempts by many mathematicians including myself.

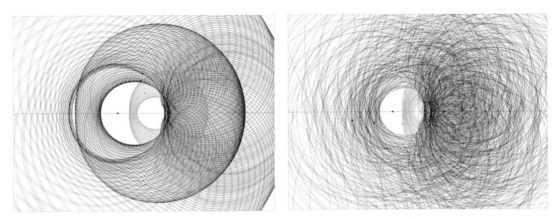

FIGURE 17.1

Three orbits ($\sigma = 0.5, 0.75, 1.25$) with finite Euler product: $P = \{2, 3\}$ (left) vs $\{2, 3, 5\}$ (right).

17.2.1.1 *Generalization using Dirichlet characters*

Formula (17.1) can be generalized as follows:

$$\eta_P(z, \chi) = \sum_{k=1}^{\infty} (-1)^{\Omega(q_k)} q_k^{-z} = (1 - 2^{1-z}) \prod_{p \in P} \frac{1}{1 - \chi(p) p^{-z}}, \tag{17.4}$$

where $\chi(p) \in \{-1, +1\}$. The product and the series may have different domains of convergence. However, on the domain where both converge, they have the same roots (except when $2^{1-z} = 1$, that is, when $\sigma = 1$ and $t = 2m\pi / \log 2$ with m an integer).

The generalized **Omega function** [Wiki] is defined as follows: if the prime factorization of q_k is $q_k = p_1^{a_1} p_2^{a_2} \cdots p_d^{a_d}$, then $\Omega(q_k) = a_1 \chi(p_1) + \cdots + a_d \chi(p_d)$. The function $(-1)^{\Omega(q_k)}$ is denoted as $\lambda(q_k)$ and referred to as the generalized **Liouville function** [Wiki]. The series in formula (17.4) is called a **Dirichlet-L function** [Wiki]. The function χ can be extended to all strictly positive integers as follows: $\chi(1) = 1$, $\chi(p) = 0$ if $p \notin P$, and $\chi(ab) = \chi(a)\chi(b)$. Then $\chi(q_k) = \lambda(q_k)$ is a **completely multiplicative function** [Wiki].

From now on, all functions denoted as $\chi(\cdot)$ are assumed to be completely multiplicative, and thus uniquely characterized by the values they take on prime arguments. Now, let $L_P(z, \chi) = (1 - 2^{1-z})^{-1} \eta_P(z, \chi)$. Then we have:

$$L_P(z, \chi) = \sum_{k=1}^{\infty} \chi(k) k^{-z}, \quad \eta_P(z, \chi) = (1 - 2^{1-z}) L_P(z, \chi) = \sum_{k=1}^{\infty} (-1)^{k+1} \chi(k) k^{-z}, \tag{17.5}$$

$$L_P(z, \chi) = \prod_{p \in P} \frac{1}{1 - \chi(p) p^{-z}}, \quad |L_P(z, \chi)| = \prod_{p \in P} |1 - \chi(p) p^{-z}|^{-1} \geq \prod_{p \in P} \frac{1}{1 + p^{-\sigma}}. \tag{17.6}$$

If for a fixed integer $m > 1$ we have $\chi(p) = \chi(q)$ whenever $p, q \in P$ are two primes with $p \equiv q \bmod m$, and if in addition $\chi(p) = 0$ if p divides m, then $\chi(\cdot)$ is called a **Dirichlet character** modulo m [Wiki]. The standard Omega and Liouville functions correspond to the case where χ is constant and equal to $+1$, and P is the set of all prime numbers. The standard Liouville function also satisfies

$$\sum_{k=1}^{n}\lambda(k)\left\lfloor\frac{n}{k}\right\rfloor=\lfloor\sqrt{n}\rfloor,\quad L(n)=\sum_{k=1}^{n}\lambda(k)=\sum_{k=1}^{n}\mu(k)\left\lfloor\sqrt{\frac{n}{k}}\right\rfloor,$$

where $\mu(k)$ is Liouville's sister function, called the **Möbius function** [Wiki]. See here for details. The brackets stand for the integer part function. The partial sums of the Liouville function are denoted as $L(n)$, while the partial sums of the Möbius function are the **Mertens function** [Wiki], and denoted as $M(n)$. If $q=q_k=p_1^{a_1}p_2^{a_2}\cdots p_d^{a_d}$, then $\mu(q_k)=(-1)^{w(q_k)}$, with $\omega(q_k)=\chi(p_1)+\cdots+\chi(p_d)$. The standard Möbius function corresponds to the case where χ is a constant function equal to 1, and P is the set of all prime numbers.

Finally, formula (17.3), providing a lower bound for the distance between the origin and any point on the orbit of $\eta_P(z,\chi)$, is still applicable and remains unchanged. In particular, if P is the set of all primes (or a big enough, infinite subset), the lower bound is zero due to divergence of the product. If that lower bound is indeed reached, even if asymptotically only, then the hope to find a hole bigger than a singleton evaporates.

17.2.2 Infinite Euler products

If P is the set of all prime numbers, the products in formula (17.1), (17.3), and (17.4) become infinite. As a result, if $0.5\leq\sigma<1$, the holes in the orbit in Fig. 17.1 may shrink to an empty set ($\sigma=0.5$) or a single point – the origin – if $0.5<\sigma<1$. Actually, it may well be an empty set too in the latter case; nobody knows. But the Riemann hypothesis states that it should be a single point. This is the situation if χ is a constant function equal to 1. This function is called **principal character** in this context. But what happens if χ is not a constant? In this latter case, depending on χ, the orbit may never get too close to the origin.

Let us consider the **completely multiplicative** function χ called nontrivial **Dirichlet character modulo** 4, and denoted as χ_4 or $\chi_{4,1}$. It is uniquely characterized by its values on prime numbers p, as follows: $\chi_4(p)=+1$ if $p\bmod 4=1$, $\chi_4(p)=-1$ if $p\bmod 4=3$, and $\chi_4(2)=0$. It satisfies $\chi_4(k+4)=\chi(k)$ for all positive integers. Again, P is the set of all primes.

Primes satisfying $p\bmod 4=3$ seem to be more numerous than the others, at least the smaller ones: they get a good head start. This is known as **Chebyshev's bias** [Wiki]. If these two types of primes are not evenly distributed, the orbit could get arbitrarily close to the origin. However, thanks to **Dirichlet's theorem** [Wiki], we know that the distribution is even. Thus one would expect that the Euler product in formulas (17.4) and (17.6) would alternate nicely between $\chi_4(p)=+1$ and $\chi_4(p)=-1$ on average, thus converging for some $\sigma=\sigma_0$ smaller than 1, and thus for all $\sigma>\sigma_0$. This is in contrast to the product in formula (17.1), corresponding to the principal character $\chi(p)=1$ for all p, denoted as $\chi_{4,0}$ and converging only for $\sigma>1$.

Having no root if $\sigma_0<\sigma<1$ due to the nonvanishing product in formula (17.4), one would conclude that the orbit of $L_P(z,\chi_4)$ never crosses the X-axis if $\sigma_0<\sigma<1$. However, to this day, nobody knows if the smallest possible value of σ_0, called the **abscissa of absolute convergence** [Wiki] is less than 1. It is conjectured to be as low as 0.5, or lower. This is part of the **Generalized Riemann Hypothesis** [Wiki], an active research topic in number theory. Yet, the associated series $L_P(z,\chi_4)$ defined in formula (17.5) is **conditionally convergent** [Wiki] if $\sigma>0$, see Example 2.39, page 36, in [4].

For a reference focusing on completely multiple functions χ in the RH context, not just Dirichlet characters, see [1]. Finally, I discuss χ_4 in more details in Section 17.3.2.3. In particular, I show the big contrast between $L_P(z, \chi_{4,1})$ and the standard Riemann zeta function $\zeta(z)$ corresponding to $L_P(z, \chi_{4,0})$.

17.2.2.1 *Special products*

Again, I investigate the infinite product $L_P(z, \chi)$ in formula (17.6), with $z = \sigma + it$. If for some $0 < \sigma_0 < 1$, the set P contains infinitely many primes, but sufficiently spaced out so that

$$\rho = \prod_{p \in P} \frac{1}{1 + p^{-\sigma_0}} > 0,$$

then the orbit of $L_P(z, \chi)$ corresponding to $\sigma = \sigma_0$ will stay away from the origin, at a distance $\geq \rho$ at all times. This is true regardless of the function χ. In particular, it means that $L_P(z, \chi)$ has no root if $\sigma = \sigma_0$.

Now, if P is the set of all primes, $\chi(p) = 1$ for all primes (the standard case) and $\sigma = 0.5$, then $\eta_P(z, \chi)$, defined in formula (17.4), has infinitely many roots. In addition, if its orbit gets too close to the origin, it gets attracted to it, otherwise it gets deflected: the origin seems to have an event horizon similar to that of a black hole. If you get too close, there is no way out, you will hit the origin very fast. See the blue curve in Fig. 17.2, where the X-axis represents the time t, and the Y-axis the distance to the location $(c, 0)$ in the complex plane. For the blue curve, $c = 0$. Note that as long as $0.5 < \sigma < 1$ and $0 < t < T$ with T finite, the (finite) portion of the orbit exhibits a hole. But the hole shrinks very slowly to a single point, as $T \to \infty$. If $\sigma < 1$, the hole encompasses the origin at all times. But its actual center is located further to the right on the X-axis. See Figs. 17.2, 17.3, and 17.4: each curve represents a distance to a specific location $(c, 0)$. The center moves to the left as T increases, or as σ decreases and gets closer to 0.5, until it merges with the origin. If $\sigma > 1$, the hole may not contain the origin, but the orbit is bounded and the origin is outside the external boundary of the orbit: see the yellow orbit in Fig. 17.1.

Finally, another case worth investigating is as follows. Let P be the set of all primes, and p_k be the kth prime with $p_1 = 2$. Define $\chi(p_{2k+1}) = +1$ and $\chi(p_{2k}) = -1$. Then the product in formula (17.4) converges if $\sigma > 0.5$ (prove it for $t = 0$, using the fact that the product is alternating; see also here). Thus the infinite product (which has no root) can be used to compute $\eta_P(z, \chi)$. But the convergence is not absolute. I expect that there is no root if $0.5 < \sigma < 1$. But I also expect that the hole is reduced to a single point (the origin), as in the standard case.

17.2.2.2 *Probabilistic properties and conjectures*

Here P is the set of all primes, and $\chi(p) = 1$ for all p. The Liouville function $\lambda(\cdot)$ and Möbius function $\mu(\cdot)$, introduced in Section 17.2.1.1, have many interesting properties and open questions. Many are equivalent to or generalizing RH. Here I present here a brief summary; more can be found here. Again, let $L(n) = \lambda(1) + \cdots + \lambda(n)$.

- The numbers $\lambda(k)$, for positive integers k, are equal to -1 or $+1$ in equal proportions, thus averaging to zero. But due to a good head start with negative values, it takes a long time for $L(n)$ to turn

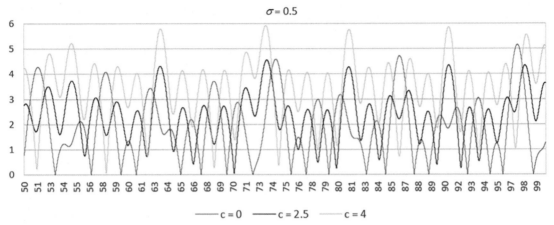

FIGURE 17.2

Distance between orbit and location $(c, 0)$ depending on t on the X-axis.

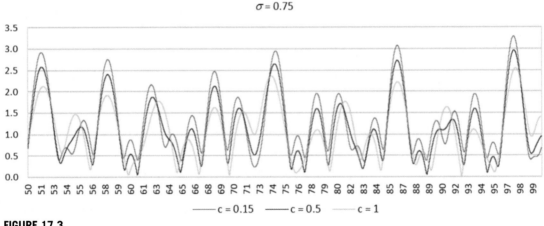

FIGURE 17.3

Distance between orbit and location $(c, 0)$ depending on t on the X-axis.

positive. In fact, the **Pólya conjecture** [Wiki] claims that $L(n)$ is always negative, but it was disproved in 1958. The smallest possible n satisfying $L(n) > 0$, namely $n = 906,180,359$, was found in 1980. The sign changes in $\lambda(k) = \pm 1$ occur somewhat randomly, as in independent Bernoulli trials. If the $+1$ and -1 were truly randomly distributed with zero mean, they would satisfy the **law of the iterated logarithm** [Wiki]:

$$\limsup_{n \to \infty} \frac{|L(n)|}{\sqrt{n \log \log n}} = C, \tag{17.7}$$

for some constant C with $0 < C < \infty$. It is conjectured that this is not the case. In fact, the $\lambda(k)$'s cannot possibly be independent, not even asymptotically, since the function is completely multi-

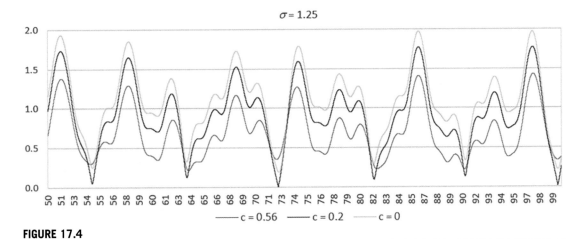

FIGURE 17.4

Distance between orbit and location $(c, 0)$ depending on t on the X-axis.

plicative. But to prove RH, all that is needed is a weaker statement, the fact $L(n)/\sqrt{n^{1+\epsilon}} \to 0$ as $n \to \infty$, for any $\epsilon > 0$. This is yet unproved. A similar conjecture exists for the Möbius function: the Mertens conjecture [Wiki], also implying RH, and thus yet unproved. See [11] for a stochastic version, based on random multiplicative **Rademacher functions** [Wiki], used as a substitute to emulate the "randomness" of the Möbius function.

- A stronger conjecture, yet not as strong as the law of the iterated logarithm, is this: the $\lambda(k)$'s behave like the binary digits of a **normal number** [Wiki]. In short, the number $v = \sum_{k=1}^{\infty} \lambda(k)2^{-k}$ is normal. Of course, v is irrational, otherwise $\lambda(\cdot)$ would be a periodic function. It is not yet known if v is transcendental, though some closely related numbers are [2]. The normality (or equivalently, ergodicity) of the sequence $\{\lambda(k)\}$ would imply that the **Chowla conjecture**, itself stronger than RH, is true; see [6]. But this is yet unproved.

- The numbers $\mu(k)$, for positive integers k, are equal to -1, 0, or $+1$. The proportion of those equal to zero is $1 - 6/\pi^2$. This is because $\mu(k) = 0$ if and only if k has a square factor. It is well known and easy to prove that the proportion of **square-free integers** [Wiki] is $6/\pi^2$. The proportions of $\mu(k)$'s equal to -1 or -1 are identical, a consequence of **Dirichlet's theorem** [Wiki].

Finally, an application of **Kronecker's theorem** [Wiki] leads to the following result: over time, for any fixed σ, the orbit of the Dirichlet L-function defined by formula (17.5) (assuming convergence) eventually fills a dense area in the complex plane. This is true whether the orbit is bounded or not, and whether it is has a "visible" hole or not. In other words, the image domain of $\eta_P(z, \chi)$ or $L_P(z, \chi)$ is a **dense set** [Wiki]. I provide an elegant proof of this fact in Exercise 17.5, using arguments similar to those used to prove its **universality property** [Wiki]. This implies that if $0.5 < \sigma < 1$, assuming P contains sufficiently many prime numbers, the Dirichlet eta function, regardless of χ, gets arbitrarily close to zero, even though it may never actually hit zero. In other words, in that case, the hole eventually shrinks to a single point.

17.3 Finite Dirichlet series and generalizations

This section covers a large class of functions, starting with truncated modified Dirichlet series to assess the status of the hole in the orbit. I then move back to infinite Euler products in Section 17.3.2, but this time not over the full set of primes as in Section 17.2.2, but instead on infinite subsets arising from additive number theory. Some of these functions have no root if $\sigma > \sigma_0$, with (say) $\sigma_0 = 5/6$. They thus satisfy a weaker version of GRH, called quasi-GRH. Section 17.3.3 covers non-Dirichlet functions that do not have an Euler product, but behave like the Dirichlet eta function $\eta(z)$ with regard to the orbit and its hole. Here P is the set of all primes, but the sine and cosine attached to $p^{-z} = \sigma^{-z}\cos(t\log p) - i\sigma^{-z}\sin(t\log p)$ are now replaced by wavelets. Section 17.3.4 deals with noninteger primes (even matrices) that mimic the behavior of prime integers, and called Beurling primes. They come with Euler products too, and the corresponding Dirichlet series is now called a Dedekind zeta (or eta) function. Section 17.3.5 deals with random Dirichlet functions: their interest lies in the fact that the corresponding (random) Euler products converge, albeit conditionally, when $\frac{1}{2} < \sigma \le 1$. Thus they satisfy a probabilistic version of GRH, in particular the absence of root if $\sigma > \frac{1}{2}$.

17.3.1 Finite Dirichlet series

Formula (17.1) features a finite (Euler) product. However, the corresponding series, on the left-hand side, is infinite. Here I discuss a different approach, using a finite version containing the first n terms of the full Dirichlet series when P is the set of all prime numbers. The new function is defined as

$$\eta(z, \beta, n) = \sum_{k=1}^{n} \delta_k \lambda_k p_k^{-z}, \tag{17.8}$$

where $\lambda_k = 1/k$ for all k except $k = 2$. The coefficient λ_2 is denoted as β. Here, $\delta_k = 1$ if k is odd, otherwise $\delta_k = -1$. If n is infinite and $\beta = 1/2$, then $\eta(z, \beta, n)$ coincides with the standard Dirichlet eta function.

Despite the finite number of terms in the series, this approach is considerably more difficult. Unlike in Section 17.2.1, there is no simple product (finite or infinite), to represent the truncated η function. While the approach in Section 17.2.1 has a strong number theory flavor, here we are dealing with approximations and numerical analysis. Yet, the case $n = 3$ is trivial: the orbit fills a ring. The hole is a circle centered at $(1, 0)$, not at the origin. Both the interior and exterior boundaries of the orbit are circles, with known radius. See Exercise 17.4 for a complete solution.

But the general case is much more complicated. Of course, the series corresponding to the finite Euler product results in an orbit with a solid hole of radius > 0, always encompassing the origin, and not shrinking to a singleton when you display the full, infinite orbit. But that series always has an infinite number of terms. As you increase the number of terms in the truncated series, keeping the first n terms only and $\beta = 1/2$, the hole disappears when $n \ge 5$ is small enough, only to reappear when $n > 50$. The hole then stays there all the way to $n = \infty$. As n increases, it eventually shifts to the left on the X-axis, to encompass the origin. For instance, at $n = 2000$, the origin is inside the hole. This is based on visually inspecting the orbit at $\sigma = 0.90$, with $0 < t < 2000$; see Fig. 17.6.

For small values of n with no hole, increasing β is one way to reintroduce the hole in the orbit, as pictured in Fig. 17.5. This leads to a possible new path to explore RH: using a large n, with $\beta > 1/2$ (the larger β, the larger the hole), and let $\beta \to 1/2$ as $n \to \infty$. In Exercise 17.4, I discuss some conditions that guarantee the presence of a hole encompassing the origin, for small values of n.

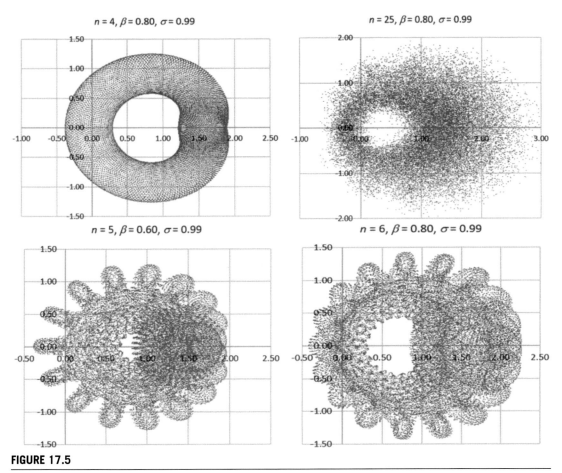

FIGURE 17.5

Four orbits where the "hole" (repulsion basin) is apparent.

The Python code in Section 17.5.1 allows you to replicate my experiments. You need to set the parameter `method` to `Eta`, and the parameter `Dirichlet` to `True`. This allows you to work with a series that converges when $\frac{1}{2} \le \sigma < 1$, as opposed to $\sigma > 1$. Of course, for finite Euler products, the infinite Dirichlet series always converges regardless of σ, with or without `Dirichlet` set to `True`.

17.3.2 Nontrivial cases with infinitely many primes and a hole

Now, let us get back to Euler products. Thus the associated Dirichlet series (the expansion of the product) always contains infinitely many terms, even if the product is finite. For a given σ, in order to get a hole encompassing the origin, with the distance between the orbit and the origin always $\ge \rho$ at all

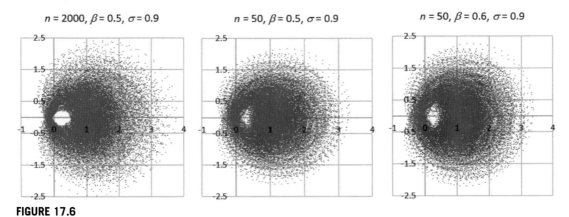

FIGURE 17.6

Three orbits with "hole" closer to the origin, showing impact of $\beta > \frac{1}{2}$ and larger n.

times t, the following must be satisfied:

$$\rho = \prod_{p \in P} \frac{1}{1 + p^{-\sigma}} > 0. \tag{17.9}$$

This is briefly discussed at the beginning of Section 17.2.2.1. Note that this requirement is independent of the function χ. It is satisfied if the product is finite (that is, if the set P is finite), or if $\sigma > 1$, or if $\sigma < 1$ and P is infinite but sparse enough so that the product converges. This section discusses the latter.

Because of the generalized **universality property** [Wiki] discussed in Exercise 17.5, the inequality $\geq \rho$ becomes an equality: the largest circle encompassing the origin, not crossed by the orbit, has radius exactly equal to ρ.

We already know that if P is the full set of primes and $\sigma < 1$, there is no hole. According to the Riemann Hypothesis, the hole at the origin is reduced to a singleton if $0.5 < \sigma < 1$, and to an empty set if $\sigma = 0.5$. The **Generalized Riemann Hypothesis** [Wiki] claims that this is true regardless of the **Dirichlet character** $\chi(\cdot)$ [Wiki]. But what if we use the set of **twin primes** [Wiki] for P? Then the product in formula (17.9) converges if $\sigma = 1$, thus there is a hole with $\rho > 0$ encompassing the origin, if $\sigma = 1$. The convergence is a direct consequence of **Brun's theorem** [Wiki]: the fact that the sum of the inverse of twin primes converges. I did not investigate the case $\sigma < 1$.

I now discuss two cases that are known to satisfy (17.9). Both illustrate methods of **additive number theory** [Wiki]. The idea is to look at two (or more) sets of integers A and B, and then check the density of integers in $A + B$. The most well-known example is **Goldbach's conjecture** [Wiki]: it states that if $A = B$ is the set of all primes, then $A + B$, defined as the set of all integers $a + b$ with $a \in A$, $b \in B$, covers all positive even integers greater than 2. The second most well-known example is when $A = B$ is the set of square integers. The problem is referred to as **sums of squares** [Wiki]. The resulting $A + B$ is too large to be of interest here. A more general version is the sum of higher powers, known as **Waring's problem** [Wiki]. If $A = B$ is the set of positive cubes, or A is the set of positive cubes and B the set of squares, then $A + B$ is small enough to lead to interesting results. Let us now investigate these popular cases.

17.3.2.1 *Sums of two cubes, or cuban primes*

Let P be the set of primes, greater than 2, that are the sum of two cubes. They are called **cuban primes** [Wiki], and featured in the OEIS list of integer sequences as entries A334520 and A002407. These primes are of the form $3x^2 + 3x + 1$ where x is a positive integer. Because cuban primes are less numerous than square integers, we have $\prod_{p \in P}(1 + p^{-\sigma})^{-1} < \infty$ if $\sigma > 0.5$. Thus, if $\sigma > 0.5$ and regardless of χ, the associated $L_P(z, \chi)$ orbit has a hole at the origin, with radius > 0 (not a single point or an empty set). In short, $L_P(z, \chi)$ never gets too close to zero if $\sigma > 0.5$. This is in stark contrast to the standard Riemann zeta function $\zeta(z)$, which has a hole of strictly positive radius only if $\sigma > 1$.

It is conjectured that there are infinitely many cuban primes. For primes of the form $x^3 + 2y^3$, a proof was published in 2001, see [12].

17.3.2.2 *Primes associated to elliptic curves*

Now, let $P = \{p_1, p_2, \dots\}$ be the set of primes of the form $x^3 + y^2$, listed in increasing order. These primes are far less numerous than primes of the form $x^2 + y^2$, but far more numerous than primes of the form $x^3 + y^3$ (the cuban primes). Here x, y are positive integers. Note that if $p \in P$, then $y^2 = x^3 + p$ for some integers $x \le 0$, $y \ge 0$. This is the equation of an **elliptic curve** [Wiki].

When n is large enough, the number of positive integers smaller than n, of the form $x^3 + y^2$, is less than $n^{5/6}$. We do not know how many of them are prime numbers, but we know that it must be less than that. Thus p_k is asymptotically larger than $k^{6/5}$. For details, see Exercise 17.6, based on a general summation formula posted here. Then, using formula (17.6), we have

$$\rho = |L_P(z, \chi)| \ge \prod_{k=1}^{\infty} \frac{1}{1 + p_k^{\sigma}} \ge \prod_{k=1}^{\infty} \frac{1}{1 + k^{6\sigma/5}}. \tag{17.10}$$

Regardless of the function $\chi(\cdot)$, the rightmost product in formula (17.10) converges (absolutely) if $6\sigma/5 > 1$, that is, if $\sigma > \frac{5}{6}$. So, not only $L_P(z, \chi)$ has no zero if $\sigma > \frac{5}{6}$, but there is a circle of radius $\rho > 0$ centered at the origin (a hole), that the orbit never crosses.

For other Dirichlet-L functions with known **abscissa of convergence** [Wiki] $\sigma < 1$, see the article "Modular Elliptic Curves", pages 14–18, in [16]. Interestingly, (conditional) convergence is proved also for $\sigma > \frac{5}{6}$, by looking at the series rather than the product. Primes of the form $x^3 + y^2$ are listed in the Encyclopedia of Integer Sequences, as entry A066649. Related entries include A022549, A055393, A173795, and A123364.

Note. The theory of elliptic curves is now a hot topic in number theory. They were used in the proof of **Fermat's last theorem** [Wiki]. The proof was published in 1995, more than 350 years after it was first conjectured. The theorem states that $x^n + y^n = z^n$ has no nontrivial solution in integer numbers if $n > 2$.

17.3.2.3 *Analytic continuation, convergence, and functional equation*

If the Euler product converges only for $\sigma > 1$, you need to find and extension to $\sigma > 0.5$ to assess whether $L_P(z, \chi)$ has roots when $0.5 < \sigma < 1$. One way to do it to get an **analytic continuation** [Wiki], at least down to $\sigma = 0.5$. If $\chi(\cdot)$ is constant and equal to 1, try using the alternating Dirichlet series $\eta_P(z, \chi)$ defined by formula (17.4), rather than the Euler product, to compute $L_P(z, \chi)$. It may converge over a larger domain. If the analytic continuation satisfies a standard **Dirichlet functional equation** [Wiki] and $z_0 = \sigma + it$ is a root with $0 < \sigma < 1$, then $1 - z_0$ is also a root. Thus in that case, if there is no root with $0.5 < \sigma < 1$, then any possible root with $0 < \sigma < 1$ must have $\sigma = 0.5$. The functional equation, when it exists, can be derived using **exponential sums** such as $\sum_{k=1}^{\infty} \exp(-\pi k^2 y)$. See Section 4.1 (page 71) in [4].

If for some σ_0 the Dirichlet series converges, then it converges for all z with $\Re(z) = \sigma > \sigma_0$. The **abscissa of conditional convergence** for the η_P series defined in formula (17.5) is denoted as σ_c. It is the minimum value satisfying

$$\sum_{k=1}^{\infty}(-1)^{k+1}\chi(k)k^{-\sigma_c} < \infty. \tag{17.11}$$

The **abscissa of absolute convergence**, denoted as σ_a, is the minimum value satisfying

$$\sum_{k=1}^{\infty}|\chi(k)|k^{-\sigma_a} < \infty.$$

Note that $\chi(k) \in \{-1, 0, +1\}$. It is equal to 0 only if k cannot be expressed as a product of elements of P. This happens when P is not the full set of primes. Similar arguments can be used to obtain the abscissa of convergence for the L_P series, or to study the convergence of the product. For instance, for the product in formula (17.4), conditional convergence is equivalent to the convergence of the series $\sum_{p\in P}\chi(p)p^{-\sigma}$. In particular, for $\chi = \chi_4$, the **Dirichlet character modulo 4** introduced at the beginning of Section 17.2.2, the series for $L_P(z, \chi)$ has $\sigma_c = 0$ because χ_4 is periodic, and thus the series in formula (17.11) is alternating.

17.3.2.4 Hybrid Dirichlet–Taylor series
An interesting generalization of the **Euler product**, with $\chi(p) = x^{\nu(p)}$, is as follows:

$$L_P(z, x, \nu) = \prod_{p\in P} \frac{1}{1 - x^{\nu(p)}p^{-z}} = \sum_{k=1}^{\infty}\varphi(k)x^{\Omega_\nu(k)}k^{-z},$$

where $\nu(p)$ is defined on the primes $p \in P$. If the unique factorization of k, using primes in P, is $k = p_1^{a_1} p_2^{a_2} p_3^{a_3} \cdots$, then $\Omega_\nu(k) = a_1\nu(p_1) + a_2\nu(p_2) + \cdots$, where the latter sum is actually finite. Here the a_i's are integers ≥ 0. If k cannot be factored in P, for instance, if P does not contain all the prime integers, then $\varphi(k) = \Omega_\nu(k) = 0$ otherwise $\varphi(k) = 1$. Note that $\Omega_\nu(\cdot)$ is a function defined on $Q = Q_P$, the multiplicative group generated by P, containing all product combinations of elements of P (including 1). In fact, $\Omega_\nu(\cdot)$ generalizes the **Omega function** [Wiki]. If the elements of Q_P are denoted (in increasing order) as q_1, q_2, and so on, then the following notation is more flexible:

$$L_P(z, x, \nu) = \prod_{p\in P}\frac{1}{1 - x^{\nu(p)}p^{-z}} = \sum_{k=1}^{\infty}x^{\Omega_\nu(q_k)}q_k^{-z}. \tag{17.12}$$

This notation works even if the p_k's (and thus the q_k's) are not integers, as in Section 17.3.4. We can also define $\eta_P(z, x, \nu)$ using the same mechanism as in formula (17.5); it may provide an analytic continuation when $x \to 1$.

Examples. Assuming P is the set of all prime integers, interesting examples include:

- If $v(p) = 1$ and $x = 1$, then $L_P(z, x, v) = \zeta(z)$, the **Riemann zeta function** [Wiki]. If $v(p) = 1$ and $x = -1$, then $L_P(z, x, v) = \zeta(2z)/\zeta(z)$. If $v(p) = \log p$ and $0 < x \leq 1$, then $L_P(z, x, v) = \zeta(z - \log x)$. If $v(p) = p$ and $-1 < x < 1$, then we have absolute convergence when $\sigma \geq 0$. In addition, the series in formula (17.12) is a Taylor series in x, and a Dirichlet series in z. This function has no roots, but it does have **poles** [Wiki]. Furthermore, $\lim_{x \to 1} L_P(z, x, v) = \zeta(z)$.
- Let $x = -1$ and $v(p) = 2d(\pi(p), \alpha) - 1$, where $\pi(\cdot)$ is the **prime-counting function** [Wiki] and $d(k, \alpha)$ is the kth binary digit of the real number $0 < \alpha < 1$. Choose α so that its binary digits are random enough, behaving like an infinite fair coin-tossing game. Then, by virtue of the **Glivenko–Cantelli theorem** [Wiki], the empirical distribution [Wiki] of the digits converge to the underlying theoretical distribution of the process described in Section 17.3.5. In particular, we have both convergence of the product and no root if $\sigma > 0.5$. Thus the **Generalized Riemann Hypothesis** [Wiki] (abbreviated as GRH) is verified in this case. You still need to find some α that works, for instance, some **normal number** [Wiki] that would fit the bill. Of course, $\alpha = \sqrt{2}/2$ is a great candidate, but no one knows if it is normal or not, despite the fact that it successfully passed all the statistical tests ever designed.
- In the previous example, if $\alpha = 2/3$, GRH is also satisfied, despite the lack of randomness: the digits alternate perfectly between 0 and 1. But $p_{2k}^{-\sigma} - p_{2k+1}^{-\sigma} \to 0$ fast enough as $k \to \infty$ (see here), thus we have convergence of the product if $\sigma > 0.5$ and therefore, no root. Now, let α be defined as follows: the first digit is zero; then $d(\pi(p), \alpha) = 1$ if $p \equiv 1 \bmod 4$ and $d(\pi(p), \alpha) = 0$ if $p \equiv 3 \bmod 4$. Then $L_P(z, x, v) = L(z, \chi_4)$ where χ_4 is the nontrivial **Dirichlet character modulo** 4. The digits have limited randomness; the proportion of zero/one is 50/50 thanks to **Dirichlet's theorem** [Wiki], and this **Dirichlet-L function** [Wiki] enjoys a number of interesting properties. If its product converges when $\sigma > 0.5$ (nobody knows), then $L(z, \chi_4)$ would also satisfy GRH. The nonrandomness of the digits (this in itself does not rule out GRH) is caused by the fact that $\chi_4(\cdot)$ is completely multiplicative and periodic. In particular, if p is a prime, then $\chi_4(p^2) = 1$ and thus $d(\pi(p^2), \alpha) = 1$.
- Let $v(p) = 1/p$ and $0 < x \leq 1$. When $v(p) = \log p$, you approach ζ (when $x \to 1$) in the exact same way as moving to the left on the real axis, from $\sigma > 0.5$ (no root if GRH is true) to $\sigma = 0.5$ (infinitely many roots). The case $v(p) = 1/p$ offers a different perspective. Also $x^{1/p} \to 1$ as $p \to \infty$, regardless of $0 < x < 1$. Thus $v(p) = 1/p$ is appealing. For instance, when $x = 0.99$ and $\sigma = 0.55$, the orbit of $\eta_P(z, x, v)$ has a small hole around the origin (if might shrink to a singleton if you display the full orbit for all $t > 0$, as it does if $x = 1$). The orbit regularly gets close to the origin before moving away again: this happens only when t is close to the imaginary part of a nontrivial root of ζ. For a fixed value of σ (say 0.5), increasing x from (say) 0.4 to 0.8 will move the hole to the left, closer to the origin as expected. Of course, $\lim_{x \to 1} L_P(z, x, v) = \zeta(z)$. For instance, let $\sigma = \frac{1}{2}$. Then if $x = 0.4$, the orbit has a massive hole centered around $(0, 1)$ on the X-axis. If $x = 0.8$, the orbit has a massive hole centered around $(0, \frac{1}{2})$.

17.3.3 Riemann Hypothesis with cosines replaced by wavelets

The standard Dirichlet eta function $\eta(z)$, with $z = \sigma + it$, can be represented by two nonperiodic trigonometric series: one for the real part involving cosine terms, and one for the imaginary part (a phase shift of the first one) involving sine terms. If you modify even very slightly the coefficients in these series, you lose the interesting properties: **Dirichlet functional equation** [Wiki], infinite number

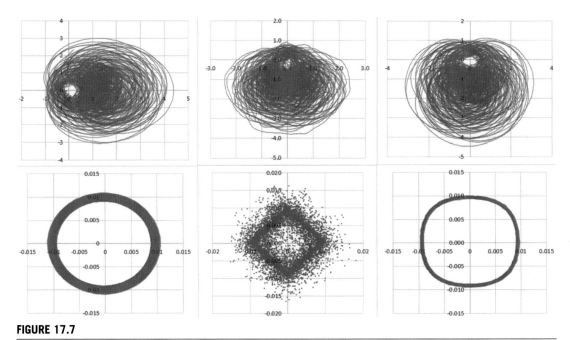

FIGURE 17.7

Orbit of Dirichlet eta $\eta(z)$ when cosines are replaced by other periodic functions.

of roots when $\sigma = \frac{1}{2}$ (in other words, the orbit passing through the origin over and over), no root and hole in the orbit when $\frac{1}{2} < \sigma < 1$.

But what about a drastic change, replacing the sine and cosine functions by other periodic functions? Depending on the replacement, this actually works (except for the functional equation and therefore the roots when $\sigma = \frac{1}{2}$), proving that there is nothing special about the sines and cosines when dealing with the Riemann Hypothesis, at least when $\frac{1}{2} < \sigma < 1$. I start by introducing the following real-valued function:

$$\varphi(z, \theta) = \sum_{k=1}^{\infty} (-1)^{k+1} \frac{W(\theta + t \log k)}{k^{\sigma}}, \tag{17.13}$$

where $z = \sigma + it$, $0 \le \theta < 2\pi$, and W is a periodic function of period 2π, to be defined later. I also use the notation $\varphi_1(z) = \varphi(z, 0)$ and $\varphi_2(z) = \varphi(z, \pi/2)$. In particular, if $W(x) = \cos x$, then $\varphi_1(z)$ is the real part of $\eta(z)$, and $\varphi_2(z)$ is the imaginary part. Also, here P is the full set of prime integers and $\chi(\cdot)$ is the constant function equal to 1.

The top part of Fig. 17.7 shows the orbit of the modified $\eta(z)$ function for $\sigma = 0.75$ and $0 < t < 200$, using the three functions W discussed in this section. The left plot corresponds to the cosine wave (in this case $\eta(z)$ is the standard Dirichlet function), the middle plot to the triangular wave, and the right plot to the alternating quadratic wave.

- Triangular wave

$$W(x) = \begin{cases} -2x/\pi, & \text{if } 0 \le x \le \pi/2, \\ -2 + 2x/\pi, & \text{if } \pi/2 \le x \le 3\pi/2, \\ 4 - 2x/\pi & \text{if } 3\pi/2 \le x \le 2\pi; \end{cases}$$

- Alternating quadratic wave

$$W(x) = \begin{cases} -4x(x-\pi)/\pi^2, & \text{if } 0 \le x \le \pi, \\ 4(x-\pi)(x-2\pi)/\pi^2 & \text{if } \pi \le x \le 2\pi; \end{cases}$$

- Cosine wave

$$W(x) = \cos x.$$

I used the first 20,000 terms in formula (17.13). In each case, the origin is inside the hole, clearly showing the absence of roots when $0 < t < 200$. Other waves tested do not exhibit a hole. The bottom plots show the corresponding errors, magnified by a factor 20: they represent the difference between the approximate computations based on 2000 terms, and the more accurate results based on 20,000 terms.

17.3.4 Riemann Hypothesis for Beurling primes

Beurling primes are real or complex numbers used to mimic and study distributions related to prime integers. A Beurling prime set $P = \{p_1, p_2, \dots\}$ is any set of real or complex numbers with the constraint that the product of elements of P cannot be an element of P. We then define $Q = Q_P$ as the set of all product combinations $q = p_1^{a_1} p_2^{a_2} \cdots$ where $a_1, a_2, \dots$ are integers ≥ 0. It is also required that the factorization of $q \in Q_P$, using Beurling primes from P, is unique.

A counterexample is the set of **Hilbert primes** [Wiki]: for instance, $1617 = 21 \times 77 = 33 \times 49$ where $21, 33, 49, 77$ are Hilbert primes (they cannot be factored as a product of Hilbert primes). A good example is when Q is the set of numbers that are sums of two square integers: if $q, q' \in Q$ then $q \cdot q' \in Q$. In this case, $P = \{2, 5, 9, 13, \dots\}$, see here. Note that $9, 49$, and 121 are primes in Q. Related to this set is the set of **Gaussian primes** [Wiki], which are complex numbers.

The Python code in Section 17.5.1 handles Beurling primes. In the current implementation, P is the set of all prime integers except that 3 is replaced by $2 + \log 3 \approx 3.0986$. When using the Beurling option, set the `Dirichlet` parameter to `True`, to get convergence when $\frac{1}{2} \le \sigma < 1$. The orbit of $\eta_P(z, \chi)$, assuming $\chi(\cdot)$ is constant and equal to 1, exhibits a hole that encompasses the origin if $\frac{1}{2} < \sigma < 1$. The hole shrinks to a point (the origin) if the full, infinite orbit is plotted, pointing to the absence of roots, just like for the standard Dirichlet eta function $\eta(z)$. Of course, this is part of the GRH conjecture, not a proven fact. Likewise, if $\sigma = \frac{1}{2}$, there are infinitely many roots. In the context of Beurling numbers, the associated Dirichlet function $L_P(z, \chi)$ is called a **Dedekind zeta function** [Wiki], and Dedekind eta for the alternating series $\eta_P(z, \chi)$.

Beurling primes can be defined for objects other than numbers, like polynomials or matrices. For instance, let A be a square matrix, and define $p_k = \exp(\mu_k A)$, where the μ_k's are distinct, strictly positive real numbers ordered by increasing values, and linearly independent over the set of positive integers, so that the factorization in Q_P is unique. For instance, μ_k is the logarithm of the kth prime integer. Any element (matrix) $q \in Q_P$ can be written as

$$q = p_1^{a_1} p_2^{a_2} \cdots = \exp(|q|A) = \sum_{k=0}^{\infty} |q|^k \frac{A^k}{k!}, \quad \text{with } |q| = \sum_{k=1}^{\infty} a_k \mu_k.$$

Here $a_1, a_2, \ldots$ are integers ≥ 0 and $|q|$ is called the norm. We can define an order on Q as follows: if $q, q' \in Q$, then $q < q'$ if and only if $|q| < |q'|$. Note that q, q', and the p_k's are matrices. We can build Dirichlet series and Euler products for these primes, and study properties when $\frac{1}{2} \leq \sigma < 1$, as we do for standard prime integers. For more on Beurling primes, see [5] and [13].

17.3.5 Stochastic Euler products

There are different ways to randomize functions related to Euler products. You may want to randomize $L_P(z, \chi)$ or $\eta_P(z, \chi)$ using **complex random variables** [Wiki]. Or you may want to randomize the real or imaginary parts of these functions, or their norm. These random products have gained a lot of interest recently, at they provide insights about RH and its generalized version, GRH. For a recent reference on **random Euler products**, see [15]. I briefly discussed randomized multiplicative functions such as random **Rademacher functions** [Wiki] in Section 17.2.2.2. More on this topic can be found in Chapter 11 and in [9–11,15]. My recent book on stochastic processes [8] discusses tiny random perturbations applied to Dirichlet series: it shows that the hole at the origin, observed on any finite portion of the orbit if $0.5 < \sigma < 1$, quickly vanishes if you slightly modify the series.

Here I focus on randomizing $L_P(z, \chi)$. Let $z = \sigma + it$ be fixed, $0.5 < \sigma < 1$, and for each prime $p \in P$, $\chi(p)$ be a random variable equal to $+1$ or -1 with probability 0.5. The $\chi(p)$'s are assumed to be independent. It follows immediately that

$$E[L_P(z, \chi)] = \prod_{p \in P} E\left[\frac{1}{1 - \chi(p)p^{-z}}\right] = \prod_{p \in P} \frac{1}{1 - p^{-2z}} = L_P(2z, \chi_0),$$

where $\chi_0(\cdot)$ is the constant function equal to one. Note that the product converges if $\sigma > 0.5$. So this type of randomization extents the abscissa of convergence from $\sigma > 1$ to $\sigma > 0.5$. Now let the random variable ρ^2 be the square of the distance to the origin:

$$\rho^2 = |L_P(z, \chi)|^2 = \prod_{p \in P} |1 - \chi(p)p^{-z}|^{-2} = \prod_{p \in P} \frac{1}{1 - 2p^{-\sigma}\chi(p)\cos(t \log p) + p^{-2\sigma}}. \tag{17.14}$$

We have

$$E[\rho^2] = \prod_{p \in P} E\left[|1 - \chi(p)p^{-z}|^{-2}\right] = \prod_{p \in P} \frac{1 + p^{-2\sigma}}{(1 + p^{-2\sigma})^2 - 4p^{-2\sigma}\cos^2(t \log p)}.$$

In particular,

$$\prod_{p \in P} \frac{1}{1 + p^{-2\sigma}} = \frac{L_P(4\sigma, \chi_0)}{L_P(2\sigma, \chi_0)} \leq E[\rho^2] \leq \prod_{p \in P} \frac{1 + p^{-2\sigma}}{(1 - p^{-2\sigma})^2} = \frac{L_P^3(2\sigma, \chi_0)}{L_P(4\sigma, \chi_0)}. \tag{17.15}$$

Again, $\chi_0(\cdot)$ is the constant function equal to 1. The maximum is attained when $t = 0$. If P is the full set of primes, formula (17.15) becomes $\zeta(4\sigma)/\zeta(2\sigma) \leq E[\rho^2] \leq \zeta^3(2\sigma)/\zeta(4\sigma)$, where ζ is the

Riemann zeta function [Wiki]. Similar bounds are available for E[ρ]. It is interesting to note that by averaging over all potential $\chi(\cdot)$'s, the orbit has a hole encompassing the origin, with a strictly positive radius. This is in contrast to the nonrandom case, where the hole is reduced to a point regardless of χ (assuming $0.5 < \sigma < 1$).

Let $P = \{p_1, p_2, \dots\}$ with the primes listed in increasing order. Now let us define the random variable $L_\chi(n) = \sum_{k=1}^n \chi(p_k)$. It satisfies the **law of the iterated logarithm** [Wiki], stated in formula (17.7), and translating here to

$$\limsup_{n \to \infty} \frac{|L_\chi(n)|}{\sqrt{n \log \log n}} = C,$$

for some constant C with $0 < C < \infty$. But the prime numbers are not perfectly random, and one would expect $\sqrt{n \log \log n}$ to be replaced by (say) $\sqrt{n^{1+\epsilon}}$ for any arbitrary small $\epsilon > 0$. This may be the case in the deterministic example where $\chi(p) = +1$ if $p \equiv 1 \bmod 4$ and $\chi(p) = -1$ if $p \equiv 3 \bmod 4$. One way to make the random Euler product more realistic is to introduce weak dependencies among the $\chi(p)$'s. Then one can test whether the improved stochastic model (with weak dependencies) is a better fit to the observed data – the actual $\chi(p)$'s. The weak dependencies can be introduced as follows, when simulating $\chi(p_{n+1})$ for n large enough:

- If $|L_\chi(n)| < \beta\sqrt{n(\log \log \log n)^\nu}$, then $P[\chi(p_{n+1}) = 1] = \frac{1}{2} + \mu n^{-\alpha}$, $P[\chi(p_{n+1}) = -1] = \frac{1}{2} - \mu n^{-\alpha}$.
- Otherwise choose between $+1$ and -1 so that $|L_\chi(n+1)| < |L_\chi(n)|$.

You may try with various values of α, β, $\nu > 0$ and μ to see which ones provide the best fit for very large n, say $n > 10^{15}$. You could also change the sign of μ every now and then. The choice of $\log \log \log n$ is inspired by Gonek's conjecture; see [14] page 29.

Finally, another random Euler product also investigated in [15] is the following:

$$\rho^2 = \prod_{p \in P} \frac{1}{1 - 2p^{-\sigma} \cos(\Theta_p) + p^{-2\sigma}}. \tag{17.16}$$

Here the Θ_p's are independent uniform deviates on $[0, 2\pi]$. Compare this to formula (17.14). Since

$$\frac{1}{2\pi} \int_0^{2\pi} \frac{1}{1 - 2p^{-\sigma} \cos \theta + p^{-2\sigma}} d\theta = \frac{1}{1 - p^{-2\sigma}},$$

we have

$$E[\rho^2] = \prod_{p \in P} E\left[\frac{1}{1 - 2p^{-\sigma} \cos(\Theta_p) + p^{-2\sigma}}\right] = \prod_{p \in P} \frac{1}{1 - p^{-2\sigma}} = L_P(2\sigma, \chi_0),$$

where again, $\chi_0(\cdot)$ is the constant function equal to 1. If P is the full set of primes, $L_P(2\sigma, \chi_0) = \zeta(2\sigma)$. The proof that the distribution attached to ρ^2 exists and is not singular can be found in [15].

17.4 Exercises

The following exercises require out-of-the-box thinking. They complement the theory or provide a proof to some of the theoretical results discussed in this chapter.

Exercise 17.1. – Asymptotic formula. Prove the asymptotic formula (17.2).

Solution

By definition, we have $q_k = p_1^{a_1} p_2^{a_2} \cdots p_d^{a_d}$ for some positive integers $a_1, \ldots, a_d$. In other words, $a_1 \log p_1 + \cdots + a_d \log p_d = \log q_k$. This is the equation of a $(d-1)$-dimensional simplex with vertices $(\log p_1, 0, \ldots, 0)$, $(0, \log p_2, \ldots, 0)$, $\ldots$, $(0, 0, \ldots, \log p_d)$. If you add the origin as a vertex, then the number of points v_k with integer coordinates, inside the newly created d-dimensional simplex, is approximately equal to the volume V_k of that **simplex** [Wiki]. Also, v_k is the number of positive integers less than or equal to q_k, since each integer has a unique factorization in (ordered) prime numbers. So, q_k is the inverse of the function v_k, which is asymptotically equal to the inverse of V_k. To complete the proof, use the well known fact that

$$V_k = \frac{1}{d!} \left(\log q_k \right)^d \prod_{p \in P} \frac{1}{\log p} = \frac{1}{d!} \prod_{p \in P} \log_p q_k,$$

where $\log_p$ stands for the logarithm in base p. The result is easy to verify if $d = 1$.

Exercise 17.2. – Equivalence between series and Euler product. Prove formula (17.1).

Solution

Expanding the product in formula (17.1), one obtains

$$\prod_{p \in P} \frac{1}{1 - p^{-z}} = \prod_{p \in P} \left(1 + p^{-z} + p^{-2z} + \cdots \right) = \sum_{a_1, a_2, \ldots, a_d} \left(p_1^{a_1} p_2^{a_2} \cdots p_d^{a_d} \right)^{-z} = \sum_{k=1}^{\infty} q_k^{-z}.$$

Let us denote the rightmost series in the above equation as $\zeta_P(z)$. To complete the proof, use the fact that

$$\sum_{k=1}^{\infty} \delta_k q_k^{-z} = \zeta_P(z) - 2 \sum_{q_k \text{ even}} q_k^{-z} = \zeta_P(z) - 2 \sum_{k=1}^{\infty} (2q_k)^{-z} = (1 - 2^{1-z}) \zeta_P(z).$$

Another interesting identity is the following:

$$(1 - 2^{1-z}) \prod_{p \in P} \frac{1}{1 + p^{-z}} = (1 - 2^{1-z}) \frac{\zeta_P(2z)}{\zeta_P(z)} = \sum_{k=1}^{\infty} \delta_k \lambda(q_k) q_k^{-z},$$

where $\lambda(\cdot)$ is the **Liouville function** [Wiki].

Exercise 17.3. – Convergence problem. If P is the set of all primes and δ_k is replaced by $+1$, then the series in formula (17.1) will not converge if $\sigma < 1$. Here, $z = \sigma + it$. That is, σ is the real part of the complex number z.

Solution

In this case $q_k = k$. Note that $k^{-z} = k^{-\sigma} \cdot [\cos(t \log k) + i \sin(t \log k)]$. It suffices to prove that the series with kth term equal to $k^{-\sigma} \cos(t \log k)$ cannot converge, even though $\cos(t \log k)$ oscillates infinitely often between positive and negative values, as k increases. The reason is because $\log k$ grows too slowly. When k is very close to a multiple of (say) 2π, too many consecutive terms are all positive, and k^{σ} does not grow fast enough (if $\sigma < 1$) to keep the partial sums bounded and converging. To the contrary, if $\log k$ is replaced by $\sqrt{k}$ in the cosine function, and $\sigma = 0.75$, then the series converge: the corresponding integral between 0 and ∞ is equal to $\sqrt{2\pi/|t|}$.

Exercise 17.4. – Truncated Dirichlet function. Determine the area covered by the orbit, for a fixed value of σ, when $n = 3$ and t runs though all the positive real numbers in formula (17.8). Generalize to $n = 4$.

Solution

Let us assume that the center of the hole is $(1, 0)$ in this case. Proving it is left to the reader. Then the square of the distance between a point on the orbit at time t and the origin is equal to

$$d^2(t) = \left[\beta^{\sigma} \cos(t \log 2) - \lambda_3^{\sigma} \cos(t \log 2)\right]^2 + \left[\beta^{\sigma} \sin(t \log 2) - \lambda_3^{\sigma} \sin(t \log 2)\right]^2$$
$$= \beta^{2\sigma} + \lambda_3^{2\sigma} - 2\beta^{\sigma} \lambda_3^{\sigma} \left[\cos(t \log 2)\cos(t \log 3) + \sin(t \log 2)\sin(t \log 3)\right]$$
$$= \beta^{2\sigma} + \lambda_3^{2\sigma} - 2\beta^{\sigma} \lambda_3^{\sigma} \cos\left(t \log \frac{2}{3}\right).$$

Since the cosine takes all values between -1 and $+1$, infinitely often with period $2\pi/(\log 3 - \log 2)$, the outer boundary of the orbit is a circle of radius ρ_1 centered at $(1, 0)$, and the inner boundary (that is, the shape of the hole) is a circle of radius ρ_2 also centered at $(1, 0)$. Here

$$\rho_1 = \sqrt{\beta^{2\sigma} + \lambda_3^{2\sigma} + 2\beta^{\sigma} \lambda_3^{\sigma}} = |\beta^{\sigma} + \lambda_3^{\sigma}|, \quad \rho_2 = \sqrt{\beta^{2\sigma} + \lambda_3^{2\sigma} - 2\beta^{\sigma} \lambda_3^{\sigma}} = |\beta^{\sigma} - \lambda_3^{\sigma}|.$$

Thus the larger the β, the bigger the hole. I assumed that $\beta, \lambda_3 \geq 0$.

The case $n = 4$ is considerably more complicated. The center is no longer $(1, 0)$, but typically $(c, 0)$ with $c < 1$. Also, the shapes may no longer be circles. There may or may not be a hole. However, if β is large enough, there will be a hole, big enough to encompass $(1, 0)$. The square of the distance to $(1, 0)$ is now

$$d^2(t) = \beta^{2\sigma} + \lambda_3^{2\sigma} + \lambda_4^{2\sigma} - 2\beta^{\sigma} \lambda_3^{\sigma} \cos\left(t \log \frac{2}{3}\right) - 2\beta^{\sigma} \lambda_4^{\sigma} \cos\left(t \log \frac{2}{4}\right) - 2\lambda_3^{\sigma} \lambda_4^{\sigma} \cos\left(t \log \frac{3}{4}\right).$$

The minimum possible value for $d^2(t)$ is $d_{min} = \beta^{2\sigma} + \lambda_3^{2\sigma} + \lambda_4^{2\sigma} - 2\beta^{\sigma} \lambda_3^{\sigma} - 2\beta^{\sigma} \lambda_4^{\sigma} - 2\lambda_3^{\sigma} \lambda_4^{\sigma}$. If $d_{min} > 0$, there is a hole big enough to encompass $(1, 0)$.

Exercise 17.5. – The orbit covers a dense area in the complex plane. The purpose of this exercise is to prove a particular case: if $\sigma < 1$, then $\lim \inf |L_P(z, \chi)| = 0$ regardless of χ. The infimum [Wiki] is over all complex numbers z. Here we assume that P is an infinite subset of primes (or the full set), and that the sum of $p^{-\sigma}$ over all $p \in P$ diverges. This proves that the orbit is dense around the origin under certain conditions. It implies, under these conditions, that the hole shrinks to a singleton (the origin) if $|L_P(z, \chi)| > 0$ for all z, and to an empty set if $L_P(z, \chi) = 0$ for some z.

Solution

Assume the Euler product is finite, and contains only the first d primes $p_1, \ldots, p_d \in P$. Let $z = \sigma + it$ as usual, with t large enough so that $t \log p_k$ gets extremely close to a multiple of π, say $m_k \pi$, for all $k = 1, \ldots, d$. This is possible thanks to **Kronecker's theorem** [Wiki]. Then $\sin(t \log p_k)$ gets very close to 0, and $\cos(t \log p_k)$ gets very close to either -1 or $+1$ depending on whether m_k is odd or even. Thus, the imaginary part of $L_P(z, \chi)$, involving the sine terms only, gets very close to 0. The real part, involving the cosine terms only, gets very close to

$$S(\chi^\star) = \sum_{k=1}^{\infty} \chi^\star(k)\chi(k)k^{-\sigma},$$

where

- The function $\chi^\star$ is a **completely multiplicative** [Wiki] and thus entirely defined by its values on prime numbers,
- $\chi^\star(p_k) \in \{1, +1\}$ if $p_k \in P$ and $1 \le k \le d$, otherwise $\chi^\star(p_k) = 0$,
- $\chi^\star(p_k) = +1$ if m_k is even, otherwise $\chi^\star(p_k) = -1$.

Also, $p^{-z} = [\cos(t \log p_k) + i \sin(t \log p_k)] \cdot p^{-\sigma} \to \chi^\star(p_k)p^{-\sigma}$ as $t \to \infty$. Thus for the Euler product, with the special t discussed above (a function of $m_1, \ldots, m_d$) and $z = \sigma + it$, we have

$$L_P(z, \chi) \to \prod_{k=1}^{d} \frac{1}{1 - \chi^\star(p_k)\chi(p_k)p_k^{-\sigma}} \in \mathbb{R} \quad \text{as } t \to \infty. \tag{17.17}$$

If $\sum_{p \in P} p^{-\sigma} = \infty$, then the product in formula (17.17) can approximate any positive value arbitrarily closely, as $d \to \infty$. Indeed, $d_k = \chi^\star(p_k)$ can be seen as the kth binary digit of the (real) number $L_P(z, \chi)$ in some special numeration system. And you can compute d_k using a technique similar to that used for standard binary digits in base 2, with a version of the **greedy algorithm** [Wiki]. To get arbitrarily close to zero, one way is to choose the function $\chi^\star$ so that $\chi^\star \chi = -1$.

Note. In the computation of $S(\chi^\star)$, I implicitly used the following facts. First, if k has the prime factorization $k = p_1^{a_1} \cdots p_d^{a_d}$, then $\cos(t \log k) = \cos(a_1 t \log p_1 + \cdots + a_d t \log p_d)$. Recursively using $\cos(\alpha + \beta) = \cos \alpha \cos \beta - \sin \alpha \sin \beta$, with the fact that all the sines are zero and $\cos(a_i t \log p_i) \to \cos(a_i m_i \pi) = [\chi^\star(p_i)]^{a_i}$ as $t \to \infty$, one obtains $\cos(t \log k) \to [\chi^\star(p_1)]^{a_1} \cdots [\chi^\star(p_d)]^{a_d} = \chi^\star(k)$.

Exercise 17.6. – Density of integers of the form $x^3 + y^2$. Prove that the kth integer of the form $x^3 + y^2$ is asymptotically larger than $k^{6/5}$.

Solution

Let $v(n)$ be the number of lattice points (x, y), with x, y positive integers, satisfying $x^3 + y^2 \le n$. Estimating v_n is a classic problem in **additive number theory** [Wiki], generalizing the **Gaussian circle problem** [Wiki]. The solution to this class of problems is as follows. Let $S_1, \ldots, S_m$ be m infinite sets of positive integers, and $v_i(n)$ be the number of elements less than n in S_i. Let $v(n)$ be the number of lattice points $(x_1, \ldots, x_m)$, with $x_i \in S_i$, satisfying $x_1 + \cdots + x_m \le v(n)$. If $v_i(n) \sim a_i n^{b_i} (\log n)^{-c_i}$ with $0 < b_i \le 1$, $c_i \ge 0$ and $a_i > 0$ ($i = 1, \ldots, m$), then

$$v(n) \lesssim \frac{\prod_{i=1}^m a_i \Gamma(b_i + 1)}{\Gamma(1 + \sum_{i=1}^m b_i)} \cdot \frac{n^{b_1 + \cdots + b_m}}{(\log n)^{c_1 + \cdots + c_m}},$$

where $\lesssim$ means "asymptotically smaller", and Γ is the Gamma function. See here and here for details.

In our case, $m = 2$, $a_1 = a_2 = 1$, $c_1 = c_2 = 0$, $b_1 = 1/3$, $b_2 = 1/2$. Thus $v(n) \lesssim n^{5/6}$. Note that this method may result in double counting, for instance, $225 = 6^3 + 3^2 = 5^3 + 10^2 = 0^3 + 15^2$. Thus the actual number $w(n)$ of positive integers of the form $x^3 + y^2$ is even smaller, thus definitely smaller than $n^{5/6}$. It follows immediately, using the inverse of the function $w(n)$, that the kth element is asymptotically larger than $n^{6/5}$.

Exercise 17.7. – Strange factorization of the Dirichlet functions. Show, based on the Euler product, that $L_P(z, \chi) = L_P(z/2, \psi) L_P(z/2, -\psi)$ where $\psi^2(p) = \chi(p)$, thus $\psi(p) \in \{1, -1, i, -i\}$. In particular, if $\chi(p) = 1$, one can choose $\psi(p_{2k+1}) = 1$ and $\psi(p_{2k}) = -1$ where p_k is the kth prime. In this case, $L(z, \chi) = \zeta(z)$, and the Euler products of $L(z/2, \psi)$ and $L(z/2, -\psi)$ both converge if $\sigma > 0$. However, $L_P(z/2, \psi) L_P(z/2, -\psi) = \zeta(z)$ only if $\sigma > 1$. How can these formulas be generalized recursively?

Solution

Let $\psi_0 = \chi$ and $\psi_1 = \psi$. Using the same logic, $L(z/2, -\psi_1) = L_P(z/4, \psi_2) L_P(z/4, -\psi_2)$ where $\psi_2^2(p) = -\psi_1(p)$. Applying this method recursively, one obtains

$$L_P(z, \chi) = L(z/2^n, -\psi_n) \prod_{k=1}^n L_P(z/2^k, \psi_k),$$

where $n \ge 1$ and $\psi_{k+1}^2 = -\psi_k$ for $k = 1, 2$, and so on. For which values of σ is this formula valid? Based on the construction, all the associated Euler products must converge, suggesting $\sigma > 2^n$.

Exercise 17.8. – Roots of the Riemann zeta function. As usual, $z = \sigma + it$. Let S_0 be any open interval containing exactly one value t_0 such that $\zeta(\frac{1}{2} + it_0) = 0$, and let $\eta(z)$ be the standard **Dirichlet eta function**. Discuss the existence (or not) of roots of $\eta(z)$ if $t \in S_0$ and $\frac{1}{2} < \sigma < 1$. Show how it works when $S_0 =]199, 202[$. You can find a table of the first 100,000 nontrivial roots of $\zeta(z)$, here.

Solution

Assume σ is fixed. Let $\mu(\sigma)$ be the minimum of $|\eta(z)|$ if $t \in S_0$, and let $\tau(\sigma)$ be the value achieving the minimum. That is,

$$\mu(\sigma) = \min_{t \in S_0} |\eta(\sigma + it)|, \quad \tau(\sigma) = \arg\min_{t \in S_0} |\eta(\sigma + it)|.$$

If $S_0 =]199, 202[$ then $t_0 \approx 201.26$. Let $t_0' = 44\pi / \log 2 \approx 199.42$. We have $1 - 2^{1-z} = 0$ where $z = 1 + it_0'$, and:

- $\mu(\frac{1}{2}) = 0$ and $\tau(\frac{1}{2}) = t_0$ since $\eta(\frac{1}{2} + it_0) = 0$,

- $\mu(1) = 0$ and $\tau(1) = t_0'$, since $\eta(1 + it_0') = 0$,
- $\mu(\sigma)$ is strictly increasing and continuous if $\frac{1}{2} \leq \sigma \leq \sigma_0$ with $\sigma_0 \approx 0.75$,
- $\mu(\sigma)$ is strictly decreasing and continuous if $\sigma_0 \leq \sigma \leq 1$.

In other words, $\mu(\sigma)$ is convex. It seems to imply that there is no root if $t \in S_0$ and $\frac{1}{2} < \sigma < 1$. However, proving that $\mu(\sigma)$ is increasing or decreasing, with only one change-point at some σ_0 (depending on S_0), may be as hard as proving RH itself: it is based on empirical evidence only, and related to the (conjectured) absence of roots for the derivative of $\zeta(z)$. Indeed, it is just a consequence of the Riemann Hypothesis, see here.

There is something particularly striking though, which could prove useful to make some progress: the function $\tau(\sigma)$ is almost flat, with a single discontinuity at σ_0. Indeed, $201.26 \leq \tau(\sigma) \leq 201.29$ if $\frac{1}{2} \leq \sigma < \sigma_0$, and $199.41 \leq \tau(\sigma) \leq 199.42$ if $\sigma_0 < \sigma \leq 1$. These variations are so small that you wonder if they are real, or caused by numerical imprecision (implying the function $\tau(\sigma)$ could be perfectly flat with a single discontinuity, making it potentially easier to prove RH). If these variations really do exist, there might be a function other than $\eta(z)$ with the same roots, say a scaled version of $\eta(z)$ with a scaling factor free of roots, for which the variations are absent. Such a function may be easier to investigate.

More generally, the functions $\mu(\sigma)$ and $\tau(\sigma)$ have this same behavior whenever S_0 contains a value t_0' such that $z = 1 + it_0'$ is a root of $1 - 2^{1-z}$, and therefore a root of $\eta(z)$. Because these roots are evenly spaced by the increment $2\pi/\log 2$, and since the roots at $\sigma = \frac{1}{2}$ are closer and closer to each other as $t \to \infty$ (see [3,17]), there is either one t_0' in S_0, or none. There can't be more than one. When there is none, the situation is even easier and amounts to setting $\sigma_0 = \infty$, or at least $\sigma_0 > 1$.

Finally, if it was possible to prove the points discussed in this exercise, then, of course, RH would be proved. It suffices to consider the collection of all possible S_0 to show that there would be no root anywhere, no matter how large t is, if $\frac{1}{2} < \sigma < 1$.

Exercise 17.9. – Approximating the Dirichlet eta function. The Dirichlet series for $\eta(z)$ converges very slowly and chaotically, especially if σ is small or t is large. One way to accelerate the convergence is to use **Euler's transform** [Wiki]. See also Exercise 25 in [8]. Other approximations exist, for instance, using Dirichlet polynomials [7]. Here I investigate yet a different type of approximation. Let $z = \sigma + it$ as usual, with σ fixed, say $\sigma = 0.8$. Also assume that the values of $\eta(\sigma + ik)$ are known and denoted as $\eta_k(\sigma)$ if k is a positive integer. The approximation is as follows:

$$\eta(z) \approx \frac{\sin \pi t}{\pi} \cdot \left[\frac{\eta_0(\sigma)}{t} + 2t \sum_{k=1}^{n} (-1)^k \frac{\eta_k(\sigma)}{t^2 - k^2} \right].$$

Show how good this approximation is. For the solution, see Exercise 8.2 in Chapter 8.

17.5 Python code

The main code is in Section 17.5.1. The code in Section 17.5.2 is provided for convenience only: it does not further illustrate the theory, but instead focuses on producing beautiful videos of the orbits studied in this paper. Section 11.3.2 about the prime test for pseudorandom number generators, deeply related to the Generalized Riemann Hypothesis, has more Python code directly relevant to the topics discussed here.

17.5.1 Computing the orbit of various Dirichlet series

The code below computes $\eta_P(z, \chi)$ if the `Dirichlet` variable is set to `True`; otherwise it computes $L_P(z, \chi)$. More specifically, it computes the value of the function in question for $z = \sigma + it$, with $\sigma = \Re(z) \geq 0.5$ fixed and determined by the variable `sig`, and for equally spaced values of t between `minT` and `maxT`. The spacing is determined by the variable `increment`, typically set to 0.01. It uses the Dirichlet series expansion, with the number of terms determined by `nterms` (typically set to 2000) to get at least 2 digits of accuracy in the worse case where $\sigma = 0.5$ or t is large. The function `primes.check()` from the primePy library tests if a number is a prime. The code actually handles the more general case where $\chi(p)$ is replaced by $\chi(p) \cdot x^{\nu(p)}$, with $\nu(p) = 1/p$ as in formula (17.12) and $0 < x \leq 1$. The standard case corresponds to $x = 1$. The variable x is represented by x in the code.

The value of $\eta_P(z, \chi)$ or $L_P(z, \chi)$ is a complex number: its real and imaginary parts are respectively named `etax` and `etay` in the code. The function χ, and thus the set P, depends on the option selected in the code, determined by the variable `method`: `Zeta` (that is, $\zeta(z)$ by default), `Eta`, `Dirichlet4` (corresponding to χ_4), `Beurling`, `Alternating`, or `Random`. Please refer to the text to identify when the series converge or not: in particular, the `Zeta` method converges only if $\sigma > 1$.

The output variables `minL` and `maxL` help determine convergence status. They are discussed in more details in Section 11.2.1 on pseudorandom number generators. The parameter `beta` should be set to 0.5, unless you want to replicate the experiments discussed in Section 17.3.1, where `beta` is represented by β. Likewise, keep x set to 1, unless you want to replicate the experiments in Section 17.3.2.4. Finally, the program uses hash tables (dictionaries in Python) rather than arrays, for increased efficiency: these arrays would be quite sparse. The source code (below) is also on GitHub: look for `DirichletL.py`.

```
# DirichletL.py. Generate orbits of various Dirichlet-L and related functions
# By Vincent Granville, https://www.MLTechniques.com

import math
import random
from primePy import primes

nterms=2000 # increase to 10000 for sig = 0.5
method='Eta'
sig=0.9
Dirichlet=False
x=1        # must have 0 < x <= 1; default is x=1
beta=0.5 # beta > 0.5 magnifies the hole of the orbit

random.seed(1)
primeSign={}
start=2
if method=='Dirichlet4':
    start=3
idx=0
for k in range(start,nterms):
    if primes.check(k):
        idx=idx+1
        p=k
```

```
        xpow=x**(1/p)
        if method=='Beurling' and p==3:
            p=2+math.log(3)
        primeSign[p]=xpow
        if method=='Dirichlet4' and k%4==3:
            primeSign[p]=-xpow
        elif method=='Alternating' and idx%2==1:
            primeSign[p]=-xpow
        elif method=='Random' and random.random()>0.5:
            primeSign[p]=-xpow
        elif method=='Eta':
            Dirichlet=True

signHash={}
evenHash={}
signHash[1]=1
evenHash[1]=0 # largest power of 2 dividing k
for p in primeSign:
    if p*math.pi %1 < 0.05:
        print(p,"/",nterms) # show progress (where we are in the loop)
    oldSignHash={}
    for k in signHash:
        oldSignHash[k]=signHash[k]
    for k in oldSignHash:
        pp=1
        power=0
        localProduct=oldSignHash[k]
        while k*p*pp<nterms:
            pp=p*pp
            power=power+1
            new_k=k*pp
            localProduct=localProduct*primeSign[p]
            signHash[new_k]=localProduct
            if p==2:
                evenHash[new_k]=power
            else:
                evenHash[new_k]=evenHash[k]

for k in sorted(evenHash):
    if Dirichlet and evenHash[k]>0:
        signHash[k]=-signHash[k]

sumL=0
minL= 2*nterms
maxL=-2*nterms
argMin=-1
argMax=-1
denum={}
```

```
tlog={}
for k in sorted(signHash):
    denum[k]=signHash[k]/k**sig
    tlog[k]=math.log(k)
    sumL=sumL+signHash[k]
    if sumL<minL:
        minL=sumL
        argMin=k
    if sumL>maxL:
        maxL=sumL
        argMax=k
denum[2]=signHash[2]/(1/beta)**sig

def G(tau,sig,nterms):
    fetax=0
    fetay=0
    for j in sorted(signHash):
        fetax=fetax+math.cos(tau*tlog[j])*denum[j]
        fetay=fetay+math.sin(tau*tlog[j])*denum[j]
    return [fetax,fetay]

minT=0.0
maxT=2000.0
increment=0.05

OUT = open("dirichletL.txt", "w")
t=minT
loop=0
while t <maxT:
    if loop%100==0:
        print("t= %5.2f / %d" % (t,maxT))
    loop=loop+1
    (etax,etay)=G(t,sig,nterms)
    line=str(t)+"\t"+str(etax)+"\t"+str(etay)+"\n"
    OUT.write(line)
    t=t+increment
OUT.close()

print("\n")
print(argMin,"-->",minL)
print(argMax,"-->",maxL)
```

17.5.2 Creating videos of the orbit

The Python code in this section deals with the visualization aspects: producing data animations (MP4 videos) of three orbits of $\eta_P(z, \chi)$, when P is the full set of prime integers and $\chi(\cdot)$ is the constant function equal to 1. This is the standard Dirichlet function. The three orbits in question correspond to $\sigma = 0.5$, $\sigma = 0.75$, and $\sigma = 1.25$. These three values are set by the instructions sigma.append() in the code. In particular, $\sigma = 0.5$ reveals the infinitely many roots, while the two other values show the lack of root.

The output videos are available on my GitHub repository, here. The videos are also on YouTube, here. For convenience, the Python code is also included in this chapter. Top variables include ShowOrbit (set to True if you want to display the orbit, not just the points), dot (the size of the dots), r (when iterating over time, it outputs a video frame once every r iterations), width, and height (the dimension of the image). The final image is eventually reduced by half due to the **antialiasing** procedure used to depixelate the curves. This is performed within img.resize in the code, using the Image.LANCZOS parameter [Wiki]. Segments joining two dots on the orbit (to create the appearance of a smooth, curvy orbit) are produced using the Pillow library and its ImageDraw functions.

Reducing the size of the image and the number of frames per second (FPS) will optimize speed and disk usage. The biggest improvement, in terms of speed, is replacing all numpy calls (np.log, np.cos, and so on) by math calls (math.log, math.cos, and so on). If you use numpy for image production rather than Pillow, the opposite may be true (I did not test). The source code is also on GitHub: look for image3R_orbit_enhanced.py.

```python
# image3R_orbit_enhanced.py [www.MLTechniques.com]

from PIL import Image, ImageDraw       # ImageDraw to draw ellipses, etc.
import moviepy.video.io.ImageSequenceClip # to produce mp4 video
from moviepy.editor import VideoFileClip # to convert mp4 to gif

import numpy as np
import math
import random
random.seed(100)

#--- Global variables ---

m=3             # number of orbits (one for each value of sigma)
nframe=10000    # number of images created in memory
ShowOrbit=True
ShowDots=False
count=0         # frame counter
r=10            # one out of every r image is included in the video
dot=4           # size of a point in the picture
step=0.01       # time increment in orbit

width = 3200    # width of the image
height =2400    # length of the image

images=[]

etax=[]    # real part of Dirichlet eta function
etay=[]    # real part of Dirichlet eta function
```

```
sigma=[]     # imaginary part of argument of Dirichlet eta
x0=[]        # value of etax on last video frame
y0=[]        # value of etay on last video frame
#col=[]      # RGB color of the orbit
colp=[]      # RGP points on the orbit
t=[]         # real part of argument of Dirichlet eta (that is, time in orbit)
flist=[]     # filenames of the images representing each video frame

etax=list(map(float,etax))
etay=list(map(float,etay))
sigma=list(map(float,sigma))
x0=list(map(float,x0))
y0=list(map(float,y0))
t=list(map(float,t))
flist=list(map(str,flist))

#--- Eta function ---

def G(tau,sig,nterms):
    sign=1
    fetax=0
    fetay=0
    for j in range(1,nterms):
        fetax=fetax+sign*math.cos(tau*math.log(j))/pow(j,sig)
        fetay=fetay+sign*math.sin(tau*math.log(j))/pow(j,sig)
        sign=-sign
    return [fetax,fetay]

#--- Initializing comet parameters ---

for n in range (0,m):
    etax.append(1.0)
    etay.append(0.0)
    x0.append(1.0)
    y0.append(0.0)
    t.append(0.0) # start with t=0.0
sigma.append(0.50)
sigma.append(0.75)
sigma.append(1.25)
colp.append((255,0,0,255))
colp.append((0,0,255,255))
colp.append((255,180,0,255))

if ShowOrbit:
    minx=-2
    maxx=3
else:
    minx=-1
```

```
    maxx=2

rangex=maxx-minx
rangey=0.75*rangex
miny=-rangey/2
maxy=rangey/2
rangey=maxy-miny

img = Image.new( mode = "RGB", size = (width, height), color = (255, 255, 255) )
imgCopy=img.copy()
draw = ImageDraw.Draw(img,"RGBA")
drawCopy = ImageDraw.Draw(imgCopy,"RGBA")


gx=width*(0.0-minx)/rangex
gy=height*(0.0-miny)/rangey
hx=width*(1.0-minx)/rangex
hy=height*(0.0-miny)/rangey
draw.ellipse((gx-8, gy-8, gx+8, gy+8), fill=(0,0,0,255))
draw.ellipse((hx-8, hy-8, hx+8, hy+8), fill=(0,0,0,255))
draw.rectangle((0,0,width-1,height-1), outline ="black",width=1)
draw.line((0,gy,width-1,hy), fill ="red", width = 1)
draw.ellipse((gx-8, gy-8, gx+8, gy+8), fill=(0,0,0,255))
drawCopy.ellipse((hx-8, hy-8, hx+8, hy+8), fill=(0,0,0,255))
drawCopy.rectangle((0,0,width-1,height-1), outline ="black",width=1)
drawCopy.line((0,gy,width-1,hy), fill ="red", width = 1)
countCopy=0

#--- Main Loop ---

for k in range (2,nframe,1): # loop over time, each t corresponds to an image
    if k %10 == 0:
        string="Building frame:" + str(k) + "> "
        for n in range (0,m):
            string=string+ " | " + str(t[n])
        print(string)
    if k%r==0:
        imgCopy.paste(img, (0, 0))
    for n in range (0,m): # loop over the m orbits
        if ShowOrbit:
            # save old value of etax[n], etay[n]
            x0.insert(n,width*(etax[n]-minx)/rangex)
            y0.insert(n,height*(etay[n]-miny)/rangey)
        (etax[n],etay[n])=G(t[n],sigma[n],2000)
        x= width*(etax[n]-minx)/rangex
        y=height*(etay[n]-miny)/rangey
        if ShowOrbit:
            if k>2:
                # draw line from (x0[n],y0[n]) to (x,y)
```

```
        draw.line(((int(x0[n]),int(y0[n]),int(x),int(y)), fill =colp[n], width = 0)
        if ShowDots:
            draw.ellipse((x-dot, y-dot, x+dot, y+dot), fill =colp[n])
        else:
            copyFlag=True
            drawCopy.ellipse((x-10, y-10, x+10, y+10), fill =colp[n])
        t[n]=t[n]+step
    else:
        draw.ellipse((x-dot, y-dot, x+dot, y+dot), fill =colp[n])
        t[n]=t[n]+200*math.exp(3*sigma[n])/(1+t[n]) # 0.02
if k%r==0:    # this image gets included as a frame in the video
    draw.ellipse((gx-8, gy-8, gx+8, gy+8), fill=(0,0,0,255))
    draw.ellipse((hx-8, hy-8, hx+8, hy+8), fill=(0,0,0,255))
    drawCopy.ellipse((gx-8, gy-8, gx+8, gy+8), fill=(0,0,0,255))
    drawCopy.ellipse((hx-8, hy-8, hx+8, hy+8), fill=(0,0,0,255))
    fname='imgpy'+str(count)+'.png'
    count=count+1
    # antialiasing mechanism
    if not copyFlag:
        img2 = img.resize((width // 2, height // 2), Image.LANCZOS) #ANTIALIAS)
    else:
        img2 = imgCopy.resize((width // 2, height // 2), Image.LANCZOS) #ANTIALIAS)
    # output current frame to a png file
    img2.save(fname) # write png image on disk
    flist.append(fname) # add its filename (fname) to flist

# output video file
clip = moviepy.video.io.ImageSequenceClip.ImageSequenceClip(flist, fps=20)
clip.write_videofile('riemann.mp4')
```

References

[1] P. Borwein, S.K. Choi, M. Coons, Completely multiplicative functions taking values in {−1, 1}, Transactions of the American Mathematical Society 362 (12) (2010) 6279–6291, [Link].

[2] P. Borwein, M. Coons, Transcendence of power series for some number theoretic functions, Proceedings of the American Mathematical Society 137 (4) (2009) 1303–1305, [Link].

[3] H.M. Bui, M.B. Milinovich, Gaps between zeros of the Riemann zeta-function, Quarterly Journal of Mathematics 69 (2) (2018) 402–423, [Link].

[4] K. Conrad, L-functions and the Riemann Hypothesis, 2018 CTNT Summer School, 2018, [Link].

[5] H.G. Diamond, W.-B. Zhang, Beurling Generalized Numbers, Mathematical Surveys and Monographs, vol. 213, American Mathematical Society, 2016, [Link].

[6] N. Frantzikinakis, Ergodicity of the Liouville system implies the Chowla conjecture, Preprint, pp. 1–41, 2016, arXiv, [Link].

[7] P.M. Gauthier, Approximating the Riemann zeta-function by polynomials with restricted zeros, Canadian Mathematical Bulletin 62 (3) (2018) 475–478, [Link].

[8] V. Granville, Stochastic Processes and Simulations: A Machine Learning Perspective, MLTechniques.com, 2022, [Link].

[9] A.J. Harper, Moments of random multiplicative functions, II: high moments, Algebra and Number Theory 13 (10) (2019) 2277–2321, [Link].

[10] A.J. Harper, Moments of random multiplicative functions, I: low moments, better than square-root cancellation, and critical multiplicative chaos, Forum of Mathematics, Pi 8 (2020) 1–95, [Link].

[11] A.J. Harper, Almost sure large fluctuations of random multiplicative functions, Preprint, pp. 1–38, 2021, arXiv, [Link].

[12] D.R. Heath-Brown, Primes represented by $x^3 + 2y^3$, Acta Mathematica 186 (2001) 1–84, [Link].

[13] T.W. Hilberdink, M.L. Lapidus, Beurling zeta functions, generalised primes, and fractal membranes, Preprint, pp. 1–31, 2004, arXiv, [Link].

[14] P. Humphries, The distribution of weighted sums of the Liouville function and Pólya's conjecture, Preprint, pp. 1–33, 2011, arXiv, [Link].

[15] M. Mine, Probability density functions attached to random Euler products for automorphic L-functions, Preprint, pp. 1–38, 2020, arXiv, [Link].

[16] V. Kumar Murty, Seminar on Fermat's last theorem, in: Canadian Mathematical Society – Conference Proceedings, vol. 17, Toronto, Canada, 1995, [Link].

[17] N. Ng, Large gaps between the zeros of the Riemann zeta function, Journal of Number Theory 128 (3) (2007) 509–556, [Link].

[18] E.C. Titchmarsh, D.R. Heath-Brown, The Theory of the Riemann Zeta-Function, second edition, Oxford Science Publications, 1987.

Text, sound generation, and other topics

18

Here I review some important or interesting topics not covered in the previous chapters. I start with turning your data into music to potentially gain unusual insights. The second topic is the production of videos and high quality plots in R, using the Cairo and AV libraries. Then I move to dual confidence regions which are analogous to Bayesian credible regions. The concept is illustrated with a bivariate parameter estimated via the minimum contrast method, in the context of point processes. This procedure offers a mechanism to retrieve the parameters of interest using proxy statistics, when they are masked due to hidden layers. In the process, I show how to produce 3D contour plots. A few sections cover feature selection, natural language processing (the creation of a taxonomy with smart crawling), and automatically detecting the number of clusters in unsupervised clustering problems.

18.1 Sound generation: let your data sing!

It is common these days to read stories about the sound of black holes, deep space, or the abyss. But what if you could turn your data into music? There are a few reasons one might want to do this. First, it adds extra dimensions, on top of those displayed in a scatter plot or a video of your data. Each observation in the sound track may have its own frequency, duration, and volume. That is three more dimensions. With stereo sound, that is six dimensions. Add sound texture, and the possibilities are limitless.

Then, sound may allow the human brain to identify new patterns in your data set, not noticeable in scatterplots and other visualizations. This is similar to scatterplots allowing you to see patterns (say clusters) that tabular data is unable to render. Or to data videos, allowing you to see patterns that static visualizations are unable to render. Also, people with vision problems may find sounds more useful than images, to interpret data.

Finally, another purpose of this chapter is to introduce you to sound processing in Python, and to teach you how to generate sound and music. This basic introduction features some of the fundamental elements. Hopefully, enough to get you started if you are interested to further explore this topic.

18.1.1 From data visualizations to videos to data music

We are all familiar with static data visualizations. Animated gifs such as this one brings a new dimension, but they are not new. Then, data represented as videos is something rather new,with examples on my YouTube channel. However, I am not aware of any data set represented as a melody. This section may very well feature the first example.

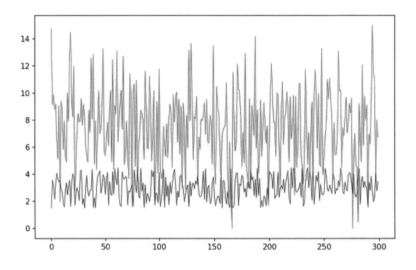

FIGURE 18.1

Data linked to the melody: red curve (dark gray in print version) for note frequencies, blue curve (dark gray in print version) for note durations.

As in data videos, time is the main component. The concept is well suited to time series. In particular, here I generated two time series each with $n = 300$ observations, equally spaced in time. It represents pure, uncorrelated noises: the first is Gaussian and represented by the sound frequencies; the second is uniform and represented by the duration of the musical notes. Each note corresponds to one observation. I used the most standard musical scale, and avoided **half-tones** [Wiki] – the black keys on a piano – to produce a pleasant melody. To listen to it, follow this GitHub link, download the WAV file, and play it. Make sure your speakers are on. You may even play it in your office, as it is work-related after all.

Since it represents noise, the melody never repeats itself and has no memory. Yet it seems to exhibit patterns, the patterns of randomness. Random data is actually the most pattern-rich data, since if large enough, it contains all the patterns that exist. If you plot random points in a square, some will appear clustered, some areas will look sparse, some points will look aligned. The same is true in random musical notes. This will be the topic of a future article, entitled "The Patterns of Randomness".

The next step is to create melodies for real life data sets, exhibiting autocorrelations and other peculiarities. The bivariate time series used here is pictured below: the red curve (light gray in print version) is the scaled Gaussian noise linked to note frequencies in the audio; the blue curve (dark gray in print version) is the scaled uniform noise linked to the note durations. As for myself, I plan to create melodies for famous functions in number theory (the Riemann function) and blend the sound with the silent videos that I have produced so far, for instance, in Fig. 18.1.

18.1.2 References

The musical scale used in my Python code is described in Wikipedia, here. An introduction to sound generation in Python can be found on StackOverFlow, here. For stereo sounds in Python, see here. A more comprehensive article featuring known melodies with all the bells and whistles, is found here (part 1) and here (part 2). However, I was not able to make the code work. See also here if you are familiar with Python classes.

I think my very short code in Section 18.1.3 offers the best bang for the buck. In particular, it assumes no music knowledge and does not use any library other than numpy and scipy.

18.1.3 Python code

In a WAV file, sounds are typically recorded as waves. These waves are produced by the get_sine_wave function, one wave per musical note. The base note has a 440 frequency. Each octave contains 12 notes including five half-tones. I skipped those to avoid dissonances. The frequencies double from one octave to the next one. I only included audible notes that can be rendered by a standard laptop, thus the instruction in range(40,65) in the code.

The last line of code turns wave values into integers, and save the whole melody as sound.wav. Now you can write your own code to listen to your data! Or you can use the code to test large sequences of random notes, to find if some short extracts might be good and original enough to integrate into your own music. You may also try nonsinusoidal waves. For instance, a mixture of waves to emulate harmonic pitches (two or more notes at the same time) and instruments other than piano.

```python
import numpy as np
import matplotlib.pyplot as plt
from scipy.io import wavfile

def get_sine_wave(frequency, duration, sample_rate=44100, amplitude=4096):
    t = np.linspace(0, duration, int(sample_rate*duration))
    wave = amplitude*np.sin(2*np.pi*frequency*t)
    return wave

# Create the list of musical notes
scale=[]
for k in range(40,65):
    note=440*2**((k-49)/12)
    if k%12 != 0 and k%12 != 2 and k%12 != 5 and k%12 != 7 and k%12 != 10:
        scale.append(note) # add musical note (skip half tones)
M=len(scale) # number of musical notes

# Generate the data
n=300
np.random.seed(101)
x=np.arange(n)
y=np.random.normal(0,1,size=n)
z=np.random.uniform(0.100,0.300,size=n)
min=min(y)
max=max(y)
y=0.999*M*(y-min)/(max-min)

plt.plot(x,y,color='red',linewidth=0.6)
plt.plot(x,15*z,color='blue',linewidth=0.6)
```

```
plt.show()

# Turn the data into music
wave=[]
for t in x: # loop over data set observations, create one note per observation
    note=int(y[t])
    duration=z[t]
    frequency=scale[note]
    new_wave = get_sine_wave(frequency, duration=duration, amplitude=2048)
    wave=np.concatenate((wave,new_wave))
wavfile.write('sound.wav', rate=44100, data=wave.astype(np.int16))
```

18.2 Data videos and enhanced visualizations in R

For a long time, charts produced by R looked pixelated and easily recognizable due to their poor quality. The problem was due to lack of **antialiasing** mechanisms [Wiki] in the graphic libraries. Now with ggplot2 [Wiki], the issue has been addressed. This package has a steep learning curve though. But if you are still using the old plot function, you still face the problem. However, there is an easy workaround, with the Cairo library. I first explain how it works, and then move to the production of videos with the AV library.

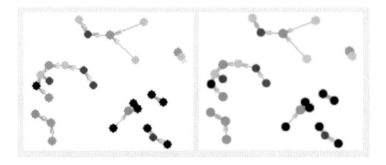

FIGURE 18.2

R plot before Cairo (left), and after (right).

18.2.1 Cairo library to produce better charts

The problem is pictured in Fig. 18.2. If you zoom in, the issue will be magnified. The fix consists of two lines of code in R. First, you need to install the Cairo library with the command install.packages('Cairo'). The first two lines in your R script would look like:

```
library('Cairo');
CairoWin(5,5);
```

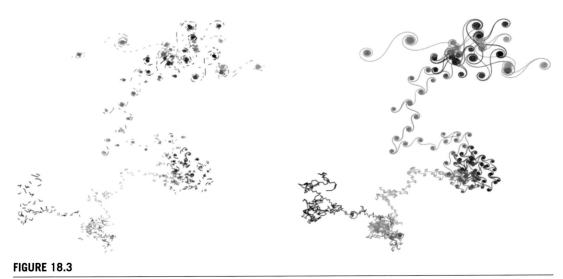

FIGURE 18.3

Intermediate (left) and last frame (right) of the video.

The second line is to create a high resolution window on your screen, to replace the standard R graphics window. For a bigger window, try `CairoWin(6,6)`. If instead you would like to save the image as a PNG file, replace the second line of code by something like

```
CairoPNG(filename="c:/Users/yourname/nice.png", width=600, height=600);
```

To actually generate the PNG image, add `dev.off()` at the bottom of your script. See CairoGraphics.org for details, or the Wikipedia entry here. The full version of my R script is available on my GitHub repository, here. It uses an input file, also available in the same repository, here.

Besides the Cairo library, you can use optimum **color palettes** in the **RGB color scheme** to further improve the visual rendering. For details about the mathematical technicalities, see here. Now, with the **RGBA color scheme**, you can also add **color transparency** [Wiki] to better visualize overlapping objects, such as in Fig. 1.5.

18.2.2 **AV library to produce videos**

The sample code below is also on my GitHub repository, here. The output videos and the data sets used to produce them are in the same folder. Look out for filenames starting with `av`. I used the Cairo library described in Section 18.2.1 for better rendering.

The input file `av_demo_vg2.txt` is a comma-separated text file. The input file has $20 \times 500 = 10,000$ rows. The R program joins (x, y) to (x_2, y_2) via the arrows function; each frame adds 20 consecutive undirected arrows to the previous frame. I chose the colors using the `rgb` parameter in the arrows function. The call to the `CairoPNG` function (requiring the Cairo library) produces the 500 PNG files (the frames) each with 600×600 pixels. Fig. 18.3 shows two of these frames. Each row in the input data set consists of

- the index k of a vector,

- the coordinates x, y of the vector in question,
- the coordinates x_2, y_2 of the next vector to be displayed,
- the index `col` of that vector (used in the randomized version).

I used cosine functions for the RGB (red/green/blue) colors, with small integer multiples of a base period. These cosine waves, called harmonics in signal processing, make the colors harmonious. The argument `framerate` specifies the number of frames per second.

```
CairoPNG(filename = "c:/Users/vince/tex/av_demo%03d.png", width = 600, height = 600);
data<-read.table("c:/Users/vince/tex/av_demo_vg2b.txt",header=TRUE);

k<-data$k;
x<-data$x;
y<-data$y;
x2<-data$x2;
y2<-data$y2;
col<-data$col;

for (n in 1:500) {
    plot(x,y,pch=20,cex=0,col=rgb(0,0,0),xlab="",ylab="",axes=FALSE );
    rect(-10, -20, 50, 50, density = NULL, angle = 45,
      col = rgb(0,0,0), border = NULL);
    a<-x[k <= n*20];
    b<-y[k <= n*20];
    a2<-x2[k <= n*20];
    b2<-y2[k <= n*20];
    c<-col[k <= n*20];
    arrows(a, b, a2, b2, length = 0, angle = 10, code = 2,
      col=rgb( 0.9*abs(sin(0.00200*col)),0.6*abs(sin(0.00150*col)),
      abs(sin(0.00300*col)) ));
}
dev.off();

png_files <- sprintf("c:/Users/vince/tex/av_demo%03d.png", 1:500)
av::av_encode_video(png_files, 'c:/Users/vince/tex/av_demo2b.mp4', framerate = 12)
```

18.3 Dual confidence regions

This tutorial explains how to build confidence regions (the 2D version of a confidence interval) using as little statistical theory as possible. I also avoid the traditional terminology and notation such as α, $Z_{1-\alpha}$, critical value, confidence level, significance level, and so on. These can be confusing to beginners and professionals alike.

Instead, I use simulations and two keywords only, confidence region and confidence level. The purpose is to explain the concept using a framework that will appeal to machine learning professionals, software engineers and nonstatisticians. My hope is that you will gain a deep understanding of the technique, without headaches. I also introduce an alternative type of confidence region, called dual confidence region. It is asymptotically equivalent to the standard definition. In my opinion, it is more intuitive.

18.3.1 Case study

This example comes from a real-life application discussed in Section 16.4.1. Here I provide the minimum amount of material necessary to illustrate the methodology. The full problem is described Section 18.3.5, for the curious reader. In its simplest form, we are dealing with independent **bivariate Bernoulli trials**. The data set has n observations. Each observation consists of two measurements (u_k, v_k), for $k = 1, \ldots, n$. Here $u_k = 1$ if some interval B_k contains zero point (otherwise $u_k = 0$). Likewise, $v_k = 1$ if the same interval contains one point (otherwise $v_k = 0$).

The interval B_k can contain more than one point, but, of course, it cannot simultaneously contain one and two points. The probability that B_k contains zero point is p; the probability that it contains one point is q, with $0 < p + q < 1$. The goal is to estimate p and q. The estimators (proportions computed on the observations) are denoted as p_0 and q_0.

Since we are dealing with Bernoulli variables, the standard deviations are $\sigma_p = \sqrt{p(1-p)}$ and $\sigma_q = \sqrt{q(1-q)}$. Also the correlation between the two components u_k, v_k of the observation vector is $\rho_{p,q} = -pq/\sigma_p\sigma_q$. Indeed, the probability to observe $(0,0)$ is $1 - p - q$, the probability to observe $(1,0)$ is p, the probability to observe $(0,1)$ is q, and the probability to observe $(1,1)$ is zero.

18.3.2 Standard confidence region

A confidence region of level γ is a domain of minimum area that contains a proportion γ of the potential values of your estimator (p_0, q_0), based on your n observations. When n is large, (p_0, q_0) approximately has a **bivariate normal distribution** (also called Gaussian), thanks to the **central limit theorem**. The **covariance matrix** of this normal distribution is specified by σ_p, σ_q and $\rho_{p,q}$ measured at $p = p_0$ and $q = q_0$. For a fixed γ, the optimum shape – the one with minimum area – necessarily has a boundary that is a contour level of the distribution in question. In our case, that distribution is bivariate Gaussian, and thus contour levels are ellipses.
Let us define

$$H_n(x, y, p, q) = \frac{2n}{1 - \rho_{p,q}^2}\left[\left(\frac{x-p}{\sigma_p}\right)^2 - 2\rho_{p,q}\left(\frac{x-p}{\sigma_p}\right)\left(\frac{y-q}{\sigma_q}\right) + \left(\frac{y-q}{\sigma_q}\right)^2\right], \tag{18.1}$$

with

$$\sigma_p = \sqrt{p(1-p)}, \quad \sigma_q = \sqrt{q(1-q)}, \quad \rho_{p,q} = -\frac{pq}{\sqrt{pq(1-p)(1-q)}}. \tag{18.2}$$

This is the general elliptic form of the contour line. Essentially, it does not depend on n, p, q when n is large. The standard confidence region is then the set of all (x, y) satisfying $H_n(x, y, p_0, q_0) \le G_\gamma$. Here you choose G_γ to guarantee that the **confidence level** is γ. Replace $\le$ by $=$ to get the boundary of that region.

In this case G_γ is a **quantile** of the **Hotelling distribution** [Wiki]. In Section 18.3.4, I show how to compute G_γ. The simulations apply to any setting, whether G_γ is a Hotelling, Fisher, or any quantile.

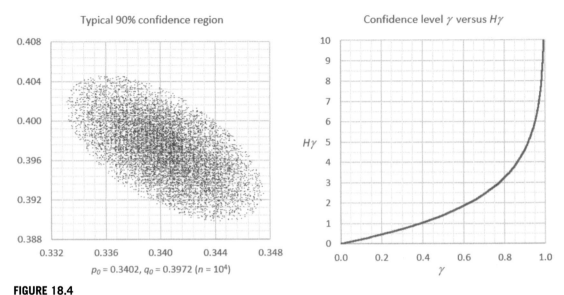

FIGURE 18.4

Example of 90% dual confidence region for (p, q).

Or whether the limit distribution of your estimator (p_0, q_0) is Gaussian or not, as n – the sample size – increases. These simulations provide a generic framework to compute confidence regions.

18.3.3 Dual confidence region

The **dual confidence region** is simply obtained by swapping the roles of (x, y) and (p, q) in $H_n(x, y, p, q)$. It is thus defined as the set of (x, y) satisfying $H_n(p, q, x, y) \leq H_\gamma$. Again, you choose H_γ to guarantee that the confidence level is γ. Also, (p, q) is replaced by (p_0, q_0). This is no longer the equation of an ellipse. In practice, both confidence regions are very similar. Also, H_γ is almost identical to G_γ. The interpretation is as follows. A point (x, y) is in the dual confidence region of (p_0, q_0) if and only if (p_0, q_0) is in the standard confidence region of (x, y). I use the same n and confidence level γ for both regions. You can use the same principle to define dual confidence intervals.

Dual confidence regions are based on the same principle as **credible regions** [Wiki] in Bayesian statistics. Other methods producing nonelliptic regions are described in [4].

18.3.4 Simulations

The simulations consist of generating N data sets, each with n observations. Use the joint Bernoulli model described in Section 18.3.1, for the simulations. The purpose is to create data sets that have the same statistical behavior as your observations: in other words, synthetic data. In particular, I simulate the bivariate Bernoulli model using some prespecified p_0, q_0, the true but unknown values that we want to estimate. I now describe how to proceed.

For each simulated data set, compute the proportions, standard deviations, and correlations. They are denoted as x, y, σ_x, σ_y, and $\rho_{x,y}$ (one set of values per data set). Use the standard formulas, but this time with x, y observed, and p_0, q_0 the variables. That is,

$$H_n(p_0, q_0, x, y) = \frac{2n}{1 - \rho_{x,y}^2} \left[\left(\frac{p_0 - x}{\sigma_x} \right)^2 - 2\rho_{x,y} \left(\frac{p_0 - x}{\sigma_x} \right) \left(\frac{q_0 - y}{\sigma_y} \right) + \left(\frac{q_0 - y}{\sigma_y} \right)^2 \right],$$

$$\sigma_x = \sqrt{x(1-x)}, \quad \sigma_y = \sqrt{y(1-y)}, \quad \rho_{x,y} = -\frac{xy}{\sqrt{xy(1-x)(1-y)}}.$$

Also compute $G(x, y) = H_n(x, y, p_0, q_0)$ and $H(x, y) = H_n(p_0, q_0, x, y)$ for each data set. Put the results in a table with N rows and 7 columns. Proceed as follows.

- **Standard confidence region** – sort the table by $G(x, y)$.
- **Dual confidence region** – sort the table by $H(x, y)$.

The first $\lfloor \gamma N \rfloor$ rows in your sorted table determine your confidence region of level γ. All the (x, y) in those rows belong to your confidence region. Here $\lfloor \cdot \rfloor$ represents the integer part function. In the first $\lfloor \gamma N \rfloor$ rows, the last value of $H(x, y)$ – if sorted by $H(x, y)$ – is H_γ. Likewise, if sorted by $G(x, y)$, the last value of $G(x, y)$ is G_γ. See example in Fig. 18.4, with $N = 10{,}000$ and $n = 20{,}000$. As N increases, your simulations yield regions closer and closer to the theoretical ones. The spreadsheet with these simulations is available on my GitHub repository, here.

18.3.5 Original problem with minimum contrast estimators

The original problem introduced in Section 18.3.1 consisted of estimating the two parameters λ, s of a perturbed-lattice point process, namely the intensity and scale. These stochastic processes have applications in sensor locations and cell network optimization. Rather than a direct estimation which is not possible in this case (these parameters are attached to a hidden lattice process), I used proxy statistics p, q instead. This method, called **minimum contrast estimation**, requires a one-to-one mapping between the original parameter space, and the proxy space. Minimum contrast estimation is a general technique encompassing **maximum likelihood estimation** [Wiki]. It is used in the context of point processes by Tilman Davies [2] and Jesper Møller [5]. See also slides 114–116 here or here.

The point count statistic discussed in Section 18.3.1 measures the number of points of this process that are in a specific interval B_k. I used n nonoverlapping intervals $B_1, \ldots, B_n$, each yielding one observation vector (u_k, v_k) for $k = 1, \ldots, n$. The observation vectors are almost identically and independently distributed across the intervals. However, the first and second components of the vectors are negatively correlated. This explains the choice of the bivariate Bernoulli distribution for the model.

More specifically, the situation is almost identical (and asymptotically identical) to the following: we observe a bivariate Bernoulli sequence of independently and identically distributed (U_k, V_k) but for each k, U_k and V_k are negatively correlated with the same correlation as in formula (18.2). The random variables have the following joint distribution:

$$P(U_k = 0, V_k = 0) = 1 - p - q,$$
$$P(U_k = 1, V_k = 0) = p,$$
$$P(U_k = 0, V_k = 1) = q,$$
$$P(U_k = 1, V_k = 1) = 0.$$

The following must be satisfied: $0 < p, q < 1$ and $p + q < 1$.

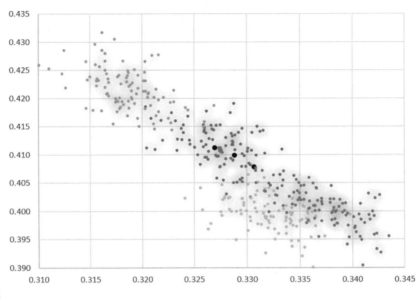

FIGURE 18.5

Minimum contrast estimation for (λ, s) using (p, q) as proxy stats.

The scatterplot in Fig. 18.5 illustrates the estimation procedure, using minimum contrast estimators. The X-axis represents p, and the Y-axis represents q. There are two main features:

- **Observed data.** The three purple dots correspond to estimated values of (p, q) derived from three sets of observations, each with $n = 10,000$.
- **Theoretical model.** The four overlapping clusters show, based on simulations, the distribution of (p, q) for four different theoretical values of (λ, s). Each cluster – identified by its color – has 100 points corresponding to 100 simulations. Each simulation within a same cluster uses the same hand-picked (λ, s). The purpose of these simulations is to find the inverse mapping $(p, q) \mapsto (\lambda, s)$ via numerical approximations, to retrieve the hidden parameter (λ, s) when (p, q) is observed. Four colors is just a small beginning. In Table 18.1, each cluster is summarized by two statistics: its computed center in the (p, q)-space, associated to the hand-picked parameter vector (λ, s).

Now let us focus on the rightmost purple dot in Fig. 18.5, corresponding to one of the three observation sets. Its coordinates vector is denoted as (p_0, q_0). The (p, q)-space is called the **proxy space**. In this case, it is a subset of $[0, 1] \times [0, 1]$. If the proxy spaced contained only the four points (p, q) listed in Table 18.1, the estimated value (λ_0, s_0) of (λ, s) would be the center of the orange cluster. That is, $(\lambda_0, s_0) = (1.4, 0.6)$ because $(0.3275, 0.4113)$ is the closest cluster center to the purple dot (p_0, q_0) in the proxy space.

But let us imagine that I hand-picked 10^5 vectors (λ, s) instead of 4, thus generating 10^5 cluster centers and a very large Table 18.1 with 10^5 entries. Then again, the best estimator of (λ, s) would still be that obtained by minimizing the distance between the purple dot (p_0, q_0) computed on the observations and the 10^5 cluster centers. In practice, the hand-picking is automated (computerized) and leads to a black-box implementation of the estimation procedure.

Table 18.1 Extract of the mapping table used to recover (λ, s) from (p, q).

Cluster	(λ, s)	(p, q)
Orange	(1.4, 0.6)	(0.3275, 0.4113)
Gray	(1.4, 0.5)	(0.3186, 0.4216)
Yellow	(1.6, 0.7)	(0.3321, 0.3995)
Blue	(1.8, 0.6)	(0.3371, 0.4007)

Finally, the glow effect in Fig. 18.5 may be used for classification or clustering purposes. It generates cluster boundaries given observed points, in a way similar to the method described in Chapter 5.

18.3.6 General shape of confidence regions

Before establishing the fundamental result, I briefly discus how to plot confidence regions in 3D. Fig. 18.6 shows an atypical nonelliptic example, arising from a **mixture model**. The **contour levels** correspond to **confidence levels**. This type of chart is called **contour plot**. However, in the literature, most contour plots are 2D. And those that are 3D usually feature vertical rather than horizontal contours, as the horizontal ones are more difficult to produce. In this case, I produced it with **Mathematica** [Wiki]. See the code below.

```
Plot3D[Exp[-(Abs[x]^3.5 + Abs[y]^3.5 )] +
   0.8*Exp[-4*(Abs[x - 1.5]^4.2 + Abs[y - 1.4]^4.2 )], {x, -2, 3},
   {y, -2, 3}, MeshFunctions -> {#3 &}, Mesh -> 25,
   Exclusions -> None, PlotRange -> {Automatic, Automatic, {0, 1}},
   ImageSize -> 600]
```

Now let us get to the core of the subject. In our particular case, the standard confidence region is asymptotically elliptic because the underlying distribution of the statistic (p, q) – itself a random vector depending on the n observations – approaches a multivariate Gaussian law as $n \to \infty$. See Exercise 27 in my book on stochastic processes [3] for details. Since contour levels of Gaussian distributions are ellipses, the result follows immediately.

More generally, the confidence region of level γ is the minimum set covering a proportion γ of a the mass of the distribution attached to the estimated parameters. Let S_γ be the set in question, and $f(x, y)$ be the density attached to the distribution. I assume that the density has one maximum only, and that it is continuous everywhere on $\mathbb{R}^2$. Thus the problem consists of finding the set S_γ of minimum area such that

$$\int\int_{S_\gamma} f(x, y)dxdy = \gamma. \tag{18.3}$$

It is easy to see that the boundary of S_γ is a contour line of $f(x, y)$. To build S_γ, you start at the maximum of the density, and to keep the area minimum, the set must progressively be expanded, strictly

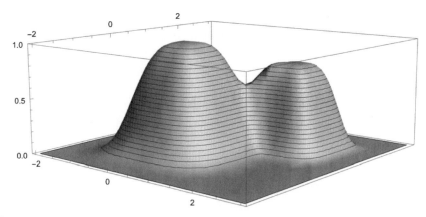

FIGURE 18.6

Nonelliptic confidence regions with various confidence levels.

following contour lines, until (18.3) is satisfied. So

$$S_\gamma = \{(x, y) \in \mathbb{R}^2 \text{ such that } f(x, y) \leq G_\gamma\},$$

where G_γ must be chosen so that (18.3) is satisfied. Assuming $\max f(x, y) = M$, the volume covered by S_γ is

$$\gamma = z_\gamma \cdot |S_\gamma| + \int_{z_\gamma}^{M} |R(z)| dz, \tag{18.4}$$

where $R(z) = \{(x, y) \in \mathbb{R}^2 \text{ such that } f(x, y) = z\}$, and $|\cdot|$ denotes the area of a 2D domain. Clearly, $|S_\gamma| = |R(z_\gamma)|$. So there is only one unknown in Eq. (18.4), namely z_γ. Finally, $G_\gamma = z_\gamma$, and thus the value of G_γ is found by solving (18.4). The area of S_γ is thus $|S_\gamma| = |R(G_\gamma)|$.

18.4 Fast feature selection based on predictive power

In all machine learning problems, deciding which metrics to use is one of the core problems. This section addresses this topic. I propose a simple metric to measure predictive power. It is used for combinatorial feature selection, when a large number of feature combinations need to be ranked automatically and very fast, for instance, in the context of transaction scoring, in order to optimize predictive models. You can easily implement it with a **parallel architecture** [Wiki], such as **Map-Reduce** [Wiki]. I used this methodology for credit card fraud detection, keyword scoring (assessing the commercial value of keyword for keyword bidding purposes), and Internet traffic quality scoring.

Feature selection is used to detect the best subset of features, out of dozens or hundreds of features (also called independent variables). By "best", I mean with highest predictive power as defined in Section 18.4.2. In short, you want to remove duplicate features, correlations between features, and features lacking predictive power, or features (sometimes called rules) that are rarely triggered – except if they are excellent predictors of rare but costly fraud, for instance.

The problem is combinatorial in nature. You want a manageable, small set of features (say 20 features) selected from (say) a set of 500 features, to run machine learning algorithms in a way that is statistically robust. But there are 2.7×10^{35} combinations of 20 features out of 500, and you need to compute all of them to find the feature set with maximum predictive power. This problem is computationally intractable, and you need to find an alternate solution. The good thing is that you do not need to find the absolute maximum; you just need to find a subset of 20 features that is good enough.

One way to proceed is to compute the predictive power of each feature. Then, add one feature at a time to the subset (starting with zero feature) until either you reach 20 features (your limit), or adding a new feature does not significantly improve the overall predictive power of the feature subset (in short, convergence has been attained). At each iteration, choose the feature to be added, among the two remaining features with the highest predictive power: you will choose (among these two features) the one that increases the overall predictive power (of the subset under construction) most. Now you have reduced your computations from 2.7×10^{35} to $40 = 2 \times 20$. A possible improvement consists in removing one feature at a time from the subset, and replace it with a feature randomly selected from the remaining features. If this new feature boosts the overall predictive power of the feature subset, keep it, and otherwise switch back to old subset. Repeat this step 10,000 times or until no more gain is achieved (whichever comes first).

Finally, you can add two or three features at a time, rather than one. Sometimes, combined features have better predictive power than isolated features. For instance, if feature A is the country, with values in {USA, UK} and feature B is the hour of the day, with values in {"Day - Pacific Time", "Night - Pacific Time"}, both features separately have little predictive power. But when you combine both of them, you have a much more powerful feature: "UK/Night" is good, "USA/Night" is bad, "UK/Day" is bad, and "USA/Day" is good, if your response (what you are predicting) is Internet traffic quality in the US. Using these two features together also reduces the risk of false positives and false negatives.

Also, in order to avoid highly granular features, use feature binning. So instead of having country as feature A (with 200 potential country values) use country group, with 3 list of countries (high risk, low risk, neutral). These groups can change over time. And instead of (say) "IP address" as feature B (with billions of potential values), use type of IP address instead, with 6 or 7 types, one being for instance "IP address is in some whitelist".

18.4.1 How cross-validation works

I illustrate the concept of predictive power on a subset of two features. Let us say that you have two binary features A and B taking two possible values 0 or 1. Also, in the context of fraud detection, one would assume that each observation in the training set is either Good (no fraud) or Bad (fraud). The fraud status (G or B) is called the response or dependent variable in statistics. The features A and B are also called rules or independent variables.

Cross-validation works as follows. First, split your **training set** (the data where the response B or G is known) into two parts: validation set and training data. Make sure that both parts are data-rich: if the validation set is big (millions of observations) but contains only one or two clients out of 200, it is data-poor and your statistical inference will be negatively impacted (low robustness) when dealing with data outside the training set. It is a good idea to use two different time periods for training and validation. You are going to compute the predictive power (including rule selection) on the training data. When you have decided on a final, optimum subset of features, you then compute the predictive power on the validation set. If the drop in predictive power is significant in the validation set (compared with training data), something is wrong with your analysis: detect the problem, fix it, start over. You can use multiple validation and training sets: this will give you an idea of how the predictive power varies from one validation set to another one. Too much variance is an issue that should be addressed.

18.4.2 Measuring the predictive power of a feature

Standard methods are based on classic goodness-of-fit metrics [Wiki], such as various ratios computed on the **confusion matrix** [Wiki]. Examples are discussed in this Wikipedia article, and include false positive and false negative rates. Here I describe an original approach to compute the **predictive power**. Using our above example with two binary features A, B taking on two values 0, 1, we can break the observations from the control data set into 8 bins. Let us denote as $n_1, n_2, \ldots, n_8$ the number of observations in each of these 8 bins shown in Table 18.2.

Table 18.2 Eight bins: 2 features (A, B) times 2 outcomes (Good/Bad).

Bin	Feature A	Feature B	Response
1	0	0	G
2	0	1	G
3	1	0	G
4	1	1	G
5	0	0	B
6	0	1	B
7	1	0	B
8	1	1	B

Now let us introduce the following quantities:

$$P_{00} = \frac{n_5}{n_1 + n_5}, \quad P_{01} = \frac{n_6}{n_2 + n_6}, \quad P_{10} = \frac{n_7}{n_3 + n_7}, \quad P_{11} = \frac{n_8}{n_4 + n_8}, \quad p = \frac{n_5 + n_6 + n_7 + n_8}{n_1 + n_2 + \cdots + n_8}.$$

Let us assume that p, measuring the overall proportion of fraud, is less than 50% (that is, $p < 0.5$, otherwise we can swap between fraud and nonfraud). For any $0 < r < 1$, define the W function (shaped like a W), based on a parameter $0 < a < 1$ (typically $a = 0.5 - p$) as follows:

$$W(r) = \begin{cases} 1 - r/p, & \text{if } 0 < r < p, \\ a(r - p)/(0.5 - p), & \text{if } p < r < 0.5, \\ a(r - 1 + p)/(p - 0.5), & \text{if } 0.5 < r < 1 - p, \\ (r - 1 + p)/p, & \text{if } 1 - p < r < 1. \end{cases}$$

Typically, $r = P_{00}, P_{01}, P_{10}$, or P_{11}. The function W has the following properties:

- It is minimum and equal to 0 when $r = p$ or $r = 1 - p$, that is, when r does not provide any information about fraud / nonfraud,

- It is maximum and equal to 1 when $r = 1$ or $r = 0$, that is, when we have perfect discrimination between fraud and nonfraud, in a given bin.
- It is symmetric: $W(r) = W(1 - r)$ if $0 < r < 1$. So if you swap Good and Bad (G and B), it still provides the same predictive power.

Now let us define the **predictive power** as

$$H = P_{00} W(P_{00}) + P_{01} W(P_{01}) + P_{10} W(P_{10}) + P_{11} W(P_{11}).$$

The function H is the predictive power for the feature subset $\{A, B\}$ with four bins "00", "01", "10", "11" corresponding to $(A = 0, B = 0)$, $(A = 0, B = 1)$, $(A = 1, B = 0)$, $(A = 1, B = 1)$. Although H is remotely related to the **entropy metric**, it has specific properties of its own. Unlike entropy, H is not based on physical concepts or models; it is actually a **synthetic metric**.

The weights $P_{00}, P_{01}, P_{1,0}, P_{11}$ guarantee that bins with low count have low impact on H. Set $W(r)$ to 0 for any bin that has less than 20 observations. For instance, the frequency of bin "00" is $(n_1 + n_5)/(n_1 + \cdots + n_8)$, its size or bin count is $n_1 + n_5$, and $r = P_{00} = n_5/(n_1 + n_5)$ for this bin. If $n_1 + n_5 = 0$, set P_{00} to 0 and $W(P_{00})$ to 0. I actually recommend doing this not just if $n_1 + n_5 = 0$, but also whenever $n_1 + n_5 < 20$, especially if p is low. If p is very low, say $p < 0.01$, you need to oversample bad transactions when building your training set, and adjust the counts accordingly. Of course, the same rules applies to P_{01}, P_{10}, and P_{11}.

Also, you should avoid feature subsets resulting in a large proportion of observations spread across a large number of almost empty bins, as well as feature subsets that produce a large number of empty bins: observations outside the training set are likely to belong to an empty or almost empty bin, and it leads to high-variance predictions. To avoid this drawback, stick to binary features and use fewer than 20 features if possible. Finally, P_{ij} is the estimator of the probability $P(A = i, B = j)$ for $i, j = 0, 1$ in **naive Bayes classification** [Wiki].

The technique easily generalizes to more than two features, and the predictive power H has interesting properties: $0 \leq H \leq 1$, with $H = 0$ if the feature subset has no predictive power, and $H = 1$ if it has maximum predictive power. If $p = 0.5$, then the function W is shaped like a V rather than a W. You may try $p = 0.5$ and check whether it provides good enough predictions.

18.4.3 Efficient implementation

Given a subset of 20 binary features, you can precompute all the bin counts in any extended **flag vector**, and store them in a hash table `Hash` – also called "associative array" or "dictionary" in Python. Such an extended vector has 21 components: 20 for the features, with value 0 or 1, and one for the response, with value G or B.

In Python, an entry in this **hash table** [Wiki] would look like `Hash[(v,y)]=56` where (say) $y =$ "G" and $v =$ "01101001010110100100". The hash table is made of **key–value pairs**. In this example, the value is 56 and the key is (v, y). It means that the flag vector v has 56 observations with response G. More precisely, a flag vector is a binary string showing which rules are triggered. Here a rule is a feature, and "triggered" means that the value of the feature in question is equal to one. Nonbinary flag vectors or responses are not discussed here, but they are also widely used. This framework is sometimes referred to as **association rule learning** [Wiki].

The hash table is produced by parsing your training set one time, sequentially: for each observation, compute the flag vector v, check if the response is Good (G) or Bad (B), and update the associated key–value pairs accordingly, with the following instruction: `Hash[(v,G)]++` if the response is Good, or `Hash[(v,B)]++` if the response is Bad.

Then whenever you need to measure the predictive power of a subset of these 20 features, you do not need to parse your big data set again (potentially billion of observations), but instead, just access this small hash table: this table contains all you need to build your flag vectors and compute predictive scores, for any combination of features that is a subset of the top 20. You can do even better than top 20, maybe top 30. While this would create a hash table with 2 billion keys, most of these keys would correspond to empty bins and thus would not be in the hash table. Your hash table might contain only 200 million keys, maybe too big to fit in memory, but easily manageable with a distributed architecture such as Map-Reduce.

Even better: build this hash table for the top 40 features. However now, your hash table could have up to 2 trillion keys. But if your data set has only 100 billion observations, then, of course, your hash table cannot have more than 100 billion keys. In this case, you create a training set with 20 million observations, so that your hash table will have at most 20 million keys (and probably less than 5 million due to empty bins). Thus, it can fit in memory, because you are working with a **sparse hash table**.

You can now estimate the predictive power of many different feature subsets. To do it, parse the hash table obtained in the previous step. For each key (v, y) in this input hash table, loop over the desired feature subsets to create new bin counts: these counts are stored / updated in an output hash table. The key in the newly created output hash table has two components: the "subset ID" (a number representing the feature subset)) and the key (v, y) of the input hash table. When the output hash table is created, you then loop over its keys to compute the predictive power for each feature subset.

18.5 NLP: taxonomy creation and text generation

This section is about structuring unstructured data. I used the techniques described in this section to automatically enhance online directories such as Wikipedia, Yelp, Amazon, or DMOZ [Wiki]. It involves extensive web crawling. One of the noteworthy results obtained by analyzing online user queries was a better breakdown of the "restaurant" category into more meaningful subcategories: romantic restaurant, dinner, wine pub, downtown or nearby restaurant, restaurant with a view or by the river, cheap, ethnic, casual or upscale restaurant, restaurant chefs, recipes, jobs, and furniture. The classic breakdown is by type of cuisine, but it does not fit as well with what users are looking for.

The technique allows you to find related keywords or synonyms, and can be combined with using a table of synonyms, to generate text in the context of **natural language generation** [Wiki]. It is one of the core components of many **large language models** [Wiki] such as **ChatGPT** [Wiki]. Here I do not cover basic steps such as cleaning the data using **stop words** [Wiki], **n-gram** permutations [Wiki], using a dictionary of synonyms, fixing typos, handling special characters, **text normalization** [Wiki] using **regular expressions** [Wiki], and so on. This can be found in any elementary introduction on natural language processing.

18.5.1 Designing a keyword taxonomy

Here I discuss an algorithm to perform fast clustering on big data sets, as well as the graphical representation of such complex clustering structures. By fast, I mean a **computational complexity** [Wiki] of order $O(n)$. This is much faster than **hierarchical agglomerative clustering** [Wiki] which are typically $O(n^2 \log n)$. By big data, I mean several millions, possibly billions of observations.

The application in mind is the creation of a keyword, product or document taxonomy. In particular, I want to create a keyword taxonomy from scratch, based on crawling billions of webpages to extract and cluster keywords into categories. This is a typical unsupervised natural language processing (NLP) problem. The proposed algorithm is as follows:

Step 1: Preprocessing
You gather billions of keywords over the Internet by crawling (say) Wikipedia or Google results, clean the results, and compute the frequencies for each keyword and for each "keyword pair". A "keyword pair" is two keywords found on the same webpage, or close to each other on the same web page. Also by keyword, I mean an entity like "California insurance", so a keyword usually contains more than one token, but rarely more than three. You then can create a keyword table, where each entry is a pair of keywords followed by three counts, such as

$$A=\text{"California insurance"}, B=\text{"home insurance"}, x = 543, y = 998, z = 11$$

where

- x is the number of occurrences of keyword A in all the web pages crawled,
- y is the number of occurrences of keyword B in all the web pages crawled,
- z is the number of occurrences where A and B form a pair (e.g., they are found on a same page).

You can build the keyword table using a distributed architecture. The vast majority of keywords A and B do not form a "keyword pair". In other words, $z = 0$ most of the time. So by ignoring these null entries, your final keyword table can be stored in memory as a **hash table** (see Section 18.4.3) where the key is (A, B) and the value attached to a key is (x, y, z). Let us name this table `Keyword`.

Step 2: Clustering
To create a taxonomy, you want to group the keywords into similar clusters. The **cosine distance** [Wiki] measuring the distance between two keywords or web pages, is popular in this context. To perform keyword clustering, I use the following **dissimilarity metric** $d(A, B)$ to compare two keywords A, B: $d(A, B) = z/\sqrt{xy}$, although other choices are possible. This metric is known as the **Otsuka–Ochiai coefficient**. Note that the denominator prevents extremely popular keywords (for instance, "free") from being close to all the keywords, and from dominating the entire keyword relationship structure: indeed, it favors better keyword bonds, such as "lemon" with "law" or "pie", rather than "lemon" with "free". The larger the $d(A, B)$, the closer the keywords A and B. I describe the clustering part in Section 18.5.2.

18.5.2 Fast clustering algorithm for keyword data

Here I have $n = 10^7$ unique keywords and $m = 10^8$ keyword pairs {A, B} where $d(A, B) > 0$. That is, an average of $r = 10$ related keywords attached to each keyword. These keyword pairs are stored in the hash table `Keyword` created in the preprocessing step in Section 18.5.1. The algorithm builds the new hash tables `Hash` (the category table) and `Weight`. It proceeds incrementally as follows:

Initialization – The small data (or seeding) step. Select 10,000 seed keywords, create (say) 100 categories, and create a hash table `Hash` where the key is one of the 10,000 seed keywords, and the value is a list of categories the keyword is assigned to. For instance,

```
Hash['cheap car insurance']={'automotive','finance'}
```

The choice of the initial 10,000 seed keywords is very important. I suggest to pick up the top 10,000 keywords, in terms of number of associations: that is, keywords A with many B's where $d(A, B) > 0$. This will speed up the convergence of the algorithm.

The big data step. Browse the hash table `Keyword` from the beginning to the end. We now build the tables `Hash` and `Weight`. Let (A, B) be the current keyword pair in `Keyword`.

If `Hash[A]` exists and `Hash[B]` does not, do:
    `Hash[B]=Hash[A]`
    `Weight[B]=d(A,B)`
Else If `Hash[A]` does not exist and `Hash[B]` exists, do:
    `Hash[A]=Hash[B]`
    `Weight[A]=d(A,B)`
Else If `Hash[A]` and `Hash[B]` exist, recategorize:
    If `d(A,B)>Weight[B]` do:
        `Hash[B]=Hash[A]`
        `Weight[B]=d(A,B)`
    Else If `d(A,B)>Weight[A]` do:
        `Hash[A]=Hash[B]`
        `Weight[A]=d(A,B)`

You could replace `Hash[A]=Hash[B]` by `Hash[A]=Concatenate(Hash[A],Hash[B])`, and the other way around. This will increase the number of categories a keyword is assigned to. I did not test that option.

The loop. Repeat the "big data step" 6 or 7 times: `Hash` and `Weight` are kept in memory and keep growing at each subsequent iteration of the loop.

18.5.2.1 *Computational complexity*

The computational complexity is asymptotically $(N + 1)m = O(n)$, where N is the number of iterations in the loop. This is very fast. However, accessing the hash tables slows it down a bit as `Hash` and `Weight` grow bigger at each new iteration.

Presorting the `Keyword` hash table by the $d(A, B)$ values allows you to reduce the number of hash table accesses, by making all the recategorizations not needed anymore. You can also improve the computational complexity by keeping the most important keys – based on count and $d(A, B)$) – and deleting the others. In practice, deleting 65% of the `Keyword` hash table (the long keyword tail) has little impact on the performance: you will have a large bucket of uncategorized keywords, but in terms of volume, these keywords might represent less than 0.1% of the Internet traffic.

Finally, one could use **Tarjan's algorithm** [Wiki] to perform the clustering, based on strongly **connected components** [Wiki]. To proceed, you first bin the distances: $d(A, B)$ is set to 1 if it is above some prespecified threshold, and to 0 otherwise. This is a graph theory algorithm: each keyword represents a node, each pair of keywords where $d(A, B) = 1$, represents an edge. The computational complexity of the algorithm is $O(n + m)$, where n is the number of keywords and m is the number of keyword pairs (edges). To take advantage of this algorithm, you might want to store the `Keyword` hash table in a **graph database** [Wiki]. For those interested in graphical representations of the cluster structure, see the **Fruchterman and Rheingold algorithm** [Wiki]. However, its computational complexity is $O(n^3)$.

18.5.2.2 *Smart crawling of the whole Internet and a bit of graph theory*

Crawling the web must be done in parallel. You need a to create a log file, updated in real time, to store all the pages that you already visited along with the status (successful crawl or not, number of bytes downloaded, domain/subdomain, and time spent to access the page). That way, if your computer crashes, you can resume from where it stopped without losing any data. You may limit the amount of data extracted by page to 16 kilobytes, and limit the number of web pages visited per website to (say) 1000. Pages that were not successfully crawled may be recrawled later at least one more time. Identify duplicate URLs such as web.com, web.com/ and web.com/?source=Facebook so you crawl only one of them.

You also need to avoid getting stuck in an infinite loop, crawling the same pages again and again. Keep a hash table of all the pages already crawled: a copy of the log file, in memory. If done well, in a few months you can crawl billions of web pages, covering (in traffic volume) most of the Internet pages ever browsed by human beings.

At level 1, you start with a list of (say) 10,000 web pages obtained by extracting data from online directories such as Wikipedia or Dmoz, or search result pages from Google, based on a list of thousands of top search keywords. All links gathered at level 1 (links found on the web pages you visited) are stored in a list used for level 2 crawling. From that list, remove links already visited at level 1. Likewise, all links found at level 2 constitute the target URLs to crawl at level 3. Again, remove from that list pages already crawled at level 1 or 2. Move on to level 4, 5, and 6 using the same principles. A practical application of this methodology is tested in my training sessions. Table 18.3 shows the amount of data (in megabytes) collected at each level. This distribution is typical.

Table 18.3 Amount of data collected at each level, when crawling the Internet.	
Level	**Data (GB)**
1	0.002877
2	0.456084
3	8.722723
4	26.942508
5	39.443366
6	42.429041
7	13.175749

It is interesting to note the connection to the **six degrees of separation** problem in graph theory [Wiki]. Most web pages with some traffic are connected to any other one by a path involving at most 6 or 7 intermediate links (called "levels" here). The **Watts and Strogatz model** [Wiki] shows that the average path length between two nodes in a random network is equal to $\log N / \log K$, where N is the number of nodes (a web page here) and K the number of acquaintances per node (that is, the number of links on any given web page).

In the case of friend connections, if $N = 3 \times 10^8$ (the US population) and $K = 30$ (the number of friends per individual), then the number of degrees of separation between any two people is 5.7.

Now if $N = 6 \times 10^9$, it is equal to 6.6. The Python code below perform the simulations to study these distributions.

The algorithm below is rudimentary and can be used for simulation purposes by any programmer: It does not even use tree or graph structures. Applied to a population of 2,000,000 people, each having 20 friends, we show that there is a path involving 6 levels or intermediaries between you and anyone else. Note that the shortest path typically involves fewer levels, as some people have far more than 20 connections. Starting with you, at level one, you have twenty friends or connections. These connections in turn have 20 friends, so at level two, you are connected to 400 people. At level 3, you are connected to 7985 people, which is a little less than 20×400, since some level-3 connections were already level-2 or level-1. And so on.

```
import random

n=2000000    # total population
nfriends=20 # number of friends per individual
ConnectedPeople={}
newConnections={}
newConnections[0]=1
TotalConnectedPeople=0

for level in range(1,8):
   newConnections[level]=0
   for k in range (0, newConnections[level-1]):
      for m in range(0, nfriends):
         human=random.randint(0,n-1)
         if human not in ConnectedPeople:
            ConnectedPeople[human]=True
            newConnections[level]=newConnections[level]+1
   TotalConnectedPeople=TotalConnectedPeople + newConnections[level]
   print("Connected people at level",level,": ",TotalConnectedPeople)
```

A previous version of this program used a faulty random generator that could not produce 2 million distinct integers. Thus I could never achieve full connectivity no matter how many levels I used. Watch out for issues like that when doing this type of simulations. You could actually use this code to test pseudorandom number generators.

18.6 Automated detection of outliers and number of clusters

In the context of unsupervised clustering, one of the most popular recipes to identify the number of clusters, is the **elbow rule** [Wiki]. It is usually performed manually. Here, I show how it can be automated and applied to other problems, such as outlier detection. The idea is a follows: a clustering algorithm (say K-means [Wiki]) can identify a cluster structure with any number of clusters on a given data set; typically, a function $v(m)$ provides a statistical summary of the best cluster structure consisting of m clusters, for $m = 1, 2, 3$, and so on. For instance, $v(m)$ is the sum of the squares of the distances from any observed point to its assigned cluster center. The function $v(m)$ is decreasing, sharply initially for small values of m, then much more slowly for larger values of m, creating an elbow in its graph. The value of m corresponding to the elbow is deemed to be the optimal number of clusters. See Fig. 18.7. Instead of $v(m)$, I use the standardized version $v'(m) = v(m)/v(1)$.

I illustrate how to use the elbow rule to detect **outliers** in Section 18.6.1. The same methodology applies to detect the number of clusters. The data consists of a realization of a 2D Brownian motion. I am interested in the increments R_k, measuring the distance between a point of the process, and the next one. For practical purposes, the simulated realization can be interpreted as a 2D random walk, and R_k is the length of the segment joining two successive points in Fig. 18.7. These segments are visible if you zoom in on the picture. The model used to produce this synthetic data is described in Section 12.2.1.

18.6.1 Black-box elbow rule to detect outliers

Fig. 18.7 shows a realization of a **Brownian motion** with 10^4 points, using $\gamma = 2$ and $\lambda = \Gamma(1 + \gamma)$ in formula (12.6). The goal is to detect the number of values, among the top R_k's, that significantly outshine all the others. Here, they are not technically outliers in the sense that they are still deviates of the same distribution; rather, they are called extremes. The first step is to rank these values. The ordered values (in reverse order) are denoted as $R_{(1)}$, $R_{(2)}$, and so on, with $R_{(1)}$ being the largest one. I used $v(m) = R_{(m)}$ as the criterion for the elbow rule, that is, after standardization, $v'(m) = v(m)/v(1)$.

On the right plot in Fig. 18.7, the Y axis on the left represents $v'(m)$, the X axis represents m, and the Y axis on the right represents the strength of the elbow signal (the height of the red bar; I discuss later how it is computed). The top 10 values of $v'(m)$ ($m = 1, \ldots, 10$) are

$$1.00, \quad 0.92, \quad 0.77, \quad 0.76, \quad 0.71, \quad 0.69, \quad 0.63, \quad 0.61, \quad 0.60, \quad 0.56, \quad 0.55, \quad 0.55.$$

Clearly, the third value 0.77 is pivotal, as the next ones stop dropping sharply, after an initial big drop at the beginning of the sequence. So the "elbow signal" is strongest at $m = 3$, and the conclusion is that the first two values ($2 = m - 1$) outshine all the others. The purpose of the black-box elbow rule algorithm is to automate the decision process: in this case deciding that the optimum is $m = 3$.

Note that in some instances, it is not obvious to detect an elbow, and there may be none. In my example, the elbow signal is very strong, because I chose a rather large value $\gamma = 2$ in formula (12.6), causing the Brownian process to exhibit an unusually strong cluster structure, and large disparities among the top $v(m)$'s. A larger γ would generate even stronger disparities. A negative value of γ, say $\gamma = -0.75$, also causes strong disparities, well separated clusters, and an easy-to-detect elbow. The resulting process is not even Brownian anymore if $\gamma = -0.75$, since in that case, $\text{Var}[R_k] = \infty$. The standard Brownian motion corresponds to $\gamma = 0$ and can still exhibit clusters depending on the realization. Finally, in our case, $m = 3$ also corresponds to the number of clusters on the left plot in Fig. 18.7. This is a coincidence, one that happens very frequently, because the top $v(m)$'s (left to the elbow) correspond to unusually large values of R_k. Each of these very large values typically gives rise to the building of a new cluster, in the simulations.

The elbow rule can be used recursively, first to detect the number of "main" clusters in the data set, then to detect the number of subclusters within each cluster. The strength of the signal (the height of the red bar) is typically very low if the $v'(m)$'s have a low variance. In that case, there is no set of values outshining all the others, that is, no true elbow. For an application of this methodology to detect the number of clusters, see a recent article of Chikumbo [1]. An alternative to the elbow rule, to detect the number of clusters, is the silhouette method [Wiki].

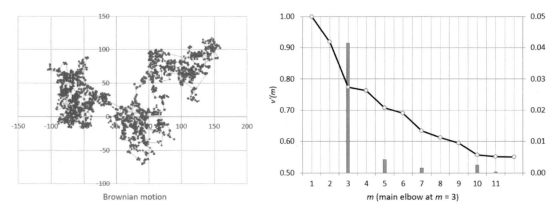

Brownian motion   m (main elbow at m = 3)

FIGURE 18.7

Elbow rule (right) finds $m = 3$ clusters in Brownian motion (left).

I now explain how the strength of the elbow signal (the height of the red bars in Fig. 18.7) is computed. First, compute the first- and second-order differences of the function $v'(m)$: $\delta_1(m) = v'(m-1) - v'(m)$ for $m > 1$, and $\delta_2(m) = \delta_1(m-1) - \delta_1(m)$ for $m > 2$. The strength of the elbow signal, at position $m > 1$, is $\rho_1(m) = \max[0, \delta_2(m+1) - \delta_1(m+1)]$. I used a dampened version of $\rho_1(m)$, namely $\rho_2(m) = \rho_1(m)/m$, to favor cluster structures with few large clusters, over many smaller clusters. Larger clusters can always be broken down into multiple clusters, using the same clustering algorithm. The data, including formulas, charts, and simulation of the Brownian motion is in the spreadsheet PB_inference.xls on my GitHub repository, here. See the Elbow_Brownian tab. You can modify the parameters highlighted in orange in the spreadsheet: in this case, γ in cell B16. Note that λ is set to $\Gamma(1 + \gamma)$ in cell B17.

18.7 Advice to beginners

In this section, I provide guidance to machine learning beginners. After finishing the reading and the accompanying classes (including successfully completing the student projects), you should have a strong exposure to the most important topics, many covered in detail in this book. At this point, you should be able to pursue the learning on your own – a never ending process even for top experts – in particular, with the advice provided in Section 18.7.1.

18.7.1 Getting started and learning how to learn

The first step is to install Python on your laptop. While it is possible to use Jupyter notebooks instead [Wiki], this option is limited and will not give you the full experience of writing and testing serious code as in a professional, business environment. Once Python is installed, you can install Notebooks from within Python, on the command prompt with the instruction python -m pip install jupyter, see here. You may want to have it installed on a virtual machine on your laptop: see VMware virtual machine installation here. Or you can access Notebooks remotely via Google Collab, see here and here.

Installing Python depends on your system. See the official Python.org website here to get started and download Python. On my Windows laptop, I first installed the Cygwin environment (see here how to install it) to emulate a Unix environment. That way, I can use Cygwin windows instead of the Windows command prompt [Wiki]. The benefits is that it recognizes Unix commands. An alternative to Cygwin is Ubuntu. You could also use the Anaconda environment.

Either way, you want to save your first Python program as a text file, say `test.py`. To run it, type in `Python test.py` in the command window. You need to be familiar with basic file management systems, to create folders and subfolders as needed. Shortly, you will need to install Python libraries on your machine. Some of the most common ones are pandas, scipy, seaborn, numpy, random, and matplotlib. You can create your own too, as illustrated in Section 5.4.3. In your Python script, only use the needed libraries. Typically, they are listed at the beginning of your code, as in the following example:

```
import numpy as np
import matplotlib.pyplot as plt
import moviepy.video.io.ImageSequenceClip # to produce mp4 video
from PIL import Image # for some basic image processing
```

To install (say) the numpy library, type in `pip install numpy` in the Windows command prompt.

18.7.1.1 *Getting help*

One of the easiest ways to learn more and solve new problems using Python or any programming language is to use the Internet. For instance, when I designed my sound generation algorithm in Python (see Section 18.1), I googled keywords such as "Python sound processing". I quickly discovered a number of libraries and tutorials, ranging from simple to advanced. Over time, you discover websites that consistently offer solutions suited to your needs, and you tend to stick with them, until you "graduate" to the next level of expertise and use new resources.

It is important to look at the qualifications of people posting their code online, and how recent these posts are. You have to discriminate between multiple sources, and identify those that are not good or outdated. Usually, the best advice comes from little comments posted in discussion forums, as a response to solutions offered by some users. Of course, you can also post your own questions. Two valuable sources here to stay are GitHub and StackExchange. There are also numerous Python groups on LinkedIn and Reddit. In the end, after spending some time searching for sound libraries in Python, I have found solutions that do not require any special library: numpy can process sound files. It took me a few hours to discover all I needed on the Internet.

Finally, the official documentation that comes with Python libraries can be useful, especially if you want to use special parameters and understand the inner workings (and limitations) rather than using them as black-boxes with the default settings. For instance, when looking at model-free parameter estimation for time series (using optimization techniques), I quickly discovered the `curve_fit` function from the Scipy library. It did not work well on my unusual data sets (see Section 1.3.3.2). I discovered, in the official online documentation, several settings to improve the performance. Still unsatisfied with the results (due to numerical instability in my case), I searched for alternatives and discovered that the swarm optimization technique (an alternative to `curve_fit`) is available in the Pyswarms library. In the end, testing these libraries on rich synthetic data allows you to find what works best for your data.

I also offer classes related to this book, see here. This is another option to learn more and get answers to your questions. See also how I solve a new problem step by step and find the relevant code, in Section 14.4.3.

18.7.1.2 *Beyond python*

Python has become the standard language for machine learning. Getting familiar with the R programming language will make you more competitive on the job market. Section 18.2 shows you how to create videos and better-looking charts in R. Finally, machine learning professionals should know at least the basics of SQL, since many jobs still involve working with traditional databases.

In particular, in one of the companies I was working for, I wrote a script that would accept SQL code as input (in text file format) to run queries against the Oracle databases, and trained analysts on how to use it in place of the dashboard they were familiar with. They were still using the dashboard (Toad in this case) to generate the SQL code, but run the actual queries with my script. The queries were now running 10 times faster: the productivity gain was tremendous.

To summarize, Python is the language of choice for machine learning, R is the language of statisticians, and SQL is the language of business and data analysts.

18.7.2 Automated data cleaning and exploratory analysis

It is said that data scientists spend 80% of their time on data cleaning and **exploratory analysis** [Wiki]. This should not be the case. To the beginner, it looks like each new data set comes with a new set of challenges. Over time, you realize that there are only so many potential issues. Automating the data cleaning step can save you a lot of time, and eliminate boring, repetitive tasks. A good Python script allows you to automatically take care of most problems. Here, I review the most common ones.

First, you need to create a summary table for all features taken separately: the type (numerical, categorical data, text, or mixed). For each feature, get the top 5 values, with their frequencies. It could reveal a wrong or unassigned zip-code such as 99999. Look for other special values such as NaN (not a number), N/A, an incorrect date format, missing values (blank), or special characters. For instance, accented characters, commas, dollar, percentage signs, and so on, can cause issues with text parsing and **regular expression** [Wiki]. Compute the minimum, maximum, median, and other percentiles for numerical features. Check for values that are out-of-range: if possible, get the expected range from your client before starting your analysis. Use **checksums** [Wiki] if possible, with encrypted fields such as credit card numbers or ID fields.

A few Python libraries can take care of this, in particular, Pandas-Profiling, Sweetviz, and D-Tale. See here for details.

The next step is to look at interactions between features. Compute all cross-correlations, and check for redundant or duplicate features that can be ignored. Look for IDs or keys that are duplicate or almost identical. Also two different IDs might have the same individual attached to them. This could reveal typos in your data. Working with a table of common typos can help. Also, collect data using prepopulated fields in web forms whenever possible, as opposed to users manually typing in their information such as state, city, zip-code, or date. Finally, check for misaligned fields. This happens frequently in NLP problems, where data such as URLs are parsed and stored in CSV files before being uploaded in databases. Now you can standardize your data.

Sometimes, the data has issues beyond your control. When I was working at Wells Fargo, internet session IDs generated by the Tealeaf software were broken down into multiple small sessions, resulting in wrong userIDs and very short Internet sessions. Manually simulating such sessions and looking how they were tracked in the database, helped solve this mystery, leading to correct analyses. Sometimes, the largest population segment is entirely missing in the database. For instance, in Covid data, people never tested who recovered on their own (the vast majority of the population in the early days) did not show up in any database, giving a lethality rate of 6% rather than the more correct 1%, with costly public policy implications. Use common sense and out-of-the-box thinking to detect such issues, and let stakeholders known about it. Alternate data sources should always be used whenever possible. In this case, sewage data – a proxy data set – provides the answer.

18.7.3 Example of simple analysis: marketing attribution

Sometimes, a simple solution that requires a few days of work as opposed to several weeks, easy to understand as in explainable AI, is good enough and makes everyone happy. When working for NBC, I was asked to perform some **marketing attribution** analysis. The project, also referred to as marketing mix modeling [Wiki] consisted of assessing the individual impact of 20 different channels – in this case specific TV shows – on Internet traffic growth.

Each week, about 12 TV shows were used to boost traffic to the target website. Collected data included the GRP (gross rating point, measuring the size of the TV audience attached to a particular TV show) and the number of unique and new users on the website. The selected TV shows were booked well in advance based on inventory availability, and could not be tested separately: in short, it was not possible to use **experimental design** techniques [Wiki] such as **A/B testing** [Wiki].

I created a **flag vector** for each week, with 20 components: one for each potential TV show. The component associated to a specific TV show was set to 1 if it was used during the week in question, and to 0 otherwise. I then compared weeks that were in a similar time period (to avoid seasonality effects) after excluding weeks with major holidays. My summary table included pairs of weeks, say weeks A and B, as well as the increase or decrease in Internet traffic between A and B. Also, I selected pairs {A, B} with the same mix of TV shows except for one that was either absent in A but not in B, or the other way around.

It was then possible, for a given TV show, to see if using it in a specific week was associated with traffic growth more frequently than traffic decline. This led to the identification of the best and worst performing TV shows. Eventually "Law & Order" was found to be the winner, and used more frequently whenever possible.

References

[1] O. Chikumbo, V. Granville, Optimal clustering and cluster identity in understanding high-dimensional data spaces with tightly distributed points, Machine Learning and Knowledge Extraction 1 (2) (2019) 715–744.

[2] T.M. Davies, M.L. Hazelton, Assessing minimum contrast parameter estimation for spatial and spatiotemporal log-Gaussian Cox processes, Statistica Neerlandica 67 (4) (2013) 355–389.

[3] V. Granville, Stochastic Processes and Simulations: A Machine Learning Perspective, MLTechniques.com, 2022, [Link].

[4] Z. Hu, R.-C. Yang, A new distribution-free approach to constructing the confidence region for multiple parameters, PLoS ONE (2013) 1–13, [Link].

[5] J. Møller, Introduction to spatial point processes and simulation-based inference, in: International Center for Pure and Applied Mathematics (Lecture Notes), Lomé, Togo, 2018, [Link], [Mirror].

Glossary

Autoregressive process	**Autocorrelated time series**, as described in Section 3.4. Time-continuous versions include **Gaussian processes** and **Brownian motions**, while **random walks** are a discrete example; two-dimensional versions exist. These processes are essentially integrated **white noise**.
Binning	Feature binning consists of aggregating the values of a feature into a small number of bins, to avoid overfitting and reduce the number of **nodes** in methods such as **naive Bayes**, neural networks, or decision tree. Binning can be applied to two or more features simultaneously. I discuss **optimum binning** in this book.
Boosted model	Blending of several models to get the best of each one, also referred to as ensemble methods. The concept is illustrated with **hidden decision trees** in this book. Other popular examples are **gradient boosting** and **AdaBoost**.
Bootstrapping	A data-driven, model-free technique to estimate parameter values, to optimize goodness-of-fit metrics. Related to resampling in the context of cross-validation. In this book, I discuss **parametric bootstrap** on synthetic data that mimics the actual observations.
Confidence Region	A confidence region of level γ is a 2D set of minimum area covering a proportion γ of the mass of a bivariate probability distribution. It is a 2D generalization of **confidence intervals**. In this book, I also discuss **dual confidence regions** – the analogous of **credible regions** in Bayesian inference.
Cross-validation	Standard procedure used in bootstrapping, and to test and validate a model, by splitting your data into training and validation sets. Parameters are estimated based on training set data. An alternative to cross-validation is testing your model on synthetic data with known response.
Decision trees	A simple, intuitive nonlinear modeling techniques used in classification problems. It can handle missing and categorical data, as well as a large number of features, but requires appropriate feature binning. Typically, one blends multiple binary trees each with a few **nodes**, to boost performance.
Dimension reduction	A technique to reduce the number of features in your dataset while minimizing the loss in predictive power. The most well known are **principal component analysis** and feature selection to maximize goodness-of-fit metrics.
Empirical distribution	Cumulative frequency histogram attached to a statistic (for instance, nearest neighbor distances), and based on observations. When the number of observations tends to infinity and the bin sizes tend to zero, this step function tends to the theoretical cumulative distribution function of the statistic in question.
Ensemble methods	A technique consisting of blending multiple models together, such as many decision trees with logistic regression, to get the best of each method and outperform each method taken separately. Examples include boosting, bagging, and AdaBoost. In this book, I discuss **hidden decision trees**.
Explainable AI	Automated machine learning techniques that are easy to interpret are referred to as interpretable machine learning or explainable artificial intelligence. As much as possible, the methods discussed in this book belong to that category. The goal is to design black-box systems less likely to generate unexpected results with unintended consequences.
Feature selection	Features – as opposed to the model response – are also called independent variables or predictors. Feature selection, akin to dimensionality reduction, aims at finding the

	minimum subset of variables with enough predictive power. It is also used to eliminate redundant features and find **causality** (typically using **hierarchical Bayesian models**), as opposed to mere correlations. Sometimes, two features have poor predictive power when taken separately, but provide improved predictions when combined together.
Generative model	Bayesian Gaussian mixtures (**GMM**) combined with kernel density estimation and the **EM algorithm** is a classic modeling tool. In this book, I used *m*-**interlacings** instead. Generative adversarial networks (**GAN**) work as follows: the generator creates new observations and the discriminator tests whether the new observations are statistically indistinguishable from training set data. When this goal is achieved, the new observations is your synthetic data. New observations can also be generated via **parametric bootstrap**.
Goodness-of-fit	A **model fitting** criterion or metric to assess how a model or sub-model fits to a dataset, or to measure its predictive power on a validation set. Examples include R-squared, Chi-squared, Kolmogorov–Smirnov, error rate such as false positives and other metrics discussed in this book.
Gradient methods	Iterative optimization techniques to find the minimum of maximum of a function, such as the **maximum likelihood**. When there are numerous local minima or maxima, use **swarm optimization**. Gradient methods (for instance, stochastic gradient descent or Newton's method) assume that the function is differentiable. If not, other techniques such as **Monte Carlo simulations** or the **fixed-point algorithm** can be used. Constrained optimization involves using **Lagrange multipliers**.
Graph structures	Graphs are found in decision trees, in neural networks (connections between **neurons**), in **nearest neighbors methods** (NN graphs), in **hierarchical Bayesian models**, and more.
Hyperparameter	An hyperparameter is used to control the learning process: for instance, the dimension, the number of features, parameters, layers (neural networks) or clusters (clustering problem), or the width of a filtering window in image processing. By contrast, the values of other parameters (typically node weights in neural networks or regression coefficients) are derived via training.
Link function	A link function maps a nonlinear relationship to a linear one so that a linear model can be fit, and then mapped back to the original form using the inverse function. For instance, the **logit link function** is used in logistic regression. Generalizations include **quantile** functions and inverse **sigmoids** in neural network to work with additive (linear) parameters.
Logistic regression	A generalized linear regression method where the binary response (fraud/nonfraud or cancer/noncancer) is modeled as a probability via the logistic link function. Alternatives to the iterative maximum likelihood solution are discussed in this book.
Neural network	A black-box system used for predictions, optimization, or pattern recognition especially in computer vision. It consists of layers, neurons in each layer, link functions to model nonlinear interactions, parameters (weights associated to the connections between neurons) and hyperparameters. Networks with several layers are called **deep neural networks**. Also, **neurons** are sometimes called nodes.
NLP	Natural language processing is a set of techniques to deal with unstructured text data, such as emails, automated customer support, or webpages downloaded with a crawler. The example discussed in Section 18.5 deals with creating a keyword taxonomy based on parsing Google search result pages. Text generation is referred to as NLG or **natural language generation**, using **large language models** (LLM).
Numerical stability	This issue occurring in unstable optimization problems typically with multiple minima or maxima is frequently overlooked and leads to poor predictions or high volatility. It

is sometimes referred to as **ill-conditioned problems**. I explain how to fix it in several examples in this book, for instance, in Section 3.4.2. Not to be confused with numerical precision.

Overfitting   Using too many unstable parameters resulting in excellent performance on the training set, but poor performance on future data or on the validation set. It typically occurs with numerically unstable procedures such as regression (especially polynomial regression) when the training set is not large enough, or in the presence of **wide data** (more features than observations) when using a method not suited to this situation. The opposite is underfitting.

Predictive power   A metric to assess the goodness-of-fit or performance of a model or subset of features, for instance, in the context of dimensionality reduction or feature selection. Typical metrics include R-squared, or **confusion matrices** in classification.

R-squared   A goodness-of-fit metric to assess the predictive power of a model, measured on a validation set. Alternatives include adjusted R-squared, mean absolute error and other metrics discussed in this book.

Random number   Pseudorandom numbers are sequences of binary digits, usually grouped into blocks, satisfying properties of independent Bernoulli trials. In this book, the concept is formally defined, and strong pseudonumber generators are built and used in computer-intensive simulations.

Regression methods   I discuss a unified approach to all regression problems in Chapter 1. Traditional techniques include linear, logistic, Bayesian, polynomial, and **Lasso regression** (to deal with numerical instability and overfitting), solved using optimization techniques, **maximum likelihood** methods, linear algebra (**eigenvalues** and **singular value decomposition**) or stepwise procedures.

Supervised learning   Techniques dealing with labeled data (**classification**) or when the response is known (regression). The opposite is **unsupervised learning**, for instance, **clustering** problems. In-between, you have **semisupervised learning** and **reinforcement learning** (favoring good decisions). The technique described in chapter 1 fits into unsupervised regression. **Adversarial learning** is testing your model against extreme cases intended to make it fail, to build better models.

Synthetic data   Artificial data simulated using a generative model, typically a **mixture model**, to enrich existing datasets and improve the quality of training sets. Called **augmented data** when blended with real data.

Tensor   Matrix generalization with three of more dimensions. A matrix is a two-dimensional tensor. A triple summation with three indices is represented by a three-dimensional tensor, while a double summation involves a standard matrix.

Training set   Data set used to train your model in supervised learning. Typically, a portion of the training set is used to train the model, the other part is used as validation set.

Validation set   A portion of your training set, typically 20%, used to measure the actual performance of your predictive algorithm outside the training set. In cross-validation and bootstrapping, the training and validation sets are split into multiple subsets to get a better sense of variations in the predictions.

Index

Symbols

α-compositing, 65

A

A/B testing, 385
Activation function, 181
AdaBoost, 35, 387
Adam gradient descent, 182
Additive number theory, 340, 350
Adversarial learning, 170, 389
Agent-based modeling, 259, 277
AI art, 170, 271
Algebraic number, 210
Algorithmic bias, 170
Analytic continuation, 332, 341
Analytic function, 207
Anisotropy, 284, 313, 320
Antialiasing, 62, 68, 356, 364
Association rule, 375
Attraction basin, 67
Attraction (point process), 299
Attractor distribution, 236, 306, 314, 325
Augmented data, 33, 110, 259, 261, 389
Autocorrelation, 53, 209
Autoregressive process, 53, 236, 387

B

Bailey–Borwein–Plouffe formulas, 210
Bayesian classification, 90
Bayesian inference, 47
    hierarchical models, 388
    naive Bayes, 375
Bernoulli trials, 367
Berry–Esseen inequality, 204
Bessel function, 322, 323
Beurling primes, 209, 345
Binning, 373
    optimum binning, 36, 387
Binomial distribution, 314
Bisection method (root finding), 247
Boosted trees, 172
Bootstrapping, 6, 123, 170, 315
    percentile method, 132
Boundary effect, 296, 297, 304, 306, 312–314, 320

Brownian motion, 56, 229, 235, 259, 260, 281, 381, 387
    Lévy flight, 236
Brun's theorem, 340

C

Cauchy distribution, 236
Cauchy–Riemann equations, 207
Causality, 388
Cayley–Hamilton theorem, 51
CDF regression, 8
Censored data, 304
Central limit theorem, 236, 294, 367
Chaotic dynamical system, 259, 281
Character
    principal, 334
Characteristic function, 322
Characteristic polynomial, 51, 53–55, 237
ChatGPT, 376
Chebyshev's bias (prime numbers), 207, 334
Checksum, 384
Chi-squared test, 296
Chowla conjecture, 337
Classification, 389
Clique (graph theory), 307
Cluster process, 298, 304, 313
Clustering, 389
Collatz conjecture, 218
Collision graph, 281
Color model
    RGB, 62, 365
    RGBA, 62, 64, 93, 365
Color opacity, 272
Color transparency, 13, 261, 365
Complex random variable, 204, 346
Computational complexity, 221, 376
Computer vision, 1, 103
Confidence band, 315
Confidence interval, 46, 312, 387
Confidence level, 367, 371
Confidence region, 5, 26, 170, 311, 313, 367
    dual region, 47, 368, 387
Conformal map, 3
Confusion matrix, 374, 389
Connected components, 186, 282, 305, 307, 313, 314, 378
Contour level, 271, 371
Contour plot, 371

Convergence
    abscissa, 334, 342
    absolute, 148, 330, 332
    acceleration, 68
    alternating series, 332
    conditional, 148, 206, 334
    Dirichlet test, 332
Convex linear combination, 140
Convolution of distributions, 323
Copula, 127, 171, 194
    Frank, 171, 178
    Gaussian, 171
Correlation matrix distance, 179, 185, 192
Cosine distance, 377
Counting measure, 294
Covariance matrix, 115, 367
Covering problem, 316
Covering (stochastic), 316
Credible interval, 47
Credible region (Bayesian), 368, 387
Critical line (number theory), 149
Cross-validation, 6, 181, 281, 373
Cuban primes, 341
Curse of dimensionality, 152
Curve fitting, 20

D

Data video, 259, 272
Decision tree, 35
Decorrelate, 192
Decorrelation, 185, 193
Dedekind zeta function, 207, 345
Deep neural network, 89, 181, 388
Dense set (topology), 337
Density estimation, 302
Diamond-square algorithm, 260
Diehard tests of randomness, 206
Dimensionality reduction, 6
Dirichlet character, 207, 209, 333, 340
    modulo 4, 334, 342, 343
Dirichlet eta function, 351
Dirichlet functional equation, 207, 341, 343
Dirichlet series, 203
Dirichlet-L function, 207, 333, 343
Dirichlet's theorem, 207, 334, 337, 343
Disaggregation, 150
Discrete Fourier series, 157
Discrete orthogonal functions, 157
Dissimilarity metric, 377
Distributed architecture, 372
Distribution
    Cauchy, 236
    Fréchet, 56, 236

    Gaussian, 367
    generalized logistic, 114, 299
    Hotelling, 367
    Laplace, 322
    Lévy, 236
    logistic, 7
    modified Bessel, 322
    Poisson–binomial, 251, 325
    Poisson–exponential, 293
    Rademacher, 203, 205
    Rayleigh, 314, 316, 324
    Weibull, 56, 236, 314
Domain of attraction, 306
Dot product, 4
Dummy variables, 36, 180
Dyadic map, 208
Dynamical systems, 208, 306
    chaotic systems, 259, 281
    dyadic map, 208
    ergodicity, 209
    logistic map, 208
    shift map, 208
    stochastic, 260

E

Edge effect (statistics), 304
Eigenvalue, 2, 58, 114, 389
    power iteration, 118
Elbow rule, 244, 304, 314, 380
Elliptic curve, 341
EM algorithm, 33, 176, 388
Empirical distribution, 7, 123, 157, 171, 293, 298, 305, 314, 320, 323, 343
    multivariate, 204
Empirical quantiles, 132, 193
Ensemble methods, 35, 103, 172
Entropy, 284, 321, 375
Epoch, 180, 185
Equidistribution modulo 1, 212
Equilibrium distribution, 260
Erdős–Rényi model, 307
Ergodicity, 209, 260, 312, 313, 322
Euler product, 203, 332, 342
    random, 346
Euler's transform, 352
Evolutionary process, 260
Experimental design, 385
Experimental math, 64, 329
Explainable AI, 3, 33, 90, 103, 114, 169, 194, 243, 264, 317
Exploratory analysis, 384
Exponential decay, 40
Exponential sums, 342

Extrapolation, 140
Extreme value theory, 236, 323

F

Feature attribution, 169
Feature clustering, 177, 185, 186, 193
Feature importance, 169
Feature selection, 6, 124, 372
Fermat's last theorem, 341
Fixed-point algorithm, 68, 114, 243, 388
Flag vector, 375, 385
Fourier series, 157
Fourier transform, 323
Fractal dimension, 56
Fractional part function, 211
Fréchet distribution, 56, 236
Frobenius norm, 114
Fruchterman and Rheingold algorithm, 378
Fuzzy classification, 64

G

Gamma function, 56, 236
GAN (generative adversarial networks), 33, 170, 176, 193, 264, 293, 388
Gaussian circle problem, 350
Gaussian distribution, 367
Gaussian mixture model, *see* GMM
Gaussian primes, 207, 345
Gaussian process, 53, 387
General linear model, 2
Generalized linear model, 2, 51
Generalized logistic distribution, 114, 312
Generative adversarial networks, *see* GAN
Generative AI, 259, 277
Generative model, 33, 58, 127, 258, 259, 261, 272, 280, 389
Geostatistics, 133
GIS, 154
Glivenko–Cantelli theorem, 343
GMM (Gaussian mixture model), 33, 83, 84, 175, 176, 193, 194, 293, 388
Goldbach's conjecture, 340
Goodness-of-fit, 64, 374
GPU-based clustering, 85
Gradient boosting, 387
Gradient operator, 5
Gradient (optimization), 243
Gram–Schmidt orthogonalization, 157
Graph, 305
    collision graph, 281
    connected components, 186, 282, 313, 378
    database, 378
    directed, 282

edge, 305
Fruchterman–Reingold, 283
nearest neighbor graph, 307, 313
node, 305, 306
random graph, 306
    random nearest neighbor graph, 306
theory, 305
tree, 283
undirected, 186, 305, 307, 314
vertex, 305
GraphViz, 283
Greedy algorithm, 147, 350
Grid search, 243, 264

H

Half-tone (music), 362
Hartman–Wintner theorem, 230
Hash table, 222, 285, 319, 375, 377
    sparse, 376
Hausdorff distance, 108
Hellinger distance, 171, 193, 195
Hermite polynomials, 157
Hexagonal lattice, 304
Hidden decision trees, 35, 37, 387
Hidden layer, 89
Hidden process, 294, 319, 323
Hierarchical clustering, 89, 186, 377
Hilbert primes, 345
Histogram equalization, 85, 89
Hoeffding inequality, 233
Homogeneity (point process), 251, 302
Hotelling distribution, 367
Hurst exponent, 56
Hyperparameter, 24, 65, 134, 179, 264

I

Identifiability, 318, 321
Ill-conditioned problem, 20, 58, 118, 389
Image segmentation, 89
Imputation (missing values), 170
Index
    index discrepancy, 320
Intensity (stochastic process), 293, 302, 313
Interarrival times, 235, 293, 306, 311, 321
    standardized, 322
Interlaced processes, 303
Internet-of-Things, 293
Inverse distance weighting, 135
Inverse square law, 277
Iterated logarithm, 205, 206, 229
Itô integral, 58

K

K-means clustering, 28, 29
Key–value pair, 36, 375
Kolmogorov–Smirnov test, 171, 204, 296, 306
Kriging, 147
Kronecker's theorem, 337, 350

L

Lagrange interpolation, 58
Lagrange multiplier, 5, 388
Laplace distribution, 322
Large language models, 376, 388
Lasso regression, 5, 389
Latent variables, 180
Lattice, 302
    perturbed lattice, 293
    shifted, 305
    stretched, 304
Law of the iterated logarithm, 205, 206, 229, 336, 347
Le Cam's theorem, 251, 295
Learning rate, 179, 185, 193
Least absolute residuals, 131
Lévy distribution, 236
Lévy flight, 236
LightGBM, 179, 193
Link function, 2, 7
Liouville function, 333, 348
LLM (large language model), 376, 388
Log-polar map, 3
Logistic distribution, 7, 303
Logistic map, 208
Logistic regression, 7
    unsupervised, 30
Logit function, 388
Loss function, 181, 185, 193

M

m-interlacing, 86, 303, 314, 318, 388
Map-reduce, 372
Marketing attribution, 385
Markov chain, 53
    MCMC, 203
Mathematica, 371
MaxCliqueDyn algorithm, 307
Maximum likelihood estimation, 369, 388, 389
Mean squared error, 5, 26
Medoid, 28
Mersenne twister, 25, 208, 212, 231
Mertens function, 334
Minimum contrast estimation, 264, 317, 321, 369
Mixture model, 24, 47, 260, 271, 303, 304, 314, 371, 389
    blending, 260

Möbius function, 334
Model fitting, 64, 388
Model identifiability, 5
Modulus (complex number), 237, 332
Monte Carlo simulations, 203, 388
Morphing (computer vision), 260
Moving average, 246
Multidimensional Fourier series, 158
Multiple root, 148
Multiplicative function
    completely multiplicative, 203, 206, 333, 334, 350
    Rademacher, 203

N

N-body problem, 277
n-gram (NLP), 376
Naive Bayes, 375, 387
Natural language generation, 376, 388
Natural language processing, 35, 377
Nearest neighbor, 293, 307, 316, 388
    interpolation, 131, 135
    nearest neighbor distances, 313, 315, 316, 318, 325
    nearest neighbor graph, 313
NetworkX, 282, 283
Neural network, 89
    activation function, 181
    epoch, 180
    hidden layer, 89
    hyperparameter, 92
    neuron, 89, 181, 388
    seq2seq, 257
    sparse, 83
    very deep, 89
Newton's method, 243
NLG (natural language generation), 376, 388
Node (decision tree), 36, 172, 387
    perfect node, 46
    usable node, 37
Node (interpolation), 148
Normal number, 204, 337, 343
    strongly normal, 206
Numerical stability, 51

O

Omega function, 333, 342
Order statistics, 323
Ordinary least squares, 54, 131, 156
Orthogonal function, 157
Otsuka–Ochiai coefficient, 377
Outliers, 323, 381
Overfitting, 5, 170, 171, 179, 321, 387

P

Palette, 260, 365
Parametric bootstrap, 12, 25, 33, 124, 170, 315, 387, 388
Partial derivative, 148
Partial least squares, 2
Path (graph theory), 305
Percentile bootstrap, 132
Permutation
    entropy, 321
    random permutation, 320
Perturbed lattices, 293
Plotly, 271
Point count distribution, 312, 316
Point process
    attractive, 313
    cluster process
        Matérn, 302
        Neyman–Scott, 302
    nonhomogeneous, 251, 302
    perturbed lattice process, 302
    radial, 302
    renewal process, 302
    repulsive, 299
Poisson point process, 235, 251, 294, 312
Poisson–binomial distribution, 251, 293, 325
Poisson–exponential distribution, 293
Pólya conjecture, 336
Positive semidefinite (matrix), 52, 115
Power iteration, 118
Preconditioning, 117
Prediction interval, 5, 123, 132
Predictive power, 36, 46, 169, 374, 375
Prime test (of randomness), 205, 221, 230
Principal character, 334
Principal component analysis, 51, 169, 387
Probability generating function, 230
Proxy space, 370
Pseudoinverse matrix, 51
Pseudorandom numbers, 231, 380
    combined generators, 226
    congruential generator, 212
    Diehard tests, 206, 223
    Mersenne twister, 212, 231, 261
    prime test, 205, 230
    strongly random, 206, 210
    TestU01, 206

Q

Quadratic irrational, 209, 213, 221
Quantile, 367, 388
    empirical, 132, 171
    function, 127, 157, 293, 299, 315

regression, 6
    weighted, 132

R

R-squared, 5, 6, 33, 264
Rademacher distribution, 205
Rademacher function, 203, 337, 346
    random, 206
Random function, 250
Random graph, 305–307
Random multiplicative function, 203
    Rademacher, 206
Random permutation, 320
Random variable
    complex, 204
Random walk, 229, 263, 387
    first hitting time, 230, 234
    zero crossing, 230
Rayleigh distribution, 314, 316, 324
Rayleigh test, 314
Records, 323
Regression splines, 2
Regular expression, 376, 384
Reinforcement learning, 186, 194, 389
Rejection sampling, 172
ReLU function, 181
Renewal process, 302
Repulsion basin, 332
Repulsion (point process), 299, 316
Resampling, 123, 315
Riemann Hypothesis, 140, 149
    Generalized, 206, 334, 340, 343
Riemann zeta function, 149, 203, 207, 343, 347
Root mean squared error, 64

S

Scaling factor, 313, 323
SDV (Python library), 177
Seed (random number generator), 172, 179, 182, 185, 222, 261
Semisupervised learning, 389
Shape signature, 105
Shapley value, 169
Shepard's method, 135
Shift map, 208
Sigmoid function, 181, 388
Simplex, 348
Singular value decomposition, 2, 389
Singularity, 284
Six degrees of separation, 379
Sklar's theorem, 171
Smoothing parameter, 134

Spatial statistics, 133, 302
Spectral domain, 260
Spline regression, 157
Square root (matrix), 52, 115, 185
Square-free integer, 205, 222, 337
Stable distribution, 236, 262, 323
State space, 260
Stationary distribution, 58
Stationary process, 53, 237, 260, 281, 295, 303, 313
Stepwise regression, 126
Stochastic convergence, 260
Stochastic function, 56
Stochastic geometry, 316
Stochastic gradient descent, 181
Stochastic process, 293
Stochastic residues, 318
Stop word (NLP), 376
Stretching (point process), 304
Sturm–Liouville theory, 157
Superimposition (point processes), 303
Supervised classification, 87
Surface plot, 271
SVD (Python library), 193
Swarm optimization, 21, 388
Synthetic data, 2, 22, 25, 58, 110, 114, 147, 155, 170, 203, 221, 231, 243, 261, 272, 281, 329, 368
Synthetic metric, 375

T

TabGAN (Python library), 178
Tarjan's algorithm, 378
Tensor, 91
TensorFlow, 178
Text normalization, 376
Theil–Sen estimator, 131

Time series, 54
    autoregressive, 55, 236
    disaggregation, 140
    Hurst exponent, 56
    nonperiodic, 19
Total least squares, 2
Training set, 131, 132, 281, 373
Transcendental number, 210
Transformer, 89, 257
Tree (graph theory), 283
Twin primes, 340

U

Universality property, 332, 337, 340
Unsupervised clustering, 86
Unsupervised learning, 30, 389

V

Validation set, 6, 63, 131, 132, 170, 171, 281, 373
Vandermonde matrix, 51, 58
Vertex, 293, 305, 306, 323
Video compression
    FFmpeg, 62, 68

W

Waring's problem, 340
Watts and Strogatz model, 379
Weibull distribution, 56, 236, 314, 325
Weighted least squares, 2
Weighted quantiles, 132
Weighted regression, 6
White noise, 22, 53, 237, 387
Wide data, 158, 186, 389

X

XOR operator, 213